PERSPECTA

URBAN DIVIDES

Contents

Preface

The network age promises an interconnected world, yet our cities are increasingly divided. Today, inequality dominates the zeitgeist, and societies are looking to architecture to relieve their anxieties: won't more walls, fences, and gates solve all our problems? If we cannot control the effects of rapid technological change, we overcompensate with obsolete physical barriers. At the same time, global communities, supposedly less fearful of the "other," are reinforcing urban partition in less obvious ways, often through their own prosperity. Gated communities, private parks, urban office-palaces, speculative luxury towers, and prohibitively expensive cafes are reinforcing inequality and exclusion in the city.

In the public imagination, urban divides are perceived as symptoms of conflict or of a failed society. Berlin, Jerusalem, and Johannesburg quickly come to mind. Yet, urban divides masquerade with architectural finesse in the places we least expect. In reality, it is the undivided city that is fictional: every city is divided, and often not by a simple line.

Perspecta 50 seeks to investigate divides as a wider mechanism of urbanism. In doing so, we explore a variety of questions facing architecture and urbanism today: How has migration due to war and global labor impacted housing and seclusion in the city? In planning for climate change, how does new infrastructure reinforce or resist inequality? How do material and social interchanges blur boundaries between the formal and informal city? How do marginalized groups resist erasure and assert their spatial narrative on the city? In this issue, we combine disparate discourses on spatial inequality, suggesting architectural comparisons that cross social and geographical boundaries. Ultimately, Perspecta 50 invites readers to interrogate the inevitability and ubiquity of urban divides.

Meghan McAllister and Mahdi Sabbagh

Foreword
by Jon Calame

»This act, be it conscious or not, undoubtedly passes the limits of human morality. Its result will sometimes be ruin, but poverty always; and the thrice-happy city is scattered abroad in obedience to a law superior to its own happiness.«

The Life of the Bee (1901),
M. Maeterlinck, Chapter 2: *The Swarm*[1]

The excitement and allure of the physically-divided city may derive from its image as a crime scene. It offers the evidence of trespass and the prospect of forensics by urban experts. Waste, suffering, decrepitude, and moaning should all be there. As a resident of Verona—Shakespeare's exquisitely divided city—Mercutio verbalizes his exasperation while bleeding to death from collateral injuries:

»A plague o' both your houses!«[2]

His exhortation brims with good sense. It would make a winning slogan for divided cities as a class, if illness were acceptable as a metaphor for urban partition. Most treatments of the subject do. A Bosnian architect I admire greatly, Amir Pasic, once explained to me that the struggle in Mostar was not between ethnicities but rather between "urban" and "anti-urban" impulses, where it was taken for granted that the nature of a healthy city is tolerant, cooperative, and efficient, and that the urban forces should prevail.

How much, and how long, I myself have wanted to believe in this dichotomy and to surrender to its tender seductions. Probably I looked at too many places and absorbed too many contradictions to keep that one together. In the end, it seemed just as likely that the city was the problem, the pox, the perp, than those actively trying to tear it into pieces. It is clear, and somewhat correct, what Amir said; there is that aspect of urban culture that we can say stands for pluralism and cooperation and synergies. Can it be, though, that even this alignment is visible only to those looking at the city from an elevated perch, a position of privilege, such that even the invocation of the term "divided" in this context is class-dependent and therefore highly problematic? Even emblematic of the conflicts themselves?

Putting these familiar assumptions on ice, it is possible to ask whether or not urban partitions are, in themselves, a fine thing. Much of the history of western cities, and several of the essays in this volume, answer in the affirmative. In a sense, the birth and growth of cities has been a love affair with walls and barriers of all kinds erected to keep unwanted elements out and stockpiled resources (talent, material, social capital, information, money, power, etc.) in. Muralophilic citizens exercised their franchise behind perimeter levees, which were usually fragile and prone to breaches. Many cities went bankrupt trying to keep the walls intact.

The inner keep of a fortified castle complex was a "citadel," shortened from "cittadella," or "little city." While there are civil rights, there are also civil wars. If we like cities and what they do, we too must like walls. Exclusionary barriers are nuclear in relation to conventional western urban development, supporting one of the city's most basic functions: to amass and retain diverse elements of concentrated wealth in:

> »... *a structure specially equipped to store and transmit the goods of civilization ... mobilized and packed together under pressure, behind the massive walls.* «[3]

Lewis Mumford asserts that the normal city, the essential city, was schizophrenic and destined for self-abnegation:

> »... *a paranoid psychal structure was preserved and transmitted by the walled city: the collective expression of a too heavily armored personality.... the very success of urban civilization gave sanction to bellicose habits and demands that continually undermined it and nullified its benefits.* «[4]

So much for the habits incubated by girdling urban walls. What about intramural partitions? These appear to be a mutation of the core program, and a genuine aberration; it is one thing to protect the integrated city, but to impose internal segregations? Is this a Freudian Slip, a repressed wish revealed? Or is it the city's attempt to molt and grow? The idea of molting, or terminal urban scale, is apparently found in both non-human cities and idealized ones. It is grounded, perhaps, in the limits of social cohesion in the face of anonymity.

When a bee hive is at the peak of its health and productivity, internal signals trigger a swarm—usually led by the old queen—that flies in search of a new hive site, to begin from scratch to form a new colony. The peak size of such a hive is estimated by Maeterlinck to be between 80-90,000 insects. Likewise, Thomas More in his Utopia, notes that the fictitious city Amaurot should not grow beyond 96,000 citizens; he provides instructions for how to siphon colonists who will establish a new city. What if a city does not molt, and continues to allow scale to weaken its social bonds? Then the unitary city may function as a cocoon, spontaneously carving more intimate and secure units out from within itself.

This can be an organic response to scale and estrangement; an affinity-based metamorphosis. Then again, it is not the biggest—or even the most ethnically diverse—cities that become partitioned, so we need a much more nuanced organizational scheme. This scheme, by the way, is almost entirely absent from the contemporary literature and very much lies ahead to be formulated and argued, perhaps by one of the more intrepid readers of this volume. For certain, anyway, ethnic partition is a response clearly subject to extreme political manipulation and sleight of hand. Many observers of coercive urban partition along ethnic lines have noted the hidden choreography that activates archaic feuds, caricatures locally despised by minorities, and provokes antagonisms that support a self-fulfilling prophecy of irreconcilable suspicion. Loic Wacquant has talked about the ghetto as "a peculiar socio-spatial contraption"—alleging a designer's keen intention in the fabrication of these barricaded spaces.

The reader of this volume might attempt to sort and compare the urban contraptions described in relation to things like sequence, thresholds, cost, porosity, precursors and authorship. There is also the question of scale, and whether some partitions work well at a neighborhood scale, but poorly at an urban or regional scale. Do the dynamics of city walls apply to the related prospect of a barrier along the United States border with Mexico, for instance?

It is worth considering the idea that partition might be part of every city's genetic inheritance, sometimes dominant but mostly recessive. Splitting, swarming, severing, reinventing bonds, resetting the scales of wealth and power and privilege and position while also resetting the physical scale of the city, or a city-within-the-city. A reader might try to ask in advance: under what circumstances does urban partition recommend itself, when should the sanctity of the established city be sacrificed to the needs of the teeming hive, and when is the cost of that sacrifice too high?

1 Maurice Maeterlinck, *The Life of the Bee* (New York: Dodd, Mead, and Company, 1917), 44.

2 William Shakespeare, *Romeo and Juliet*, Act 1, Scene 3.

3 Lewis Mumford, *The City in History* (New York: Harvest Books, 1961), 30-34.

4 Ibid, 39-53.

THE YALE ARCHITECTURAL JOURNAL

POWER LINES: Boundaries of Erasure and Expansion in Los Angeles

BY

DANA CUFF

Fig 1: Proposed site for Elysian Park Heights, ca. 1949. Courtesy of the Housing Authority of the City of Los Angeles.

The aerial photograph shows Chavez Ravine in the late 1940s, an area just north of downtown Los Angeles surrounded by the region's ubiquitous sprawl. The white line drawn over the photograph commands a disproportionate and unmistakable power: inside that line, all will be demolished; outside that line is safe. An abstraction with real and violent implications, it has not only spatial but also temporal meaning. Soon, this newly-defined territory will be scraped clean to make way for something else, something big, we know not what. The boundary line is inscribed by the same hand as the textual references to reality: the roads, cardinal directions, and by implication, the "project" named Elysian Park Heights.[1] If the text appears to inhabit a layer above the image, the boundary appears within the picture plane yet hovering slightly above the ground, as a kind of site plan to define inside from out, ours versus yours, one space of activity from another, what could be from what is present—all forms of spatial speculation. Although it may appear as though Chavez Ravine is on the city's outskirts, instead it was already by the 1940s inhabited by a longstanding community as well as ringed by even more densely populated residential fabric just beyond a band of parkland. The line creates a new and singular "here," as in "here is where we intend to build," where residents had not recognized their common fate. Encircled by a virtual net, two schools, over 1100 houses, markets, a church, some roads, a valley—all are swept into one predicament by the line.

POWER LINES

Although architecture locates its own essence in drawing, and a rich discourse about the line has evolved in art and architectural theory, there remains little extension of that discourse into either the urban condition or the realm of political action. The most relevant prior scholarship concerns the line as projective speculation, implying a translation from some existing reality (the world as it is), through a rendered abstraction (the painting; the plan, in both senses of the word), to a possible condition (the imagined world; in the case of architecture: the project). When this thinking moves into the urban condition, its potential for violence is immediate and profound. In Los Angeles, as well as other cities, that violent line is present when freeways are routed, in red-lining, and in public housing plans that require eminent domain, as in the image above.

To understand the power of the line in architecture and urbanism is to grasp its translation from real space to abstraction, to a projected real space, and finally to the violent actions the line prescribes. Any architectural drawing sits atop the palimpsest of this archaeology of lines. A place like Chavez Ravine (real space) is translated into a site or piece of property (abstraction; Fig 1), then into Elysian Park Heights (a projected real space; Figs 4-6) and lastly into the powerful actions of demolition, site preparation, and construction. In this particular case, residents were removed from their homes kicking and screaming as the bulldozers waited in the wings. At such large scales where architectural and urban projects coincide, the power of lines viscerally function to control bodies.

Los Angeles is an ideal place to examine this phenomenon, since its dominant format is a field condition. The line, particularly the encircling line, has been wielded to interrupt and mark the extended ground surface at least since the Spanish settler colonial plaza and grid were laid out according to the Laws of the Indies in the late 18th century.

The ground plane locates the plan and site plan in architectural representation, and the master plan in urban design. This plane, unlike the ground or *terra firma*, is an abstract surface, a field condition that is a construct of uninterrupted extension. Viewed from above as in the aerial photo or in a map, the actual ground of roads, buildings, vegetation and topography are already flattened by the two-dimensional image. This abstract "seeing like a state," in the words of political scientist James C. Scott, obscures the experienced reality where roads appear not as lines to follow with the white pen, but places with people, buildings, cars, landscapes, and vistas.[2] In the abstract, it is much easier to draw the outline delineating that Chavez Ravine will be cleared, its topography leveled, thousands of houses razed, and roadways redirected.

1
The author would like to thank Yang Yang and Joshua Nelson for their able research assistance.
The image comes from records kept by the Housing Authority of the City of Los Angeles, which assigned Chavez Ravine the project number Cal 4-11 and the name Elysian Park Heights to the public housing proposed for the site. See Dana Cuff, *The Provisional City* (Cambridge: MIT Press, 2000); Don Parson *Making a Better World* (Minneapolis: University of Minnesota Press, 2005).

2
James C. Scott, *Seeing Like a State* (New Haven: Yale University Press, 1998).

In fact, the undulating topographic realities of the so-called ground plane at Chavez Ravine were largely responsible for sparing this part of Los Angeles from earlier redevelopment, even though it sits just a mile and a half from the downtown business district. Rendered on the flat picture plane of the photo, it takes the form of a perspectival plan. Converted into a conventional plan (Fig 2), a title foreshadows what will come next: "The area included is inside the thick line." Only slightly altered from the aerial photo, "the area" is now even more abstract: just roads and property boundaries, flattened into plan in the plane of the drawing.

Overlaid on a larger landscape like the one above, the line on the ground foreshadows relationships between claims that are attached to property and places. The claim of a homeowner encircled by that line is threatened by its authority, their property boundaries and rights depicted as thinner than the thicker, stronger, encircling line's claim over the land. Ownership is secondary, even though all the structures located within the outline are already individually owned and only beginning to be assembled into a single parcel. The method of this essay is a close, historically-specific reading of a set of speculative projections that unleashed the line's power in Los Angeles. It weaves together discourses about the line from art, architecture, and urban planning to demonstrate the implications of their interconnectedness in the Los Angeles context. This narrative replaces the worn stereotypes about L.A. and fleshes out what I have elsewhere called convulsive urban development.[3]

Fig 2: Map of Elysian Park Heights, ca. 1950. Courtesy of the Housing Authority of the City of Los Angeles.

3 Dana Cuff, *The Provisional City*, 37–41. See note 1.

LOS ANGELES AND THE LINE

A history of the line in Los Angeles provides a context for Chavez Ravine's predicament, locating the abstraction in the city and placing it within the realm of political and spatial action. Compared to other cities, the line carries undue authority in Los Angeles, a horizontal city that is more plan than section, more extension than compression, more periphery than interior. From the dash-dot-dot-dash encircling property to the boundary-filled areas that were red-lined, graphic tools of spatial politics were anything but abstract in the development of Los Angeles. From surveys that constructed boundaries around "slums" for demolition to the recent and relatively arbitrary naming of districts as a means to attract development, the making of Los Angeles can be told through the narrative history of the line. Encircling some terrain within the larger landscape, boundaries defined inside from outside, blight from merely substandard, industrial from residential land uses, preservation-worthy from demolition-ready, and East L.A. and South L.A. from the rest of the city. Los Angeles was historically susceptible to power lines due to the vast postwar growth in the region and the dominant imaginary of a plastic city. In the twentieth century, layers of connections and divides shaped L.A.'s built environment particularly in the contested space of "downtown." This contestation has been one of erasure, protest, and violence, masked in the rhetoric of revitalization and civic betterment. The 1939 survey of neighborhood conditions (Fig 3) is one of many data maps created to study residential "blight" around downtown so that it could be razed to advance the commercial core's possibility.[4] All the neighborhoods, council districts, community plan areas, cities, and census tracts delineate, in more and less fixed manners, a topography of power in Los Angeles particularly in and around downtown. Indeed, a forceful effort was needed to generate a downtown.

From the settler colonial plaza that laid down a grid, to the Pacific Electric Red Car lines that formed an 1100-mile web across the basin, to the 527 miles of freeways built mainly in the postwar period, Los Angeles' own rules of urban growth counterpose Koolhaas' "1909 Theorem" from *Delirious New York*. In the latter, Koolhaas argues that the Flatiron Building marks the vertical reproduction of Manhattan, with each successive floor of New York's high-rises creating new territory out of thin air.[5] By contrast, according to what can be named the "1781 Theorem," in the horizontal space of Los Angeles' new territory is created only by expanding and erasing. When Governor Felipe de Neve installed the first plaza according to the Laws of the Indies in 1781, he did both: the street grid gave a new order atop existing inhabitation and farmlands, while simultaneously forecasting future development along those same streets as they moved outward from the

CONDITION OF RESIDENTIAL STRUCTURES MAP

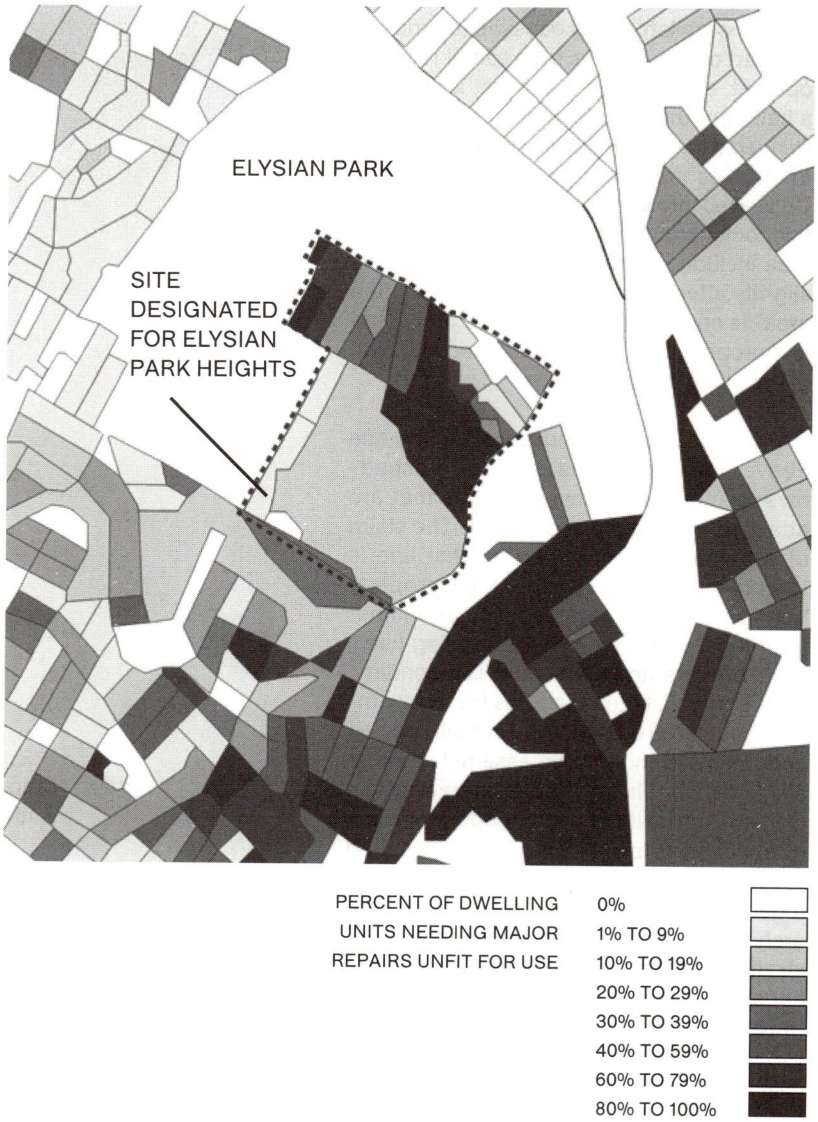

Fig 3: Condition of Residential Structures Map (modified format - original traced by Meghan McAllister). This survey, conducted in 1939, located blighted areas for the purpose of public projects and the use of eminent domain. Zones left white indicate that no housing existed in that area. Housing Survey, Housing Authority of the City of Los Angeles, August 1939. Archives of the Housing Authority of the City of Los Angeles, Files and Maps.

4
Zones left white indicate that no housing existed in that area. Housing Survey, Housing Authority of the City of Los Angeles, August 1939. Condition of Residential Structures Map. Archives of the Housing Authority of the City of Los Angeles, Files and Maps.

5
Rem Koolhaas, *Delirious New York* (New York: Oxford University Press, 1978), 69-70.

center. The violence of the colonial project has a well-established history, and the imposition of the *Laws of the Indies* in Los Angeles demonstrates that the line was its weapon of choice. L.A.'s 1781 Theorem depends upon the encircling line to erase, and a line of infrastructural mobility to expand. While much has been written about Los Angeles' unending sprawl and its concomitant infrastructures of mobility - streets, boulevards, and especially highways—this essay focuses on the flip side to examine encirclement and erasure.

Located within a basin framed by the ocean and mountains, Los Angeles' vast geography cohered in the 18th century around a core, and then around multiple centers. A city of space according to urban theorist Albert Pope,[6] L.A. adapted its Spanish colonial orthogonality to new linearities of mobility like boulevards and freeways. The 18th- and 19th-century gridiron city was followed by postwar urban plans that were rarely orthogonal. When Le Corbusier began his text, *The City of Tomorrow*, with a story of the donkey's path and man's path, he contrasted a crooked and irrational urbanism of the past with the orthogonal, rational, straight urbanism of modernity.[7] Corbusier's description of the lines inscribed on the land by humans was obviously rhetorical flourish, but it is interesting to note how donkey-like even a rational grid can be. Although the Laws of the Indies dictated that colonial street layouts should be set at a 45-degree angle from true north, situating the plaza between Bunker Hill and the river's meandering banks pushed the L.A. grid to 36 degrees. Even when the American township system arrived in the 19th century, a true north-south "rational" system was not exactly implemented.[8] Throughout the 20th century, a series of small towns and neighborhoods grew together into a network of moderately dense habitation. Today, the 4,000 square mile county of Los Angeles is comprised of eighty-eight individual cities, each linearly bounded from the other.

The basin's *terrain vague* was further carved into a new patchwork after the Second World War when freeways simultaneously linked points along their path and divided the territory through which they traversed. Appropriately, downtown Los Angeles adopted its current definition as the space between four freeways. These were exceptionally powerful lines: continuous viaducts of speed, noise, pollution, visible frame, and material topography that created political boundaries as well as real fragmentation. The federal highway system aimed for and then razed poor neighborhoods of color in its path, segregating those who remained from other parts of the city. The power to draw such lines was masked in the rhetoric of boosterism and progress: demolishing blight will revitalize the city; expanding the commercial core will strengthen the city's economic base. But behind the rhetoric are other stories of financial gain and racial discrimination, along with historically specific notions of urban betterment. Architecture was enlisted all along the way, as the material means to define otherwise invisible boundaries. The 1781 Theorem of expansion and erasure was L.A.'s postwar city-making dictum.

L.A.'s advancing sprawl proceeded at first in reference to the downtown core, but its magnetic force weakened as infrastructure moved outward. Subcenters grew stronger, like Santa Monica and Culver City, just as new ones like Century City emerged. Without a Chicago School-style diagram of concentric growth outward from a downtown, development instead occurred where subcenters could be delineated to attract development and capital. Parts of the city like Westwood Village in the 1920s or Silicon Beach after the new millennium, established boundaries that reinforced identity branding. At the same time, however, further growth congealed along lines linking these subcenters, that is, along L.A.'s characteristic corridors like Wilshire, Olympic, Pico, Hollywood, and Santa Monica Boulevards. Even along these passageways, boundaries carve out districts like "The Miracle Mile," a one-and-a-half-mile stretch of Wilshire Boulevard planned as a commercial district to rival downtown L.A.[9] Thus, Los Angeles's field-like condition is divided into bounded clusters of identity if not cities in their own right. At any point in time, the clusters represent forms of power that have erased, restructured, colonized, preserved, or otherwise overtaken preceding communities of identity.

There is no official count of these clusters, but the best estimate is offered by the *Los Angeles Times* "neighborhood map" for L.A. County. Within the county, it tallies 158 cities and unincorporated places and 272 neighborhoods; it counts 114 neighborhoods within the City of L.A.[10] These neighborhoods are marked by hundreds of blue signs posted along streets that mark one's entry into or departure from places ranging from Filipinotown and Los Feliz Village to the Furniture and Fine Arts District. Even though there are no official boundaries for those places, the political repercussions of these invisible and moving lines remain. Consider the renaming of South-Central to South L.A. in April 2003 by L.A. City Council to rid the community of its negative stigma, or the portion of Compton that rebranded itself as "Crystal Park." The name changes were intended "to distance themselves from areas with bad reputations."[11] These are attempts to erase narratives, stained story lines, without necessarily changing anything else. As one councilman said, "It's meaningless and won't really change a thing. What is really needed is a comprehensive program to address crime, unemployment, education and drug abuse."[12] The inarguable truth in

6
Albert Pope, "From Form to Space," in *Fast-Forward Urbanism*, ed. Dana Cuff and Roger Sherman. (New York: Princeton Architectural Press, 2011), 143-175.

7
See Catherine Ingraham, *Architecture and the Burdens of Linearity* (New Haven: Yale University Press, 1998); "The Burdens of Linearity: Donkey Urbanism," in *Architecture Theory Since 1968*, ed. K M. Hays (Cambridge, Mass: The MIT Press, 1998), 642-657.

8
Waldie, D.J. "L.A.'s Crooked Heart." *Los Angeles Times*, October 24, 2010. Accessed 5 May 2016. http://articles.latimes.com/2010/oct/24/opinion/la-oe-waldie-maps-20101024.

9
Eric Avila, *The Folklore of the Freeway: Race and Revolt in the Modernist City* (Minneapolis: University of Minnesota Press, 2014).

10
"Mapping L.A. Neighborhoods," *Los Angeles Times*, accessed 13 May 2016, http://maps.latimes.com/neighborhoods/.

11
Calvin Sims, "In Los Angeles, It's South-Central No More," *The New York Times*, 10 April 2003, http://nyti.ms/2ejsSk7.

that statement is countered by the historical power of such explicit or implied boundaries, if not the name.

The work of cultural geographer Denis Cosgrove suggests that the spatial history of Los Angeles was especially ripe for abstract yet violent boundaries. The public conception of major environmental transformations in Los Angeles was in fact shaped by the same hand that documented battles in the Pacific Theater during World War II. In the first half of the 20th century, the *Los Angeles Times* employed Charles Owens to render large-scale spatial news through bird's eye drawings that resided somewhere between a map and a graphic novel. Owens depicted complicated geographic narratives like the San Francisco earthquake of 1906 and the sinking of the Titanic in 1910, as well as later events when aerial photographs were readily available. Drawings like Owens' were not only less expensive to print, they were better able to tell a story than aerial photographs. His depictions of the Pacific Ocean as a space of violent wartime exchange and subsequent portrayal of the L.A. Basin's real estate fronts were rendered from the omniscient aerial view to explain the strategic plans and violent realities of war and development alike. Indeed, the first aerial photographs were shot from airplanes during World War I to produce battle maps as well as to document the front. After the war, aerial photography shifted to commercial uses, when Sherman Fairchild invented the means to overlap photographs shot from a plane to create an aerial "photomap" of Manhattan in 1921. In the next decades, the Fairchild Aerial Surveys, both direct overhead shots and oblique or bird's eye photographs, would be completed for the Los Angeles region.[13]

It is not by chance that the hybrid aerial photo-plus-drawing was the preferred technique for proposing a major convulsion in Los Angeles in the late 1940s and early 1950s. The Chavez Ravine story was about the land captured by the photograph, which was overlaid with a single boundary line to tell a simple narrative: here is the chosen site. Los Angeles was as much an inhabited *landscape* as a city, and in the ravine, two types of surfaces were patched together so unevenly that nearly 300 acres of fields and small houses sat within; even the name came from the landform. No other space for development that large existed within a 40-mile radius of downtown. In the late 40s, photographs of the area in the *Los Angeles Times* showed dirt roads, horses, small grocery stores, and self-built houses, constructing the public imaginary of a rural Mexican village. In fact, more than three thousand people lived in a small portion of the ravine, but all of them would have to move if the city were to pursue its progressive redevelopment agenda. A series of surveys were conducted inside that white boundary, finding about ninety percent of the homes had at least one basic deficiency (major structural problems or inadequate sanitary facilities), and two-thirds had two or more.[14] The demarcating white line produced a site for Los Angeles, setting the stage for a new narrative: a hillside utopia with 3,360 units of public housing designed by architect Richard Neutra and planner Robert Alexander. Inside the line, the Housing Authority of the City of Los Angeles used eminent domain to purchase every last piece of property, exchanging the rural village for a modern dream.

Henri Lefebvre argues that the representation of urban space abstracts the human body and everyday life to actualize that space for exchange or consumption. "Through its control, the state tends to accentuate the homogeneous character of space, which is fractured by exchange. This space of state control can also be defined as being optical and visual."[15] The line renders urban space, actualizing it for consumption and construction. Here again, Los Angeles' long dominance by real estate speculation would welcome representational techniques that illuminated spatial control. In the case of Chavez Ravine, that drawing laid down the political lines of battle between the City and its Housing Authority, the homebuilders who fought to keep public housing production from competing with the private residential construction industry, the residents of Chavez Ravine (a full third of whom refused to sell and others who fought for at least a fair price), and the wider citizenry who wanted nothing more to do with low-income housing.

12
Quote is from then Councilman Nate Holden; see Calvin Sims, "In Los Angeles, It's South-Central No More," *The New York Times*, 10 April 2003, http://nyti.ms/2ejsSk7.

13
Denis E. Cosgrove and Veronica della Dora, "Mapping Global War: Los Angeles, the Pacific, and Charles Owens's Pictorial Cartography." *Annals of the Association of American Geographers*, v 95 no 2 (June 2005), 373–390.

14
Dana Cuff, *The Provisional City*, 272–281.

15
Henri Lefebvre, "Space and the State," in *State/Space: a reader*, ed. N.B. Brenner, B. Jessop, M. Jones, and G. Macleod. (Malden, MA: Blackwell, 2003), 84–88.

THE LINE IN SPACE

Beyond the boundary line that defined the battle at Chavez Ravine, there were numerous schematic architectural drawings that rendered ideas of possible futures. At least since Alberti, drawing has been perceived as the repository for and instantiation of architectural ideas. Although diagrams and conceptual drawings might stand without reference to an imagined future, measured drawings and the descriptive geometry on which they are based have a predictive quality that imbues them with an authority about the real. They indicate a future state that bears a supposed one-to-one correspondence with the drawings. According to architectural theorists Perez-Gomez and Pelletier, the "enigmatic distance between the reality of the world and its projection" has a revelatory dimension that is quashed by an "assumption of literal relationship between the project and the building [that] is basic to industrial production in the modern city..."[16] The ambiguous intersection between drawings and buildings, however, leaves the space of interpretation that powerlines depend upon.

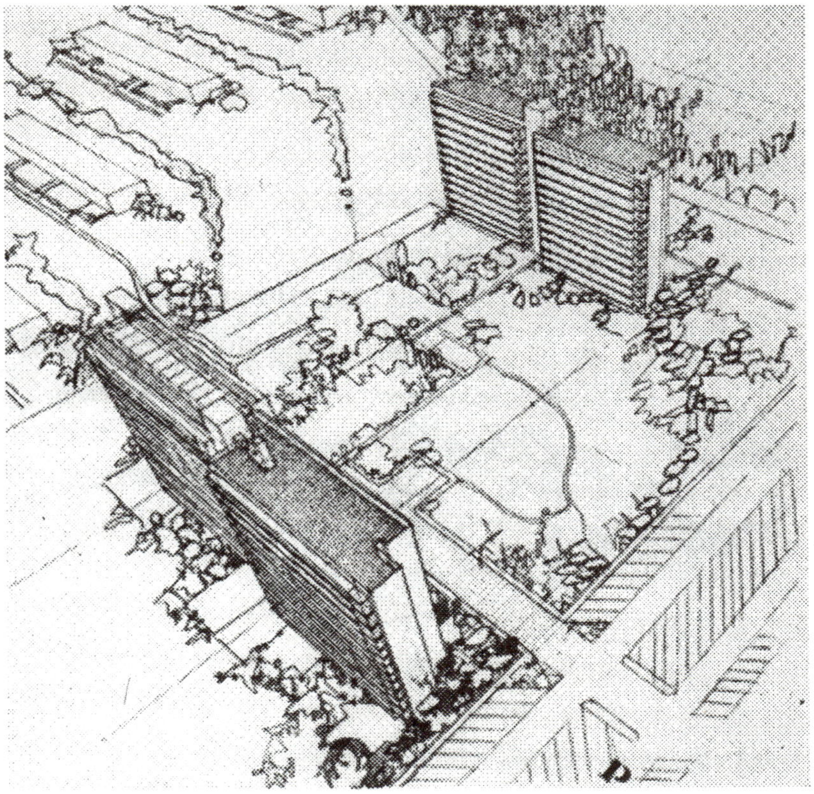

Fig 4: Richard Neutra, Elysian Park Heights public housing towers, ca. early 1950s.

Neutra's drawings (Figs 4 and 5) maintain a degree of the enigmatic distance from reality that Perez Gomez and Pelletier seek. The line work is open and without much shading, creating a constructed perspective *sketch* of the Elysian Park Heights buildings and landscape. Slightly articulated masses sit on a field of paving, planting, parking, and roadways. The consistent bird's eye view maintains the distance from experience on the ground plane, while the constructed, hard-lined perspective intimates a measured precision. Neutra's line drawings give us an illusion of reality simultaneous with a vision of future possibility.[17] The actual Chavez Ravine exists in limbo in these drawings; it remains present in the real world and its existing state is no longer in the imaginary.

The history of drawing in art and architecture contains a long discourse about the abstraction of the line and its ambiguous relationship to the real. "With the line as the prime element of a language concerned with the imitation of reality, drawing could be both a reliably accurate representation of objects as seen in reality and a poetically inspired representation conceived in the imagination."[18] In this second sense, architecture's lines delineate an imagined future reality, not the documentation of some existing observation but a representation of things to come. A line in this sense is always *about* something, as well as a thing in and of itself. It is both a sign of intention as well as an empirical object since it is substantively present in the form of graphite or ink. Today, material lines in architecture are replaced with digital vectors which are much more like their mathematical progenitors. Even though they remain visible on screen, they are another step more remote from the real.

16
Perez-Gomez, Alberto Pelletier, and Louise Pelletier, "Architectural Representation Beyond Perspectivism," Perspecta 27 (1992): 34, 39.

17
For more discussion of Neutra, his drawings, and Elysian Park Heights, see Thomas S. Hines, *Richard Neutra and the Search for Modern Architecture* (New York: Oxford University Press, 1982).

18
Catherine De Zegher, "A Century Under the Sign of Line: Drawing and Its Extension (1910-2010)," in *On Line: Drawing Through the Twentieth Century*, ed. Cornelia H. Butler and C. de Zegher (New York: Museum of Modern Art, 2010), 23.

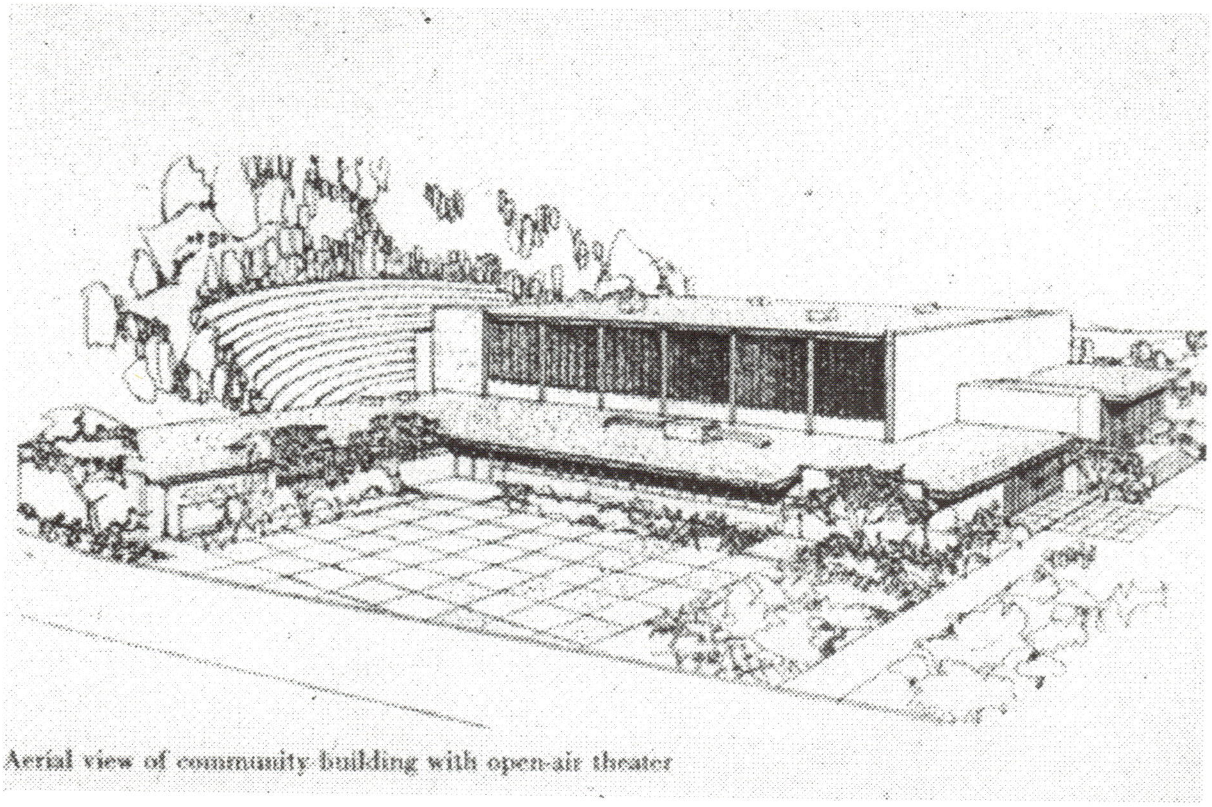

Fig 5: Richard Neutra, Elysian Park Heights community building proposal, ca. early 1950s.

The light-handedness in Neutra's drawings conceals their power, suggesting poetic ideas rather than outlining construction instructions. The line drawings are a type of architectural drawing akin to painting, at least in terms of what the philosopher Hubert Damisch calls a "semblance of presence on the absent."[19] The illusion is doubled in drawings like Neutra's, where the proposed residential towers and community building give the semblance of presence in relation to their own yet-to-exist state, but also in relation to the erased existing inhabitation on the site. These drawings carry a speculative power that helps to suppress the present.

In contrast to Neutra's perspectival renderings in which abstract distancing and erasure effect their authority, the architectural plan holds a different power. The plan documents the plane of action through program, land use, or bodily movement, establishing relationships that separate one set of situated actions from another. In a building, lines on a plan drawing foretell where occupants may enter, congregate, meet, sleep, and dine. Crossing the line can be imperceptible or it can be life-threatening, as evident in the "stand-your-ground" (sometimes referred to as "line in the sand") laws. The line in architecture is only occasionally acknowledged as being imbued with power. In his graphic novel on the politics of the line, Léopold Lambert argues that when a line becomes a wall it violently splits territories and controls bodies. "Lines of property are being virtually traced and architecture materializes them into violent devices actively controlling bodies. The wall is quintessential and paradigmatic in this regard and is operating at every scale, from the domestic wall of an apartment to the United States' border with Mexico via various scales of gated communities."[20]

The line in architecture is not only plan-based; indeed the "regulating line" establishes geometric proportion to resolve formal composition in plan and especially in elevation. In buildings, care with geometric relations would confer a sense of order, harmony, and beauty, and at the same time guard against capriciousness.[21] Regulation and control, in contrast to capricious behavior, were functions of the line. As the architect's drawing began to pale in relation to computer-aided design, architectural theorist Catherine Ingraham considered a full spectrum of drawing's functions. She states that the geometric line "...sets in motion an entire range of practices. It organizes structure, resolves the play of forces, inscribes the design, upholds a system of meaning and ontology in the profession, defines an arena of composition and aesthetics, and exhibits the skill of the architect."[22] The present essay argues that from the first aerial photograph to the preliminary drawings for Elysian Park Heights, lines inscribe all the practices Ingraham names and then some; they also inscribe power, control, and violence.

19
Hubert Damisch, *Noah's Ark: Essays on Architecture* (Cambridge: MIT Press, 2016).

20
Léopold Lambert, *Weaponized Architecture: The Impossibility of Innocence* (New York: dpr-barcelona, 2012), 44.

21
Le Corbusier, *Toward an Architecture* (London: Frances Lincoln, 2008; John Goodman, translator; Jean-Louis Cohen, introduction) 133-135.

22
Catherine Ingraham, "The Problem of Distinction," *Assemblage* 14 (Apr 1991), 24, 26.

Richard Neutra's site perspective drawing of Elysian Park Heights (Fig 6) buries the landscape that was visible in the opening aerial photograph. On the razed ground, he portrays building blocks on a hill covered with dense vegetation bisected by roadways. The drawing relies on the outline of the buildings' volumes to delineate the future, "for the outline represents nothing other than the line of demarcation, of separation, the hinge between two surfaces."[23] Hubert Damisch's description applies to the towers and garden apartments in this descriptive view of Elysian Park Heights, whose bold white forms seem to wring themselves out of the dark foliage. The drawing uses the line to hinge each structure upward at right angles from its implied footprint on the ground. While the buildings are transparently speculative, the vegetation erases the past with an opaque ground cover. The way the roadways seem to hover over rather than weave their way through the foliage appears to be an inconsistency in the elegant drawing. However, their treatment is entirely consistent with a reading of the ground plane as an abstraction. Both the aerial photograph and the site perspective obscure the plane of inhabitation, where a lived reality will be violently removed to create a surface for the future. In different ways, both equate the ground's surface with the plane of the representation, be it photo or drawing, to compose what Damisch would call the "projective dimension." In fact, erasure was the only thing that was real at Chavez Ravine. In the late 1950s, bulldozers cleared the land and its inhabitants, while voters rejected Elysian Park Heights' public housing, and backroom politics replaced it with a newly forged, speculative project: Dodger Stadium. The baseball field and its parking lots forget the past that Ry Cooder recalled in the lyrics of his song "Third Base, Dodger Stadium:"[24]

> *In the middle of the 1st base line,*
> *got my first kiss, Florencia was kind.*
> *Now, if the dozer hadn't taken my yard,*
> *you'd see the tree with our initials*
> *carved.*
>
> *... Just a place you don't know,*
> *up a road you can't go.*

23 Hubert Damisch, *Noah's Ark: Essays on Architecture*, 73.

Fig 6: Richard Neutra, Elysian Park Heights site perspective, ca. early 1950s.

Fig 7: Dodger Stadium on the Chavez Ravine site, where Elysian Park Heights had been planned. From 1962 Fairchild Aerial Survey. Courtesy of the Housing Authority of the City of Los Angeles.

One might conclude that power lines do their dirty work in the site plan, and indeed this was the case in postwar Los Angeles. At that time, the city's dominant horizontality was its primary projective dimension: a surface pictured with multiple futures, a plane that begged for limits to demarcate stable forms, a landscape from which to create places in the field. But the historical specificity of the violent line is no longer the province of plan alone. As Los Angeles begins to grow up rather than out, taking on sectional qualities along with planar ones, perhaps the 1781 Theorem will have run its course. With virtually no further lines for horizontal expansion, a twenty-first century Los Angeles is finding that erasure as well as vertical growth are both politically embroiled. Instead, current power lines are wedging new programs into forgotten and overlooked spaces, on tight infill sites where every available surface will be deployed. Concomitant forms of violence, including gentrification, extreme densification, and displacement haunt the architect's speculations. Today, as always, architects hold power in the lines they make, whether rendered or built. It is time to recognize this politically and embodied complexity so that the next generation of architectural city-making is cognizant of its power.

24 Ry Cooder, W. Garcia, and J. Kevany with Bla Pahinui (vocals, guitar, ukulele), "Third Base, Dodger Stadium," in *Chavez Ravine: A Record*, by Ry Cooder, et al. (New York: Nonesuch, 2005).

{DIS}INCORPORATION: FURTHER NOTES ON THE CITY AS A LEGAL CONCEPT

Jesse Vogler

In 2015 State Representative Bob Burns of Missouri, representing District 93 in the St. Louis area, initiated House Bill No. 1686, a measure to enact "fourteen new sections relating to disincorporation of certain cities" within the Revised Statutes of Missouri.[1] A year earlier, State Senator Jamilah Nasheed introduced Senate Bill No. 72, calling for the immediate disincorporation of all villages in counties with greater than 950,000 inhabitants.[2] These acts—championed in the wake of Michael Brown's death at the hand of a Ferguson, Missouri police offer—were were meant to ease and expedite the dissolution of municipal entities in Missouri, with a particular focus on the cities that form the metropolitan area of Greater St. Louis. Neither bill passed. But as symptom and roadmap, these and similar efforts point to what is a growing movement and discourse around the country: disincorporation.

What does it mean to disincorporate?[3] To loosen the bonds of municipal incorporation? To effect the dissolution and erasure of a municipal entity—its boundaries, its administrative structure, and its social and economic imperatives? Disincorporation is the non-spectacular, administrative cousin to the more material urban destruction and reconstruction that has come to occupy the disciplinary imagination whenever questions of shrinkage, decay, and population loss are invoked.[4] Disincorporation, of course, brings us into the field of urban eschatology, with all the concerns of judgment and final destiny this may imply. That the call for the dissolution of a city—what some call a form of urbicide—strikes mightily at the heart of an urban discourse makes sense; we essentially do not have a language for thinking otherwise—for thinking outside of a capitalist logic of continuous growth.

If incorporation is a prelude to *the urban*, then we might understand disincorporation as a prelude to *territory*. It is a becoming-landscape of an administrative ordering of lower energetics. A deterritorialization of the city, where excess, expenditure, and senescence are constituent processes in a more general theory of urbanization.[5] At stake in disincorporation is the diagram linking territory, sovereignty, and governance in their numerous imbrications—where cities and citizens are no longer found to be addressable.

As a body of legal theory, disincorporation is the less elaborated twin of municipal incorporation law. As a category of urban theory, disincorporation is rarely if ever even invoked; a range of other rhetorical and descriptive language is often inserted instead. What the language of disincorporation provides that, say, the language of shrinking cities does not, is a merging of concrete administrative procedures with a theoretical framework for thinking differently about the political stakes of a growth model of urbanism. For the leading legal scholar on municipal disincorporation, "Dissolution opens a new chapter in understanding shrinking cities, a chapter we can think of as shrinking governance."[6] So where the shrinking cities discourse tends to merge radically different political, economic, and social contexts under a single, formal category of description, the discourse around disincorporation refers to a very specific administrative operation and its socio-spatial effects.[7]

To understand disincorporation, we must also understand its necessary prelude—municipal incorporation. Municipal incorporation is the explicit provisioning of powers, privileges, and immunities—the power to designate inclusions and exclusions, and the capacity to dictate how land is zoned, used, and ultimately valued. Additionally, incorporation explicitly provides for the mobilization of a police force, drafting of regulations, establishment of permanent administrative bureaucracies, procedures for taxation, and the development of unique codified law—the primary building blocks of a much broader capitalist state. In short, incorporation marshalls the city as agent, as instrument, and, perhaps, as weapon.

At work in municipal (dis)incorporation is an understanding of the city as a legal and regulatory instrument—as a *territorial technology* for the sorting, recording, and processing of populations and property.[8] This sorting has often adopted particularly racialized and class-based mechanisms; it shows the ways that difference, privilege, and identity in the American context are not simply descriptive but constitutive factors of our urban imaginations. Marking an important historical transition in the segregative technologies of the city, political scientist Gregory Weiher maps the ways that, "while neighborhood level segregative mechanisms have been fitfully removed, municipal level segregative mechanisms

1 Missouri House Bill No. 1686, 98th General Assembly, Second Regular Session (2016).

2 Missouri Senate Bill No. 72, 98th General Assembly, First Regular Session (2014). It should be noted that the only county in Missouri with close to this population is St. Louis County. The roundabout language follows from a prohibition against special laws, targeting specific populations—only laws that cover general interests or a range of municipalities. "Villages" in Missouri law refer to towns that, at the time of incorporation, had fewer than 500 inhabitants —which at the time this bill was advanced numbered 22, or nearly a quarter of the incorporated municipalities in the county.

3 Michelle Wilde Anderson, "The New Minimal Cities," *Yale Law Journal* 123 (2014): 1118; and Michelle Wilde Anderson, "Dissolving Cities," *Yale Law Journal* 121, no. 6 (April 2012): 1364.

4 For example, see Keller Easterling, "Subtraction," *Perspecta* 34 (2003): 80–90.

5 A reading of disincorporation in light of George Bataille's notions of productive expenditure and excess energetics is forthcoming by author. See George Bataille, *The Accursed Share: An Essay on General Economy*, vol. 1 (New York: Zone, 1988).

6 Anderson, "Dissolving Cities," 1431.

7 See, for example, Philipp Oswalt ed., *Shrinking Cities*, vol. 1 and 2 (Stuttgart: Hatje Cantz, 2005 and 2006).

8 For more on the idea of "cultural technologies," see Bernhard Siegert, "Cacography or Communication? Cultural Techniques in German Media Studies," *Grey Room* 29 (2007): 26–47.

have remained intact,"[9] in the post-war American city. Our cities are explicitly incorporated to mark difference—to render inclusions and exclusions—rather than following from any sort of assumed benevolent right of self-governance. As the contemptible range of intra-city regulatory and exclusionary practices were slowly eradicated in law and in practice, exclusion and regulation fell upon the category of the city unit itself. Through a range of zoning mechanisms—nominally structured around land use, housing types, family structures, and density—the incorporated city itself took on the role of restricting entire categories of citizens from living within its boundaries. As one author explains, "With the outlawing of racially restrictive deed covenants in 1948 (with the passing of Shelley v. Kraemer), cities themselves were the only legal means of ensuring racial homogeneity," with the expected result that city borders have gradually become racial and class borders as well.[10]

At stake in this diagram, then, is the abiding, but under-theorized, imbrications of landscape and law. In bringing a cross-disciplinary reading to the political geography of space, we are caught, on the one hand, with an architectural/urban discourse that prioritizes formal qualities, and, on the other, a legal discourse that focuses almost exclusively on the relationship between individuals and the state. The result is that a self-conscious legal conception of space is slow to emerge, a conception that would go a long way toward addressing Foucault's solicitation: "A whole history remains to be written of *spaces*—which would at the same time be the history of *powers*—from the great strategies of geo-politics to the little tactics of the habitat ... passing via economic and political installations." Installations, we might argue, such as the incorporated municipality itself. With this, we could begin to argue for a design discourse not of form but of processes that have formal, social, and economic *effects*. This shift marks a turn from the design of specific cities, to the territorial fact of the city *per se*. It marks a shift in the register of analysis—from form and fabric to boundary delineation and boundary maintenance—where perhaps we can see the typical variables of urban analysis as epiphenomenon of a more general principle: incorporation.

What this paper addresses, then, are the often-overlooked processes of municipal incorporation and disincorporation—the founding and dissolution of cities and towns—as a creative agent in the spatial history of territory. Through a reading of American municipal (dis)incorporation law, this paper will chart an historical and theoretical genealogy of the legal concept of the city. While there is a small but growing field of critical legal geography addressing the imbrications of landscape and law, this way of understanding cities and landscapes has been slow to enter into architectural discourse. This paper is structured in two parallel strands: a theoretical framing of the spatial and legal implications of (dis)incorporation and a historical study of (dis)incorporation in St. Louis, one of the most fragmented metropolitan regions in the country. Both are central, just as each is a footnote to the other—theory and its instantiation flickering across a divide.

9 Gregory Weiher, "Public Policy and Patterns of Residential Segregation," *Western Political Quarterly* 42, no. 4, (1989): 651.

10 Nancy Burns, *The Formation of Local American Governments: Private Values in Public Institutions* (New York: Oxford, 1994), 57; Weiher, "Public Policy and Patterns of Residential Segregation," 651.

INCORPORATION

From the early nineteenth century onward, incorporation has been the sole regulatory and legal mechanism by which American cities come into being; yet, as the leading legal scholar on municipal corporations, John Dillon, humbly admits, "There is nothing in the law more complex and abstruse."[11]

In the first theoretical reflection on incorporation, his 1872 *Treatise on the Law of Municipal Corporations*, Dillon explains that municipal incorporation is "a legal institution, devised to confer upon the individuals of whom it is composed powers, privileges, and immunities which they would not otherwise possess."[12] A legal institution, we must add, that counts among its powers the direct or indirect capacity to bracket out a whole range of cultural practices, land uses, economic classes, and populations.

Historicizing the patterns of inclusion and exclusion that lie at the heart of American town formation, political scholar Nancy Burns writes:

> Exclusionary zeal in various forms has been a part of American local institutions from their beginning... The earliest tradition is the establishment of towns that create economic homogeneity... In the seventeenth century this process was led by English merchants who planned the colonization of New England. The resulting communities are exemplified by the founding of Watertown, Massachusetts, in the late 1630s: Everyone hoped that there would be no poor, and Watertown had made special provisions to exclude them. To that end, they established that anyone who "may prove chargeable to the town" could be ordered to leave.[13]

In this description, we can see the ways that popular sovereignty and administrative autonomy are mobilized as technologies of negation—where seemingly benevolent notions of community and belonging are defined and patrolled precisely through the privilege of exclusion.

11 John Dillon, *Treatise on the Law of Municipal Corporations* (Chicago: James Cockcroft & Company, 1872), 29.

12 Ibid., 27.

13 Burns, *The Formation of Local American Governments*, 35.

How might we more fully understand the geography of this exclusion? To begin, let us remember that to incorporate is to first, and crucially, divide by a line.[14] The construction and constitution of the city boundary is the founding act of contemporary municipal incorporation law[15]—a bounding that is also a binding. A binding of certain legal rights and responsibilities, of "powers, privileges, and immunities," to a specific territorial unit and to the bodies that inhabit that territory. It is a seemingly prosaic and unremarkable diagram of bio-power operating within a milieu of dividing practices. To incorporate is to provide for a boundary of governance, within which these rights and responsibilities can be guaranteed and policed. It is here where municipal division—distinction, separation, and enforcement—both announces an abiding value system and perpetuates those values through enforcement and the persistence of built form. In the ritualized act of municipal demarcation, the history of architectural thought gives us a rich set of ways to think the founding of a city. Alberti, in a section covering public works in his *Ten Books on Architecture*, includes the textured material practices associated with defining the city boundary:

> The ancients, Varro and Plutarch among others, mention that our ancestors used to set out the wall of their cities according to religious rite and custom. On an auspicious day they would yoke together a bull and cow, to draw a bronze ploughshare and run the first furrow, which would establish the course of the town walls. The fathers of the settlement would follow the plough, the cow on the inside and the bull on the outside, turning any uprooted and scattered clods back into the furrowed line, and piling them up to prevent their being dispersed. When they reached the point where the gates were to be, they carried the plough by hand, leaving the threshold of the gate untouched. By this means they deemed the whole course and fabric of the walls consecrated, and with the exception of the gates, which could not rightly be called sacred.[16]

In the simultaneous yoking and distancing suggested in Alberti's bovine surveyors—held apart, as it were, by the line of the city boundary—we might read any one of the shames of municipal boundary production throughout the course of American urban history—race, class, ethnicity, and so on. While the motivations of exclusion often take on the common scapegoats of formal urban concerns—public health, nuisance, density—the most fundamental mechanism of exclusion has long been the construction and maintenance of boundaries. For in the post–Shelley v. Kraemer American context, the adjustment of city boundaries to achieve exclusionary ends—what Justice Frankfurter described as an "essay in geometry and geography to despoil colored citizens"—has been the operative mechanism in the divisive technology of the city.[17] One must only think of the sundown towns of post-Reconstruction America or the gerrymandering of city and voting districts today to find the exclusionary power of boundary maintenance at work. With municipal incorporation, then, we can see a specific administrative production of scale. To incorporate is to summon *the city* out of the territorial field and to make concrete a bounded entity that might otherwise have little perceptible distinction from its surrounding landscape. As a leading legal theorist of the city, Gerald Frug acknowledges the fundamental distinction of municipal incorporation law is *geographic*, noting "territoriality is to some extent the basis of city organization."[18] In this, he is echoing Dillon's forceful coupling of populations and geography: "Persons residing in or inhabiting a place to be incorporated, as well as the place itself, are—both *the persons* and *the place*—indispensable to the constitution of a municipal corporation."[19] In this twinning of persons and place, then, we can see the conceptual flicker by which cities are addressed as spatial entities, on the one hand, and as bodies politic on the other. So while we can read the city boundary as the legal definition of place, we will see how the rights conveyed within this boundary include the authority to define the constitution of domestic diagrams, such as what constitutes a family, a legal household, and the broader body politic of their citizenry.

There remained within the fantasy of municipal identity a popular notion of cities forming autonomous "Local Republics"[20] of a sort of *imperium in imperio*—a state within a state. And it was with this

14 State laws govern city, town, or village incorporation in the United States, so there are many different parameters around how such places are established, modified, or dissolved. As such, there is no single formula or threshold for incorporation. For example, while Illinois requires a minimum population of fifty prior to incorporation, Maine does not. And while Mississippi automatically begins the disincorporation process when an entity slips below the minimum population threshold, many other states with population limits do not initiate such processes and rely on the municipal corporation to initiate the legal process of disincorporation. The result is numerous "zombie" towns—bereft of a governing body and its population, but administratively accounted for. See Chester James Antieau, *Municipal Corporation Law: Antieau's Local Government Law* (New York: Matthew Bender, 1955), chapters 1–3, for a range of physical constraints on municipal boundary construction and annexation.

15 See, for example, Missouri Revised Statutes Chapter 72: Classification and Consolidation of Cities, Towns and Villages, 72.080.1, August 28, 2016: "such petition shall describe, by metes and bounds, the area to be incorporated and be accompanied by a plat thereof."

16 Leon Battista Alberti, *On the Art of Building in Ten Books*, translated by Joseph Rykwert et. al., (Cambridge: MIT Press, 1988), 101.

17 For example, in the 1960 *Gomillion v. Lightfoot* case, the US Supreme Court found that the city of Tuskegee, Alabama, violated the Fifteenth Amendment when it adjusted the city boundaries from a simple square figure to a 28-sided polygon that effectively disenfranchised 90% of the black population by gerrymandering entire African-American residential districts out of the city. Justice Felix Frankfurter, in arguments during the case, speaks directly to the disciplinary geography of this boundary when he states: "While in form this is merely an act redefining metes and bounds, if the allegations are established, the inescapable human effect of this essay in geometry and geography is to despoil colored citizens, and only colored citizens, of their theretofore enjoyed voting rights." Geometry and geography here combine to form the operative mechanism of an exclusionary and divisive technology—the technology of municipal boundary production itself. See C. G. Gomillion et al., Petitioners, v. Phil M. Lightfoot, as Mayor of the City of Tuskegee, et al. 364 U.S. 339 (81 S.Ct. 125, 5 L.Ed.2d 110).

18 Gerald Frug, "The City as a Legal Concept," *Harvard Law Review* 93, no. 6 (April 1980): 1057–1154.

19 Emphasis original. Dillon, Treatise on the Law of Municipal Corporations, 29.

20 Ibid., 18.

autonomy in view that Missouri and St. Louis pioneered the idea of a city freed from state mediation with Missouri's passage of the country's first municipal home rule constitution in 1875.[21] As a legal concept, the basic function of home rule is to redistribute and realign power between the state and local municipal governments. It is a flexible granting of powers from the state to a municipality, where certain rights and responsibilities surrounding the exercise of police powers, otherwise granted to the state through the Tenth Amendment of the US Constitution, are shifted and bequeathed to the city. In freeing the city from legislative oversight by the state and encouraging local experimentation, it represents the most autonomous form of municipal governance. In the discourse around home rule there is, after all, a certain dream of the autarchic metropolis.[22]

In the July 3, 1876, meeting by the St. Louis Board of Freeholders, it was resolved that the then all-encompassing St. Louis County "shall be divided into two districts by a line."[23] From this, a distinct entity called St. Louis, a figure against the territorial background of county, was summoned.[24] The line establishing the city of St. Louis extracted an entity that was almost immediately to stand in antagonistic relationship with its ground.[25] Importantly, this boundary was agreed to be durable and indelible—the city of St. Louis could not enter annexation proceedings of adjacent territories or subdivisions.

This great city/county divorce set in motion the conditions of possibility for a whole set of extra-urban incorporation strategies, and their concomitant exclusionary mechanisms, that continue to haunt greater St. Louis today. For without the possibility of annexation, a procedure dictating much of American city growth, the result has been a proliferation of municipalities, many no larger than a traditional subdivision with few inhabitants, in which we can locate an object-case of the divided city.[26] Studies have found in St. Louis County's sclerotic municipal boundaries, the second most fragmented metropolitan region in the country.[27] Greater St. Louis is a landscape of divisions—296 incorporated entities, twelve counties, two states; 91 municipalities, 82 of which hold under 25,000 people.[28] It is in this fragmented periphery where the stakes of incorporation and disincorporation are daily being tested.

21 Article IX, § 16 of the 1875 Missouri Constitution: "Any city having more than 10,000 inhabitants may frame and adopt a charter for its own government, consistent with and subject to the Constitution and laws of the state."

22 As a legal concept, there remains considerable disagreement as to home rule's meaning and the horizon of powers granted to the city through home rule statutes. Home rule has been described as a messy meeting of political symbol and legal concept that functions as much as metaphor as it does a meaningful and legal administrative unit. One legal scholar has described home rule as one of the most "startling" innovations in American institutional history, "something of the pioneer's daring originality of spirit in the matter of political institutions;" while another has explained, "it has proven almost impossible to draw a firm, clear line between local or municipal affairs and matters of statewide or general concern." See, respectively, Kenneth E. Vanlandingham, "Municipal Home Rule in the United States," William & Mary Law Review 10, no. 2 (1968): 269; Howard Lee McBain, The Law and the Practice of Municipal Home Rule (New York: Columbia University Press, 1916); James E. Westbrook, "Municipal Home Rule: An Evaluation of the Missouri Experience," Missouri Law Review 33, no. 1 (1968): 27.

23 Scheme for the Government of the County and City of St. Louis and Charter for the City of St. Louis, as Proposed by the Board of Freeholders, Acting under and in Pursuance of Section 20, Article IX of the Constitution of the State of Missouri (Saint Louis (Mo.), Saint Louis County (Mo.), Saint Louis (Mo.) Board of Freeholders, 1876).

24 In the spirit of the city as a summoning, I would like to propose a municipal incantation of the city's metes and bounds: "Beginning at a point in the middle of the main channel of the Mississippi river, and running thence westwardly at right angles to said channel, to a point on the west bank of said river 200 feet south of the center of the mouth of the river Des Peres; thence westwardly and parallel to the center of the river Des Peres, and 200 feet south thereof, to the eastern line of the Lemay Ferry road; thence westwardly to a point in the west line of said Lemay Ferry road at its intersection with the center of the Weber road; thence westwardly along the center of the Weber road to its intersection of the east line of lot (1) one of the Carondelet Commons, south of the river Des Peres; thence westwardly to the southeast corner of Rudolph Overman's, or northeast corner of B. H. Haar's land; thence westwardly to said Haar's northwest corner; thence northwestwardly to a point in the center of the Gravois road (600) six hundred feet southwardly from the center of the bridge across the river Des Peres; thence northwestwardly to the southeast corner of lot (31) thirty-one of the subdivision of the Mackenzie tract in U. S. Survey 1,953; thence northwestwardly in continuance of said last-mentioned line to the southern line of lot (21) twenty-one of the sub-division of the said Mackenzie tract; thence northwestwardly to a point in the southern line of United States Survey 2,035 (26) twenty-six chains eastward from the southwest corner of said survey; thence northerly to a point in the north line of the subdivision of East Laclede, (600) feet west of the McCausland road; thence northwardly and parallel to the center of the McCausland Road, to a point on the Clayton road (600) six hundred feet west of its intersection with the McCausland road; thence northerly and parallel with the Skinker road, and (600) six hundred feet west thereof, to its intersection with the old Bonhomme road; thence northeasterly to the intersection of the center lines of McLaren avenue and Mead street; thence in a northeasterly direction to a point in the Bellefontaine road (600) six hundred feet north of its intersection with the Columbia Bottom road; thence northerly, and parallel with the center line of the Columbia Bottom road to the northern boundary line of United States Survey number (114) one hundred and fourteen; thence easterly along said line to the center of the main channel of the Mississippi river; thence with the meanderings of said channel southwardly to the point of beginning."

25 Peter W. Salsich and Samantha Caluori, "Can St. Louis City and County Get Back Together? (Do Municipal Boundaries Matter Today?)," *Saint Louis University Public Law Review* 34 (2014): 13–49.

26 Advisory Commission on Intergovernmental Relations, *Metropolitan Organization: The St. Louis* Case (Washington, D.C.: GPO, 1988); Colin Gordon, "Patchwork Metropolis: Fragmented Governance and Urban Decline in Greater St. Louis," *Saint Louis University Public Law Review* 34, no. 1 (2014): 51–71; E. Terrence Jones, *Fragmented By Design: Why St. Louis Has So Many Governments* (St. Louis: Palmerston & Reed, 2000); and Salsich and Caluori, "Can St. Louis City and County Get Back Together?"

27 Rebecca Hendrick and Yu Shi, "Macro-Level Determinants of Local Government Interaction: How Metropolitan Regions in the United States Compare," *Urban Affairs Review* 51, no. 3 (2015): 414–38.

Municipalities in St. Louis, based on map by St. Louis County GIS Service Center (2012).

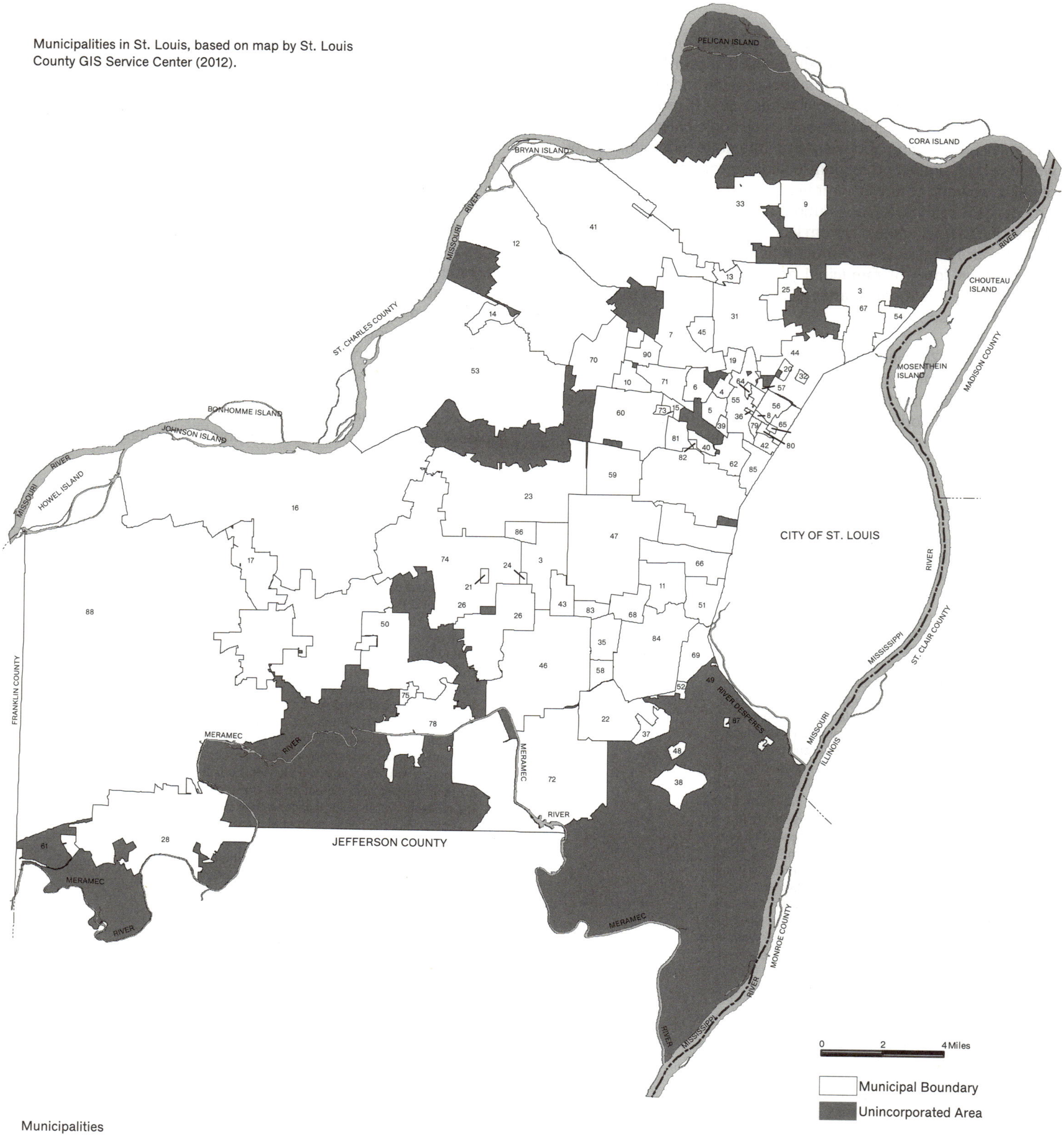

Municipalities

1 Ballwin
2 Bella Villa
3 Bellefontaine Neighbors
4 Bellerive
5 Bel-Nor
6 Bel-Ridge
7 Berkeley
8 Beverly Hills
9 Black Jack
10 Breckenridge Hills
11 Brentwood
12 Bridgeton
13 Calverton Park
14 Champ
15 Charlack
16 Chesterfield
17 Clarkson Valley
18 Clayton
19 Cool Valley
20 Country Club Hills
21 Country Life Acres
22 Crestwood
23 Creve Coeur
24 Crystal Lake Park
25 Dellwood
26 Des Peres
27 Edmundson
28 Ellisville
29 Eureka
30 Fenton
31 Ferguson
32 Flordell Hills
33 Florissant
34 Frontenac
35 Glendale
36 Glen Echo Park
37 Grantwood Village
38 Green Park
39 Greendale
40 Hanley Hills
41 Hazelwood
42 Hillsdale
43 Huntleigh
44 Jennings
45 Kinloch
46 Kirkwood
47 Ladue
48 Lakeshire
49 Mackenzie
50 Manchester
51 Maplewood
52 Marlborough
53 Maryland Heights
54 Moline Acres
55 Normandy
56 Northwoods
57 Norwood Court
58 Oakland
59 Olivette
60 Overland
61 Pacific
62 Pagedale
63 Pasadena Hills
64 Pasadena Park
65 Pine Lawn
66 Richmond Heights
67 Riverview
68 Rock Hill
69 Shrewsbu
70 St. Ann
71 St. John
72 Sunset Hills
73 Sycamore Hills
74 Town & Country
75 Twin Oaks
76 University City
77 Uplands Park
78 Valley Park
79 Velda City
80 Velda Village Hills
81 Vinita Park
82 Vinita Terrace
83 Warson Woods
84 Webster Groves
85 Wellston
86 Westwood
87 Wilbur Park
88 Wildwood
89 Winchester
90 Woodson Terrace

As the recent report by the Ferguson Commission in the aftermath of Michael Brown's killing makes abundantly clear, in the disastrous matrix of culpability surrounding aggressive police tactics, much can be attributed to municipal fragmentation and the concomitant pressure to balance small, municipal budgets through routine police stops.[29] As a recurring variable in the cycle of economic and racial violence, then, it should come as no surprise that municipal divisions play a key role in the spatial articulation of power.

One example from the St. Louis region evidences a range of strategic, instrumental motives for municipal incorporation—where exclusionary zoning and the biopolitics of citizenship were recently tested. Adjacent to Ferguson, and among the fractured constellation of municipalities that constitute St. Louis County, is the relatively new town of Black Jack. Founded in 1970, the town openly incorporated as a defensive measure in order to impose zoning regulations preventing multifamily housing—specifically a new low-income, federally subsidized housing project, Parkview Heights—from being developed in the area. In a case brought that year by the US Attorney General, the plaintiff alleged that the city engaged in racially discriminatory housing practices in seeking to block the construction of Parkview Heights, in violation of the Federal Fair Housing Act of 1968.[30] Attempting to draw out a statistical understanding of the structural racism that both plaintiff and defendant agreed existed in regional housing practices on the part of the real-estate industry, as well as agencies of the federal, state, and local governments, the US Attorney went further in alleging that the zoning regulations precipitating incorporation were "motivated by the racial prejudices of its citizens."[31] The Court nonetheless ruled in favor of Black Jack, citing a lack of concrete evidence to support a charge of racial motivation, purpose, or intent in the incorporation of the city. This was in spite of the slippery testimony of a former mayor noting that "in his opinion race was one factor, albeit 'very insignificant' and only in some people."[32] So while the burden of proof of institutional racism proved too high in this case, the powers of incorporation nonetheless allowed and in fact encouraged the recapitulation of economic and racial divisions that mark St. Louis's fragmented periphery.

Thirty-six years later, Black Jack was again the stage where a particular diagram of incorporation, domesticity, and biopower was tested. An unmarried couple and their three children were removed from their own home on the grounds that they were not sufficiently related to satisfy the parameter of "family" as defined by municipal ordinances. This time, at issue was a question of what constitutes the horizon of the domestic unit, and who has the right to live together in the same house. As part of the already notorious zoning regulations outlined above, the city used the powers vested in their corporate charter to define a legitimate family as, among other things, "A group of not more than three (3) persons who need not be related by blood, marriage or adoption."[33] Following a lawsuit brought by the American Civil Liberties Union, the City Council eventually overturned the ruling, allowed the family to return to their home, and changed the city charter—but not before effectively carrying out this exercise in municipal biopower and exclusionary geography.

DISINCORPORATION

While the city has long held a unique and well-recognized position in the political geography of statecraft, a history of the concerted, intentional, and organized dissolution of the city is rarely, if ever, addressed.[34] In the processes of disincorporation, we can see a form of *anti-sovereignty,* an abdication of the authority to govern. While the reasons for dissolution, extinguishment, or termination are various,[35] all evidence an acknowledgement of administrative entropy—an instauration of a lower level of territorial and admin-

28 See Gordon, "Patchwork Metropolis"; Advisory Commission on Intergovernmental Relations, "Metropolitan Organization: The St. Louis Case," (Washington, D.C.: ACIR, 1988); Rolf Pendall, Robert Puentes, and Jonathan Martin. "From Traditional to Reformed: A Review of the Land Use Regulations in the Nation's 50 largest Metropolitan Areas," (Washington, D.C.: The Brookings Institution, 2006); The Missouri Council for a Better Economy, "Better Together: General Administration Study #2: Municipal Structure, Powers, Funding, and Operations," December 2015, accessed December 3, 2016, http://www.bettertogetherstl.com/wp-content/uploads/2015/12/Better-Together-General-Administration-Report-2-FINAL-.pdf.

29 The Ferguson Commission (Mo.), "Forward through Ferguson: a path toward racial equity," October 14, 2015, accessed Dec 3, 2016, http://3680or2khmk3bzkp33juiea1.wpengine.netdna-cdn.com/wp-content/uploads/2015/09/101415_FergusonCommissionReport.pdf.

30 UNITED STATES v. CITY OF BLACK JACK, MISSOURI. No. 71 C 372 (1). 372 F.Supp. 319 (1974).

31 The US Attorney noted the mixed racial make up of St. Louis City proper (approx. 60% white and 40% black at time of incorporation) vis-à-vis Black Jack (approx. 99% white and 1% black at time of incorporation), the concentration of black families in overcrowded or substandard accommodations (40% of black families as compared with 14% of white families), and the potential racialized makeup of those eligible for low-income housing earning less than $10,000 (approx. 80% of black families and 50% of white families) in arguing that the zoning regulations were in fact racially motivated.

32 UNITED STATES v. CITY OF BLACK JACK, MISSOURI. No. 71 C 372 (1). 372 F.Supp. 319 (1974), 325.

33 *Black Jack, Missouri, Code of Ordinances, Appendix C - Zoning, Sec. 030. - Definitions, 03.27: Family. 2006.*

34 Anderson provides a useful, if extremely short, bibliography on the sum total of texts addressing disincorporation. Anderson, "Dissolving Cities," 1366.

35 Anderson notes: "Dissolution can serve many purposes. Yet across this varied terrain, five themes emerge repeatedly: economic collapse, rebellion against taxes, corruption and mismanagement, race, and the link between legal independence and community. Each theme constitutes a hypothesis for why dissolutions do or do not occur, providing a foundation for scholars of law, sociology, urban theory, and political science who turn their attention to dissolution." Anderson, "Dissolving Cities," 1418.

istrative energetics. To disincorporate is to undergo a process of de-specification—a dissolution of a figure into its background—where boundaries, difference, and specificity, are sifted and erased into the background of the county or township.[36]

There are, of course, instructive examples, language, and practices of municipal dissolution that help historicize the explicit administrative and bureaucratic concerns of this essay—cases that fall outside the more common tropes of shrinkage, disaster, or imperial decay. For example, we may turn to the seventeenth-century British pivot in which the Corporate Charter of the City of London was revoked and the city was disincorporated, coming under direct control of the crown. In what has been called "the most important case in English history,"[37] the *quo warranto* taken against the Corporation of London by King Charles II in 1683 asked "by what warrant"—by whose authority—does the city exist? With his sovereignty challenged by the growing economic power of London, the fear expressed in this case was that of the cities becoming "so many commonwealths by themselves,"[38] powerful entities independent from their territorial setting and able to empower an extraterritorial population outside the centralized control of the king. As Frug argues through a recapitulation of Thomas Hobbes, what is at stake in the *quo warranto* proceedings is "the immoderate greatness of a Town,"[39] a growing understanding of the town as a center of popular sovereignty and self-government. And while London's charter was to be reinstated in 1688 with the successes of the Glorious Revolution, the *quo warranto* continues to haunt municipal incorporation law to this day.[40]

More than half of the disincorporations ever recorded in the United States have taken place since 2000, with nearly as many dissolutions as incorporations in that period nationwide.[41] In this present context, legal scholar Michelle Wilde Anderson provides a useful framework for understanding disincorporation by outlining three modalities—passive, involuntary, voluntary—that might be pursued in understanding the practice. Passive disincorporation can be found in fifteen state statutes that allow the state or a receiving county to dissolve a city if its population passes below a minimum threshold, or for failure to elect or appoint municipal officers, levy and collect taxes, or provide basic services. This is a typical ghost town scenario, where the basic charge is that the town has stopped *acting* like a town. While rarely invoked without outside impetus, passive dissolution laws nonetheless acknowledge the municipal lifecycle as immanent to the constitution of the territory.

Involuntary disincorporation, as its name suggests, is the much more contentious practice of a state or county forcing municipal dissolution (or at least initiating disincorporation proceedings) based on factors usually related to chronic mismanagement. Many cases arising in California in recent decades hinge on such arguments, with, for example, a Grand Jury of Santa Barbara County urging the City of Guadalupe to disincorporate, citing a decade of financial mismanagement, a declining tax base, and the city's rising debt obligations.[42] In a hybrid practice combining the inevitability of passive disincorporation with the more politically aggressive practice of involuntary disincorporation, Los Angeles County prosecutors cited a growing pattern of municipal malfeasance when drafting legislation for the automatic disincorporation of cities with fewer than 500 inhabitants and encompassing a territory smaller than ten square miles.[43]

36 "Municipal corporations proper are called into existence, either at the direct solicitation or by the free consent of the persons composing them, for the promotion of their own local and private advantage and convenience... On the other had, Counties are at most but local organizations, which, for the purposes of civil administration, are invested with a few functions characteristic of a corporate existence. They are local sub-divisions of a state, created by the sovereign power of the state, of its own sovereign will, without the particular solicitation, consent, or concurrent action of the people who inhabit them. The former (municipal) organization is asked for, or at least assented to, by the people it embraces; the latter organization (counties) is superimposed by a sovereign and paramount authority." Hamilton County v. Mighels, 7 Ohio St. 109, 1857.

37 Jennifer Levin. The Charter Controversy in the City Of London 1660–1688, and its Consequences. (London: The Athlone Press, 1969), 80.

38 Ibid., 48.

39 Frug, "City as a Legal Concept", 1091.

40 As evidence, in one of the more cited legal cases regarding incorporation in the American context, the Supreme Court found in Meriwether v. Garrett that "The right of the State to repeal the charter of Memphis cannot be questioned. Municipal corporations are mere instrumentalities of the State for the more convenient administration of local government. Their powers are such as the legislature may confer, and these may be enlarged, abridged, or entirely withdrawn at its pleasure." A threat of withdrawal that may come to be known as the great mediatization of Memphis. Meriwether v. Garrett, 102 U.S. 472 (1880) 102 U.S. 472, 26 L. Ed. 197, 1880 U.S. LEXIS 2056.

41 Anderson identifies the number of disincorporations nationwide as at least 130 between 2000 and 2012. "Dissolving Cities," 1366.

42 Matt Hamilton, "Grand Jury Urges Central Coast City of Guadalupe to Dissolve," *Los Angeles Times*, April 14, 2015.

43 Hector Becerra, Sam Allen, and Kim Christensen, "Vernon a Tightly Controlled Fortress," *Los Angeles Times,* September 18, 2010.

Finally, in what is the most common dissolution practice (if still comparatively rare), voluntary disincorporation relies on a local body or voter block to initiate and carry out disincorporation proceedings. In a pattern seen through depopulating medium to small towns across the rural, suburban, and urban spectrum, voluntary disincorporation is often a way for smaller communities to avoid tax increases, attend to infrastructure deterioration, and avoid compounding financial difficulties associated with local municipal offices. As the title of a recent *New York Times* article on the widespread "deorganization" of towns in Maine recently summarized, "local control is a luxury fewer towns can afford."[44] Disincorporation, here, is a preemptory move toward joining what Maine officially calls its Unorganized Territory—toward an administrative assimilation of town and territory.

While the California cases of involuntary disincorporation are particular responses to mismanagement, and the deorganization of small-town Maine points to a growing pattern of depopulation throughout the country, the recent calls for widespread disincorporation in St. Louis County that began this essay are based on a fundamentally different argument. In essence, the motions for disincorporation witnessed in Greater St. Louis cut to the heart of the municipal corporation itself. They argue that there is something intrinsically flawed in the municipal model of incorporation *per se*, citing the ways that in the divided metropolis "new boundaries, created mostly along race and class lines, determine access to education, housing, and basic services, allowing the privilege of exclusion to accompany the privilege of municipal management."[45] So while the Missouri congressional bills for disincorporation do not target Ferguson and its disastrous municipal court system in particular, they do target the effect that dozens of Fergusons have on the St. Louis metro region. In these bills and in the legitimate anger that attends them, we can hear an echo of the *quo warranto*—but here a body politic asking "by what warrant" do these cities have to define whose bodies and what practices matter.

However, what the St. Louis context reminds us, in addition, are the ways we must be attentive to the double exclusioning that disincorporation might inflict. For in the years between the first order suburbs and the massive exurban growth beyond, many of the original, majority-white municipal enclaves have become majority-black—many with African-American leaders in positions of power. So in this recent charge to disincorporate, many of these leaders see yet another move toward the disenfranchisement of black America, and a new challenge to the structures of self-governance that have been so long in the making. Highlighting a pattern of disregard toward St. Louis' African-American community, Mayor Viola Murphy of Cool Valley, Missouri, speaks of the ways "people are making decisions concerning our cities without even having a conversation with any of us before decisions are being made,"[46] an echo and reminder of the many ways marginalized communities can be silenced and disintegrated.

Given the widespread proliferation of incorporated towns giving shape to the fragmented American municipal landscape of the twentieth century, the discourse around the dissolution of cities is all the more startling. Virtually all our theories of city transformation rely on an unquestioned model of growth. Ivan Illich memorably summons our very unfamiliarity with this improbable practice of undoing a city in his invocation of Alberti's boundary furrow:

> Once inaugurated, a city is almost impossible to get rid of. The ideal space of a town cannot be eradicated; it survives the leveling of its walls, the burning of its buildings, and the enslavement of its inhabitants. After Scipio, the Roman general in the Third Punic War of 146 B.C., had desolated Carthage, he had by no means completed its destruction. He had not undone its foundations until Carthage was "plowed under." Its sacred furrow had to be reversed: those clods that in the foundation ritual had been carefully heaped toward the inside had to be returned to the outside.[47]

For it is precisely in these clods—in house setbacks, minimum lot sizes, regulation of how yards are used, and the definition of what constitutes a family–where the social and political stakes of this reversal can be measured.

While disincorporation may, in practice, simply be the first step in a multistage process of annexation and reincorporation, this should not dissuade us from thinking about what disincorporation means, as well as its possible implications. Design has still not developed a meaningful way to work within a non-growth model of being. Design and senescence are, it seems, if not fundamentally at odds, then at least strange bedfellows. In disincorporation, we can see a choreographed withdrawal of the ordering principles that have come to define design in all of its manifestations. Perhaps we can look forward to a discipline of critical, creative geography that can take a more active and projective stance toward (dis)incorporation—to rethink what the *unincorporated urban*, or the *incorporated wilderness*, might mean. Which is to say, a new framing of nonutilitarian, extralegal, and, perhaps, less exclusionary attitudes toward landscapes and territories.

So, in reading the city as a technology of territory, it remains to ask what sort of operations disincorporation performs. Perhaps here, following media theorist Bernhard Siegert, we would do well to remind ourselves that technologies simply house other technologies. As such, the kinds of landscape transformations that disincorporation effects are those at the level of processing bodies and territories. Speed limits change, traffic lights and stop signs disappear, roads are alternately eroded or repaired, and mailboxes change their addresses. And it is perhaps here, in the addressability of subjects—of populations, people, citizens, territorial identities —where the work of disincorporation is most readily felt. For to disincorporate is to find oneself no longer addressable by the same means—to find the territory, once well-defined and divided from its neighbors, softened and withdrawn into the broader contours of its surroundings. With this, we might say, disincorporation brings with it a concrete administrative structure for the withdrawal of concern.

I am grateful to Jesse LeCavalier for this reference and his insightful and committed reading of this essay.

44 Jess Bidgood, "In Maine, Local Control Is a Luxury Fewer Towns Can Afford," *The New York Times*, January 16, 2016.

45 Burns, The Formation of Local American Governments, 117.

46 Jason Rosenbaum, "African-American Mayors are Wary of Push for Municipal Consolidation in St. Louis County," St. Louis Public Radio, January 11, 2015.

47 Ivan Illich, *H2O and the Waters of Forgetfulness* (Berkeley: Heyday Books, 1985), 18.

(Re)Connecting Belfast: Mobility Justice in Divided Cities

Mark Hackett and Ken Sterrett
City Reparo

Much of the analysis of Northern Ireland's governance for the last fifty years has neglected to highlight the damaging effects of the silo mentality of the various departments and agencies. This distinctive bureaucratic culture is understood as part of the legacy of direct rule from Westminster and the ongoing sectarian politics. This article examines the consequences of this culture for Belfast's built environment. It does so, first, by examining the development of the city over the last fifty years; and second, by offering a critical account of the process of planning, designing, and developing a major road scheme in the north of the city, known as the York Street Interchange. As a case study, it attempts to unravel not only the administrative and professional processes, but also, critically, the lost opportunities for the city and particularly for those working-class communities who have suffered most from poor planning and infrastructure decisions.

Throughout this article references are made to the "conflict" and to the ongoing political differences that play out in governance structures and in spatial segregations. A century ago, Belfast was in many respects a global city, but debilitated internally by a parochial contest around ethno-national identity between its two main communities: Protestant (Unionist with Great Britain) and Catholic (Nationalist with the Republic of Ireland). Largely these divisions have sustained and indeed were at the center of the violent conflict that stretched from the late sixties to the mid nineties.

BACKGROUND

The so-called "peace walls" across the Belfast landscape may be the most visible manifestations of division in the city. Indeed, many of these ten to thirty-foot walls or fences that divide mostly working-class residential areas, have become the iconic images of sustained separation between the two conflicted communities. Arguably, it is the visibility of these structures that has prompted the government's initiative TBUC (Together: Building a United Community) for them to be removed by 2022.[1] And yet, when we look at how the spatial environment of Belfast has been manipulated, we can see barriers of other various shapes and forms. Roads, car parks, blighted land, gates, fences, buffer buildings, and other bulwarks all contribute to sustaining a city divided on socio-economic grounds as much as the better known ethno-religious divisions.

The physical configuration of Belfast is similar to other cities in many respects. It nestles in a valley between hills to the west and east; it has a starfish arrangement of radial roads stretching out from the city center; and it has a commercial core that has since expanded along the reclaimed riverfront (the Laganside developments) and into the former shipyard area known as the Titanic Quarter. Both the Laganside and Titanic Quarter regeneration initiatives were modeled after similar waterfront schemes such as the Baltimore Inner Harbor and London Docklands. However, this urban structure needs further analysis and understanding. The city has been planned and designed, at different times during its relatively recent history, to meet what we might call socio-political objectives.

However, in Belfast many of these planning initiatives were undertaken during the period of the conflict, and have, in many respects, contributed to a problematic city layout and urban structure. Many developments in the city were purposefully employed to create barriers between communities in conflict or to manipulate the spatial environment to exclude problematic community areas. Most notably in 1970–71 the planned Belfast Urban Motorway was noted in official minutes as a chance to create a "cordon sanitaire" between the west (and north) of the city and the commercial core.[2] Further examples include two areas in North Belfast which were deliberately planned as "buffer zones" between communities in conflict. The business park on the north side of the main road, Duncairn Gardens, was planned and designed as a built environmental response to a very violent interface between the Catholic New Lodge neighborhood and Protestant Tiger's Bay. A decline in the demand for housing in Tiger's Bay facilitated the demolishing of about two hundred houses, a church, and other commercial premises to be demolished. In their place, a site was created for businesses claiming to be neutral. Similarly, the Hillview Retail Park was planned as a buffer between the Protestant Oldpark and Catholic Oldpark/Ardoyne neighborhoods. Set back off the Crumlin Road with a large gated parking lot, this complex has only served to sterilize neighborhood development in favor of outside car users.

While these and similar initiatives were designed with deliberate political intent, others, such as the many road infrastructure projects, continued to pursue the modernist vision of a city designed for the car. Of course, a number of these also brought beneficial political effects in the form of barriers or buffer zones. However, a core issue that permeated a range of spatial reconfigurations was the protection, enhancement, and fortification of the central commercial city. As urban commentators Frank Gaffikin and Mike Morrissey note, this modernization was part of a wider initiative to prepare the regional environment for new inward investment following the weakening of the traditional industrial base after World War II.[3] This started in the late 1960s and early 1970s with an elevated urban motorway proposal, which was downgraded to the Westlink, and then purposefully developed in the 1980s as a strategy to help create a vibrant commercial core and cut off troublesome West Belfast.[4] The decanting

1. Northern Ireland Executive Office, Together: Building a United Community Strategy, May 23, 2015, https://www.executiveoffice-ni.gov.uk/publications/together-building-united-community-strategy.
2. Tim Cunningham, "Cutting with the Grain: Human Rights, Conflict Transformation and the Urban Planning System—Lessons from Northern Ireland, *Human Rights Review* 17, no. 3 (September 2016): 329–47.
3. Frank Gaffikin and Mike Morrissey, "Planning in Divided Cities; collaborative shaping of contested cities," Wiley-Blackwell, 2011.

4. Cunningham, "Cutting with the Grain."
5. Building Design Partnership with Travers Morgan and Partners, *City of Belfast: Planning Aspects of the Belfast Urban Motorway* (Belfast: Building Design Partnership, 1968), 18.
6. Belfast City Council, Belfast Masterplan 2004, http://www.belfastcity.gov.uk/buildingcontrol-environment/regeneration/belfastmasterplan.aspx.
7. Belfast City Council, "Local Development Plan, 2020-2035, Topic Paper: Transportation," accessed February 2, 2017, http://www.belfastcity.gov.uk/nmsruntime/saveasdialog.aspx?lID=20507&sID=18628.
8. Northern Ireland Assembly, Research and Information Briefing Paper. Des McKibben, "Transport governance and the management of car dependency in Belfast," 2011.
9. Rowland Atkinson and John Flint, "Fortress UK? Gated Communities, the Spatial Revolt of the Elites and Time-Space Trajectories of Segregation," *Housing Studies* 19, no. 6 (2004): 875–92.
10. Planning for Spatial Reconciliation Research Group, *Making Space for Each Other: Civic Place-Making in a Divided Society*, (Belfast: Queen's University Belfast, 2016), 44.

of civil servants from suburban locations to offices in the city center together with massive subsidies to new commercial developments created a retail recovery during the late 1980s into the 1990s, as well as the symbolism of defiance against the Irish Republican Army (IRA) bombing campaign. A ring of temporary security barriers including pedestrian control, known as the "ring of steel," from the early 1970's to the mid 1990's, also helped to protect the core commercial city from bombs and incendiary devices.

This deliberate strategy of creating a protected node of commercial activity was further supported by a range of developments that reinforced the insularity of the center. These include buildings, such as the downtown shopping center Castle Court that turns its back to North and West Belfast; the Gasworks that has been renovated into a corporate campus and sealed off from adjacent working-class neighborhoods, such as the Markets, Lower Ormeau, and Donegall Pass; and, of course, the new quarters of Laganside and the Titanic Quarter, which are socially and physically detached from the historically residential areas the of city.

Previously a densely populated inner-city with shop-lined arterial routes, the center now depends on car commuters for commercial viability. This, in turn, has created a need for cheap car parking and a supportive road network. Of course, the expectation in the 1960s was that everyone would aspire to be a car owner; consequently, investment in public transport was less important. In the original reports on the new road transport proposals by consultants Building Design Partnership and Travers Morgan, even the aesthetics of the proposed motorway experience were considered: "In the twilight areas 'facial cosmetics' of buildings beside the motorway which are left may be necessary so that a good front is presented to the motorway."[5] To complement this, car parking was to become a major feature for the new modern city. The contemporary spatial result is a core city effectively disconnected from the surrounding inner-city neighborhoods but highly connected for the 100,000+ car commuters who enter the city every day.[6]

This commuting culture can be traced back to the development of Belfast's suburbs and the surrounding satellite towns, particularly during the 1970s when the conflict was at its most intense. At its peak in 1951, Belfast had a population of 444,000. By 2011 it had shrunk to around 281,000, with much of this loss due to Protestants moving out of the city to suburban locations. A recent publication by Belfast City Council offers some recognition of past mistakes: "Belfast is a city that has historically been dependent on the private car and the streetscape has evolved to cater to these demands, resulting in road infrastructure that is oversized, overcomplicated and a barrier to non-motorised accessibility."[7] Indeed, Belfast is now regarded as being "the third most congested city in Great Britain and the tenth most congested in Europe."[8]

The devastation of the inner-city through the remodeling of urban space for the car had a major impact on most of the inner North Belfast, which is now isolated from an nascent vibrant core. The historical grid layout that characterized Belfast's inner-city since the nineteenth century connected neighborhood streets to the main arterial thoroughfares and to the city center. These thoroughfares which acted as spokes from the central core were significantly disrupted by the Westlink and "inner box" roads which effectively formed a wide ring road around the core. In consequence, many buildings and existing street fabric was cleared to form a sea of fractured developments and spaces. All of this affected the general mobility of communities and reinforced their isolation, both physically and psychologically, from the rest of the city. This breakdown in the structure and layout of the inner-city and the spatial privilege given to the car had widespread consequences, particularly for communities with low car ownership rates.

Indeed, it is possible to track two distinctive patterns of movement within the city. One, referred to as "urban bubbling" by Rowland Atkinson and John Flint, captures the way in which the middle classes use the entire city and its environment as their neighborhood.[9] The key to this level of access is the car—or metaphorically, "the bubble." Working, shopping, pursuing leisure, and so on throughout the city is very much the middle-class lifestyle. For working-class neighborhoods, on the other hand, movement is largely limited to walking and public transport. Local facilities are therefore more important, as are safe walking environments that allow access to other parts of the city. However, in inner-city Belfast there is a double bind.

First, working-class communities are largely territorialized. In 2011, 56 percent of the population in Belfast lived in a single-identity neighborhood—a neighborhood that was at least 70 percent Protestant or Catholic.[10] During the conflict, these single-identity communities became very insular and self-reliant. While this offered a degree of safety and protection, it also reduced contact with the rest of the city and between communities. Moreover, out of necessity at the time, new facilities, such as leisure centers, health centers, grocery stores, and post offices were often located in the heart of a community area, which inevitably excluded their use by others.

Fig 1. Map illustrating areas of high deprivation in darker gray tones. Note that highest levels of deprivation are on the west and north sides of the city center. Deprivation indicators include income, employments, health and disability, education, skills and training, proximity to services, living environment, crime and disorder. Data is based on the Northern Ireland Multiple Deprivation Measure from the 2010 Census.

11. Jörg Plöger, *Belfast City Report*, Centre for Analysis of Social Exclusion (2007), 16.
12. Ralf Brand, "Written and Unwritten Building Conventions in a Contested City: The Case of Belfast," *Urban Studies* 46, no. 12 (November 2009): 2669–89.
13. Jane Jacobs, *The Death and Life of Great American Cities* (New York: Modern Library, New York, 1993), 146–52.
14. The Forum was a not-for-profit organisation that campaigned for a better and more equitable built environment in Belfast. It was launched in June 2009 by a group of architects, planners, and others who came together to explore alternative ways to develop the city. The Forum ended in July 2015 and was, in part, replaced by City Reparo.

Undoubtedly, the remodeled layout of the physical environment undertaken during the housing redevelopment schemes of the 1970s and 1980s helped to reinforce this insularity. The traditional grid street pattern offered permeability, which facilitated wider social interactions and connections to services and employment. In contrast, much inner-city redevelopment employed "defensive planning," with cul-de-sac layouts that lowered densities and reduced connectivity. The cul-de-sac layout was initially developed in the late 1970s and early 1980s for a new suburban Catholic housing neighborhood in the west of the city known as Poleglass, but was then imported into inner-city redevelopment projects on both sides of the sectarian divide. The overall process saw the loss of over 55 percent of the inner city's population.[11]

Second, it is also important to note that patterns of movement in Belfast have a certain peculiarity, particularly in and around segregated residential areas. An ongoing legacy of the conflict is what might be termed an "inbuilt psyche" of knowing how to traverse the city.[12] In the north and west of the city, for example, many pedestrian spaces along the arterial routes are still almost exclusively used by one community or the other. While this sensitivity to community geography is also evident in how communities use public transport, it does not overly affect the behavior of commuting car traffic. Of course, the real and psychological constraints of territory, and how this plays out in terms of movement and access, is made worse by this car-dominated environment, which not only favors the middle class, but also allows all car owners to largely avoid any interaction with communities or territory perceived as other.

While community territory is an important dimension of the inner-city geography of Belfast, it is also significant that many of these communities, irrespective of political or religious hue, share similar problems and characteristics, such as high levels of deprivation and marginalization from the wider city. Within the inner-city's working-class areas, both communities, Catholic and Protestant, have very limited access to private cars. Relative mobility and access to urban amenities are, therefore, significantly differentiated on a socioeconomic basis. While the residents of the inner-city ethno-religious territories continue to live in tension with each other, the middle classes of both political hues can, and do, use the wider city, but they do so in Belfast by largely using private car transport. Until relatively recently, there were very few middle-class citizens living in the inner or core city. However, a small number of mostly gated private apartment developments have been built that cater for singles and couples, which further illustrates socio-economic divisions.

While the comfort of territory has been important for communities, it should not distract from the need, in this post-violent conflict time, to open up the city to local neighborhoods and to encourage the development of a shared urban environment. In the early 1960s, Jane Jacobs was making a similar point about American cities. She argued that the notion of neighborhood was a somewhat sentimental concept that was ultimately "harmful to city planning." For her, the city is the neighborhood, offering its citizens "wide choice and rich opportunities... Whatever city neighborhoods may be, or may not be, and whatever usefulness they may have, or may be coaxed into having, their qualities cannot work at cross-purposes to thoroughgoing city mobility and fluidity of use, without economically weakening the city of which they are a part."[13]

In Belfast, the "city mobility and fluidity" has been severely undermined by urban blight associated with the restructuring and widening of the city roads and the housing redevelopment outlined above. Notably a wide space of vacant sites lie in a doughnut-shaped zone around the city core. These mainly commercial sites have never been redeveloped once the associated hinterlands of housing were cleared and ring roads were widened. In 2009–10, our organization formerly called the Forum for Alternative Belfast (the Forum), captured the extent of vacant lots in a publication named the "Missing City Map." The title was coined after noting that the extent of these fragmented vacant sites, if brought together, would approximate the area of the city's entire current commercial core—these sites were a part of the city that had essentially gone missing (Fig 10).[14]

In 2011 the city was mapped again, this time concentrating on the land dedicated to commuter and regional car access around the core along with its associated car parking space. Mapped in these terms, a doughnut of urban motorway, blighted sites, and car parks becomes more explicit as a perimeter zone around the core. The Forum emphasized the impact these shatter-zones had on pedestrian access to the central city. Moreover, these vacancies led formerly active streets to become dead with building frontage-free roads devoid of the qualities needed to sustain urban walking. Not only are inner-city neighborhoods dislocated from the economic center and its services, but so are the outer areas of the city, doubly cut off from walking and cycling into and through the city. Viewed objectively and, indeed, quantifiably, these maps document the primary barriers to people traversing the city. And yet today, three decades after their implementation, these zones are not questioned by many who now wholly accept the dominance of the car in the city, its inevitability and desirability from an socio-economic perspective. In Belfast the overriding socio-economic division has arguably surpassed the older ethnic divisions, and yet the city seems more able to discuss the latter rather than the more obvious issue of where efforts and regeneration should be targeted, namely re-stitching

Fig 2. These so-called "peacelines" were built throughout city neighborhoods as "protection" barriers between the two ethno-religious communities. Photograph by author.

15. Department of the Environment Northern Ireland, *Draft Belfast Metropolitan Area Plan* (Belfast: Department of the Environment), 2004.
16. Belfast City Council, Belfast City Centre Regeneration and Investment Strategy, 2015, accessed March 1, 2017, http://www.belfastcity.gov.uk/buildingcontrol-environment/regeneration/Regenerationandinvestmentplan.aspx.
17. Heather Smith, "Even Detroit is Hatin' on Freeways Now," *Grist*, January 9, 2015.
18. Conflict in Cities and the Contested State, "Briefing Paper 2: Rethinking Conflict Infrastructure: How the Built Environment Sustains Divisions in Contested Cities," 2012, 1, http://www.urbanconflicts.arct.cam.ac.uk/downloads/briefing-paper-2.

the city core to its arterial routes, and reconnecting the working-class neighborhoods to the wider city.

CONNECTIVITY AND EXCLUSION

Belfast city center, the Queen's University campus, Laganside, and the Titanic Quarter provide a range of services and facilities that are at the heart of the city's economy. Indeed, this is recognized in the Belfast Metropolitan Area Plan, which states that "the promotion of Belfast City Centre and the development opportunities within the Belfast Harbour will support the provision of new job opportunities in central locations accessible to all sections of the community."[15] Moreover, much of the planning and regeneration emphasis over the last thirty years has been on these areas because they function as neutral, if not shared, spaces. However, many of these areas are not socio-economically inclusive and are often seen by working class communities as inaccessible and unwelcoming. There is no doubt that, at least in part, this is because these neutral spaces and events are consumption-oriented. Genuine civic spaces that offer public amenity are very limited in number and in scope.

All of this suggests that facilitating direct and pedestrian-friendly access to key areas of the city should be a planning and regeneration priority. Promoting connectivity and accessibility has not been a priority of the planning and regeneration projects in Belfast. Rather, single function planning and single site-focused investment has largely ignored the broader spatial and social needs of the city. The underpinning assumption, explicitly mentioned in the current Belfast City Centre Regeneration Strategy, is that the private market will generate activity and, in turn, that activity will bring economic benefit to the city.[16] However, this scenario implies that if new educational and vocational training facilities exist in the Titanic Quarter or if job opportunities are available in Laganside, then it is up to individuals to overcome any issues of access. In other words, the focus is on the individual rather than on any collective concerns.

Prioritizing collective needs is especially critical in a context where exclusive ethnic and social-class space often triumphs over the civic. Rather, every major development decision contributes to the future of the city, both economically and socially. Successful city form is not only created through aesthetics; the outcome of good urban design is a place that everyone can share and access. A key question for city planners, therefore, is how all major development proposals can respond to and address the fractured and divided city. Moreover, prioritizing a re-stitching agenda would allow the development of a vision for the city that recognizes that spatial fracture and disconnection help sustain social and ethno-religious fracture and disconnection.

While acknowledging that dysfunctional city form and structure is only one dimension of a deeper set of problems, it is, nevertheless, a significant issue. Creating the potential for shared space and services requires thoughtful street design and layout; it requires walkable, safe, and interesting connections. New or revitalized streets can offer opportunities to locate services that can be accessed by both sides of the community and all classes. The perceived neutrality of the city center has the potential to be expanded along arterial routes and connecting streets. Not only might this improve the neighborhoods, but it might also help the city center become more socioeconomically inclusive.

The harmfulness that major ring roads cause to social and economic activities is not particular to Belfast. On an international level, there is growing recognition of the role that infrastructure can play in cementing division. In the United States, for example, Detroit's mayor, Mike Duggan, acknowledged that the freeways that encircle the Detroit metropolitan area have had a negative impact on the city and have contributed significantly to Detroit's steep economic decline. In his view, "Freeways cut off and isolate neighborhoods. We are still trying to recover from that."[17] Similarly, in the United Kingdom, a major Economic and Social Research Council (ESRC) project, Conflict in Cities and the Contested State, concluded in 2012 that social and political divisions can be exacerbated by a range of long term physical barriers:

> Walls, buffer zones, checkpoints, urban enclaves, and even large roads, tramways and motorways — continue to play a major role in dividing cities… Mobility, or lack of it, is often used as a tool of conflict. Interventions in the physical environment can overtly further the interests of certain groups, whilst seemingly well-intentioned and apparently benign encroachments on the landscape can create or sustain inequalities in ways that are hard to reverse.[18]

This raises a number of key questions:

- How can Belfast's urban structure be redesigned, repaired, and managed to create a more accessible city for those communities who largely depend on public transport and walking?
- How does the structure and layout of roads affect the potential of creating a more connected and shared city?
- How can all of this be delivered in the context of a political administrative culture characterized by separate silos of responsibility?

CASE STUDY: YORK STREET INTERCHANGE

In 2010 the Forum for Alternative Belfast focused its Summer School on inner North Belfast, and more specifically, on a major proposed road interchange for the

Fig 3. The Westlink cuts dramatically through the city.

The connected terrace streets of the 1965 map were comprehensively redeveloped into isolating cul-de-sacs which further reinforce the perception and creation of urban ghettos.

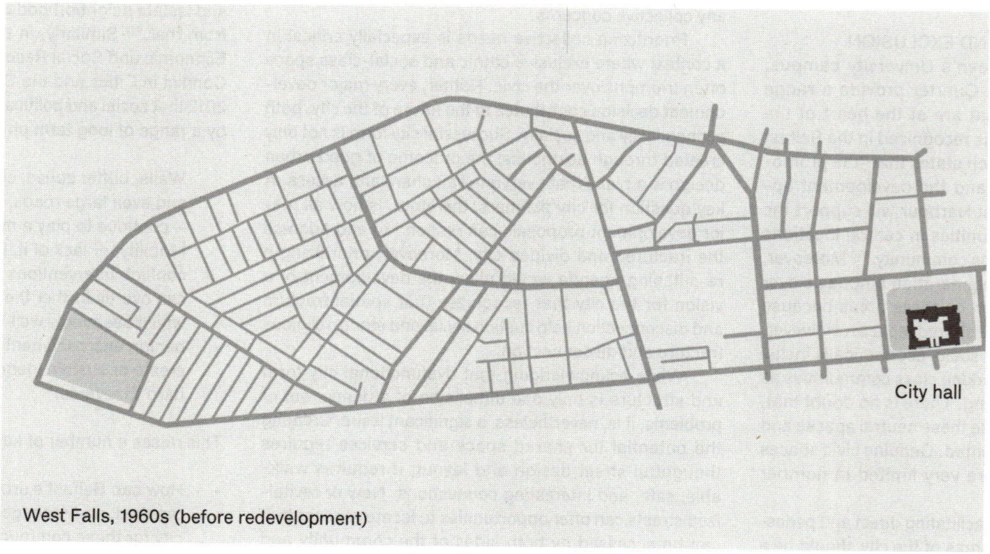

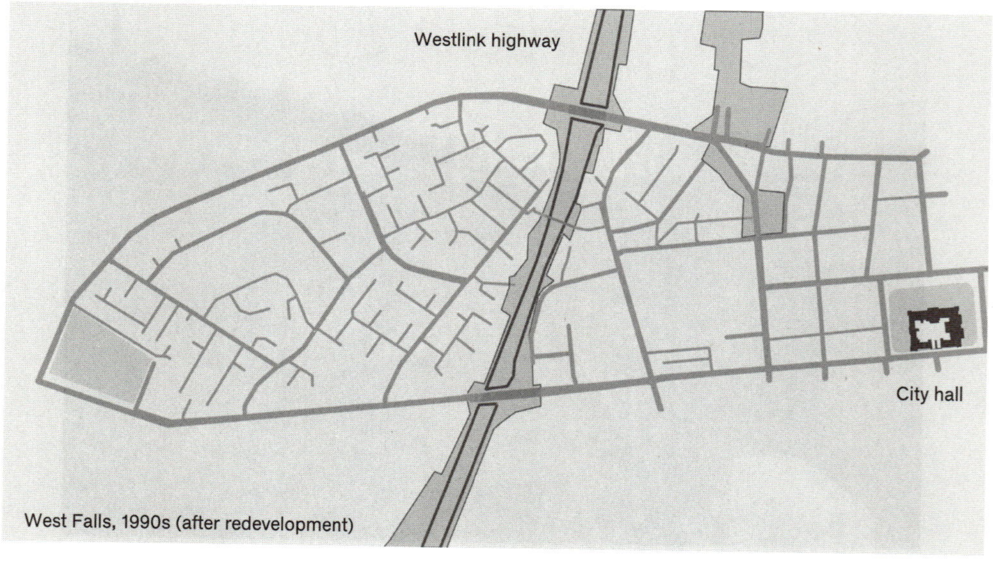

Fig 4a and 4b. These maps indicate the west side of the city from City Hall to Falls Road and Grosvenor Road. The motorway was built to create a 'cordon sanitaire' to separate the west and north of the city, the sectors which also suffer high deprivation compared to the south and east.

Fig 5. The Westlink as it passes Falls Road, West Belfast. The Roads Department neglects the blighted zones they created, the right side is maintained by the NIHE and City Council.

Westlink motorway, known as the York Street Interchange (YSI). The proposal was to create an interchange on the northern section of the network that would allow an uninterrupted flow of regional and national traffic along the south-to-north corridor within the city and with the M3 motorway, which connects to the eastern suburbs of Belfast. Together with the already implemented road schemes in the area, this proposal, particularly its footprint, would effectively destroy the existing street pattern and create even more barriers for pedestrian movement to and from inner North Belfast.

It is important to note that inner North Belfast has a high concentration of the most deprived communities in Belfast, both Catholic and Protestant. It also has the highest number of peace lines or interfaces in the city; its geography is often described as a patchwork of territories.

In addition to the York Street Interchange, there were a number of other developments planned for the north side of the city center. These included a new Ulster University campus, a number of student housing schemes, and two major mixed-use regeneration developments, City Quays and Royal Exchange (forthcoming).[19] Responsibility for these extended across five government departments, and there was little or no evidence of any coordination.

In this context, it is also significant that inner North Belfast is geographically positioned to connect to many economic opportunities. A North Belfast study by Queen's University students showed that the city center and the Titanic Quarter were, potentially, within five to ten minutes walking distance of Duncairn Gardens, in the heart of inner North Belfast.[20] However, the route to the city center is frustrated by road barriers and poor quality frontage environments, and the route to the Titanic Quarter is circuitous by both bus and walking.

The Forum's 2010 Summer School brought together a range of groups from both local community organizations and government agencies. The Summer School also engaged with the road engineers who were overseeing the engineering solutions for the interchange. The geographical boundaries for the project were loosely agreed upon with local communities to allow scope for creative outcomes. While accepting that the interchange would, at some stage, be implemented, the overriding aim was to explore opportunities for how the overall urban design scheme could be used to meet the needs of disconnected local communities.

During discussions and research, a number of more specific objectives emerged. First, the issue of disconnection had to be addressed. The participants examined ways to connect inner North Belfast to the city's nearby sites of employment and services such as the city center and Titanic Quarter. It was also crucially important that such connections would be pedestrian-friendly. Second, the issue of vacant land in the fracture zone had to be addressed. This was particularly important for local communities who needed land for housing and who were fearful about the impact that an impending new Ulster University campus in the north city center would have on the local housing land supply. At the time of writing, the development of the new campus is underway. Tall blocks of student housing associated with it are causing some consternation with local communities. In anticipation of this, the Summer School's objective was to identify what land would be available for a range of developments, including residential components.

The outcome of the Summer School's investigation was a scheme titled the "Six Links." As illustrated, the road interchange at the center of the proposed York Street Interchange was enclosed by a number of building blocks that have dual design functions. On the one hand, they help reduce the visual impact of the road interchange, while on the other, they contribute to the recreation of street structure on the west, north, and east.

Three key links are created on a west-east basis. The most northerly link connects the street known as Duncairn Gardens, across the river via a new bridge to the Titanic Quarter. Duncairn Gardens is effectively an interface between the Catholic New Lodge to the south and the Protestant Tiger's Bay to the north. This tree-lined street was the site of intense violence during the conflict, but is now gradually assuming a more peaceful role, connecting both communities to a shopping center at its eastern end. The second link also reinforces the possibility of connecting to the Titanic Quarter but additionally creates a potential corridor for the new University of Ulster campus. A third west-east link is a cultural corridor stretching from the now closed and historic prison, Crumlin Road Gaol, to an area it the city center known as Cathedral Quarter. This corridor would help connect local historic landmarks to the emerging cultural hub of the city around St Anne's Cathedral.

The north-south links are an attempt to reinstall, and indeed strengthen, the historic street structure. New buildings along the frontages would help create urban streets replete with pedestrian space and, where possible, animated ground floors. Overall, the framework is an attempt to repair the broken structure of this part of the city—but it goes beyond this, to connect the disadvantaged communities of inner North Belfast to the employment and education facilities being developed in the Titanic Quarter. In addition, it identifies a range of sites that can offer space for new housing as well as other compatible uses.

19. City Quays master plan by Grimshaw is intended to connect the Titanic Quarter back to the city center, see: "Planning application lodged for City Quays," October 21, 2011, Belfast Harbour News, accessed April 15, 2017, https://www.belfast-harbour.co.uk/news/planning-application-lodged-for-city-quays-42. Royal Exchange is a proposed twelve-acre mixed-use "shopping village." John Mulgrew, "Royal Exchange plans revealed for Belfast project," *Belfast Telegraph*, August 26, 2016, accessed December 12, 2016, http://www.belfasttelegraph.co.uk/business/news/royal-exchange-plans-revealed-for-belfast-project-34993186.html.
20. Queen's University Belfast, "North Belfast Report" (MSc Urban Design and Spatial Regeneration, School of Planning, Architecture & Civil Engineering, 2014).

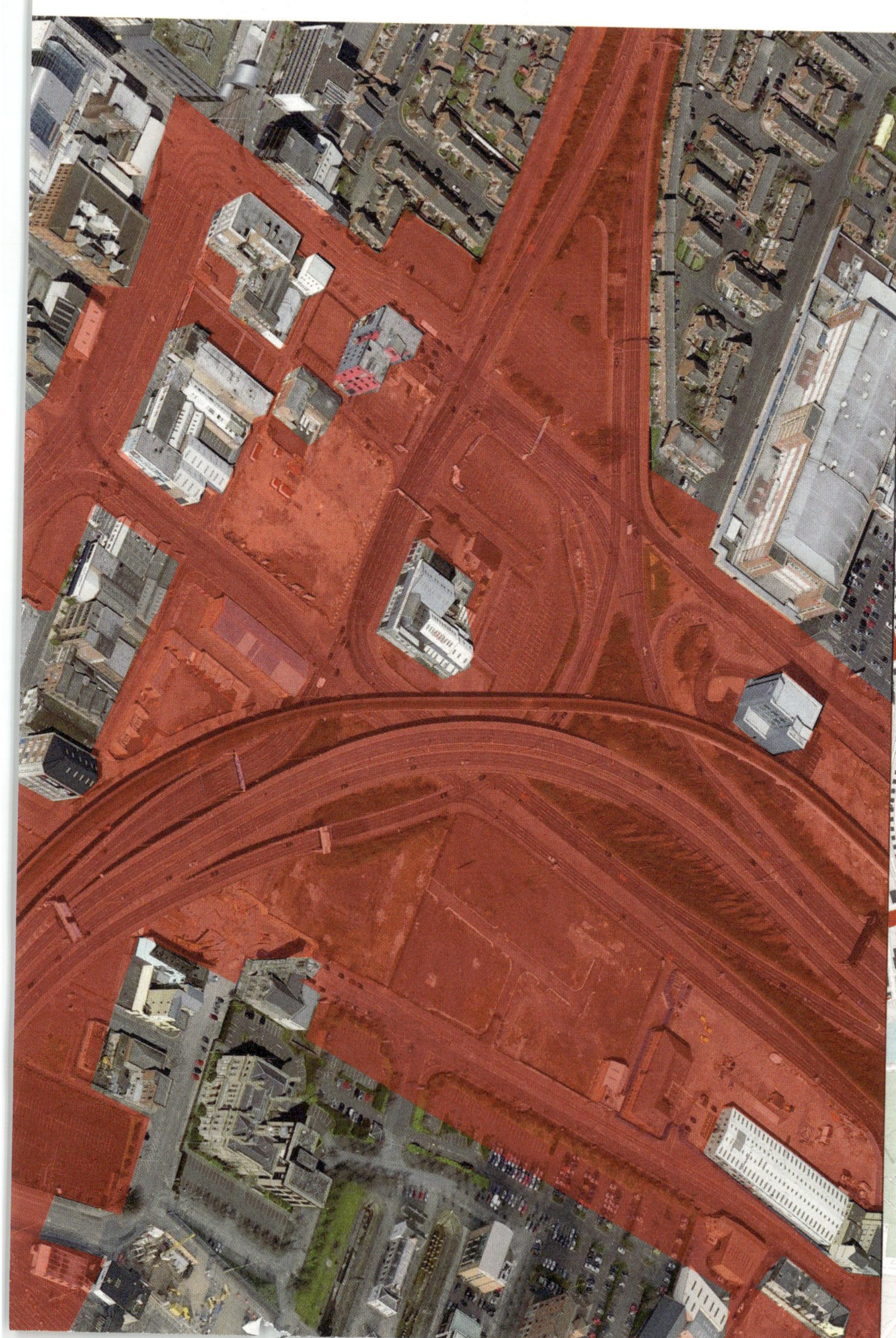

Fig 11. "Shatterzones" of urban blight by the longrunning construction of the urban motorway. First planned in the 1960s, this junction at York Street to the North of the city core will not be complete before 2023 causing over half a century of development uncertainty. The large zone is difficult to traverse by pedestrians and effectively creates a cordon sanitaire to exclude North and West Belfast.

Fig 10. The Missing City (2009). This map was produced by the Forum for Alternative Belfast to illustrate comprehensively the vacant land and development sites around the city core.

21. Wesley Johnston, "Northern Ireland Roads Site," accessed March 1, 2017, http://www.wesleyjohnston.com/roads/m2m3westlink.html.
22. Alex Lord, Phil O'Brien, Olivier Sykes, and John Sturzaker, "Planning as 'Market Maker': How Planning is Used to Stimulate Development in Germany, France and the Netherlands" *RTPI Research Report* no. 11 (November 2015).

The Six Links proposal was formally launched in May 2011. Following this, the Forum worked with local community activists in presenting the material to a wider set of community players. In addition, the Forum met with the Minister for the Environment, Belfast City Council, and senior officials in other government departments. The Minister for the Environment then convened a joint ministerial meeting to look at cooperation around a number of inner north projects, including the Six Links. In turn, this led the Forum to organize a Winter School involving all the key stakeholders, including local communities and government departments.

The argument the Forum presented is that economic, social, and physical design benefits can come from a more coordinated, holistic, and coherent approach to the development of inner north Belfast. More specifically, it pointed out that traditional practices would typically see roads, regeneration initiatives, and urban planning as separate and unrelated endeavours without explicit social purpose for disadvantaged communities. At the heart of this argument is the need to see roads and streets as public places in their own right.

While the arguments and alternative design solutions were winning over local communities and other built environment activists, the bulwark of silo governance still prevailed. A preliminary set of four options, published in 2009 by the Department for Regional Development, exclusively focused on road engineering solutions.[21] It was in this context that Forum pressed a version of the Six Links proposal that incorporated an underpass solution.

Efforts successfully persuaded the Department for Regional Development to select this option and then set up an advisory group known as the Strategic Advisory Group (SAG). However, the brief for SAG was limited to some aspects of the aesthetics and offered only a minimal urban remit to oversee the development of the proposal as it moved towards a public inquiry. Moreover, it was evident during the SAG meetings that a fairly passive, non-interventionist approach to urban development opportunities was observed by the other participating government departments as well as the City Council.

All major planning and road schemes are required by legislation to be examined at a public inquiry where objectors and others can contribute their views on the published proposals. The public inquiry was held in November 2015. City Reparo presented alternative designs that met the needs of both the regional roads scheme and the local re-stitching objectives. Moreover, Reparo's research demonstrated that much of the leftover land was publicly owned and that their scheme could have a substantial financial return, while also reducing overall costs, currently estimated to be £165m.

OVERALL REFLECTIONS

At the time of writing, the first stage of the York Street Interchange has gone out to tender for a first detailed design phase. This was the scheme presented and defended by the government at the public inquiry. The Brexit vote of June 2016 has brought another development; a large portion of the project required European funds, and it is likely these may not be fully secured by the central UK government. The current minister favors other projects for road building to connect the neglected west of Northern Ireland. In this context, there is some opportunity for reflection. City Reparo continues to lobby the new political administration to consider the social, physical, and financial value of its alternative scheme.

In many respects the York Street Interchange case study captures and expresses a wider set of issues that relate to the legacy of silo governance. This confirms the view held by many that the lack of coordination between government departments and agencies has had a detrimental impact on planning and regeneration. In April 2015 local government in Northern Ireland was reorganized. Twenty-six local councils were reconfigured into eleven and given additional powers. There is some hope that this shift of responsibilities to the eleven new local authorities may bring some possibility of dealing with this, at least in part. Spatial planning as a local government responsibility can become a key mechanism for better coordination. However, a number of key services, such as housing, regeneration, education, health, and transport will remain the responsibility of the central government.

Belfast City Council has the authority and agency to achieve positive change in the city, but some fundamental bureaucratic changes in project implementation must take place first. Developers, including public sector agencies, need to have in place the confidence of a planned context. This includes a coordination agency such as the City Council. There is growing evidence that a more proactive form of planning can induce developer confidence and achieve significant socioeconomic outcomes.[22]

At present a local development plan is being prepared for the city by the City Council. This is the first time since the 1960s that the council will have the opportunity to shape its own city. City Reparo has urged the planners and the councillors to prioritize the re-stitching of the city; in other words, to fix a city broken and fragmented by road infrastructure, surface car parks, derelict sites, and so-called peace walls. An important part of City Reparo's vision is to repopulate the inner and central city. Breaking down barriers and reconnecting the city would facilitate this and help integrate the inner-city working-class neighborhoods into of the city. At the City Council level, it is difficult to promote the civic over the ethnic. And yet this is what the city needs to do in shaping its future. A local phrase used to describe the current situation refers to a "shared out future," rather than a "shared future."

Fig 6. An example of inner-city housing after redevelopment in 1970-90s. Its design as low density, often in cul-de-sacs with back-to-front layouts, entrenches isolation and division.

Fig 8. Travers Morgan and Building Design Partnership (BDP) plan in 1967, illustrating the range of urban motorway options being considered. R. Travers Morgan & Partners (NI) for Ministry of Development Belfast Corporation, *Report on Belfast Urban Motorway* (Belfast: Belfast Corporation, 1967), 46.

Fig 9. The proposed urban motorway plan overlaid on the existing city, reproduced (with notations by author) from *The Rape and Plunder of the Shankill* by Ron Weiner (Belfast: Notaems Press, 1975).

Fig 14. Sketch view from 2010 of the Six Links proposal with a new square in the foreground and bridges connecting North Belfast to East Belfast and the Titanic Quarter.

Fig 13. A plan of the Six Links proposal shows new connections from North Belfast to the city center to the south and to the Titanic Quarter across the water to the east.

Fig 7a and 7b. These sketch maps imagine the city trajectory unless comprehensive efforts are made to restitch the city.

The first map indicates residential neighborhoods with their original arterial streets largely broken as they pass through "shatterzones" of empty or incoherent city fabric created by road engineering. One connection exists leading south from the city core which remains largely unpopulated and is seen as a utility space for shopping and office use, but rarely as a civic or connected center for residents.

The second map indicates mixed-use development remaking urban arterial routes and stitching the core into the residential areas. The multiplier effect of repaired walkable connections allows vitality and commerce to grow—a new vision for a connected city.

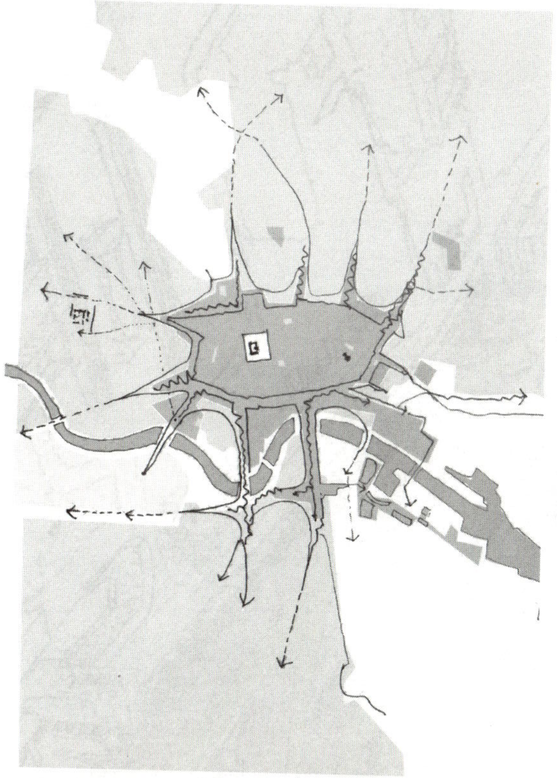

Figs 12a and 12b. These figure-gound maps show North Belfast in 1965 and 2000. They indicate the loss of density and connective street fabric caused by the motorways and rehousing at low density.

W A T E R C R A F T :

DETROIT WATER INFRASTRUCTURE AND ITS PROTOCOLS OF SPRAWL AND DISPLACEMENT

BY MITCH MCEWEN

The state of Michigan surrounds the Great Lakes, the largest surface freshwater system on the planet, spanning 94,000 square miles of surface freshwater.[1] After Chicago and Toronto, Detroit is the third largest metropolitan area of the Great Lakes megaregion. Yet, since 2014, over 50,000 households in Detroit have had their water service shut off by Detroit's Water and Sewerage Department (DWSD).[2] Detroit residents, within miles of the largest freshwater system on earth, are denied access to running water. This article investigates how this paradox operates as a mode of infrastructure management and how, since the 1940s, the growth of regionally managed water filtration and centralized sewage infrastructure has enabled and subsidized the sprawl of the suburbs.[3]

This article traces the protocols of water and sewage infrastructure—and the consequent forms of citizenship and displacement—along the divide of Detroit and its suburbs. While the article delves into municipal infrastructure pricing, federal environmental policy, regional planning, and infrastructure financing, the disciplines of architecture and urban design remain crucial. It is through architecture that we can make comparisons of urban water management to other spatial patterns. These patterns include slum clearance, highway expansion and subsidizing of the American suburban house. Also relevant are the concepts in service of these operations (such as blight) and the effects of information technologies on land-use and spatial practices. This analysis hopes to open up a more nuanced discourse around urban housing, infrastructure, and precarity—beyond the staid binaries of formal/informal and developed/developing.

The Detroit system intake of freshwater has not changed much in over one hundred years. Two out of the three current system intakes were active by the end of the 19th century. Not surprisingly, these nodes of infrastructure still work completely fine, given that they effectively have unlimited access to eighteen percent of the world's surface freshwater.[4] What has changed, and is still changing, is the system's processing of sewage. The functions of intake and sewage processing are coupled together for disciplinary, bureaucratic, and historical reasons. The coupling enables the co-allocation and co-management of a set of infrastructure practices.

The cost for Southeast Michigan's regional water and sewage infrastructure, as it cuts through and moves under various boundaries of governance and property, is not paid for by any form of taxes, municipal budget, or ongoing infrastructure fund. The revenue model of a private company with individual customer accounts (for Detroit) and wholesale accounts (for suburban counties) was baked into this infrastructure from the height of its suburban expansion.[5] The pricing runs counter to the reality that sewage processing becomes inseparable from drainage for much of the network. In the past five years, this private user model of financing and its failure to meet system costs has become the justification for shutting off water to tens of thousands of Detroit residents—an operation that many consider a twenty-first-century version of slum clearance.

These water shutoff procedures and their enabling algorithms of pricing and payment generate an instance of the contemporary urban divide. This divide is no longer one of borders. The suburb/inner city distinction continues to generate socioeconomic effects, but its effects do not coalesce in the same mid-twentieth-century pattern of center and periphery.[6] In Detroit we see the emergence of infrastructure and resource management to accompany this new divide, a new spatial order within the city. I call this new infrastructure logic *watercraft*, building off of Keller Easterling's notion of *extrastatecraft*.[7] Like *extrastatecraft*, *watercraft* is beyond the governance of statecraft; it is the management of privatizing and re-spatializing

1 *The Great Lakes: An Environmental Atlas and Resource Book*, 3rd ed. (Toronto: Government of Canada, 1995), 3.

2 Joel Kurth, "Detroit Hits Residents on Water Shut-offs as Businesses Slide," *Detroit News*, April 1, 2016, accessed October 1, 2016, http://www.detroitnews.com/story/news/local/detroit-city/2016/03/31/detroit-water-shutoffs/82497496/.

3 In the case of Detroit, the water infrastructure has been managed by a series of boards and departments, culminating recently with the post-bankruptcy lease of Detroit Water and Sewerage Department assets to the regional Great Lakes Water Authority.

4 *The Great Lakes*, 3.

5 Early managers of DWSD lobbied for expansion of system into the suburbs in order to lower overhead costs; see Detroit Water and Sewerage Department, "In the Spotlight – Remus' vision created today's Detroit Water System." *In the Flow* 9, no. 2 (2009), accessed October 15, 2009, http://www.dwsd.org/downloads_n/announcements/in_the_flow/itf_2009/InTheFlow_spring_2009.pdf.

6 See Gerald D. Suttles, *The Social Order of the Slum: Ethnicity and Territory in the Inner City* (Chicago: University of Chicago Press, 1968).

7 Keller Easterling, *Extrastatecraft: The Power of Infrastructure Space* (London: Verso, 2014).

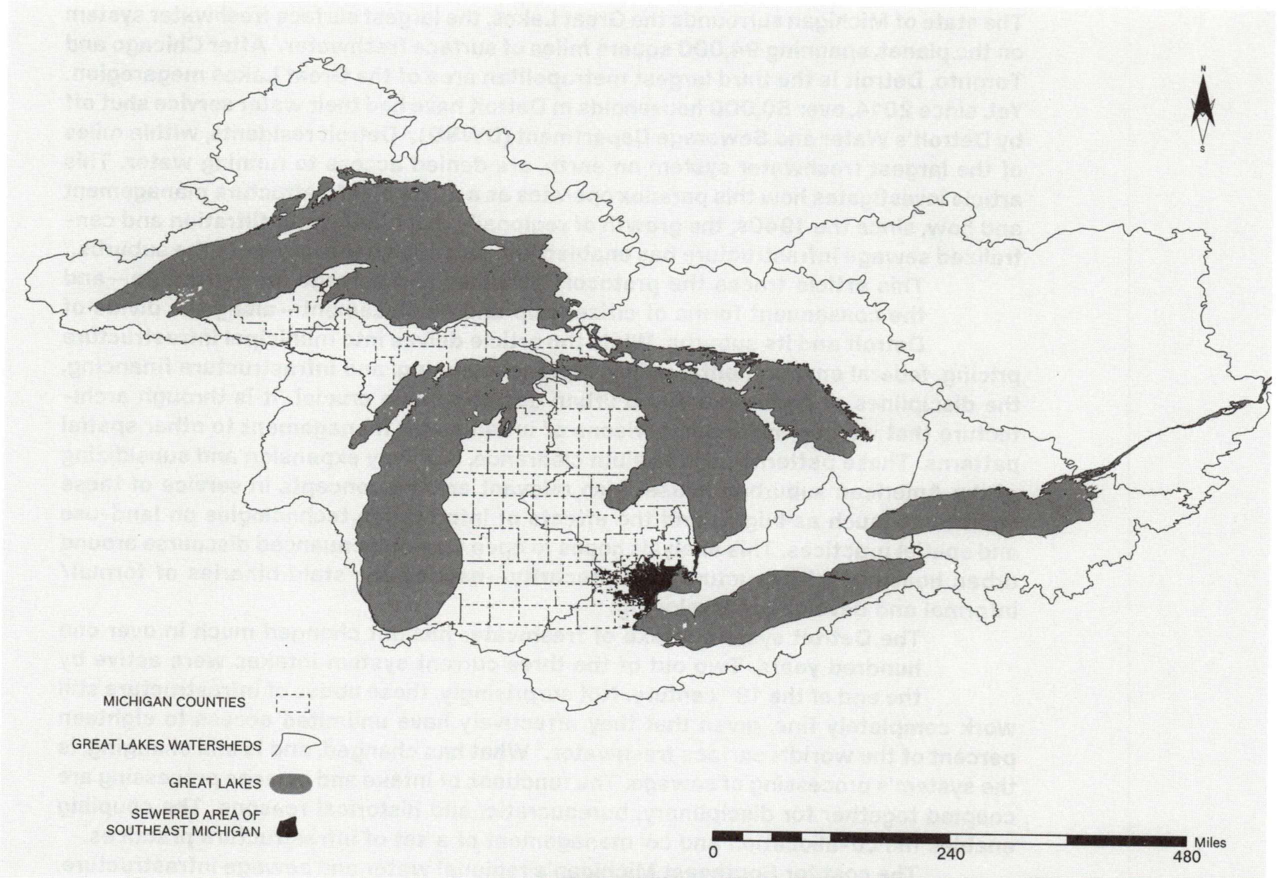

Fig 1. Great Lakes region, Michigan counties, and surrounding landmasses. By author.

Fig 2. Hurlbut Gate at entrance to Water Works Park when it was a publicly-accessible park at the end of the 19th century. Originally published by Detroit Publishing Co., c. 1890 - 1901.

Fig 3. Gate and sign at fence of Water Works Park, Detroit. Photo by author, 2016.

resources. It is fluid, yet it is capable of evicting residents, criminalizing households, and rendering faucets, fixtures, and toilets useless—all from the manipulation of a spreadsheet.

TESTING PUMPS, FILTERS, AND CONCRETE

In 1912, following a typhoid epidemic, Detroit's Board of Water Commissioners organized an event for the residents of Detroit to participate in a taste test.[8] The taste test took place at Chauncey Hurlbut Memorial Gate, the entrance to a 56-acre farm that had been purchased by the Board of Water Commissioners and opened as a public park in 1893.[9] The point of the taste test was to audition public filtered freshwater pumped from the intake pipe in Lake St. Clair, a filtration system engineered by local engineering talent Charles Hubbell to take advantage of recent innovations in both concrete and calcium hypochlorite.[10]

Soon after this 1912 taste test, the city commissioned Hubbell to undertake a research project on sewage measurement and processing. The mega-infrastructure project that became the Detroit Wastewater Treatment Plant (WWTP) started with Hubbell's measurement of feces solids, population, and intake, culminating decades later in the design of the WWTP collection structure.[11] Construction of the Detroit WWTP was finalized on New Year's Day in 1940, financed largely on a complex loan from the federal government.[12] Eventually, over seven thousand miles of sewage and stormwater pipe, both combined and separated, would fork from this plant to the suburbs like data trees.[13]

A century after that 1912 taste test, a network of concrete eight-inch mains for filtered water has rooted itself in the ground and extended across thousands of pipe miles to serve the water and waste processing for roughly three million people, constituting one of the most extensive water and sewage systems in the United States, collected into one of the largest wastewater treatment plants in the world.[14] Located in southwest Detroit near the confluence of the Rouge River and Detroit River, this wastewater plant was built and paid for by the City of Detroit. Yet Detroit residents today have a precarious relationship to the plant and its integrated water service network. Residents who live next to the Detroit WWTP find their water bills routinely higher than the value of their homes.[15]

TOO BIG TO FAIL

Today the DWSD network, leased to the Great Lakes Water Authority, serves 3.2 million residents. Less than 700,000 of those serviced residents live in the City of Detroit, but the sewage processing occurs entirely within the city.[16] There is no one definitive way to calculate the cost of serving each node in the system. The further

8 On December 2, 1923, DWSD formally opened the largest filtration plant in the world; see Michael Daisy and Richard Hughes, *The First 300 Years*, The Detroit Water and Sewerage Department, accessed October 15, 2016, http://dwsd.org/downloads_n/about_dwsd/history/complete_history.pdf.

9 City of Detroit, *Journal of the Common Council of the City of Detroit: From the Time of Its First Organization* (1895), accessed December 4, 2016, 590. https://catalog.hathitrust.org/Record/008607297.

10 "History of the Detroit Water and Sewage Department (DWSD) 1900 to present," *Glow Bass*, February 5, 2011, http://glowbass.com/history-of-the-detroit-water-and-sewage-department-dwsd-1900-to-present/; see also Daisy and Hughes, *The First 300 Years*.

11 The plant is located at 9300 W. Jefferson Avenue in Detroit.

12 Hubbell, Roth & Clark, Inc., *The First 30 Years: 1915–1945*, 2015, accessed October 15, 2016, http://www.hrc-engr.com/pubs/hrc_first_30.pdf.

13 As of 2015, the Wastewater Treatment Plant serviced the needs of 35 percent of the state's population contained within Detroit and 76 other communities in a service area of more than 946 square miles. See "Wastewater Treatment Plant," Detroit Water and Sewerage Department, accessed December 4, 2016, http://archive.dwsd.org/pages_n/facilities_wastewater.html. Based on the mapping analysis included here by author, sewered roads that are directly served by the WWTP add up to approximately 7,125 linear miles.

14 "Wastewater Treatment Plant Fact Sheet," City of Detroit Water and Sewerage Department, 2013, accessed October 15, 2016, http://www.michigan.gov/documents/deq/deq-wrd-npdes-DetroitWWTP_FS_415425_7.pdf.

15 Minimum bid on a Wayne County tax foreclosure auction is $500. As of 2015, the average debt of Detroit water customers is $663; see Ryan Felton, "Detroit Water Shut-offs Resume—and Residents Continue to Struggle with Bills," *Metro Times*, July 6, 2016, http://www.metrotimes.com/Blogs/archives/2016/07/06/detroit-water-shut-offs-resume-and-residents-continue-to-struggle-with-bills.

16 Sewage processing is located at the Jefferson Waste Water Treatment Plant; see V. Farr, "Sewer Map," Detroit Water and Sewage Department IT-GIS, September 6, 2014, accessed October 15, 2016, http://www.detroitmi.gov/Portals/0/docs/GLWA/Water_Sewer_Maps_Guide_1.pdf.

away a node is from the source of intake or processing, the more line it takes to connect and the more maintenance along the length of the line. Conversely, the side effects of sewage processing—smells and potential overflows, including the bacterial risk of exposure during overflows—are borne most heavily by those who are proximate to the processing facilities.

Both these direct relationships—the increased cost of service based on distance from the water source and the side effects of proximity to sewage—suggest that suburban points of access cost more to maintain and incur less of the direct detriments.

Despite this, the DWSD funding model was developed based on revenue from individual consumption, even though the consumption data for both intake and sewage resist consistent measurement. To fulfill the consumer model of pricing, the monitoring of usage and estimates of drainage at each point of use creates an expense itself, a kind of built-in maintenance of information. As the system expanded into the suburbs from the 1940s through the 1970s, the management of the water and sewage infrastructure shifted from an engineering model to a revenue model—aping the management of private business—despite there being no market established for determining water prices.

To analyze the spatial assets and risks managed by Detroit's *watercraft*, the coupling of water filtration and sewage under a joint authority are key. This dual authority was formalized at the height of the Department of Water Service's suburban expansion in 1966, but its potential can be traced back to the nineteenth century in relation to Detroit's position on an international border.[17] While the processes of water intake have remained unencumbered since the late nineteenth century, the processing of sewage has consistently failed to maintain clean waterways, from the city's first sewer in 1836 to the present day. This is largely due to Detroit's combined sewer system,[18] but cannot be disassociated from the suburban service expansion.

The consolidation of sewer management with water management in 1966 coincided with the implementation of telemetered sensing devices for monitoring water levels in sewers and the centralization of stormwater treatment. Thus, a larger part of the runoff from storms, including the entire runoff from small storms and the highly contaminated first flush of the very large storms, would be retained in the system for complete treatment at the regional wastewater plant. An additional benefit of this stormwater monitoring and remote control system would be the potential reduction of basement flooding, thereby preserving the value of single-family homes that found themselves connected to an overflowing sewer line during heavy rain events.[19] This consolidation centralized the effects of flooding in a way that would shift the risk impacts of heavy rain events from the metro-area single-family house to the City of Detroit.

With the emergence of the Environmental Protection Agency (EPA) and the Clean Water Act of 1972, the federal government sued the state of Michigan for its combined sewer overflow (CSO) into the freshwater of the Detroit River.[20] This lawsuit continued for decades, giving the state's judicial courts—neither engineers nor planners, nor democratically elected officials—a leading role in the management of Detroit's urban and suburban *watercraft*.

Despite the longstanding coupling of sewage processing and water delivery,[21] the constellation of *watercraft* infrastructure owned by the City of Detroit remains legally blocked from charging suburban customers for the full

17 Gerald Remus, DWSD Director, led the expansion into the suburbs in Robert Moses fashion. Remus, September 8, 1966: "The program calls for the development of an area-wide waste collection system, tighter stormwater control and beautification of our lakes and rivers. It also eliminates the need for small, ineffective and costly waste treatment plants which have sprung up in the area." City of Detroit, Department of Water Service, Agency Report (archive material), 1966.

18 A combined sewer system collects rainwater runoff, domestic sewage, and industrial wastewater into one pipe that, in normal conditions, is all delivered to a Wastewater Treatment Plant. Combined sewers can cause serious water pollution problems during combined sewer overflow (CSO) events when wet weather flows exceed the sewage treatment plant capacity, and untreated storm water and wastewater discharges directly to nearby bodies of water. See EPA, "Combined Sewer Overflows (CSOs), October 16, 2016, https://www.epa.gov/npdes/combined-sewer-overflows-csos.

19 Pollution Control Program for the Detroit Regional Watershed 1966, Section VIII, Stormwater Overflow Control, 21.

20 "In 1977, the Environmental Protection Agency (EPA) sued the City of Detroit, DWSD, and the State of Michigan, alleging that Detroit's sewage system did not satisfy the requirements of the FWPCA. Following negotiations between the parties, a consent judgment was entered by this court, requiring the City to adopt a user charge system and have it fully implemented and effective on all bills after January 1, 1980." CITY OF DETROIT, BY DETROIT WATER v. STATE. 594 F. Supp. 574 (E.D. Michigan. September 28, 1984), accessed February 14, 2017, http://law.justia.com/cases/federal/district-courts/FSupp/594/574/1900910.

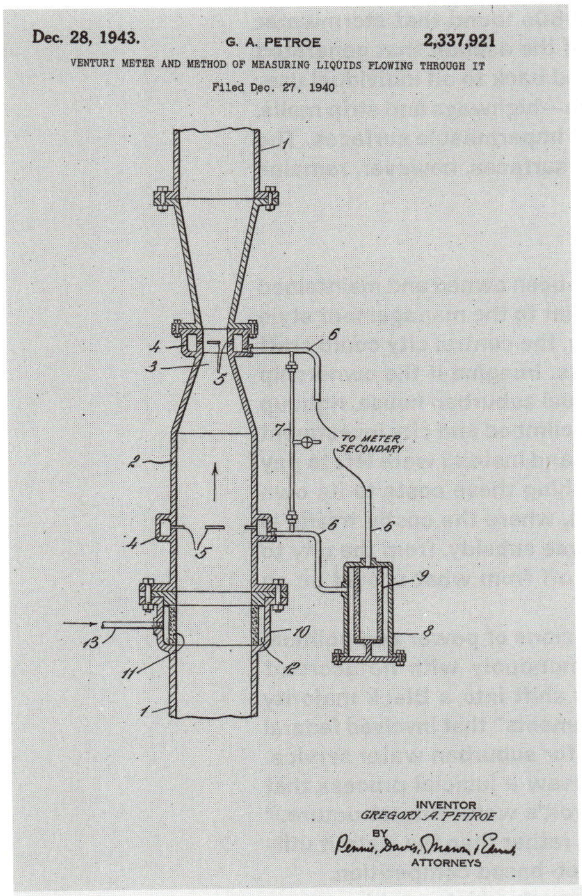

Fig 4. Meter invention used for measuring sewage flows by Gregory A. Petroe, 1943, US Patent Publication Number US2337921 A.

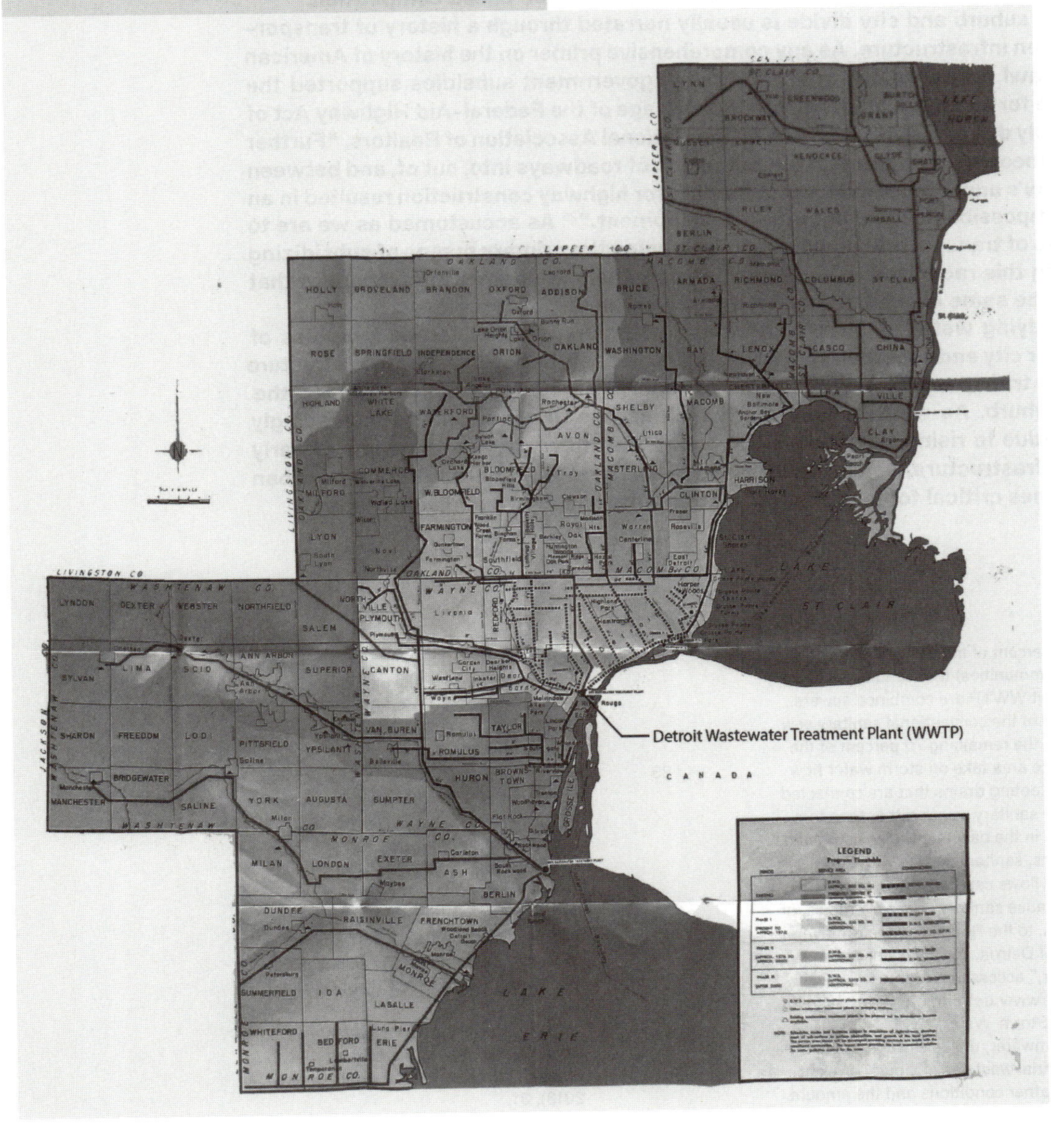

Fig 5. Map of pollution control program for the Detroit regional watershed, 1966, Detroit Department of Water Service.

centralized infrastructure cost. Judicial rulings in the 1980s found that stormwater could not be considered a cost allocated to the owners of the asphalt that generated the run-off because stormwater, itself, could not be traced back to an individual user or customer.[22] The repeated spatial patterns of the suburb—highways and strip malls, parking lots and grass lawns—tend toward the spread of impermeable surfaces. The infrastructural cost of the stormwater running off these surfaces, however, remains centralized in the City of Detroit.

SCALE PROBLEM

Imagine if the highway system of a metropolitan region had been owned and maintained by the core city at the height of suburban expansion. Similar to the management style of Robert Moses in mid-twentieth-century New York City, the central city could craft tolls to cover operating costs and even generate a surplus. Imagine if the ownership was so robust that it included the lanes up to each individual suburban house, right up to the garage door. Now, imagine that as suburban wealth climbed and city investment fell, the city failed to wield its power to demand any tolls, and instead were left to pay for every pothole along thousands of miles of roads, pushing these costs to its own residents. That is, effectively, the Detroit water situation, where the costly traffic is sewage, not automobiles. The result is decades of a reverse subsidy, from the city to the suburbs, culminating recently in urban residents cut off from what should be an abundant—even free—water supply.

Sociologists have begun tracing the racial dimensions of power and political influence that engendered this paradox of a monopoly with no accrued benefit.[23] The decades of Detroit's demographic shift into a Black majority correspond to the same decades of "Rate Settlement Agreements" that involved federal court intervention and consistently beneficial rate terms for suburban water service. For decades, beginning in the 1970s, a single judge oversaw a judicial process that set water rates for each suburban county served by Detroit's water infrastructure.[24] These rates were reached through structured negotiation, rather than the Detroit utility charging rates as a monopoly or pricing through market-based competition.

The suburb and city divide is usually narrated through a history of transportation infrastructure. As any comprehensive primer on the history of American sprawl notes, following World War II, government subsidies supported the marketplace for suburban housing with the passage of the Federal-Aid Highway Act of 1956, partially due to intense lobbying by the National Association of Realtors. "Further enabling homeownership through the expansion of roadways into, out of, and between cities, the law's unprecedented level of funding for highway construction resulted in an otherwise impossible level of suburban development."[25] As accustomed as we are to the narrative of transportation and mortgages being the primary means of subsidizing and enabling this racialized suburban expansion, there is another infrastructure that subsidized the same development pattern: sewer lines and water lines.

Studying water in Detroit and its intersection of racialized geographies of inner city and suburban sprawl uncovers parallels between water infrastructure and transportation planning as expensive enablers of white flight to the American suburb. As we face an era in which access to water will be increasingly important—due to rising flood levels, increased storm events, and the aging of early industrial infrastructure, among other issues—analyzing the infrastructure of urban water becomes critical for locating the spatial protocols of urban divides today.

21 "30 percent of the sewer systems (26 of 77 communities) that send flows to the Detroit WWTP are combined sewers... Many of the conventional sanitary sewers in the remaining 70 percent of the service area take on storm water flow from footing drains that are connected to the sanitary sewer rather than to a sump in the basement. Like combined sewers, sanitary sewers with storm water flows can become overloaded and cause sanitary sewer overflows, or SSOs, to the Rouge and Detroit rivers." City of Detroit, "Overview of Storm Water," accessed November 21, 2016, http://www.detroitmi.gov/How-Do-I/Find/Storm-Water.

22 "Stormwater, unlike sewage or other industrial waste, is obviously a result of weather conditions and the amount of rainfall treated and therefore is not a waste created by any particular user or recipient of services." CITY OF DETROIT, BY DETROIT WATER, § 2(A) (1984).

23 Dana Kornberg, "The Structural Origins of Territorial Stigma: Water and Racial Politics in Metropolitan Detroit, 1950s to 2010s," *International Journal of Urban and Regional Research* 40 (2016): 263–84, doi: 10.1111/1468-2427.12343.

24 Judge John Feikens of the United States District Court, Eastern District of Michigan, Southern Division, United States of America. See City of Detroit, 1984.

25 Vishaan Chakrabarti, *A Country of Cities: A Manifesto for an Urban America* (New York: Metropolis Books, 2013), 31.

WATERCRAFT —STATE OF EMERGENCY MANAGEMENT

Despite the City of Detroit's coordinated planning and urban design efforts to support neighborhoods outside the privately capitalized downtown, water shutoffs continue to act as a more direct lever to displace residents. At its peak in fall 2015, the city averaged 2,000 residential shutoffs per week.[26] Indeed, the focus of Detroit's *watercraft* has been on displacing non-paying residents more than businesses—the number of residential shutoffs exceeds four times that of businesses. While 2015 saw Detroit water service shut off to approximately 23,300 homes, water service continued for thousands of businesses that owed millions of dollars to DWSD.[27]

***The Nation* magazine, prior to the atrocity of poisoned water in Flint, Michigan, called Detroit "ground zero" in the new fight for water rights.[28] The state of Michigan appointed an Emergency Manager in Detroit in 2013 to oversee financial operations, effectively seizing legal authority from the mayor and City Council for two years. Water shutoffs in Detroit started getting local media attention in 2014, and Detroit activists even successfully involved the United Nations in the human rights aspects of the water shutoffs.[29] More than half of Detroit's 200,000 households with water accounts had bills at least sixty days past due, and the DWSD announced water service shutoffs for those who were sixty days delinquent and owing more than $150.[30] Within a year, national public health officials and international human rights organizations became critical of the situation, even calling it a "possible public health catastrophe."[31]**

Yet, the DWSD continued to shut off water to thousands of residents. Detroit residents and activists point out DWSD's accounting-based service stoppages can be compared to previous modes of displacement and urban land clearing, including blight removal and eminent domain. One Highland Park resident organizing protests in that municipality called water shutoffs "the newest form of urban renewal."[32] Since the Emergency Management period, water bills in the inner city have become data in a point-based algorithm of urban desertification. Based on real-time monitoring of outstanding water bills, the DWSD disperses a fleet of contractors to shut off water service, point by point.

When a resident's water is shut off, he or she is not only rendered bereft of flushing toilets or bathing water, but also risks child protective services taking away children due to the reduced sanitation. A precarious situation becomes more precarious, placing more pressure on city services in health, foster care, and social work. The ease of turning water back on masks the real issue, which is in the relationship between service disruption and implicit criminalization of those who disrupt the disruption (by, for instance, blocking contractor trucks from accessing a street or directly manipulating the shutoff valve with a wrench).[33]

Despite the fact that the majority of households served by DWSD infrastructure are in the suburbs, the water shutoffs have occurred almost exclusively within city limits.[34] After declaring bankruptcy in the City of Detroit, Emergency Management rule in Detroit extended into the governance of the DWSD. In this way, Emergency Management operated comparably to the zone in Easterling's analysis:

> [T]he zone embodies bifurcated or multiple forms of sovereignty that leverage the state to relinquish its resources in exchange for

26 Kurth, "Detroit Hits Residents on Water Shut-offs as Businesses Slide."

27 Ibid.

28 Laura Gottesdiener, "Detroit Is Ground Zero in the New Fight for Water Rights," *Nation*, July 15, 2015, accessed October 15, 2016, http://www.thenation.com/article/detroit-is-ground-zero-in-the-new-fight-for-water-rights/.

29 "Detroit's Water Shut-Offs Target the Poor, Vulnerable and African Americans." United Nations Human Rights Office of the High Commissioner, October 20, 2014, accessed October 15, 2016, http://www.ohchr.org/EN/NewsEvents/Pages/DisplayNews.aspx?NewsID=15190&LangID=E.

30 Joel Kurth, "Detroiters Struggle to Survive Without City Water," *Detroit News*, December 14, 2015, accessed October 15, 2016, http://www.detroitnews.com/story/news/local/detroit-city/2015/12/14/detroiters-struggle-survive-without-city-water/77263784/.

31 Full quote from Dr. Wendy Johnson, the former medical director of the Cleveland Department of Public Health: "I was shocked by the draconian measures employed by the Detroit Water Department... Water shutoffs set-up the possibility of public health catastrophe—that's what we see in poor African and Central American countries." In Martina Guzmán, "Exploring the Public Health Consequences of Detroit's Water Shutoffs," *Model D*, October 6, 2015, accessed October 16, 2016, http://www.modeldmedia.com/features/water-shut-offs-100615.aspx.

32 *The Water Front*, directed by Liz Miller (Reading, Penn.: Bullfrog Films, 2007), DVD.

33 Clinton Kirby, "Detroit: Got a Wrench? Turn Your Water Back On," *Liberty Road Media*, July 1, 2014, accessed October 16, 2016, https://libertyroadmedia.wordpress.com/2014/07/01/detroit-got-a-wrench-turn-your-water-back-on.

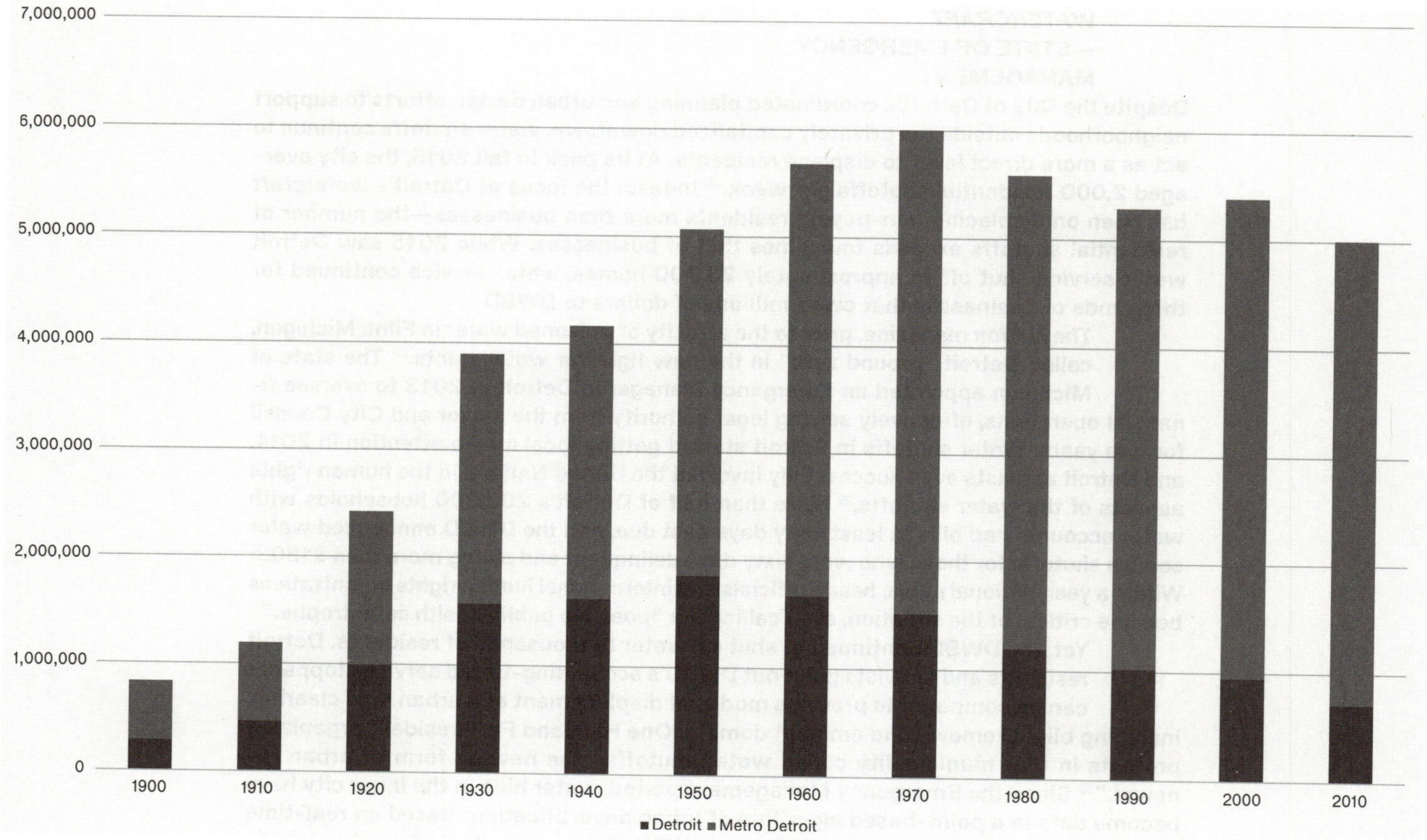

Fig 6. As the city's population continues to decline, the suburban population stays relatively stable. Chart by author based on U.S. Census Data; see U.S. Bureau of the Census, "Census of Population and Housing: Decenial Census," accessed January 20, 2017, https://www.census.gov/prod/www/decennial.html.

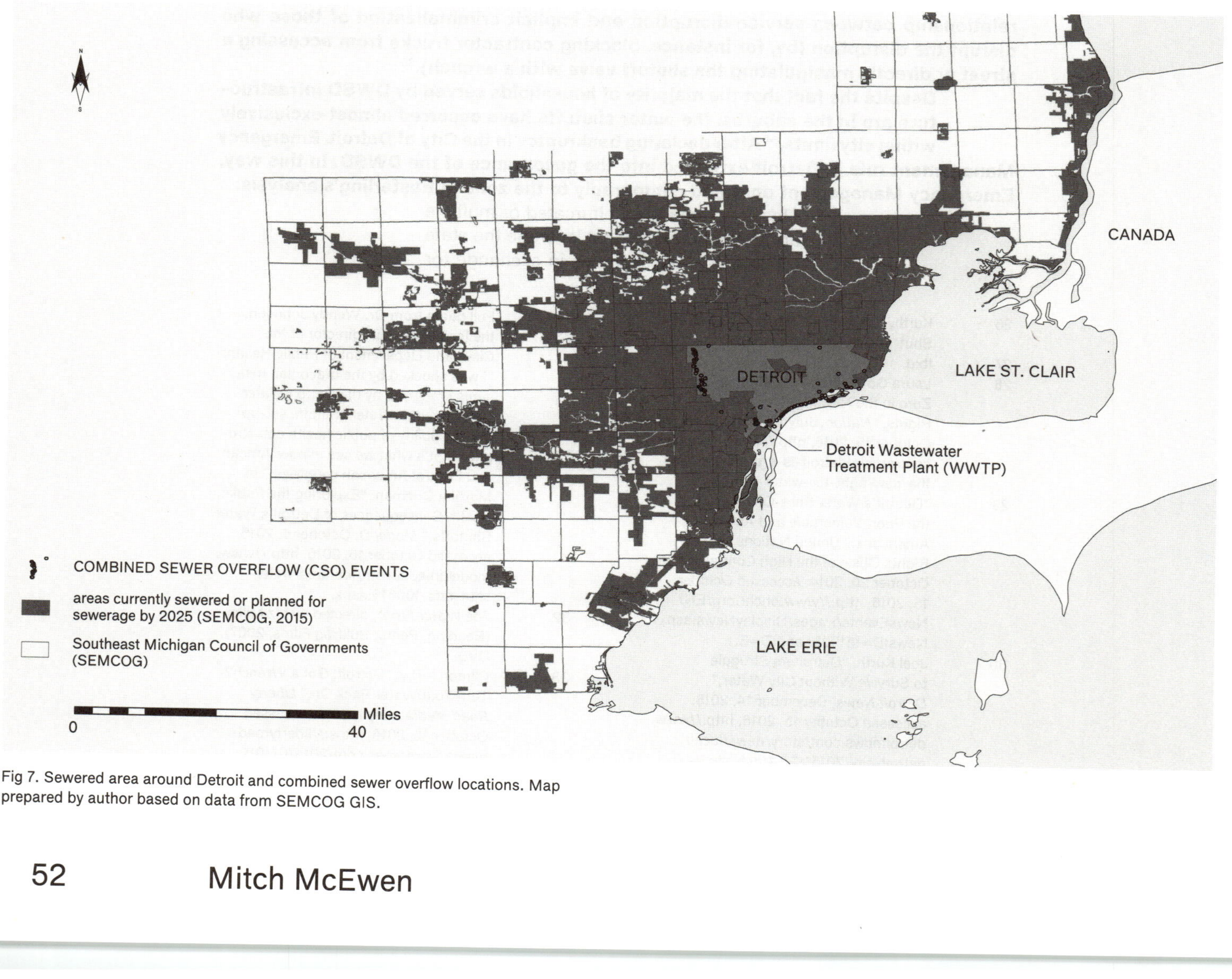

Fig 7. Sewered area around Detroit and combined sewer overflow locations. Map prepared by author based on data from SEMCOG GIS.

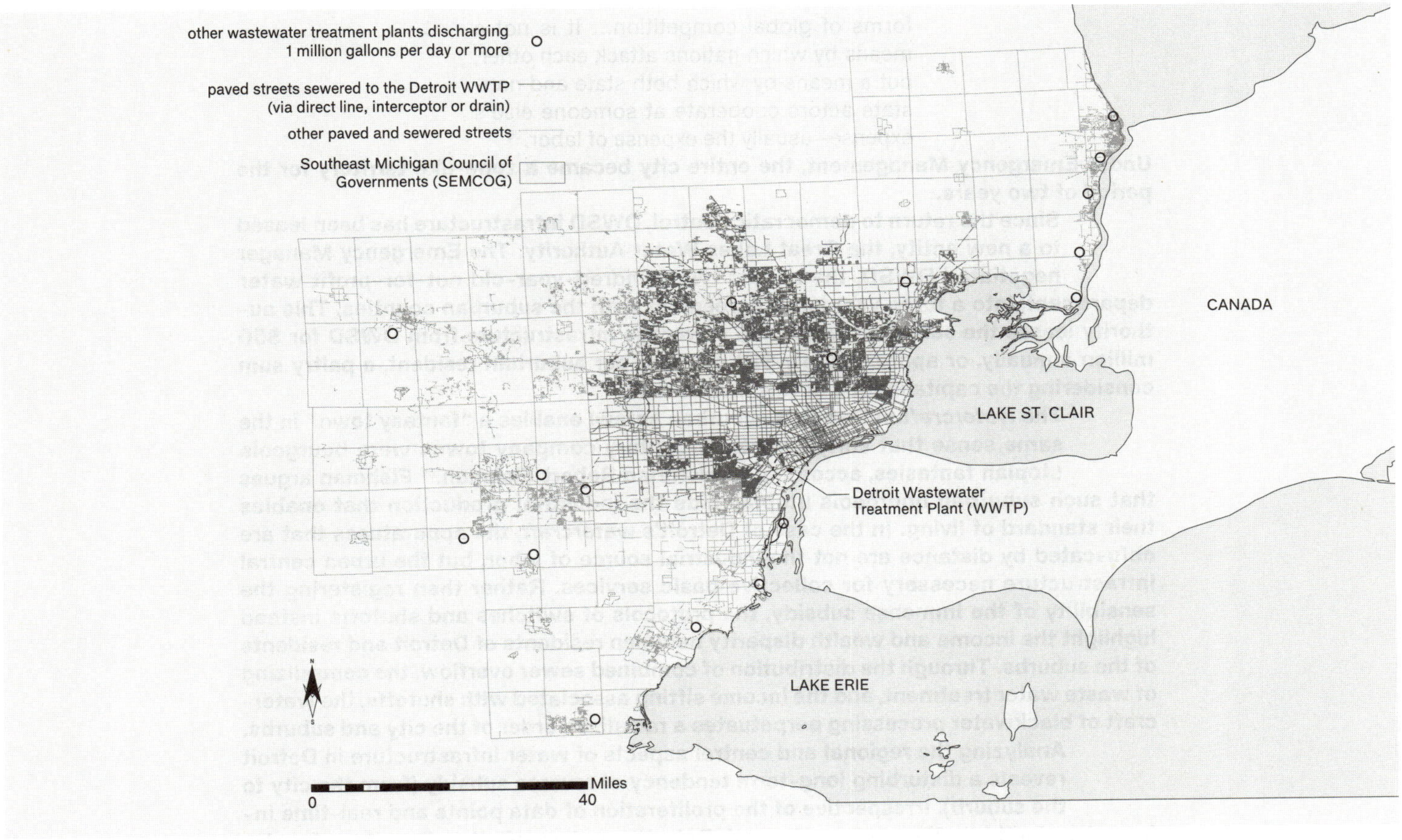

Fig 8. Paved streets serviced directly by the Detroit WasteWater Treatment Plant on Jefferson (denoted by dashed circle). Facilities that support grey streets are noted with a black circle. Many of these facilities also discharge sediment dewatering wastewater into the Detroit WWTP.

Map prepared by author based on Detroit Water and Sewerage Department GIS, SEMCOG GIS, and Wastewater Master Plan, Executive Summary, October 2003, 132. Note: The dark gray streets are the minimum serviced currently by the Detroit WWTP. Many facilites that support streets coded as light gray also discharge sediment dewatering wastewater to the Detroit WWTP.

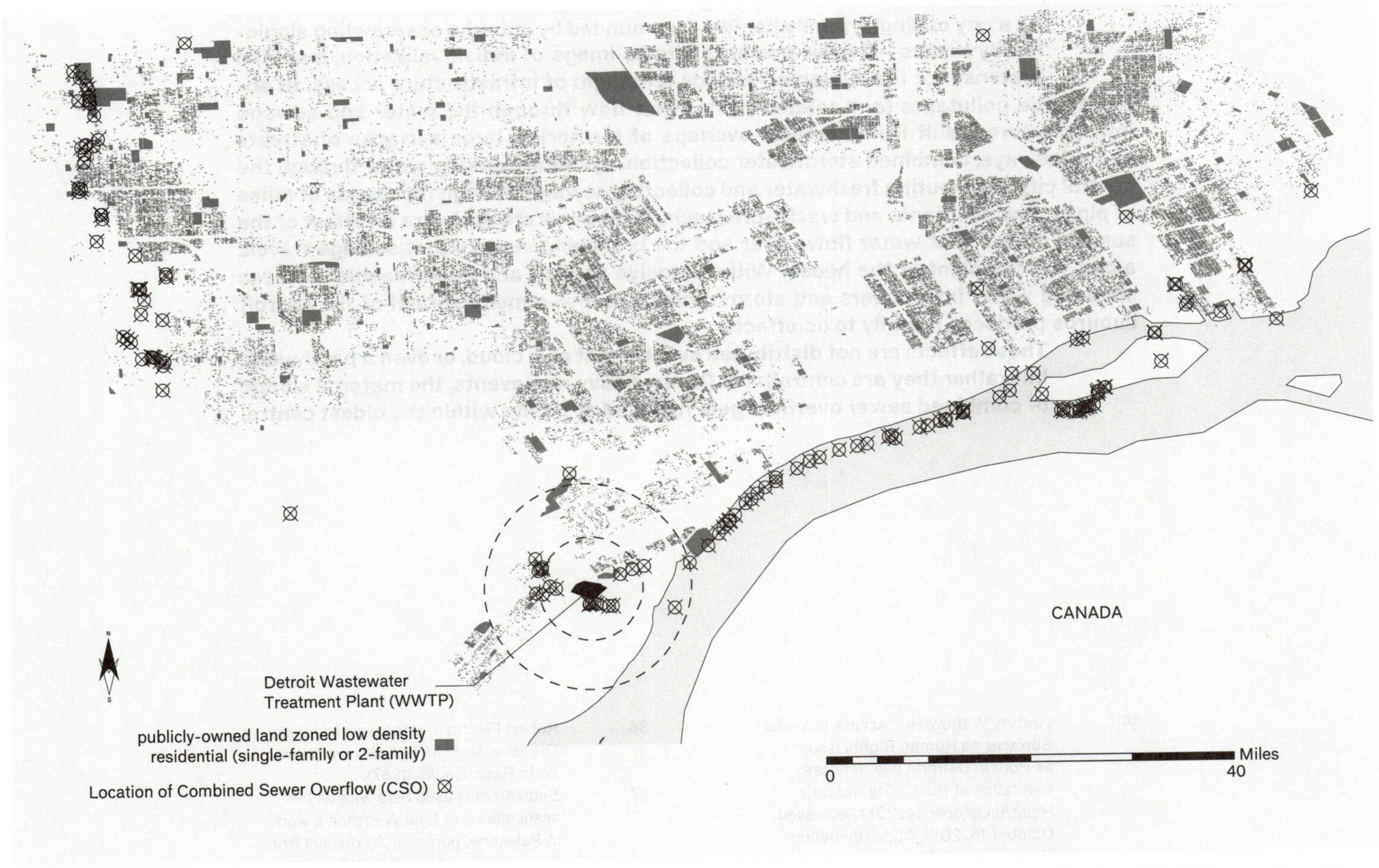

Fig 9. Residential land becomes publicly owned for many reasons, including tax liens, vacancy, and water bill foreclosures. This map shows the extent of publicly-owned low-density residential land in Detroit (zoned for 1- or 2-family houses, shown in gray) and its relationship to combined sewer overflow locations (in black).

> forms of global competition... It is not a means by which nations attack each other, but a means by which both state and non-state actors cooperate at someone else's expense—usually the expense of labor.[35]

Under Emergency Management, the entire city became a zone-like territory for the period of two years.

Since the return to democratic control, DWSD infrastructure has been leased to a new entity, the Great Lakes Water Authority. The Emergency Manager negotiated DWSD, the almost two-hundred-year-old not-for-profit water department, into a forty-year lease agreement with the suburban counties. This authority leases the suburban water and sewerage infrastructure from DWSD for $50 million annually, or approximately $21 per year per suburban resident, a paltry sum considering the capitalization of this investment.

The *watercraft* of Detroit's suburban sprawl enables a "fantasy town" in the same sense that early-twentieth-century company towns were bourgeois utopian fantasies, according to historian Robert Fishman.[36] Fishman argues that such suburban bourgeois utopias hide the industrial production that enables their standard of living. In the case of Detroit's *watercraft*, the apparatuses that are obfuscated by distance are not the industrial source of labor, but the urban central infrastructure necessary for collective basic services. Rather than registering the sensibility of the immense subsidy, the protocols of switches and shutoffs instead highlight the income and wealth disparity between residents of Detroit and residents of the suburbs. Through the distribution of combined sewer overflow, the centralizing of waste water treatment, and the income sifting associated with shutoffs, the watercraft of blackwater processing perpetuates a racialized order of the city and suburbs.

Analyzing the regional and central aspects of water infrastructure in Detroit reveals a disturbing long-term tendency of reverse subsidy (from the city to the suburb), irrespective of the proliferation of data points and real-time information built into the system. Through Detroit's *watercraft*, the allocation of water becomes not a resource but a service, comparable to wireless telephones. This field of resource allocation evolves the urban divide from a geometry of lines (redlining) to one of points (on/off). These are points of service blockage and desertification. This emergence of a new urban divide as a scattering of control points reveals a matrix of resources and crises managed in service of suburban sprawl and white middle-class settlement and at the detriment of a largely Black city.[37]

As a city of single-family homes—surrounded by suburbs of sprawling single-family homes—Detroit presents a false image of individualization, a spatial pretense for the customer-service paradigm of infrastructure access. In actuality, the pollutants (and related costs) that flow through the water and sewage infrastructure result from complex overlaps of territories, large surfaces of streets and driveways, combined stormwater collection, systems intaking water through the central city, distributing freshwater and collecting sewage through thousands of miles of pipes. The pollutants and waste-processing that generate costs are an effect of the surface matter that water flows over and the branching vectors that sewage travels along, not the point of the house. With extensive asphalt and impermeable surfaces shedding water into sewers and storm drains, the low-density sprawl of the Detroit suburbs produces literally toxic effects.

These effects are not distributed evenly—not as a cloud, or even a patchwork, but rather they are centralized. During heavy rain events, the material sludge of combined sewer overflow gets released at points within the oldest central

34 Lindsey Wahowiak, "Access to Water Surfaces as Human Rights Issue as Poor in Detroit Lose Services: Sanitation at Risk," *The Nation's Health*, October 14, 2014, accessed October 16, 2015, http://thenationshealth.aphapublications.org/content/44/8/1.3.full.

35 Easterling, *Extrastatecraft*, 148.

36 Robert Fishman, *Bourgeois Utopias: The Rise And Fall of Suburbia* (New York: Basic Books, 1987).

37 Settlement is used here with all the associations of Eyal Weizman's work in Palestine, purposefully distinct from "gentrification." See Eyal Weizman, *Hollow Land: Israel's Architecture of Occupation* (London: Verso, 2007).

areas of Detroit, points plotting a line at the Detroit river, as well as the border between Detroit and its western suburbs. It is important to understand that these points have environmental qualities and risks that cannot be separated from the suburban geography that the watercraft infrastructure serves.

EMERGENCY MANAGEMENT AND THE "BLUE ECONOMY"

Today metropolitan Detroit's management of water operates as a showcase of new modes of infrastructure, a just-in-time deployment of switches through wrenches and spreadsheets. A choreography of spatial controls has evolved quickly in Detroit through innovations in management, governance, and resource control, as the city has shifted from democracy to Emergency Management and back. Throughout these shifts, water has been a medium for an intense and radical set of protocols—whether in data gathering through pumps and monitors, price setting through closed-door agreements, or shutting off service to residents.

Since the mid-twentieth century, water infrastructure has evolved from a centralized resource for an industrializing city into a sprawling regional network. In studying this territory of water management around Detroit and its suburbs, one finds ongoing protocols of suburban expansion and environmental ghettoization of the urban Black poor. From Detroit to the suburbs, water access and sewage processing are subsidized by the poor for the wealthy and by majority Black American and Latino neighborhoods to enhance capacity in majority white enclaves.

The most nationally recognized tragedy around water allocation from the Great Lakes has been the state-managed poisoning of Flint. While that instance involved a poisonous allocation of water temporarily from the Flint River, the circumstances are not unrelated. The impetus to craft a temporary water source arose from the transition from the Detroit-based DWSD water system to a new pipeline – the Karegnondi Water Authority (KWA). After having been served by DWSD water since 1967, Flint's Emergency Management signed on to receive untreated water from KWA in 2013.[38] This new KWA pipeline was not planned by Flint to serve Flint residents. It was planned by Genesee County to open that suburban county to the 'Blue economy'—namely development sites for industrial use of untreated water, primarily for water bottling plants and fracking.[39]

WATERCRAFT AS EXTRASTATECRAFT

Keller Easterling's notion of *extrastatecraft* becomes especially useful in understanding the regional water system as "infrastructure space"—as something shaped by geology, urban form, socioeconomics, and policy. In the crafting of water resources and policy, there is no neutral ground. As Easterling notes, "The aggressions within infrastructure space often occur with no defining moments and no satisfying declaration of an enemy. The consequential evidence may be found in the innocuous details—an invisible buildup of neglect or a silent form of attrition."[40]

Key to the contemporary effects is the network of resources, protocols, and switches (what Easterling terms *active forms*) deployed in the DWSD's self-proclaimed "shut-off procedures."[41] Rather than considering the shutoffs as a rupture in infrastructure, this analysis considers the termination of running water to selected nodes in the city as a performance of a mode of urban infrastructure, itself. In tracing such banalities as stormwater runoff and sewage handling, the resource protocols at work in the dialectic between Detroit and its suburbs become legible as processes for transferring risk and, even, displacing residents.

It is within the terrain of this water network, splaying out across over a thousand

38 Diane Bukowski, "Bi-Partisan Deal Led to Flint Water Poisoning for Profit: The Karegnondi Water Authority (KWA)," *Voice of Detroit*, February 15, 2016, accessed October 16, 2016, http://voiceofdetroit.net/2016/02/15/bi-partisan-deal-led-to-flint-water-poisoning-for-profit-the-karegnondi-water-authority-kwa/.

39 Allie Gross, "Emails Reveal Flint EM and State Advised Not to Join the KWA—It Was Never about Saving Money," *Detroit Metro Times*, February 13, 2016, accessed October 15, 2016, http://www.metrotimes.com/Blogs/archives/2016/02/13/emails-reveal-flint-should-never-have-joined-kwa-andnbspit-was-never-about-saving-money#.

40 Easterling, *Extrastatecraft*, 149.

41 "Shut-off procedures begin if payment has not been received by the due date stated in the Final Notice. If service is terminated, full payment of the past due balance is required and a deposit may also be required." DWSD, "Customer Service: Past Due Accounts and Shutoffs," accessed February 14, 2017, http://archive.dwsd.org/pages_n/customer_service.html.

square miles—the urban and the formerly urban, the suburban, the formerly agricultural turned urban sprawl, and the newly pastoral of Detroit—that a new form of urban renewal emerges. Like previous forms of urban renewal, these processes require displacements of some residents to make way for new development. Unlike the last century's forms, which produced a *tabula rasa* defined by a closed polygon, these operations proceed from point to point, parcel to parcel, household to household. The geometry is more dot matrix or cellular automata than bounded Euclidian form. A line is formed from interceptor to suburban house, and the risks associated with that line are transferred to the single point of wastewater processing, the centralized points of CSO, and the dispersed points of houses belonging to individual customers who face water shutoffs.

The cellular point of the inner city house denied water services is linked to the infrastructural space of *watercraft* via remote control. As Easterling explains in *Extrastatecraft*:

> A remote control effects change indirectly or from some distance away, often without being detected... [A] nation indirectly floods a city when it builds a dam downstream... A mass-produced suburb, remote from the center, drains the city of its population. Any switch in any of the networks of infrastructure space can act like a remote—as a valve that may control flows of cars, electricity, microwaves, or broadband capacity somewhere down the line.[42]

In the case of the desertification of points via Detroit's *watercraft*, it is important to note that the remote control in effect here does not begin with water. The data feeding into the algorithm of shutoffs becomes binary in relation to a temporality—currently forty-five days late payment—and a numerical figure: the monetary amount owed.[43] This numerical figure is based on a calculated cost for water and sewage service. The monetary cost bundles together water and sewage as dual services of an authority that, itself, is subject to negotiations and control of rates by the judiciary. In other words, at no point is a market involved, despite the monetization and bundling of the resources. At no point does demand exceed supply. The customer service mode of infrastructure management and the remote control switch of shutoffs have been layered over a delivery of resources that is highly centralized and controlled.

In an ominous way, Detroit's *watercraft* could be considered a pioneer in US evolution of smart infrastructure. DWSD's systems were partially computerized to monitor CSO failure as early as 1980, as part of a restitution for a 1966 EPA finding.[44] Point-by-point water shutoffs might be considered the culmination of decades of sensor-based monitoring and data collection, which could not have existed in the era of paper files and printed Sanborn Maps. Only the instant transfer of data between agencies, searchable databases, and information-based systems mapping (such as GIS) could make this house-by-house switch infrastructure possible.

The water shutoffs in Detroit complete a computerization of the city that dates back in Detroit to the 1980s, but can be compared to Reyner Banham's reading of Archigram decades prior. As architectural theorist Anthony Vidler provides in a meta-reading of Archigram, "'Zoom City,' 'Computer City,' 'Off-the-Peg City,' 'Completely Expendable City,' and 'Plug-in City' were important as much for the technology on which they were predicated as for their aesthetic qualities."[45]

42 Easterling, *Extrastatecraft*, 227.
43 DWSD, "Customer Service."
44 Michigan Department of Natural Resources, *Detroit River Remedial Action Plan, Stage 1* (1991), 3-7, https://www.epa.gov/sites/production/files/2013-12/documents/1991_detroitriverrapstg1.pdf.

The *watercraft* of Detroit is, likewise, able to render the city "completely expendable," perhaps because there is no image of what its machinations look like. In this operation, the "computer city" becomes aformal. Its illegibility makes it politically inaccessible. Philosopher Slavoj Žižek asserts that hegemony directs us toward false points of binary decisions that render the operations of ideology illegible. The inner city house is this false point in space, rendering the ideology of *watercraft* illegible. The focus on the individual switch obscures the larger public investment and ownership of thousands of miles of sewer and water lines, more than a thousand square miles of territory feeding stormwater into the network, and the ongoing centralized points of sewage impact—whether CSO or the stench of almost a billion gallons per day of wastewater treatment at one centralized facility.

FIELD OF SWITCHES

The water shutoffs and the *watercraft* that enable them draws separation, not between city and suburb, but within the line that connects the two, creating an autonomous authority of customer service that can be deployed to transfer risk from one point on the line toward another. This might even, tragically, be considered an anti-democratic enactment of the interdependent active form. As Easterling notes, "broadband urbanists might offer an alternative organ of design—not an object form like a master plan, but an active form or an interplay of spatial variables... Broadband space can similarly be redesigned as a kind of software or a machine of interdependencies."[46] With Detroit's *watercraft*, the open public resource of the Great Lakes becomes a service, turned off as easily as a Netflix account. The water authority operates like a communications provider. Over time, with health impacts and threats of child protective services around water access issues, the house without water access can be rendered unlivable. The house becomes a dumb vessel, similar to the cellphone known as "bricked," an inert object.

The spatial variables at play in Detroit's *watercraft* include allocation of large landscape projects for water catchment and the accounting of those costs, the calculation of flow for ever-escalating peak rain events and the distribution of excess capacity across thousands of miles of pipe and sewer-lines. Across all of that, the single detached house becomes a node and symbol for the distribution of resources across a territory of over a thousand square miles. Broadband urbanism here appears as a tool of neoliberalism and even a means of criminalizing the Black urban poor.

The logic and language of customer service is, itself, a form of *extrastatecraft* that shapes infrastructural space.[47] Through Detroit's *watercraft*, the entire nonhomeless population of the city can be recast as customers. The water delivery network is wielded as an instrument of debt collection. *Watercraft* participates in the shift from a political paradigm of citizens with access to public resources to a paradigm of customers being served.

THE COMING STATE OF ECOLOGICAL EMERGENCY

This paper aims to participate in the dissensus of the demands for water access in Detroit, not by staking claims of rights or speech, but through making visible that which was not visible, namely the territories and spatial economies of *watercraft*. As Jacques Rancière states, "Dissensus is not the confrontation between interests or opinions. It is the manifestation of a distance of the sensible from itself."[48] Here the sensible includes the asphalt of suburban sprawl, the topography of stormwater runoff, the vectors of processing sewage and stormwater, the thousands of miles of sewer and water lines sprawling into the suburbs. There is a distance between these spatial

45 Anthony Vidler, "Cities of Tomorrow: Technology, Ecology, and Architecture," *Artforum* 51, no. 1 (September 2012): 134.

46 Easterling, *Extrastatecraft*, 133.

47 Ibid., 177.

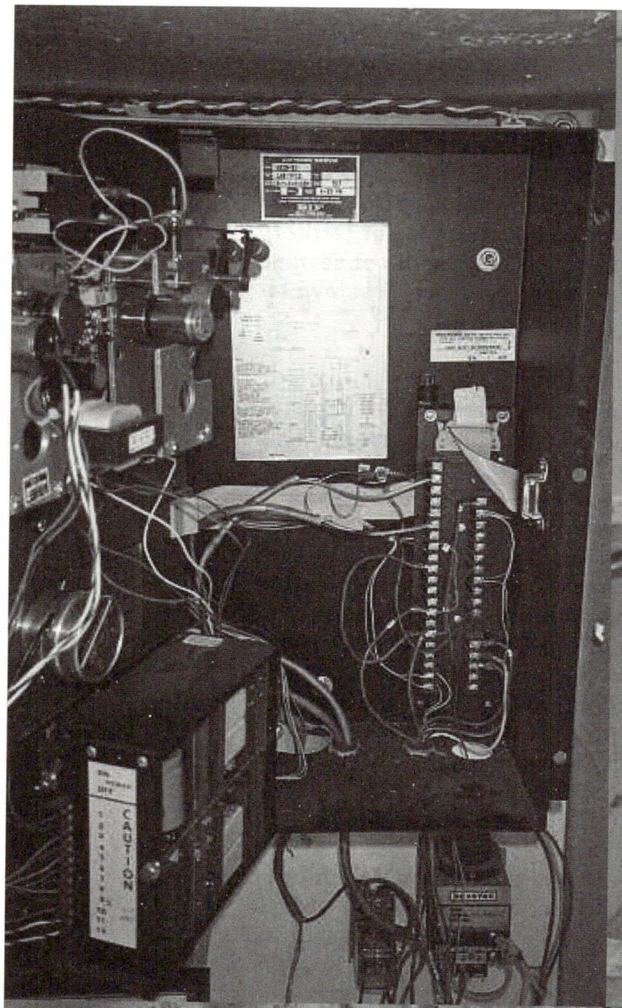
CAUTION

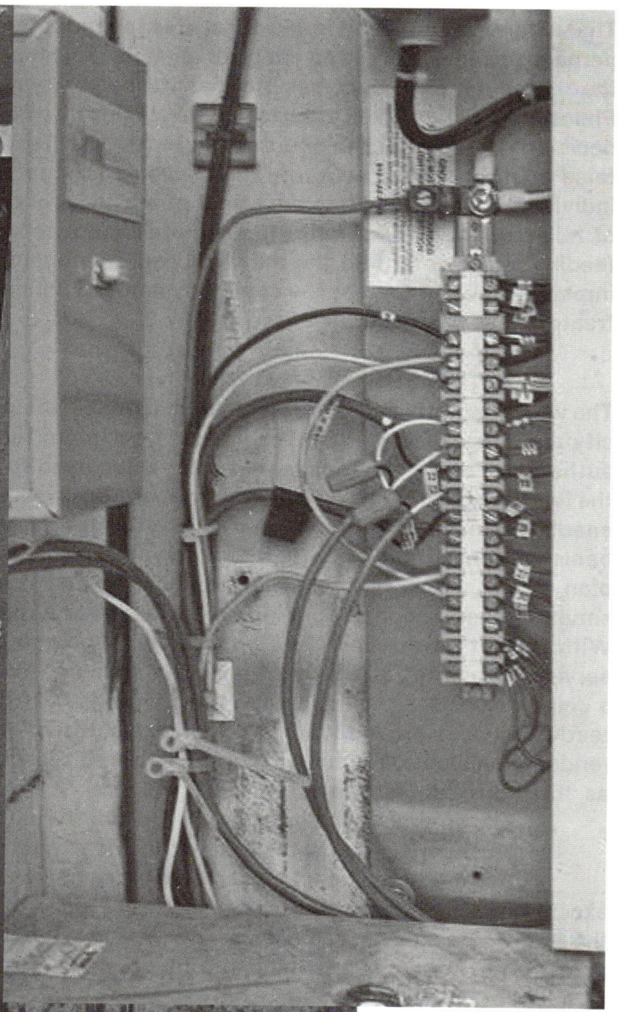

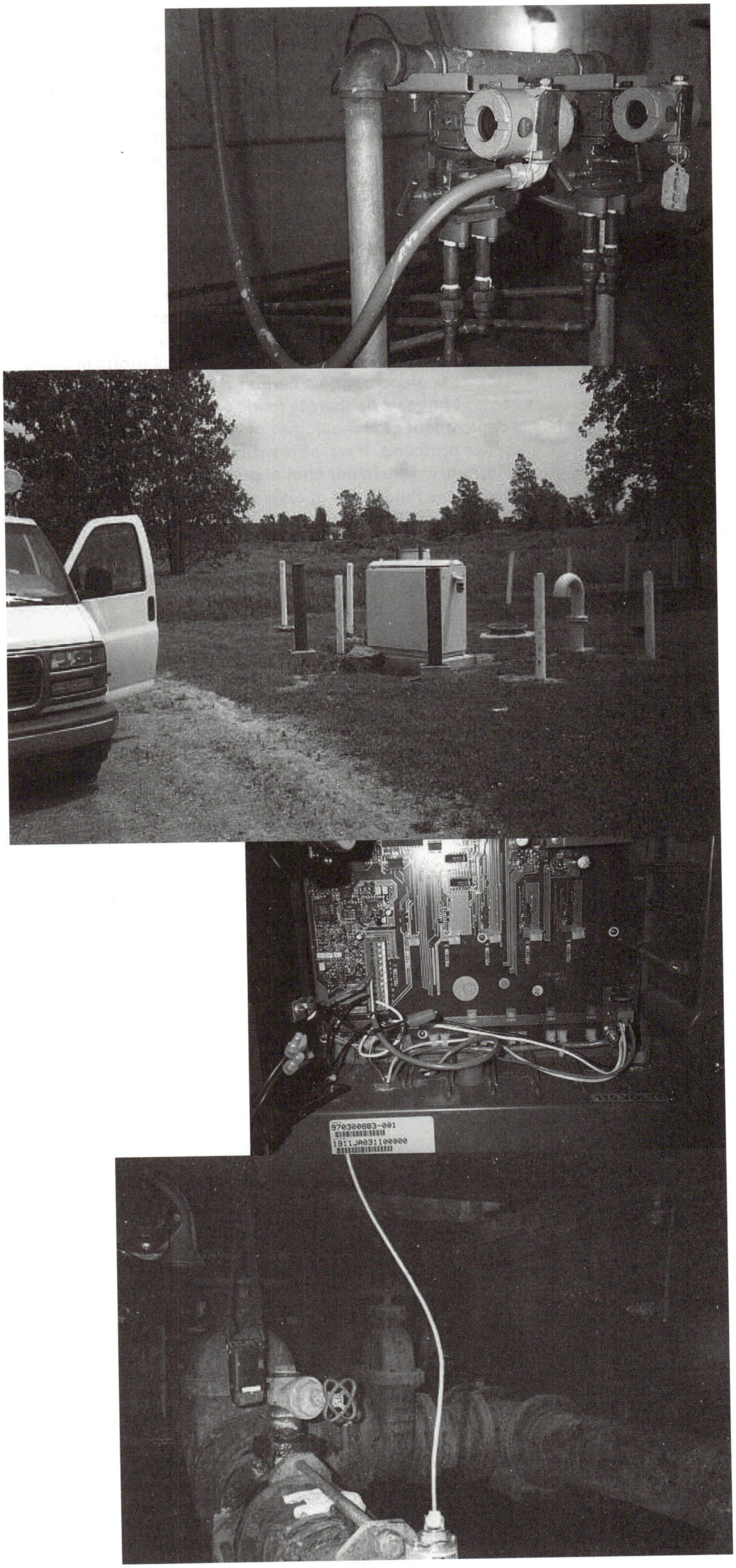

Fig 10. Meter pits, data-loggers, venturi meters, and other devices for measuring the flow of water and sewage between counties, primarily for the purposes of rate setting. Photos from DWSD online archive, DWSD, "Comprehensive Water Master Plan: Appendixes," accessed March 10, 2017, http://archive.dwsd.org/pages_n/task_g_appendix_d.html.

facts and the houses shut off from the water network due to the private matter of bill collections. Visualizing the spatial effects produced by these resource allocations—via remote controls and switches—becomes both a design problem and a politics.

It is important to note that this analysis of *watercraft* and urban desertification cannot be reduced into a nostalgia for the natural or an awareness of ecology.

As international activists and critics of globalization have noted, ecological emergency can be wielded as both cause and effect of austerity policy. As the collective authors of *The Coming Insurrection* state, "Tracking, transparency, certification, eco-taxes, environmental excellence, and the policing of water, all give us an idea of the coming state of ecological emergency."[49] Economist Thomas Piketty makes the parallel observation: "[I]t is important, I think, to insist that one form of the most important issues in coming years will be the development of new forms of property and democratic control of capital."[50] Via *watercraft*, the management of water and sewage infrastructure becomes an orchestration of displacement and urban renewal, unmediated by the conventional spatial practices of planning and urban design.

It is crucial to consider the water shutoffs in Detroit, ongoing since Emergency Management, as neither a failure of infrastructure nor a natural occurrence, but as a deliberate mode of infrastructure deployment. The shutoffs arrive as a deployment of technologies of switches, real-time data management, and customer service protocols. If we, as practitioners of the built environment, seek to engage modes of infrastructure in our spatial practices, we must develop new methods to reveal and counter the fluid forms of reverse subsidy, displacement, and non-market privatization of resources. This is the work of discerning and drawing *watercraft*—for it to become accessible and legible to dissensus.

48 Jacques Rancière and Steve Corcoran, *Dissensus: On Politics And Aesthetics* (London: Continuum, 2010), 7.

49 Comité Invisible, *The Coming Insurrection* (Los Angeles: Semiotext(e), 2009), 79.

50 Thomas Piketty and Arthur Goldhammer, *Capital in the Twenty-First Century* (Cambridge, Mass.: Belknap Press of Harvard University Press, 2014), 569.

Terrains of Contestation:

The Politics of Designing Urban Adaptation

Kian Goh

1. Maplecroft, "Climate Change Vulnerability Index 2013—Most at Risk Cities," 2013, http://maplecroft.com/about/news/ccvi_2013.html.

2. Directedly translated as "village," *kampungs* in urban centers such as Jakarta are informally constructed settlements, with varying degrees of land tenureship. Some of the kampungs in Jakarta have existed since Dutch colonial times, with rural-to-urban migration and urban redevelopment alternately adding and subtracting to their extent and density.

Fig. 1. Ciliwung River at Kampung Pulo, Central Jakarta.

From hurricanes along the U.S. Eastern Seaboard and Gulf Coast to chronic flooding in the megacities of Southeast Asia, the impacts of climate change on cities are becoming more clear and alarming. City and national governments around the world are proposing ambitious urban infrastructural and environmental projects to protect against sea level rise, stronger and more frequent storms, increasingly unpredictable precipitation, and heat waves. These projects promise safety from climate impacts and the perpetuation of economic growth, but they also bring up social questions—who and what to protect in cities that already confront spatial and social inequities.

Architects, landscape architects, and urban designers are central to these initiatives, which involve scientific knowledge, environmental transformation, urban design and policy, and sociopolitical change. But while urban resilience and adaptation has emerged as a focus of architectural exploration, the ways in which design methods, practices, and outcomes intersect with urban governance and sociopolitical processes remain neglected and misunderstood. This paper, part of a broader study of the urban spatial politics of climate change adaptation, explores the multiple dimensions of design in urban adaptation.

In this essay, I investigate large-scale urban design initiatives for protection from flooding and storms in two cities, the Giant Sea Wall master plan in Jakarta, and Rebuild by Design in New York. I explore the interconnected actors and institutions, concepts and ideas, and motivations across the sites and strategies. In particular, I focus on design as a form of policy mobilized through global-urban networks, and as a site of on-the-ground contestation. I ask, in the context of climate change and uneven social and spatial urban development, how does envisioning urban futures express and privilege contested urban politics?

3. There were 925 households evicted in August 2015, according to an account in Agung Wasono, "Violent Eviction in Kampung Pulo Jakarta: The Need of Community Development Approach," November 2015, http://www.agungwasono.com/2015/12/violent-eviction-in-kampung-pulo.html.

4. See City of New York, "PlaNYC: A Greener, Greater New York," rev. ed. (New York: Office of the Mayor, 2011); and New York City Panel on Climate Change (NPCC), "Climate Change Adaptation in New York City: Building a Risk Management Response, New York City Panel on Climate Change 2010 Report," ed. Cynthia Rosenzweig and William Solecki, *Annals of the New York Academy of Sciences* 1196, rev. ed. (Boston: Blackwell on behalf of the New York Academy of Sciences, 2015).

5. See Hurricane Sandy Rebuilding Task Force, "Hurricane Sandy Rebuilding Strategy: Stronger Communities, A Resilient Region," August 2013; and "Executive Order -- Establishing the Hurricane Sandy Rebuilding Task Force" [Press release], White House, Office of the Press Secretary, December 7, 2012, https://www.whitehouse.gov/the-press-office/2012/12/07/executive-order-establishing-hurricane-sandy-rebuilding-task-force.

6. Rebuild by Design, "Promoting Resilience Post-Sandy Through Innovative Planning and Design," U.S. Department of Housing and Urban Development, June 21, 2013, https://portal.hud.gov/hudportal/documents/huddoc?id=REBUILDBYDESIGNBrief.pdf.

Fig. 2. Rendering of Jakarta NCICD Master Plan.

JAKARTA

Jakarta, the capital city of Indonesia, is considered one of the five cities that are most vulnerable to climate change globally.[1] In January 2013, massive floods hit Jakarta. The event captivated a global audience as prominent landmarks such as the Bunderan HI (Hotel Indonesia roundabout) were subsumed under water. The floods highlighted the city's failing infrastructure, and the plight of residents, particularly those living in the informal *kampung*[2] settlements along the city's coastline and its thirteen rivers.(Fig. 1)

Jakarta's predicament precipitated a medley of action. Then-city governor Joko Widodo, newly elected and popularly known as Jokowi, promised change and enlisted the help of the South Korean government and engineering conglomerates to re-envision the future of the notoriously flood-prone Ciliwung River, which flows through the heart of Jakarta. River dredging projects by the World Bank and the Japan International Cooperation Agency (JICA), took on renewed importance. Researchers from Singapore-ETH Centre sent drones down the river to capture point cloud data for three-dimensional hydrological models. World-renowned architects joined efforts to design "vertical kampungs."

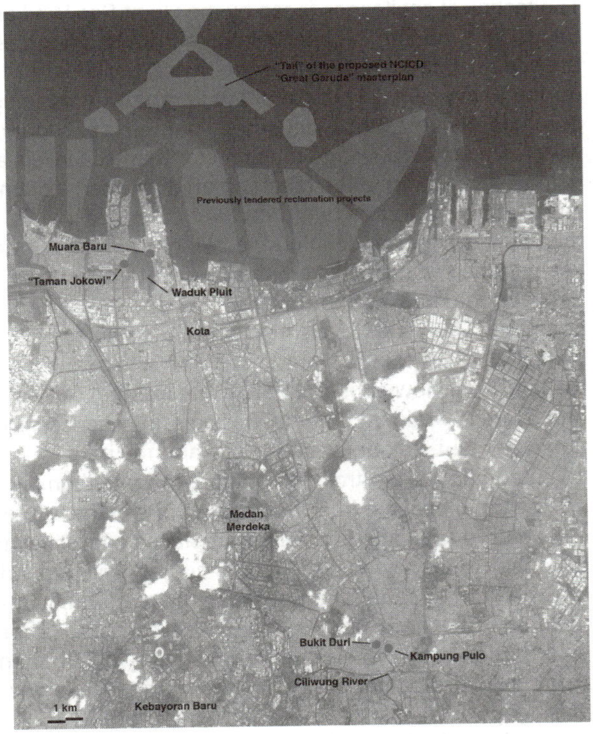

Fig. 3. Map of kampungs discussed in relation to Jakarta landmarks and the proposed NCICD Master Plan.

On a visit to Jakarta in April 2014, Melanie Schultz, Minister of Infrastructure and the Environment for the Netherlands, announced the masterplan for a massive new sea wall. In itself a new city for 1.5 million people to be built on reclaimed land in the Jakarta Bay, the National Capital Integrated Coastal Development (NCICD) masterplan is colloquially known as the "Giant Sea Wall" or the "Great Garuda," and from the air resembles the mythical bird that is Indonesia's national symbol.(Fig. 2)

But on the ground, kampung activists were fighting to keep their homes. The dredging projects entail the eviction of poor urban residents from settlements along coastlines and river edges. In some of the threatened kampung areas, community organizations have resisted, organizing and proposing alternatives to business-as-usual eviction and displacement. Mass evictions and demolitions took place in August 2015 and January 2016 in the Kampung Pulo and Bukit Duri areas[3] in the face of strident protest and continued negotiations.(Fig. 3)

NEW YORK

On October 29, 2012, Hurricane Sandy hit the New York City region. Arriving one year after Hurricane Irene, Sandy cemented in popular imagination the vulnerability of the metropolitan region. Images of a darkened lower Manhattan, rows of houses destroyed by fire in the Rockaways, and cars floating in underground garages turned into pools all turned public and municipal attention to the issue. The city had already formed a Climate Change Adaptation Task Force in 2008, part of PlaNYC, the city's sustainability plan.[4] In the wake of Sandy, this foundation was reinforced with the formation of the Hurricane Sandy Rebuilding Task Force.[5]

The Hurricane Sandy Rebuilding Task Force launched Rebuild by Design in June 2013, a high-profile competition tasked with finding "innovative, implementable proposals that promote resilience in the Sandy-affected region."[6] Led by the U.S. Department of Housing and Urban Development (HUD), and largely supported by a private philanthropic organization, the Rockefeller Foundation, Rebuild by Design selected ten multidisciplinary, designer-led teams to conduct research and produce proposals for localities in New York, New Jersey, and Connecticut. In June 2014, one year later, six winning teams and projects were announced, with $930 million in federal Community Development Block Grant Disaster Recovery (CDBG-DR) funds allocated to implementation.

Hurricane Sandy also exposed the unevenness of vulnerability in the urban region, what researchers have called a "tale of two Sandys."[7] Systemic inequities continue to affect the speed and scope of recovery. Grassroots groups such as Occupy Sandy organized to address what was seen as an institutional void.[8] The immediate post-Sandy period also suggested the ways in which

7. "A Tale of Two Sandys," Superstorm Research Lab, 2013, http://superstormresearchlab.org/white-paper/. This paper, produced collaboratively by researchers, activists, and community leaders, contends that the impacts and responses to Superstorm Sandy exacerbated long-standing inequities in the New York region. For example, the paper finds that government officials were more focused on short-term responses to direct storm damage, neglecting the systemic inequities that adversely impacted historically-marginalized communities in the aftermath.

8. Peter Marcuse, "Blog #23 – Occupy Sandy: Social Change through Prefiguring Action," *Peter Marcuse's Blog*, November 15, 2012, https://pmarcuse.wordpress.com/2012/11/15/blog-23-occupy-sandy-social-change-through-prefiguring-action/.

9. Intergovernmental Panel on Climate Change (IPCC), *Climate Change 2013: The Physical Science Basis. Contribution of Working Group I to the Fifth Assessment Report of the Intergovernmental Panel on Climate Change*, ed. T.F. Stocker et al. (Cambridge, U.K.: Cambridge University Press, 2013).

community social relationships are linked to environmental resilience. In places like Red Hook, Brooklyn, and the Lower East Side, Manhattan—coastal, low-lying areas with substantial populations of low-income residents in public housing—community organizations such as the Red Hook Initiative and Good Old Lower East Side played key, leading roles in post-storm recovery.

The events in Jakarta and New York have three things in common. First, they both resulted in a state-led emphasis on the design of large-scale urban development in order to address climate change impacts. Second, the planning and design processes exhibit a notably high degree of global interconnections—particularly with actors and institutions related to environmental planning and water management in the Netherlands. Third, in both locations, the planning of high-profile environmental and development projects reveals the disparate struggles faced by marginalized residents in vulnerable, low-lying urban areas.

DESIGN AND CLIMATE CHANGE ADAPTATION

The impacts of climate change present a number of key risks to urban centers. These include health impacts and disrupted livelihoods in low-lying coastal zones due to storm surges, coastal flooding, and sea level rise; the breakdown of infrastructure networks and critical services due to extreme weather events; mortality and morbidity during periods of extreme heat, particularly for vulnerable urban populations; and food insecurity linked to warming, drought, flooding, and precipitation variability and extremes, particularly for poorer populations.[9] Recent studies project that even if we stopped rising greenhouse gas emissions now, the planet would continue to grow warmer.[10] Adaptation, previously seen as a "dirty word" in global climate discussions, has now been given emphasis, primarily due to the increase of climate-related disasters and inadequate global action on mitigation.[11]

The scholarly field of urban climate change adaptation—generally developed in the social sciences and in policy research and practice—has tended not to focus on the design of spaces in the city. It has generally drawn distinction between physical, engineered infrastructure and measures that are more social and political in focus,[12] using classifications that differentiate spatial/nonspatial and physical/nonphysical categories of analysis and action.[13]

The complicity of design and the role of agents and institutions responsible for designing the systems at play seem to be ignored altogether. Initiatives to design urban adaptation present opportunities to form integral connections between the social and the spatial. Design, whether viewed as a process, a practice, or an outcome, presumably involves the capacity to bridge competing claims. While designers—urban, environmental, architectural—are certainly practicing in cities like New York and Jakarta, the design fields have not yet stepped up to reflect on this work and to situate it within other relevant fields and practices.

Design for adaptation is still under-theorized. Proponents of the design practices variously termed ecological urbanism are seemingly suited to address climate change adaptation.[14] But they have, to date, not engaged fully with climate change scenarios, especially in consideration with the levers of policy change, social change, or urban governance. Other theories of ecological urban design that directly respond to climate change, on the other hand, have tended to neglect sustained engagement with social and political issues.[15] An emerging set of studies that bridge climate science and design have produced helpful contributions.[16]

DESIGN IN JAKARTA *THE GREAT GARUDA*

The symbolic, formal qualities of the NCICD Giant Sea Wall plan rival its infrastructural ambitions. Aerial renderings by Rotterdam-based urban design and landscape architecture firm KuiperCompagnons show a bright bird with open wings protecting the dark city behind it.(Fig. 4) The initial sketches of the Garuda design are large, immediate, and gestural, broad marker strokes smoothing over the contradictions of scale, ecology, and politics.(Fig. 5) Its form evokes the winged Brasília—the Brazilian capital city—and the history of utopian modernism.

> Formed by the laws of nature, flow and efficiency, this elegant foil-shaped waterfront city resembles a great bird, an eagle spreading its great wings to protect the people of Jakarta, the national capital.
> –NCICD Master Plan[17]

The technical challenges faced by the Giant Sea Wall are daunting. Flooding in Jakarta comes from two sources: the sea, during high tide, and the rivers, particularly during heavy rains. This condition is rapidly worsening due to land subsidence, caused by pumping of groundwater. The city is sinking—much faster than sea levels are rising.[18] According to the master plan, the inner, existing sea wall would first be reinforced. An outer sea wall is then built in the bay, defining the "wings" of the Garuda, keeping the sea out. This creates large retention lakes between the outer wall of the new city and the current coastline. The water levels in the retention lakes will be controlled, with excess water pumped out to sea, keeping the lake levels low enough to allow the existing canals and rivers to drain into them. The lakes, in essence, function as a giant sink between the city and the bay.

In addition to controlling flooding, the retention lakes are meant to become freshwater reservoirs in the future, as captured seawater is gradually replaced by freshwater from the canals and rivers. This, of course, will depend on whether the canal and river waters are suitably unpolluted. The Giant Sea Wall marries large-scale, iconic reclamation projects like the Palm Islands in Dubai and complex hydrological works like the Marina Reservoir in Singapore.

For hydrologists and engineers, design comes after the engineering decisions. In a video describing the

10. See, for example, Thomas Lukas Frölicher, Michael Winton, and Jorge Louis Sarmiento, "Continued Global Warming after CO2 Emissions Stoppage," *Nature Climate Change* 4 (January 2014); and Veerabhadran Ramanathan and Yan Feng, "On Avoiding Dangerous Anthropogenic Interference with the Climate System: Formidable Challenges Ahead," *Proceedings of the National Academy of Sciences* 105, no. 38 (2008): 14245–14250.

11. Mizan R. Khan and J. Timmons Roberts, "Adaptation and International Climate Policy," *Wiley Interdisciplinary Reviews: Climate Change* 4, no. 3 (2013): 171–89.

12. For example, in Jörn Birkmann et al., "Adaptive Urban Governance: New Challenges for the Second Generation of Urban Adaptation Strategies to Climate Change," *Sustainability Science* 5, no. 2 (2010): 185–206; and Matthias Garschagen and Frauke Kraas, "Urban Climate Change Adaptation in the Context of Transformation: Lessons from Vietnam," in *Resilient Cities: Cities and Adaptation to Climate Change – Proceedings of the Global Forum 2010*, ed. Konrad Otto-Zimmermann (Dordrecht: Springer, 2011), 131–39. See also JoAnn Carmin, David Dodman, and Eric Chu, "Urban Climate Adaptation and Leadership," *OECD Regional Development Working Papers* (Paris: OECD Publishing, 2013).

13. For example, in Stephen Tyler and Marcus Moench, "A Framework for Urban Climate Resilience," *Climate and Development* 4 (2012): 311–26.

14. See Mohsen Mostafavi, "Why Ecological Urbanism? Why Now?," *Harvard Design Magazine* 32 (Spring/Summer 2010): 1–12; Anne Whiston Spirn, "Ecological Urbanism: A Framework for the Design of Resilient Cities," 2012, http://annewhistonspirn.com/pdf/spirn_ecological_urbanism-2011.pdf; and Charles Waldheim, ed., *The Landscape Urbanism Reader* (New York: Princeton Architectural Press, 2006).

15. See, for example, Alisdair McGregor, Cole Roberts, and Fiona Cousins, *Two Degrees: The Built Environment and Our Changing Climate* (New York: Routledge, 2013); and Peter Newman, Timothy Beatley, and Heather Boyer, *Resilient Cities: Responding to Peak Oil and Climate Change* (Washington, DC: Island Press, 2009).

Fig. 4. Rendering of Jakarta NCICD Master Plan.

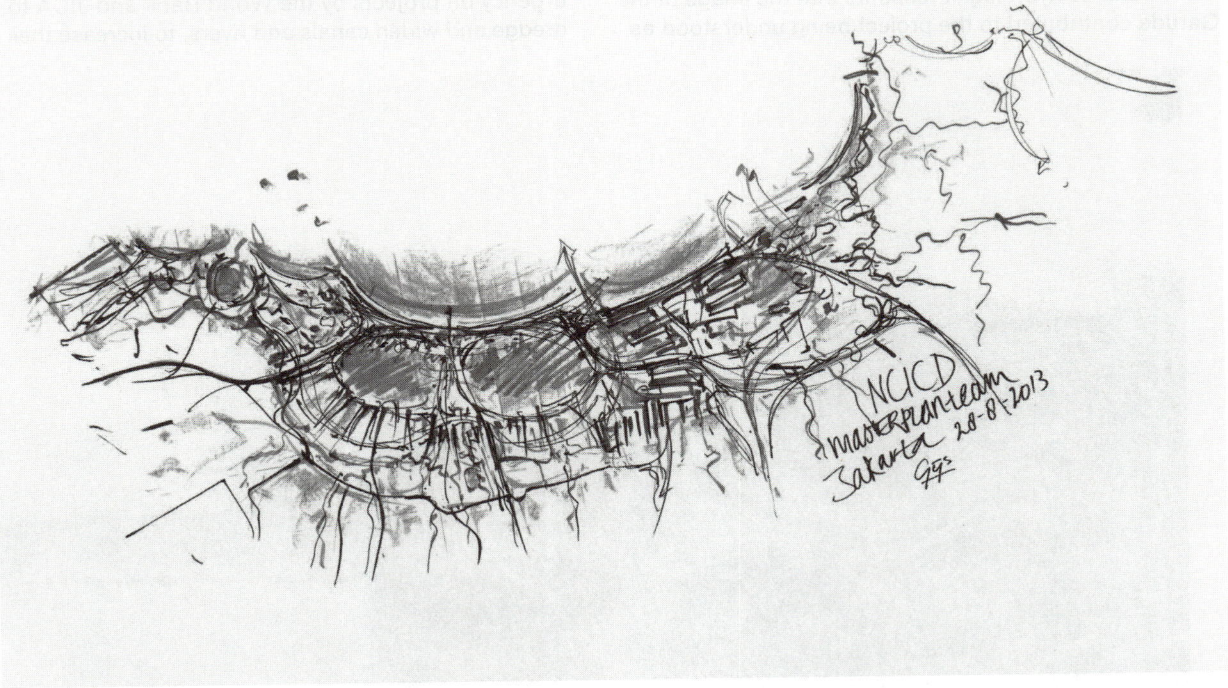

Fig. 5. Sketch of Jakarta NCICD Master Plan.

16 These include Guy Nordenson, Catherine Seavitt, and Adam Yarinsky, *On the Water: Palisade Bay* (New York: Museum of Modern Art, 2010), a study of the New York-New Jersey Upper Bay two years before Hurricane Sandy, illustrating methods of spatial research and design speculations on the role of soft, hybrid infrastructure in coastal protection; and Steward T. Pickett, Mary L. Cadenasso, and Brian McGrath, eds., *Resilience in Ecology and Urban Design: Linking Theory and Practice for Sustainable Cities* (Dordrecht: Springer, 2013), an edited volume connecting concepts in ecology and urban design.

17. Indonesia, Coordinating Ministry for Economic Affairs (MENKO), "National Capital Integrated Coastal Development Master Plan," October 1, 2014, http://ncicd.com/wp-content/uploads/2014/10/MP-final-NCICD-LR.pdf.

18. Hasanuddin Z. Abidin et al., "Land Subsidence of Jakarta (Indonesia) and Its Relation with Urban Development," *Natural Hazards* 59, no. 3 (2011): 1753–71; Jan Jaap Brinkman and Marco Hartman, "Jakarta Flood Hazard Mapping Framework," International Conference on Urban Flood Management, 2009, http://www.hkv.nl/upload/publication/Jakarta_Flood_Hazard_Mapping_Framework_MH.pdf.

19. Deltares, "Jakarta Sinking City," shown at *International Architecture Biennale Rotterdam 2014—Urban By Nature*, Rotterdam, 2014, https://www.youtube.com/watch?v=Amkyt1SMKPc.

20. KuiperCompagnons principal, interview with the author, Rotterdam, October 1, 2014.

21. Ibid.

Jakarta project, a hydrologist with Dutch research institute Deltares talks about how "bright architects came in and they thought about how this dike should look ... they saw wings in the form of the Jakarta coast."[19] The designer himself —in his office in Rotterdam's Van Nelle Factory building, an icon of modernism—speaks about how he literally demolished his hotel room in Jakarta making the sketches, covering the walls with large sheets of paper and going at it freehand.[20] He strongly emphasizes the necessity of local stakeholders in Indonesia to embrace the Giant Sea Wall, for it to be an Indonesian project. For him, the role of the designer was to take the technological requirements and "integrally shape" them so that the Jakarta residents could become excited about the project. Well aware of the parallels to Brasília—also "winged" and built on *tabula rasa* conditions—the designer brings up the comparison himself, posing the question to Jakarta officials: How will Jakarta be different?[21]

So if anthropologist James Holston, in his influential study of Brasília,[22] asserted that modernist design did not take seriously existing social relationships, then what the designer of the Giant Sea Wall is advocating for is a particular kind of *post*-modernist design. Designers, so mindful of modernism's checkered history, have themselves adapted to a new global environment. This new design doctrine negotiates capital, authority, and participation. It will no longer, for example, be Le Corbusier proclaiming the "prodigiously true" nature of his Plan for Algiers,[23] but the Dutch urban designer inviting a shared possession of the legitimacy of his vision. As if to ask, why wouldn't you want to be behind the vision of a new kind of city?

A Deltares hydrologist recounts that the image of the Garuda contributed to the project being understood as something beyond a collection of technical objectives. The Garuda design, the hydrologist stresses, turned a "Dutch development aid project into a national ambition."[24]

At its most basic, the Giant Sea Wall is merely that, a wall. It is an engineering project, a "defense strategy" —born out of disaster and motivated by the specter of worse disasters. It is an expensive fix for decades, if not centuries, of bad decisions. But, formulated as the Great Garuda, it is proposed to be a national development plan—a step into a different kind of world citizenship. Design here connects the pragmatic to the emotional.

KAMPUNG DESIGN ACTIVISM

But design can also connect the emotional to the pragmatic. Residents most vulnerable to floods in Jakarta live in the informal kampung settlements, especially along the north coastline and the Ciliwung River. Kampung residents, essentially synonymous with the urban poor in Jakarta, are plainly called "illegal" by city officials.[25] These officials blame kampung residents for the floods, saying that their actions degrade the waterways, while ignoring illegal garbage dumping and uncontrolled urban development.

The Giant Sea Wall proposal to create large retention lakes between the new sea wall city and the current coastline, and to turn them into freshwater reservoirs, counts on clean rivers and canals flowing into the retention lakes. These rivers and canals have long been clogged by sediment and refuse, and increasingly overstressed by runoff caused by rapid urban development.[26] This places urgency on projects by the World Bank and JICA to dredge and widen canals and rivers, to increase their flow

22. James Holston, "Spaces of Insurgent Citizenship," in *Cities and Citizenship* (Durham, N.C: Duke University Press, 1999), 155–74.

23. As recounted in James C. Scott, *Seeing like a State: How Certain Schemes to Improve the Human Condition Have Failed* (New Haven, Conn.: Yale University Press, 1998).

Fig. 6. Houses in Muara Baru, on the edge of Waduk Pluit in Jakarta. Photograph by author, July 2014.

26. Contributing to decreased ground permeability and increasing stormwater runoff to drains and canals. See Grace Susetyo, "Once Upon a Sinking City: The Perpetual Floods of Jakarta," Rujak, May 6, 2013, http://rujak.org/2013/05/once-upon-a-sinking-city-the-perpetual-floods-of-jakarta/ for a discussion on causes of flooding in Jakarta by Marco Kusumawijaya, director of Rujak, an urban research and advocacy organization.

24. Deltares hydrologist, interview with the author, Jakarta, July 11, 2014.

25. Representative of Jakarta DKI government, interview with the author, Jakarta, July 16, 2014.

27. See Kian Goh, "Making Room for Water? Urban Adaptation and Uneven Development in Jakarta," (under review), for elaboration on these issues.

28. See Lawrence J. Vale, Shomon Shamsuddin, and Kian Goh, "Tsunami + 10: Housing Banda Aceh after Disaster," *Places Journal* (December 2014), for more information on rebuilding in Banda Aceh, ten years after the tsunami, including the work of Uplink.

29. Ciliwung Merdeka, "Kampung Susun Manusiawi Bukit Duri," (Microsoft Powerpoint, Jakarta, Indonesia, n.d.).

30. Architecture for Humanity, *Design like You Give a Damn: Architectural Responses to Humanitarian Crises* (New York: Metropolis Books, 2006).

Fig. 7. Organizers from Urban Poor Consortium (UPC) and Muara Baru kampung residents in Jakarta. Photograph by author, July 2013.

and "normalize" them, in the words of city officials. The dredging and widening projects directly threaten the displacement of kampung settlements, many of which sit directly on the water's edge.(Fig. 6)

The work on the Giant Sea Wall masterplan coincided with a number of resistance initiatives on the ground in the kampungs. Both the Urban Poor Consortium (UPC) and Ciliwung Merdeka (Free Ciliwung), two community-based organizations, succeeded in forging working agreements with city officials for alternatives to the forced evictions and displacement that have characterized recent struggles in Jakarta. They both achieved this with innovative design initiatives and coalitions.[27]

In the Muara Baru area, in North Jakarta, UPC's coalition includes community architects, students from University of Indonesia, and researchers from Rujak Center for Urban Studies, an urban advocacy and research organization.(Fig. 7) A UPC coordinator recounts how its organizing strategy and its use of broad-based coalitions, including designers, started in the aftermath of the Indian Ocean tsunami in 2004, during which the organization worked with architects and local community network Uplink Banda Aceh to help design and rebuild communities.[28] In Jakarta, faced with the threat of eviction, UPC's coalition proposed designs for a new typology of social housing, comprising five-story apartment blocks, with collective spaces for economic and social uses on each floor.(Fig. 8) Organizers also secured promises from Governor Jokowi that the new housing would be built on nearby land.

In Bukit Duri and Kampung Pulo, two of the most threatened kampungs along the Ciliwung, Ciliwung Merdeka built a coalition that included, at one time, Kota Kita, a citizen planning group, designers and planners from Harvard University and the Bartlett School of Architecture and Planning, and housing advocacy organizations like the Asian Coalition for Housing Rights. Ciliwung Merdeka has also been in talks with city officials and has continued to press its case for alternative solutions, including designs for new typologies of river-edge housing and rehousing in place. In their vision for a "humanitarian vertical kampung" for Bukit Duri, they conducted community-led mapping of the kampung and river, determined a preferred course for river widening, and designed new stacked, higher density kampung dwellings to house selectively relocated residents within the existing area, maintaining neighborhoods and livelihoods.[29] (Fig. 9)

These initiatives by kampung activist coalitions bring up clear provocations and questions about the relationship between design and social justice. In recent years, there has been a fair amount of attention paid to humanitarian design—*Design Like You Give a Damn,* in the words of the founders of the recently shuttered Architecture for Humanity.[30] These efforts are motivated, in large part, by the premise that the skills of professional designers are much needed, and often neglected, in the places with the most pressing social and environmental problems.

But these alternate visions in Jakarta—these counter-plans—are not just examples of humanitarian design. Nor are they a form of post-Hernando de Soto design-driven "entrepreneurial" slum dweller.[31] They are more coherent and multilevel. Kampung organizers build on the exigency of real, shared struggles, conditions of notoriety, a history of political activism, and the vision and ability to form new coalitions.

Design becomes part of a platform for organizing. Design makes political vision tangible and credible—using documents, data, and drawings of urban and architectural

31. Hernando de Soto, *The Mystery of Capital: Why Capitalism Triumphs in the West and Fails Everywhere Else* (New York: Basic Books, 2000). See also Colin McFarlane, "The Entrepreneurial Slum: Civil Society, Mobility and the Co-Production of Urban Development," *Urban Studies* 49, no. 13 (2012): 2795–2816.

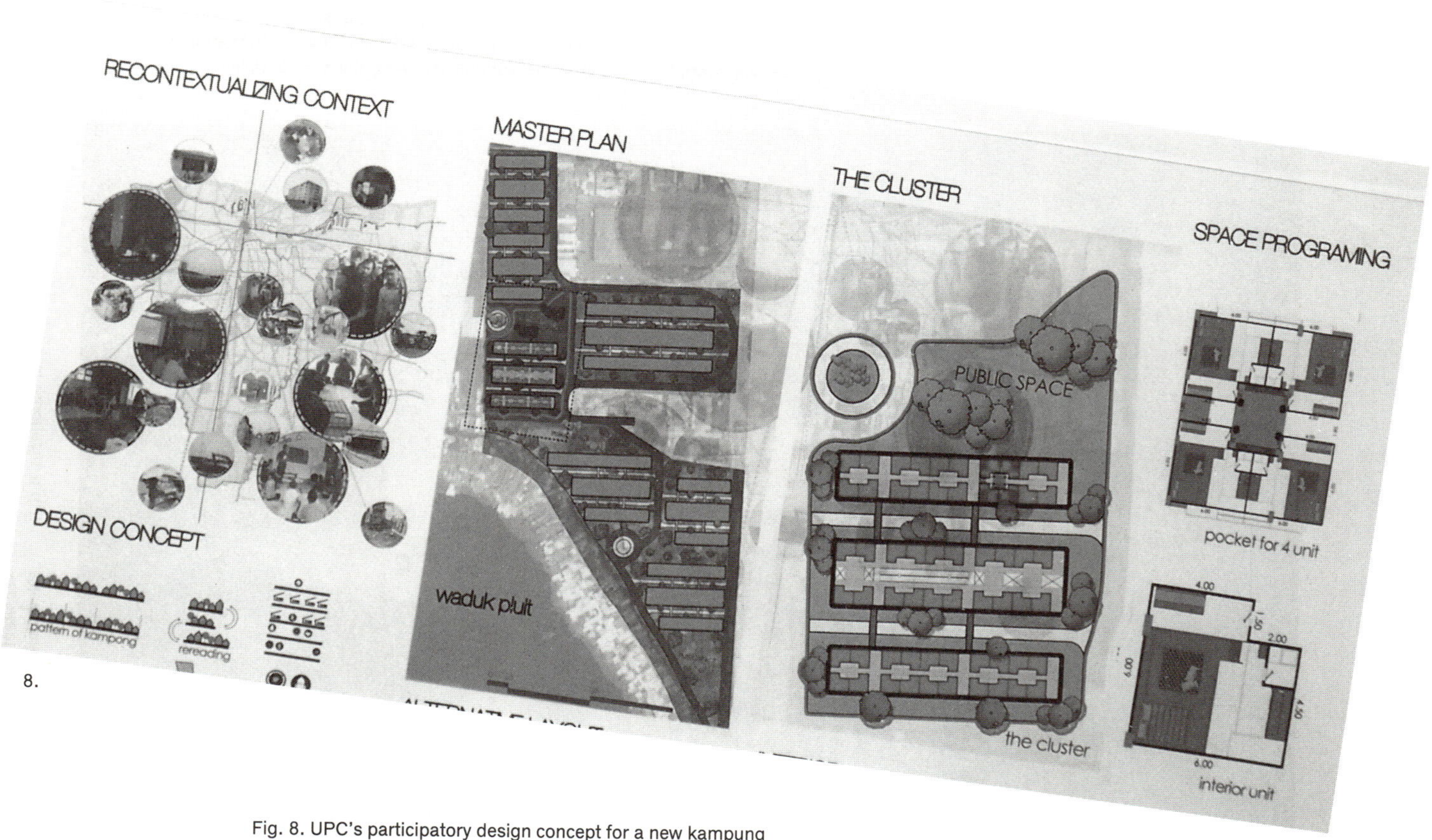

8.

Fig. 8. UPC's participatory design concept for a new kampung typology at Muara Baru, exhibited at the Jakarta Vertical Kampung exhibition at the Dutch Embassy in Jakarta, July 2013.

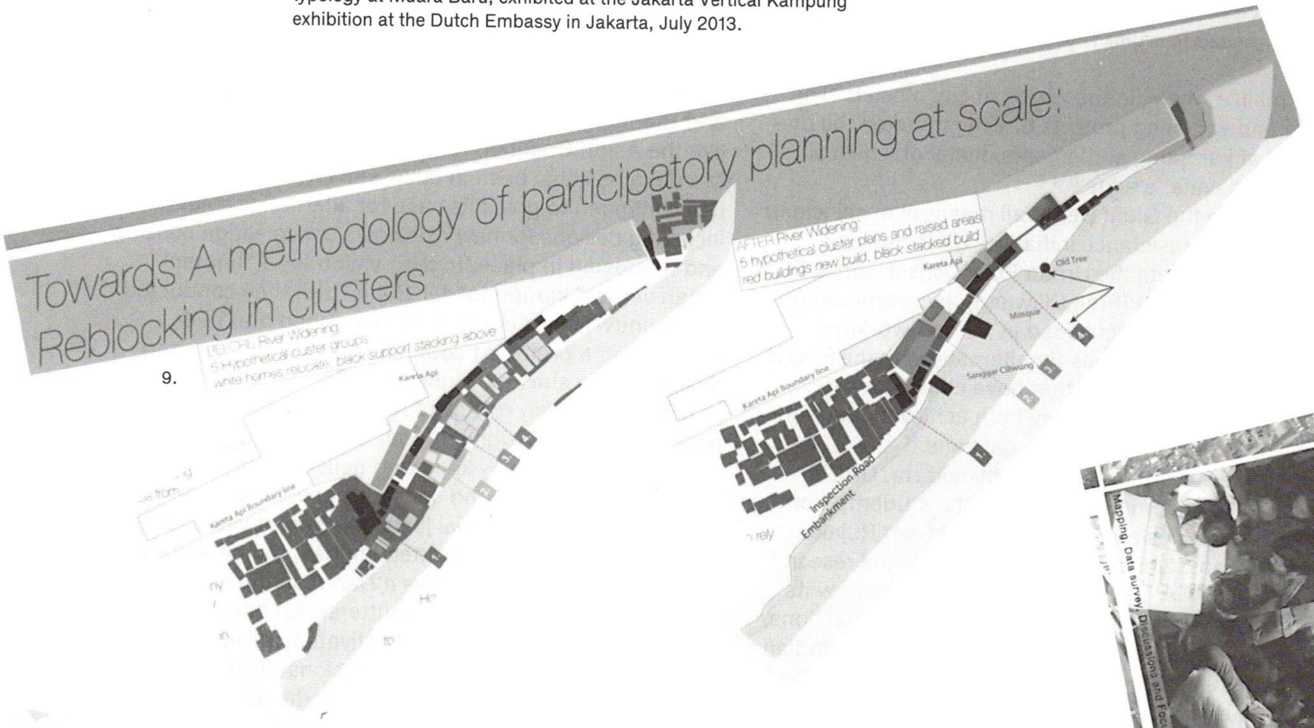

9.

Fig. 9. Ciliwung Merdeka's design for a "humanitarian vertical kampung," exhibited at the Jakarta Vertical Kampung exhibition at the Dutch Embassy in Jakarta, July 2013.

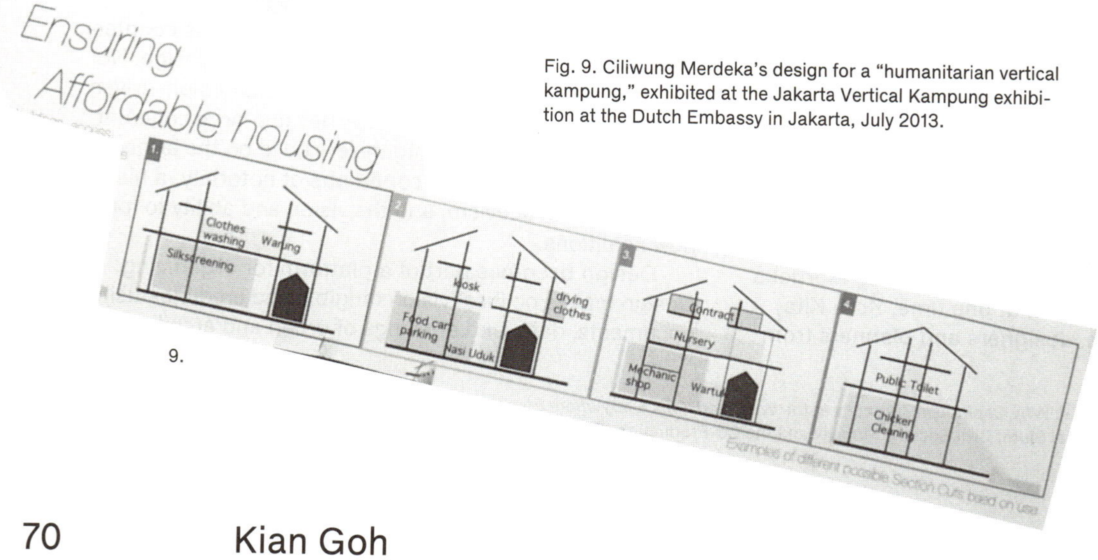

9.

9.

32. Ciliwung Merdeka activist, interview by the author (translated from Bahasa Indonesia), Jakarta, July 18, 2014.

forms to explain and negotiate. It gives form to what might have been summarily dismissed as emotional appeals or fought off as political activism. Both coalitions' visions were presented in an exhibition titled *Jakarta Vertical Kampung* at the Dutch embassy in Jakarta in 2013, and they have succeeded in building a working, if tenuous, relationship with city officials. Says a Ciliwung Merdeka activist:

> For years, the urban poor in Jakarta had a very negative stigma, that they were lazy, passive, illegal, only taking welfare, and didn't want to participate, didn't want to be organized. We proved that a collective planning process, with plans and mappings, could be made by the community themselves ... that they had the imagination to form the ideals for their own kampung, in ways that were concrete.[32]

Design connects the emotional to the pragmatic.

DESIGN IN NEW YORK
REBUILD BY DESIGN

In New York, timing (after two major storms, Sandy and, the year after, Irene), prior initiatives (such as the formation of the New York City Panel on Climate Change in 2008, and the Museum of Modern Art's *Rising Currents* exhibition in 2010), and the fortuitous connections of powerful individuals (primarily HUD Secretary Shaun Donovan, Rockefeller Foundation president Judith Rodin, and Dutch director of spatial planning and water affairs Henk Ovink) opened the possibilities for an innovative response. This alignment of federal and state governments, international relationships, and nonprofit philanthropy brought the issue of design into prominence. Design, after all, had not been a central concern in federal environmental programs. Rebuild by Design organizers envisioned bringing the design process in line with the outcome and building an effort for comprehensive planning that has been neglected in U.S. urban development. Six teams were declared winners of the competition, and awarded implementation funds:

- The BIG team proposed "The Big U," a series of buildings, landscape elements, and demountable protections that wraps around the southern tip of Manhattan.(Fig. 10) The team's design documents stress the "needs and concerns of the island's diverse communities" and "integrated social and community planning." (Awarded $335 million.)[33]

Fig. 10. Rendering of "The Big U" at the south tip of Manhattan by BIG team.

- The Interboro team stresses a comprehensive, regional view of Nassau County's South Shore.(Fig. 11) The team proposal, titled "Living with the Bay," emphasizes a process that intersects a "systems approach," and a "community approach," and is explicitly ecological in strategy while also taking on issues of racial segregation. ($125 million.)

Fig. 11. Aerial rendering of "Living with the Bay" proposal by the Interboro team.

- The MIT CAU + ZUS + URBANISTEN team's "New Meadowlands" project in New Jersey is set in a context in which fragile wetlands ecosystems abruptly meet expanses of concrete, asphalt, and steel—the support systems for the New York City urban region. The team's strategy encompasses the environmental and the economic, including nature reserve, transportation networks, and urban densification.(Fig. 12) ($150 million.)

Fig. 12. Concept drawing of "New Meadowlands" proposal by MIT CAU + ZUS + URBANISTEN team.

- The OMA team, addressing Hoboken, New Jersey, proposed a strategy to "resist, delay, store, discharge" water.(Fig. 13) The plan proposes a series of enhanced hard and soft infrastructure protections along the coast (resist), permeable areas within the city (delay), a set of storm water holding areas within the city (store), and pumps and drains (discharge). ($230 million.)

33. This amount, like the other winning team awards, is less than necessary to complete the designs as proposed. The "BIG U" proposal, according to the design team, is projected to cost $1.09 billion.

34. Rebuild by Design principal, interview by the author, November 24, 2014.

35. U.S. Department of Housing and Urban Development (HUD), "CDBG-DR: Community Development Block Grant Disaster Recovery Program," HUD Exchange, accessed June 10, 2015, https://www.hudexchange.info/programs/cdbg-dr/.

Fig. 13. Rendering of "Resist, Delay, Store, Discharge" plan for Hoboken by OMA team.

- The PennDesign/OLIN team, proposing "Hunts Point Lifelines" for the Bronx, zeroes in on the challenges of poverty, environmental vulnerability, and undesirable land uses, while also stressing the strengths of local activism, including the work of groups like Sustainable South Bronx.(Fig. 14) The proposal highlights opportunities for community-based planning, new jobs, new methods of intermodal food and supply distribution, and local economic development. ($20 million.)

Fig. 14. Aerial rendering of "Hunts Point Lifelines," South Bronx, proposal by PennDesign/OLIN team.

- The SCAPE/Landscape Architecture team proposed "Living Breakwaters" for the eastern coastline of Staten Island.(Fig. 15) Eschewing conventional "hard" protections, the proposal entails storm-dissipating breakwaters built of hybrid construction, blocks, and gabions to encourage oyster habitats and other marine life. SCAPE/Landscape Architecture also stresses community links and educational and cultural opportunities for local residents. ($60 million.)

Fig. 15. Rendering of "Living Breakwaters" proposal by SCAPE team.

Each of the design teams emphasizes community engagement—in line with Rebuild by Design's explicit direction. With the possible exception of the OMA team, each tries to show how this engagement is an integral part of its design process. But the scale and scope of the projects sometimes brings up clear issues in terms of engagement objectives. In the case of the BIG team, the list of stakeholders includes ten municipal departments, four city council districts, four state senate districts, six state assembly districts, eight U.S. congressional districts, three New York State departments, numerous federal agencies and departments, as well as various real estate developers, property managers, nonprofit organizations, and community groups. The BIG team's attempt to be all inclusive also reveals the complex nature of a site like Lower Manhattan. When you try to include all stakeholders in such a contentious setting, what, actually, are the stakes? The key question is whether this kind of participation is able to transform existing power dynamics.

Rebuild by Design attempted to bridge two cultures, merging the entrepreneurship, individualism, and competition of the United States with a more collaborative approach and focus on the common, as emphasized in Dutch precedents.[34] This is an ambitious objective, particularly within the context of New York City urban spatial politics.

PROCESS

The Rebuild by Design award process was set up in a very specific way. The CDBG-DR federal community development block grants targeted toward disaster recovery were assigned to local municipalities. The CDBG-DR funds are specifically meant to aid low-income communities after disaster.[35] The Rebuild by Design organizers were explicit that design teams had to win the backing of a broad group of local stakeholders in order to win the award. Designers, then, worked in a relatively communicative fashion. This is in line with normative planning principles.

For example, in the proposal by the BIG team for Lower Manhattan, designers attempted to hybridize Robert Moses and Jane Jacobs[36]—meshing top-down and bottom-up, large-scale infrastructure and community relationships. One could argue that the designers attempted this Moses-Jacobs meshing on two levels—in terms of the spatial objectives of the design itself, combining waterfront infrastructure, prominent cultural buildings, and spaces for local gathering, and in terms of their own practice, necessarily engaging with a broader "public" on a city-scale, and attempting to bring community groups on board with their proposal.

The community stakeholders here, including Lower East Side affordable housing advocates, ended up quite happy with the vision and their participation. It did not start out that way. A longtime local housing activist, now with community organizing coalition LES Ready,[37] cited the long history of beautification projects exacerbating gentrification, as well as the unequal attention to east and west sides of Lower Manhattan.[38] These concerns echo longstanding issues in Manhattan urban politics. The west side of Lower Manhattan, including the West

36. Robert Moses was the New York City planner responsible for large-scale transformations of the city, particularly infrastructural projects, park expansions, and slum clearances. Jane Jacobs is most well-known for her book *The Death and Life of Great American Cities* and her activism against the Moses-conceived Lower Manhattan Expressway, proposed to cut through large swaths of the Lower East Side. Moses' and Jacobs's positions have come to stand in, somewhat simplistically, for the conflict between large-scale, top-down, state-led urban interventions and small-scale, historically-attuned community-based development.

37. Lower East Side Long Term Recovery Group (http://lesready.org), a coalition of community groups and institutions coordinating our response and preparedness planning and training for future disasters, formed in the wake of Hurricane Sandy. See also LES Ready et al., "Getting LES Ready: Learning from Hurricane Sandy to Create a Community-Based Disaster Plan for the Future," Urban Justice Center, 2014, https://cdp.urbanjustice.org/sites/default/files/CDP.WEB.doc_Report_LESready_20141117.pdf.

38. Community activist, member of LES Ready, interview by the author, New York, December 18, 2014.

39. Kevin Fox Gotham and Miriam Greenberg, "From 9/11 to 8/29: Post-Disaster Recovery and Rebuilding in New York and New Orleans," *Social Forces* 87, no. 2 (2008): 1039–62.

40. Asian American Federation of New York, "Chinatown after September 11th: An Economic Impact Study," Asian American Federation of New York, April 4, 2002, www.aafny.org/doc/ChinatownAfter911.pdf.

41. Community activist, member of LES Ready, interview by the author, New York, December 18, 2014.

42. Member of Rebuild by Design's management team, interview by the author, New York, June 19, 2014.

Village, Tribeca, and Battery Park City neighborhoods, has long since become affluent. The dismantling of the elevated West Side Highway made way for the new Hudson River Park; yet the FDR Drive on the east side remains, and community and recreational uses are much less developed, even after multiple planning initiatives. After the September 11, 2001 attacks, the Chinatown area of the Lower East Side was hit particularly hard, first by the immediate economic impact, then by inequitable distribution of housing and job-creation funds[39] and spatial segregation by security barriers and rerouted transportation from the Wall Street area.[40]

So, the fact that the design team was focusing on LES Ready's constituents and neighborhood was not immediately seen as a positive. Yet, the activists were heartened by the Rebuild by Design management team's attention to the participatory design process.[41] A key member of the management team acknowledged the challenge of connecting designers and community stakeholders, recalling their continual efforts to make the audiences aware that their feedback was central to the success of the design proposals.[42] Rebuild by Design ensured a level of community engagement on the part of the design teams by asserting this link between the outcome of the competition and community support. After a process that was, to local activists, both contentious and productive, LES Ready convinced elected officials to support the BIG team's plan.[43]

Two of the challenges to the Rebuild by Design strategy are tied to the very innovation for which it is credited. The first is the organization of the competition structure and the uncertain relationship between the competition phase and the implementation phase. After HUD released the CDBG-DR funds, each local city or state authority began its own program to advance the projects. These projects are now atomized into separate procurement and public review processes. By mid-2015, a fragmented picture of this situation had emerged across the chosen localities, with varying degrees of progress and success.[44]

The second challenge concerns the source and amount of funding. In the case of Lower Manhattan, the BIG team's proposal was awarded $335 million—a lot of money, but only a fraction of what it would take to build defenses surrounding Manhattan, midtown-down. The initial award is meant to spur further private funding, to create a "new form of public-private financing mechanism."[45] After the competition phase, HUD released the funds to the city, which then started its own proposal process for what is now called the East Side Coastal Resiliency project. In this case, the design team members were retained largely intact.

Early in the implementation phase, in the fall of 2014, there was already debate and contestation over which areas would be protected first.[46] The first section to be built excludes several public housing developments in the Lower East Side hit hard by the storm, and residents there contend that they are not being prioritized, even though their neighborhoods were the worst impacted and the lowest lying.[47] This emerging situation, ongoing as of mid-2015 as the city begins new public meetings for this project, illustrates very well what is perhaps the key obstacle of the Rebuild by Design initiative.

Design here works to engage communities, win block grants, and capture imaginations. In this case, however, it is not necessarily part of a broader effort to change social relationships and political structures.

ANALYSIS AND CONCLUSION

In Jakarta, the Giant Sea Wall master plan is unapologetically figural, the symbol of the Garuda masking, in some ways, the sophistication of the hydrological plan and the complexity of the existing conditions. Negotiating between Dutch vision and Indonesian aspirations, the design achieved an important goal. It won the political support of city and national government officials. The design gave form to a previously technical process. It allowed officials to see beyond an engineered wall, even beyond a real estate development project, to national ambition. But the design was also part of a process that prompted the foreclosure of alternate options. It posed an ideal, technological, and infrastructural solution to what, in many ways, is a sociopolitical and urban governance problem.

Conversely, in the kampungs of Muara Baru, Bukit Duri, and Kampung Pulo, community organizations along with their coalitions have marshaled design toward productive agreements with then governor Jokowi. Design here enabled kampung residents to give form to a sociopolitical campaign. The visions and the measures afforded by the design process and documents enabled new platforms for negotiation between organizers and city officials. Such efforts are proving, at best, partially successful. The more socially attuned "humanitarian vertical kampungs," advocated for by community groups, has not yet come to fruition. And the continuing evictions and destruction of settlements in the following years demonstrate the entrenched power of systemic relationships in the city.

In New York, organizers for Rebuild by Design intently foregrounded community participation, ensuring, in its best cases, a high level of engagement between design teams and community stakeholders. At the same time, each of the winning teams' designs reveals priorities that reflect both the local sites and the makeup of their team. But the broader ambitions of Rebuild by Design—comprehensive and regional-scale planning, an innovative merging of competition with collaboration—face serious challenges in the implementation phase, confronted by fragmented administrative jurisdiction at the local level.

The post-competition contestation also reveals the limitations of design strategies that strive for inclusiveness but, ultimately, inadequately support the possibilities for social and political change, particularly in the context of contested urban politics. In the Lower East Side, community stakeholders in LES Ready felt included and listened to during the competition phase. But bureaucratic procurement processes and continuing unequal power relationships in the city now threaten to replicate historical patterns of marginalization.[48]

Design presents visions of alternate futures and brings choices and motivations to the foreground. The maneuverings and contestation around design exposes sociopolitical motivations and power relationships in cities. We see that design plays multiple roles in the production and

43. The BIG team's "BIG U" project is arguably the most high-profile of the Rebuild by Design proposals, and LES Ready's experiences during the competition phase and beyond present an important assessment of community engagement. One can find alternative opinions of community participation in the case of the OMA team's Hoboken proposal. See Ron Hine, "State Takes Control of Hoboken's Rebuild by Design Project; Estimated Start Date for Construction 2019," Fund for a Better Waterfront, May 21, 2015, http://betterwaterfront.org/njdep-takes-control-of-hoboken-rebuild-by-design-project-estimated-start-date-for-construction-2019/.

44. "Projects Are Moving Forward," Rebuild by Design, June 3, 2015, http://www.rebuildbydesign.org/update/projects-are-moving-forward/. In early 2016, a Hoboken, New Jersey, resident group rejected the plan, citing concerns about a sea wall blocking their views. See Patrick McGeehan, "Plan to Flood-Proof Hoboken Runs Into a Wall," *New York Times*, February 7, 2016.

45. "HUD Announces Winning Proposals from the 'Rebuild by Design' Competition," [Press release], U.S. Department of Housing and Urban Development, June 2, 2014, http://portal.hud.gov/hudportal/HUD?src=/press/press_releases_media_advisories/2014/HUDNo_14-063.

46. This was before the starting of the city's own community engagement process, to begin in December 2014. "East Side Coastal Resiliency Project," City of New York, March 19, 2015, http://www.nyc.gov/html/planyc/downloads/pdf/150319_ESCR_FINAL.pdf.

47. Dusica Sue Malesevic, "2 Years after Sandy, Who Will Get Shelter from the Storm? Only Some Downtown," *Downtown Express*, October 29, 2014.

48. It bears restating that this discussion elaborates on the specifics of one site, and one group of stakeholders. But the primary conclusion about the fragmentation of the process holds true when assessing other Rebuild by Design cases. For further illustration, as of early 2016, the implementation process appears to be moving more smoothly for the SCAPE/Landscape Architecture team's Staten Island proposal, and much less so for the OMA team's Hoboken proposal.

legitimization of adaptation plans. Design connects the pragmatic and the emotional. The marshaling of design can be used to connect a more technocratic process of planning with the messier, more unpredictable priorities of communities on the ground. This is what the Great Garuda vision attempts in Jakarta; it is what Rebuild by Design's participatory process is meant to accomplish in New York. Inversely, design—and the production of the documents of design—can give measurable weight to what might be dismissed as emotional appeals. This is what UPC in Muara Baru and Ciliwung Merdeka in Bukit Duri and Kampung Pulo have been able to do.

Design is political. It is intertwined with foundational ideas about society, concerning symbol, image, identity, and legitimacy. Critically, design can also be a part of resistance, a mode of political organizing. Design opens terrains of contestation.

AN ALTERNATIVE? RED HOOK INITIATIVE

To end, I offer another example as an alternative. In 2010, I designed a community center for the Red Hook Initiative (RHI). The RHI space was designed in a collaborative process, by and for the community. (Fig. 16) We prioritized a collective sense of ownership by participants. When Hurricane Sandy hit the New York region, Red Hook was one of the worst hit neighborhoods in the city. RHI's space survived the storm, and in the days after emerged as a hub of grassroots recovery efforts.[49]

The RHI community center stayed dry in part due to luck and topography. The flooding reached the streets adjacent to the RHI space, but did not go beyond. It was also a matter of architectural design and economy. The building was built as a warehouse space, with a concrete, slab-on-grade floor. It does not have a basement. All the mechanical systems were placed on the roof or mounted on the walls, out of the way of floodwaters. (Mounting critical equipment above the ground floor is now a standard architectural design recommendation for storm surge and flood resilience. The Red Hook Houses, a NYCHA housing project, just across the street, do have basements, and did not fare quite as well.)

Fig. 16. Red Hook Initiative, March 2010.

How did the space, along with the staff members and volunteers, become a recovery hub in the wake of Sandy? In my view, three points stand out: First, our design team paid particular attention to the relationship between spatial design and social organization. We prioritized openness, transparency, and accessibility, aligned with RHI's approach as a community space, as well as a diversity of spaces to account for the fast-changing and often unpredictable uses. This included leaving the large warehouse doors as glazed, roll-up doors. In the days after the storm, this enabled volunteers to set up soup kitchen service just inside the doors, with lines spilling out the sidewalks. Second, the location of the building, catty-corner to the Red Hook Houses, allowed the RHI space to function as it was intended—as a place for the community. Third, there had been "buy-in" from the community members—the staff and participants, almost all who have ties to public housing. The RHI space, completed only two years before the storm, had become a center of social life, a building belonging to its community.

In Red Hook, community building, social and environmental resilience, and space and design were inextricably intertwined. It serves as an example for how designers can engage with deeper aspects of justice and equity. Eric Klinenberg, a sociologist at New York University and research advisor for Rebuild by Design, explicitly made this connection when he brought members of the selected design teams to the RHI space, asking: "Can we design spaces like this?"[50]

A project like the Red Hook Initiative does not replace the kind of large-scale infrastructural and landscape design projects that Rebuild by Design envisions. There is a space for big plans like that, especially in circumstances in which there is broad consensus for high levels of physical protection, embraced as part of the sociocultural and economic lives of residents. But the RHI project allows us to consider that crucial weaving of social and spatial, in particular the place of agency of marginalized residents.

It is not that one project changes much—but that one project is successfully embedded in a broader process of organizing for social and political change. In the words of the executive director of RHI, "People from the community have the power to create their own social change ... you have to create opportunities for people to take action ahead of time."[51]

AUTHOR'S NOTE

This paper is based on research and findings conducted for the author's doctoral dissertation on the urban spatial politics of climate change adaptation. This research was funded in part by the Center for International Studies, the Aga Khan Program for Islamic Architecture, the William Emerson Travel Fund, and the Harold Horowitz Research Fund, all at the Massachusetts Institute of Technology.

49. See Red Hook Initiative, "Red Hook Initiative: A Community Response to Hurricane Sandy," (Brooklyn, NY: Red Hook Initiative, June 2013).

50. Michael Kimmelman, "Next Time, Libraries Could Be Our Shelters from the Storm," *New York Times*, October 2, 2013.

51. Red Hook Initiative executive director, interview by the author, Brooklyn, NY, September 13, 2014.

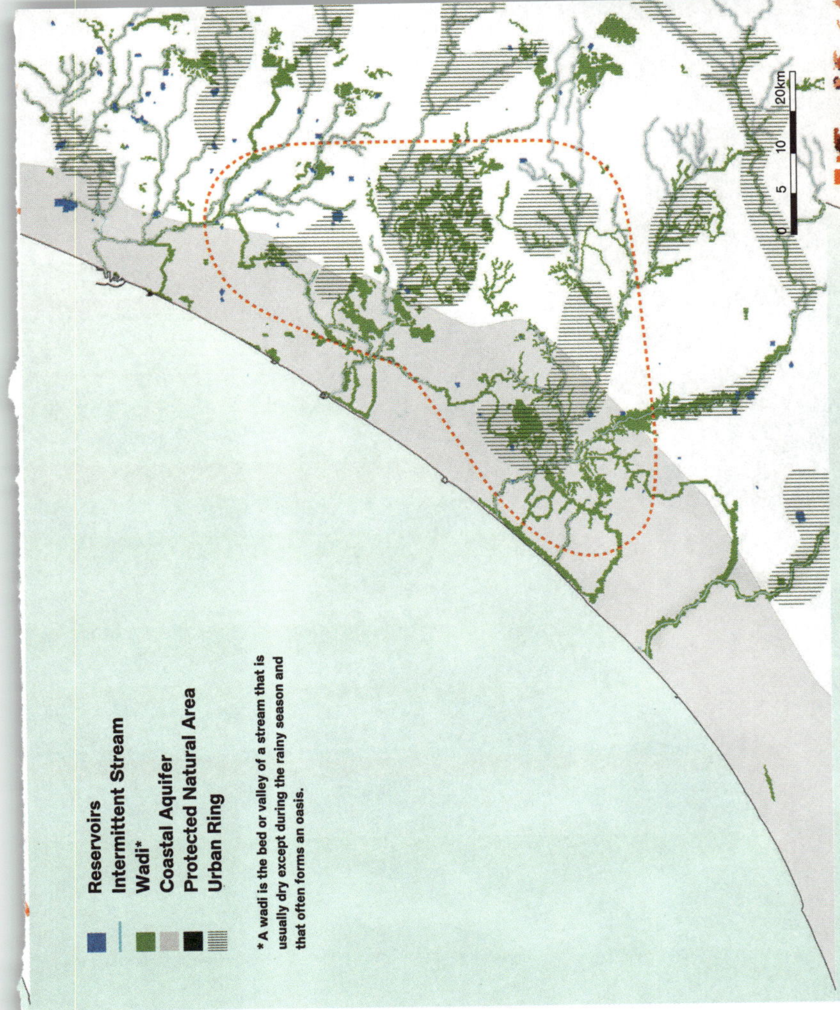

NATURAL SYSTEMS PRESERVATION AND ENHANCEMENT

URBAN GROWTH (2066)

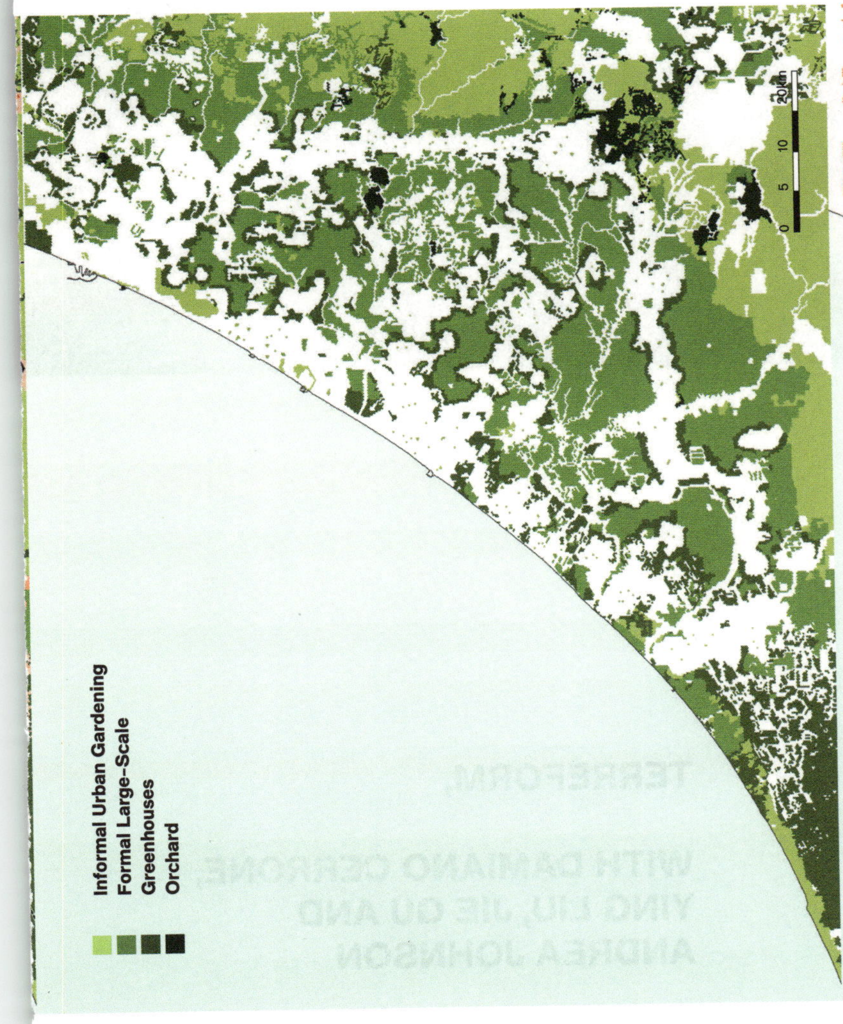

AGRICULTURE

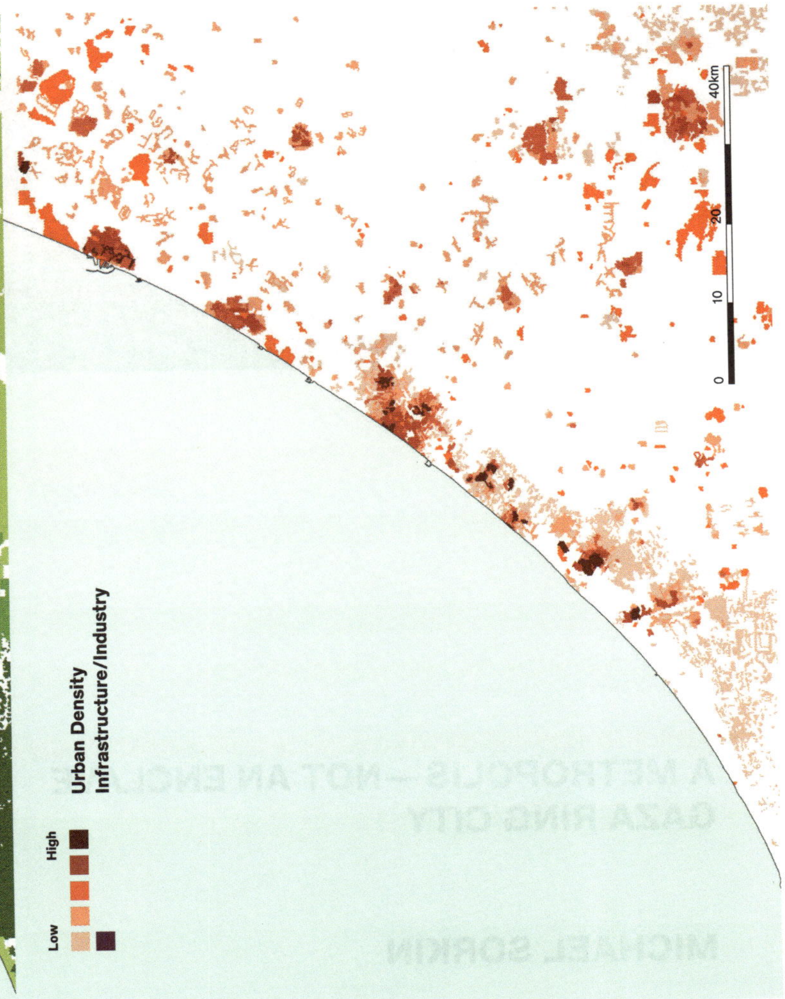

URBAN GROWTH (2016)

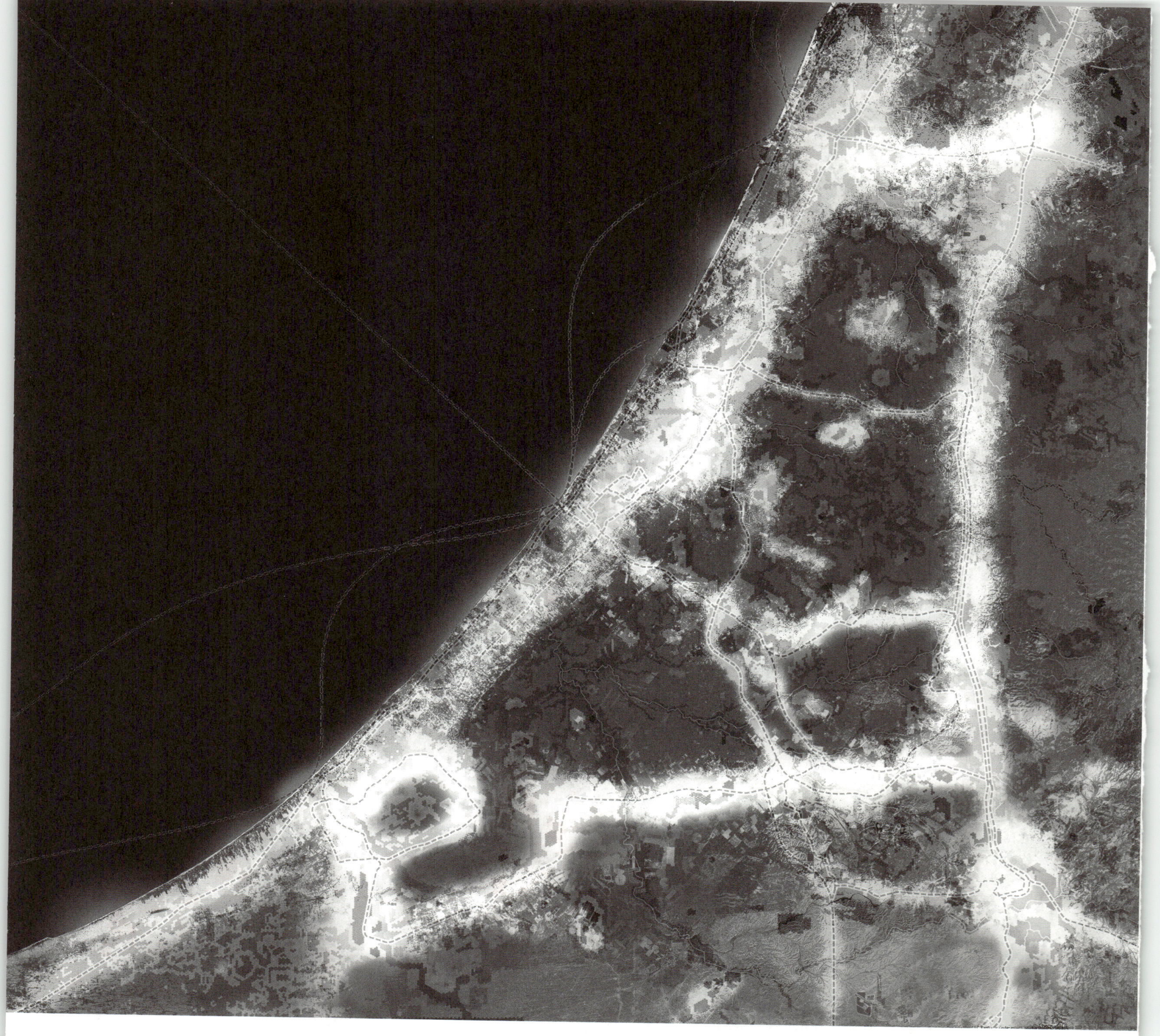

A METROPOLIS—NOT AN ENCLAVE
GAZA RING CITY

MICHAEL SORKIN

TERREFORM,

WITH DAMIANO CERRONE,
YING LIU, JIE GU AND
ANDREA JOHNSON

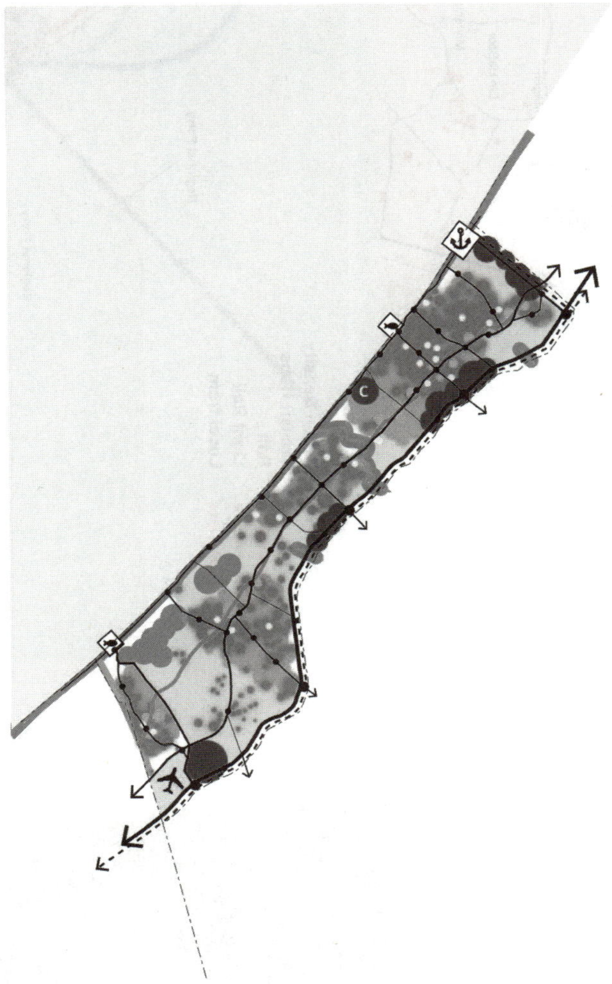

1. ISOCARP Gaza & West Bank Urban Planning Advisory Team, *Ideas for Palestine's Gaza Coast*, 2015. In ISOCARP Gaza & West Bank Urban Planning Advisory Team, "Spatial Visioning Reflections: Gaza.", *PLAN 2* (2015): 32–36. Copyright 2015 with ISOCARP.

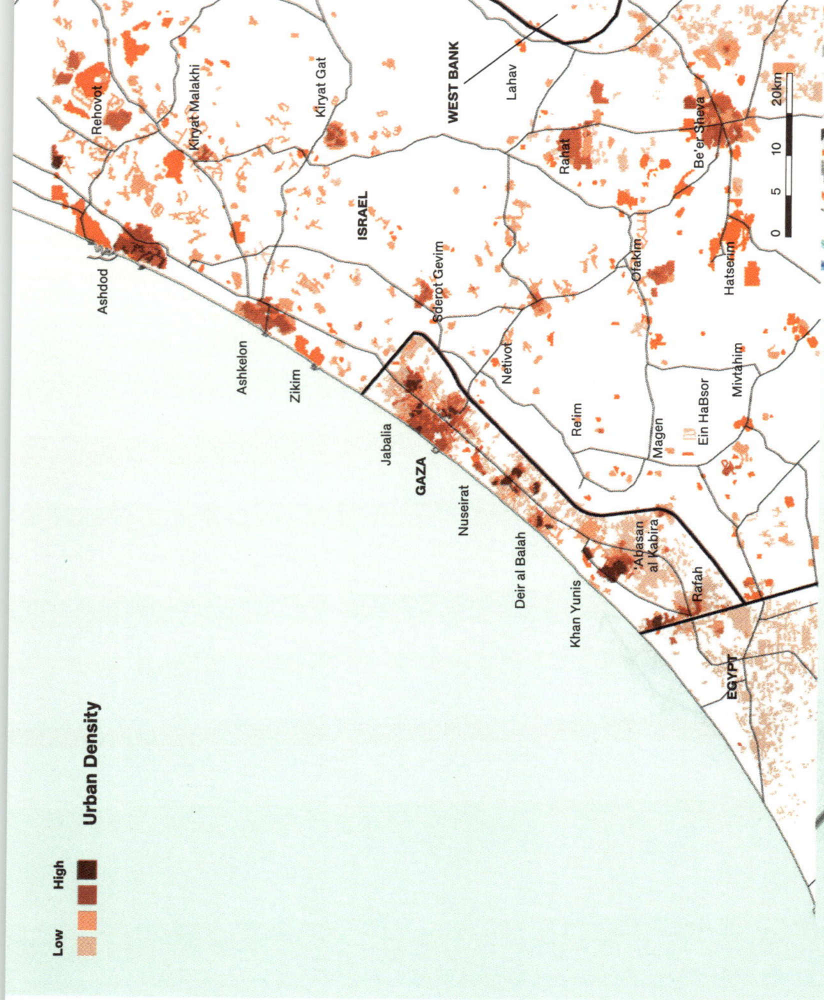

EXISTING BORDERS AND SETTLEMENTS

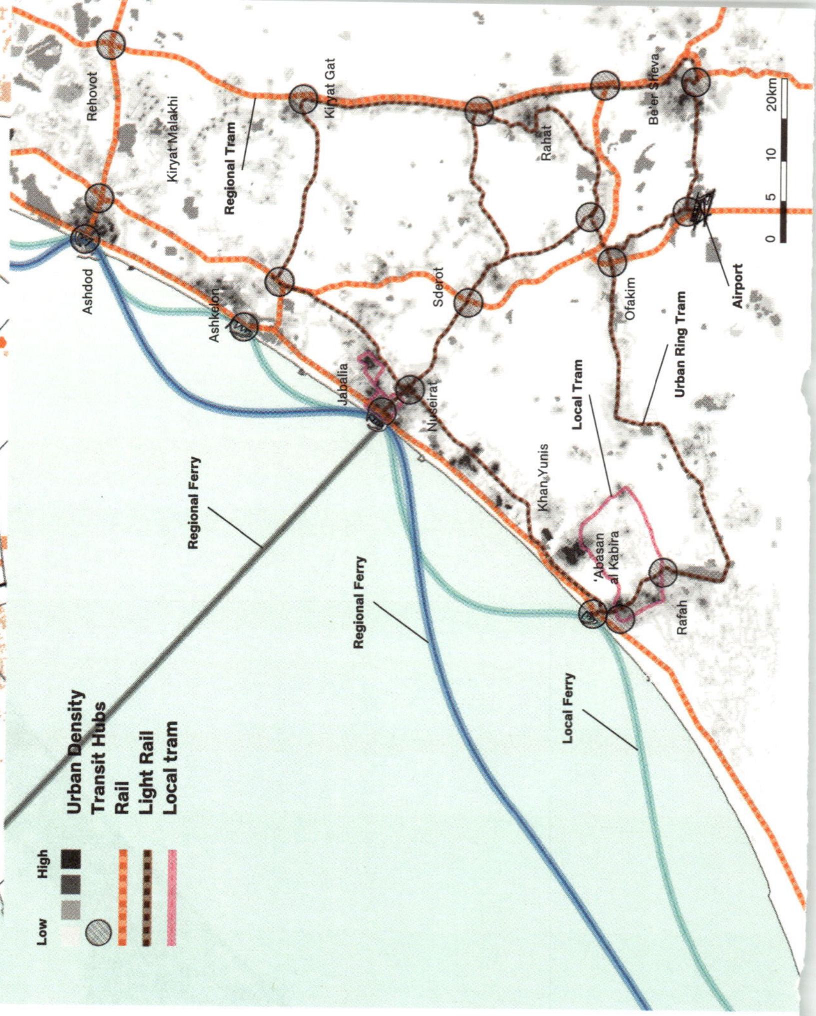

TRANSPORTATION

AREA OF FOCUS

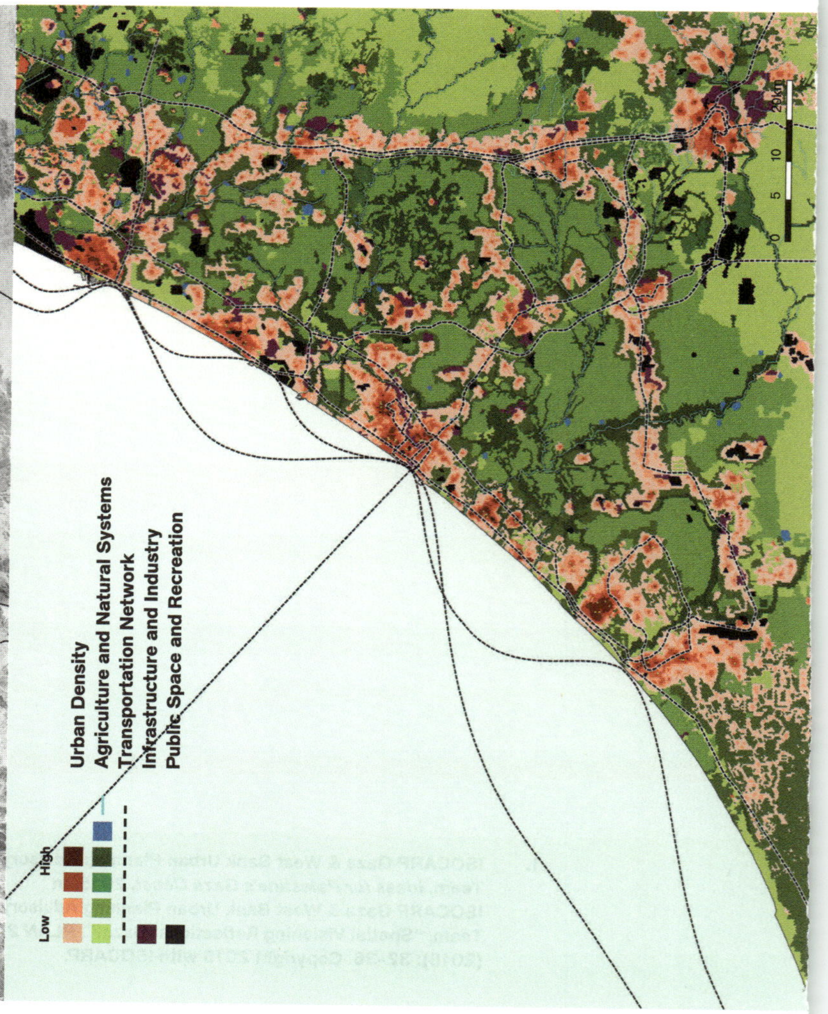

RING CITY 2066

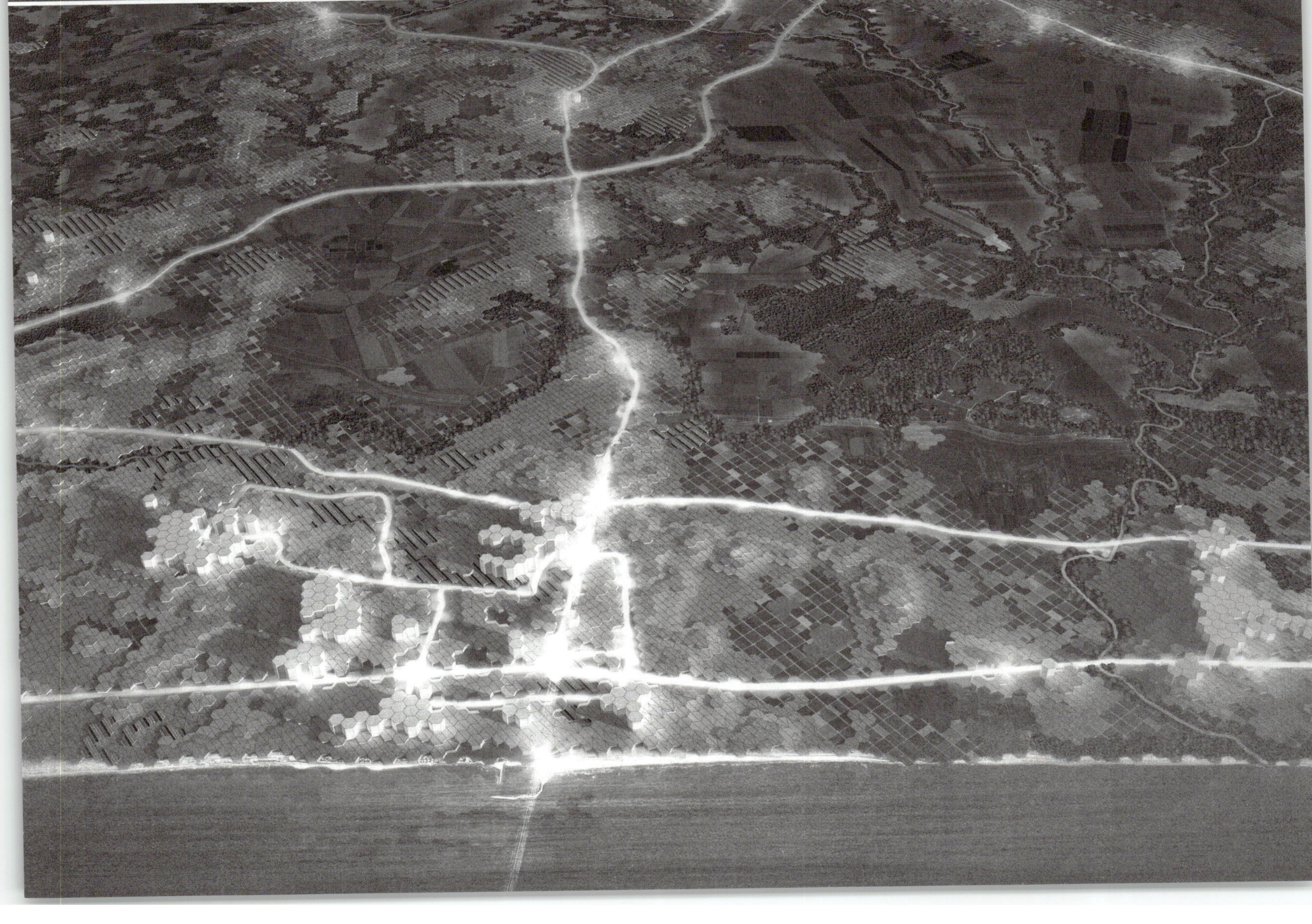

BEFORE

AFTER

groves, modern greenhouses, large-scale and low-water fields, to grazing land and domestic gardens.

TRANSPORTATION

An efficient transit system is based on universal convenience and equitable access. The linearity of the densest portions of the "strip" enable a double tram line to place all residents within close proximity to public means of movement. A variety of "last mile" possibilities, including bicycles, shared cars and taxis, and enhanced pedestrian ways, would be provided at each tram stop. The system also encompasses the larger loop that forms the expanded city and this light rail would be augmented by a regional heavy rail network extending to towns and cities in Egypt, Israel, Palestine, Jordan, Lebanon, Syria, and beyond.

Taking advantage of Gaza's proximity to the sea, we have also suggested a coastal ferry system for both local and regional transit, as well as enhancements to the port. This would allow for travel around the Mediterranean to the innumerable cities on its shores – Haifa, Izmir, Brindisi, Marseilles, Tangier – that are not under siege. This water-born system would join the heavy rail and enhanced roadways to enable site saturation by a multi-modal logistics system.

Finally, we have suggested the conversion of the Hatzerim Military Airbase, west of Beersheba, to an international civilian airport. This more capacious site would be served by both the light and heavy rail systems and would be located in a more favorable acoustic environment than the now destroyed Gaza airport. Additionally, it can offer greater flexibility for expansion, cargo handling, and other ancillary facilities, including storage, manufacture, and aerospace.

CULTURAL, EDUCATIONAL, AND RECREATIONAL FACILITIES

Mapping the density of existing facilities reveals patterns of concentration and sparseness that can be read for both access and deprivation. Our solution is gestural: to harmonize the numbers of facilities with the presence of populations. The placement of shared facilities is rooted in the idea of local access. We do not seek the even densities of sprawl: on the contrary, the morphology we propose is one in which the thickness of urbanity is seen as the material condition of both sociability and sustainability. In this proposal, we are working at a grain where a mosque is indistinguishable from a football field but we are certain that all such facilities should be both accessible to all who would use them. By zooming out from the familiar scale of the strip, we seek to use the representational valence of the map to foreground forms of subjectivity that are shared.

Again, we identify this most important subdivision of the city in a notional rather than specific way. Were we to actually design the future of a Ring City neighborhood, we would think about the provision of all needed facilities for happily living everyday life, about open space, about styles of gathering, about decent housing for all inhabitants, about services and infrastructure, about transportation and walkability. Categories that are inevitably mapped under a political frame – refugee camps, military bases, settlements – would surrender these descriptors to become mere places in the city. The striking material similarity between prosperous and tractable environments throughout the region suggests the grounds for a certain kind of convergence, based on both shared and elected affinities. We thus identify occurring and prospective urban structures that can be traversed in twenty minutes and house populations invested in their own neighborliness. Of course, there must be that imperative universal right to the city and this will surely bring about changes, including dramatic ones. This right – in its classic articulation by Henri Lefebvre, David Harvey, and others – is fundamental and to be understood not simply in terms of freedom of movement, safety from surveillance, or access to services but – and crucially – in the right to imagine and demand a city that is most deeply rooted in individual dreams and desires.

ACCESSIBILITY

A spatial syntax model used to analyze street and path segments and their inter-accessibility within the network reveals Gaza's limited interconnection. A lighter line signifies greater difficulty to reach that segment from all other segments and less likelihood that movement between different parts of the network will pass along that segment.

We have enhanced and extended the pattern of roadways to increase ease of movement, to increase choices in moving about the city, and to strategically locate uses that are contingent on high levels of traffic and access. An improved street hierarchy and an abundance of public transportation options, including "last mile" bike and pedestrian paths, augment and distribute accessibility and connection throughout the region.

ECOLOGICAL FOOTPRINT

A simple Ecological Footprint (EF) calculation is imprecise until fleshed out with local particulars but it can be a very useful medium of articulation and situation. Using Israel's current EF – 6.2 global hectares (gha) per capita (i.e. the average Israeli requires 6.2 hectares to produce their resources), the 2016 image reveals the actual "size" of Gaza if the calculus includes the full

– if abstracted – extent of the territory required to provision the entire population of this newly – and otherly – understood town at the same rates of consumption currently enjoyed by Israelis.

Despite a widening gap between the EF and biocapacity, we believe that the use of rational technologies can simultaneously shrink environmental demand even as expectations for quality of life are raised. If resource demands were reduced to meet the biologically productive area available in the region, the EF would shrink to twenty-seven times the area of its current political boundary, shown as the smallest footprint on our 2066 plan. This would – again at current Israeli rates of consumption – only support 161,000 people, well under one-tenth the current population of Gaza.

It is unrealistic, however, that Palestine or Israel could ever operate in an ecological reserve due to their high population densities and harsh climate, marked by water scarcity and limited fertile land. We've therefore also shown the dimensions of a footprint for the proposed Ring City at a population of 2.5 million based on a somewhat different perspective. This has been calculated not at Israeli rates but at the current world average of 2.7 gha which would have the effect of cutting the current footprint almost in half, even accounting for population increases. This scenario would allow for a comfortable standard of living, but drastically reduce the cumulative impacts of human activities on natural systems and allow for a greater degree of regional autonomy.

While recognizing that ecological footprint calculations are fuzzy, fraught, and reductive, they can, nevertheless, be usefully revelatory. To begin, they measure inequality with great precision and map embedded global injustice at every scale. Gaza, walled from its sustaining hinterland and obliged to beg, fight, or smuggle to maintain its cruel subsistence is fundamentally unsustainable. To a planner operating with justice – both local and planetary – as a basis for design, this calculus obliges the infusion of the procedures of physical distribution with an ethical standard. While mathematical formulae for human equality are perilous things, especially when it comes to the recognition and defense of difference, the idea of equalizing access to both sustenance and opportunity is at the vital center of what it means to plan.

This proposal stages a confrontation between representation and justice. In an environment that lives in a permanent state of exception, the tools of "normal" planning suggest not only the degree to which human rights – including the right to the city – are impossible under the carceral regime that governs Gaza, but also that a literal reframing of the situation points to imperative political logics to which urban and environmental design arc. Strategies and styles of redress directed to the situation on the ground in Gaza – however urgent in the immediate term – also have the effect of reifying a nightmare. A few calories added to the prison meal will not hasten the break-out.

A version of this essay is also published in:
Terreform, Open Gaza
(New York: UR Books, forthcoming).
www.urpub.org

ECOLOGICAL FOOTPRINT (2016)

ECOLOGICAL FOOTPRINT (2066)

ECOLOGICAL FOOTPRINT

Ecological Footprint (EF) measures the land and water area a population requires to produce the resources it consumes and absorb the carbon dioxide emissions it generates. A population whose EF is higher than its biocapacity, defined as the biologically productive area required to generate an ongoing supply of renewable resources, must import biocapacity through trade. Israel has an ecological deficit of -5.9 global hectares per capita (gha) and a low biocapacity at 0.4 gha (compared to the world average of 1.7, the U.S.' 3.8, and Brazil's 9.1), due to water scarcity and limited fertile land. As consumption increases and land availability shrinks, the gap between supply and demand, or biocapacity and EF, widens.[1]

To visualize Gaza's EF if every resident consumed at the Israeli level of 6.2 gha (i.e. the average person requires 6.2 hectares to produce its resources), Gaza's EF would encompass an area 305 times its actual size.

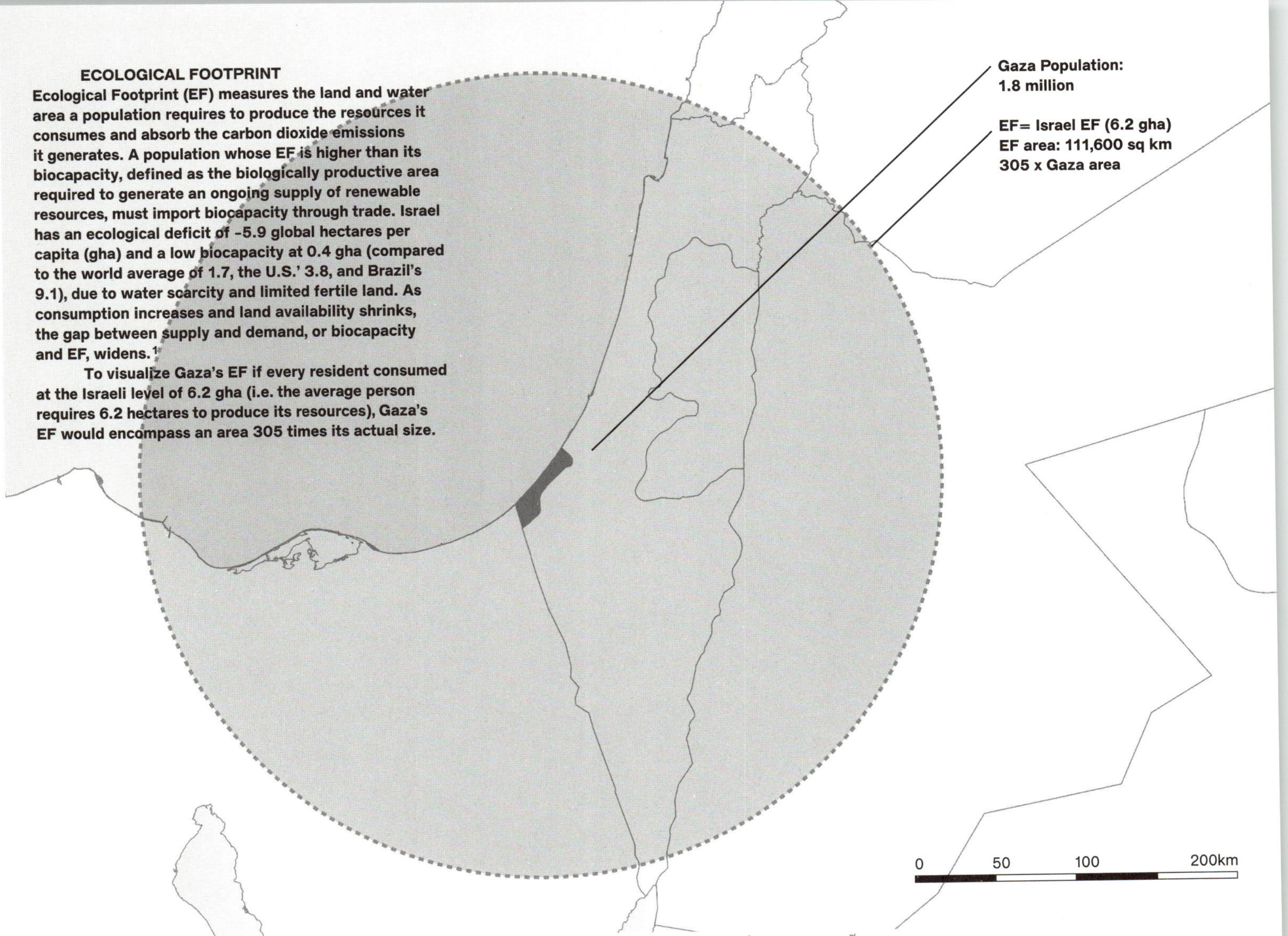

This proposal suggests that through renewable energy production, an efficient transport system, desalinization of the aquifer, reduction of waste, local processing, and protection of natural resources and agriculture land it is possible to significantly reduce the EF while increasing biocapacity.

An extreme scenario, utilizing an EF equivalent to Israel's biocapacity of 0.4 gha would drastically shrink the Ring City's footprint to five times its actual size. Accepting, however, the region's unlikelihood of ever operating in ecological reserve due to its high population density and harsh climate, we consider a more realistic EF equivalent to the world average of 2.7 gha. This scenario almost cuts in half the current footprint, and would allow for a comfortable standard of living, but would drastically reduce the cumulative impacts of human activities on natural systems and allow for a greater degree of self-sufficiency in the region.

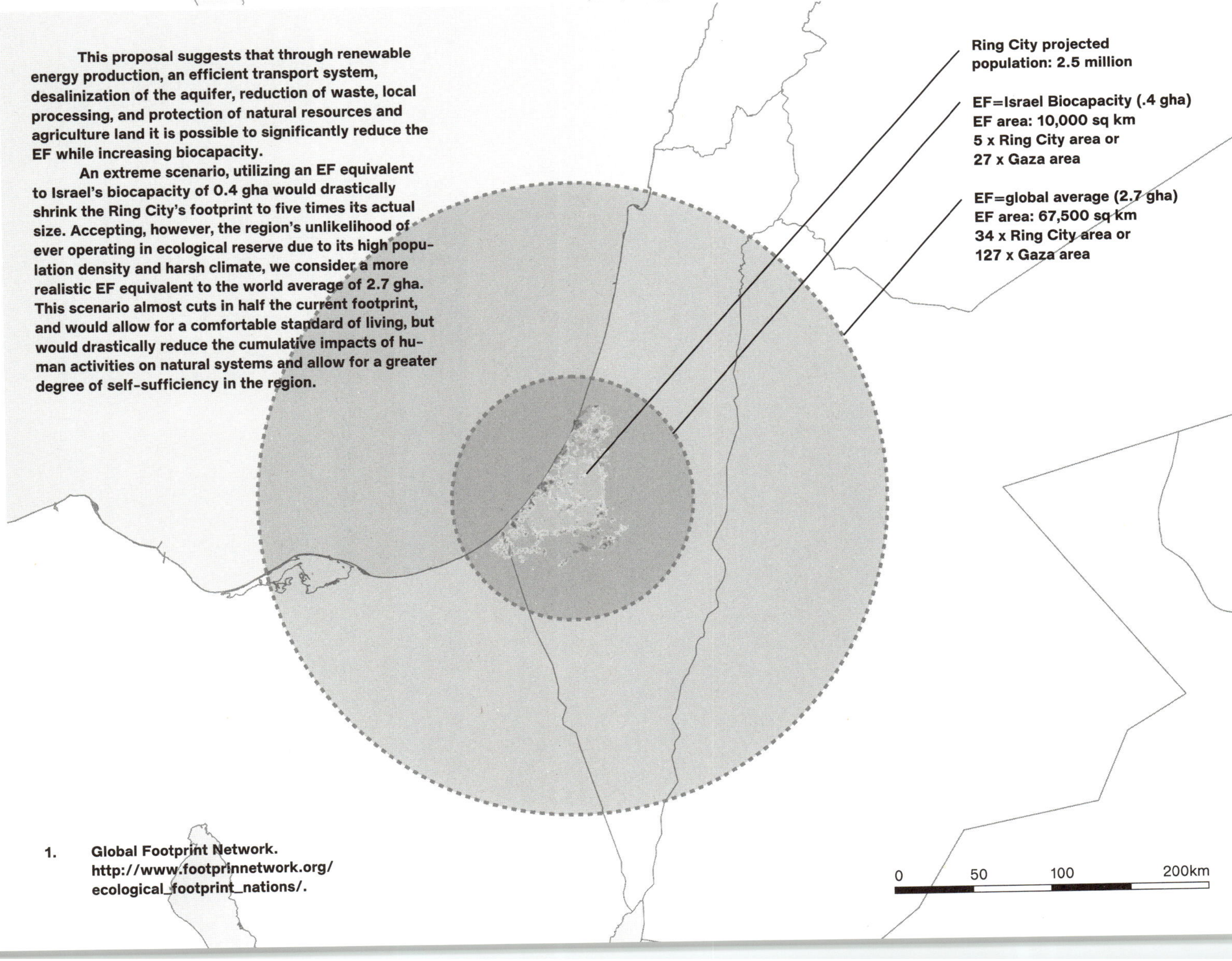

1. Global Footprint Network. http://www.footprinnetwork.org/ecological_footprint_nations/.

FOREVER TRANSIENT:

LIFE AT THE "AFFORDABLE" MEXICAN PERIPHERY

By Tatiana Bilbao
Photographs by Onnis Luque

These photographs tell the story of someone trying to live in Mexico City, a metropolis with 20 million inhabitants in a country of 120 million people. This is the all-too-common tale of a woman owning a house that is so far removed from the city and employment that she suffers just from trying to live in it. It is the story of owning a house that is now only half of its initial worth. It is a tale where owning a house is a burden as well as a luxury in a country where nearly 9 million households are in need of adequate housing. This is the story of Fabi, a working woman who lives in Chalco, the farthest settlement in Mexico City's periphery, and works in Polanco, the city's most prestigious and affluent area. Hers is a story shared in some form or another by nearly 40 million others living in the suburban ghettos of Mexico.

5:30 Wake up. On a Tuesday morning, the weather in Chalco is brisk and it still smells of rain from the evening before. Along with the scent of wet dirt and moist pine, a waft of sewage lingers—the street drainage hasn't functioned properly for some time. As I get dressed and prepare to head to work, life in these housing projects seems still-born. A silence fills the air. The twinkling lights from the identical houses across the street seem to mirror my own and are the only reminder that others inhabit this neighborhood.

6:35 Upon leaving the house, a hush stillness lies over the neighborhood. The streets, vast and empty, would seem surreal but they won't be any livelier tomorrow or even the day after that. Everything is always the same. Almost. A stray dog wanders around. Overgrown grass has taken over neglected gardens that just a few years ago were neatly trimmed as the houses were being sold. Graffiti half-heartedly covers some of the walls. These imperfections, come to think of it, weren't present in the model at the sales office.

6:42 After some time walking, I've reached my favorite part. The walls lining the streetscape of Lote 3 are painted murals. I must have walked past here thousands of times but today I look up and around. I'm curious how, amidst all the sameness, this block has gotten to be so different. For some time we've talked about adding a third story to our house but we haven't been able to save up for it.

7:05 It's still some ways to go before reaching the bus stop. To my left, the sound of flapping plastic in the wind calls attention to bright polyester pennants stretched on the string. The new housing development is finally going on sale. The little tan boxes so neatly arranged, their *tinacos*[1] and orange accent walls give rhythm to the composition. As *peseros*[2] drive along the road I stick my hand out hoping to catch a ride on one, but they are all full this morning, as they are most mornings. I always try anyways.

1 *Tinacos* are water cisterns, often installed on the roof of a house.

2 *Peseros*, or microbuses are one of the most recognizable features of the urban landscape in Mexico City, their green-grey color scheme synonymous with mass transit. The buses are able to go into narrow streets that larger buses cannot. In the urban periphery, such as Chalco, even these smaller buses are too large and thus the microbus fleets there are usually composed of VW Combis or Transporters. This privately-owned fleet of over 29,000 buses provides rides to neighborhoods disconnected from public transport. The buses are cheaper than taxis and operate along an informal network which does not have marked routes but accounts for nearly 60% of all transit in Mexico City. See Zoe Mendelson, "Mapping Mexico City's Vast, Informal Transit System," *Fast Company*, April 08, 2016, accessed October 10, 2016, https://www.fastcoexist.com/3058475/mapping-mexico-citys-vast-informal-transit-system.

7:33 It's getting cold while standing in line, but the next two *peseros* have arrived. The sounds of employees at the corner store, conveniently set up beside the bus stop, fill in for small talk.

The drivers get out quickly. "*Un sandwich de pollo*," says one; the other is buying snacks. The attendant shuffles awkwardly between those of us lined up, bumping into every person. There isn't enough space; the stands with candy and chips have taken up half of the sidewalk. Finally on the bus, the silence doesn't break, but there is a shared conviviality amongst this group of strangers.

9:02 It's the end of the line, but the start of another. Underneath the overpass, the overbearing smell of burnt diesel fills the air. Beyond the river of *peseros*, trucks, and *mexibúses*,[3] pink tarps line both sides of the road, soon to be overflowing with goods for sale: knock-off Barbies, CD Players, *gorditas*, *flautas*, flowers, among an assortment of many more shops. It is strange: I always thought that the nature of a *tianguis*[4] was to be temporary, but this one seems to always be here.

3 *Mexibús* is a bus rapid transit system (BRT) in Greater Mexico City.

4 A *tianguis* is an open-air market.

9:07 Beneath this underpass, unseen, it is time to descend further below. The sign for the metro station is hardly visible. The handrail along the stairs is missing and the marble floor tiles, the ones that become dangerously slippery in the rain, are chipped. Once again, I almost didn't notice the plywood construction shacks in the background. They've been there for a while.

9:10 One doesn’t often equate holiness with public transport but today the match seems made in heaven. Beneath the chaos of above, buried into the darkness, here at the unfinished periphery, I’m not quite sure transcendence is in order, but, surely, we are all in need of some guidance.

9:36 Bold colors and strong shapes that, I can't help but think, were traced to inspire vigor in us. But it's dark and the paint has faded and the lights are harsh and most of them are broken. The myth of Mexican nationalism lies here, buried, as if it had been replaced by a new vision above, built in sheet-rock, lined in glass, and ornamented with boutique chain stores that are too expensive anyway.

9:53 The metro seems dictated only by one rule: the brief, terse, pneumatic whoosh. Whoosh. The train breaks as it pulls into the station. Whoosh. The doors open as people burst from the inside of the car, always in a hurry. Whoosh. The doors close. Whoosh. They reopen. Whoosh. They close. Whoosh. The doors once again reopen: as people look around confused, I notice the kid to my right finally managed to pry his backpack from the jammed doors. Whoosh. They close. Whoosh. The brakes are released and the train zips away.

9:57 A breeze of cool air drafts from above. As we near the surface, the street begins to overflow with people from below. A stray car horn faintly heard, the street talk resumes outside the darkness, the grey walls encasing the stairs shine a bit brighter from the daylight that previously got away. One last look down. The small portal where two worlds merge. I notice the marble tiles, the ones that become dangerously slippery in the rain; they seem more at home here than in Ciudad Neza. At least they aren't chipped.

9:59 In Polanco at last. Lush green expanses and cafe-lined avenues percolate through Mexico City's most privileged neighborhood. One journey gives way to another. But no time to think of it. Off to work. Besides, later tonight I still have to make the return trip home. Plenty of time to dream then.

Since the 1990's, the high demand for housing, combined with the privatization of communal farmland on urban peripheries and incentives for developers to build subsidized housing, has created an unsustainable growth of remote and vast social housing developments.[5] Hoping to optimize financial and material resources, many developers have simplified their designs, creating a repetitive architecture that lacks identity and belonging and that indiscriminately spreads over the territory. These neighborhoods can contain up to 25,000 identical units each.[6] Ninety percent are built far outside the major city limits and have serious connectivity issues, creating isolated environments where there is lack of services and a poor quality of life.[7] Millions of residents, like Fabi, spend all their savings obtaining their houses, use half of their salary to keep them, and then suffer from simply trying to live in them.

The story of Fabi is not an outlier, it is lived every day by thousands of others in countless variations. The root of the problem is political and economic, but its deployment is also spatial and architectural. It is clear that replicating a housing type helps to solve the immediate housing backlog problems, but, on the other hand, it creates urban issues of another kind. As architects, we must challenge the idea of social housing developments as rigid, unspecific and anachronistic spaces. And we must challenge the notion that the success or failure of a housing program can be measured by the number of units constructed, or even judged based on the design of a unit on its own. The importance of large-scale planning and infrastructure is clear, as well as the limits of what architecture can achieve on its own. Regardless, we must aim to better understand the everyday plight of people, like Fabi, whose interactions with our designs might enrich their lives, even if momentarily. Through projects at all scales, from exhibitions to master plans, we must push decision-makers to reevaluate the status quo of social housing today.

5 Christopher E. Herbert et. al, "The State of Mexico's Housing – Recent Progress and Continued Challenges," *Joint Center for Housing Studies Harvard University,* accessed December 6, 2016, http://www.jchs.harvard.edu/sites/jchs.harvard.edu/files/w12-8_mexico.pdf.

6 Livia Corona Benjamin, "Two Million Homes for Mexico," *Mascontext,* accessed May 2, 2016, http://www.mascontext.com/issues/21-repetition-spring-14/two-million-homes-for-mexico.

7 Fundación CIDOC and Sociedad Hipotecaria Federal, "Current housing situation in Mexico 2009," Factors to Analyze the Price Formation in the Formal and Informal Markets Table, accessed December 6, 2016, http://www.shf.gob.mx/English/Press/Publications/Documents/EAVM%202009-VINGLES.pdf; Andres G. Blanco et. al, "Rental Housing Wanted: Options for Expanding Housing Policy," *Inter-American Development Bank,* 209, accessed December 6, 2016. https://publications.iadb.org/bitstream/handle/11319/6730/Rental-Housing-Wanted-Options-for-Expanding-Housing-Policy.pdf?sequence=4.

Deepening Divisions in Johannesburg

Guy Trangoš

Global cities are fraught with divisions at a variety of intensities and scales. Many sites face deepening division today as evidenced by heightened anti-immigration sentiment in Europe, a politics of polarization in the United States,[1] increasingly unaffordable city centers in New York and London,[2] and the construction of global border walls.[3]

Despite decades of post-apartheid nation building and a respected and inclusive constitution, South Africa has seen increased forms of division emerge. Its most populous city, Johannesburg, is notoriously revered as one of the most divided cities in the world, a reputation made possible by more than a century of social, economic, and racial division. As such, the city has become regarded as a litmus test for uniting divided cities.[4] Located in Gauteng Province, South Africa's smallest, densest, and most economically active province, Johannesburg together with the cities of Tshwane (Pretoria) and Ekurhuleni form an integrated conurbation known as the Gauteng City-Region.

Forged by labor exploitation and resource extraction, Johannesburg's fate as a segregated city was almost sealed. Mining brought class and income inequality structured along racial and ethnic lines. British colonialism that followed further engrained racial division and, importantly, set in place the foundations of a racialized spatial geography.

01
Nate Cohn, "Polarization Is Dividing American Society, Not Just Politics," *New York Times,* June 12, 2014, http://www.nytimes.com/2014/06/12/upshot/polarization-is-dividing-american-society-not-just-politics.html.

02
Richard Florida, "Class-Divided Cities: New York Edition," *CityLab,* January 24, 2013, http://www.citylab.com/housing/2013/01/class-divided-cities-new-york-edition/3819/.

03
Mark Rice-Oxley, Paul Torpey, Seán Clarke, Ranjit Dhaliwal, "Walled World," *The Guardian*, 19 November 2013, accessed 2 April 2015, http://www.theguardian.com/world/ng-interactive/2013/nov/walls#outro.

04
Jo Beall, Owen Crankshaw, and Susan Parnell, *Uniting a Divided City: Governance and Social Exclusion in Johannesburg,* (London: Earthscan, 2002).

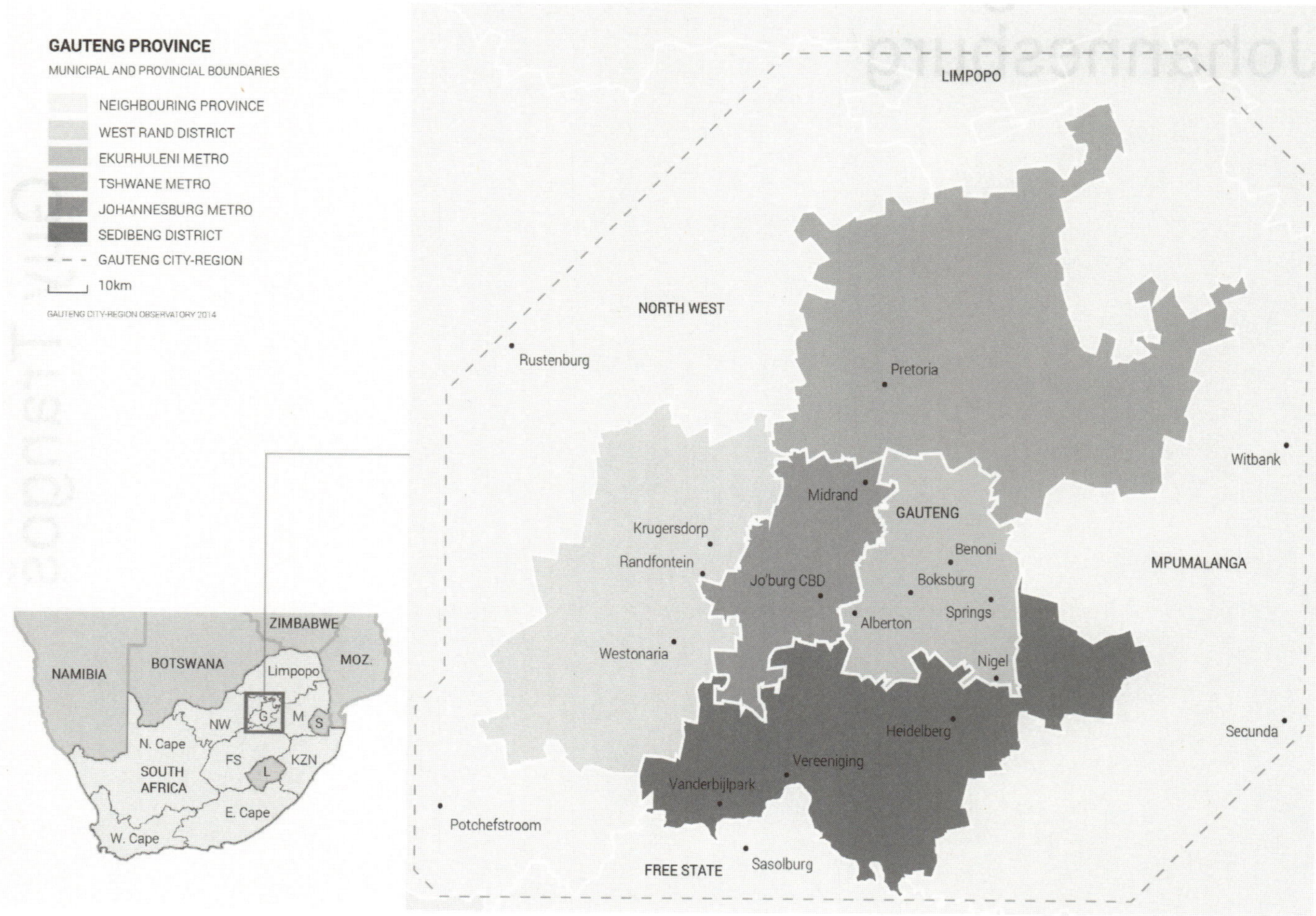

Fig. 01
Locating Johannesburg within Gauteng Province. Map by author.

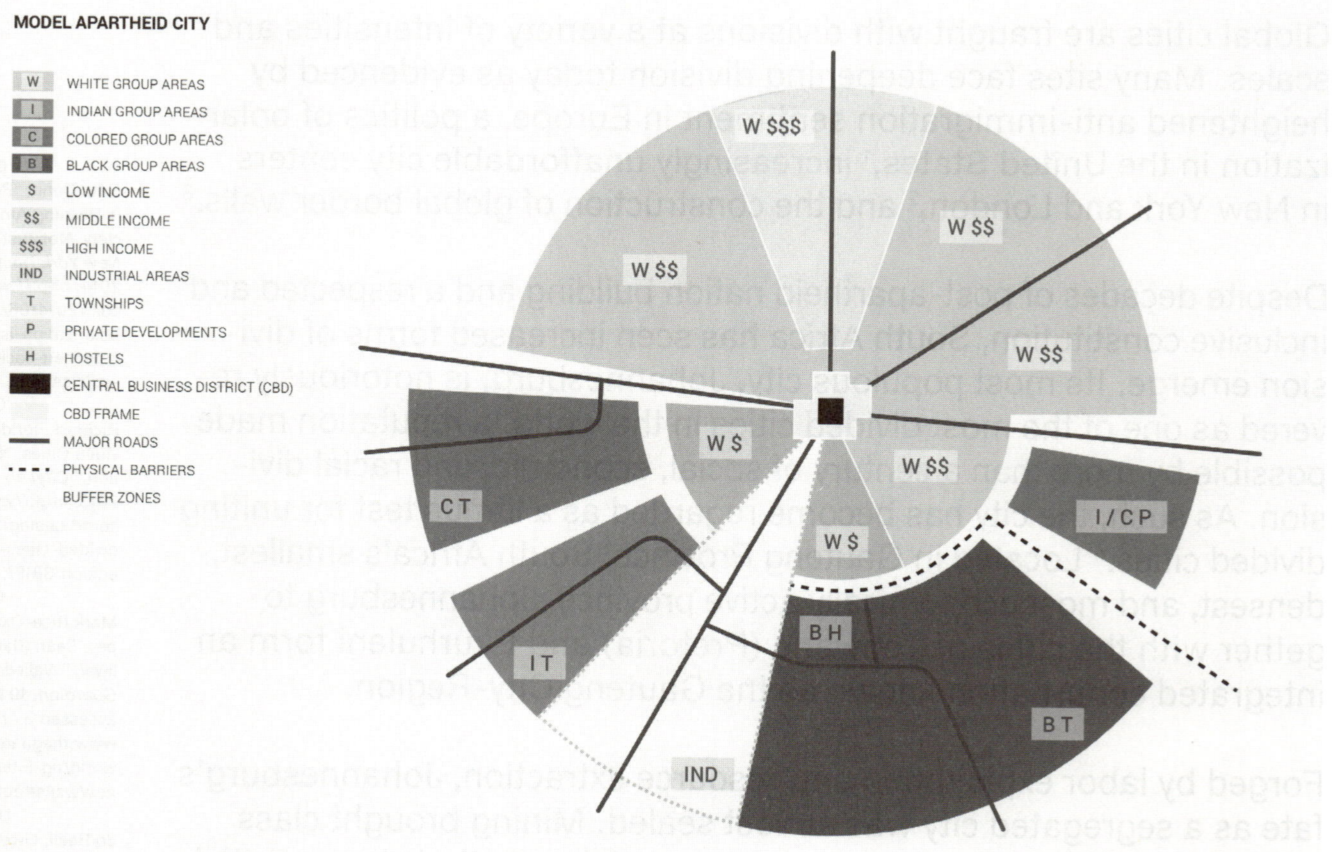

Fig. 02
The apartheid city plan as modeled on Johannesburg. Diagram by author, based on David Kay, *South African City Planning in a Post Apartheid Era* (Johannesburg: David Kay, 2007).

While the black population[5] was disenfranchised under British colonialism, so too were the Afrikaner people, mainly of Dutch decent.[6] This fueled a surge in Afrikaner nationalism across South Africa in the early twentieth century that escalated after World War II and led to the election of the National Party, which instituted apartheid.

Through a series of policies and laws, the apartheid government mechanically denied black South Africans rights, such as the ability to own property, start businesses, move freely, and receive a quality education. Cities, built on the backs of black labor, were carved in particularly menacing ways by the forced removal and resettlement of black residents. While very few black and mixed-race communities lived in close proximity to the city, many black residents were formally displaced to apartheid township areas located in the distant urban periphery.[7] Well-known apartheid townships include Soweto (established from 1934), KwaThema (1951), and Thembisa (1957). Townships were erased from the daily experience of white people, their names were absent from road signs, and their enormous and sprawling forms were hidden behind mining waste and the horizon.

Fig. 03
Soweto in the 1960s. Photograph by Martin West. Courtesy of UCT Libraries, C Kirkwood.

Fig. 04
Soweto (west) behind mine residue areas and freeways. Google Maps, 2016.

05
Black is used to denote people of all races and ethnicities who were marginalized by apartheid. It is used instead of the problematic alternative *non-whites*. These are imposed racial classifications, which are nonetheless constituent parts of South African identity and culture. Steve Biko, *I Write What I Like: Selected Writings* (Chicago: University of Chicago Press, 2002).

06
Albert Grundlingh, "Afrikaner Nationalism in the 1930s and 1940s," in *Turning Points in History, Book 4: Industrialisation, Rural Change and Nationalism* (Pretoria: Department of Education, 2004).

07
The Native (Black) Urban Areas Act of 1923 made municipalities responsible for housing the black population in reserved areas away from the white population, with controls placed on their movement. This materialized in the notorious passbook system.

The end of apartheid came in the early 1990s following successful international sanctions, increased political pressure, protests, and sustained campaigns by civic movements and political parties. South Africa held its first democratic elections in 1994. The social democratic party, African National Congress (ANC), was elected and remains in power today.

South African cities have seen a remarkable transformation since the end of apartheid. Millions of black South Africans have received quality schooling and benefitted economically from government redistribution policies, housing, and social services. White South Africans have also benefitted from the removal of apartheid sanctions and the economic growth that followed.[8] However, while the percentage of South Africans who fall below the national poverty line has decreased, economic inequality has increased since the end of apartheid, caused in part by the neoliberal turn of the post-apartheid economy.[9]

These economic changes continue to have profound effects on South Africa's cities, most notably Johannesburg. Here inequality manifests spatially and physically at both ends of the spectrum. It can be seen in the form of high-security complexes, walled residential estates, and the privatized policing of wealthy suburbs, as well as in makeshift and over-crowded inner city housing and distant dormitory suburbs, where low-income earners remain confined.

Numerous contemporary urban processes have evolved to support division in the city. As such, this research proposes a scaled approach to understanding these processes and how they are deepening division in Johannesburg. This is achieved through an analysis of the region, the neighborhood, and the body—as governed through municipal bylaws. Recognizing the dynamic rescaling of urban and social process, which is constantly challenging old amalgams such as *city*, *urban*, and *national*,[10] this enquiry reflects on the notion that spatial scales are never fixed.[11] It builds an argument detailing the entangled nature of social, economic, and political process as enacted in multiple scales and spaces.

POST-APARTHEID HUMAN SETTLEMENT PLANNING

In the run up to the first democratic elections, the country began strategizing a national post-apartheid housing plan. The National Housing Forum (NHF) was created in 1992 as a temporary platform to negotiate social housing strategies. Funded by a government grant,[12] the forum aimed to "address historical imbalances, eradicate the enormous backlog, and prepare for future demands."[13]

08
Haydn Cornish-Jenkins, "Despite the 1994 Political Victory against Apartheid, Its Economic Legacy Persists," *South African History Online* (2015), http://www.sahistory.org.za/article/despite-1994-political-victory-against-apartheid-its-economic-legacy-persists -haydn-cornish-#sthash.zQAEiQjm.dpuf.

09
"Economic Inequality in South Africa," Chartbook of Economic Inequality (CEI) (2014), http://www.chartbookofeconomicinequality.com/inequality-by-country/south-africa/.

10
Neil Smith, "New Globalism, New Urbanism: Gentrification as Global Urban Strategy," *Antipode* 34, no. 3 (2002): 427–50.

11
Gordon MacLeod and Mark Goodwin, "Space, Scale and State Strategy: Rethinking Urban and Regional Governance," *Progress in Human Geography* 23, no. 4 (1999): 503–27.

12
Marie Huchzermeyer, "Housing for the Poor? Negotiated Housing Policy in South Africa," *Habitat International* 25 (2001): 303–31.

13
Matthew Nell and Kecia Rust, "The National Housing Forum: Consensus Based Policy Making During Political Transition in South Africa," *Housing Finance International* (June 1993): 8–34.

14
Kiran Lalloo, "Arenas of Contested Citizenship: Housing Policy in South Africa" *Habitat International* 23 (1998): 35–47; Huchzermeyer, "Housing for the Poor?: Negotiated housing policy in South Africa," 303-331.

15
Lalloo, "Arenas of Contested Citizenship," 35-47.

16
Ibid.

17
Ibid.

18
Kate Tissington, *A Resource Guide to Housing in South Africa 1994–2010: Legislation, Policy, Programmes and Practice*, (Johannesburg: Socio Economic Rights Institute of South Africa, 2011).

19
Ibid. Actual figures are contested.

While the NHF was established as a representative platform, business interests had significant dominance over the negotiations.[14] This put the focus on nominally modifying imbalances without disrupting economic activity.[15] Also partially influenced by the apartheid state that was still in power,[16] the policies emphasized short-term housing delivery over creating a long-term housing strategy based on equality and participation.[17] The ANC's own Reconstruction and Development Program (RDP), introduced following their election to power in 1994, was strongly influenced by the NHF approach. In particular, private developers were incentivized to construct large social housing developments using state-financed capital subsidy schemes.[18]

The impact of this early policy formation on the spatial structure of South African cities has been profound. While millions of people were provided with single-family houses in the twenty-two years of democracy,[19] these have largely been in satellite dormitory developments on the edges of township areas. Far removed from the city, residents have a place to live but little economic opportunity. The policy makers failed to truly grapple with the geography of the property market, and without regulation, developers built on the most inexpensive land with little regard to location, mobility, or access.[20] The poor quality of life in these developments was exacerbated by a lack of services and substandard construction quality.[21] Largely resembling the apartheid-era townships, these newer developments continue to perpetuate the spatial, social, and economic divisions of apartheid. As stated by Deputy Minister of Cooperative Governance and Traditional Affairs, Andries Nel, "In some ways the success that we have achieved in providing basic services such as housing has had unintended consequences of strengthening that apartheid geography."[22] This approach has also been critiqued by South Africa's lauded National Develoment Plan 2030,[23] which calls for government to "develop a strategy for densification of cities and resource allocation to promote better-located housing and settlements."[24]

Despite these governmental acknowledgements, the Gauteng Provincial Government is currently planning to build new post-apartheid cities similarly disconnected from Johannesburg.[25] These new cities will be relatively low-density, sprawling semi-suburban areas. At least five of the cities will each host over 22,000 housing units.[26]

These megaprojects, as trumpeted by Human Settlements Minister Lindiwe Sisulu,[27] are inherently unsustainable. While their planning documents routinely describe them as integrated, mixed-use and mixed-tenure, these projects do not have viable plans to draw in the investment and economic activity that would make them sustainable. In addition, much research has shown that people do not readily move to new cities, and that new cities often signal separation and enclosure.[28]

20
Sarah Charlton and Caroline Kihato, "Reaching the Poor? An Analysis of the Influences on the Evolution of South Africa's Housing Programme," in *Democracy and Delivery: Urban Policy in South Africa*, eds. UdeshPillay, Richard Tomlinson, and Jacques Du Toit (Cape Town: HSRC Press, 2006): 268.

21
Centre on Housing Rights and Evictions, *Business as Usual? Housing Rights and 'Slum Eradication' in Durban, South Africa* (Geneva: COHRE, 2008).

22
Penwell Dlamini, "State Urged to Abandon RDP Houses as It Reshapes Future of South African Cities," *Business Day*, March 6, 2014, http://www.bdlive.co.za/national/2014/03/06/state-urged-to-abandon-rdp-houses-as-it-reshapes-future-of-south-african-cities.

23
The National Development Plan 2030 was developed and funded by the National Planning Commission under the Ministry in the Presidency. National Development Plan (NDP), The Presidency of the Republic of South Africa: National Planning Commission (2013).

24
Ibid., 58.

25
In 2014, new Gauteng Premier David Makhura, a seasoned ANC politician and previous ANC provincial secretary, was elected. His major policy directive included the implementation of "Ten Pillars of Radical Transformation," one of the major action items is new "post-apartheid" cities. Gauteng Provincial Government (GPG), *Gauteng Pillars of Radical Transformation*, (Johannesburg: Gauteng Provincial Government, 2014).

26
Gauteng City-Region Observatory (GCRO), *Map of the Month: The Location of Planned Mega Housing Projects in Context* (Johannesburg: GCRO, 2015).

27
Lindiwe Sisulu, "Speech by L N Sisulu, Minister of Human Settlements on the Occasion of the Budget Vote of the Ministry of Human Settlements," *Housing Finance Africa*, July 2014, http://www.housingfinanceafrica.org/wp-content/uploads/2014/07/budget-vote-speech-by-minister-of-human-settlements-hon-l-sisulu-15-July-2014.pdf.

28
Lauren Royston and Yahia Shawkat, "The Idea of New Cities May Be Folly," *Business Day*, September 11, 2015, http://www.bdlive.co.za/opinion/2015/09/11/the-idea-of-new-cities-may-be-folly.

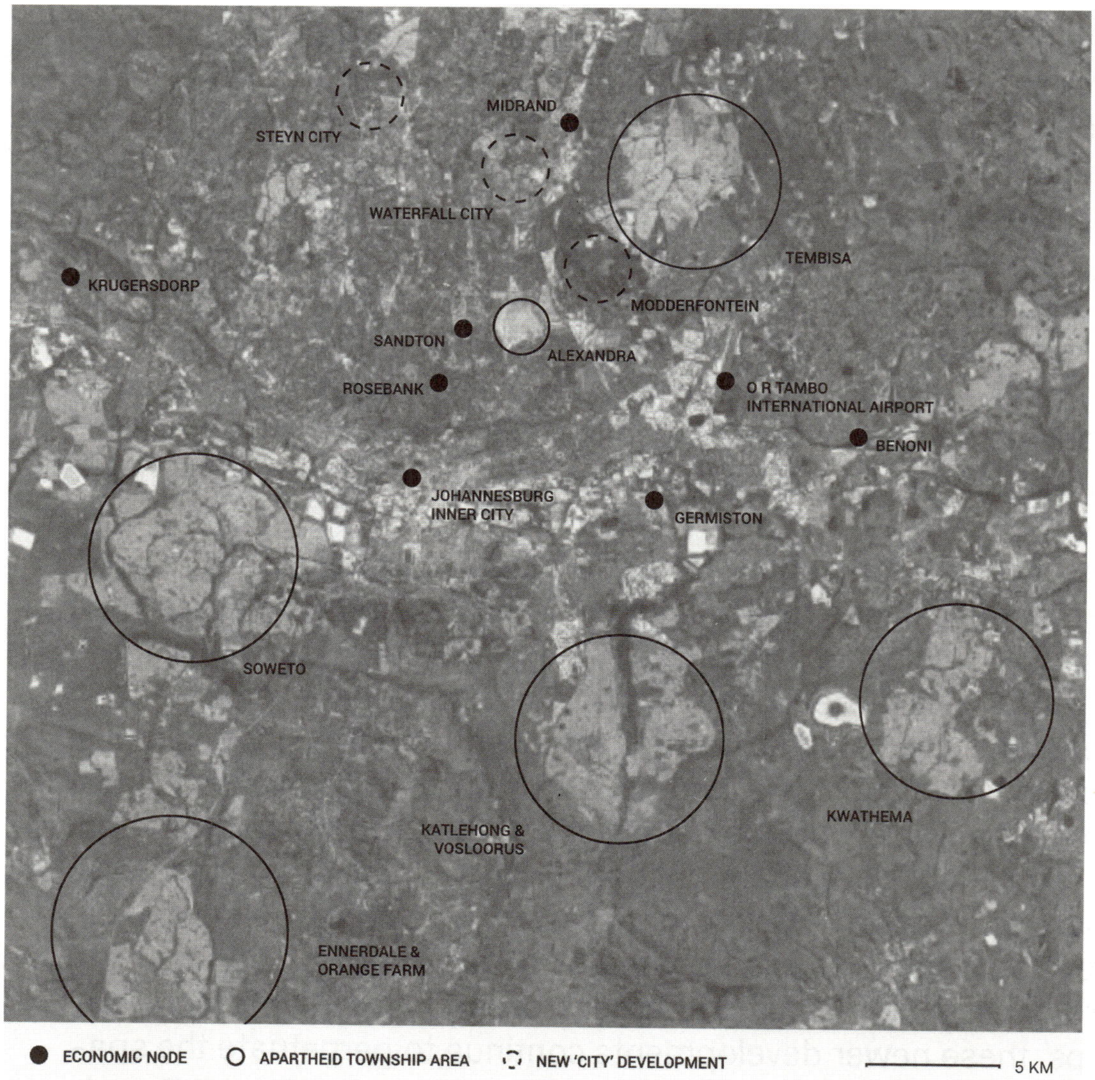

Fig. 05
Apartheid townships and their new post-apartheid extensions with new private "cities" north and east of Johannesburg in relation to economic centers in Johannesburg and Ekurhuleni, 2015. Google Maps, 2015 with notations by author.

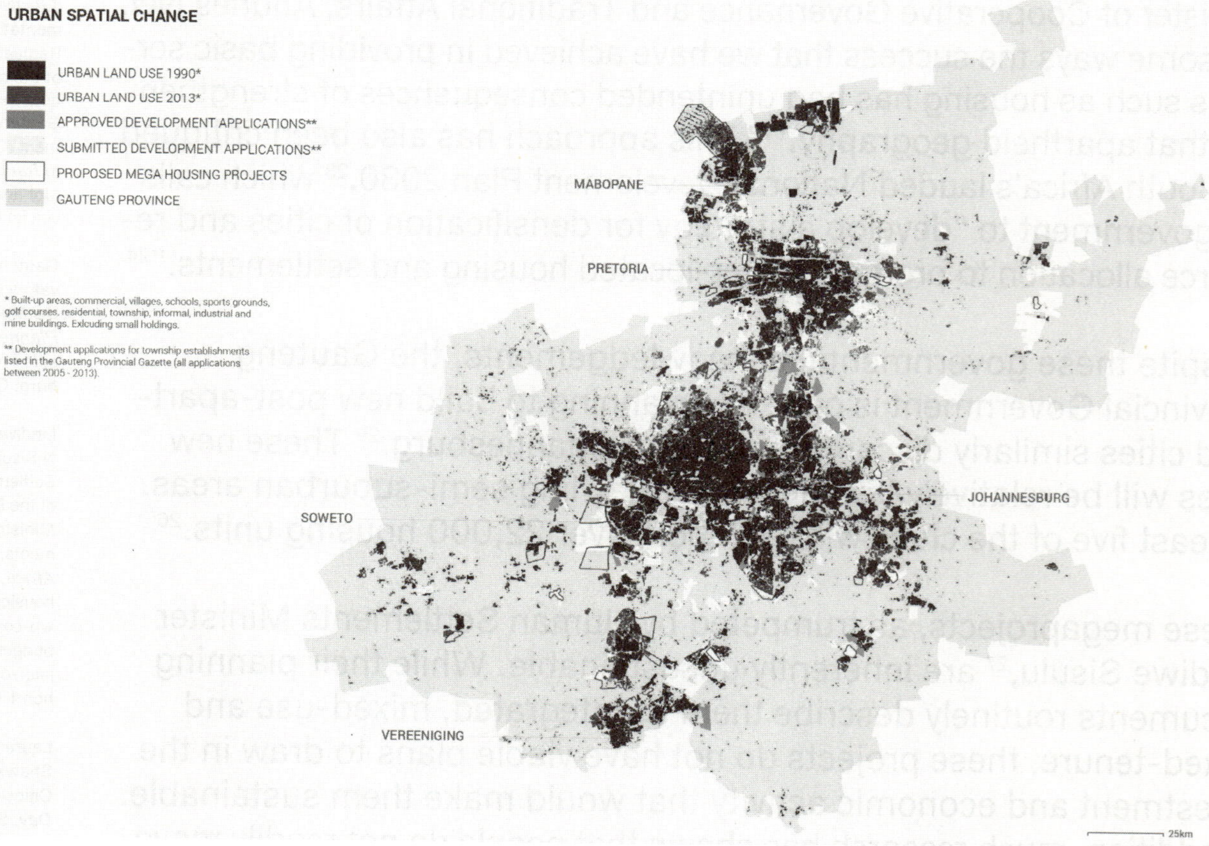

Fig. 07
Urban spatial change in Gauteng from 1990 to 2013. Map by author, based on data from: Gauteng Department of Human Settlements (GDHS), Mega Projects (Pretoria: GDHS, 2015). GeoTerra Image, Land use change (1990 and 2013); MetroGIS: Development applications (Pretoria: GeoTerra Image, 2013).

Fig. 06
Westonaria Borwa Mega Project is currently under construction and mimics apartheid township development in its distance from economic activity and sprawling suburban form. WBMP, Westonaria Borwa Mega Project (2015), https://westonariaborwa.co.za/housing-2/.

Fig. 08
Plans for a new "integrated human settlement," as part of the Gauteng "Mega-Human Settlements," demonstrate no true integration across income groups and uses. Instead, the plan mirrors traditional development typologies not too different from those with a segregationist focus. Gauteng Department of Human Settlements (GDHS), Mega Projects: Clusters and New Cities (Pretoria: GDHS, 2015) with notations by author.

While social housing developments led by the public sector run the risk of further deepening division in Gauteng, numerous local and international property investment companies are also building a number of their own "cities" across the province. These have little to no engagement with new public sector–led cities. With names such as Steyn City, Waterfall City, Modderfontein City and Hazeldean, these multibillion rand mixed-use developments primarily target middle-class property buyers seeking urban convenience and outdoor lifestyles.[29] Many include private schools, private hospitals, business centers, shopping centers, and their own private security and services. These estates are under construction in opportune edge-land near transport hubs and economic activity, but are entirely walled, their entrances controlled. The deepening of division in Gauteng is thus aggressively exercised from both ends; the poor are to be further accommodated in economic dead zones surrounded by failing public infrastructure, while the wealthy retreat to private Elysiums.

29
"Five Multi-Billion-Rand Cities Being Built in Gauteng," *Business Tech*, November 8, 2015, http://*businesstech.*co.za/news/general/104473/five-multi-billion-rand-cities-being-built-in-gauteng/.

Despite the challenges inherent in both the public and private new cities, the City of Johannesburg has already initiated a spatial planning strategy, known as Corridors of Freedom, which has seen key arterial routes re-zoned to mixed-use high density along a Bus Rapid Transit backbone.[30] This innovative strategy can be read in opposition to edge development and stitches together Johannesburg's disparate parts through a corridor of economic activity and residential advantage. The new city projects in Gauteng, driven by the Province and not the City of Johannesburg, undermine these efforts and dilute their impact. Instead of using new development to stitch together the Province, division in the city-region will again be exacerbated.

INNER CITY REGENERATION

Given the large expanse of dislocated suburban fabric that comprises Johannesburg, the city's historical inner city only occupies a small southern portion of the city's footprint. While in some places the inner city's tight grid, corporate architecture, and tall buildings evoke other global city centers, the inner city as a whole has developed its own hybrid form: a mix of repurposed historical buildings, high residential densities, and old industrial warehouses.

Change is perhaps the city's most constant feature. Sustained economic flight from the inner city during the 1980s and 1990s occurred as building stock aged, traffic congestion increased, car ownership soared, and decentralized suburban office parks and shopping malls became more desirable. This flight paralleled the final days of apartheid, when urban prospects became increasingly more accessible to those previously denied them.

These economic and demographic shifts have produced an inner city absent from the lives and culture of the city's largely white middle-class suburban dwellers. As a result, the inner city is traditionally fictionalized and othered as a dangerous, no-go zone. The last decade, however, has seen an increasing interest in the inner city by the middle class, which is shifting urban culture, but thus far has failed to induce much significant change in class mixing or inequality. Cities across the world are witnessing what geographer Neil Smith terms "the globalization of gentrification."[31] Governmental and corporate interests today drive gentrification processes, unlike the slow accrual of middle-class migrants into neighborhoods that once attracted the label.[32] Johannesburg actively pursues inner city regeneration through governmental organizations such as the Johannesburg Development Agency, often in partnership with the private sector.[33] To entice investment, the city has instituted tax incentives within a defined Urban Development Zone (UDZ), which includes most of the inner city.

30
Corridors of Freedom was developed by the City of Johannesburg as a policy remedy to decentralized apartheid and post-apartheid development. The basic drivers for Corridors of Freedom are Transit Oriented Design (TOD) and urban compaction. A number of corridors were identified as linear urban zones for mixed-use and mixed-income high-density development, in close proximity to central economic nodes, and along Bus Rapid Transit (BRT) routes. These are currently being implemented.

31
Smith, "New Globalism, New Urbanism," 427-50.

32
Ibid.

33
The Johannesburg Development Agency was established in 2001 as an agency of the City of Johannesburg to stimulate and support area-based economic development initiatives throughout the Johannesburg metropolitan area. Their core operational modes include the administration and management of development projects and development facilitation. City of Johannesburg (CoJ), "Johannesburg Development Agency" (2007), http://joburg.org.za/index.php?option=comcontttent&task=view&id=121&Itemid=9#ixzz47lfDQXPt;Johannesburg Development Agency (JDA), "About the JDA" (2016), http://www.ida.org.za/index.php/who-we-are/about-the-jda.

Fig. 09
New privatized cities being planned and built in Gauteng. From top: Vaal River City (Vaal River City Consortium, DBM Architects, Johannesburg), Modderfontein City (Zendai Group, Atkins, Colliers International, Arup), Waterfall City (Attacq, Johannesburg), and Modderfontein City as first imagined.

In the east of the inner city and within the UDZ, a private development zone branded Maboneng, a Sotho word meaning "Place of Light," has seen a number of warehouse buildings converted into apartment buildings, restaurants, shops, studio spaces, art galleries, and coworking spaces. Propertuity, Maboneng's developer, brand themselves as "Bringing City Back."[34] They have invested over one billion rand into buying and renovating over forty properties in adjacent areas such as Jeppestown, an old warehousing district now home to new lower income communities, and the neighborhood confusingly known as "City and Suburban" in the inner city.[35] Their main ambition is to create a slice of Johannesburg's inner city that is palatable to middle-class tastes and located in an urban fabric that

Fig. 10
Remodeled industrial architecture, lively street corners and pristine sidewalks define Maboneng. SA Tourism.

34
Propertuity, *Bringing City Back* (2016), http://propertuity.co.za/.

35
Palesa V. Tshandu, "Developers Move on Investment-Free CBDs," *Sunday Times*, September 6, 2015, http://www.timeslive.co.za/sundaytimes/businesstimes/2015/09/06/Developers-move-on-investment-free-CBDs.

evokes loft and studio living as popularized in Williamsburg in Brooklyn or Shoreditch in London. As such, the development has not only become a destination for urban lattés, but a middle-class outpost in the eastern inner city.

Maboneng is fraught with contrasts. An architectural language of patina, urban accumulation, hard surfaces, and tough facades conceal elegantly spartan interiors, industrial lighting, and austere furniture. On the street, narrow sidewalks are planted with small trees, and recent paving demarcates those areas that fall within the unfenced development. Chairs and tables occupy the public realm, protected by private security guards stationed on corners. Just outside Maboneng's vague borders—which in many instances involves crossing a nondescript road—Johannesburg's underserviced and seemingly forgotten eastern edge remains. Here, public infrastructure and private buildings require significant maintenance and renovation, shops serve patrons through security bars for fear of crime, and overcrowding is palpable.

During March 2015, residents of buildings in Jeppestown, the neighborhood just to the east of Maboneng, were forcibly evicted by a private eviction and security service known as the Red Ants.[36] Evicted residents demonstrated and the eviction turned violent, with 22 residents being arrested.[37] Propertuity CEO Jonathan Liebmann denied early reports that evicted buildings were earmarked for development and inclusion into Maboneng and stated, "We are not responsible for any evictions. We have never done any gentrification."[38] Whether or not Propertuity was planning to develop the buildings under eviction is inconsequential given that the Maboneng development has fueled property price increases and speculation across the east of the inner city.[39]

Although Maboneng could not be directly implicated in the evictions, the protesting residents held signs stating "Fusegi Maboneng" and chanted "Sifuna ukudla iSushi noMaboneng!"—*Go Away Maboneng*, and *We want to eat sushi in Maboneng!* [40] Advanced by litigation,[41] municipalities are mandated by the court to provide alternative temporary accommodation for evicted residents in close proximity to the site of the eviction. Attorney Teboho Mosikili, representing evicted Jeppestown residents, notes that the city's actions do not signal a commitment to finding alternative accommodation—if so evicted residents would not have to keep applying for court orders.[42] Throughout the Jeppestown protests, and as demonstrated in similar inner city evictions,[43] low-income residents are further marginalized through the actions of private actors and the inefficiencies of the public sector to support them, even in times of crisis.

36
Jesse D. Mulder, "Red Ants March through Jeppestown," *eNCA*, March 19, 2015, https://www.enca.com/south-africa/red-ants-march-through-jeppestown.

37
"Maboneng Eviction Protest Turns Violent," *eNCA*, March 18, 2015, https://www.enca.com/south-africa/residents-protest-over-maboneng-evictions.

38
Ibid.; "Uncertainty as to Who Ordered Jeppestown Evictions," *eNCA*, March 18, 2015, https://www.enca.com/south-africa/uncertainty-who-ordered-evictions-residents-continue-clash-cops.

39
Stefanie Jason, "Urban Renewal's Bourgeois Curse," *Mail & Guardian*, August 8, 2014, http://mg.co.za/article/2014-08-08-urban-renewals-bourgeois-curse-1.

40
eNCA, "Maboneng Eviction Protest Turns Violent,"; Andrew Levy, "We Want to Eat Sushi in Maboneng!" *Umuzi Photo Club*, March 18, 2015, http://umuziphotoclubnews.blogspot.co.za/2015/03/we-want-to-eat-sushi-in-maboneng.html.

41
Most notably the famous Blue Moonlight and Olivia Road cases. Michael Clark, *Evictions and Alternative Accommodation in South Africa: An Analysis of the Jurisprudence and Implications for Local Government*, (Johannesburg: Socio-Economic Rights Institute of South Africa, 2013): 1-63.

Johannesburg's inner city remains a fraught and divided terrain. Private investment has improved service delivery and amenities in specific areas, but this is usually achieved through the privatization of these services. Other improvements have been made possible through the creation of private sector–led City Improvement Districts (CIDs) in areas with significant business interests. Here service provision can be seen to deliberately better serve wealthier neighborhoods. While the City of Johannesburg is quick to highlight numerous inner city investments as examples of its commitment to creating a livable inner city for all, a lack of maintenance, public realm management, policing, and innovative approaches to housing have resulted in the proliferation of low-income ghettos. In contrast, private-led developments, such as Maboneng, entrench the retreat of public service provision through their own urban management and service provision. The resulting neighborhoods are intrinsically divided along income lines.

Fig. 11
Jeppestown evictions. Photographs by Khotso Mahlangu, 2015.

While investment in Johannesburg's inner city is important to improving the lives of all its residents, this often happens at the expense of those communities already living in the city. Geographer Aidan Mosselson notes, "Multiple readings and interpretations of urban renewal processes ... are not only possible, but necessary."[44] He accurately identifies the complexity of competing interests in any urban environment, and, like urban and regional planner Ares Kalandides, he calls for the considered use of terms such as gentrification and regeneration (which Neil Smith warns as being misidentified as a "natural process").[45]

42
Alex Eliseev, "New Twist in Jeppestown Evictions," *Eyewitness News*, March 19, 2015, http://ewn.co.za/2015/03/19/New-twist-in-the-Jeppestown-evictions.

43
Clark, *Evictions and Alternative Accommodation in South Africa*, 1-63.

44
Aidan Mosselson, "Vernacular Regeneration: Low-Income Housing, Private Security and Urban Transformation in Inner-City Johannesburg," (PhD diss., University College London 2015): 11.

45
Ares Kalandides, "If Everything is Gentrification then What Is Gentrification?" *Inpolis*, June 6, 2011, http://blog.inpolis.com/2011/06/06/if-everything-is-gentrification-then-what-is-gentrification/; Smith, "New Globalism, New Urbanism," 455.

Johannesburg's inner city has seen increased public and private investment, and this, as with most neoliberal urban restructuring, has come with economic exclusion, increased controls over public space, and an increased private security presence.

ANTI-POOR 'OPERATIONS'

Beyond urban planning and investment strategies, in the past few years division has been enacted on the bodies of Johannesburg's poor. Michel Foucault describes the ascent of the bourgeoisie class in the eighteenth century as being supported through the guise of democratic and egalitarian judicial and political systems.[46] He refers to these asymmetrical systems as "the disciplines." This term finds new meaning today in the neoliberal state's governance of the poor. In Johannesburg during the first half of 2015, the poor once again found themselves on the receiving end of aggressive municipal policy. This was largely inspired by the U.S. "War on Crime" rhetoric,[47] which supports the notion that criminality is the product of personal failings, and not a much larger political and economic system.

Unlike many other global cities with a strong public space and public transport infrastructure, Johannesburg provides severely limited opportunities for different income groups to even interact. This two-tier city is enforced by the privatization of public functions such as security services and public transport. For example, South Africa had 2.57 private security personnel to every police employee in 2011,[48] and in 2013, 65% of Gauteng's population used private mini-bus taxis, and 32% used private cars, for their daily transit requirements.[49]

Given this spatial separation, one of the few opportunities for beggars and micro-entrepreneurs to access middle- to high-income earners is at busy traffic intersections. In largely middle-class suburban areas, traders, beggars, and window washers ply their trade. While many are able to make a living this way, they are often mistrusted and vilified by motorists as criminals. With a national unemployment rate of 26.4% in early 2015,[50] and the inability of recent cross-border migrants to work legally in the country, many people turn to begging. Jetro Gonese, a recent Zimbabwean immigrant and blind beggar, who managed to keep his daughter in school through begging at intersections, notes, "banning people from begging would eliminate the only income that many unemployable people have."[51]

In recent years, the Johannesburg Metropolitan Police Department (JMPD) ran two citywide "operations" to remove street traders from the streets. These initiatives were called "Operation Clean Sweep," followed by "Operation Ke Molao" ("*It's the law*"). Orchestrated in

46
Michel Foucault, *Discipline and Punish* (New York: Pantheon, 1977).

47
Loïc Wacquant, *Punishing the Poor: The Neoliberal Government of Social Insecurity* (Durham, N.C.: Duke University Press, 2009).

48
Kate Wilkinson, "Does SA Have the Largest Private Security Industry in the World?" *Africa Check*, January 23, 2015, https://africacheck.org/reports/does-sa-have-the-largest-private-security-industry-in-the-world/.

49
GCRO, *Quality of Life Survey 2013* (Johannesburg: GCRO, 2013).

50
Trading Economics, "South Africa Unemployment Rate" (2016), http://www.tradingeconomics.com/south-africa/unemployment-rate.

51
Guy Trangoš, "Is it the Law?" *Lawyers for Human Rights* (2015), http://www.lhr.org.za/news/2015/it-law.

52
Greg Nicolson and Thapelo Lekgowa, "Operation Clean Sweep: Johannesburg Metro Police Arrests Human Rights Lawyer," *Daily Maverick*, December 6, 2013, http://www.dailymaverick.co.za/article/2013-12-06-operation-clean-sweep-johannesburg-metro-police-arrests-human-rights-lawyer/#.Vq9Hg7B96Rs; Nomzamo Zondo, "ConCourt Slams JMPD's Operation Clean Sweep – SERI," *PoliticsWeb*, April 4, 2014, http://www.politicsweb.co.za/party/concourt-slams-jmpds-operation-clean-sweep--seri; Tanya Zack, "Tanya Zack's Open Letter to the City of Johannesburg," *UrbanAfrica.net*, (2013), http://www.urbanafrica.net/news/informal-traders-take-city-johannesburg-court-0/.

late 2013, Operation Clean Sweep was violent by many accounts.[52] After immediate court action, the operation was found to be in violation of the South African Constitution, with Acting Chief Justice Dikgang Moseneke describing it as an act of "humiliation and degradation."[53] Much has been written on Operation Clean Sweep,[54] and despite condemnation and legal battles from interest groups, the JMPD initiated Operation Ke Molao little over a year later.[55]

By July 2015, over 550 "illegal" window washers had been arrested[56] by specially deployed "ghost squads."[57] Here there is little differentiation between the crime of theft and a number of other perceived crimes. These perceived crimes are often so vague that those arrested are only charged with loitering.[58]

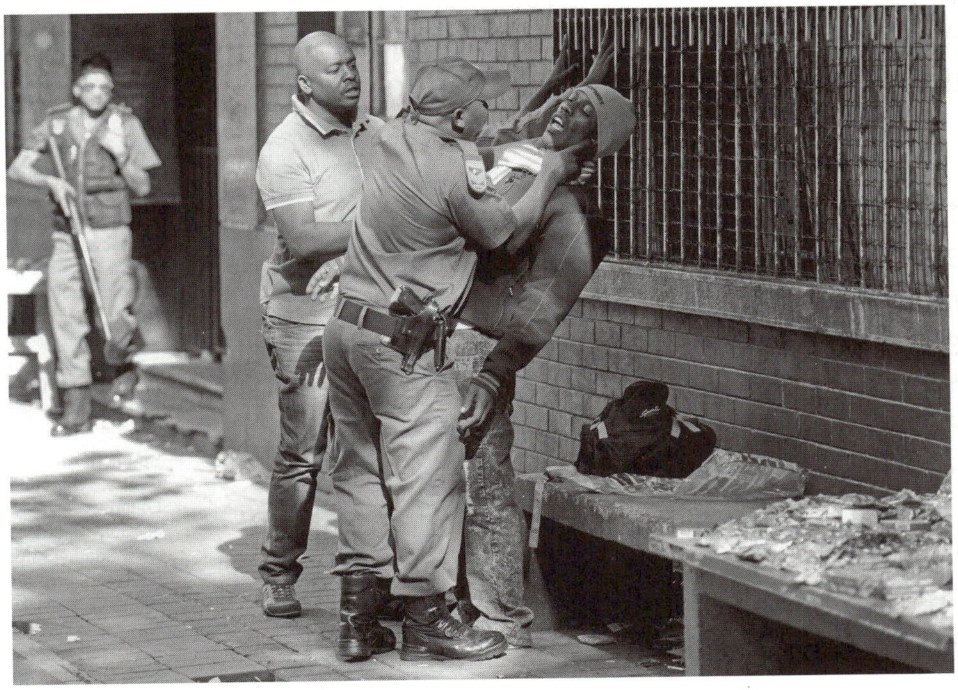

Fig. 12
Operation Clean Sweep. Photograph by Khotso Mahlangu, 2013.

In 2009, the Southern Africa Litigation Centre deemed anti-loitering bylaws to be "unconstitutional," "vague," and "over breath,"[59] since the oppressive apartheid government the laws had been used mostly as a means to keep black people out of urban areas.[60] They have not been updated in line with the new South African Constitution and today have taken the form of easy charges against those suspected as illegal immigrants by the democratic government, who ironically fought against these very laws during apartheid.[61]

While the abuse of antiquated bylaws instills an anti-poor sentiment, the use of terminology such as "operation," "illegal," and "zero tolerance" echoes what sociologist Loïc Wacquant describes as "the rampant gesticulation over law and order ... conceived and carried out not so much for its own sake as for *the express purpose of being exhibited and seen,* scrutinized, ogled: the absolute priority is to put

53
Socio-Economic Rights Institute of South Africa (SERI), "South African Informal Traders Forum and Others v City of Johannesburg and Others ('SAITF')," (2014), http://www.seri-sa.org/index.php/19-litigation/case-entries/206-south-african-informal-traders-forum-and-others-v-city-of-johannesburg-and-oters-saitf.

54
Daniel K. Thompson and Richard Grant, "Enclaves on Edge: Strategy and Tactics in Immigrant Business Spaces of Johannesburg," *Urban Forum* 26 (2015): 243–62; Chris Rogerson, "Progressive Rhetoric, Ambiguous Policy Pathways: Street Trading in Inner-City Johannesburg, South Africa," *Local Economy* (31(1-2), 2015): 204-218; Claire Bénit-Gbaffou, *In Quest for Sustainable Models of Street Trading Management: Lessons for Johannesburg after Operation Clean Sweep* (Johannesburg: Centre for Urbanism and Built Environment Studies and School of Architecture and Planning, University of the Witwatersrand, 2015); Zack, "Open Letter,"

55
The action, while initiated by the Johannesburg Metropolitan Police Department (JMPD), was supported by the ANC, who holds control over the City of Johannesburg municipality. JMPD Spokesperson Wayne Minnaar explained the operation as being, "established to clear intersections and freeways of window washers, street traders, smash-and-grabbers, hijackers and all other offenders, including beggars." Lerato Mbangeni, "Outcry over Window Washers' Arrests," *IOL*, February 17, 2015, http://www.iol.co.za/news/crime-courts/outcry-over-window-washers-arrests-1819367.

56
Marelise van der Merwe, "Washing Hands of the Window Washers," *Daily Maverick*, July 16, 2015, http://www.dailymaverick.co.za/opinionista/2015-07-16-washing-hands-of-the-window-washers/#.Vq9I0r-B96Rs.

57
Dennis Webster, "Ke Molao Wa Rona: Joburg Continues Its Anti-Poor Approach," *Daily Maverick*, February 27, 2015, http://www.dailymaverick.co.za/opinionista/2015-02-27-ke-molao-wa-rona-joburg-continues-its-anti-poor-approach/#.Vq9UtE7aKI.

on a spectacle, in the literal sense of the term."[62] These actions trump up media coverage to demonstrate the police's commitment to improving society.[63] At the same time, they draw on long-engrained and institutionalized language that serves to elevate these operations into "low-intensity wars against perceived 'disorder.'"[64] When defending Operation Ke Molao, a city official emphasized the importance of people feeling safe to move about the streets, clearly referring to "people" as those who own private vehicles, and urban mobility as solely vehicular.[65]

In August 2016, South Africa held local elections and the ANC lost control of the city to the opposition Democratic Alliance for the first time in the country's democratic history. While many saw this as an important moment for change, the city's new mayor, Herman Mashaba—a successful businessman—continued an anti-poor discourse and called for "claiming the city back" from informal traders and criminals.[66]

Operation Ke Molao and the sentiments of Johannesburg's new mayor have demonstrated the degree to which an anti-poverty bias continues to plague the city. The challenges that underpin homelessness, begging, and street trade need to be properly understood and remedied by all sectors of society in a concerted manner. As Wacquant states, "The law-and-order merry-go-round is ... a mirror deforming reality to the point of the grotesque that artificially extracts delinquent behaviors from the fabric of social relations in which they take root and make sense, deliberately ignores their causes and their meanings, and reduces their treatment to a series of conspicuous position-takings, often acrobatic, sometimes properly unreal...."[67]

CONCLUSION

The deepening division in Johannesburg is occurring at a number of scales through numerous political and economic processes. This is not merely a maintenance of a status quo. Rather, a gulf continues to widen between those who have benefitted economically in the post-apartheid age and those who have not. While economic measures prove this,[68] the daily actions, strategies, cultures, and processes that influence the spatial form of Johannesburg need to also be carefully analyzed and understood.

Importantly, the urban configuration of post-apartheid Johannesburg still underpins strong cultural and language divides between population groups and incomes. This dual city is implicit in both the daily interactions of residents and the larger flows of capital that continue to shape the conurbation.

58
News24, "Window-Washers, Hawkers Arrested in Johannesburg," February 14, 2015, http://www.news24.com/SouthAfrica/News/Window-washers-hawkers-arrest-in-Johannesburg-20150214; Karishma Dipa, "Window Washers Arrested, Then What?" *IOL*, February 13, 2015, http://www.iol.co.za/news/crime-courts/window-washers-arrested-then-what-1.1817684; Some are asked to pay an admission of guilt fine of R300, or $20: Lerato Mbangeni, "Outcry over Window Washers' Arrests," *IOL*, February 17, 2015, http://www.iol.co.za/news/crime-courts/outcry-over-window-washers-arrests-1819367; Some are handed over to the government-funded National Prosecuting Authority (NPA), who are then required to, and often cannot, prove beyond reasonable doubt with the aid of witnesses that the arrested party was indeed guilty: Dipa, "Window Washers Arrested."

59
Southern Africa Litigation Centre, "Litigating against Loitering Laws – PILG Panel," July 13, 2012, http://www.southernafricalitigationcentre.org/2012/07/13/litigating-against-loitering-laws-pilg-panel/.

60
Choe Griffiths, "Bizarre Apartheid Law Stops Job Creation," *IOL*, July 21, 2003, http://www.iol.co.za/news/south-africa/bizarre-apartheid-law-stops-job-creation-1.110124.

61
Redi Direko, "What Constitutes Loitering, and Is It Illegal?" *Redi Direko Show*, 702 Talk Radio, July 23, 2009, 11:05am.

62
Wacquant, *Punishing the Poor*, 1-408.

63
Raymond Joseph, "South Africa's Very Own Superman," *Daily Maverick*, March 19, 2012, http://www.dailymaverick.co.za/opinionista/2012-03-19-south-africas-very-own-superman/#.Vq9HKbB96Rs.

64
Christopher McMichael, "Urban Pacification and 'Blitzes' in Contemporary Johannesburg," *Antipode* 47, no. 5 (November 2015): 1261–78.

First, Gauteng's new cities present a worrying future scenario for spatial integration and the remedying of Gauteng's divided apartheid landscape. A number of lessons can be drawn from previous failings. Apartheid townships were designed to be stores of dormitory labor in order to support the mining industry. They were not developed as economic nodes. Any further such development will serve to worsen levels of unemployment in the periphery and deepen economic division. In addition, the significant distance that residents of the new cities would be required to travel in order to access economic opportunity is debilitating financially and socially. Second, for inner city development, a hybrid approach is essential to ensure that investment occurs at a sustainable rate, but also that social, low-income, gap market, emergency, and mixed-tenure housing is integrated into these developments to enable mixed-income and integrated communities. Third, the continued marginalization of low- or no-income earners in Johannesburg, who due to historical process are generally black residents, perpetuates the unequal city.

The result of these three processes is a city spatially dictated by thresholds of various thicknesses and intensities, with some more visible than others, enforced by difference, exclusion, and separation. For example, the window of a private car negotiates the relationship between the street trader and the driver; the more modern and expensive the car the more likely the window will be closed, sealing an air-conditioned cell of commuter comfort, denying the street trader any means to interact. Similarly, the roads that define the periphery of inner city development in areas such as Maboneng are styled and managed to flaunt their difference as sites of wealth and exchange value, and in doing so make the precinct inaccessible and unaffordable to neighboring communities who might feel foreign in its spaces. In addition, the walls of new private cities separate these enclaved environments from the rest of the city. They are islands of wealth, privilege, and exclusion. Finally, the gulfs of space and physical infrastructural barriers that continue to embed divisions between former township areas and middle-class suburbs remain in place. New connections have been made to unite these, and physical divisions such as old mine-dumps have been reprocessed and removed, but ultimately the integration of urban areas across these divides remains one of the greatest challenges and opportunities for the spatial restructuring of Johannesburg.

The neoliberal economic focus of South Africa hands us an additional challenge. While it is important to build the country's fiscal base, the dependence on neoliberal policies, once heralded as essential to a new democracy, has resulted in the entrenching of economic power by those already well positioned to benefit, and the growth of a propor-

65 City of Johannesburg Member of the Mayoral Committee (MMC) Sello Lemao, who oversees the city's Public Safety portfolio, noted that Operation Ke Molao was launched in a "climate of current lawlessness," and must "be understood and accepted as the basis of people feeling safe to move about through the streets and roadways of our city and not feel vulnerable to strangers approaching their vehicles." Sello Lemao, "Opinion: Operation Ke Molao in Context," *Eyewitness News*, March 20, 2015, http://ewn.co.za/2015/03/20/OPINION-Sello-Lemao-Operation-ke-molao-in-context.

66 Penwell Dlamini, "Mahaba says his focus is on claiming back Joburg's inner city," *Sowetan*, October 5, 2016, http://www.sowetanlive.co.za/news/2016/10/05/mashaba-says-his-focus-is-on-claiming-back-joburgs-inner-city-.

67 Wacquant, *Punishing the Poor,* xii–xiii.

68 The Gini coefficient provides an index through which inequality can be measured (BBC, 2015). South Africa currently had a GINI index rating of 62.5 in 2013, which makes it the fourth most unequal country in the world (CIA, 2016). Magazine Monitor, "Who, What, Why: What Is the Gini Coefficient?" BBC, March 12, 2015, http://www.bbc.com/news/blogs-magazine-monitor-31847943; U.S. Central Intelligence Agency, *The World Factbook*, 2016, https://www.cia.gov/library/publications/the-world-factbook/rankorder/2172rank.html.

tionately small urban black middle class.[69] The post-apartheid era has been characterized by freedom, democracy, and opportunity, but also inequality, civil frustration, and privatization. Its complexities and contradictions are laid bare in the daily experience of Johannesburg. While residents may be free to move, systemic apparatuses ensure their peripherality and poverty through policing, private security, social housing policy, displacement, and forms of gentrification.

In seeking a means to circumvent the deepening of division in South African cities, a number of trends and policy considerations can be synthesized from this research. Most prolific is perhaps the silo approach with which both the private and public sector approach development in Johannesburg. Very little space is created for nuance, hybridity, innovation, and exploration. As such, the cogs of the economy continue to turn in very similar and divisive ways. Implicit in an economic restructuring is a spatial restructuring. Both are entangled and support each other. Less public and private edge-city construction and more integrated development in commercial cores with strong public management and guidelines will ensure a socio-economic knitting together of the fragmented city. Similarly, the city's diverse and multi-scalar economies need a means to be better recognized and supported; the poor cannot be simply wished away by public safety policy, or "handed over to social services."[70] These actions call for a more active and accountable public sector, a private sector with greater awareness of its duties to assist South Africa in its economic transformation, and residents who are committed to inclusivity, diversity, and structural reform.

Johannesburg offers the world a compelling site for the further analysis of the impacts of neoliberal economic structuring of urban space, which, due to the inhumane aftershocks of apartheid, continues to carve up and divide Johannesburg's urban form. Innovative policy responses from the City of Johannesburg in the shape of the Corridors of Freedom project have the potential to positively restructure space in the city, but only if these efforts remain focused on creating intensely integrated, multi-use, and centralized neighborhoods. Creating societies that are more equal requires radical foundational shifts, necessary to spark the structural reform required. Few cities in the world offer meaningful examples of where this has been achieved. However, while more equitable urban environments are planned and imagined, any process or action that serves to impede this goal needs to be urgently remedied. Fractious polarization as forged by greater global inequality offers a bleak future for humanity.

69
BusinessTech, "How Big Is South Africa's Black Middle Class?" August 4, 2015, http://businesstech.co.za/news/wealth/94987/how-big-is-south-africas-black-middle-class/.

70
Lemao, "Opinion: Operation Ke Molao in Context."

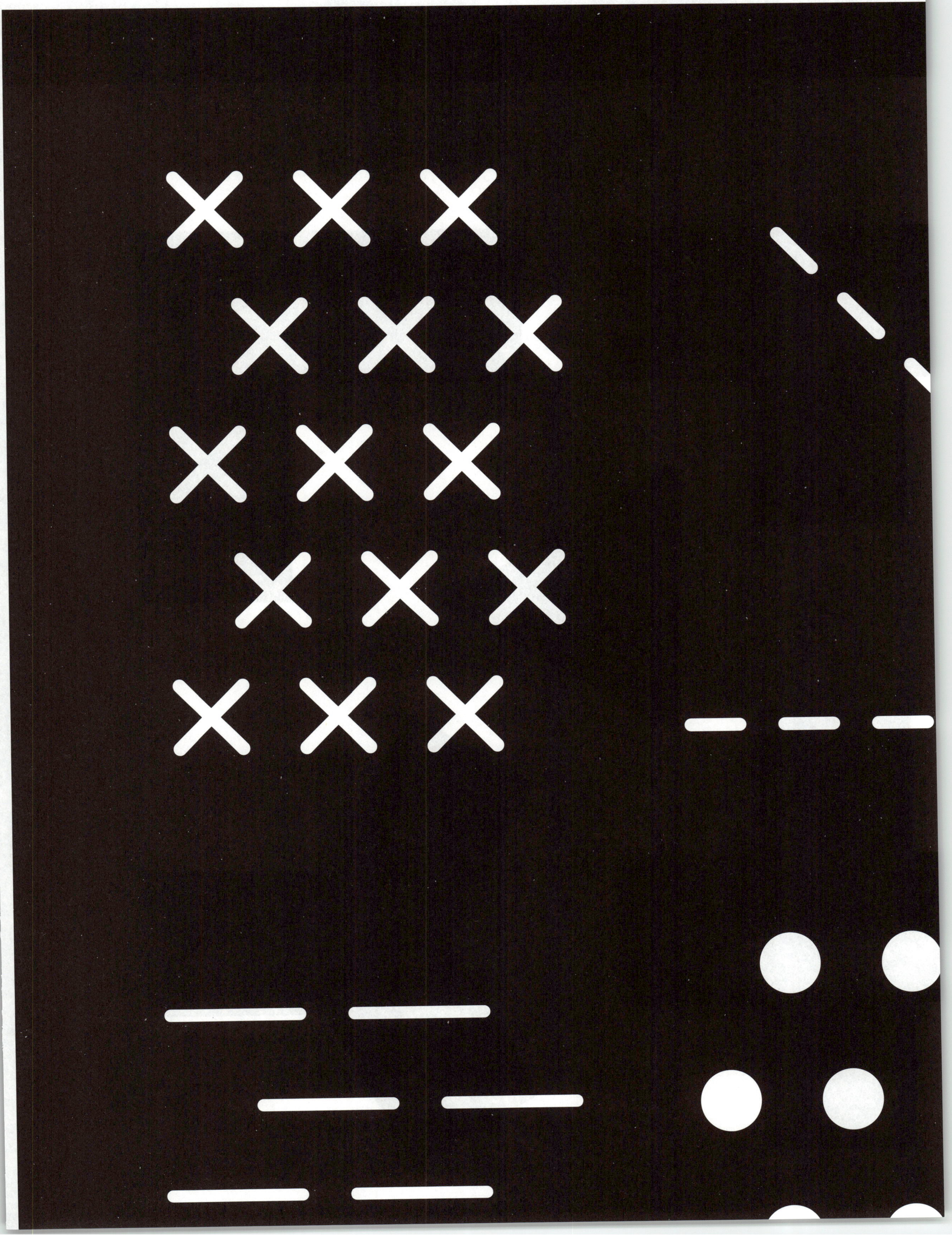

SEPARATION ANXIETY: INEQUALITY AND EXCLUSION IN ATHENS AND CAPE TOWN

by
Alfredo Brillembourg,
Hubert Klumpner
& Alexis Kalagas

*The frontier of our world is not far away;
it doesn't run along the horizon
or in the depths.*

*It glimmers faintly close by, in the twilight
of our nearest surroundings.*[1]

Fig 1.
A newly built state-subsidized housing development in Khayelitsha, Cape Town.
Courtesy of Daniel Schwartz/U-TT.

Fig 3.
A predominantly white suburban neighborhood southeast of central Cape Town. Courtesy of Daniel Schwartz/U-TT.

Speaking to reporters in Zürich in May 2004, just after FIFA had awarded the 2010 World Cup to South Africa, bid chairman Irvin Khoza declared euphorically, "this is the people of the world voting for Africa's renewal."[2] Four months later, the country's Minister of Housing, Lindiwe Sisulu, announced the N2 Gateway Project—an ambitious initiative bringing actual renewal to impoverished informal settlements along a ten-kilometer strip of the "Settlers Way" N2 motorway connecting Cape Town's airport to downtown.[3] Though couched in the rhetoric of a policy pivot towards *in situ* upgrading, the more pressing goal was to "clean up" the city's main transit route for the passing eyes of World Cup visitors.[4] After a devastating shack fire the following year, thousands of squatters were removed to distant "temporary relocation areas." Further forced evictions were threatened, as development was fast-tracked. Tensions climaxed in September 2007, when indignant residents blockaded the highway in protest.[5]

As Peter Marcuse asked more than two decades ago, "what's so new about divided cities?"[6] The built environment is an often discomfiting mirror of the society that produces it. Rising inequality has captured the zeitgeist. But inequality is a fluid phenomenon, and its experience in an urban setting is about far more than economics. Social and political structures can exacerbate, or alleviate, material disparities. While the (relatively) fixed physical form of a city can slow the pace of change, urban environments are malleable.[7] At Urban-Think Tank, we harbor few illusions about the power of heroic architects to single-handedly reduce inequality. At the same time, when looking at cities, we agree with Marcuse that it is "much more important to locate the breaks, the basic lines of cleavage, than... measure the extent of the differences."[8] Space does matter because spatial legacies, especially in the case of housing and infrastructure, can constrain the purported trickle down benefits that might otherwise boost opportunity.

NO CITY LEFT BEHIND

When it comes to how inequality impacts the lives of city dwellers, what most interests us is the possibility of change. In other words, whether urban divides represent insurmountable boundary conditions, or whether these physical and figurative cleavages are permeable and shifting. We have recently engaged in long-term research and design projects in two very different cities: Athens and Cape Town. Both are arenas where the inherited built form of the city is being reshaped by powerful global forces. They are also both places where historic spatial development patterns influence present-day efforts to address symptoms of economic turbulence and exclusionary growth. The profession has rightfully moved on from a hubristic belief in the ability of designers to "correct society on the drawing board."[9] But as social architects focused on catalyzing positive transformation in marginalized or distressed communities, the spatialization of uneven development forces us to rethink how we can intervene within the city.

In the case of the N2 in Cape Town, deprived residents abutting the "gateway" stretch of the highway seemed to benefit due to their visibility. Unlike the millions of poor South Africans languishing on the waiting list for government housing, they were being accelerated into subsidized units in a new development. Yet many were pressured to accede to an unpalatable bargain: eventually receive a home, but only after relocating indeterminately to a makeshift camp on the city periphery. For the majority, this meant severe disruption to critical social and economic networks. Many lost their jobs due to poor transport links, or had to increase their commuting costs fivefold despite already stretched household budgets.[10] Residents had been acutely sensitive to this threat to their livelihoods. The location of the informal settlement adjacent to a key transport artery was no accident. Far from a pathway out of poverty, the promise of a real house actually deepened the urban divide.

Surveys conducted in a number of developed countries have suggested that people find economic inequality fair, but only if equal opportunities exist.[11] Expressed another way, we are frequently willing to tolerate unequal outcomes, so long as we still believe in intergenerational social mobility—the prospect of individual self-betterment that lies at the heart of aspirational ideals like the American Dream. The Organization for Economic Co-operation and Development (OECD) has warned, however, that inequality can stifle social mobility.[12] An era of rising inequality is more likely to heighten differences than diminish them. In an urban context, socio-spatial segregation compounds this problem. The crowding together of poor or low-income communities in segregated areas in cities reduces chances of upward social mobility.[13] Spatial inequality contributes to social exclusion, limits access to important services, feeds stigmatization and discrimination in the job market, weakens political representation, and often goes hand in hand with patterns of disinvestment and decline in the built environment.

Like Caracas, a place Urban-Think Tank knows intimately, Athens and Cape Town are both unequal cities. According to international indices, Greece suffers from one of the highest levels of inequality among all developed countries, while South Africa is plagued by perhaps the most extreme levels of inequality worldwide due to its apartheid legacy.[14] Moving from the national to urban

1 Michal Ajvaz, *The Other City* (London: Dalkey Archive Press, 2009), 2.

2 Jere Longman, "South Africa is Named Host of 2010 World Cup," *New York Times*, May 16, 2004.

3 See Department of Housing, *"Breaking New Ground": The Comprehensive Plan for the Development of Sustainable Human Settlements* (Pretoria: Department of Housing, 2005).

4 Caroline Newton, "The Reverse Side of the Medal: About the 2010 FIFA World Cup and Beautification of the N2 in Cape Town," *Urban Forum* 20 (2009): 101.

5 David Jordhus-Lier, "Community Resistance to Megaprojects: The Case of the N2 Gateway Project in Joe Slovo Informal Settlement, Cape Town," *Habitat International* 45 (2015): 173.

6 Peter Marcuse, "What's So New About Divided Cities?" *International Journal of Urban and Regional Research* 17 (1993): 357.

7 Robert A. Beauregard and Anne Haila, "The Unavoidable Incompleteness of the City," *American Behavioral Scientist* 41 (1997): 328.

8 Marcuse, 357.

9 Meyer Schapiro, "Architect's Utopia: Review of *Architecture and Modern Life*," *Partisan Review* 4 (1938): 89-92.

10 Warren Smit et al, *Living on the Edge: A Study of the Delft Temporary Relocation Area* (Cape Town: Development Action Group, 2007): 4.

Fig 2
An informal settlement adjacent to subsidized housing in Khayelitsha, Cape Town.
Courtesy of Daniel Schwartz/U-TT.

scale, Cape Town—alongside its domestic counterparts Johannesburg, East London, Bloemfontein, Pretoria, Port Elizabeth, and Durban—is one of the most unequal cities on earth.[15] Similarly, in a recent study of inequality in thirteen European cities, Athens was only narrowly outstripped by London, Madrid, and Riga.[16] Longer-term trends offer little relief. Inequality has continued to increase in both countries, despite the considerable economic spoils of post-apartheid growth in South Africa, and the leveling effect of the prolonged debt crisis that has ravaged Greece since 2008.

To be clear, Athens and Cape Town are not directly comparable. Vast disparities in per capita wealth are only the most recent chapter in complex histories of urban development linked by violence and displacement, but separated by politics, economics, and culture. Yet they both offer object lessons in how the evolving geography of the contemporary city can amplify or mitigate the effects of inequality. Unlike in the gilded waterfront retreats and sprawling townships of Cape Town, inequality in Athens is not inscribed in the spatial order. The built form and organization of each city continues to influence its ability to deal with inequality without segregation. For many in Cape Town, economic apartheid has survived the system of racial apartheid officially dismantled over two decades ago. Meanwhile, despite economic polarization and waves of immigration, social fissures in Athens are yet to calcify into visible spatial divides. The reasons why provide lessons for architects and policymakers alike.

THERE SHALL BE HOUSES, SECURITY, AND COMFORT!

"Now my life has changed, and I can be happy. But if all the time in your life you stay in one place, that is not life."[17] Richard is a community leader in BT Section, a triangular pocket of approximately seventy self-built shacks within the largest township in South Africa, Khayelitsha. When he first arrived in Cape Town in search of a job in 1974, leaving his young family behind in the Eastern Cape, he was required by law to reside in an all-male hostel. After a stint squatting near what became the township Crossroads, he fled growing violence in the early 1980s and was one of the first to settle informally in Khayelitsha, then a haphazard cluster of pitched tents and empty fields. Three decades later, Richard remains. His home has grown into a mazy 117 square-meter structure, from which he once operated a popular *shebeen* (informal bar), but electricity only came in 2010, and onsite water and sanitation is still a literal pipe dream.

The interior of a self-built shack in Khayelitsha, Cape Town. Courtesy of Daniel Schwartz/U-TT. Fig 4.

It is impossible to discuss inequality in Cape Town without reflecting on the systems of territorial control that culminated in apartheid. And it is impossible to comprehend the post-apartheid city without recognizing the persistent spatial logic of segregationist planning. As architectural historian Nicholas Coetzer suggests, "where and how people live in and around cities was the battleground on which the contradictions of the apartheid fantasy raged."[18] The 1913 Natives Land Act and 1923 Natives (Urban Areas) Act first legislated for segregated urban environments and instituted a restrictive migrant labor scheme. The 1950 Group Areas Act further enforced residential segregation by dividing South African cities into race-based sectors. Freehold settlements were destroyed, and "Africans" living in "white" areas were forcibly removed to vast, peripheral townships with restricted tenure rights. In parallel, the 1951 Prevention of Illegal Squatting Act prevented new rural migrants from settling through strict influx control measures and the clearance of squatter communities.

Street view of a typical detached "RDP" house in Khayelitsha, Cape Town. Courtesy of Daniel Schwartz/U-TT. Fig 5.

Housing was a principal means through which urban space was reorganized. Cape Town's urban areas near the commercial center and waterfront were set aside as enclaves for the development of an exclusive white property market.[19] Planned townships, and bands of overflow informal development that emerged in liminal buffer strips established as "ideological friction-prevention zones," created a sharp racial divide between black and colored communities banished to the floodprone sands of the Cape Flats, and the white southern and northern neighborhoods skirting the sea and Table Mountain.[20] Townships comprised of endless rows of uniform low-rise dwellings were denied industrial and commercial development, preserving their limited function as poorly maintained dormitory settlements for a tightly controlled labor pool. Additional land-use planning and morphological features, such as rail lines, highways, rivers, scrubland, and industrial facilities, were rigorously employed by the state to further separate and contain these "group areas."

Over time, selective rights to the city were granted through a hierarchy of non-white accommodation: from leased public housing to single-sex hostels, infill backyard shacks, and shacks on occupied land.[21] Cape Town's distance from the bantustans established as rural "homelands" for black migrant workers, as well as a government freeze on family housing production, led to the rapid expansion of informal settlements in the 1970s, as marginalized groups sought an urban foothold. Informal development exploded after the 1986 abandonment of influx controls, even as the state simultaneously attempted to seize on nascent economic stratification to divide black communities and promote preferential homeownership for an emerging middle class.[22] This period of privatization in housing delivery coincided with a final wave of rudimentary sites-and-services construction—"toilet towns"—on the city's periphery, intended as a pressure valve to relieve tensions fueled by overcrowding, neglect, organized resistance, and escalating violence between "shacklords" contesting territorial control.[23]

After 1994, house building bore the weight of nation building.[24] The state was ill-equipped, however, to deal with the flood of rural migrants from the Eastern Cape. Authorities prioritized the mass delivery of low-cost housing, but even today—and despite more central public land holdings—most new development is located in the underserved townships and cheap land of the Cape Flats.[25] Desegregation of formerly whites-only neighborhoods is beginning to erode the city's racialized geography, but rising inequality within the labor market has created a new division between racially mixed middle class areas, and isolated black neighborhoods grappling with persistently high unemployment.[26] The dispersed and fragmented spatial legacy of apartheid

11 See Christopher Jencks and Laura Tach, "Would Equal Opportunity Mean More Mobility?" in *Mobility and Inequality: Frontiers of Research in Sociology and Economics*, ed. Stephen L Morgan et al. (Stanford: Stanford University Press, 2006).

12 OECD, *Divided We Stand: Why Inequality Keeps Rising* (Paris: OECD, 2011), 40.

13 Tim Cassiers and Christian Kesteloot, "Socio-Spatial Inequalities and Social Cohesion in European Cities," *Urban Studies* 49 (2012), 1913.

14 See OECD, *In It Together: Why Less Inequality Benefits All* (Paris: OECD, 2015).

15 UN-HABITAT, *State of the World's Cities 2010/2011: Bridging the Urban Divide* (London: Earthscan, 2010), 73.

16 See Tiit Tammaru et al, "A Multi-Factor Approach to Understanding Socio-Economic Segregation in European Capital Cities," in *Socio-Economic Segregation in European Capital Cities: East Meets West*, ed. Tiit Tammaru et al. (New York: Routledge, 2015).

17 In discussion with the author, Cape Town, 4 November 2015.

18 Nicholas Coetzer, *Building Apartheid: On Architecture and Order in Imperial Cape Town* (Surrey: Ashgate Publishing, 2013), 135.

19 Marie Huchzermeyer, *Unlawful Occupation: Informal Settlements and Urban Policy in South Africa and Brazil* (Trenton: Africa World Press, 2004), 96.

20 Skip Krige, "Bloemfontein," in *Homes Apart: South Africa's Segregated Cities*, ed. Anthony Lemon (Bloomington: Indiana University Press, 1991), 109; Owen Crankshaw, "Deindustrialization, Professionalization, and Racial Inequality in Cape Town," *Urban Affairs Review* 48 (2012): 854.

21 Huchzermeyer, *Unlawful Occupation*, 85.

22 Susan Parnell, "State Intervention in Housing Provision in the 1980s," in *The Apartheid City and Beyond: Urbanization and Social Change in South Africa*, ed. David Marshall Smith (London: Routledge, 1992), 58.

23 Arnold H. Isaacs, "Crossroads: The Rise and Fall of a Squatter Movement in Cape Town, South Africa," in *Urban Social Movements in the Third World*, ed. Frans Schuurman and Ton Van Naerssen (London: Routledge, 1989), 114.

24 First articulated in the African National Congress' Reconstruction and Development Program (RDP) in 1994, the right to adequate housing was subsequently enshrined in the 1996 Constitution.

25 Marie Huchzermeyer, "Housing for the Poor? Negotiated Housing Policy in South Africa," *Habitat International* 25 (2001): 303.

26 Crankshaw, *Deindustrialization, Professionalization, and Racial Inequality in Cape Town*, 857.

Fig 10.
View from the street. Courtesy of U-TT.

Fig 9.
Digital tools ensure the new site plan is minimally disruptive and incorporates resident preferences. Courtesy of U-TT.

Fig 8.
Integrated urban water management and solar feed-in tariff systems are intended to relieve stressed municipal infrastructures. Courtesy of U-TT.

A post-war *polykatoikia* in central Athens. Courtesy of Daniel Schwartz/U-TT. Fig 6.

ensures vulnerable communities are still stranded far from Cape Town's main employment centers.[27] Inadequate and costly public transport creates daily hardships for those residents lucky enough to have low-paid jobs, even as the government spends more on transport subsidies than housing, artificially sustaining a polarized spatial economy.[28]

The state of low-income housing is another residual brake on social mobility. Past government policies of first monopolizing, then limiting, the production of affordable housing meant that the city was completely unprepared to absorb a surge of newcomers, but committed to denying title to those settling informally. Despite the mobilization of large scale capital subsidies for turnkey developments, informal settlements have continued to mushroom. This has created further divides between residents gifted freehold property titles and a low-grade house by the state, and those living for years in precarious conditions of tenure insecurity. The latter group are damned if they do and damned if they don't. The private housing market remains weak as a result of uncertainty over property rights and limited access to financing—also discouraging lasting upgrades—while a steep price gradient and shortage of appropriate rental accommodation excludes moves to better located neighborhoods for those with stable employment.[29]

The design of housing in Cape Town has also contributed to persistent segregation. For rich and poor alike, the dominant typology is the single family detached unit surrounded by a yard or garden. The Garden City movement of the 1920s heavily influenced the low-density, anti-urban character of much residential development.[30] However, as Coetzer notes, a brief burst in the construction of mixed high-rise apartment blocks at the time was seen as a direct threat to a White national identity.[31] The spatial proximity of tenement living allowed for contact across color lines, and the possibility of working class solidarity. Policing the density of dwellings had an exclusionary effect, both by making certain areas of the city unaffordable, as well as generating sprawl that increased spatial separation. This same typology was reproduced on a modest scale in both apartheid and post-apartheid housing—initially, as a way to capitalize on cheap, unskilled construction labor, and later as an enduring symbol of middle-class aspiration.

Housing still embodies South African dreams of social transformation. But Cape Town's development has reproduced a painfully familiar urban structure, where large swathes of the population are "thoroughly dependent on the city's economy and deeply marginalized within it."[32] Widening intraracial inequality is an especially stark reminder of how spatialized forms of exclusion have created place-based poverty traps that are stubbornly resistant to redistributive social programs. Even more confronting is the recognition that a highly segregated urban environment, once maintained through careful design and an elaborate system of oppression, is now being reinforced through the interplay of market forces. Most residents of Cape Town today live where and how they do because they have no other choice. In the meantime, poor rural migrants continue to gravitate to the city out of aspiration or desperation. What they find is a place where deep-rooted inequalities still deny them spatial justice.

NEVER LET A CRISIS GO TO WASTE

"I've never seen in another European capital what we are witnessing here in Athens."[33] Gesturing at the buildings around him, Thanos, a 35-year-old teacher we met on the street in the neighborhood of Exarcheia, explained how mass vacancy and abandonment were distorting the urban environment. He could just as easily have been remarking on how swiftly the Greek debt crisis had morphed into a deeper social crisis—a collective trauma that was leaving physical scars on the city. Thanos used to live in the southern suburbs, but had relocated with his unemployed wife to a smaller apartment in central Athens so they could survive on his reduced income. He volunteered regularly in a municipal soup kitchen near Omonoia Square, where he served many people, mostly women. More than half of the apartments in their building were vacant. Despite the immense challenges Athens faced, Thanos was convinced change had to start "from the bottom."[34]

Like Cape Town, Athens has also been indelibly shaped by patterns of internal migration. Unlike in Cape Town, however, these inflows did not create an enduring divide between areas of orderly and disorderly urbanization, but instead defined the spatial character of the city from the ground up. Two major crises were pivotal. In 1923, the Treaty of Lausanne agreed at the end of the GrecoTurkish War formalized a mass population transfer already underway, with more than 1.3 million Orthodox Greeks uprooted from Anatolia. Thirty years later, the hostilities of World War II and the subsequent Civil War left a country in ruins. As the epicenter of the interwar resettlement process, greater Athens doubled its population from 1920 to 1928.[35] By 1951, when the Marshall Plan ended, the original refugee housing question was still unresolved, even as the Civil War generated an entirely new group of internally displaced people. Again, Athens emerged as the primary pole of attraction.

After almost a decade of conflict, much of the country's housing stock and infrastructure was either destroyed, or had fallen into disrepair.[36] Faced with escalating need, and the failure or conscious retreat of the state, the Athenian population responded to both crises with self-help strategies. Modern Athens already had a history of unplanned growth and illegal or arbitrary building.[37] The slow pace of official refugee resettlement programs in the 1920s led to a spontaneous movement of informal construction on the city's margins, resulting in numerous overnight *tenekedoupoli* (tinplate cities). In time, these temporary structures acquired a degree of permanence, and the state's willful blindness gave way to retrospective legalization. Beginning in the 1930s, but taking off during the postwar reconstruction era, the *antiparochi* system supplanted low density incremental development on small, subdivided lots. Developers acquired houses for free and compensated landowners with units in the multistory *polykatoikies* (apartment blocks) built in their place.[38]

During both crises, the unmet housing demands of new arrivals triggered an inventiveness based around self-serving, but synergistic, private systems of exchange, which were not capital intensive. Emboldened by a permissive building code and laissez-faire regulation, rapid urban expansion resulted in a fragmentation of construction responsibility and ownership—initially at the household level, and later among a vast class of self-financed petty developers swept up in the speculative property boom. Illegal building and pirate subdivisions initially acted as a shock absorber, determining the pace and frontiers of interwar urban growth, while the fragmented postwar housing market led to increased sprawl and uncontrolled densification. Crisis conditions were resolved in the built environment, which was produced through an irregular pattern of bottom-up development that also addressed broader livelihood needs by birthing a light industry centered on the manufacture of housing-related consumer goods and building materials.[39]

By the mid 1970s, deteriorating and congested conditions in the overbuilt central municipality began to trigger a middle class suburban exodus. But the disintegration of the Communist Bloc in the early 1990s resulted in an unexpected and rapid new inflow of migrants, the majority crossing into Greece from neighboring Albania.[40] Because most areas of the city were now dominated by homeownership—and in the absence of social housing—the few affordable rental options for immigrants were largely found in the vacated basements or lower floors of *polykatoikies*, with the spacious upper floor apartments occupied by

27 Ken Sinclair Smith and Ivan Turok, "The Changing Spatial Economy of Cities: An Exploratory Analysis," *Development Southern Africa* 29 (2012): 392.

28 Ivan Turok, "Persistent Polarization Post-Apartheid? Progress Towards Urban Integration in Cape Town," *Urban Studies* 38 (2001): 2351-2352.

29 Ibid., 2360.

30 Coetzer, *Building Apartheid*, 130.

31 Ibid., 146.

32 Cobus de Swardt et al, "Urban Poverty in Cape Town," *Environment & Urbanization* 17 (2005): 101.

33 In discussion with the author, Athens, 17 November 2014.

34 Ibid.

35 See Alexander Tzonis and Alcestis P Rodi, *Greece: Modern Architectures in History* (London: Reaktion Books, 2013), 76.

36 Approximately 25-30 percent of the built environment was in ruins: Lila Leontidou, *The Mediterranean City in Transition* (Cambridge: Cambridge University Press, 1990), 139.

37 Indeed, one of the first settlements of this kind sprung up without permission on the side of the Acropolis hill in the mid-19th century: Tzonis and Rodi, *Greece: Modern Architectures*, 37.

38 Maria Mantouvalou et al, "Processes of Social Integration and Urban Development in Greece: Southern Challenges to European Unification," *European Planning Studies* 3 (1995): 192-193.

39 Leontidou, *The Mediterranean City*, 102.

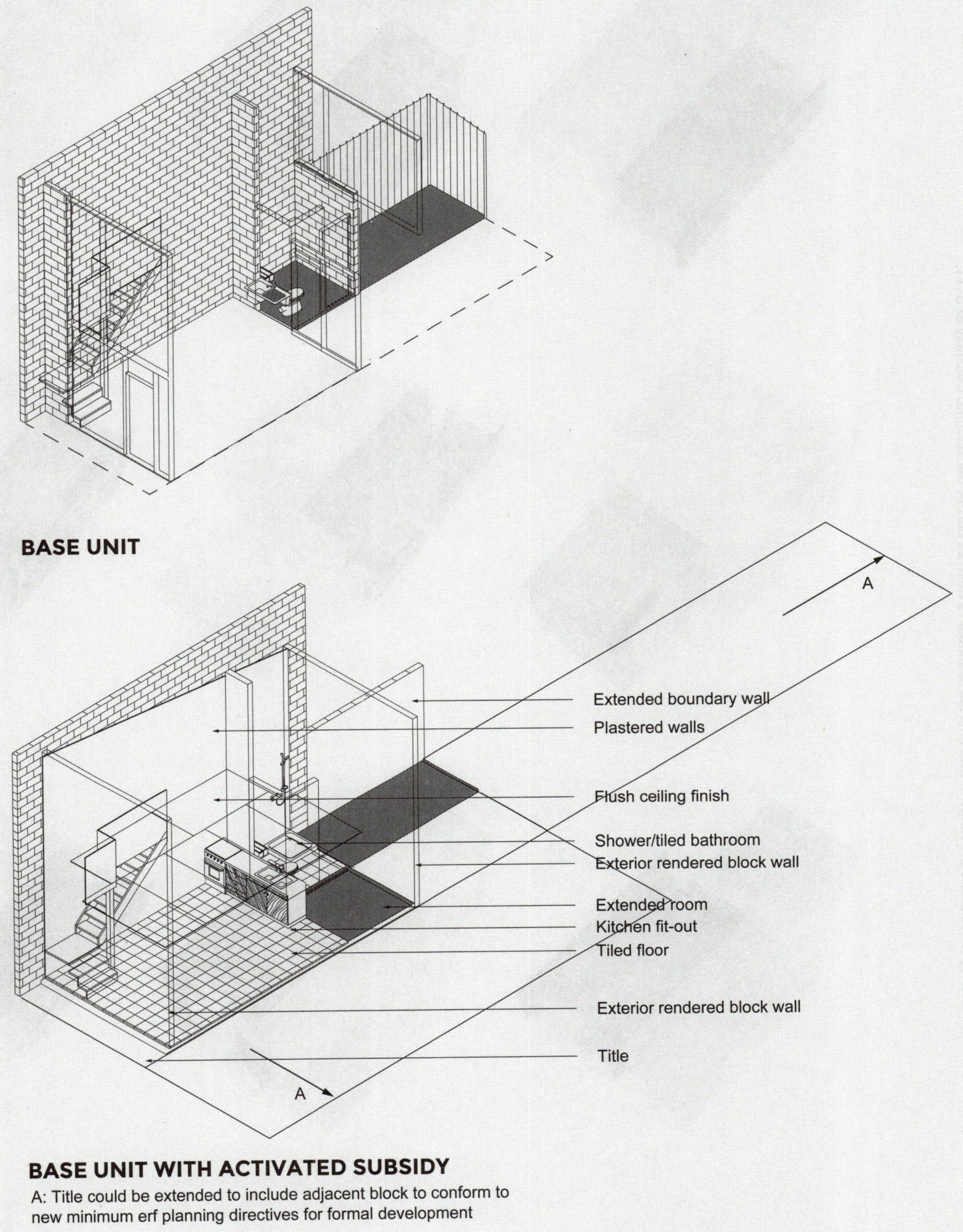

Fig 7.
Axonometric diagram illustrating the incremental upgrading possibilities of the Empower Shack base unit. Courtesy of U-TT.

Fig 12.
Floorplan renders illustrating to residents the range of unit choices available to them as part of the scheme. Courtesy of U-TT.

Fig 11.
Diagram illustrating the incremental upgrading possibilities of the Empower Shack base unit.

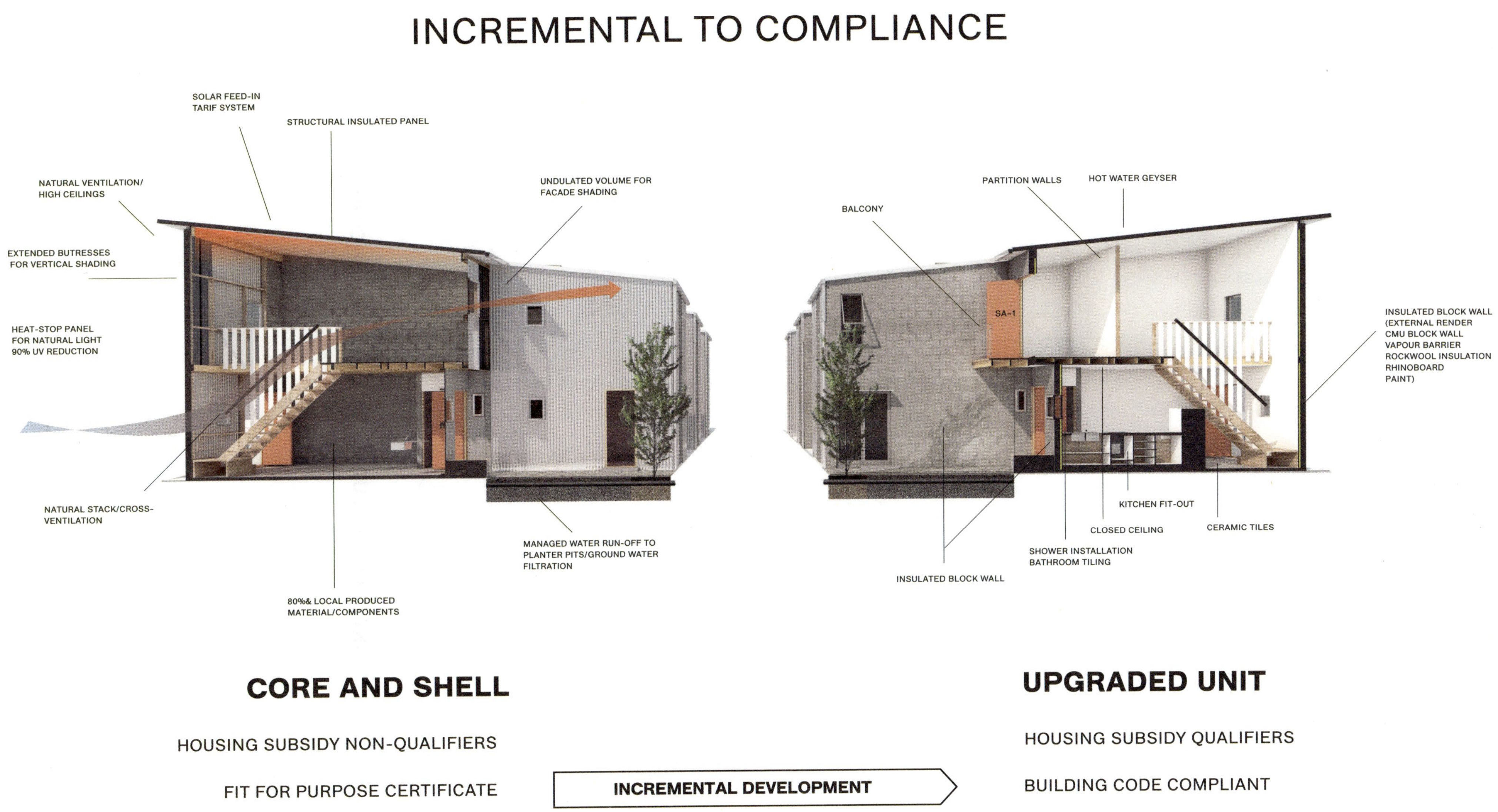

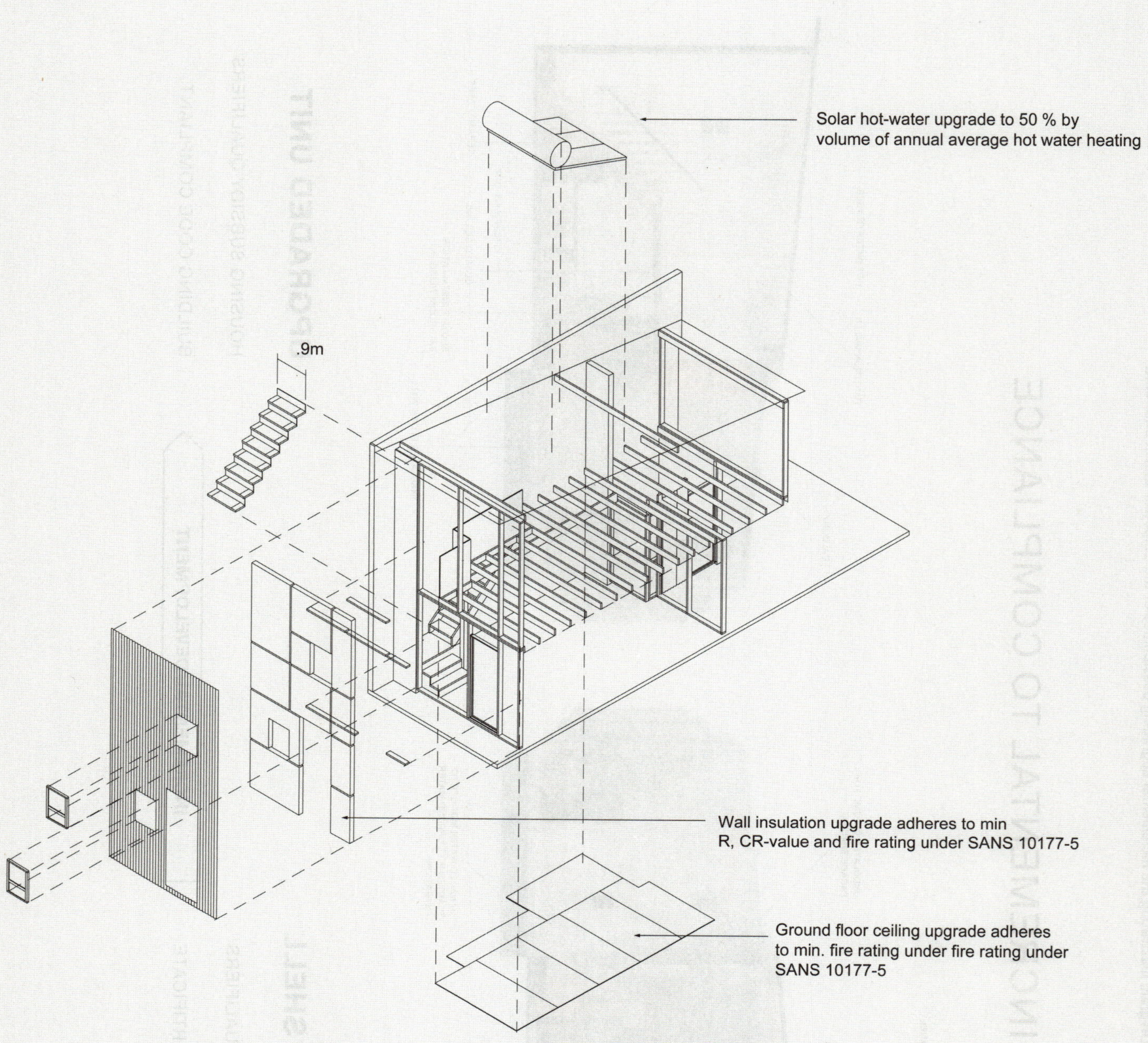

INCREMENTAL UPGRADE TO COMPLIANCE (UNIT D3)

wealthier and more established residents.[41] As a result, a distinct form of vertically segregated cohabitation emerged.[42] While Athens has since become a primary gateway to Europe for vast numbers of migrants from Central Asia, the Middle East, and Africa who face housing discrimination, this system of vertical segregation has prevented outright ghettoization.

Since 2008, soaring unemployment, dwindling incomes, and small landlords reluctant to sell idle properties at a significant loss have led to a growing web of vacancy.[43] But despite worsening inequality and deepening marginalization, the availability of cheap apartments in mixed-income areas due to the state's tacit support of the *polykatoikia* boom helps to restrict segregation. Equally, that same construction boom (between 1950 and 1980), together with the preceding period of informal development, was responsible for extending property titles to millions of Athenians. The spatial effects have echoed through the generations. Even before the collapse of the housing market and retreat to family solidarity, limited access to financing meant that property inheritance was crucial to many young couples meeting the societal expectation of homeownership. Rather than forming enclaves of concentrated wealth, higher-earning children of working class parents often remained in the neighborhoods where they grew up.[44] Social mobility did not result in residential mobility, but instead a form of intergenerational gentrification.

Perhaps ironically for a process that shaped the sustained postwar Greek economic miracle, Athens' radical form of user-generated urbanism eroded the city's resilience to future economic shocks. But it also left three important legacies that counteracted potential forces of segregation. First, a largely self-financed housing system characterized by high rates of homeownership, a complex and fragmented title structure, intergenerational transfers of property, limited access to mortgage credit, and an absence of social housing.[45] Second, the endless repetition of a generic architectural typology—the *polykatoikia*—that democratized urban space for all socioeconomic groups in a sea of mid-rise apartment buildings.[46] And third, an unplanned, mixed-use urban fabric without the concentrations of industrial activity and functional distinctions produced by stricter zoning regimes. Despite the impact of immigration and the economic crisis, different segments of the population continue to live in relative proximity. Inequality has not erased diversity.

DESIGNING FOR DIVERSITY

The examples of Cape Town and Athens point to the futility of isolated architectural interventions in the absence of structural change. Nonetheless, our desire to understand how economic inequality translates into a more frozen form of spatial inequality goes beyond the academic. Architects and designers have an urgent role to play in identifying and addressing the spatial practices that fuel and perpetuate segregation, threatening the prospects of social mobility for future generations. We must contribute to a more fundamental vision of the city as a place of equal opportunity, employing "design as the first signal of human intention."[47] The experiences of Athens and Cape Town also serve as a timely warning. As the wage differentials between countryside and city continue to widen, rural-to-urban migration will remain a defining issue of our time. How a city copes with rapid urbanization is tantamount to how it addresses spatial patterns of inequality through inclusive development.

Fig 13.
Recently arrived migrants at the Praksis Day Center, Athens. Courtesy of Daniel Schwartz/U-TT.

Fig 14.
The dense urban blocks surrounding Victoria Square in central Athens. Courtesy of Daniel Schwartz/U-TT.

Our Empower Shack project in Khayelitsha was conceived in this spirit. While seeking to improve the lives of the BT Section community through higher quality dwellings, it also reflects our conviction that an innovative pilot scheme can influence a new direction for housing policy and delivery nationwide. We wish to reshape informal settlements in South Africa by offering an integrated methodology for the fair distribution of public space, a safer urban environment, improved infrastructure and services, and an urbanization scheme that combines dignified housing with new economic and social possibilities for residents. The initial phase, consisting of four adjoining houses to the south of the main site, was completed in December 2015 and is currently undergoing user evaluation. The next phase began in February 2017, including the roll out of 72 additional units, a community center, a greywater management system, and a feed-in tariff solar installation.

Empower Shack has been designed with a commitment to *in situ* upgrading. We have prioritized the preservation of communities over more quixotic attempts to challenge the spatial legacy of apartheid that would result in their displacement. Equally, however, the project targets some of the key underlying processes that make places like BT Section persistent poverty traps. It has three core components: a modular two-story housing prototype built with prefabricated local components, an inclusive spatial planning process—supported by new digital tools—that offers a controlled path to densification, and a range of integrated programming that responds to broader social, environmental, and economic dynamics within the surrounding settlement. This includes a micro-finance scheme, an income generating renewable energy pilot, an urban agriculture initiative, and an apprenticeship program focused on the development of

40 Gabriella Lazaridis and Joanna Poyago-Theotoky, "Undocumented Migrants in Greece: Issues of Regularization," *International Migration* 37 (1999): 715; Colin Williams and Jan Windebank, "Black Market Work in the European Community: Peripheral Work for Peripheral Localities?" *International Journal of Urban and Regional Research* 19 (1995): 22.

41 Thomas Maloutas, "Segregation, Social Polarization and Immigration in Athens During the 1990s: Theoretical Expectations and Contextual Difference," *International Journal of Urban and Regional Research* 31 (2007): 748.

42 Thomas Maloutas and Nikos Karadimitriou, "Vertical Social Differentiation in Athens: Alternative or Complement to Community Segregation," *International Journal of Urban and Regional Research* 25 (2001): 699.

43 Bank of Greece, *Summary Table of Short-Term Indicators for the Real Estate Market* (Athens: Bank of Greece, 2015).

44 Thomas Maloutas, "Socio-Economic Segregation in Athens at the Beginning of the Twenty-First Century," in *Socio-Economic Segregation in European Capital Cities: East Meets West*, ed. Tiit Tammaru et al. (New York: Routledge, 2015), 179.

45 George Donatos, "A Quantitative Analysis of Investment in New Housing in Greece," *Urban Studies* 32 (1995): 1475.

46 Thomas Maloutas, "Social Segregation in Athens," *Antipode* 25 (1993): 235.

47 William McDonough, "Design, Ecology, Ethics, and the Making of Things," *Colonnade* 10 (1994): 9.

Fig 15.
An aerial view of the Empower Shack scheme, which will include new public and shared spaces. Courtesy of U-TT.

marketable construction and community facilitation skills. From the outset, the process has involved active participation from all community members.

Two aspects of the Empower Shack strategy stand out when it comes to resisting spatial drivers of inequality and segregation. First, we believe that densification and the introduction of mixed-use structures will transform the area. By distributing the existing residential footprint over multiple floors, the urbanization plan frees up land within the settlement. This will allow for the introduction of additional housing stock for rental and sale at multiple price points, as well as the clustering of buildings to create new common spaces and retrofit missing infrastructure. The plan also envisages commercial zones within what is now largely a dormitory suburb suffering from high unemployment rates. The housing prototype's adaptable floor plan and exposed, modular internal services, allows for a diverse range of ground-level commercial uses supporting local entrepreneurial activity. Rather than replacing shacks with mono-functional sprawl, the project opens up space for vibrant, community-driven urban development.

Second, we believe that stimulating a more diverse and dynamic housing market in the area will accelerate the upgrading process and unlock latent potential. Central to this strategy is designing in a pathway to formalization—what we term "incremental to compliance." Greater certainty about tenure security and future adherence to housing codes will not only overcome the paralyzing effect of permanent impermanence, but also encourage incremental investment in an asset now recognized by financial institutions. The micro-finance scheme facilitates the repayment of resident contributions, while a land release credit provides an incentive rewarding the transfer of unused occupied land to the wider development. The prototype caters to shifting spatial needs by offering demand-driven unit sizes. This will allow for households from a broader segment of the economic spectrum to coexist in the community as it evolves, while at the same time acknowledging (and integrating) the stepping-stone role played by the informal "backyard shack" rental market.

Rear view of the "BT South" Empower Shack pilot, was completed in December 2015. Courtesy of Jan Ras/U-TT. Fig 16.

With Empower Shack, we are committed to transcending the formal-informal binary through which housing in South Africa tends to be viewed. Rather than erecting a bridge, we are questioning the fundamental assumptions of official planning policy. Visiting Khayelitsha, it becomes immediately apparent that the lived experience of most South Africans is not reflected in existing approaches. Until now, the residents of BT Section have had no dialogue with formal planning provisions. By accepting the need to work with what already exists—however shaped by a history of discrimination—we have been able to negotiate with the City of Cape Town to employ more permanent construction techniques and materials, allowing the upgraded homes to eventually join the formal housing stock. More importantly, through our willingness to engage at the level of laws and procedures, we have been able to influence the formulation of new planning directives that promise a far wider impact.

At Urban-Think Tank, we have argued consistently for the need for a different kind of architect—open to new ways of thinking both about design, and about the role and responsibilities of the profession in the social, economic, and political arenas. The complex challenge of inequality in cities demands exactly this kind of expanded definition of our work. It demands that architects and designers take a moral position and be prepared to venture into the realm of social and political action. As the examples of Athens and Cape Town show, even a basic residential unit—a home—cannot be divorced from the context in which it was produced. Equally, the two cities show how the design of that home, and the systems that sustain it, can continue to influence the experience of spatial inequality down through the generations. To paraphrase Slavoj Žižek, what cannot be spoken of speaks through architecture.[48] It is about time we brought these conversations out into the open.

48 See Adrian Lahoud, "Architecture, Contingency and Crisis: An Interview With Slavoj Žižek," *Architectural Design* 207 (2010): 112.

"Along Sound Lines": Drawing up Dubai's Labor Camps from 1950 to 2008

Todd Reisz

1

Fig. 1 Tweet from the account of the Government of Dubai Media Office announces that Dubai Police were able to "resolve the issue in less than an hour." In the image an officer from Dubai Police calls out instructions to the builders at the Fountain Views construction site after police had corralled them into a semi-enclosed area nearby. Dubai Media Office, Twitter post, March 10, 2015, 6:49am (ECT), https://twitter.com/DXBMediaOffice.

On March 10, 2015, news outlets worldwide reported that several hundred construction workers had protested their labor conditions in Dubai.[1] The action took place in an area of the city often considered to be the center of "New Dubai." Workers streamed out of the construction site for the Fountain Views residences, a tower selling vistas looking over the world's largest choreographed fountain. Without a choreography of their own, the protesting workers wandered somewhat diffidently into morning traffic. Described as a "rare" event, this was not the first labor demonstration in Dubai. That said, such demonstrations—let alone strikes—are illegal in the United Arab Emirates. The workers likely knew this: there were no signs, no rote chants. They did not so much demonstrate as just leave work. They could only exploit their en masse attire of mint-green coveralls and company-issued fluorescent yellow vests, which did what they were designed to do: alert attention to the wearer. One might surmise that the employees did not select their stage based on its central or dramatic location in Dubai; they chose it because that is where they worked, not where they lived.

There were very few photographs of the protest published online, an indication that media representatives were not alerted prior to protest.[2] Press did not respond as quickly as Dubai's police and media teams, which together executed speedy, successful emergency plans in "less than an hour."[3] Some news sources called the demonstration a "sit-in," which is more or less what the situation became once police, some in riot gear, shepherded the men into a partially enclosed area of a construction site. That was where a photograph was taken of a Dubai police officer issuing commands through a megaphone to the corralled workers. After Dubai officials released the image—with the world's tallest skyscraper, Burj Khalifa, featured as a cropped backdrop—it was picked up by newspapers ranging from local government-owned newspapers to such internationally reputed outlets as the BBC. The photograph these news sources used to accompany the article about disobedience was a government-delivered impression.

Aside from one Reuters article, none of the English-language reporting captured a statement from any of the protesters. State-supported newspapers and international news sources alike relied upon statements issued later by city officials and representatives of the employer, who all claimed that there had been no pay withheld, but rather the overtime "incentives" paid to encourage speedier work. Those incentives apparently more than doubled the workers' monthly salaries from 500 dirhams to 1100 dirhams.[4]

TRACKING THE LEGACY OF DUBAI'S LABOR HOUSING

A poignant message from the Fountain Views demonstration is that workers' demands were about withheld weekly pay that the workers expected to receive. They were not about living conditions, impossible debt burdens, withheld passports, or the inequities embedded in the worker sponsorship system known as the *kafala* system.[5] Attempts to reform employment conditions for workers like those at Fountain Views, nevertheless, have confronted the longer list of grievances with great difficulty. The system, for lack of a better term, is designed to refract blame so that there is no clear accountable agent. Many activist proposals demand that the host countries or companies cover the extortionate recruitment fees that burden workers with significant debt even before they begin their jobs. Though with noble intentions, such a simplistic suggestion ignores the complexity of markets and geopolitical forces—above and under the table—at hand. There has been little to no speculation, for example, on how labor brokers who finance the travels and contracts of South Asian workers, often at extortionate levels, would respond to higher salaries for their prospective clients. There have been calls for abolishing the role of these intermediaries, not only by outside activist groups but also national governments who represent many of these laborers, but no specific proposal convincingly demonstrates how to remove the bribery and corruption that bleeds into and out of the notorious labor contracts that distance international building industry companies and their locally based clients from the spurious process.[6]

Activist groups and media outlets have also focused on the physical conditions of workers in Dubai. This might seem a more direct, and visible, way of effecting improvements than, for example, trying to reform the ways men and women have been recruited across national borders. Though living conditions were a less significant component of the 2006 Human Rights Watch report described below, it did observe "decrepit conditions" at one site with overflowing toilets and no electricity. Without any easy images of decrepitude in other arenas, such as the more elusive structures of hiring and pay, there has been much emphasis on labor housing. Consequently, for the very reason of visual perception, private and government officials have chosen to respond to outside activist groups' accusations in this realm.[7] Whether or not outside observers want to place a focus on housing, a continuing media focus remains set on the housing, and government officials respond in ways that alter how Dubai's least-paid workers live in the city.

To perceive the effects of outside publishing on labor conditions in Dubai, it is essential to understand current laborers' housing as a historically shaped condition since the city's earliest modernization programs. Dubai has long been a home to a migrating and destitute labor force, much longer than it has accommodated labor camps. The labor camp is a relatively recent spatial product in Dubai that aided the city's development goals from the mid-1990s onward.[8] It continues to be reformulated based on concerns about efficiency and hygiene and about Dubai's outward image.

A 2006 report by Human Rights Watch (HRW) titled "Building Towers, Cheating Workers" can be credited for instigating a global interest in who was building Dubai's boom. The HRW report and accompanying media campaign forced the the UAE government's first on-record response to allegations of inhumane treatment. As discussed below, long before the HRW report, Dubai's leadership had sought ways to respond to labor conditions in ways that ensured safety and responded to concerns about how Dubai was perceived by a potentially critical outsider observer. Nevertheless, the HRW report shaped how many in the Western hemisphere and beyond perceived this specific topic and the city in general. The HRW report and the media storm that cited it resulted in palpable changes within Dubai's borders and promises for further improvement. Despite the report's greater focus on other aspects of workers' lives, those improvements most often addressed the physical and spatial conditions of housing.

A typical rebuttal to the HRW report begs a comparison of circumstances in Dubai to those the workers left behind in towns and cities of, for example, India or Pakistan. Rarely, if ever, is there an attempt to place current conditions in Dubai in the context of the city's own history of labor housing.[9] Acquiring and understanding that urban history, specifically a history of managing the living conditions and location of Dubai's least-paid workers, clarifies how ongoing changes to housing formats are a result of the merging interests of the city's economic planning and its public image. Fastening together disparate archival documents with journalistic reporting about the city's development since the early 1950s provides a representation of how millions of people have lived and worked in Dubai, many of whom risked their lives just to arrive there. It also illuminates how Dubai's employers and government officials have sought to accommodate these migrant workers. Consideration of such an urban history might, first, give us some clues about how such a contemporary living condition for Dubai's least-paid workers came about, and, second, begin to demonstrate how the private and public sectors have responded to public criticism over the course of a much broader stretch of time than usually considered in recent media coverage.

BUILDING THE LABOR CAMP

Today Dubai's low-wage labor force is characteristically associated with the labor camp, a barracks-style housing type that is walled, gated, and likely managed by yet another subcontractor.[10] A labor camp houses only men or only women. Further, it is most often surrounded by other labor camps, therefore suggesting that there are designated and delineated locations in the city for this kind of housing, such as in the districts al-Quoz and al-Muhaisnah.[11] These areas of Dubai are often misleadingly portrayed as a hidden or dark side of Dubai. Quite the contrary, designated locations of labor camps are easily accessible from Dubai's most traveled roadways, with some in al-Quoz mere minutes away from one of the city's most popular shopping malls. Until 2010, most labor camps had empty guard houses, and anyone could enter.[12] Presumably as a result of increased media coverage, entry to the labor camps is now more often secured, but it takes no great effort to walk around the labor camp districts and to eat in the cafes and shop in the stores that serve the camps' residents.

A good year to start a history of labor housing in Dubai is 1950, when the city was still a protected state under the British government. At that time the city housed only about 30,000 residents, but a British official noted that the city had reached a major milestone: its population was defined more by its immigrants—or, more accurately, those people passing through—than by its local population. Dubai's population would dramatically increase over the coming decades, and the foreign majority would continue to constitute an even larger percentage of the city's population, resting today between 80 and 90 percent, according to some sources.[13] As today, the foreign majority in the 1950s was made up of people from all levels of income. At the top were a handful of Europeans, but mostly Iranians and South Asians, and those at the bottom were also Iranians and South Asians. Fine-grain data did not exist, yet it is fair to say that Dubai had its share of indigent individuals and families, who might have relocated from the desert hinterlands or from foreign shores somewhere between Bushehr in Iran and Kozhikode in India. Migrant laborers had been in Dubai well before the 1930s, when the city's pearl-trading economy collapsed. That economic crash, considered Dubai's first, did not result in a wholesale departure of those foreign pearl

2

◇ A Omran Workers Accommodation
◆ B Al Safa
◆ C Al Quoz
◆ D Third-class "lodging area," 1960 master plan
◆ E Carton
◆ F Al Muhaisnah
◆ G Al Awir

Fig. 2 Map indicates where housing has been designated for Dubai's lowest-paid workers, beginning with the 1960 plan's designation of "third-class lodging." Labor housing is divided into three chronological categories:

1. Black. Cordoned areas where workers and their families built barasti-style housing for themselves. Informal housing was regulated in the sense that rectilinear right-of-ways were maintained for fire safety (see Figures 3-4).
2. Grey. Designated areas for labor housing were set further out as the city expanded in areas that were also designed for industry. Early barracks-style housing was first built. Eventually these were demolished as they became dilapidated, and they were replaced by multi-story slab building (see Figures 6-7).
3. White. Omran Workforce Accommodations represent the latest versions in labor housing seen throughout the United Arab Emirates and the Gulf. More services are provided to residents; however, the securitized site's distance from city center makes it more difficult for residents to partake in the city. (see Figures 8-9). Map drawn by Mahdi Sabbagh.

workers, mainly because no one could afford to send them back. Dubai's eventual postwar development would be thankful for their destitute presence years later.[14]

Despite its ramshackle appearance in the 1950s, Dubai exhibited great potential as a regional commercial center. To exploit the port's increasing relevance in regional trade, British officials implemented early development schemes to bring administrative and financial order to the city.[15] While these schemes would have lasting ramifications for all of Dubai's residents, they were not so much far-sighted, long-ranging planning policies as they were an amalgamation of hodgepodge dictates with plenty of fumbles. How Dubai's poorest residents were housed was one topic of discursive decision making.

At the start of Dubai's accelerated modernization in the 1950s, Dubai's poorest residents arriving from inland or from overseas were most often living in what were called *barastis*.[16] An idealized form of the *barasti* is made from fastened palm fronds and might be considered a traditional building style, connected to Dubai's desert landscape. In reality, it was a less-than-pure, informal housing type, often reinforced with packing materials scavenged from Dubai's increasingly globalized port. In 1957, during the hot month of August, a fire broke out across an expanse of *barastis* on the city's edge. The fire started with an "overturned prius stove" and "was quickly fanned by a strong wind, and within half an hour had swept over a large area, consuming approximately 400 [*barastis*]."[17] No death toll was reported. Dubai leaders and merchants responded by offering aid in the form of food and money. After sending in some extra supplies "to show good will," British officials used the moment to push their agenda: more municipal organization. The *barastis* had to be spaced apart from one another and from the city. Division began to be formalized.

Less than two years after the fire, the political agent, the highest ranking British official in Dubai, called for the wholesale demolition and abolition of the housing type that sheltered the city's poorest families. The officer's report stated that a *barasti* could "burn to the ground in less than one minute." To supplant the *barasti*, the British official wanted to replace the huts with "light, cheap steel or asbestos and steel buildings."[18] The funding would have to come from the British government. That he received no response from his superiors in London was as good as a "no."

The proposed *barasti* ban was forgotten, and this expedient housing type endured well through the 1970s as an accepted, if informal, way of living. Rather than the rural-to-urban migration that often characterizes urban growth in many expanding cities, Dubai's growth was mostly generated by boatloads of people coming from abroad—for example, Pakistan, India, and Palestine.[19] As early as the 1950s, there were concerns about Dubai's expensive housing market, a fact that only made it more likely that newcomers would find themselves in this primitive housing type.[20] The *barasti's* flexibility meant it could be constructed almost as quickly as it could burn down. It could be found just about anywhere in Dubai, but always at the edge of a building or town. It could perform as a provisional attachment to the outer walls of a more permanent coral and mud house where a wealthier employer lived. It could also be found on a rooftop, or, in much larger numbers, on the edges of the city.[21] Dubai's communities of low-paid workers and their families inhabited *barastis* in the expanding and expected shantytowns of a developing city.[22] As Dubai grew, so did these districts. And they could be dismantled seemingly overnight. In 1970, a British political agent reported a "shantytown" of *barastis* had "vanished altogether" when notices announcing that a campaign to round up undocumented workers was about to begin.[23]

Two years after the deadly fire, control of the *barastis* and therefore the lives of Dubai's poorest was further regularized by the political agent in a document he titled "Dubai Lands," which sketched out how Dubai would develop "along sound lines." The document later functioned as the brief for Dubai's first master plan delivered in 1960, which cited the former document's three "classes" of housing, a ranking that would endure into the 1970s. There was no explicit mention of ethnic or racial segregation—only economic. The first two classes of housing were prescribed as concrete buildings. The third class, also called the "lodging area," was reserved for "the poorer classes, who would normally build on it buildings of the '*barasti*' type or other light edifices."[24] Officially recognized in Dubai's first urban planning document as the housing type of the "third class," *barastis* were now officially banished to outside the city center in a delineated district beyond the city's outer ring road. British officials had once attempted to ban the building type altogether, but now professional British consulting legitimated it by displacing it. The "third class" district is the only designated area of the plan that did not have a finite edge, suggesting an infinitely expanding grid of *barastis* away from the city. For the first time, an incalculable part of the population, often referred to as "illegal immigrants" when an official immigration service was not in full operation, could now be collected and counted. Development blocks measuring 540 by 240 feet were made up of three rows of *barastis*, each apportioned a 180-square-foot lot. Encircling each block was an unpaved passage, purposefully wide enough to be traversable by a fire brigade, although no fire brigade existed yet in Dubai. If the *barasti* could not be replaced, then regulated positioning would prevent more than a block of housing from being engulfed in flames in a matter of minutes.

With Dubai's continuing expansion, the labor area was eventually pushed further out to a designated and delineated area that came to be known as "Carton," a name which referred to the cardboard and plywood used to construct these homes. Employers, including the British political agency, complained of losing access to their workers who were forced to move en masse further outside the city.[25] Palm fronds were all but entirely replaced as a building material by port debris, no longer found but bartered for at the port. Salvaged cargo packaging was in character with the forces that were creating Dubai—a network of people, materials, and systems brought in from somewhere else. The architecture could be considered vernacular, especially when the *barasti* builders began to improvise wind towers. Reminiscent of the traditional *barjeel* towers of the older homes of Dubai's wealthier families, the contraption pulled cooling wind through homes. In the third-class-lodging areas they were made of canvas and (valuable) tree branches. The houses may have seemed slipshod to an outsider, but their irregularity was in direct contrast to the strict orthogonal layout enforced by the municipality. These lodging areas continued to grow in size and in numbers.

Unlike in today's labor camps, there was no clear organization of who lived where, though people tended to live among their own kind. British documents observe, for example, that Pakistanis lived in a certain part of town, and Indian Buddhists in another. Any given nationality was associated with a slot or slots on the income index, thereby reinforcing how nationalities were easily grouped into Dubai's three categories of housing. While earlier planning initiatives in Kuwait or Saudi Arabia were more explicit in ethnically dividing the population, Dubai's planning allowed residents more room to organize themselves within assumed relationships between ethnicity and salary. Similar to other reporting on the topic, the *Chicago Tribune* described Dubai society in 1968: "Each week brings more American and British oilmen, Greek and Lebanese traders, Iranian and Pakistani laborers."[26] Segregation was therefore implicit through the everyday talk of job assignments and nationality. Dubai's residents obeyed particular racial and ethnic lines, while the Dubai Municipality's surveyors, almost always South Asian, were apparently policing district lines for the sake of safety and hygiene.

3

4

Fig. 3 By the late 1970s, the term *barasti* was still used to describe the houses that Dubai's lowest-paid workers were building in areas of the city designated for them. Palm fronds were still an observable building material, but they were being quickly replaced by salvaged materials from Dubai's port. Photograph by Mark Harris, [c. 1978].

Fig. 4 Dubai's Carton district seen from a helicopter in February 1974. Except for the mosque, every building in this district was made of salvaged materials, usually from Dubai's port. As prescribed in the 1960 master plan, Dubai's "third-class" housing strictly obeyed an orthogonal grid as a fire-safety measure. Photograph by Peter Jackson, [1974].

CONTROLLING THE FLUX OF WORKERS

Lines, often marked with flagsticks before tarmac discerned one district from another, offered the means by which Dubai and British officials could measure the flux of people migrating to Dubai in the hope of finding work. The fledgling Dubai Municipality attempted a census in 1960, but beyond just the general misgiving residents expressed toward the surveyors, it was almost impossible to measure how many people were moving to Dubai while also accounting for how many people were leaving. What qualified as residence: one day, one week, one year? Even before the 1960s, British officials were concerned about undocumented immigrants. Dubai's port officials would sometimes refuse entry to a boat of migrants if they could not provide proper paperwork. To avoid this risk, boatmen were known to dump their human cargo farther than a day's walk away from Dubai's shore, sometimes on a deceptive shoal from which an encroaching current would wipe away unwitting travelers.[27] There were stories of boats stopping a mile or two away from the shore and passengers being ordered to jump ship and swim the rest of the way. If they made it to land, they were dehydrated, vomiting, and at the mercy of whoever might come across them. The question of whether or not they could find work would only gain importance once they had recuperated from the tragedy of migration.

In 1968 a British official convinced Dubai's ruler to sign a decree that warned local sea merchants against delivering undocumented migrants.[28] It must not have been enforced because Dubai's economic growth needed the seemingly endless supply of low-cost labor. British officials, until their departure in 1971, expressed concern about the livelihood of these boatloads of people, if only to protect the British government from regional outcry. News of deaths in the Gulf's waters incriminated the overseeing British, not the absconding boatmen. The British political departure meant that there was no longer a single entity to blame. Throughout the 1970s, once Dubai had become a city within the United Arab Emirates, news outlets based in South Asia expressed concern about the exploitation of poor men from India and Pakistan who were driven to find work in the Gulf. The *Times of India* reported in June 1976 on the first arrest of someone accused of duping indigent villagers into paying for forged paperwork and passage to Dubai. Police officials arrested the culprit before the launch took off.[29] A story in the same newspaper a few months beforehand had estimated that for every three who "prosper" in the Gulf, five "don't make it."[30]

Until the 1990s, English-language newspapers covered both how Indian families were dependent on money transfers from relatives in the Gulf and how Indian migrant workers were being treated abroad. One article cites a study that found a village of 18,000 people in southwest India where every household relied on at least one emigrant in the Gulf for necessary income.[31] Confronted with tales of deplorable conditions in the daily press, one Indian reporter went to see Dubai for himself in 1978. He reported that "facilities provided to Indian labor can even euphemistically be described as enviable. None of the workers I met had any serious complaints.... They live in plywood houses and about three to five workers share a room provided with a fan. In every room I found radios and cassette recorders. Adjoining the quarters is a row of specially constructed toilets for the workers."[32] The use of plywood suggests that this housing was not very different from the *barastis*, but that it was now provided by the employer. While there would have still been examples of more shantytown-style housing as late as 1979, it is fair to say that the visiting reporter witnessed the early semblance of a labor camp in Dubai, even though by the late 1960s construction workers were known to be housed in tent camps.[33]

Without a petroleum-rich future, Dubai never experienced the same influx of large-scale Western operatives who housed workers in vast military-style camps in Saudi Arabia, Kuwait, and Bahrain.[34] Dubai's economy, based more on aspects of trade, was less systematic, more gradual, and more spastic. It was not until the 1990s that English-language papers used the term "labor camp" to describe Dubai's worker accommodations. This suggests that by then more workers were starting to be segregated according to their specific jobs and employers in labor camp housing modeled after those in petroleum-rich countries.[35]

In a 1995 article by its seasoned Middle East correspondent Robin Allen, the *Financial Times*, which had regularly reported on Dubai as a cheap-labor option for Western companies, delivered one of the earliest accounts of how Gulf cities' poorest migrants were at high risk of being exploited by spurious middlemen and legal systems that did not protect them.[36] In the following year, the Dubai government began an aggressive campaign to expel unregistered foreign workers. At that time, in the entire UAE, there were officially 1.8 million nonresidents, of which 200,000 were expected to leave either voluntarily on chartered flights or by force.[37] The *Financial Times*, which also reported that the "huge airlift" would result in higher labor costs, reported that workers in Dubai were in a catch-22. Many were reported to have employers who had not paid them for months. Even if they could afford the departure without due wages, leaving Dubai would eliminate any chance of ever collecting that due pay. UAE officials claimed that more than 160,000 left by the deadline; 1,300 alone left in the dank and windowless hull of a cargo ship outfitted with twenty wooden boxes as makeshift toilets.[38]

There was no economic crisis that necessitated this evacuation. Quite the contrary, Dubai's economy was healthy. Public officials described the mass deportations as a means to "streamline" the labor force. Mere weeks after the departure deadline in early November 1996, Dubai unveiled its first ever "strategic development plan." The future was to be defined not by feats of infrastructure but instead by achievement of GDP benchmarks. Officials prescribed that future in charts and forecasts. The focus would be on "capital—rather than labour—intensive industries."[39] Lines drawn in Dubai now designated which rules applied to which zones. It cannot be overlooked that, within a year of the strategic plan's release, a coauthor of the plan, Mohammed al-Abbar, helped found Emaar, one of Dubai's largest real estate firms and the developer of Fountain Views where the 2015 demonstration occurred. In May 2002, Dubai's crown prince Sheikh Mohammed bin Rashid Al Maktoum designated parts of Dubai's real estate market as open to foreign ownership. The decree launched the building boom that jolted the city's develoment pace. Emaar and other major Dubai developers were already in operation to supply the boom.[40] Their development projects demanded as much labor as Dubai could obtain from where it had traditionally come (Pakistan, India, and Bangladesh) and from new places (Philippines, Sri Lanka, Nepal, and China). Now with the advantage of a more controlled system of labor immigration, "lodging areas" were replaced with labor camps, where the "labour-intensive" parts of urban development and real estate speculation would be more controlled and formalized than ever. Workers arrived on airplanes, no longer boats, and were checked in accordingly at customs. By this time, male migrant laborers were even less likely to come with their wives and families to Dubai.

Like the major local developers, the barracks-style labor camps were in operation in time for the boom of the early 2000s. While one 2006 article in the Glasgow *Herald* reported that some construction workers were living in the basement of the tower they were building, the most common practice was for construction workers to reside in clearly delineated labor camps with the name of the employer emblazoned on a gate house.[41] Labor camps

Fig. 5 An earlier type of labor housing in Dubai's Al Muhaisan district, one-story barracks-style housing allowed for communal exterior spaces where workers could socialize and cook in the warm months. Photograph by author, [2007].

were located in sections of the city designated for them. By 2006, it seemed that every camp was being run by, or for, a particular company. Company buses ushered workers between work and employer-regulated residences. Well before these new working conditions, the *kafala* system, described earlier, was already the established set of guidelines linking migrant workers to their employers, who were granted the right and responsibility to disburse government-allocated visa quotas. Workers were less residents of a city than workers whose lives, inside and outside work hours, were ensconced in companies' twenty-four-hour organization charts. The labor camp helped make that relationship even more explicit. All scales of a labor camp's development were linked to the employer, from the site they obtained from the government to the construction of the building to the provision of mattresses.[42]

During site visits to labor camps in the al-Quoz and al-Muhaisnah districts of Dubai in 2006, I found conditions of labor camp housing in transition. Conversations with nearby residents revealed that dormitories had to be demolished about every five or six years as it was cheaper to build a new camp than maintain an old one. Decommissioned older barracks were single-level concrete block structures, often with shared outdoor courtyards. Some of the early examples were constructed of less durable materials and with leftover building supplies, such as tile and doors from the construction sites where the residents worked. Shading was offered by planted trees and by terraces that residents built out of found materials. The exposed courtyards were usually filled with shared kitchens and appliances salvaged by residents. From observations, it seemed there was a low standard of living but at least a sense of community that was not so present in later renditions of the labor camp.

RESPONDING TO HUMAN RIGHTS WATCH

Published in 2006, "Building Towers, Cheating Workers" was Human Rights Watch's first published treatment of Dubai and the UAE since it had begun covering topics in the Middle East and Asia in the 1980s. The report claimed that 800 migrant construction workers had died in Dubai in 2004. With statistics like this one, the report is arguably credited for an ensuing cascade of journalistic articles about deplorable conditions in Dubai's labor camps, which has become a regularly covered topic about Dubai.[43] Public officials were called upon to answer to accusations of maintaining low health and safety standards, forbidding the creation of organized trade unions, and doing nothing to protect workers from the exorbitant fees demanded by recruiting agencies.[44] Dubai's planners responded by instituting more controls on how and where migrant laborers live in the city. They encouraged denser and higher-built districts for laborers that looked more like apartment buildings than barracks. More controls resulted in more accurate ways to measure this sector of the population (and to make potential deportation programs easier). However, it could be seen as a strange turn of events that once planners had begun to formalize such controls, there would be more of a chance for laborers to be seen. Clearly demarcated labor camps made it easy for foreign watchdog groups and press to assess the conditions themselves.

While organizing laborers into camps made them more apparent to external observers, it also set up a more convincing means of responding to outside criticism. In January 2008, UAE labor officials held a forum with their counterparts from the Asian countries where most low-pay laborers hailed. Recommendations were made: Dubai's workers were to be better protected by a new "raft of regulations."[45] In October 2008, Dubai's health director reported to the *Financial Times* that a total of 159 labor camps had been forced to close, out of a total of nearly 1,500; 4,953 inspections had been carried through, a 35 percent increase from the previous year. The ability to track progress was delivered as a confidence booster in Dubai authorities' ability to monitor problems. Dubai officials responded with clear, if sparse, "municipality rules" prescribed for labor camps: a minimum of forty square feet of residential space per worker, a maximum of eight people assigned to a room, at least one shower for every ten residents, sanitary eating areas, a first aid room, adequate fire exits, and proper drainage systems. As stated earlier, these proposed regulations did little to address the major focuses of the HRW report.

Already in 2006, one-story camps were being replaced by multistory, single-loaded buildings with outdoor corridors. The new camps were even more regularized, with selfsame rooms and evenly dispersed toilets and kitchens. Based on consistent designs shared among labor camps, it seemed there was a more coordinated service in providing turnkey camps for employers. It is understood that the municipality leased much of the land designated for these camps to labor housing providers, often companies with recognizable Dubai family names. Most buildings were lifted atop columns so that the ground plane remained outdoors for laundry washing, maintenance access, and gathering space to await work shuttle buses. This new multilevel housing separated workers from the ground, thereby making it less likely they would cook outside and claim outdoor space for recreation. In exchange, each room included an air conditioner and a window, usually blacked out by the residents. These newer buildings, often brightly painted maritime blue or tangerine orange, were shrouded with clean laundry drying over the exterior banisters. One might observe that the laborers' standard of living was increasing, in that achievable standards were being met: regularized number of beds in a room, air conditioning, newer premises. However, the quality of living is up for question: cooking had to happen indoors in less-than-ideal conditions, bedrooms lost outdoor access, and workers had less say in the shaping of their surroundings. Denser living also required new sewage and septic systems, which were continuously underperforming.

In anticipation of the release of the HRW's report, the British weekly *Observer* reported that there was a rising revolution of Dubai's laborers that threatened to make tourists "targets." The article cited a brief strike near the Burj Khalifa, not far from the site of the 2015 demonstration, and quoted an alleged organizer of the protest, who warned of future protests in shopping malls and at beaches.[46] Such a series of actions did not materialize, but several months later there was another protest at Port Jebel Ali, more than twenty miles away from the previous demonstration and far from anyone who might have reported on the matter. As with the Fountain Views protest, the preferred audience was the employer. Far away from the city proper, the protesters had no traffic to disturb, only the logistical smoothness of port operations. Their demands were described to the press by representatives of the employer, who blamed the situation on diminishing value of the UAE dirham in relation to the Indian rupee, a financial situation that slashed the value of salaries wire-transferred back home to workers' families. Employers placed blame on something beyond their control: the larger forces of global markets.

"WELCOMED AND LAUDABLE"

While there was neither a reported resolution to the workers' grievances nor subsequent protests at Port Jebel Ali, these outskirts of Dubai would be again in the news in 2008. In October the *Financial Times* referred to "workforce accommodations," no longer labor camps, being proposed by Nakheel, one of Dubai's largest developers founded in anticipation of the opening of the real estate market. Mirroring development projects throughout Dubai, the workers' complex was given a proper name: Omran, an Arabic word that can be translated as "solid structure." The Omran Work

6

7

Fig. 6 This later version of labor housing in Dubai's district of Al Muhaisnah (sometimes referred to as Sonapur, or "city of gold") materialized certain requirements, including air conditioning and minimal living area per person. Residents use the outer railing to dry their laundry, which is washed in sinks or machines installed in communal spaces on the ground level. Photograph by author, [2009].

Fig. 7 By the early 2000s, labor camps were being built three- to four-stories high, taking residents' access to the ground away. Communal contact is restricted to the narrow gangways along room entries and to unenclosed and unpaved areas between the slabs of housing. All furniture and utilities are supplied by the employer's camp management. This photograph was also taken in the district of Al Muhaisnah. Photograph by author, [2009].

force Accommodations opened in the summer 2008 and, in addition to comfortable accommodation, it offered "outdoor sports facilities, swimming pools, communal IT resources, retail space, a canteen providing three meals a day, and even a professional laundry service."[47] The *Financial Times* reported that HRW found the private-sector response "welcomed and laudable," but needed to see structural changes from the government.

"Welcomed and laudable" might characterize the improvement in the spaces and furnishings provided by the complex, but one might question just how improved living was for the workers. Arriving at the vast complex of the first 5,000 beds (a total of 60,000 were planned), I could not help but notice the impenetrability of the site. A guardhouse almost three miles from the site along pock-marked road keeps away any unregistered visitors. If you are able to get close enough to see it, a barbed-wire perimeter contains the housing much like a low-security prison. One needed an identity card to get in (and out) or clearance from the twenty-four-hour administration. The swimming pool had yet to be filled.[48] There was a basketball court, but the daytime heat made it useless. Although this first phase of Omran was rented to capacity, a Nakheel employee was available for informational tours for those interested in securing space for their laborer in upcoming phases. The grounds were neat and manicured, if sparse, with a sampling of fragile saplings and kit-of-parts gazebos. The buildings were all the same type of prefab construction in a medical green color. There were unoccupied one-or two-person "executive" rooms available for viewing. The guide confirmed that a maximum of four persons shared a single room. An executive room had the feel of a room in a brand-new hostel, or maybe a halfway house. They were outfitted with veneered furniture, a tray of glasses and a water cooker, overhead lighting, and an illuminated mirror.

Residents at Omran can only cook water in their rooms for tea and instant coffee; other than that, they have to rely on meals at scheduled times in the canteen. They do not, and cannot, wash their own laundry. Each resident is issued a color-coded laundry bag and an ID card. There are communal rooms: a library with few books, a giant flatscreen television with planted rows of chairs (a rope line discourages standing), a billiards table, and a gym. I was told that there was an ATM machine and a bus that would shuttle workers to the city on their days off. I didn't see the bus. Omran lies about thirty miles from Dubai's older districts, where low-paid workers might find shops and cafes that they could afford to frequent. In the older labor camps much closer to these districts, there were regular bus routes and opportunities to share a cab into town. Isolated in the desert, those options are not available in newer camps like Omran. Additionally, this isolation makes it almost impossible for residents to be observed by anyone not involved with running the camp. The experience of utter isolation might be the most troublesome condition.

In the end, one might ascertain a trend in Dubai's labor housing, from *barastis* to labor camps to workforce accommodations. There has been a gradual appreciation of living standards and architectural standardization: space is legally apportioned, air conditioning is assured, health and safety regulated. The checklist is delivered, and it can be quoted to the reporter and to the visiting observer. Furthermore, these living conditions, including the security apparatuses and the mandatory laundry service, are presumably incorporated into the workers' pay. One might wonder whether, given the option to be responsible for one's own laundry or receive more pay, a worker would prefer to have more money to spend in the city or to send home. As a response to outside criticism, laborers have been pulled farther away from the city that they are employed to sustain. Regulation has become an instrument of message control. If they were able to speak for themselves from out of this securitized complex to the global press, workers at Omran might have descriptions for their accommodation that veer from "welcomed and laudable."

A CONCLUDING PARABLE

As Nakheel opened the Omran Workers Accommodation to the first residents, the Dubai developer launched the adjacent 50-hectare Waterfront Landscape Nursery. There, more than 156,000 plants, shrubs, and trees were being grown to provide future landscaping throughout the city of Dubai and, as one trade magazine described it, "to create a pleasant, community-driven environment for the end-user." In 2008 the project was "flourishing amidst the desert," as a Nakheel executive stated, and had the ambition to produce four million plants every year.[49] Touted as a sustainability project by Nakheel, the nursery conserved water and energy by employing treated effluent collected from the adjoining Omran Workforce Accommodation's sewage system. There is no longer mention of the nursery on Nakheel's website, though it still appears to be in operation according to Google Earth. It seemed a telling plan at the time: human waste and water collected from laborers resting at home were feeding the nursery's plants. Even when they were at rest, workers continued to help beautify the faraway shopping malls, boulevards, and traffic circles. Dubai's adaptive approach to labor housing, which has seen a gradual displacement of workers not only to increasingly distanced edges but also into tightly secured premises, will make it less likely Omran's residents will ever witness the city that they, at work and at rest, have made possible.

8

9

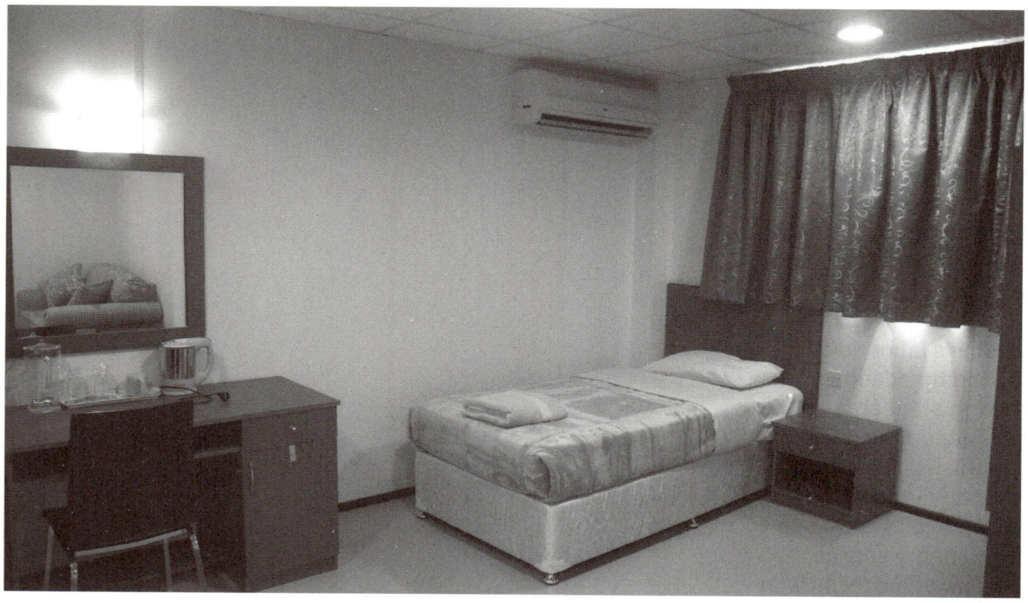

10

Fig. 8 Entry to the Omran Workforce Accommodations, just after the guard house and barbed wire-topped fencing. Photograph by author, [2008].

Fig. 9 The rear side of a row of housing at the Omran Workforce Accommodations near Dubai's Port Jebel Ali. At time of visit, there was evidence of a modest effort to begin landscaping the site. Photograph by author, [2008].

Fig. 10 Interior of an "executive room" at the Omran Workforce Accomodations. Workers are not allowed to cook anything other than water in their rooms. Furniture, bedclothes, and other amenities are supplied by the accommodation's management office. Bedclothes and workers' clothing is also cleaned by management. Photograph by author, [2008].

Notes

1
See "Construction Workers Stage Protest in Dubai Over Pay," *Daily Star* (Beirut), March 11, 2015; "Foreign Construction Workers Stage Rare Protest in Dubai Over Pay," *Guardian*, March 10, 2015; "Video: Workers Stage Strike In Downtown Dubai Over Wage Issues," *Gulf Business* (Dubai), March 10, 2015; "Dubai Foreign Workers Stage Rare Strike," NDTV (Delhi), March 11, 2015.

2
Dubai Media Office, Twitter post, March 10, 2015, 6:49am (ECT), https://twitter.com/DXBMediaOffice. One video made by a bystander, uploaded to an account called "will iam," was sourced by several news sources; it was removed from YouTube shortly after the incident. Stills from the video remain online.

3
"Dubai protest: Workers stage rare sit-in over pay," *BBC News*, March 10, 2015.

4
"UPDATE 1-Construction Workers Stage Rare Protest in Dubai Over Pay," *Reuters*, March 10, 2015, http://www.reuters.com/article/2015/03/10/emirates-workers-protest-idUSL5N0W-C2X920150310. 500 dirhams is about $136. It was not clear in the article whether the quoted laborer was involved in the demonstration.

5
In Dubai and throughout the Persian Gulf, the worker sponsorship system is referred to as the *kafala* system. The term can have a sinister, if catchy, ring to it. *Kafala* is, however, no clearly defined notion. Sponsorship laws vary throughout the Gulf. Robert Vitalis's book makes it clear that such contract-based existence is a system practiced in more places than the Persian Gulf. Vitalis, *America's Kingdom: Mythmaking on the Saudi Oil Frontier* (London: Verso, 2009).

6
On a construction site or in a labor camp, it is rare to see the name of recognizable contracting companies emblazoned on buildings and uniforms.

7
Architects have also chosen this as a venue for their own design activism.

8
In the decades before, the labor camp was more prevalent in Gulf cities like Kuwait City, Dhahran, and Abu Dhabi, where they were used to contain and control the much-larger fluxes of laborers arriving to work in oil production.

9
Human Rights Watch, "Building Towers, Cheating Workers: Exploitation of Migrant Construction Workers in the United Arab Emirates," November 11, 2006, https://www.hrw.org/report/2006/11/11/building-towers-cheating-workers/exploitation-migrant-construction-workers-united.

10
Many of Dubai's low-wage workers occupy shared apartments and retrofitted villas in the city's older districts. This article does not consider these types of housing, which have been the sites of renewal efforts to remove residents to more formalized and controllable premises.

11
While labor camps are a prevalent and obvious form of housing for Dubai's poorest migrant workers, others live in less discrete forms of housing, mostly older multi-unit buildings and villas in Dubai's older districts. Most often the buildings have been retrofitted into dorm-like facilities for workers. Other low-wage workers live in the houses of employees, such as domestic servants. There are also higher-paid workers in Dubai, for example, employees of the Dubai airline Emirates, who live in barracks-style company housing with better furnishings and more on-site amenities.

12
Based on the author's regular visits to labor camps between 2005 and 2016.

13
The International Organization for Migration has recently published the number as 83%. "Where Are the World's Most Cosmopolitan Cities?" *CityMetric*, February 19, 2016, http://www.citymetric.com/politics/where-are-worlds-most-cosmopolitan-cities-1851.

14
Aqil Kazim, *The United Arab Emirates A.D. 600 to the Present: A Socio-Discursive Transformation in the Arabian Gulf* (Dubai: Gulf Books Centre, 2000), 225.

15
Dubai was among other sheikhdoms, including Abu Dhabi, that made up what was then called the Trucial States and would later become known as the United Arab Emirates when the British government departed in 1971.

16
Barasti is a Hindi word and is most commonly used in historical British government documents to describe this kind of housing. In Arabic, the word used is *arish* (pl. *orosh*).

17
Anita L.P. Burdett, ed., "Dubai and the Northern Trucial States Review of the Year 1969," *Records of Dubai 1761–1960*, vol. 7 (Cambridge: Archive Editions, 2000), 253.

18
FO 371/140144, Kew Gardens (UK), The National Archives.

19
See, for example: Anita L.P. Burdett, ed., "Dubai and the Northern Trucial States Review of the Year 1969," *Records of the Emirates* 1966–1971, vol. 4 (Cambridge: Archive Editions, 2002), 19-25.

20
"Dubai Lands," FO 371/140222, Kew Gardens (UK), *The National Archives*.

21
Today shantytowns are no longer found within Dubai's city limits. Their erasure from Dubai's urban landscape was made possible by administrative implementations that eventually included the labor camp.

22
Christine Buckley, "Golden Souk, Golden Sands," *Financial Times*, August 26, 1995.

23
"Letter from Julian Bullard," *Records of the Emirates 1966–1971*, vol. 5, 479–80.

24
"Dubai Lands," FO 371/140222.

25
"Dubai and the Northern Trucial States Review of the Year 1969," *Records of the Emirates 1966–1971*, vol. 4, 22.

26
Eldon Griffiths, "Britain to Run Out on Obligation to Defend Seven Trucial Coast Sheiks," *Chicago Tribune*, February 4, 1968.

27
Michael Tomkinson, *The United Arab Emirates: An Insight and a Guide* (London: Michael Tomkinson Publishing, 1975), 58.

28
"Illegal Immigration," January 6, 1968, FCO 8/911, Kew Gardens (UK), *The National Archives*.

29
"Man Who Promised Jobs in Dubai Lands in Lock-Up," *Times of India*, June 18, 1976.

30
"An Arabian Night's Dream?," *Times of India*, April 4, 1976.

31
"Kerala Thrives on Gulf Wages," *Guardian*, September 11, 1978.

32
"Prospering in The Gulf," *Times of India*, January 28, 1978.

33
"Project Close-Up: Rashid Hospital Dubai," *Building* (London), January 21, 1977.

34
Regarding the effects of oil extraction efforts on urbanization efforts, see Vitalis, *America's Kingdom*, and Richard Lawless and Ian Seccombe, "Impact of the Oil Industry on Urbanization in the Persian Gulf Region," *Urban Development in the Muslim World* (New Brunswick, N.J. : Center for Urban Policy Research, 1993), 233-252.

35
Such a housing format might have been new to Dubai, but it was not new to the Persian Gulf region and other parts of the world. Labor camps were a staple housing type in the oil-producing parts of the Persian Gulf. In his book about the practices of American oil companies in Saudi Arabia, *America's Kingdom*, Robert Vitalis provides an incisive account of not only these kinds of camps but also their lineage of planning techniques by U.S. company towns set up for extraction (mining) missions in South and Central America. Vitalis makes only slight reference to another source of precedent not only for the companies in Saudi Arabia but also for Dubai: the manipulation of British town-planning practices in oil camps in Iran and Kuwait. By the late 1950s, similar camps were being built in Abu Dhabi on Das Island, where South Asian laborers lived in housing distinctly worse than that offered to the British and European employees on the same island.

36
Robin Allen, "Imported Labour May Not Be Cheap for Gulf States," *Financial Times*, October 13, 1995.

37
The Emirati historian Fatma Al Sayegh put the total number at one million foreigners who had to leave. Fatma Al Sayegh, "Post-9/11 Changes in the Gulf: the Case of the UAE," *Middle East Policy* 11, no. 2 (2004): 107–24.

38
Caroline Drees, "Illegal Aliens in UAE Crowd on Cargo Ship Home," *Reuters*, October 1, 1996.

39
Angus Hindley, "Dubai Unveils First Strategic Development Plan," *Middle East Economic Digest*, November 25, 1996.

40
Dubai Holding Group was founded in 2000. Nakheel was founded in 2002.

41
Michael Tierney, "The Dream Makers; Every Day Hundreds of Migrant Workers Arrive in the Glittering Emirate of Dubai, Thirsty for Work and a Future," *Herald* (Glasgow), May 27, 2006.

42
While this relationship might seem very clear, development contracts often allow for a particular developer or contractor to work with a multitude of subcontractors, making it very difficult to find out with which building project or developer a labor camp was associated.

43
See, for example, Gulf Labor Artist Coalition, http://gulflabor.org; Nesrine Malik, "Dubai's Skyscrapers, Stained by the Blood of Migrant Workers," *Guardian,* May 27, 2011, http://www.theguardian.com/commentisfree/2011/may/27/dubai-migrant-worker-deaths; "Conditions of Dubai's Immigrant Workers Highlighted," *BBC News*, January 20, 2011, http://www.bbc.com/news/world-middle-east-12246979.

44
Roula Khalaf, "UAE Pledges to Improve Plight of Migrant Workers," *Financial Times*, March 31, 2006.

45
Simeon Kerr, "UAE Push to Bolster Rights of Workers," *Financial Times*, January 25, 2008.

46
Dan McDougall, "Tourists Become Targets as Dubai's Workers Take Revolt to the Beaches," *Observer*, April 9, 2006.

47
Nada El Sawy, "Labour Camps Under Scrutiny," *Financial Times*, October 21, 2008.

48
The pool is photographed without water in Google Earth's 2016 image.

49
Lauren Hills, "Landscape Nursery Flourishes at Nakheel's Waterfront," *Construction Week Online*, January 4, 2009, http://www.constructionweekonline.com/article-4099-landscape-nursery-flourishes-at-nakheels-waterfront/.

JERUSALEM'S DIVISIONS: *ARCHITECTURES AND TOPOGRAPHIES OF URBAN VIOLENCE*[1]

Annabel Jane Wharton

> It is a well known fact that not many people can endure living in Jerusalem any length of time.... The Holy City makes them morose or drives them insane; yes, and it even kills them outright. You cannot stop there a fortnight without hearing people say of this or that person, who has passed away: "Jerusalem has killed him."
>
> Selma Lagerlöf, *The Holy City*, 1918[2]

Division is always a disposition of power, sometimes equal but more often not. Few cities in the world have been more riven by division than Jerusalem. This essay poses a primitive question: How do divisions inscribed in Jerusalem by its geo-architectural topography contribute to its pathological violence? It offers a heuristic model for an answer, anticipating that the model might help better understand other urban landscapes, increasingly marked by fragmentation. Jerusalem performs well as an archetype. Its scale is comprehensible. The Old City occupies a mere 220 acres; urban expansion beyond its Ottoman walls occurred only in the 1860s. Its topography and architecture are hyperbolic. The mountainous terrain of the site lends a peculiar prominence to its monuments. Its violence is chronic and notorious. From the Babylonians through the Romans and Persians to the Crusaders, it has been subjected to horrific violence. That violence has become endemic, embedded in the geo-architectural anatomy of the city. The heights, warrens, peripheries, and breaks in the city enact distinct forms of coercion. All social orders contribute to the violence of a fragmented topography, although the state, the state's religious proxies, and foreign elites are its greatest perpetrators.

In Jerusalem, the violence of urban divisions is deeply historical. It is articulated in rivalries among the ancient hills of the city, within the medieval mazes of its depressions, through the modern colonization of its circumference, and by the post-human barriers of the present. Architects and urban planners regularly map both the physical and sociological geographies of cities, but two-dimensional cartography masks the unevenness of planes that contributes to urban violence. Perhaps the schematic scaffolding that I propose—heights, warrens, peripheries, and breaks—will provide those who construct the urban with a different view of the ways in which their own production perpetrates or remedies spatial inflammations.

HEIGHTS

Heights define the boundary between those who are above and those who are below. That division is powerfully metaphorical, as well as patently physical and political. Heights tend to be coveted by elites. Heights can be effectively fortified and extended; they facilitate surveillance. Heights abet the manifestation of power; those who occupy the heights commonly supplement their social dominance within the city through construction, monumentalizing their authority. Where heights are absent, they may well be produced—as on the island of Manhattan or the flatlands of Mesopotamia. High places, however, often don't play nicely together. They incline towards a divisive mutual enmity, competing for attention.

In Jerusalem the competition among heights is conspicuous. The careful archaeological model of Jerusalem built in 1964 at the Holyland Hotel in the suburbs of Jerusalem, now relocated on the grounds of the Israel Museum, provides an accessible rendering of the topography of the city *(Fig. 1)*.[3] It offers its observers a view of the Old City and its vicinity as a *whole*. Seen from the raised ramp that surrounds it, the city appears comprehensible—framed, ordered, under control. Its landscape is legible. But the sense of comprehensible wholeness conveyed by the model is not just visual. It is also historical: the observer assumes that the model, like a timeline, offers mastery of the deep past in a glance. The model represents the Jerusalem of Herod the Great at the turn of the first millennium. It was then a world-class city, the flourishing, undivided center of Jewish Judea, a prosperous Roman client state.[4]

Dominant is the Temple Mount occupying the northern prominence of the long eastern ridge. That ridge is defined on the east by Kidron Valley and the slopes of the Mount of Olives and on the west by the Tyropoeon Valley, bridged by Wilson's and Robinson's arches. At the time of David and Solomon (tenth century BCE), the authority of the two heights of the eastern ridge were unchallenged. Solomon's famous temple adorned the northern outcrop; the royal palace and its dynastic tombs occupied its southern elevation. This height was Zion, a title that functioned both as a toponym for Solomon's auratic precinct and as a synecdoche for Jerusalem itself as a holy city. Ten centuries later, Herod the Great constructed a grand new temple on the same outcrop as its predecessors. He aggrandized not just the ancient *temenos*, but also its topography by engineering one of the great podiums of the ancient world, now al-Haram al-Sharif.

Higher, if less prominent, in the model is the southwest hill. Herod constructed a new, luxurious, fortified royal residence opposite the Temple Mount on the northern ridge of that more elevated hill, vacating the old site of kingship and its royal sepulchers. But the original Zion was not to be left behind. By the first century CE, the toponym Zion had moved to the southern end of the southwest ridge. Later, even a faux tomb of David was invented for the new location.[5] Zion retained its traditional proximity to kingship. Less salient in the Holyland Hotel Model is the northwest hill, just outside the city's "Second Wall." The site is rendered there as a quarry, though many archaeologists identify it as a place of execution and burial *(Fig. 2)*.[6]

The apparent wholeness of Jerusalem represented by the model was momentary: Herod completed the great temple complex in about 62 CE; it was despoiled in 70 CE by the Roman emperor Titus during the suppression of the First Jewish Revolt. A more thorough demolition of Jerusalem and the expulsion of its Jewish population occurred with Hadrian's defeat of the Second Jewish Revolt in 135 CE. The imposition of Roman control also initiated a more spectacular and deadly competition among the heights of the city. Hadrian reconfigured Jerusalem as Aelia Capitolina. He left the Temple Mount in ruins as proof of Roman military superiority and constructed a new city with a forum and *temenos* on the northwest hill. This hill, previously marginalized by its location outside the walls as a quarry and place of execution, was transformed into the privileged core of the city. The prominence of this new center was further aggrandized with the Christianization of the city under Constantine in the fourth century CE. It was elevated by a new icon of imperial power, the cathedral, known later as the Church of the Holy Sepulchre *(Fig. 3)*. The ascendant height and its disempowered counterpart traded places: the northwest hill, earlier a place of death and pollution outside the walls of the city, displaced the once glorious center of the eastern hill, now a site of desecration and corruption.

The relative status of the two hills was again reversed three centuries later with the conquest of Palestine by Caliph Omar. From the seventh through the eleventh centuries, the Temple Mount, identified as al-Haram al-Sharif, once more became the dominant focus of the city while the Church of the Holy Sepulchre decayed. The new, resplendent architecture of the northeast height—the Dome of the Rock and al-Aqsa Mosque—embodied the new sovereignty of the Islamic state.[7]

(Fig. 1) Jerusalem, Israel Museum, Model of Jerusalem, Avi Yonah and Yoram Tsafrir, begun in 1956 with topographic labels. Photograph by author, 2006.

(Fig. 2) Jerusalem, Holy Land Hotel, Model of Jerusalem, Golgotha. *Pictorial Guide to the Model of Ancient Jerusalem*, Paiphot, Ltd, Jerusalem (n.d.). The site, though still marked, was given less prominence in the model after its removal to the Israel Museum.

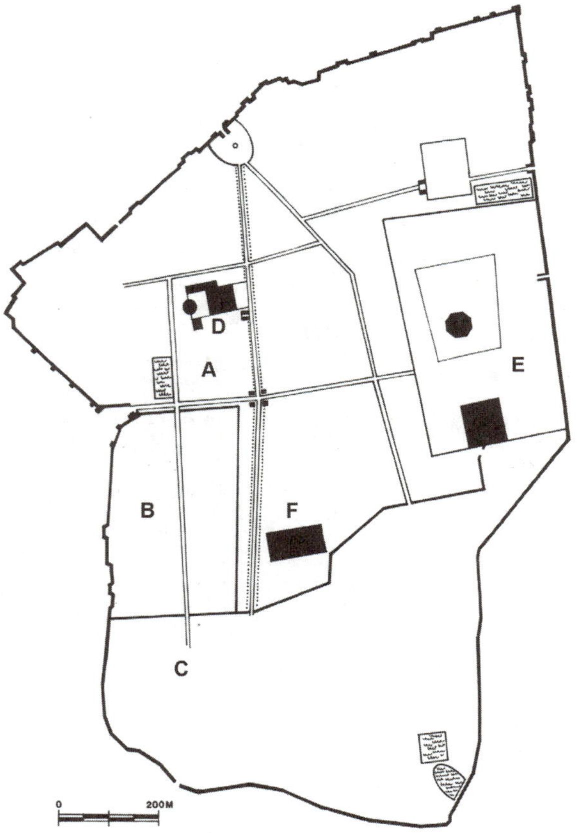

(Fig. 3) Jerusalem, sketch plan of the early medieval city. *A*. Hadrian's Arch and Forum (after 135 CE); *B*. Possible site of Hadrian's military encampment; *C*. new Zion; *D*. Constantine's Church of the Holy Sepulchre and the remains of a Hadrianic arch; *E*. al-Haram al-Sharif (Temple Mount) with the Dome of the Rock and al-Aqsa Mosque; *F*. Justinian's New Church of the Virgin (543 CE). Drawing by the author, modified from Tsafrir.

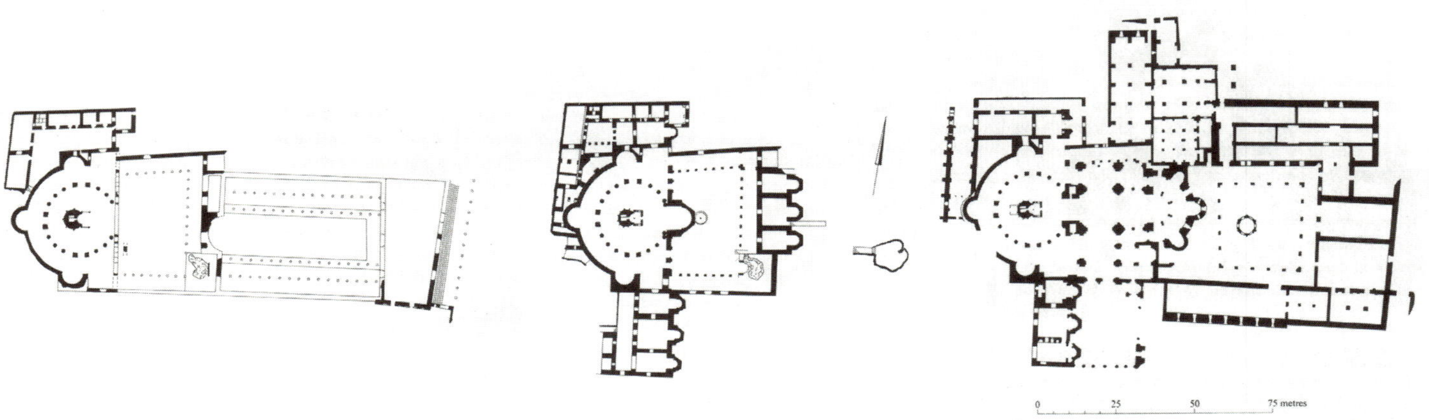

(Fig. 4) Series of plans of the Holy Sepulchre. From left to right: Fourth century: basilica, rotunda, baptistery and episcopal palace; Eleventh century: Byzantine reconstruction after the Fatamid Caliph, al-Hakim, destroyed the building in 1009; Twelfth century: Crusader reconstruction.

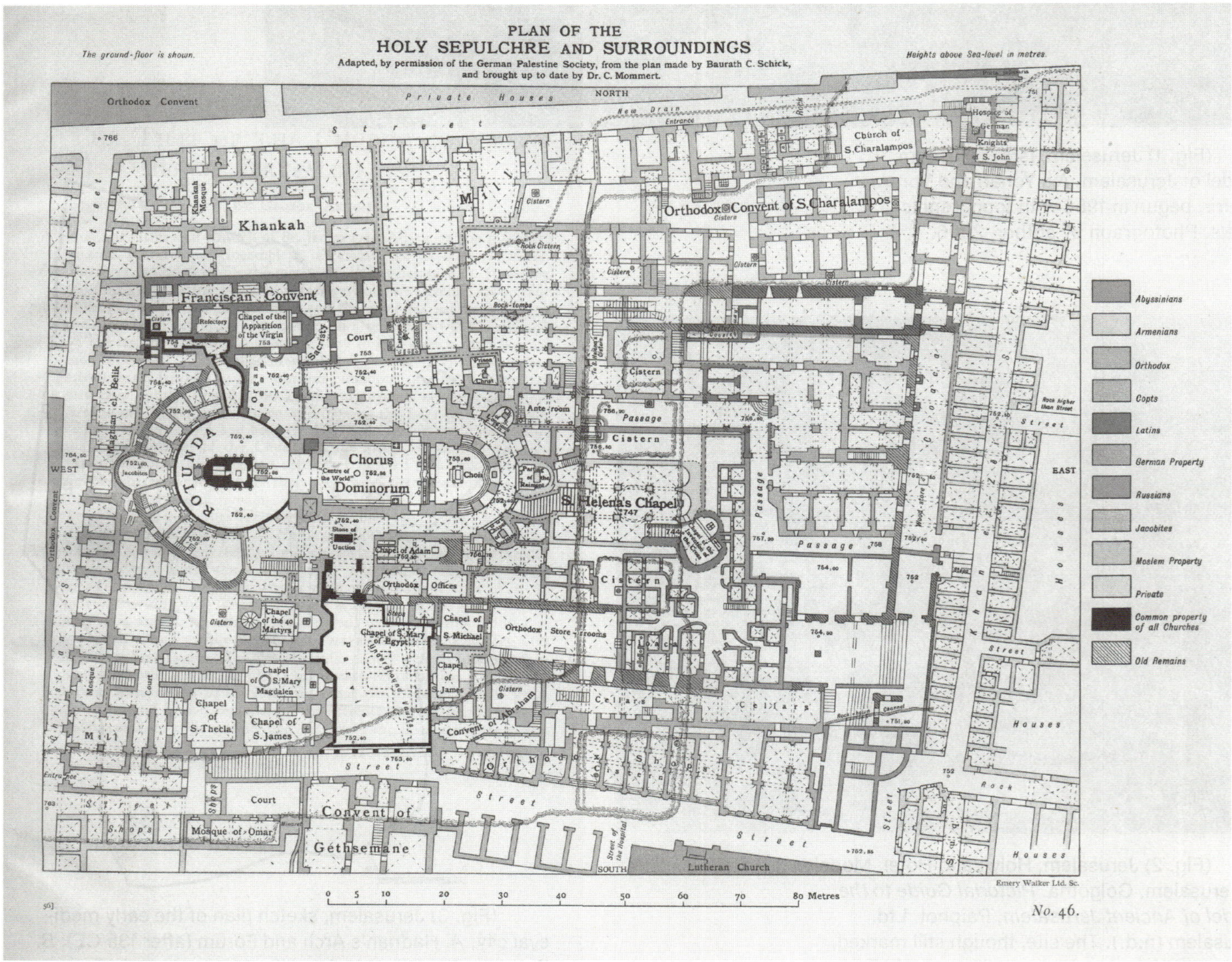

(Fig. 5) Church of the Holy Sepulchre, plan by C. R. Ashbee (1924), fig. 46.

In Jerusalem and elsewhere, the critical role of heights in defining hegemony is revealed in the brutality of the attacks made upon them. The destruction of New York's World Trade Center towers in 2001 offers an obvious case. The ideological force of heights is also exemplified in the anxiety caused by the continued prominence of patently Muslim structures in a city under Jewish military control. In 2000, in an explicit enactment of sovereignty, Ariel Sharon (the Israeli Defense Minister held by many to be responsible for the civilian massacres at the Sabra and Shatila refugee camps in Israel's 1982 invasion of Lebanon) entered al-Haram al-Sharif with hundreds of Israeli riot police. The incident ignited the Second or al-Aqsa Intifada, in which over three thousand Palestinians and hundreds of Israelis died.[8] The Dome of the Rock and al-Aqsa Mosque remain under constant threat from Jewish and evangelical extremists.[9] The prominence of the Holyland Hotel Model on the websites of those promoting the construction of the Third Temple on the Temple Mount demonstrates the power of a model to predict the future as well as represent the past. Implicit is the annihilation of the existing Islamic structures on the site. The topographic and historical conditioning of contemporary violence is manifest.

Topography remains a tactical tool of violence today, though the relief of the modern landscape is less dramatic than it was in antiquity. Debris of the violent destructions of the city has filled in its valleys, eroding the differences between the city's heights and its depths.[10] Despite the modified geological anatomy of Jerusalem, heights continue to contribute to the city's deadly divisions.

WARREN

Less obvious than heights, the warren also inscribes divisions within the city. "Warren" appears in the late Middle Ages as a legal term for a bounded site granted to wealthy landowners for breeding animals—primarily rabbits: "Warren is a place privileged by prescription or grant of the King, for the preservation of hares, conies [rabbits], partridges and pheasants."[11] The land appropriated for warrens was that least useful for agriculture—dry, sandy, barren.[12] Animals were enclosed to protect them from unauthorized predators, human and animal, as well as to expedite their reproduction and harvesting.[13] Within their compound, the animals ordered their lives as best they could—digging their burrows, mating, skirmishing in the establishment of their social hierarchies—as they would in nature, but under the particular coercion of spatial restriction.[14]

The term "warren" is now applied to places where humans rather than animals are constrained (ghettos, slums, favelas, barrios, camps). The warren is sometimes confused with a maze or a labyrinth, but it shouldn't be.[15] A maze—as in amazement—is not the material site so much as the emotional state of astonished bewilderment that it induces. The confusion of the maze's complexity is more conceptual than somatic. Indeed, a maze may well be seductive. The warren, in contrast to the maze, does not bedazzle, but rather benumbs. The warren has more in common with the labyrinth, which is designed for entrapment. The prototype of the labyrinth was constructed by Daedalus to ensnare Greek youths and maidens extorted by King Minos to feed the Cretan Minotaur: its partitions physically frustrate the escape of those imprisoned within it. The warren's internal complexities, however—in contrast to those of the labyrinth or, for that matter, the prison—are not externally designed, but internally generated.

"Warren" in modern usage retains many of the implications of its late medieval source. It is a circumscribed locus of the disempowered Other. Although its boundaries are determined from the outside by those in authority, its internal order is generally produced by those enclosed. The interior space of the warren—in contrast to the prison—is never entirely externally controlled; its complexities are commonly constructed from within. Arrangements tend to evolve through expedience, not programmatically. The domain of the warren is not readily understood by outsiders; it is fully comprehensible only to its inhabitants. Warrens are spaces under compression. The macro violence involved in the external imposition of boundaries affects the micro violence of the sequestered. Heights exert their power strategically; warrens evolve tactically.[16] Late medieval animal warrens were rural; modern human ones are urban. All cities have them. Some are constructed on the margins of the metropolis or in abandoned sites within them—Ciudad Nezahualcóyotl in Mexico City, the ghetto in Venice, the Robert Taylor Homes in Chicago.[17] Jerusalem certainly has its diverse share of warrens, among them Meah Shearim, Silwan and other East Jerusalem neighborhoods, the Shu'fat Refugee Camp, and the Church of the Holy Sepulchre.

The Holy Sepulchre serves here as an example. The emperor Constantine constructed the Holy Sepulchre as a spectacular complex, including a great basilica for the celebration of the liturgy, a massive rotunda monumentally enclosing the empty tomb identified as that of the risen Jesus, a baptistery, and a bishop's palace. From the time of the Islamic conquest of Jerusalem, the revivification of al-Haram al-Sharif (Temple Mount) depleted the life of the Holy Sepulchre. The site was segregated and controlled but not maintained by successive sovereign powers. It degenerated; its structures decayed. The buildings were occasionally abused and episodically rebuilt *(Fig. 4)*.[18] The space became increasingly incoherent. This complexity was intensified by the power residing in the building's fragments: each niche and crevice that was revealed in the process of atrophy or produced in the conduct of reconstruction generated a sacred narrative or a physical relic. Hallowed spaces proliferated—not just the tomb of Jesus and the site of his execution, Golgotha, but his prison, the Stone of Unction, the site of Melchizedek's offering of bread and wine to Abraham, the cave of Saint Helena's finding of the True Cross, and so on.

By early modernity, the site of the Holy Sepulchre was a warren. Ottoman authorities certainly controlled the structure. Like the Jews of the Ghetto in Venice or the Italians of the Genoese *fondaco* in Alexandria, the Christians occupying the Church of the Holy Sepulchre were locked in at night.[19] The state also mediated which spaces within the building belonged to which Christianity, but only upon petition from those involved. Like the warren, internal activities were determined from within. The messy division of space, negotiated by the Ottomans with local elites and foreign powers, was inherited by the British with the establishment of the Mandate for Palestine in 1923 and codified as the status quo.[20] Of course, a mess is best experienced directly; texts, photographs, and diagrams inevitably rationalize clutter. But as a surrogate for an actual encounter with the interior of the Church of the Holy Sepulchre, the plan by C. R. Ashbee, friend and follower of William Morris and civic advisor in Jerusalem during the British Mandate, will do *(Fig. 5)*.[21] In Ashbee's plan, the divisions of the church's fragmented interior space among its various Christian stakeholders are color-coded in sympathetic pastels.[22] In practice, those boundaries had been enacted by violence from early modernity to the present.[23] John Stoddard, like other nineteenth-century western Protestant travelers, commented on the occupants' belligerence:

> The "Holy Sites" are owned by various Christian sects, who hate each other cordially; ... officers, appointed by the Turkish Government, are always present to protect the property, and to prevent the owners from flying at one another's throats. This is, alas! no exaggeration.... Not long ago, during Holy Week, a priest of the Greek Church hurled a bottle of ink at the head of the Franciscan Superior who was conducting a procession round the Holy Sepulchre. [Though the mark was missed], it created a disturbance which Turkish soldiers were obliged to quell.[24]

Violence continues.[25] The spatial/social complexity of the church promotes its disintegration. Each of the multiple parts of the building has its own aura, its own compelling integrity, its own possessor. Each of the Christianities in the Holy Sepulchre assumes that it is the only true Christianity and that it alone should possess the site. The Greek writer and philosopher, Nikos Kazantzakis, recounted a comment made to him by a Greek Orthodox priest in the early twentieth century:

> This entire church belongs to us, the Orthodox. All the sacred shrines are ours. The heretics, whom God has damned, want to take them from us; but we're fencing off the disputed areas with iron bars and won't let anyone set foot inside! Look at what we gave the Abyssinians, a rock. Come what may, we're not giving them another inch. Now we're going to throw the Armenians out; they've over-stepped their boundaries and are standing on our ground. Whatever the Latins tell you is a lie. All their shrines are fakes. I hope to God the day comes when we can throw them out![26]

Each Christianity with a stake in the Holy Sepulchre accedes to the division of the church's real estate not because it acknowledges the legitimacy of the others' traditions, but only because state power—Ottoman, British, Jordanian, and now Israeli—has so dictated. The Holy Sepulchre, once whole, is now a warren of separate identities, each of which arrogantly denies the rights of existence to all of the others.[27] The violence of the warren is less spectacular than that of the heights, but it is, at least sometimes, even more disquieting.

PERIPHERY

"Periphery" is another urban division. It is a late ancient Latinate word derived from the Greek περιφέρω, meaning to carry or move around or to bring to an end, to reduce, to subject.[28] In common language, "periphery" retains both its weak and its strong senses. It refers to the passive outside edges that delimit a space or object. It commonly labels those territories that are most distant from their cultural or political center, provinces exploited to maintain the wealth of the capital. But periphery may also refer to those zones that define the center and challenge its power. In pre-modern cities, the periphery was the defensive wall that defined the relation between the safe and the dangerous, the indweller and the invader, the living and the dead. Jerusalem retains its great Ottoman city wall and is still surrounded by graveyards—Jewish tombs crowd the Mount of Olives to the east; Palestinian burials lie under the proposed Museum of Tolerance to the west.[29]

Certainly peripheries have always been militarily critical—whether in the disintegration of the Roman Empire or in the American Cold War policy of containment. In a Deleuzian sense, the periphery is the zone where the smooth and striated overlap, where nomadic forces gather to challenge established state control.[30] There the alien acts to subvert the familiar. This is the periphery of violence. Jerusalem has experienced that violence often—Egyptian, Philistine, Babylonian, Roman, Persian, and Crusaders martialed troops on the periphery of the city before conquering it. But not all invasions are, at least initially, overtly military. Some occupations from the periphery begin culturally and economically: the Genoese in Pera across the Golden Horn in Istanbul in the thirteenth century, the Jews on the outskirts of Jaffa in the early twentieth.

In the mid-nineteenth century, with the industrial revolution and the inklings of globalization, urban peripheries developed in the form of suburbs. In Jerusalem, that periphery was, and still remains, the principal site of colonizing ambition. The Western investment of the city began with the expansion of neighborhoods outside the city walls in the 1850s.[31] Most like their Western counterparts were the new well-to-do Palestinian suburbs, notably the Husseini neighborhood in the Sheikh Jarrah area to the northeast. More prominently, enclaves of foreigners encircled Jerusalem with architectures imported in their programming and even in some cases in their materials from the homeland: Russians in the Russian Compound (later a British, then an Israeli prison) to the northwest, Jews in enclaves like Mishkenot Sha'ananim to the southwest and Meah Shearim to the north, Germans in the German Colony to the southwest *(Fig. 6)*. Foreign ecclesiastical, missionary, and cultural institutions proliferated on the periphery: the Scottish Church of St. Andrew, the German Churches of the Dormition of the Virgin and Augusta Victoria, and the English Cathedral of St. George; the American School of Oriental Research, École biblique et archéologique française, and the British School of Archaeology. Though a relatively late addition to this series, the Palestine Archaeological Museum exemplifies the performance of colonialism on the periphery of Jerusalem.[32]

The Palestine Archaeological Museum was programmed by James Henry Breasted, America's foremost Egyptologist and founder of the Oriental Institute of the University of Chicago, funded by the American oil magnate and philanthropist John D. Rockefeller, Jr., owned by the British Mandate government, and administered by a board elected from the local Western archaeological institutions. It opened in 1938. The structure was designed with handsome austerity in a Neo-Islamic form by the Mandate's official British architect, Austen St. Barbe Harrison *(Fig. 7)*. The museum reveals its Orientalist operation not only in its architectural style, but also in its symbolically charged location: it occupies the rise east of Damascus Gate, from which the Crusaders first breached the walls of Jerusalem.

The museum consummated the long tradition of Western archaeological investigation of the Holy City at the same time that it represented a dramatic shift in its direction. The archaeological exploration of biblical truth—"scientific" archaeology in the service of religion—had begun at the end of the sixteenth century and continued as the dominant mode of archaeological inquiry through the early twentieth century.[33] For Breasted, archaeology's mission was not to confirm religious convictions, but rather to identify and trace the origins of (Western) man's cultural advance. Like its funding and its administration, the project of the museum was Western: the museum's artifacts were ordered not to prove the truth of the Hebrew Bible, but rather to track the West's teleological ascent to modernity. In the chronological arrangement of the museum's wealth of artifacts, the Hebrew phase of history was documented, but received no special attention—it was just one of a succession of societies from the Mesopotamian and Egyptian to the Ottoman, which provided the foundations for the cultural achievements of Euro-American man. The political climate has changed again since the museum's construction. The Palestine Archaeological Museum and the particular history that was exhibited there have been displaced by the Israel Museum, with its emphasis on the region's religious-national Jewish heritage.

The Palestine Archaeological Museum, officially renamed the Rockefeller Museum by the Israelis, has been left for dead along with the rest of Palestinian East Jerusalem. The museum is pitifully neglected—no parking is available, the galleries are unheated in the winter, and toilet facilities are primitive *(Fig. 8)*. Its collections have been pillaged; the once great repository of the Dead Sea Scrolls is now empty. Even its own past is misrepresented.[34] Visiting has been successfully discouraged; the museum is deserted. The fate of the Palestine Archaeological Museum reveals two conditions of the colonized periphery. First, alien powers on the periphery of a city displace and dispossess one another. The locus of power has shifted from the north of the Old City to Givat Ram to its west. The Israel Museum, where the Dead Sea Scrolls and other objects from the collections of the Palestine Archaeological Museum are now

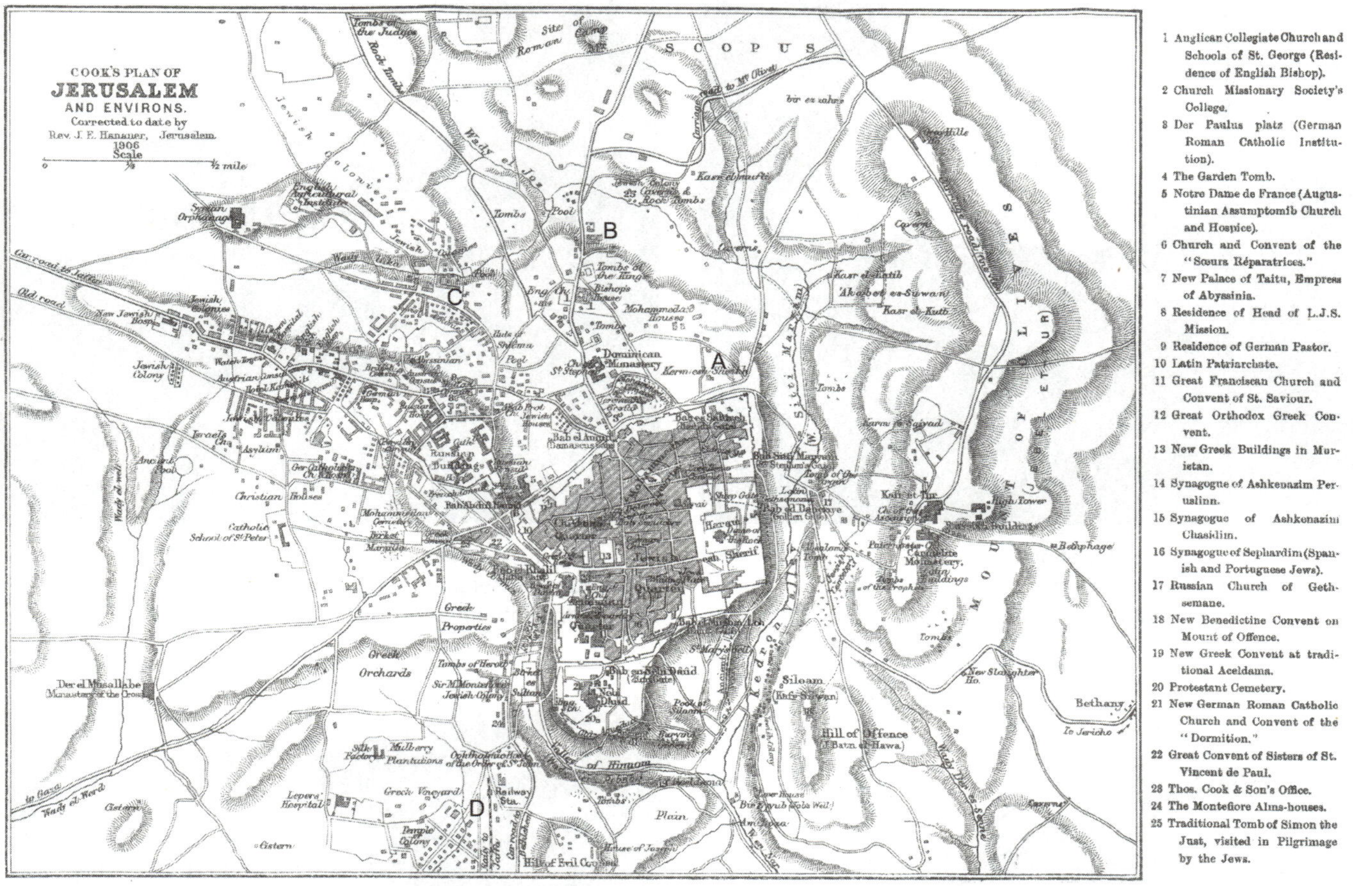

(Fig. 6) Jerusalem, Cook's 1905 Plan of Jerusalem. Author's collection.
A. Palestine Archaeological Museum;
B. Husseini neighborhood/Sheikh Jarrah;
C. Meah Shearim;
D. German Colony.

(Fig.7) Jerusalem, Palestine Archaeological Museum, courtyard. Photograph by author, 2008.

(Fig. 8) Jerusalem, Palestine Archaeological Museum, toilets. Photograph by author.

(Fig. 9) Jerusalem, separation wall in the Abu Dis neighborhood. Photograph by Mahdi Sabbagh, 2016.

(Fig. 10) Jerusalem, house in the Sheikh Jarrah neighborhood. Photograph by Mahdi Sabbagh, 2015.

(Fig. 11) Jerusalem, Meah Shearim, plan. Modified from David Kroyanker's drawings. Drawn by author.

(Fig. 12) Jerusalem, Mandelbaum Gate, 1950.

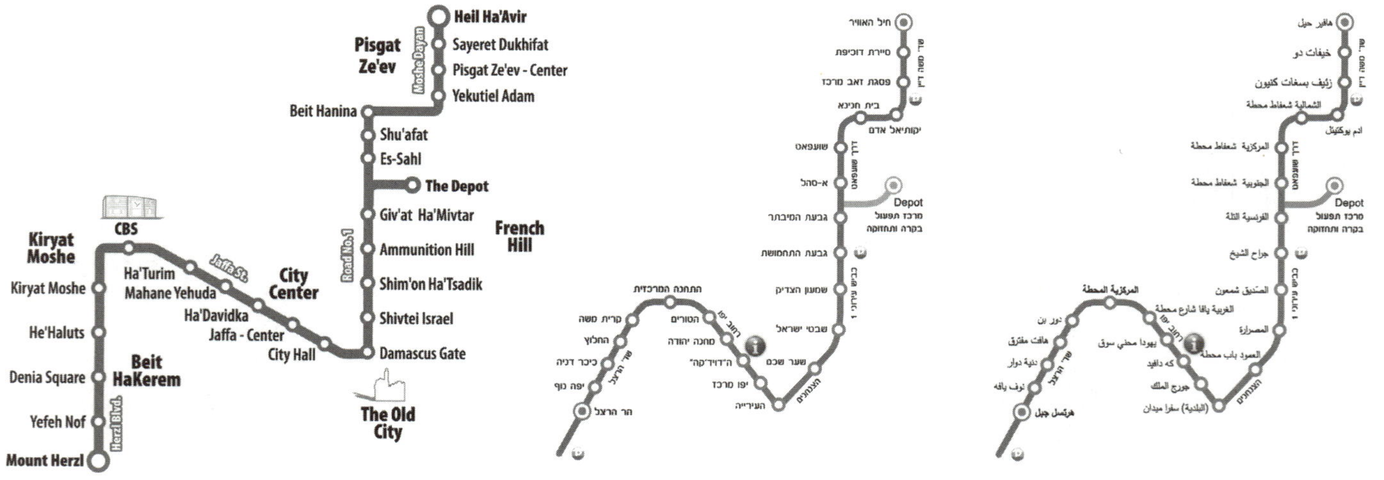

(Fig. 13) Jerusalem, light rail system, from "City Pass - Jerusalem's Light Rail," accessed October 2016, http://www.citypass.co.il/.

held, the Knesset, the Supreme Court, and the Hilton Hotel (now the Crowne Plaza) are all located in Givat Ram. Second, the projects of colonization are legitimated by the cultural institutions established in the periphery. The Israel Museum's archaeological celebration of the Jewishness of the region's history supersedes the Palestine Archaeological Museum's authorization of the evolution of Western culture. The exhibitions of the two museums present ideologically burdened narratives of hegemony. Both institutions disclose the enduring importance of the role of archaeology in establishing the West's political authority as the basis of its cultural ascendancy. ISIS' iconoclasm is certainly a response to Koranic and biblically proscribed figuration, as well as a sign of the organization's barbarity. But it may also be an index of the sectarian Arab identification of the archaeological project as a particularly Western and colonial one.

BREAK

"Break" describes the spatial and social division of communities within a single urban domain. The word "break" implies a violent separation, but, in contrast to "tear" or "rend," one that does not necessarily involve intention. A break may be accidental, but it is a human accident, not, as with the case of "rupture," a natural one. "Break" suggests a wholeness that has been lost, in contrast to "border" or "edge," which mark the limits of a privileged space or thing and neglect what lies beyond. "Break" names a gap between fragments, in contrast to "seam," which records an effort to put pieces back together. The West Bank is riven with divisions imposed by the state: the highways above and below Palestinian villages that are accessible only by Israelis, the disfiguring separation walls, the brutally intrusive tunnels through Palestinian homes *(Fig. 9)*.[35]

Jerusalem also has its state-sponsored divisions, but some breaks in the fabric of the city first occurred independently of direct state intervention. One such break began as a crack in the second half of the nineteenth century. Separate spheres emerged as neighborhoods developed to the north of the Old City. Palestinian businesses flourished outside the walls near Damascus Gate; middle-class Palestinian suburbs expanded to the north along Saladin Street and Nablus Road, the principal route north. Sheikh Jarrah was well-known for its handsome two-story, single-family dwellings, set in beautiful gardens *(Fig. 10)*.[36] Jewish neighborhoods occupied the vicinities to the west, along Shivtei Israel Street, north of the Russian Compound, sheltering in the past as they do in the present the less-prosperous ultra-Orthodox. Meah Shearim is characteristic of the architecture of these neighborhoods: small row houses are tightly organized around a central courtyard, turning their inhospitable backs to the broader community.[37] Each apartment's entrance, along with its latrine, was encountered from the interior courtyard *(Fig. 11)*.[38] That courtyard, though planned as a garden, was soon claustrophobically crowded with more buildings. It became a warren.

Between these two spheres, with their different densities, architectures, prosperities, ethnicities, and religions, was a relative emptiness that became a void: the no-man's-land of the 1948 War that subsequently became the barricaded border between Jordan and Israel. The one opening between the two sovereignties along this otherwise hermetically sealed boundary was the Mandelbaum Gate, Jerusalem's equivalent of divided Berlin's Checkpoint Charlie *(Fig. 12)*. A military trauma converted a topographically articulated but porous separation into a break. That break was not sutured back together in the aftermath of the Six-Day War in 1967, when the territories north, south, and east of Jerusalem all came under Israeli control. Rather, the impervious border wall was remodeled as a different form of break: the four-to-six lane Road 1, connecting Jerusalem to the principal highway to Tel Aviv.[39]

The use of urban throughways as a means of isolating minorities and ensuring their continued economic deprivation was a common strategy of urban planners in the United States from the 1950s through the 1980s. The deployment of the highway as a barrier has new life now in Israel. Road 1 is one example of that manipulation. As Wendy Pullan, principal investigator for "Conflict in Cities and the Contested State" at the University of Cambridge's Centre for Urban Conflicts Research, observed with her co-authors, "Road 1 shares many characteristics, in strategy, function and design, with the bypass roads of the Occupied Territories... Our maps show that its connections and junctions, speed controls and the shape of the road itself, facilitate travel to Israeli destinations and privilege Israeli needs: the overall flow of traffic is an Israeli one."[40] The political and social inequities of the break are further demonstrated by its reinforcement with a light rail system completed in 2010. That light rail links the illegal Israeli settlements of the north of Jerusalem with the west of the city, reconstituting them as suburbs rather than as outposts. The signage posted by the operator reveals the light rail's politics.[41] Names of the stops are coherently written in Hebrew and English, but they are incoherently presented in Arabic: the word order is inverted. For example, Sheikh Jarrah is displayed as Jarrah Sheikh and Bab al-Amud as al-Amud Bab *(Fig. 13)*. The offensive character of this signage cannot be ascribed to mere incompetence. It is too resonant with the attacks on Palestinians for their use of Arabic in public.[42] The intrusion of this Israeli-reinforced break in the fabric of the city has made the light rail another instrument of abuse of the disenfranchised.[43] Road 1 and its adjunct, the light rail train, demonstrate how cracks in the urban fabric mutate over time and with state collusion into catastrophic breaks.

CONCLUSIONS

From this analysis of the geo-architectural order of Jerusalem I draw two conclusions. The first relates to the city: Jerusalem is hard on the soul. Even the casual observer is witness there to the routinized exercise of naked power. The episodes that I chose to present here, however, are meant as reminders that the state is not the only perpetrator of institutional urban violence in Jerusalem. Nor is the current violence an exclusively Palestinian vs. Israeli phenomenon. Christianity, at the present moment, seems to think of itself as a peaceful religion. Those who work on the history of Jerusalem know better.

Second, in relation to architecture and urbanism more generally: different divisions in the urban landscape of Jerusalem can be associated with different forms of violence—"height" with the power of the dominant state, "warren" with sectarian rivalry, "periphery" with the incremental authority of aliens, and "break" with economic, ethnic, and political difference. Whether this observation allows us a better grasp on the current conditions of the city or whether the lessons learned from the physical environment of Jerusalem are applicable to any other urban condition remain open questions. One thing is clear: the life and actions of geo-architectural features in the urban landscape should be carefully scrutinized. If the addictions, obsessions, and diseases of sites are not treated, their pathologies will continue to infect their occupants.

1 I am grateful to this year's editors of *Perspecta*, Mahdi Sabbagh and Meghan McAllister, for their invitation to contribute to the "Urban Divides" issue. I am also indebted to the students of my graduate seminars on Jerusalem both at the Yale School of Architecture and in the Department of Art, Art History, and Visual Studies of Duke University.

2 Selma Lagerlöf, *The Holy City: Jerusalem II*, trans. Velma Swanston Howard (Garden City, NY: Doubleday, Page and Company, [1902] 1918), 67.

3 Work on this replica was begun by the distinguished Israeli archaeologist Michael Avi-Yonah in 1964. The model was later kept archaeologically current by another eminent Israeli archaeologist, Yoram Tsafrir. The model was transferred from its original site at the Holyland Hotel on the periphery of the city to the Israel Museum at its new core in 2006. For the most recent guidebook to the model, see, David Amit, *Model of Jerusalem in the Second Temple Period* (Jerusalem: Israel Museum, 2009).

4 Pliny describes Jerusalem as "by far the most famous city of the East and not of Judaea only" ("longe clarissima urbium Orientis, non Iudaeae modo.") Pliny, *Natural History*, trans. H. Rackham, Loeb Classical Library 2 (Cambridge, Mass.: Harvard University Press, 1942), 272–75.

5 Annabel Jane Wharton, "Jerusalem's Zions," *Material Religion* 9, no. 2 (2013), 218–43.

6 For a summary of the evidence, see Martin Biddle, *The Tomb of Christ* (Stroud, UK: Sutton, 1999), 54–58.

7 See, for example, Oleg Grabar, *The Dome of the Rock* (Cambridge, Mass.: Harvard University Press, 2006).

8 "Intifada Toll 2000–2005," *BBC News*, February 8, 2005, http://news.bbc.co.uk/2/hi/middle_east/3694350.stm.

9 For a Dan Brown-like television-series version of the extremist threat to the Temple Mount, see Tim Kring and Gideon Raff, *Dig*, (USA TV, 2015).

10 For the earliest "scientific" discussion of the city's original topography, see Sir Charles Warren, *The Temple or the Tomb: Giving further Evidence in Favour of the Authenticity of the Present Site of the Holy Sepulchre, and Pointing Out Some of the Principal Misconceptions Contained in Fergusson's 'Holy Sepulchre' and 'The Temples of the Jews'* (London: Richard Bentley, 1880), 32–35.

11 John Rastell, *Les termes de la ley; or, Certain difficult and obscure words and terms of the common laws and statutes of this realm now in use, expounded and explained* (London: W. Rawlins, et al., 1536), 667.

12 Mark Bailey, "The Rabbit and the Medieval East Anglian Economy," *British Agricultural History Society* 36, no. 1 (1988).

13 A legal dictionary of the early eighteenth century indicates the resentment with which such enclosures were regarded by the common man. "Rebellious Assembly is a gathering together of twelve persons, or more, intending or going about, practicing or putting in use, unlawfully, of their own authority, to change any laws or statues of the realm, or to destroy the enclosure of any park or ground enclosed, or banks of any fish ponds, pool or conduit, to the intent the same shall remain void, or to the intent unlawfully to have common or way in any of the said grounds, or to destroy the deer in any park, or any warren of coneys [rabbits], dove-houses or bays, or to burn stacks of corn, or to abate rents or prices of victuals." Thomas Blount, *A Law-Dictionary and Glossary*, 3rd ed. (London: Nutt and Gosling, 1717), 256.

14 Dietrich von Holst et al., "Social Rank, Fecundity and Lifetime Reproductive Success in Wild European Rabbits," *Behavioral Ecology and Sociobiology* 51 (2002).

15 This reading is a variation on that of Umberto Eco, *Semiotics and the Philosophy of Language* (Bloomington: University of Indiana Press, 1984), 81-82.

16 Michel de Certeau, *The Practice of Everyday Life*, trans. Steven F. Rendall (Berkeley: University of California Press, 1984), 36–37.

17 Sudhir Venkatesh, *Gang Leader for a Day* (New York: Penguin, 2008); Robert C. Davis and Benjamin Ravid, *The Jews of Early Modern Venice* (Baltimore: Johns Hopkins University Press, 2001); Mike Davis, *Planet of the Slums* (London: Verso, 2006); Ennio Concina, Ugo Camerino, and Donatella Calabi, *La città degli ebrei. Il Ghetto di Venezia: Architettura e urbanistica* (Venice: Albrizzi 1991).

18 For a summary of the building's complex history, see, Robert Ousterhout, "Architecture as Relic and the Construction of Sanctity: The Stones of the Holy Sepulchre," *Journal of the Society of Architectural Historians* 62, no. 1 (2003), 4–23.

19 Olivia Remie Constable, "*Funduq*, *Fondaco*, and *Khan* in the Wake of Christian Commerce and Crusade," in *The Crusades from the Perspective of Byzantium and the Muslim World*, ed. Angeliki Laiou and Roy Parviz Mottahedeh (Washington, D.C.: Dumbarton Oaks, 2001).

20 L. G. A. Cust, *The Status Quo in the Holy Places* (1929; repr. Jerusalem: Ariel, 1980).

21 C. R. Ashbee, ed. *Jerusalem, 1918–1920: Being the Records of the Pro-Jerusalem Council during the Period of the British Military Administration* (London: John Murray, 1921).

22 Armenians, Greek Orthodox, Copts, Roman Catholics, Russian Orthodox, and Jacobites all claim specific sacred sites within the compound. As complex as it appears, the plan is a simplification, as it does not include much of the upper elevation of the building. C. R. Ashbee, ed., *Jerusalem, 1920–1922: Being the Records of the Pro-Jerusalem Council during the First Two Years of the Civil Administration* (London: John Murray, 1924), plate 46.

23 Fighting over territory in the Holy Sepulchre was not limited to its precincts. Disputes over the keys to different bits of the building became international incidents in Europe. For example, see, "French Intervention," *Times*, October 27, 1852; "Russian Intervention," *London Times*, February 21, 1854.

24 John L. Stoddard, *Lectures: Constantinople, Jerusalem, Egypt*, John L. Stoddard's Lectures, vol. 2 (Boston: Balch Brothers, 1897), 154–55.

25 For a vigorous early-twentieth-century denunciation of the warring Christian factions in the Holy Sepulchre and Church of the Nativity, see, James Creelman, "The Profanation of the Holy Sepulchre," *New York Times*, October 24, 1909. For a summary, see, Glenn Bowman, "'In Dubious Battle on the Plains of Heav'n': The Politics of Possession in Jerusalem's Holy Sepulchre," *History and Anthropology* 22, no. 3 (2011).

26 Nikos Kazantzakis, *Journeying: Travels in Italy, Egypt, Sinai, Jerusalem and Cyprus*, trans. Themi Vasils and Theodora Vasils (1926; Boston: Little, Brown and Company, 1975), 153.

27 The Christian clergy beat up one another; through the nineteenth century, Christian pilgrims also thrashed Jews who mistakenly walked in the passage in front of the entrance to the Holy Sepulchre.

28 *Oxford English Dictionary*, s.v. "periphery."

29 Rory McCarthy, "Row Over Plan to Build Jewish Museum of Tolerance on Site of Muslim Cemetery," *Guardian*, February 10, 2010.

30 Gilles Deleuze and Félix Guattari, *A Thousand Plateaus: Capitalism and Schizophrenia*, trans. Brian Massumi (Minneapolis: University of Minnesota Press, 1987), 474–500.

31 Yehoshua Ben-Arieh, "The Growth of Jerusalem in the Nineteenth Century," *Annals of the Association of American Geographers* 65, no. 2 (1975) 252–69.

32 Annabel Jane Wharton, *Architectural Agents: The Delusional, Abusive, Addictive Lives of Buildings* (Minneapolis: University of Minnesota Press, 2015), 31–56.

33 Perhaps the first "archaeologist" to work in Jerusalem was Bernardino Amico, who completed his research in the last years of the sixteenth century. Amico, *Plans of the Sacred Edifices of the Holy Land*, trans. Theophilus Bellorini and Eugene Hoade (1610; Jerusalem: Franciscan Press, 1953). Archaeology is, of course, never free from ideological involvement—controlling history is too important to be objective. Isaiah Silver, "Digging the Occupation: The Politics of Boycotts and Archaeology in Israel," *Savage Minds*, July 6, 2014, http://savageminds.org/2014/07/06/digging-the-occupation-the-politics-of-boycotts-and-archeology-in-israel-bds-pt-3/.

34 In his endowment, Rockefeller specified that the museum was to be the property of the legally constituted government of Palestine, administered by a Board of Directors made up of scholars appointed by that government. Under the Mandate, it was British Mandate Property. When the British evacuated Palestine in 1948, instead of ceding ownership to the government of Jordan, they contravened the founder's provisions by precipitously enacting legislation that transferred ownership of the museum to its Board of Directors. High Commissioner and Council of Ministers, "Order of Transfer of Ownership of the Museum," *Palestine Gazette* 1663 (1948). Jordan renationalized the museum a few months before the outbreak of the Six-Day War in 1967, with the strong support of a number of board members. Jordan retained the board, as under the Mandate, to administer the museum. With the Six-Day War, the museum became part of the Occupied Territories. Against international law, Israel took possession of the property, dissolving the museum's board. The museum once had the largest collection of Dead Sea Scrolls in the world. Now it has none. Many of its other artifacts are now on display at the Israel Museum in West Jerusalem.

35 Eyal Weizman, "Seeing through Walls: The Split Sovereign and the One-Way Mirror," *Grey Room* 24 (Summer 2006), 88–99; Weizman, *Hollow Land: Israel's Architecture of Occupation* (New York: Verso, 2007); and Philipp Misselwitz and Tim Rienits, eds., *City of Collision: Jerusalem and the Principles of Conflict Urbanism* (Basel: Birkhäuser, 2006).

36 For a detailed consideration of one such home, see, Annabel Wharton and Avner Amiri, "Home in Jerusalem: The American Colony and Palestinian Suburban Architecture," *Post-Medieval Archaeology* 45, no. 2 (2011), 237–65. The Palestinian neighborhoods of Jerusalem, in contrast to the Jewish and German ones, have received little serious scholarly attention. That Mahdi Sabbagh may remedy this situation was evidenced in his excellent paper for our Jerusalem seminar at Yale.

37 By the 1890s the non-ultra-Orthodox Jews of the community, including some of its founding members, had been evicted. Meah Shearim's restrictive covenants make the later racial ones of the United States seem benign. David Kroyanker and Dror Wahrman, *Jerusalem Architecture: Periods and Styles--The Jewish Quarters and Public Buildings Outside the Old City* (Jerusalem: Jerusalem Institute for Israel Studies and Domino Press, 1983), 133.

38 Ringing the common space with toilets had its unpleasentness, as noted of a similar arrangement in Jaffa by a Jewish settler, Ze'ev Smilansky, in 1907:

> *It is saddening and shaming to find something akin to a new version of the ghetto.... Because the houses were so close together, the toilets were built one beside the other and, what is more, the houses are at the back of the courtyard and the toilets at the front.... Thus in walking... one passes a long row of outhouses.*

Quoted by Ruth Kark, *Jaffa: A City in Evolution, 1799–1917*, trans. Gila Brand (Jerusalem: Yad Izhak Ben-Zvi, 1990), 115.

39 Wendy Pullan, et al., "Jerusalem's Road 1: An Inner City Frontier?," *City* 11, no. 2 (2007).

40 Ibid., 182–83.

41 These observations on naming were stimulated by a paper for our Jerusalem seminar presented by Raphael de la Fontaine, "The Light Rail of Jerusalem: A Contemporary Agent of Control Over Space," School of Architecture (Yale University, 2014). I want to thank Professor Kalman Bland for the comparative assessment of the three separate maps of the light rail that appear on the operator's website, http://www.citypass.co.il. I am also indebted to Mahdi Sabbagh for his confirmation of the Arabic irregularities.

42 Elhanan Miller, "Jewish Students to Protest Violence by Speaking Arabic on Jerusalem Tram," *Times of Israel*, April 27, 2015.

43 Joshua Mitnick and Nicholas Casey, "Israel Erects Train-Station Barriers in Wake of Attacks," *Wall Street Journal*, November 13, 2014.

EVIDENCE: VISUALIZING URBAN DIVIDES

A CROWDSOURCED PHOTO ESSAY BY

MEGHAN McALLISTER AND MAHDI SABBAGH

The grotesque, the mutant, the "other" has piqued the fascination of society for centuries. As architects and urbanists, this often translates to the deviant in built form—a pre-occupation with the divided city. We ogle over photographs of divisive walls, fences, gates, a certain violence and power inherent to these forms. But what if the most powerful societal divisions are actually much more subtle? What if it is more often a slow-moving virus than a catastrophe, deliberately affecting some people more than others, creeping below the surface until we become so used to it that we think it is normal?

Or perhaps it's not even a disorder at all? Rather, is it more like a genetically modified fruit—a purposeful mutant to arguably aid society—to keep communities together through a sense of identity and place?

Regardless of any value judgment, a better understanding of what type of virus this is and how it behaves could be a valuable tool for any practitioner of the built environment. In the following photo essay, we catalogue visual evidence of urban divides. Collected over a period of two years, the crowdsourced photographs juxtapose iconic divisions with more mundane, everyday urban conditions. Identifying the architectural devices and the urban types used within each scene reveals further unanticipated comparisons. Spatial cues mark the exclusion of the disenfranchised at times, and the empowered in others. Crossing social and geographical boundaries, we interrogate the inequities inherent to architecture, and challenge readers to recognize the ubiquity of urban divides.

Type: affordable housing
Device: wall
Location: Juarez

Photograph by
Aanya Chugh

Mexican social housing pushes up against the border, allowing residents easy access to jobs in the border zone.

Type: walled city
Device: wall
Location: Thessaloniki

Photograph by
Palmyra Geraki

A house is built out of the adjacent defensive city wall, merging the wall into the town's urban fabric.

Device: highway
Location: Seattle

Photograph from the Seattle Municipal Archives, [1966].

Interstate 5 cuts through Seattle, bounding its city center.

Type: walled city
Device: wall
Location: Dubrovnik

Photograph by
Denis Schofield

Dubrovnik's historic stone walls encircle the Old Town, while the city has expanded beyond.

Type: affordable housing
Location: Fayum

Photograph by
Denis Schofield

Built of concrete block, new housing in Fayum, Egypt resembles many affordable low-rise projects globally.

Type: affordable housing
Location: Houston

Photograph by
David Lee

Low-rise public housing in Houston's Greater 5th Ward is in poor condition despite being in close proximity to downtown.

Type: camp
Location: Dheisheh refugee camp

Photograph by
Mahdi Sabbagh

The density and extents of the camp resembles a city, yet the camp lacks the institutions, rights, and planned permanence of a city.

Type: camp
Location: Filippiada refugee camp

Photograph by Camilla Wasserman and the Filippiada camp residents in October 2016

Refugee camps across Greece, intended to be provisional, were often erected in remote regions, resulting in controlled make-shift environments that the residents struggle to make habitable.

Type: affordable housing
Location: Cairo

Photograph by
Denis Schofield

Popularly known as “Garbage City,” Manshiyat Nasser, a neighborhood on the outskirts of Cairo, houses many inhabitants who work as garbage collectors for the larger city.

Type: affordable housing
Location: Queens

Public domain

Among the oldest public housing in the U.S., the Queensbridge Housing Projects were built on the water with views to the wealthier Upper East Side.

Type: affordable housing
Location: Collingwood

Photograph by
Nick Carson

In an inner suburb of Melbourne, a 1960’s era public housing project abuts the older low-rise urban fabric.

Type: upscale towers
Location: Ho Chi Minh City

Photograph by
Andy Sternad

High-rise towers replace mangroves and informal settlements in a peripheral master planned district across the river from the historic downtown.

Device: security checkpoint
Location: New York City

Photograph by
Craig Rosman

Sections of Wall Street are secured using automatic traffic barriers.

Device: security checkpoint
Location: Berlin

Public domain

Security infrastructure at Checkpoint Charlie is preserved to memorialize the historic divide.

Device: security checkpoint
Location: Nicosia

Photograph by
Gérard Janot

From this security barrier and platform on the Greek Cypriot side of Nicosia, pedestrians can look beyond the UN-administered Green Line.

Type: enclave
Device: gate, ornament
Location: San Francisco

Photograph by
Meghan McAllister

An ornamented gate celebrates the threshold to Chinatown in San Francisco.

Type: upscale housing
Location: New York City

Photograph by
Mahdi Sabbagh

Like other luxury buildings in Manhattan, the Plaza Hotel boasts a driveway, awning and doormen, reinforcing its exclusivity.

Type: affordable housing, enclave
Device: gate, ornament
Location: San Francisco

Photograph by
Meghan McAllister

With an ornamental gate at its center, the Ping Yuen public housing complex in Chinatown uses distinct architectural ornamentation to identify with its projected population.

Device: poor door
Location: London

Public domain

This London apartment building is designed with two entrances, one for the wealthy residents and one for the tenants of affordable units.

Device: gate
Location: Dheisheh refugee camp

Photograph by
Mahdi Sabbagh

A former gate to the camp is preserved as a memorial to its fenced past when the turnstile acted as the camp's sole entry.

Type: campus
Device: wall, gate
Location: New Haven

Photograph by
Maggie Tsang

Yale University campus is surrounded by fences, walls, and landscaped trenches, differentiating its space from the rest of the city.

Type: security fence
Location: Mexico City

Photograph by
Meghan McAllister

Security infrastructure blocks off an ordinary street that is within a few blocks of a government building.

Type: campus
Location: Cupertino

Photograph by
Jean Ahn

A new corporate campus is inserted as an large-scale object into a more finely-grained urban fabric, completely internal to itself.

Type: affordable housing
Location: Saint Louis

Photograph courtesy of
U.S. Geological Survey,
[c. 1963-72].

An iconic public housing project of the post-war era, the Pruitt-Igoe complex facilitated the seclusion of lower-income communities.

Type: gated community
Device: gate
Location: Los Angeles

Photograph by
Meghan McAllister

The oldest gated community in Los Angeles, Fremont Place, boasts a classical entrance with a gatekeeper beyond.

Type: gated community
Device: gate
Location: Gurgaon

Photograph by
Swarnabh Ghosh

Elaborate security gates announce the entrance to a luxurious golf community in India.

Type: camp
Device: gate
Location: Filippiada refugee camp

Photograph by Camilla Wasserman and the Filippiada camp residents in October 2016

The entrance to the camp in northern Greece allows unrestricted access for its residents, yet it still resembles a border control point.

Type: camp
Device: fence
Location: Dubai

Photograph by
Todd Reisz

Workers' camps in Dubai are often fenced, gated and increasingly isolated from the city.

Device: wall
Location: Muhlhausen

Photograph by
Eckehard Jagdmann

A medieval center for trade, this German town utlized its secure stone walls to regulate tariffs and the flow of goods.

Type: upscale mall
Location: Jerusalem

Photograph by
Mahdi Sabbagh

The Mamilla mall occupies the former buffer zone between East and West Jerusalem, introducing mechanisms of gentrification and policing to the nearby impoverished Old City.

Type: special economic zone (SEZ)
Location: Gurgaon

Photograph by
Swarnabh Ghosh

A dirt embankment and security fence separates a new private development from main thoroughfare in this Special Economic Zone (SEZ) in India.

Type: trade zone
Device: wall
Location: Nogales

Photograph by
Walker Oleson

Economic policy enables commercial and industrial pockets along US-Mexico border.

Type: upscale housing
Location: Brooklyn

Photograph by
Nizar Harake

New market-rate housing in Brooklyn is unaffordable to most longtime residents of the neighborhood.

Type: upscale market
Location: Mexico City

Photograph by
Meghan McAllister

A new upscale market in Mexico City is popular for tourists and local elite, but cost prohibitive to many who live in the surrounding neighborhood.

Type: special economic zone (SEZ)
Device: wall
Location: Gurgaon

Photograph by
Swarnabh Ghosh

High-end luxury condominiums of a Special Economic Zone (SEZ) can be seen from an adjacent urban village, separated by a wall.

Type: informal settlement, olympic zone
Location: Rio De Janeiro

Photograph courtesy of
Catalytic Communities

A historic favela, Autodromo, was cleared in order to make way for a high-rise complex that served the 2016 Summer Olympics.

Type: upscale housing
Location: Tianjin

Photograph by
Jonathan Sun

New high-rise housing outside of Tianjin is often fenced off and disconnected from nearby urban villages and industrial areas.

Type: informal settlement
Location: Mumbai

Photograph by
Jensie Gheest

High-rise construction is seen from the informal neighborhood of Dhobi Ghat, known as the laundry district.

Type: gated community
Location: Hanoi

Photograph by
Gabriel Hurtado

A new gated development outside of Hanoi brands itself as "International City."

Type: affordable housing
Location: Philadelphia

Photograph by
Michael McAllister

Inner city public housing projects mimic suburban cul-de-sac layouts, in sharp contrast to adjacent rowhomes and the office towers viewed beyond.

Type: informal settlement
Device: topography
Location: Rio de Janeiro

Photograph courtesy of
Catalytic Communities

The Santa Marta favela, secluded up on a hill, offers sweeping views of the wealthy housing and tall office buildings in the formal city below.

Type: upscale housing
Device: height
Location: New York City

Photograph by
Pavel Bendov

The proportions of pencil towers creates a new condition of vertical segregation, as the small footprints can only accomodate private apartments for the super wealthy.

Type: upscale housing
Device: topography
Location: San Francisco

Photograph by
Meghan McAllister

Just across the bay from San Francisco, expensive private homes sprinkle the hillside with waterfront views.

Type: enclave
Device: topography
Location: Har Homa settlement

Public domain

North of Bethlehem, the Israeli settlement of Har Homa takes advantage of its hilltop topography.

Type: enclave
Device: ornament
Location: Buzescu

Photograph by
Andreea Cojocaru

In this Romanian town, gypsy communities employ architectural motifs of extravagance to symbolize and assert their identity and newfound wealth.

Type: enclave
Device: signage
Location: New York City

Photograph by
Mahdi Sabbagh

Once ostracized, the Italian immigrants in this enclave now use symbols of their cultural heritage to assert their identity and to attract tourists.

Type: enclave
Device: mural
Location: Belfast

Photograph by
Meghan McAllister

An inner-city enclave asserts its ethno-political association in a mural, rendering others unwelcome.

Device: mural
Location: Detroit

Photograph by
Meghan Lewis

A neighborhood in Detroit paints a mural to create identity and community in hopes of breathing life back into the dilapidated area.

Type: affordable housing
Device: infrastructure
Location: New York City

Photograph by
Mahdi Sabbagh

A public housing project in Manhattanville abuts an elevated rail line and the new campus expansion of Columbia University.

Type: informal settlement
Device: topography, infrastructure
Location: Jakarta

Photograph by
Andy Sternad

Threatened by rising sea levels, informal settlements cluster along the water, while wealthier neighborhoods seek higher ground.

Device: wall
Location: Nogales

Photograph by
Peggy Deamer

A metal wall marks the U.S.-Mexican border, regardless of natural topographic conditions.

Device: railway, park
Location: New York

Photograph by
Mahdi Sabbagh

The Highline, an iconic railroad-turned-park, still cuts through Manhattan, but now leaves wealth and gentrification along its path.

Device: signage
Location: New York City

Photograph by
Mahdi Sabbagh

In Manhattan, land owners demarcate their property from public space using plaques embedded in the sidewalk.

Type: olympic zone
Device: vacancy
Location: Nanjing

Photograph by
Sheena Zhang

Plazas and other facilities from the 2005 Olympics sit disused while other areas of the city are in dire need of reinvestment.

Device: vacancy
Location: Detroit

Photograph by
Meghan Lewis

The dilapidation of this public park reflects larger issues of poverty and abandonment in the neighborhood, while the commercial towers of downtown carry on in the distance.

Type: exclusive park
Device: gate
Location: New York City

Photograph by
Mahdi Sabbagh

Gramercy Park is a gated private park that only adjacent neighbors can access with a key.

Type: camp
Location: Los Angeles

Photograph courtesy of
Outside Development

Skid Row has one of the largest populations of homeless people in the U.S. and its encampments often take over the sidewalks.

Type: informal settlement
Location: Manila

Photograph by
John Tubles

This Manila cemetery is used as a makeshift residential area, with people living in the spaces between tomb structures.

Type: parklet
Location: San Francisco

Photograph by
Perry Wexelberg

Intended as public space, many parklets appear increasingly exclusive as they are used by adjacent restaurants in gentrifying neighborhoods.

Type: informal market
Location: Mexico City

Photograph by
Meghan McAllister

La Merced Market is known for its great produce but also crime and prostitution, leaving it often avoided by the wealthier population.

Device: wall
Location: Jerusalem

Photograph by
Mahdi Sabbagh

The separation wall slices through previously cohesive neighborhoods in East Jerusalem.

Device: river, rail tracks
Location: Saint Louis

Photograph by
Jesse Vogler

A railway and the Mississippi river separate East St. Louis from a once bustling downtown.

Device: highway
Location: Brooklyn

Photograph by
Mahdi Sabbagh

The elevated Brooklyn Queens Expressway turns into a grade level divide in this section of South Williamsburg.

Device: wall
Location: Baghdad

Photograph by
Caecilia Pieri

Various parts of Baghdad are Sealed off with walls and fenses, giving the appearance of multiple cities within the city.

The photographs presented here were taken by 33 photographers in 20 countries. We would like to thank the following individuals for sharing their work with us:

Jean Ahn
Pavel Bendov
Nick Carson
Aanya Chugh
Andreea Cojocaru
Catalytic Communities
Peggy Deamer
Outside Development
Palmyra Geraki
Jensie Gheest
Swarnabh Ghosh
Nizar Harake
Gabriel Hurtado
Eckehard Jagdmann
Gérard Janot
David Lee
Meghan Lewis
Meghan McAllister
Michael McAllister
Walker Oleson
Caecilia Pieri
Todd Reisz
Craig Rosman
Mahdi Sabbagh
Denis Schofield
Andy Sternad
Jonathan Sun
Maggie Tsang
John Tubles
Jesse Vogler
Camilla Wasserman
Perry Wexelberg
Sheena Zhang

Traversals:

In and Out of the Dadaab Refugee Camps

Anooradha Iyer Siddiqi

and

Alishine Hussein Osman

In 1991, in response to a civil war, drought, and famine in Somalia that displaced 1.7 million people, four hundred thousand asylum seekers fled to Kenya by boat from the Mombasa or Kismayo seaports, or on foot through the western border into Kenya's Garissa District.[1] That same year, several boys and young men fleeing Sudan crossed borders to enter the country on the other side, arriving in the Turkana District on foot, many from camps in Ethiopia. In response to these influxes, the Kenyan government requested United Nations assistance and began designating land for refugee encampments.[2]

On Kenya's border with Somalia, The United Nations High Commissioner for Refugees (UNHCR) set up a reception station and temporary settlement in a town called Liboi. This makeshift camp was reported to have such poor shelter quality that international staff preferred to sleep outdoors.[3] The government of Kenya provided a site to house these refugees for the longer term, one hundred kilometers from the border, just north of a village on the unpaved highway that connected Nairobi and Mogadishu.[4] The village, called Dadaab, had a population of five thousand and was not yet electrified when the UNHCR set up its field office.[5] Ground clearing and construction of a new camp for thirty thousand inhabitants began in October of 1991.[6] It was called Ifo. That field office and refugee camp underwent a material and morphological transformation as they expanded into a system of three designated settlements sheltering nearly one half million inhabitants by 2011, with two additional camps added later.[7]

Although international refugee law guarantees refugees the right to work and education, the Kenyan state's enforcement of an encampment policy curtailed these rights by restricting refugee movement outside designated settlements.

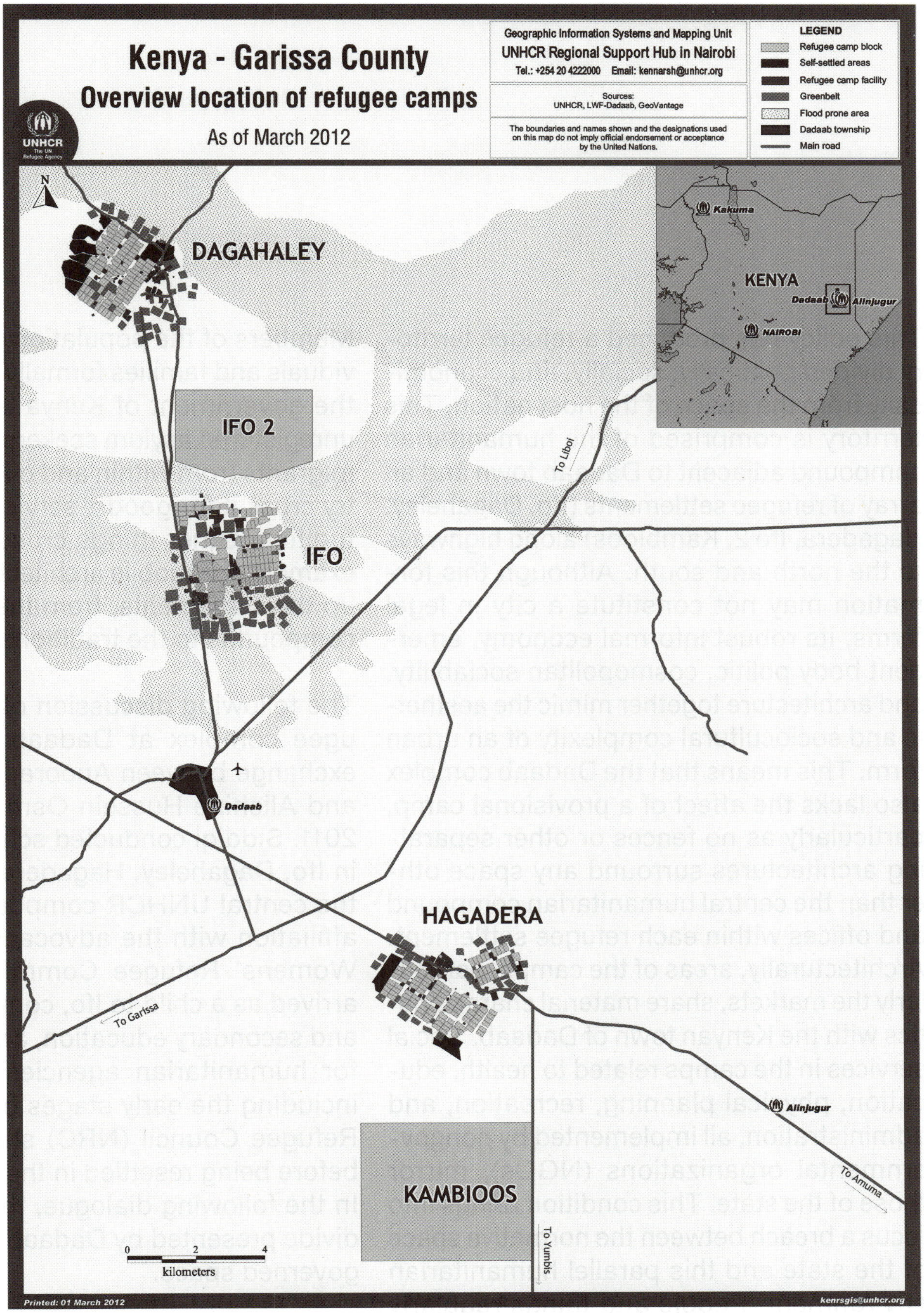

Fig. 1 **UNHCR overview map of Dadaab refugee camps, 2012.**

This policy has produced a refugee territory divided politically, socially, and economically from the space of the host nation. This territory is comprised of the humanitarian compound adjacent to Dadaab town and an array of refugee settlements (Ifo, Dagaheley, Hagadera, Ifo 2, Kambioos) along highways to the north and south. Although this formation may not constitute a city in legal terms, its robust informal economy, emergent body politic, cosmopolitan sociability, and architecture together mimic the aesthetic and sociocultural complexity of an urban form. This means that the Dadaab complex also lacks the affect of a provisional camp, particularly as no fences or other separating architectures surround any space other than the central humanitarian compound and offices within each refugee settlement. Architecturally, areas of the camps, particularly the markets, share material characteristics with the Kenyan town of Dadaab. Social services in the camps related to health, education, physical planning, recreation, and administration, all implemented by nongovernmental organizations (NGOs), mirror those of the state. This condition brings into focus a breach between the normative space of the state and this parallel humanitarian environment. People and things regularly traverse this surveilled and policed breach. Members of the population, including individuals and families formally registered with the government of Kenya or the UNHCR, unregistered asylum seekers, and economic migrants from within and outside the country cross it for goods, services, and opportunities. Other things cross it as well: for example, the mobile architectures that make up the settlements, from the humanitarian compounds to the traditional dwellings.

The following discussion of life in the refugee complex at Dadaab is part of an exchange between Anooradha Iyer Siddiqi and Alishine Hussein Osman, initiated in 2011. Siddiqi conducted scholarly research in Ifo, Dagaheley, Hagadera, Dadaab, and the central UNHCR compound, visiting in affiliation with the advocacy organization Womens' Refugee Commission. Osman arrived as a child to Ifo, completed primary and secondary education, and later worked for humanitarian agencies in the camp, including the early stages of a Norwegian Refugee Council (NRC) shelter initiative, before being resettled in the United States. In the following dialogue, they discuss the divide presented by Dadaab within a larger governed space.

Anooradha Iyer Siddiqi (AIS):

Let's talk about how we each first entered the refugee settlements at Dadaab. It may begin to explain the spatial separation it presents. I am a United States citizen, and as part of my scholarly research, I worked with the Women's Refugee Commission under the aegis of the International Rescue Committee (IRC). I traveled on the UNHCR chartered plane from the Wilson airport in Nairobi to the Dadaab airport, where the IRC driver took us to our base in the humanitarian compound across the highway from Dadaab town.

Alishine Hussein Osman (AHO):

I first arrived in Ifo refugee camp with my family in 1991. After the civil war erupted in Somalia, my family had to flee the country. We arrived at the Kenya-Somalia border, where there were lots of other refugees. We were received by the UNHCR and screened. We entered Kenya by vehicle and were settled at Liboi. Because Liboi was close to Somalia, the UNHCR decided to relocate the refugees to Dadaab a few months later. We were transported by vehicles operated by the UNHCR, and moved to newly established blocks with empty tents, which would become our first home as refugees. That tent in Ifo camp became my home for the next seventeen years. I graduated from high school in 2003, and worked in many jobs there, including in more than one NGO. I left the camp in 2007 for the United States. I got a Bachelor's degree from Pennsylvania State University, and I also became a United States citizen.

It makes me emotional whenever I talk about this, particularly when I compare my seventeen years in Dadaab with my five years here, and think about the time that was lost. I first traveled back in 2009 and met some of my old friends, some of them my classmates in first and second grades. They still live in the refugee camp.

I have visited the camps three times since I moved away, to see my family and friends. During each visit, I was either a citizen or permanent resident of the United States. When traveling to the camp, I usually take the bus from Eastleigh in Nairobi, via Garissa, to the Dadaab camps; the bus station is in the central market in Ifo.[8] Occasionally I take a bus that terminates in Garissa, and catch another one to Dadaab. It is a long trip and sometimes I want to spend a night in Garissa to rest.

AIS:

I have always been curious: when you applied to go to college, who wrote your recommendation letters?

AHO:

Nobody. I went to Harrisburg Area Community College in Pennsylvania, and took the assessment test for English and math. Based on the results, I was placed in classes in the community college, where I spent a couple of years. When I accumulated enough credits, I transferred to Penn State. The university requested a high school transcript, and they accepted the one issued by Ifo Secondary School. I now work in Harrisburg for a nonprofit social service organization.

When I think about where I grew up, I believe the Dadaab settlements are geographically and politically segregated from the rest of the world. Refugees do not have legal rights to move outside of the camp. Now when I travel there, I am aware that there are numerous checkpoints, in both directions. On the way back to Nairobi, there are many more checkpoints than on the way into the camps. The police check your bags, the photos on your phones, your calls. If you hold a foreign passport with a Kenyan visa, the police capture your biometrics. Even if the UNHCR gave identification cards to the refugees, they could not use them to travel to other parts of Kenya. They need to have an identity document that is called *kipande*, or *kitambulisho*.[9]

As time went on, things changed, but initially we lacked means of communication. We didn't have television or telephones. We could not go to Nairobi, or even Garissa. We could not go to Somalia because of the conflict there. We could not go to Ethiopia or other neighboring countries. After nearly seventeen years, I was among a tiny population of refugees offered a resettlement opportunity.

When you live in a refugee camp for twenty-five years, you are not the same as others who have identity, education, and legal rights to move around the country or from one country to another, and so on.

AIS: *Kipande* divides people inside the camps and outside the camps. It is a material object that makes spaces and borders, and dictates much larger zones. Can you describe it? Is it a piece of paper, or something else? Is it something that could fit in a wallet, like a ration card?

AHO: It is a document, which looks almost like a driver's license that we have here in the United States. But to acquire one is not a simple process. You have to have at least one parent who is a Kenyan. So, how is a refugee going to get that document? A lot of my immediate family members, born in the refugee camp, cannot get Kenyan citizenship.

One of the functions of *kipande*, from a refugee's perspective, is that it enables travel around the country. In very limited situations, when a person needs medical attention, the UNHCR issues travel documents. Some students are also issued travel documents so they can go to school for higher education. In 2006, the United Nations started giving an alien card. At the beginning, we refugees thought it would allow us travel privileges, but it did not. *Kipande* was what was required, which was issued to Kenyans only. Kenyans can travel, but the refugees cannot.

AIS: Can you describe how the government issues it?

AHO: The Kenyan government and the UNHCR take biometrics—fingerprints and a photo—to capture the vital information of refugees over the age of eighteen. Once they capture that, they put it in a database. Persons in the database may not apply for Kenyan identification. People in the refugee camps in Kenya cannot acquire that identification, and therefore cannot engage in business outside of the camps.

AIS: If you are born in the refugee camps, what country are you a citizen of?

AHO: Somalia. Or Ethiopia. Wherever your parents are from.

AIS: You are recognized as a Somali citizen if you were born to Somali parents in the camps in Kenya?

AHO: Yes, the Somali government will not decline citizenship rights because of being born in the refugee camps; they acknowledge that the parents are Somalis.

AIS: So, people born in the camps are not actually stateless. If being born in the camps meant that a person didn't have citizenship of any country at all, that would be one form of social and political separation from the general population, meaning that the population produced inside the camps exists outside national space. But to be born in the camps and to inherit the citizenship of your parents raises other questions. What if one of your parents is an Ethiopian refugee and another is a Somali refugee? It creates a different form of citizenship and social space.

AHO: Well, let's say a child is born in the refugee camp, and one of the parents is a Kenyan citizen but the other parent is a Somali refugee. Logically, that child should be a Kenyan citizen.

AIS: If so, the Kenyan law could be seen as generous, in that way.

AHO: The problem is that this is not really something that can be implemented. If a Kenyan citizen marries someone of another nationality, then the spouse may become a Kenyan citizen through marriage. But that is just on paper. I know a Somali refugee who has applied for a Kenyan identification card several times, but was denied. The government has her fingerprints and photos; the system record shows that she is a refugee. This woman has one child, and has been married to a Kenyan citizen for over five years, and lives in Kenya with her husband, but she is still a refugee, and was never able to get a Kenyan citizenship.

AIS: On what grounds was she denied?

AHO: It is not really clear on what grounds she was denied. Even though one can apply for citizenship through marriage under Kenyan law, the process typically ends when the authorities find out the applicant is a refugee. Rather than requesting further evidence of proof of relationship, such as a marriage certificate, to determine the eligibility of the claim, the government usually neglects to make the request.

AIS: Does she live in the camps?

AHO: No, she lives in Garissa.

AIS: Does her child have a Kenyan birth certificate?

AHO: Yes. At age eighteen, he will either register as a refugee, or apply for citizenship through his father. And let me explain the process of applying for identification cards, at least what I remember; things may have changed. First of all, the process doesn't happen every day. The opportunity comes along two to three times a year. There is a clerk from the central government who goes to one part of the city or to one village, with the biometrics equipment. That person waits for the elders to come. Then they gather the local government employees and people from the community. If I were the applicant, I would say: my name is so-and-so, and I am the son of so-and-so. Now, the community would have to say: Oh, we know him! They would have to identify me and verify whether I was the person I said I was. They would have to identify where I was born, and when I was born.

AIS: Is it done in a public place?

AHO: They might do it in a school. And that's just the first part of it. These two or three government representatives collect all the biometric data, and they process it. After processing the application, if they find out that the applicant was once a refugee, it would likely be denied. If not, in about three to four months, the applicant would acquire *kipande*.

Now, the child I was talking about earlier is currently four years old. After he finishes high school, if he doesn't go through the refugee registration process, he should be able to apply for *kipande*, or *kitambulisho*, and would most likely have no problem acquiring it.

AIS: Why would he apply to be a refugee if he could become a citizen?

AHO: Some people make a claim to refugee status to receive different forms of aid from the camps, including food. Some local citizens are able to register as refugees and come twice a month during the aid distributions to collect food, along with what the agencies call "non-food items," like plastic sheeting and other materials. Relatives and friends update them with phone calls or text messages as goods become available.

AIS: At age eighteen, he could go through the process of registering as a refugee or a citizen. In your experience, one is not necessarily more beneficial than the other?

AHO: Not necessarily. But I never applied for *kipande*. Anyway, if I went to the committee, who would recognize me? It is unlikely that someone would apply without a strong case.

AIS: The processes that produce these divisions begin earlier than age eighteen. When did you get a refugee card?

AHO: Age five or six.

AIS: Were you on your parents' card or did you have your own?

AHO: When we first came, we were head-counted. Our names were put in a book, and entered in a computer record later on. We were given a small card, for a family of one to twelve.

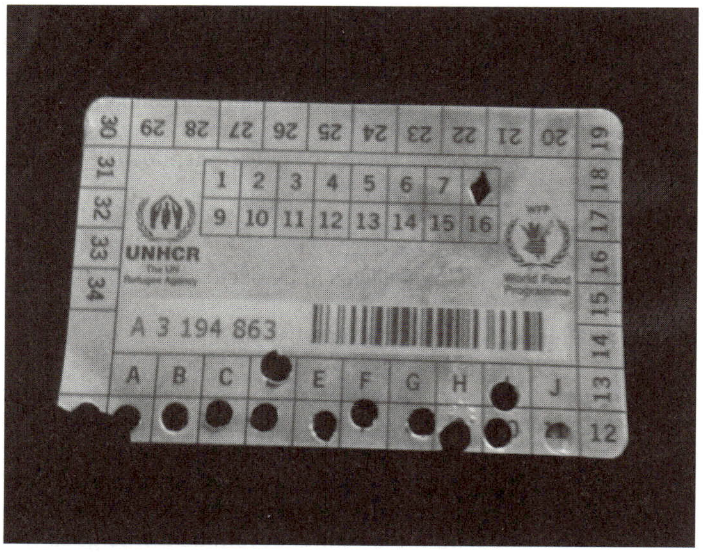

Fig. 2 **UNHCR ration card, photo courtesy of Alishine Osman.**

AIS: Were your parents with you?

AHO: Yes, one of my parents was there. There were seven of us at the time, but they punched number six. When we went to the ration distribution center, we were given rations for six.

AIS: But the cards are in categories, and one of the cards is for a family size of one to twelve. Is there a family size category larger than that?

AHO: At the beginning, the maximum family size on the cards was twelve. Some families had two cards: one was punched for twelve and another for the remaining number. Today the ration cards can be punched for up to sixteen.

AIS: I suppose the number of dependents becomes crucial on distribution days, and even one extra ration can reverse a family's fortunes. When I visited the food distribution center in Ifo, I began to realize how it enacted power dynamics through architecture alone, by controlling the material flow of goods. There is a visible threshold that you can see in the photo, between the person receiving aid and the person placed in the position to distribute it. But this architecture

Fig. 3 **Food distribution point, Ifo camp, photo by Anooradha Iyer Siddiqi.**

represents boundaries between these two people and the agencies or donors as well. I remember the World Food Programme officer describing a refugee dispute over who was selected to distribute rations. It puts into play incredible power differences.

The donkey carts lined up outside the distribution point also spoke to the existence of differentiated economic zones in the camp and the possibility of a real socio-economic gradient from the camp interior to the perimeter. Aid recipients in Dadaab generally sell portions of their ration at the market just after distribution days. The donkey carts facilitated the sale of rations by people in the camp to people at the camp exterior. If you live close to the food distribution point, you can transport rations to your domicile without this additional expenditure. If you live outside the camp, you are likely an unregistered asylum-seeker, do not receive rations like a registered refugee, and have to buy food and hire transport to move it from the center. For me, the image of the donkey carts suggested a disaggregation of the informal economy: there are the wholesalers, the delivery people, the cart owners and renters, the local retailers, and the consumers. They each occupy coordinates in space that can be mapped in relation to the distribution center. Here, the design of the camp matters, as does the allocation of plots, especially in terms of the proximity of all points to the aid distribution point.

Fig. 4 **Secondary distributors outside food distribution point, Ifo camp, photo by Anooradha Iyer Siddiqi.**

Fig. 5 **Market, Ifo camp, photo by Anooradha Iyer Siddiqi.**

AIS: I was also amazed by the markets; I saw everything being sold, from goat meat and camel's milk, to construction supplies, to bed frames and mattresses, to televisions and cellphones. And the markets in the camps do not look different from the market in Dadaab town. But because of the informal economy, you could exchange hundreds of U.S. dollars in the camps; you couldn't do that in town.

Fig. 6 **Market, Dadaab, photo by Anooradha Iyer Siddiqi.**

And the food distribution points and markets were not the only charged spaces. The water distribution points seemed even more volatile. I took this photo at a tap stand that had been fenced off by one of the refugees.

Fig. 7 **Water distribution point, Ifo camp, photo courtesy of Bethany Young.**

AHO: This photo looks like the tap stand where I used to live, in sector A in Ifo camp. Somebody built a fence around it. Twice a month, when we received the food ration, we would sell some flour and give that person a portion of our ration—equivalent to one dollar—to protect the water. It was a mutual agreement; otherwise, people would misuse the water equipment, or even break the tap. Water usually runs from 7:30 A.M. to 11:30 A.M., and again after 2 P.M. This photo was probably taken at around 1 P.M. People bring water cans, and put them in line. They put them in order on a first-come, first-serve basis, and over time, they have worked out a particular order. That's the system, but sometimes people breach the system, and you'll find people fighting over this. Once we had to move from Block B to another block in Ifo because of water scarcity. Some blocks had more water than other blocks. There were no individual pipes or water storage systems for families. So if the water source equipment was broken or the pump was out of fuel then there would be no water for the families until it got fixed. We experienced this several times. This may be one of the biggest differences between life in the camps and in nearby towns like Dadaab or Garissa. The Kenyans have water running in their individual households or a system that reserves water in case of a shortage. That is not the case for the refugees.

AIS: It's very difficult. In addition to the harshness of this life, the problems are based on certain forms of resource scarcity that Kenyans also feel. At this stage, the situation is also predicated on a politically awkward condition. After twenty-five years, with many refugees intermarried or in the same clan as members of the host community, divisions like these are in many ways *only* political—not social, or anything else.

I want to return to this question of how you were able to move around on a regular basis. Were you able to leave Ifo, other than in extreme circumstances?

AHO: I could not leave permanently, but I could go to other camps temporarily.

AIS: What about when you were working for the NRC?

AHO: Not unless I had a requirement for something official and had to travel for the organization, in which case I had to arrange for travel documents and paperwork. I couldn't just travel. But remember, this is Africa, there's a lot of corruption. If you have money, you can definitely travel.

AIS: As an employee of the NRC, could you go to its office in the UNHCR compound in Dadaab?

AHO: Yes, but not beyond Dadaab.

AIS: Could you go to the central humanitarian compound before you started working for the NRC?

AHO: Yes. Even as a regular refugee you could travel to the UNHCR compound in Dadaab. Beyond Dadaab is where the problem is.

AIS: If you lived in Ifo, how would you get to the other camps, Hagadera or Dagaheley, which are far away by foot? Would you take a vehicle, or would you walk? It's about thirteen kilometers, and took us a little over twenty minutes in a car. Do people take *matatus* [shared minibuses]?[10]

AHO: There are not a lot of people taking *matatus*. You have to wait until enough people are on the *matatu* for it to go, and instead of waiting, people would walk. I would often walk to Dagaheley. I have walked so many times from Ifo to Dadaab to Hagadera.

Fig. 8 **Highway from Dadaab to Ifo, photo by Anooradha Iyer Siddiqi.**

AIS: The crossing between camps makes you aware of the great deal of space that a few kilometers can create. The landscape is very harsh, with red dust and scrub as far as you can see, the occasional tree, and those ominous marabou storks looming everywhere! The highways are unpaved. And when you leave a camp, there is no entry or exit; there are no gates. Except in certain places, the boundary is existential: there is simply nowhere to go. Of course, you can see the edges and the density of the built fabric from above. But on the ground, it seems that it would be easy to be on the road, and in areas where the acacia bushes are high, you could miss the camps entirely if you weren't directed to them. As an international visitor, as you know, I traveled in the UN convoys to move between camps. Because of the security issues, these all-terrain vehicles were required to travel together at set times of the day. Every morning, we would leave the UNHCR compound and stop by the police station in Dadaab to pick up our police escort. I wasn't allowed to walk anywhere because the agencies had to assume responsibility for me, and they wouldn't let me do my work unless I remained with a police escort. It felt overblown at the time, but the agencies have been reacting to regular threats against aid workers since the camps were established in 1991. After the kidnapping of the aid workers and the bombings in the camps in 2011, they stopped allowing non-essential personnel or visitors on site.[11] I had never worked in a context like that before, and often felt a combination of shame and anxiety. It put into context how very different my status was from that of the refugees, how my life was protected. I felt the contrast especially when I would watch women set out from the camps alone and unprotected to collect firewood.

AHO: That's true. The agencies are dealing with security on one level, but for the refugees, the security problem is very different. Walking outside the camps can be very risky. There are bandits. There are hyenas. I have seen a lot of people robbed. Some people would hide their money in their shoes. A lot of women are also raped, especially when collecting firewood for cooking fuel. Either bandits are trying to steal from them, or they are attacked because local people resent the refugees.

AIS: The lack of safety ties into the problem of work, especially because livelihoods are related to new power dynamics.[12] Through my research, I became very interested in informal work and the economies that structure life in the camps. Even in the safest of conditions, the architecture of the camp complex seems to inscribe certain inequalities; for example, the distance of your dwelling from the food distribution impacts your income, or the distance of a dwelling from a school impacts whether children will be educated. It seemed systemic, in spite of good intentions.

I did a close study of the NRC's shelter initiative, as you know, which is the project you worked on with them, and I looked at the ways in which it tied into a tradition of self-help and development discourses, which had been picked up by architects and planners working with the UNHCR and the NRC. In their pilot initiative in Ifo, the NRC provided materials for one-story mud brick shelters with tin roofs, and asked the beneficiaries to do the construction, so that they would take ownership of the dwellings, and not just trade the shelter materials. Certain refugees did that work and developed skills around it: in masonry building, construction management, and design. I studied one woman's process of designing a shelter to accommodate a

Fig. 9 **Norwegian Refugee Council mud brick shelter, photo by Anooradha Iyer Siddiqi.**

stock and sales room for a shop, which enabled her some economic freedom to conduct petty trade, and also put her in a new social role. Your role was different, though. Perhaps it was awkward as well; you were neither an NGO project manager nor an end-user. You were employed by the NRC to organize refugees to receive and participate in this form of aid, as well as to direct construction on site. Your position probably did not come automatically with the respect that a Kenyan or international aid worker would receive.

AHO:

That's right. There is this inequality in refugee employment. But think of the other end of the spectrum. Your photo of a *tuqul* explains it. When refugees come to the camps they usually have nothing,

Fig. 10 **Tuquls surrounded by branches for protection against animals, Ifo camp, Hawa Jube outskirts, photo by Anooradha Iyer Siddiqi.**

and cannot get immediate attention from the agencies. They have to find shelter. That's the initial stage that every refugee goes through. Most of us had to build a *tuqul*: a small dwelling made of sticks and pieces of cloth. I lived in one. We had to cut down trees and whatever branches we could find. Agencies give away extra materials, trying to provide shelter and satisfy secondary needs whenever they can. I think they do a great job, but the system has these inequalities built in. As a refugee, I might have a co-worker who is a Kenyan citizen, doing the same job. I might have a high school diploma, and he might not. Even so, he might make five hundred dollars, and I might make one hundred dollars.

AIS:

These jobs for refugees, which the agencies call "incentive" work, evolved because refugees could not legally be employed, and organizations were trying to legitimately hire and pay them, as well as help them build transferable skills. They are positions that would typically be salaried, but instead refugees are paid a small wage; they are often trained and expected to take on responsibility. In addition to perpetuating inequality on a larger level, these jobs create frustration for the workers on both sides. Refugees don't tend to stay in these positions because they can't advance, and NGOs lose trained workers. At the time that the Kenyan government acceded to the Convention Relating to the Status of Refugees, it took exceptions to the right to work, specifically so that the Kenyan citizen's ability to earn would not be diminished by the presence of refugees.[13] It was intended to discourage refugees from making inroads into the labor market and capitalizing on the resources of the state from their position in the camps. A lot of developing countries did this, and the divisions created by the exceptions are in place in legal structures all over the world; they exist in different refugee contexts for different historic reasons.

I am interested in the history behind this, and also what we make of it. There is a whole generation that has now grown up in Dadaab. It is important to start talking differently about this place, in terms of a broader history of colonial, imperial, and post-imperial land use and settlement in Kenya. It is also important to note the ways that Dadaab is and is not ephemeral. Claims are made on it being temporary, but it is more accurate to say that it is forced to *behave* as temporary. Also, after so much time sustaining such a large population and the deliberate structuring of territory, it is important to acknowledge Dadaab as possessing potential that is not only economic but also political. I believe the government's announcement to close the camps has caused so much speculation, in part, because of this political potency.[14]

AHO: Speaking of politics, why don't we talk about the elections? In my experience, at Dadaab, each of the camps—Ifo, Dagaheley, and Hagadera—had its own administration. In each camp, refugees elected one male and one female chairperson every two years. The camps were divided into sector, designated as A, B, C, and so on, and chairpersons were elected by sector leaders. The sectors were divided into blocks, which were designated as A1, A2, A3, and so on, and sector leaders—again, one male and one female—were elected by the block leaders. Each family unit—about ninety to two hundred total—elected the two leaders of each block, one male and one female. Block leaders were elected by a process that varied across the camp, and also changed over time. Sometimes block leaders were elected by direct vote and sometimes they were appointed by a selected few. Many years ago, the position was simply held by volunteers, maybe because there was less incentive to become a block leader in the past.

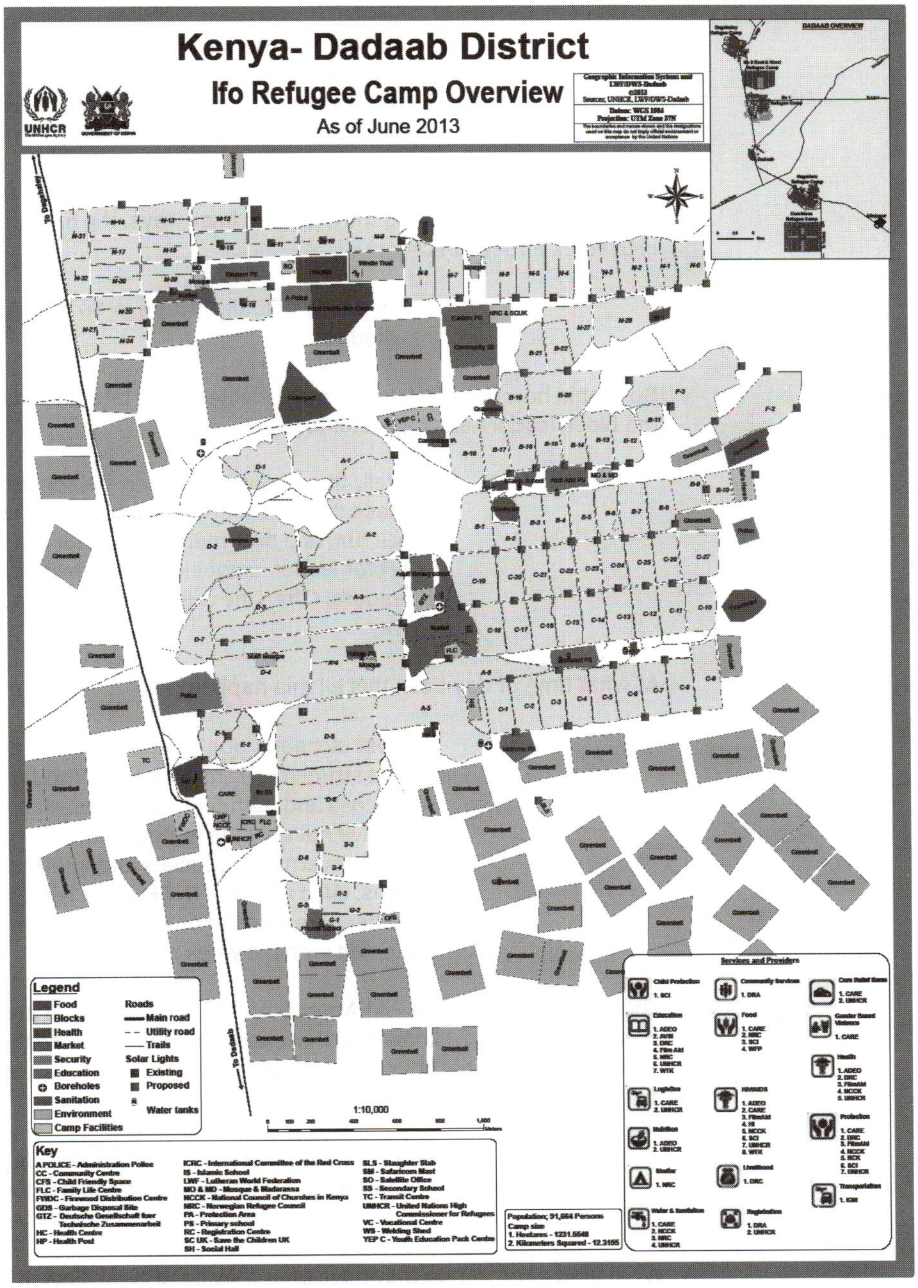

Fig. 11 **UNHCR overview map of Ifo, 2013.**

AIS: These block and sector divisions are standard in UNHCR camps. Can you talk about who would vote? Was it only the head of household, or each family member?

AHO: Anyone over the age of eighteen. And since I left, a lot of things have changed. In 2011, the refugee camps reached a population of a half million, and there were bomb explosions in the market that changed the security status and the political status of different leaders.

AIS: Can you describe the election process? Does everyone meet in one place? Does the UNHCR census and block-and-sector partitioning drive the voting?

AHO: Well, during an election year, there is campaigning in the camps. There is a lot of corruption in the election of the sector leaders; again, they control voting for the chairpersons. There is influence over the process through the distribution of *khat*.[15] The election begins over the course of one day. People line up somewhere inside the block. The person who gets the longest line gets elected. If the lines are equal, they recount them.

AIS: Who does the counting?

AHO: Members of the community, with members of the social service agencies involved. For example, CARE, one of the social service agencies, was involved. If the lines are equal—well, the lines are never equal!—but if the two lines are too close in length, they may recount.

AIS: This is a very physical and spatial process. It also depends on the eyes of whoever is making the decision. In all ways, the human body is used as a measure.

AHO: It's crazy, actually. There is no ballot, and everyone sees who you voted for.

AIS: So that is how the block leaders are elected. And later that day, do the block leaders elect a sector leader?

AHO: Well, the sector leader can be someone already in office. Most of these things are predetermined. We know how many block leaders will run, and how many will run for the sector leader. Remember, the sector leader is not elected by the people; he is chosen by the block leaders. Often, he will buy them *miraa*;[15] he may influence them that way.

AIS: At what time of day does this all this happen?

AHO: Most elections don't happen in one day because there is a lack of infrastructure, transportation, and technology, and because of the process and number of agencies and people involved. The elections involve not only the refugees at the sector and block levels, but also local government officials and international agencies and organizations, such as the UNHCR and CARE, who keep the peace. So, block leaders are voted in one day, sector leaders the next. All of them are elected within a week or so.

AIS: That is a very exciting week! After all of this happens, what are they governing, exactly? I know that the leaders are representing the refugees to the national government and to the UNHCR, but what else are they doing?

AHO: The refugees have a lot of issues! Say they need bathrooms, and don't have materials. They contact the block leaders, who contact the social service agencies. They are facilitators; that's what they do.

AIS: What kind of power do they have after they have been elected? Can they affect who gets *kipande* or a travel permit? Do they control the flow of money or goods?

AHO: I don't think they have power in those direct ways. They go to conferences. They go to the agencies and raise issues. They help families with their problems. But as you said, they do attend meetings with the Kenyan government and the UNHCR. And they do represent something bigger than just the day-to-day management of the camps.

AIS: Why would someone want to be elected?

AHO: They are the first people to hear an issue in the community. They are representing many people; there is a sense of pride in that. Also, their election demonstrates clan support.[16] Winning is based on affiliations. A chairperson cannot become a chairperson unless he has the support of all those block leaders.

AIS: And so the social capital translates into the political. I think the emergent body politic and spatial politics are remarkably uncanny, especially because they have emerged in a closed space.[17] I think some of the social spaces in the camps bring this representative, political world into view, particularly now, under the threat of the camps being decommissioned. The documentation of this built environment has become even more important as an element of a disappearing heritage.

AHO: Yes, for example, I took this photo when I went back to the refugee camp in 2009. I saw a lot of people turn out to watch this soccer

Fig. 12 **Spectators at a soccer match, Ifo camp, photo by Alishine Osman.**

match! An overwhelming number of people there were under the age of twenty-five, which is interesting, because this younger generation has access to the internet and television, and they are using this media to watch soccer! People would come out wearing jerseys from teams around the world: Arsenal, Brazil... Even though this camp is a contained space, people have access to this information. A crowd like this wouldn't have appeared in 1994. This photo captures a big change in the social life of the camp over twenty years. Cellphones and Facebook have also had a significant influence in the refugee camps, just the same way they have had in developed countries.

AIS: Ifo cemetery captures another significant aspect of life in the camps, social as well as material. Dadaab has been discussed as approaching something urban, in terms of both social complexity and form. But I believe the cultural space and spatial designation for lives to end ceremoniously speaks most clearly to the ways in which this place is and is not urban, even as it is a home to many people. A burial ground in a refugee camp may not be unique to Ifo, but, in a context where the spatial separation for the living has been so acute, it represents a very different traversal out of the camps. The irony, especially if we think of the possibility of the Dadaab settlements being closed, is that this way out of the camps is actually an anchor within them, and within the state as well.

Fig. 13 **Cemetery, Ifo camp, photo by Alishine Osman.**

NOTES

1

For information on displacement in Somalia, see Ismail I. Ahmed and Reginald Herbold Green, "The Heritage of War and State Collapse in Somalia and Somaliland: Local-Level Effects, External Interventions and Reconstruction," *Third World Quarterly* 20 (1999): 113-127, 121. For information on arrival of refugees in Kenya, see Cindy Horst, *Transnational Nomads: How Somalis Cope with Refugee Life in the Dadaab Camps of Kenya* (New York: Berghahn Books, 2006), 19.

2

Guglielmo Verdirame, "Human Rights and Refugees: The Case of Kenya," *Journal of Refugee Studies* 12 (1999): 56-57.

3

M. Dualeh, D. Mora-Castro, and S. Wähning, Programme and Technical Support Sector (PTSS) Mission Report 91/14, "Kenya: Technical Mission for Site Selection and Planning of Ifo and Walde Camps for Ethiopian and Somali Refugees. 10-28 June 1991," 1-2, UNHCR archive, Geneva.

4

M. Dualeh, D. Mora-Castro, and S. Wähning, Programme and Technical Support Sector (PTSS) Mission Report 91/14, "Kenya: Technical Mission for Site Selection and Planning of Ifo and Walde Camps for Ethiopian and Somali Refugees, 10-28 June 1991," 1, 8, UNHCR archive, Geneva; Martin J. Taylor, "Refugees in Kenya: Current Status," Lutheran Federation of World Service Report (November 1991), 11.

5

Tom Corsellis, "The selection of sites for temporary settlements for forced migrants" (Ph.D. dissertation, King's College, University of Cambridge, 2001), 150. See also Cindy Horst, *Transnational Nomads*.

6

S. Wähning, "Kenya: Technical Follow-Up Mission for the Planning of Ifo and Walde Camps for Somali and Ethiopian Refugees, 2-28 October 1991," Programme and Technical Support Sector (PTSS) Mission Report 91/28, 2, UNHCR archive, Geneva.

7

This essay focuses on the Dadaab refugee settlements in the Garissa District on the border of Somalia. Kakuma, the other major encampment in Kenya, which is in the Turkana District near the borders of Ethiopia, South Sudan, and Uganda, is also still in operation as of this writing.

8

Garissa is the capital of the district where the camps are located. Eastleigh is a primarily Somali suburb of Nairobi. The central market in Ifo is called "Bosnia," named after a place in the news at the time the market was established.

9

The *kipande* system was used in various British colonies during the late empire to control the movement of people, and perhaps most notoriously as a tool of apartheid in South Africa during much of the twentieth century. In Kenya, the system carried over into the independence period. *Kipande* may be understood as an element of material culture and infrastructure that reproduces forms of division.

10

A *matatu* is a minibus frequently used in East African cities as a shared taxi.

11

Damien Mc Sweeney, "Conflict and Deteriorating Security in Dadaab," *Humanitarian Exchange* 53 (2012): 26-27.

12

My research in the camps included several individual and focus group interviews for the 2012 Womens' Refugee Commission Report, "Preventing Gender-based Violence, Building Livelihoods: Guidance and Tools for Improved Programming." December 2011, https://www.womensrefugeecommission.org/images/zdocs/preventing_gbv,_building_livelihoods_12.2011-1.pdf.

13

Kenya acceded to the 1951 United Nations Convention Relating to the Status of Refugees in 1966.

14

"Kenya to close all refugee camps and displace 600,000 people," *The Independent*, May 9, 2016, accessed December 15, 2016, http://www.independent.co.uk/news/world/africa/kenya-refugee-camp-closure-dadaab-worlds-largest-a7019461.html; "UNHCR appeals to Kenya over decision to end refugee hosting," *UNHCR News*, May 9, 2016, accessed December 15, 2016, http://www.unhcr.org/news/latest/2016/5/5730b5f36/unhcr-appeals-kenya-decision-end-refugee-hosting.html; Nanjala Nyabola, "Closing Dadaab," *Rift Valley Institute Nairobi Forum Meeting Report,* September 2015, accessed December 15, 2016, http://riftvalley.net/publication/closing-dadaab#.WIVzVLYrJE5.

15

Khat, also known as *miraa*, is a narcotic, often traded informally.

16

Somali society is based upon a familial clan system. From the outset, the UNHCR settled refugees in blocks and sectors according to clan affiliation for protection and security. Whether Somali or not, in practical terms, refugees must receive clan support in order to win elections. For more on Somali society, see I.M. Lewis, *Understanding Somalia and Somaliland: Culture, History, Society* (New York: Columbia University Press, 1893).

17

"Kenya says go home," *The Economist*, May 14, 2016.

The Concrete Tent:
A Paradox of Permanent Temporality

A project by Decolonizing Architecture Art Residency (DAAR)
with an introduction by the editors

A mere two kilometers from Bethlehem, the Dheisheh refugee camp feels worlds away. Housing roughly fifteen thousand people on one-third of a square kilometer, its designation as a camp has more to do with its legal-political condition than its appearance. Predominantly cast-in-place concrete, the buildings vary in height and appearance as they cluster close to each other. The dense streets of Dheisheh meander in an ad hoc fashion, and are often only wide enough for pedestrian traffic. The camp appears as haphazard vertically as it does in plan. Many families have built upwards since they cannot build outwards—the camp's built-out area was maximized years ago. It is difficult to imagine that the entire site once held uniform, repetitive shelter units laid out by the United Nations Relief and Work Agency (UNRWA).

Almost seventy years after its establishment, Dheisheh is most certainly urban, yet it significantly differs from a city. The dichotomy between city and camp highlights a struggle that is widely understood in terms of access to resources and freedom of movement. Yet, the more ephemeral, psychological differences between the city and the camp pose additional challenges related to architecture and urbanism. The camp's separation strains the community's overall sense of agency and its perception of both history and the future, which in turn can have a very material impact. Compounded with scarcity of space and resources, some of these more nuanced challenges can be overlooked when approached by well-intentioned architects, who often focus on designing individual shelters.

The following collaborative project by Decolonizing Art and Architecture Residency (DAAR), the educational non-profit Campus in Camps, and the Dheisheh refugee community, takes a step back to evaluate a need for community space that takes history and place into account.[1] Over a period of two years, DAAR worked with Campus in Camps to investigate issues of temporality, history and agency in Dheisheh through the lens of architecture and public space. The resulting project, the Concrete Tent, materializes their collaborative provocations, and is especially powerful in highlighting the paradox of the camp's "permanent temporality."

1 Campus in Camps is an experimental educational program that brings elements of the city into the camp and allows the camp to reciprocally teach the city. Programs include lectures, workshops and discussions, all held in the Dheisheh refugee camp. For more information: http://www.campusincamps.ps/about.

The following excerpts are from a talk given by Alessandro Petti for Campus in Camps, in the Dheisheh refugee camp, 26 June 2015.

"In December 2013, after two years of investigation, Campus in Camps' participants found a plot of land in Dheisheh refugee camp called the "three shelters." The three shelters' site consisted of three original 1950s UNRWA-built structures (three rooms, one communal toilet and a water reservoir) that were still standing. The plot, no longer in use and closed behind a gate, narrates the camp's foundation and its history. But how can a space that is supposed to be dismantled and disappear actually even have a history?"

"The Concrete Tent is a gathering space for communal learning. It hosts cultural activities, a working area and an open space for social meetings. The urgency and idea of such a space has emerged in discussion with the participants of Campus in Camps who saw a possibility to materialize, to give architectural form to narrations and representations of camps and refugees beyond the idea of poverty, marginalization and victimization."

"The Concrete Tent deals with the paradox of a permanent temporality. It solidifies a mobile tent into a concrete house. The result is a hybrid between a tent and a concrete house, temporality and permanency, soft and hard, movement and stillness. Importantly, the Concrete Tent does not offer a solution. Rather, it embraces the contradiction of an architectural form emerged from a life in exile."

"Architecture is able to register various transformations that make the camp a heritage site. And in camps every single architectural transformation is a political statement. Therefore architecture registers political changes.

When refugees, during the first rigid winters in the early fifties, decided to replace the tent with concrete walls, they were forced to confront the necessity to protect their family from the adverse conditions and provide more decent living conditions. They were forced to accept the risk of making life in exile more stable and permanent."

"The project tries to inhabit the paradox of how to preserve the very idea of the tent as symbolic and historically valuable. Because of the degradability of the material of the tents, these structures simply do not exist any more. And so, the recreation of a tent made of concrete today is an attempt to preserve the cultural and symbolic importance of this archetype for the narration of the Nakba."[2]

2 Nakba, literally "disaster," refers to the 1948 Palestinian exodus when Palestinians were expelled from their homes during the war.

"Claiming that life in exile is historically meaningful is a way to understand refugeehood not only as a passive production of an absolute form of state violence, but also as a way to recognize refugees as subjects of history, as makers of history and not simply victims of it. Claiming the camp as a heritage site is a way to avoid the trap of being stuck either in the commemoration of the past or in a projection into an abstract messianic future that is constantly postponed and presented as salvation."

captions

01 Overlooking the Dheisheh Refugee Camp from nearby buildings. Photograph by Alaa Abu Asad
02 The Dheisheh Refugee Camp. Photograph by Alaa Abu Asad
03 The Concrete Tent, Exterior View. Photograph by Alaa Abu Asad
04 The Concrete Tent, Interior View. Photograph by Dima Srouji
05 The Concrete Tent, Exterior View. Photograph by Alaa Abu Asad
06 The Concrete Tent, Exterior View. Photograph by Alaa Abu Asad
07 The Concrete Tent, Exterior View. Image courtesy of Campus in Camps/Sara Anna
08 Girl attending the opening event of the Concrete Tent. Image courtesy of Campus in Camps/Sara Anna
09 Opening event of the Concrete Tent. Image courtesy of Campus in Camps/Sara Anna

01

02

03

04

05

07

08

09

Heritage, Modernity, and Difference in Contemporary Indian Urbanism

Jyoti Hosagrahar

Upon becoming an independent republic in 1950, India sought to shed its legacy of two hundred years of colonial rule under the British to embark on a path of technology, modernization, and nation-building with grand industrial projects. New industrial policies in 1991 set in motion economic reforms and liberalization that transformed India's development by opening up pathways to information technology and globalization with cities as the loci of development. Cities in India today are evidence to these economic reforms. Glass-and steel-skyscrapers of their central business districts dominate the skylines. Signs of a global modernity are everywhere: Special Economic Zones (SEZ) for multinational corporations, exuberant shopping malls, and vast gated communities. With a flourishing steel industry and expertise in telecommunications, information, and biotechnology, India today hopes to claim global leadership in technological services. From grandiose infrastructure schemes to the conversion of vast tracts of agricultural land into IT centers and SEZ areas, development policies in India have offered technology as panacea for many of India's urban problems.

Since 1992 India has been racing ahead on a path to modernization and development. On the road to nuclear technology, an unmanned mission to establish Indian presence on the moon, and a new 24/7 culture of global communication technology, the nationalist narratives of India's modernity seem to have been realized. Yet, in the popular imagination India has remained an exotic land of temples, colorful festivals, and dire poverty. Globalization has been as much a universalizing force as it has been a polarizing one: exaggerating difference, fragmenting experiences, emphasizing locality even while rendering geographies irrelevant.

During this same period of technological advancement in India, heritage has experienced the contradictory forces of rampant destruction and selective preservation. Rejecting history and tradition, speed, simultaneity, and homogenization have accompanied urban transformations in the race to modernity. Traditions encountering this bewildering rejection and transformation have negotiated with modernity to persist—even if transformed. Yet South Asia's urban history, going back over four thousand years, and a vibrant heterogeneity have made heritage an important aspect of urban development in the region. Fragmented urban landscapes have emerged with contrasting visions of productive industrial utopias of mass production intersected by ethnic landscapes of seemingly unique local culture. On the one hand, it is India's constitutional mandate to preserve its cultural heritage, and international standards also call for protecting heritage and diversity.[1] On the other, there has been a drive to commodify and commercialize cultural heritage to make culture and history attractive products for global consumption. While built forms rooted in tradition and history have been and continue to be rapidly lost, new fictions of heritage now flourish as the cultural accompaniment to India's technological achievements.

The past two decades have also been remarkable in seeing unprecedented growth in the tourism industry. A media campaign launched in 2002 has promoted images of an "Incredible India" that insist the country is a kaleidoscope of colorful traditions and stunning heritage, where boundless forms of religion and spirituality as well as arts and crafts thrive.[2] Seemingly isolated from the global flows of technology and information, the places, their unique culture and locality, are celebrated for their authenticity. Corporate marketing efforts aimed at increasing tourism systematically promote places, people, and cultural expressions unsullied by the homogenizing influences of a universal modern. Similarly, an effort to promote cultural heritage weaves together history, myth, and technology in the staged landscapes of Bollywood-influenced orchestration of an ensemble of historical fragments from different eras and places put together to create a pleasing and romanticized experience that I call "heritage entertainment." What room do these interpretations of heritage and modernity leave for the ordinary built forms of the farmers and artisans now impoverished and marginalized by new technologies?

In this paper, I take a historical perspective on India's development after its mid-twentieth-century independence, with particular attention on the rapid transformations since 1990, to look at some of the

1 Constitution of India, Article 49, emphasizes "Protection of monuments and places and objects of national importance." "It shall be the obligation of the State to protect every monument or place or object of artistic or historic interest, declared by or under law made by Parliament to be of national importance, from spoliation, disfigurement, destruction, removal, disposal or export, as the case may be." Article 51A (f) directs every citizen "to value and preserve the rich heritage of our composite culture." For international norms and standards, see for instance UNESCO, Convention concerning the Protection of the World Cultural and Natural Heritage (1972); UNESCO, Convention for the Safeguarding of the Intangible Cultural Heritage (2003); and UNESCO, Convention on the Protection and Promotion of the Diversity of Cultural Expressions (2005).

2 The "Incredible India!" campaign was the first marketing initiative of its kind. The primary objective of this branding exercise was to create a distinctive identity for the country. The campaign successfully established India as a high-end tourist destination, generating a 16% increase in tourist traffic in the first year. See Amitabh Kant Sunil, *Branding India: An Incredible Story* (Noida, India: Collins Business, 2009).

A view of the glass and steel towers of Gurgaon, 2011

Villagers and migrants in Gurgaon outside the office-parks and gated communities, 2011

ways that history, place, and heritage have engaged with modernity and globalization. I focus specifically on an investigation of Gurgaon, a city in the metropolitan region of New Delhi that is a hub and a designated SEZ for the information technology industry and multinational corporations.

In looking at the interpenetrations of history and modernity, I examine the role of heritage and identity in India's built environment as it races to be at the forefront of high technology. Meanwhile, far from the globalized world of information technology, countless historic towns—with their palaces, mosques, temples, lively bazaars, traditional neighborhoods, and living heritage—make up the fabric of urban India. I use a seemingly quintessential historic city, the old walled city of Delhi, as a counterpoint to understand the place of heritage in India's modernity.[3]

HERITAGE IN THE NEW REPUBLIC

The rise of nationalism and anti-imperialist sentiments during the twentieth century fueled the idea of reclaiming a pristine and glorious precolonial past. In the process of nation building immediately after independence in 1947, heritage served as a significant identifier to construct an alternative to the Western imagery of modernism. Postcolonial countries wanted to define themselves in their own terms as modern. This meant a rejection of colonial and Western architectural forms and associations. In India, two models of modernity were most powerful. The first was the Gandhian view of agrarian, self-sufficient villages, which referred to simplicity and an imagined tranquility of rural life as the essence of Indian modernity. A second model was that of an India leading in science and technology premised on an ancient heritage of astronomy and mathematics. India's first prime minister Jawaharlal Nehru was one of the strongest proponents of the latter view and was instrumental in the construction of Chandigarh as an icon of Indian modernity.

In the postcolonial nationalistic rush to erase the wounds of colonialism, the government adapted imperial buildings and reused them, and by renaming cities, streets, and landmarks hoped to reclaim them. Statues of Gandhi or other nationalist heroes replaced those of Queen Victoria or the viceroys. In many instances, the structures and spaces remained but their uses and meanings transformed. This is most evident in the reappropriation of the viceregal palace in Delhi, built by the British colonial rulers, and designed by Edwin Lutyens in the Indo-Saracenic style, as the presidential residence and secretariat complex in the new republic. The grand avenue of Kings' Way, intended for imperial processions, was reinterpreted as the space of the national Republic Day parade.

In part because the monuments were not central to the construction of Indian modernity, those glorified under British colonial rule simply became absorbed into the new nation state as national heritage. Under Nehru, India focused on building a narrative of India that celebrated accomplishments in science, technology, and industry rather than art and heritage as a way for India to claim modernity. The Archaeological Survey of India, an agency established under British rule, continued in the new republic with a charge to protect monuments and archaeological sites that it declared to be of national importance.

THE MAKING OF COSMOPOLITAN GURGAON

Starting in 1990, Gurgaon saw a dramatic transformation from a sleepy village in a largely agricultural state into a global space of multinational corporate parks, IT offices, megamalls, and gated complexes that are more like cities within a city. Gurgaon is home to a variety of huge multinational companies such as Motorola, Dell, Microsoft, and Maruti Suzuki, India's first private automobile manufacturer. It is also home to DLF City and a 600-acre project for an International Industrial Model Township. For many this world of air-conditioned glass-and-steel office towers and wide straight streets, epitomizes modernity in India.

Everything in Gurgaon is intended to convey a placeless cosmopolitanism that, despite its apparent similarity to North American suburban office-park landscapes, has come to represent global modernity. Companies like Hewlett Packard and Cisco, malls called Sigma and Central, and gated residential complexes with names like Bellaire, Summit, and President, signify connections to a world far beyond Gurgaon, Haryana State, and India.[4] Their international appeal is intended to attract worldwide customers who can identify with it as "home" rather than particularly Indian or local. At work, a majority of young and upwardly mobile Indians communicate in English with partners and clients globally, operating on clocks set to New York, London, Singapore, and Tokyo time.

Gurgaon's built form and homogenized global culture seemingly renders history and locality irrelevant. Gurgaon's development is associated with the career trajectory of Kushal Pal Singh of Delhi Land and Finance (DLF), a key property developer responsible for its dramatic transformation. Singh joined the real estate firm of DLF in 1954 only to find that, on the passing of the Delhi Development Act in 1957, the development of any land in Delhi was controlled by a state monopoly. This inhibited land speculation and private development. Singh was forced out of business in Delhi.

By the mid 1970s Maruti Udyog had been set up in Gurgaon as the first private car manufacturer in India. Singh and DLF began to buy land in Gurgaon in Haryana State, on the outskirts of New Delhi, at a

3 Research for this paper is drawn from a larger body of work on historic Delhi that has been ongoing for the last several years, as well as more recent primary research and field work on the development of Gurgaon and other SEZ areas in India.

4 Seth Schindler, *A 21st Century Urban Landscape: The Emergence of New Socio-Spatial Formations in Gurgaon* (New Delhi: Sarai Reader, 2007).

5 Sanjay Sharma, "How K.P. Singh of DLF Group Helped Build Gurgaon into one of Asia's Largest Private Townships," *Gurgaonscoop*, (New Delhi, March 21, 2005).
6 Ibid.
7 Charles Detilleux, "En Marchant dans Gurgaon," *Urbanisme* no. 355 (July-August 2007): 78–79.
8 The sale of the agricultural land only happened in areas where developers were pushing to buy up the land for real estate development. In the vicinity of metropolitan cities, this has become prevalent despite regulatory efforts to prevent conversion of agricultural land to commercial purposes.
9 A village *panchayat* is the cornerstone of the *panchayati raj* system in India, a local self-governing organization at the village or small town level, and has a *sarpanch* as its elected head.

time when it was still largely agricultural. Land ownership and titles were complicated by the traditional patriarchal patterns of family and inheritance so that farms of even a few acres had multiple owners who needed to reach consensus before sale. The average size of the farms was four to five acres, owned by large extended families headed by a patriarch (under the Hindu Undivided Family Act), so Singh visited homes to establish personal relationships with the farmers and their families, earned their trust, and convinced each adult to obtain their legal consent for the sale.[5] With no access to large-scale credit to undertake the property purchases, he borrowed from one farmer to pay the other, so that the farmers themselves served as bankers for the DLF. He finally acquired about 3,500 acres, with more than half the land on credit. They developed the property with the concepts of "walk to work" and "walk to leisure"—the developments were conceived as complete townships with offices, leisure facilities, schools, hospitals, and shopping complexes as a way to persuade people to move out of the congested metropolis.[6] By 2005, DLF City was Asia's largest private township, and DLF had developed twenty million square feet of residential space, three million square feet of commercial space, and one million square feet of retail space in Haryana.

THE OTHER GURGAON

Outside the gated complexes of sparkling towers, paved paths, tidy hedges, and manicured lawns lies the "other" Gurgaon, amid wide treeless streets, nondescript intersections, and whirling clouds of dust under a relentless sun. Motley groups can be spotted taking refuge in shadowy fringes vending *chai,* cigarettes, cane juice, tire repair services, ice-lollies and fruits.[7] Vegetable and fruit vendors negotiate vehicular traffic at the edges of the roads and intersections, their wares on carts or makeshift shelves, protected from the harsh sun or the monsoon rains by a piece of plastic or tarpaulin supported on a bamboo pole. Sprawling masses of slums are obscured from view in shadowy spaces behind the colorful billboards and architect-designed towers.

Beyond ceaseless construction activity, the expansive glass-and-steel towers also demand services and upkeep. Migrants from Bihar and Bangladesh have arrived here since the beginning of the construction work in the mid-1990s, seeking jobs as maids, drivers, gardeners, office errand boys, and the like. Every middle-class apartment and house within the gated complexes has generated employment for a cleaning maid, a cook, a driver, and often an *ayah* for childcare. Glass fitters, carpenters and woodworkers, cane and bamboo workers, goatherds, and welders have all found niches in the otherwise ordered and planned developments that had made no room for them. In the lost spaces beneath overpasses and on construction sites, they have made homes in shacks amid piles of construction material and debris. Filling the interstices between the precise and geometric compounds are the fluid, flexible, and spontaneous landscapes of the villagers who inhabit the surroundings of Gurgaon. Urban villages with entirely different land use and ownership patterns have, over time, become completely hemmed in by new developments that have taken over their agricultural lands.

The older settlements of Gurgaon, Manesar and Farukh Nagar, have also been overwhelmed and squeezed into the narrow confines of their built properties by the new developments. The typical pattern of agricultural settlement in the region had been that of nucleated settlements, a village, surrounded by agricultural lands. Farmers and agricultural workers lived in the village and owned agricultural land surrounding the village. What DLF and other developers bought up was the agricultural land, which means that the farmers and workers could keep their village homes if they owned one. The sale of their holdings at nominal sums left inhabitants with only their homes in the villages—most villagers had a home, whether grand or humble.[8] The marginal, the outcaste, and the landless in the villages, otherwise not eligible for compensations or proceeds from sales, were, in some cases, relocated. One small neighborhood, Harijan Basti, for instance, houses rickshaw pullers, goat herders, welders, and other outcastes of a nearby village. However, neglected by municipal development authorities as well as the village *panchayat,* even today, are without infrastructure facilities like roads, sewer lines, and water supply. Heritage for these villagers was the houses they lived in and streets they had inherited; not some grand monument or palace.[9]

HERITAGE OR ENTERTAINMENT?

Many heritage sites have been driven by the possibilities of attracting more visitors from around the world. Numerous programs of the local, provincial, and national governments, along with investors and hoteliers, have rushed to capitalize on burgeoning global tourism. Forts and palatial residences have been retrofitted to function as hotels. Turbaned waiters and sumptuous decorations offer visitors the opportunity to temporarily live opulent fantasies from the fabled Indian Maharajas. Colorful fairs, houseboats, hand-crafted memorabilia, temple processions, and camel rides are made available to eager tourists in search of an imaginary "real" India. Colonial estates and bungalows have become upscale resorts. They too stand for luxury, spaciousness, and the airy life of masters. With enthusiasm, officials and entrepreneurs embrace India's exoticism and connive in its construction.

A paradoxical inversion of familiar forms, spaces, and identities are evident in

A view of Nautanki Mahal, 2011

A view of the indoor Culture Gully, 2011

Gurgaon's relationship to history and preservation. The amusement park Kingdom of Dreams, opened in September 2010, is one dramatic example of India's new relationship to history and heritage. An international event management and entertainment company conceived Kingdom of Dreams as a "heritage" themed amusement park for live theatrical entertainment and a marketplace to showcase Indian culture, including craft, performing arts, and food from all over India. The complex spreads over six acres and was built at a cost of over $43 million USD.

Inside the park, Nautanki Mahal is a state-of-the-art 850-seat theater for live theatrical entertainment and music shows based on Bollywood-style entertainment. Its façade has been designed to capture the nostalgic elements of north Indian palace architecture.

Culture Gully is a lavishly designed marketplace for artisanal goods and handicrafts from all over India. Street performers and regional cuisines epitomize the theatrical packaging and presentation of India's heritage as an exotic commodity that corporate capital makes available in plush surroundings. Omung Kumar, a masterful Bollywood set designer and art director, has designed the street façade of Culture Gully to capture both the grandeur of India as well as its exotic flavors and festivity. In a single sanitized and air-conditioned structure, Culture Gully houses an indoor boulevard lined with architectural fronts representing fourteen different regions and states in India, with the interiors set up as craft showrooms and themed restaurants serving regional cuisine. Traditional street performers and folk artists lend color and festivity that is reminiscent of a village fair—albeit dust free. A 350-seat amphitheater and a Bollywood-themed restaurant-bar are also part of the Kingdom of Dreams complex. As Viraf Sarkari, director of Wizcraft International Entertainment, a leading communication and entertainment company in India, observed:

> Kingdom of Dreams will offer an experience that has never been experienced in our subcontinent before. This is a milestone in the history of India's entertainment industry and will leave Indians and foreign visitors completely spellbound. We are immensely proud to have been involved in the creation of something so beautiful that brings alive the richness and opulence of India's cultural heritage.[10]

Another type of heritage-themed entertainment that has enjoyed a growing popularity in India in recent years is heritage hotels. Luxury hotels vie with each other to promise distinctive and memorable experiences and conjure tantalizing visions of the pleasure and decadence of a mythical orient. Heritage Village Manesar, also on the outskirts of Gurgaon, has been conceived and promoted as "a Rajasthani haveli style palatial resort" that invites guests to experience a world of ethnic grandeur.[11] They claim with pride that what they offer is a "stupendous fusion of vibrant colours and landscapes of Indian ethnicity and International eloquence."[12] This ethnic-themed hotel is a pristine white structure with frescoes, cobbled pathways, and flamboyantly colorful décor.

NEGOTIATING MODERNITY IN A HISTORIC CITY

In contrast to the global space of Gurgaon, historic cities like Old Delhi represent the quintessentially provincial. Defined by difference, they represent everything Gurgaon is not. Old Delhi was incrementally built over centuries and celebrates community and handicrafts rooted in tradition. Developed by kings, Old Delhi today has also inherited distinctive neighborhoods identified by traditional occupations rather than economic strata that seems antithetical to the organization of contemporary cities. Yet Old Delhi is also a hybrid, layered with both history and globalism despite its dominant visual identity as a historic place.

Delhi was established in 1658 as a sovereign city of the vast Mughal Empire by the Emperor Shahjahan. It was a walled city by the Yamuna River that had a palace, city walls and gates, mosques, temples, bazaars, squares, and well-defined neighborhoods. Until the middle of the nineteenth century, Mughal elite lived in extensive mansions that were almost self-contained neighborhoods. The streets were walled, narrow, and winding, but inside the compounds were airy pavilions arranged around green and paved courtyards. The vast retinue in service of the nobility or under their patronage lived in or around the mansions in smaller units that also had access to private open spaces.[13]

After the conquest of the city in 1857, British colonial rulers set about deliberately modernizing the walled Mughal city—by reshaping spatial patterns but also by redefining the economic, innovative, cultural, and social roles of the city in the region. The ubiquitous mansions and courtyard houses had, at one time, formed a primary unit of the urban fabric. By the early twentieth century, many of these elegant and sprawling mansions had suffered dilapidation and had been converted into overcrowded multifamily tenements, warehouses, and specialty markets.

In the contemporary city, through appropriation of sidewalks for hawking and vending and extending private homes over public walkways, citizens have flouted building bylaws for decades. They have done so not through confrontation with officials or blatant disregard, but through subversion, nonconformity with new regulations, and countless numerous quiet rebellions that have undermined the power of a modern municipality. The residents of Delhi—at once members of a neighborhood and citizens of a boundary-less global world—have nego-

10 Viraf Sarkari as quoted in Sian Dissan, "New Theme Park Is Dream Come True," *World Architecture News,* August 19, 2010, http://www.worldarchitecturenews.com/project/2010/14525/wan-editorial/kingdom-of-dreams-in-gurgaon.html.

11 Heritage Village Resort and Spa, Manesar, January 26, 2017, http://gurgaon.selecthotels.co.in.

12 Ibid.

13 For a detailed analysis of historic Delhi see Jyoti Hosagrahar, *Indigenous Modernities: Negotiating Architecture and Urbanism* (London, New Delhi, New York: Routledge, 2005).

14 In his book, V. S. Naipaul refers to a million mutinies as revolutions within a revolution in a complex society layered and fragmented by difference in every aspect. V. S. Naipaul, *India: A Million Mutinies Now* (1990; repr. New York: Vintage International, 2011).

15 Hosagrahar, *Indigenous Modernities*.

Note: The ideas and opinions expressed in this article are those of the author and do not necessarily represent the views of UNESCO and do not commit the Organization.

tiated multiple identities and geographies. Neither trenchantly traditional nor fervent converts to someone else's version of globalization, for them modernity is "a million mutinies," as renowned writer V.S. Naipaul put it.[14]

HETEROGENEITY AND DIFFERENCE IN HERITAGE AND MODERNITY

In the newly-formed republic, national policies indicated that the heritage of grand monuments and landmarks is at odds with a national identity driven by science and technology. Heritage sites and structures labeled as such were thus caught in a dilemma of being fixedly historical. Once designated as a repository of culture, they were historical and denied modernity. Also by default, being a part of modern economic, social, and cultural networks, they were not authentically historical in many regards. At the same time, many colonial structures and institutions persisted through independence and were adapted for new uses that were similar, but that transformed the meanings of their historic forms.

Out of the new era of globalization and technology has arisen a new kind of heritage-themed built forms that celebrate India's exoticness. Neither national pride nor community outrage at the loss of cultural heritage has motivated the sponsors and promoters of the new heritage-themed places: rather they seek to commodify and market colorful festivity, artisanal products and a nostalgic image of a seemingly medieval royal life that together construct heritage as entertainment.

Historic cities like Old Delhi, on the other hand, represent local identities (and a less idealized heritage) in urban forms and meanings. The discourse of globalization, however, defines their identities based on difference: the antithesis of universal modernism; they stand for everything Gurgaon is not. In the idealized opposition, one is new, the other old; the one instantly developed, the other incrementally built and rebuilt over centuries; the one a temple to modern commerce and consumption, the other a place of ancient religion and ritual; the one built by multinational corporate capital, and the other by the wealth and benevolence of Kings and the modest investments of ordinary residents; the one a casteless society where anyone could make it to the top, and the other a place where a complex web of caste, community, and gender determined one's position in society.

The apparent cosmopolitanism of Gurgaon then is more mythical than real; its seemingly universal form has been constructed on and interwoven with the particularities of the local. Despite the dominant visual identity of its historic sites, Old Delhi too can be similarly read, as a hybrid landscape interpenetrated and layered by globalism. Despite being a homogenizing and universalizing force, globalization has been as much about polarizing and fragmenting. The utopian visions of technology and tradition are further complicated by mythical landscapes of an idealized Indian grandeur that fluidly merge heterogeneous localities with insidious globalism.

Elsewhere I have developed the concept of *indigenous modernities* to denote the paradoxical features of modernities rooted in their particular conditions and located outside the dominant discourse of a universal paradigm centered on an imagined ideal of the West.[15] As a seemingly coherent traditional built environment ruptures, *indigenous modernities* are expressed in the irregular, the uneven, and the unexpected. In the actualization of universal agendas, these traditional moderns negotiate the uniqueness of a region and its history to create multiple *indigenous modernities.* Against the rigid opposition and monolithic identities of traditional and modern, West and non-West, the concept of *indigenous modernities* celebrates simultaneity and engagement. The categories infiltrate each other so that neither form is completely one or the other. Identities are neither entirely global and modern nor completely local and traditional, but simultaneously contain the oppositions within them in an ever-shifting landscape.

Indigenous modernities acknowledge instead the multiple dimensions of subordinate experiences, appropriating the right to define fundamental values, policies, operations, and identities. In so doing, they particularize universal narratives and globalize narrowly parochial ones. In Gurgaon as much as in Old Delhi, traditional social structures and particular histories have shaped its seemingly global modernism. Equally, global flows of capital, information, and communication transformed the cultural landscape of Old Delhi, seemingly steeped in history and tradition. Together these have given rise to a multiplicity of histories and heritages where truth and fiction, entertainment and history, science and mythology, authenticity and fanciful design have merged to create complex narratives of heritage, history, and modernity in post-independence India.

RIO'S FAVELAS: THE POWER OF INFORMAL URBANISM

BY THERESA WILLIAMSON

View of Cantagalo, overlooking Pavão-Pavãosinho

Colorful pedestrian street in Rocinha

It was Saturday March 10, 2012, an hour before sunset, and I had offered David Fortin, an architecture professor from Montana State University, a visit to Cantagalo, a favela overlooking Rio de Janeiro's iconic Ipanema beach. I had been working in the favelas of Rio since 2000, when I founded a small NGO called Catalytic Communities that supports Rio's favelas by highlighting and building on their existing social assets. Over the years we have supported over 250 of Rio's one thousand such communities.

David and I met at the southernmost metro station of General Osório Square, amid shiny new cafés, expensive restaurants, twenty-story buildings, banks, and a prime tourist destination of Rio's elite South Zone. In a matter of seconds, we had traveled up the new, flashy state-sponsored glass elevator from the metro station to the top of Cantagalo and walked out into another world. The atmosphere of the square below—a feeling of isolation among strangers passing by, the emphasis on commerce, the intensity of modern construction, and the noise of car traffic —had, in seconds, given way to a vision of human-scale development, earthen materials, light bouncing off textured surfaces and colored tiles, the buzz of intense social interaction, and music at every corner. Children were playing freely in alleys. Cats lay on steps. Dogs watched from roofs. Chickens were plucking along. It was, after all, a late summer Saturday afternoon.

The visual and sensorial experience was overwhelming. David, turned and said a long, slow, "Wow," as I experienced the same sense of awe at the energetic rush of this moment in this time and place. As we walked through Cantagalo's alleys, the feeling intensified with every turn, with each visible color pattern grabbing our attention anew, due to the diverse improvised lighting fixtures and doors left wide open as residents chatted in front of their homes. External textured walls carved their marks into our senses, driving home that there can be intense beauty in the "unfinished" exteriors of Rio's favelas. Barbecues were set up. On this day, a feeling of ease and celebration dominated the community. A world apart from the formal city, visible below.

This was not the first time I had visited Cantagalo, nor would it be the last. But that experience never repeated itself, there or elsewhere. Not because my other experiences of Rio's favelas have been less or

View of Cantagalo, overlooking Ipanema

A trash pile in a narrow street of Cantagalo

more impactful, but because, with their informal nature and iterative development, Rio's favelas are constantly changing, and every experience of them is unique. Due to the variety of circumstances that produce them—some are on hills, others in low-lying areas; some were settled one hundred years ago, others in recent decades; some are favored by abundant local employment or easier access to public services, others are not; some are shaped by the cultures from which residents migrated or the personalities of leaders during the community's evolution; some have become easy targets for organized crime, while others resisted—the experience of each of these communities is completely and utterly unique.

A close study and appreciation of the tremendous diversity of Rio's favelas is thus in order—in our narrow perspectives on what constitutes "good" planning, architecture, and design, have our stigmatizing and stereotyped views led us to overlook a source of insight for cities around the world?

Cities globally have a stake in what happens in the laboratory that is Rio de Janeiro. Rapidly urbanizing, nearly one third of all humanity will live in informal settlements, mostly new ones, by 2050.[1] Rio's favelas, some of the oldest such settlements in the world, offer a unique window into informality when left to flourish, yielding not only well-known challenges but also essential lessons in urban resiliency, which could inspire new approaches to urbanism not only in developing contexts, but for cities around the world. Despite being marginalized, Rio's favelas, a fruit of *and* engine in the city's well-loved culture of informality, are essential to Rio de Janeiro's history and its future.

SLAVERY, COLONIALISM, AND THE BIRTH OF FAVELAS

The *New York Times* recently reported on a Dixie town in rural São Paulo that was established after the American Civil War when confederate families were invited to Brazil, where slavery was still prospering.[2] In fact, the slave trade in Brazil sped up during the nineteenth century as the rest of the world closed shop on one of the most despicable practices in history, and Rio de Janeiro solidified its position as the largest port-of-entry to enslaved

The Favela of Providência in 1927

View from Rocinha, overlooking São Conrado

peoples in world history.[3] Over nearly four hundred years, Rio received two million Africans forced to the New World, by some accounts more than four times those received in the entire United States.[4] Brazil as a whole received 4.8 million.[5]

Reflective of the Brazilian elite's unshakable commitment to slavery is the term "É para inglês ver," or "It's for the English to see," which came into popular usage after an 1831 Brazilian law that declared Africans arriving into the nation's ports free. It was passed due to pressure from England to abolish slavery, but the law was not intended to be implemented. It served only on paper as an instrument for convincing the British that a law existed, while ultimately allowing those in positions of power to maintain the status quo. Ultimately, in 1888, Brazil was the last country in the western hemisphere to abolish slavery, just as it was about to assume a republican constitution in 1891.[6] By the late 1800s and into the early 1900s, Rio was not only a federal capital, but also a prospering world city, recognized for one of the first sewerage systems and tram lines, among many other developments leading it to be selected to host the 1922 World Expo.[7] Much of this was built on the backs of delayed abolition. At the same time, when Brazil was first established as a colony, the entire territory was owned and managed by just twelve families. Descendants of such colonial elites are still closely associated with power in Brazil today, ownership of massive tracts of land is still centralized, and powerful interests benefiting from modern-day slavery remain.[8] This elite perceives low-income Brazilians' socioeconomic rise as a direct affront to their culture and status.[9] In the early twenty-first century, Brazil remains among the world's most extreme in land inequality.[10]

These three conditions—severe land inequality, combined with the delayed end to a voluminous slave trade, during a period of early and intense urbanization relative to other developing contexts —produced the settlements that have become known as favelas. Rio's favelas were born within ten years of abolition, as former slaves and their descendants, along with rural migrants, made their way to the then federal capital and largest city in Brazil. The first favela, today known as Providência, appeared in 1897. Though they were the majority, Afro-Brazilians and laborers were disempowered politically and arguably still are to this day.[11]

Providência's story is emblematic of the treatment of favelas historically. It was formed when veterans of the Canudos War in Brazil's northeast were promised land in Rio as payment for serving battle, but upon arriving, found no such land available. They awaited their promise by squatting in front of the Ministry of War in Rio's downtown. As a way to keep them at bay, a colonel gave the veterans permission to occupy a nearby hill, which they named "Morro da Favela" after the robust and spiny favela plant typical of the Canudos hills where they had spent many nights in battle. Over the following decades the community grew as freed slaves and new European migrants joined the early settlers. The various new informal settlements that appeared across the city became known generically as *favelas*.[12] This eventually led the community to be renamed Morro da Providência, or Providence Hill. Now one hundred twenty years later, Providência is still chronically under-serviced, and residents suffer regular eviction threats.[13]

FAVELAS AND THE DIVIDED CITY

While North American and European cities instituted slum clearance policies at the height of the industrial revolution and later developed comprehensive master planning strategies, Rio de Janeiro did nothing about its slums nor planned for affordability. Favelas were deemed convenient, because they provided cheap nearby labor without requiring public investment. Since 1890, the dominant policy has thus been neglect and avoidance of Rio's favelas, leaving them to develop on their own. This policy was broken for short intense and traumatic periods of forced evictions in the name of urban renewal, most notably during the early 1900s, the 1960s and 1970s, and during the most recent Olympic administration.[14]

Simultaneously, a lack of investment in public housing has made favelas the default option.[15] Favelas often are even preferable because residents are able to slowly invest in their homes. The formal housing market, even today, is incredibly exclusive and unaffordable.[16] This exclusivity, combined with yet another policy —the criminalization of poverty—has exacerbated the proliferation of favelas.[17] The stigma generated by favela residents' historic criminalization is frequently used as justification for maintaining these neighborhoods that are precarious and underserved by public services. Rio today has over 1.4 million citizens living in favelas, comprising nearly twenty-four percent of the city's population.[18]

To this day Rio is clearly segregated along racial lines, with favelas housing the

Guerrilla infrastructure in Pica-Pau

Precarious Cantagalo houses and pedestrian street

majority of the city's black residents and racial maps showing clear delineations where favelas begin and the formal city ends.[19] The psychological damage of such a system must be contemplated. To historian Katiuscia Barbosa the challenge of fighting racism in Brazil stems from the "job very well done" by established sectors of society that result in Afro-Brazilians rejecting their own culture such that "the oppressed wants to be the oppressor and wants to occupy the spaces of the oppressor, even though they will never be theirs."[20] Hence, favela residents have also been led to look down upon themselves, their own spaces, communities, customs, and history.

The deep rift that is perceived as dividing Rio—between formal and informal, beauty and blight, what is good and what is bad in the city—has led locals to refer to Rio as the *cidade partida*, or "divided city," with Rio's beach-facing formal South Zone neighborhoods on one end and the city's approximately one thousand informal favelas on the other.[21]

This divide is reinforced by local labels and colloquialisms. In popular usage, when *cariocas* (Rio natives) describe informal and formal areas of the city, they use the terms *favela* and *asfalto*, or "asphalt." Favelas are understood as areas where public services, including paved roads, do not reach. Not coincidentally, the main declared legacies of the 2016 Rio Olympic Games have been enormous investments in transport, requiring the removal of tens of thousands of people from their homes.[22] These investments have yet to produce savings in the most important indicator, home-to-work commutes.[23] Instead, the long bus corridors allowed the government to relocate a huge portion of Rio's low-income residents significantly further to the west, in poorly-built and militia-controlled public housing.[24]

This lopsided view of development happily serves the construction and real estate sectors while depriving communities of crucial public services. Sadly and ironically, "asphalt" has been associated with deaths in favelas, where paving works have resulted in increased erosion and landslides.[25]

The topic of planned roads has arisen numerous times during my visits with favela community leaders since 2000. A new road can dramatically change a community, slicing through it and thus removing homes and pedestrian areas, or traveling past it with immense volumes of traffic. Rarely has one of the community leaders denied the right of a road, no matter the negative consequences it would bring. "Progress is progress, who am I to get in the way of progress," Carlos Alberto "Bezerra" da Silva, President of the Asa Branca Residents' Association in the West Zone, once told me about such a road. I have heard this echoed numerous times, from Cantagalo in the South Zone to Pica-Pau in the North.

This concept of a deep divide, accentuated by planning policies, continues to dominate public opinion to the present day. Yet recognition of favelas as legitimate parts of the city dates back to when Brazil re-democratized in the 1980s. Following many decades of favela development in the face of government neglect, housing rights groups successfully lobbied for the federal constitution to recognize urban squatters' rights, or adverse possession.[26] The new Brazilian constitution of 1988 established the right to adverse possession, so that after occupying land without contestation for five years, citizens in Brazilian cities gain the right to acquire or inhabit that land.[27]

By the 1990s, favelas achieved recognition within the architectural, engineering, and legal establishments. From the Brazilian Regional Council of Engineering and Architecture (CREA) to the Brazilian Institute of Architects (IAB), technical experts have recommended favela upgrading as a primary solution.[28]

In 1994 Rio began implementing a large-scale informal settlement upgrading program called Favela-Bairro. Under the program, 140 favelas received upgrades.[29] It was predicated on Rio's 1992 master plan with its goal of "integrating the favelas into the formal city" and "preserving their local character." These laws and others were a far cry from the "favela as aberration" language of Rio's 1937 building code.[30]

CHALLENGING THE BINARY OF INFORMAL VS FORMAL

My British aunt, a lifelong social worker who worked with refugees to the United Kingdom, recently commented about how wonderful she found the "flexibility" on my family's Brazilian side. When a family friend's child needed a home, my Brazilian mother was simply able to "adopt" him, take him under her wing, and raise him as her own. Whenever a problem emerged, a solution was at hand. My aunt reminisced about the days when, as a social worker, she would take groups of refugee youth on holiday to the Welsh seashore. She would persuade local businesses to provide the children with free canoeing and cheap boat rides around the islands, where they would swim, climb, and play football. Today, she sadly explains, the same kids would be stuck in an apartment, because the permissions to do such a trip would be too costly, and their social workers would not approve it. Today, in the hyper-regulated context that is much of the developed world, informality has been banished. Could it be that the broad assumptions we make in applying anti-informality principles, often blindly, are lacking in common sense? Might we benefit from a dose of *gambiarra*, a local Rio term for "improvised solution"?

Generally, there is an implicit assumption that formalization is good, and informality is bad. This assumption has been used to legitimize a number of policies in recent years, from cracking down on street vendors to impeding *cariocas* from dribbling footballs and eating traditional cheese sticks on the beach, from blocking improvised favela connections to the energy grid to forcing favela businesses to close if they cannot afford the bureaucratic requirements of the formal market.[31]

Ironically, Rio's culture as a whole hinges on informality. Not only in the favelas, but in the formal city as well. The *jeitinho*, for example, is a widely used and basic cultural practice, relying on informal relationships and strategies to get by. Brazilian studies professors Stephanie Dennison and Lisa Shaw reflect on this term:

> Although similar mechanisms exist throughout the world, in Brazil the *jeitinho* has become an accepted feature of everyday life, which helps to eliminate hierarchies of ethnicity, gender or class. As [anthropologist] Livia Neves de H. Barbosa says 'the *jeitinho* is a flexible way of dealing with the surprises of daily life, a way of humanising the rules that takes into account the moral equality and social inequalities of persons in the society... [it] works as an equalizing ritual... It also emphasizes the side of Brazilian society that privileges the *human* and *natural* aspects of social reality over the legal, political and institutional ones.'[32]

The *jeitinho* is used equally by all Brazilians. It is learned in childhood and applied throughout life. The assumption is made that "there is always a way." Creativity is the most important ingredient.[33] It is most closely associated with the brand of acceptable informality described by economist Ravi Kanbur as adjusting activity to move out of the ambit of regulation, though not necessarily applying to regulation, but certainly involving adjustment to assumptions or rules that are initially held.[34]

Favelas and the formal city of Rio are not two separate worlds, but rather two sides of the same coin. Informality is seen in everything, from the chronic and accepted tardiness of *cariocas* to the frightening vigilante police mafias, known as *militas*, that run huge swaths of the city today. Yet there is consistently a general rejection of this in others and an acceptance of it in oneself (such as with home extensions, a common practice in formal and informal neighborhoods), either because "everybody does it" or because it is simply the best way to do something.

Beyond recognizing informality's role in the culture of the formal city, there are daily physical exchanges between the formal and informal city, mostly at the scale of the body. Many favela residents work in the construction of the formal city; they provide the inexpensive labor for many businesses in the formal city. The drug trade also has a complex network that surpasses the formal/informal divide. Residents of the formal city rarely set foot in favelas, but some have rental properties or businesses that benefit from the favela economy, while others run businesses based on favela tourism.

At the same time, favela culture itself is increasingly appropriated by other parts of society, such as in funk-themed parties or expensive T-shirts featuring the word "favela," and even in the visuals of the 2016 Olympic Opening Ceremony.[35]

In response to a quick recent survey on Facebook, thirty-one expats who live in Rio, along with a few *cariocas*, gave the following words they use when broadly describing Rio to friends abroad (see facing page):

PLAYFUL
FUN-LOVING
SPONTANEOUS
JOIE DE VIVRE
VIVACIOUS

FUN
JOYOUS
EXTRAVAGANT
CHILL
EXCESSIVELY INDULGENT

RELAXED
EASYGOING
COOL
LAID-BACK
CASUAL

HEALTHY
BEACH-GOING
DANCING
INCONSIDERATE
NONPUNCTUAL

FLAKY
FICKLE
CONTRADICTORY
JEITINHO
CREATIVE

TRICKSTER
OVERCOMING
MAKING A PLAN B
FATALISTIC
DELIGHTFULLY CHAOTIC

ILLOGICAL
ENERGETIC
VIBRANT
PASSIONATE
COLORFUL

WARM
AFFECTIONATE
FRIENDLY
CORDIAL
EMOTIONAL

INTELLIGENT
HELPFUL
KIND

Simply defined, informality refers to "the state or quality of being informal," which in turn hinges on not being "ceremonious," on being "casual," and on "not being in accord with prescribed regulations or forms."[36] What could be more Rio? And why is it presumed bad?

Some informal behavior is incredibly productive (responding to basic needs as they arise), and other informal behavior is not (enacting laws you have no intention of implementing simply to maintain the status quo). In other cases it may or may not be socially productive (*jeitinho*). While formalization in developed contexts is now being criticized at times for lacking in common sense, informality is criticized for its association with illegality. This binary ignores the potentially healthy role of informality, as well as how integral informality is to local Brazilian culture in all parts of the nation's cities.

A HEALTHY DOSE OF INFORMALITY

The question then arises, when and where should we encourage healthy informality? Does this vary from society to society, depending on context and conditions? That is, perhaps each place could have a continuum of its own, integrating a certain amount of both healthy formalization and healthy informality.

Rio's favelas have been a practical laboratory for such nuances since 2008, when programs began to be implemented by the city and state governments aimed to formalize the favelas, either by granting them business and land rights, or by relocating residents to formal public housing. The programs were seen as positive, given the widely held assumption that formalization is in and of itself a positive trend. This process would begin with the arrival of at times violent Police Pacification Units, followed by the arrival of paid cable television, water, and electricity. Lastly, the formalization of community businesses would begin, requiring owners to pay to register their businesses and meet legal and tax requirements. This would sometimes be followed by land titling and subsequent property tax payments.

A study conducted in Santa Marta, the first favela to pass through this formalization process, is telling. It found that the rise in numerous expenses associated with this process made business costlier, and that families' limited budgets were now overtaken by such costs, leaving fewer resources to spend in the community.[37] Additionally, to make up for increased costs, informal local family businesses were forced to raise prices. As a result, residents could no longer afford to frequent their own community's business, opening the floodgates for gentrification. According to the study's authors, this policy "gives the community an ambiguous sentiment of pride that they are part of a formalized space, next to a great insecurity generated in relation to the consequences of this process over the lives of each individual and the community as a whole."[38] As if this is not enough, cost increases led to rent increases, which generated insecurity among renters: a 200 percent increase in prices at the top of the vertical community, and 74 percent at the bottom.[39] Formalization is thus not a panacea, and can ultimately be an instrument of social exclusion, not to mention denying a society of the inherent qualities of its culture.

This was more visibly the case with efforts to formalize favelas by demolishing them and relocating their residents to public housing. Jane, a resident of Vila Autódromo, fought vehemently, but was ultimately removed from her community in the name of Olympic redevelopment. Nearly a year following her relocation to

Precarious Cantagalo houses and pedestrian street

Street barber in Asa Branca

Boys on bikes in the street of Asa Branca

public housing, she told me: "What I most miss about living in the favela is the freedom. The freedom to get together with my neighbors and create a Christmas tree on the main street. The freedom to join the association and work together to build a daycare center. Now, in public housing, there is no freedom. When we came together to erect a Christmas tree last year, security came in and told us we couldn't do it."[40]

FAVELA ASSETS? YES!

The idea that favelas have assets worthy of recognizing, strengthening, supporting, and preserving is slowly—but increasingly—gaining traction.[41] Rio's 1992 master plan recommendation to "preserve their local character" was somewhat visionary. Despite the widespread agreement to not tear down favelas, many organizations and governments promoting slum upgrades do not publicly recognize the assets of informal settlements—beyond their affordability. This goes for the World Bank and the United Nations, whose websites discuss "rights and needs" but not assets.[42]

Despite this, favelas do have a significant and growing number of well-documented assets, both sociocultural and economic/urbanistic.[43] Those which I have identified so far, in seventeen years of work in over a hundred of Rio's favelas,[44] can be broken down as follows:

SOCIOCULTURAL ASSETS OF FAVELAS

In comparison with the formal city, Rio's favelas exhibit greater:

- Cultural production[45]
- Sociability[46]
- Atmosphere of play[47]
- Strong undeniable sense of community
- Culture of collective action, or *mutirão*[48]
- Intricacy in solidarity networks[49]
- Use and early adoption of social media[50] [51]
- Adaptivity and talent for improvisation[52]

Rio's favelas also dramatically further the city's:

- Aesthetic qualities[53]
- Linguistic and musical production[54]
- Independence from the media monopoly[55]

URBANISTIC AND ECONOMIC QUALITIES OF FAVELAS

Rio's favelas exhibit a number of qualities that the urban planning and development fields today advocate for:

- Affordable housing in central areas, providing residences close to workplaces[56]
- Low-rise, high density, mixed-use neighborhoods[57]
- Flexible and need-based architecture[58]
- Narrow streetscape favoring pedestrians and engendering safe leisure spaces
- High usage of bicycles and public transportation
- Creative and adaptive, cutting-edge use of technology[59]
- Economies generated through mutual support
- High rate of entrepreneurship and growing upward mobility[60]
- Improvisation of public services at times, making them more affordable than public provision[61]

These are assets uncovered in our own research to date at Catalytic Communities,[62] which can be generally observed in most favelas in Rio. Furthermore, each specific favela reflects individual assets due to a unique compilation of factors.

Recognizing and applying such criteria across favelas has recently been made easier through the actions of architect Eliot Allen of Criterion Planners in Portland, Oregon. Allen worked with a Catalytic Communities intern, Julia Jones, to evaluate the favela Asa Branca in terms of LEED ND criteria (LEED for Neighborhood Development, a formal certification system for sustainable neighborhoods), and compare it to Ilha Pura, the Rio de Janeiro Olympic Village, which had acquired LEED ND status. As it turns out, the Asa Branca favela ranked higher: it claimed 60 of 110 possible points (gold status) compared to Ilha Pura's 47 (barely certified).[63] Similar ranking systems that take into account all favela assets and challenges could provide a fantastic starting point for the sustainable upgrading of such communities through community-led design.

INFORMALITY AND THE FUTURE OF CITIES

Rio's favelas offer a vantage point from which to reflect on what we want urbanization to look like, and how we want to view informality and its role in developing cities.

Rio's favelas are not to be seen as a temporary, ahistorical problem to fix; they have a long and deep history, as Providência's approaching 120th-anniversary celebrations attest. Given their age and history, Rio's favelas teach us that informality is the engine on which developing cities prosper. it is on informal businesses that new migrants depend; it is in informal housing that they raise their families and design their environment to suit their needs. It is in informal neighborhoods that they build a sense of common purpose, and as Providência community organizer and photographer Maurício Hora often comments, it is thanks to the economies generated through neighborhood solidarity that "no beggars live here." This has all led—despite systemic marginalization—to a growing middle class in these communities, along with a growing number of residents who feel proud of their communities.[64]

Looking deeper, informality provides a laboratory, which fosters and enables creativity, experimentation, responsivity to needs, freedom from bureaucracy and patriarchal approaches, low-cost solutions, and non-monetary-dependent development. Informality allows for a lifestyle defined by strong social capital, which includes developing skills associated with social intelligence (*jeitinho*), a sense of solidarity, and social networks that encourage collective cultural production. It is not a coincidence that cultural practices bred in Rio's favelas are socially interdependent—they thrive on informal exchange between performers and their audience to a greater degree than more formal cultural practices.

There is a growing recognition within the urban planning field, in light of the dramatic changes cities face today—migration, climate change, financial crisis, and cities' growing, central role—that too much planning and regulation may be an impediment to development and the resiliency cities need going forward.[65] The fact is that informality is essential to healthy community building and vital to urban planning. Many progressive planning ideas come from observing informal, organic use of space and engaging citizens in spontaneous and lively dialogue

Community protest against evictions and demolitions in Vila Autódromo, 2014

about priorities and preferences.[66] This includes informal housing.

Resilience is one of today's essential buzzwords given rapidly escalating threats—from climate change to violence. Resiliency represents the ability to absorb chaotic and unpredicted incidents and bounce back, or to be prepared outright in a way that reduces the impact of such threats. Whether in humans, neighborhoods, cities or ecosystems, the value of diversity and widespread experimentation is a basic premise of resilience.[67]

Favelas are inherently resilient. They are in and of themselves versatile, organic, and responsive. Residents are free to develop solutions to problems as they arise, without having to engage in formal processes, bureaucracy, or complicated rituals. Their built environment—low-rise, high-density, mixed-use, resourceful and highly interdependent—fosters large-scale cultural production and entrepreneurship. The more control people have over their own space in a collective environment of support, the more resilient they are.[68]

As a community journalist from Complexo do Alemão, Daiene Mendes, put it recently, "Favelas should not be thought about as something exotic, distanced from reality or pitiable. Favela residents carry with them the strength and energy to transform realities. I like to say that almost every favela resident is an activist, because resistance precedes activism, and the only thing that defines the favela context is struggle and resistance."[69]

Thus, the city of tomorrow, a great city, embraces informality. It experiments to discover the right balance between informal and formal, which continually changes due to context and situation. That flexibility is what the future calls for. We should look to Rio's favelas as signposts to tomorrow's city.

ENDNOTES

1 The United Nations predicts 3 billion will live in informal settlements by 2050 if current settlement patterns do not change. United Nations Department of Economics and Social Affairs, "Sustainable Development Challenges," *World Economic and Social Survey 2013* (2013), http://www.un.org/en/development/desa/policy/wess/wess_current/wess2013/WESS2013.pdf.

2 Simon Romero, "A Slice of the Confederacy in the Interior of Brazil," *New York Times*, May 8, 2016, http://www.nytimes.com/2016/05/09/world/americas/a-slice-of-the-confederacy-in-the-interior-of-brazil.html.

3 Stephanie Reist, "Mapping the Slave Trade and Growing Black Awareness in Brazil," *RioOnWatch*, November 20, 2015, http://www.rioonwatch.org/?p=25458.

4 Renan França, "Pesquisa americana indica que o Rio recebeu 2 milhões de escravos africanos," *O Globo*, April 5, 2015, http://oglobo.globo.com/rio/pesquisa-americana-indica-que-rio-recebeu-2-milhoes-de-escravos-africanos-15784551; Henry Louis Gates Jr., "How Many Slaves Landed in the US?" *The Root*, January 6, 2014, http://www.theroot.com/how-many-slaves-landed-in-the-us-1790873989.

5 França, "Pesquisa americana indica que o Rio recebeu 2 milhões de escravos africanos."

6 Gabriela Elena Weldon, "PARA INGLÊS VER: Rio de Janeiro's Conception of Self and the Contestation of the Favela," (BA thesis, Harvard College, March 1, 2016), 4–5.

7 Olga Khazan, "What Happens When There's Sewage in the Water?" *Atlantic*, March 31, 2016, http://www.theatlantic.com/health/archive/2016/03/what-happens-when-theres-sewage-in-the-water/476013/; Allen Morrison, "The Tramways of Latin America," http://www.tramz.com/tw/la.html; "1922 Rio de Janeiro World Expo – Brazilian Centennial Exposition," World Exhibitions, http://www.worldexhibition.org/1922-rio-de-janeiro/.

8 "Quinze famílias mais ricas do Brasil são donas de 5% do PIB," *Estado de São Paulo*, May 15, 2014, http://economia.estadao.com.br/noticias/geral,quinze-familias-mais-ricas-do-brasil-sao-donas-de-5-do-pib,184946e.

9 "Danuza lamenta que todos possam ir a Paris ou NY," *Brasil247*, November 26, 2012, http://www.brasil247.com/pt/247/cultura/86189/Danuza-lamenta-que-todos-possam-ir-a-Paris-ou-NY.htm.

10 Michael Albertus, "Land and Conflict in Brazil," *Security Watch*, The International Relations and Security Network, ETH Zürich, September 2, 2014, accessed January 15, 2017, http://e-citations.ethbib.ethz.ch/view/pub:142910.

11 Thamyra Thamara de Araújo, "Impeachment: Brazil Shows Its Face (Oops!) [OPINION]," *RioOnWatch*, April 29, 2016, http://www.rioonwatch.org/?p=28480.

12 Rio On Watch TV, "What is a Favela?" video by Catalytic Communities, YouTube, July 18, 2016, https://www.youtube.com/watch?v=Evd6ryt3YgA.

13 Theresa Williamson and Maurício Hora, "In the Name of the Future, Rio Is Destroying Its Past," *New York Times*, August 12, 2012, http://www.nytimes.com/2012/08/13/opinion/in-the-name-of-the-future-rio-is-destroying-its-past.html.

14 Maria Eduarda Chagas, "Book Maps Forced Eviction of Residents During Eduardo Paes Administration," *RioOnWatch*, May 5, 2015, http://www.rioonwatch.org/?p=21863.

15 A few limited experiences with upgrading of favelas did happen during the twentieth century. Catherine Osborne, "A History of Favela Upgrades Part I (1897–1988)," *RioOnWatch*, September 27, 2012, http://www.rioonwatch.org/?p=5295.

16 Camila Nobrega and Rogério Daflon, "A explosão do déficit habitacional no Rio," *Canal Ibase*, April 19, 2014, www.canalibase.org.br/a-explosao-do-deficit-habitacional-no-rio-de-janeiro.

17 Alex Besser, Alix Vadot, Ava Rose Hoffman, Eli Nemzer, and Nashwa Al-Sharki, "Understanding Rio's Violence: The Criminalization of Poverty," *RioOnWatch*, August 1, 2016, http://www.rioonwatch.org/?p=30636.

18 Rafael Galdo, "Rio é a cidade com maior população em favelas do Brasil," *O Globo*, December 21, 2011, http://oglobo.globo.com/brasil/rio-a-cidade-com-maior-populacao-em-favelas-do-brasil-3489272.

19 Felicity Clarke, "Maps Show Racial Segregation in Rio de Janeiro," *RioOnWatch*, November 12, 2015, http://www.rioonwatch.org/?p=25311.

20 Stephanie Reist, "Heloisa Helena of Vila Autódromo Receives First Ever Dandara Award," *RioOnWatch*, May 17, 2016, http://www.rioonwatch.org/?p=28902.

21 Zuenir Ventura, *Cidade Partida* (São Paulo: Companhia das Letras, 2006); Jean Wyllys, "A cidade continua partida," *Carta Capital*, September 23, 2015, http://www.cartacapital.com.br/sociedade/a-cidade-continua-partida-5856.html.

22 Adam Talbot and Cerianne Robertson, "Three Months to Go: Checking in on Rio's Olympic Legacy Promises," *RioOnWatch*, May 5, 2016, http://www.rioonwatch.org/?p=28371; "*JR* mostra como políticos fluminenses conseguem prosperar com o Estado falido," *R7*, November 23, 2015, http://noticias.r7.com/jornal-da-record/videos/jr-mostra-como-politicos-fluminenses-conseguem-prosperar-com-o-estado-falido-23112015.

23 Eva Kassens-Noor, Christopher Gaffney, Joe Messina, and Eric Phillips, "Olympic Transport Legacies: The Case of Rio de Janeiro's BRT System," *Journal of Planning Education and Research* (December 19, 2016), doi: 10.1177/0739456X16683228.

24 Giulia Afiune, Jessica Mota, and Natalia Viana, "The Legacy of Olympic Evictions: A Multitude in the Hands of the Militias," *RioOnWatch*, August 4, 2016, http://www.rioonwatch.org/?p=30919.

25 Felicity Clarke, "Community Organizations Respond to Rains Disaster and Denounce Government Works," *RioOnWatch*, December 19, 2013, http://www.rioonwatch.org/?p=12819.

26 "Primary Housing and Property Laws in Brazil–Rio de Janeiro's *Favelas*," memorandum prepared by Mattos Filho Advogados for Cyrus R. Vance Center and Catalytic Communities, January 24, 2014, http://catcomm.org/wp-content/uploads/2016/05/Mattos_Filho_Memo_24-01-14_final.pdf.

27 "Primary Housing and Property Laws in Brazil–Rio de Janeiro's Favelas," Catalytic Communities, http://catcomm.org/law-housing/.

28 Upgrading is the technical term for bringing communities up to standard in terms of infrastructure and public services, in sharp contrast to policies of renewal or removal. "Crea critica como é feita a reurbanização de favelas do Rio," Folha de São Paulo, May 22, 2000, http://www1.folha.uol.com.br/fol/geral/ult22052000012.htm.

29 Andressa Cabral, "Favela-Bairro: 20 anos depois," Viva Favela, June 12, 2014, http://viva-favela.com.br/513-favela-bairro-20-anos-depois.

30 Catherine Osborn, "A History of Favela Upgrades Part II: Introducing Favela-Bairro (1988–2008)," RioOnWatch, November 26, 2012, http://www.rioonwatch.org/?p=5931.

31 Isabela Bastos, "Prefeitura fará choque de ordem 24 horas no Centro," O Globo, September 2, 2011, http://oglobo.globo.com/rio/prefeitura-fara-choque-de-ordem-24-horas-no-centro-2668321; "Rio veta futebol, churrasco e queijo coalho nas praias no verão," Exame, December 9, 2011, http://exame.abril.com.br/brasil/noticias/rio-veta-futebol-churrasco-e-queijo-coalho-nas-praias-no-verao; "Light faz operação contra 'gatos' na Zona Oeste do Rio," G1, January 28, 2016, http://g1.globo.com/rio-de-janeiro/noticia/2016/01/light-faz-operacao-contra-gatos-na-zona-oeste-do-rio.html; Bernardo Tabak, "Pacificação abre caminho para formalização nas favelas do Rio," *G1*, July 12, 2011, http://g1.globo.com/economia/pme/noticia/2011/07/pacifica-cao-abre-caminho-para-formalizacao-nas-favel-as-do-rio.html.

32 Stephanie Dennison and Lisa Shaw, *Popular Cinema in Brazil, 1930–2001* (Manchester: Manchester University Press, 2004).

33 Juliana Mello, "The Brazilian Way of Doing Things," *Brazil Business*, March 26, 2012, http://thebrazilbusiness.com/article/the-brazilian-way-of-doing-things.

34 In his article "Conceptualising Informality: Regulation and Enforcement," Ravi Kanbur articulates the difference between four clearly delineated situations, those that are: formal (in the ambit of regulation and comply); informal-illegal (within the ambit of regulation but do not comply); and informal, of which there are two scenarios (adjust activity to move out of the ambit of regulation, or are outside the ambit of regulation in the first place). Ravi Kanbur, "Conceptualising Informality: Regulation and Enforcement," Cornell University, February 2009, http://www.arts.cornell.edu/poverty/kanbur/Conceptualizinginformality.pdf.

35 Natalie Southwick, "'We Verify the Truth They Leave Out': Favela Journalists Speak at First Communication Congress," *RioOnWatch*, August 31, 2016, http://www.rioonwatch.org/?p=32373.

36 See "Informality" in William Morris, *The American Heritage Dictionary* (Boston: Houghton Mifflin, 1992), 986.

37 If one lives in a favela in the first place, it is almost always in part due to holding insufficient income to shoulder the costs of a formal market.

38 Again, the psychological factor is important. Formalization as implemented under the pacification policy can be seen as constituting a tenet of this "space of the oppressor." Stephanie Reist, "Heloisa Helena of Vila Autódromo Receives First Ever Dandara Award," *RioOnWatch*, May 17, 2016, http://www.rioonwatch.org/?p=28902.

39 Sabrina Ostl and Sonia Fleuryll, "The Market Goes to the Gavela. Do Citizens Come Back? Socioeconomic Effects of Pacification of the Santa Marta Favela," *Dados* 56, no. 3 (September 2013): 635–71.

40 Former Vila Autódromo resident, Jane Nascimento, communication with author, February 2, 2016.

41 Patricia Sendin, "10 Great Things About Rocinha, Rio's Notorious Favela," *not only about architecture*, February 17, 2014, http://www.patriciasendin.com/2014/02/10-great-things-about-rocinha-rios.html.

42 "Participatory Slum Upgrading Programme (PSUP)," *UN-Habitat*, http://unhabitat.org/urban-initiatives/initiatives-programmes/participatory-slum-upgrading/; "Slum Upgrading Overview," *World Bank*, http://web.worldbank.org/WBSITE/EXTERNAL/TOPICS/EXTURBANDEVELOPMENT/EXTURBANPOVERTY/0,,contentMDK:22628486~menuPK:7199077~pagePK:210058~piPK:210062~theSitePK:341325,00.html.

43 Michel Jaquet, "Qualities of Urban Informality: Case Study of Rio's Favelas," *RioOnWatch*, July 23, 2014, http://www.rioonwatch.org/?p=16678.

44 Theresa Williamson, "Building the Singular City: Land Tenure and Urban Planning in Rio de Janeiro's Favelas," *RioOnWatch*, August 7, 2013, http://www.rioonwatch.org/?p=11075.

45 Jorge Barbosa, "Cultura da favela é cidade," *Observatório de Favelas*, August 8, 2012, http://of.org.br/noticias-analises/cultura-da-favela-e-cidade/.

46 Madison Tolleson, "My Experience in Rio de Janeiro 2015," Field School in Applied Anthropology (Georgia State University), July 27, 2015, http://sites.gsu.edu/anthro-rio-2015/2015/07/27/my-experience-in-rio-de-janeiro-2015/.

47 Caitlin Dixon, "Engaging Play in Rio's Favelas," *RioOnWatch*, October 22, 2014, http://www.rioonwatch.org/?p=18351.

48 Brooke Parkin, "'Militant' Favela Activist Wins Historic Election in Babilônia," *RioOnWatch*, June 18, 2015, http://www.rioonwatch.org/?p=22424.

49 RioOnWatchTV, "Favela as a Sustainable Model," video by Catalytic Communities, YouTube, June 26, 2012, https://www.youtube.com/watch?v=2sT8rhhbCUA.

50 Alana Gandra, "Study Shows Favela Residents Use Technology More than Those in the Formal City," *RioOnWatch*, September 30, 2015, http://www.rioonwatch.org/?p=24466.

51 Ruth Faulkner, "Favelas' Love Affair with Social Media: 2015 Roundup and Predictions for 2016," *RioOnWatch*, January 25, 2016, http://www.rioonwatch.org/?p=26474.

52 Debora Pio, "Favelados 2.0: The Importance of Maker Culture in Favelas," *RioOnWatch*, February 16, 2016, http://www.rioonwatch.org/?p=26854.

53 Jaquet, "Qualities of Urban Informality."

54 Gitanjali Patel, "The Language of the Favela," *RioOnWatch* (2015–16), http://www.rioonwatch.org/?tag=series-favela-language.

55 Raull Santiago, "What's Your Narrative? Alemão's Raull Santiago on the Future of Media," *RioOnWatch*, December 9, 2015, http://www.rioonwatch.org/?p=25510.

56 Williamson, "Building the Singular City."

57 Comunidades Catalisadoras, "Lance Brown on Community, Sustainability and New Urbanism," YouTube, June 11, 2011, https://www.youtube.com/watch?v=3TZZU1YSEP8.

58 Jaquet, "Qualities of Urban Informality."

59 Felicity Clarke, "GatoMÍDIA Host Favelado 2.0 Media and Technology Residency in Complexo do Alemão," *RioOnWatch*, March 17, 2016, http://www.rioonwatch.org/?p=27513; Jody van Mastrigt and Stephanie Reist, "Youth Forum Launches 'Nós por Nós' Application to Denounce Police Violence," *RioOnWatch*, March 24, 2016, http://www.rioonwatch.org/?p=27670.

60 Alice Wakai, "Pesquisa revela dados sobre empreendedorismo nas favelas," *E-Commerce Brasil*, March 3, 2015, https://www.ecommerce-brasil.com.br/eblog/2015/03/03/pesquisa-revela-dados-sobre-empreendedorismo-nas-favelas; "Unidas, favelas e comunidades formariam o 5° maior estado do País," *Carta Capital*, February 20, 2013, http://www.cartacapital.com.br/sociedade/unidas-favelas-e-comunidades-formariam-o-5o-maior-estado-do-pais/.

61 Claire Lepercq, Lovinia Reynolds, and Nia McAllister, "Water Societies and Other Sustainability Initiatives Thrive in Morro da Formiga," *RioOnWatch*, October 10, 2015, http://www.rioonwatch.org/?p=24637.

62 Based in Rio de Janeiro and with a US 501(c)(3) charitable status, Catalytic Communities (CatComm) is an empowerment, communications, think tank, and advocacy NGO working since 2000 on behalf of Rio's favelas at the intersection of sustainable community development, human rights, local-global networks, communications, and urban planning. CatComm supports and empowers residents of informal settlements, evolving strategically to support their needs as they arise. http://catcomm.org/about/. The author is the organization's founder and executive director.

63 Eliot Allen and Julia Jones, "Asa Branca Wins the Gold! Is a Rio Favela Greener Than the LEED-Certified Olympic Village?," *RioOnWatch*, August 3, 2016, http://www.rioonwatch.org/?p=30968.

64 "Pesquisa mostra que 94% dos moradores de favela são felizes," *G1*, February 23, 2014, http://g1.globo.com/fantastico/noticia/2014/02/pesquisa-mostra-que-94-dos-moradores-de-favela-sao-felizes.html.

65 Benjamin Barber, "Why mayors should rule the world," *TED*, June 2013, https://www.ted.com/talks/benjamin_barber_why_mayors_should_rule_the_world?language=en.

66 Daniel Campo, *The Accidental Playground*, Fordham University Press, 2013.

67 Paul van Helden, "Adaptation, redundancy or resilience," *European Molecular Biology Association* 12, no. 9 (September 2011), http://www.ncbi.nlm.nih.gov/pmc/articles/PMC3166466/; Recently, this potential of community-led planning was illustrated by the community NGO Raízes em Movimento, in Rio's Complexo do Alemão favela. The government had left a mess there, demolishing homes and leaving debris without creating publicly useful infrastructure, even after a community consultation process. The government argued it did what it did because what the community wanted was "not technically viable... it's not possible to do that here." In response, Raízes took matters into their own hands. They took over the empty lot left by the government's haphazard demolitions and with design help from the architecture program at a local university "prove[d] that it is possible to achieve technical quality while at the same time taking into consideration what residents want for the space. The result will also be a political weapon," explained community leader Alan Brum, "to be able to say, 'You told us that it's not possible to take into account what residents want—and how they want things—and at the same time maintain technical quality. *It is possible*.'" Ava Rose Hoffman, "Knowledge to Create Solutions in Complexo do Alemão: Instituto Raízes em Movimento," July 11, 2016, *RioOnWatch*, http://www.rioonwatch.org/?p=30158.

68 Julie Beck, "Study: Feeling In Control Prolongs Life," *Atlantic*, February 7, 2014, http://www.theatlantic.com/health/archive/2014/02/study-feeling-in-control-prolongs-life/283657; Fatih Ozbay, MD, Douglas C. Johnson, PhD, Eleni Dimoulas, PhD, C.A. Morgan, III, MD, MA, Dennis Charney, MD, and Steven Southwick, MD, "Social Support and Resilience to Stress: From Neurobiology to Clinical Practice," *Psychiatry* (Edgmont). 2007 May; 4(5): 35–40; https://www.ncbi.nlm.nih.gov/pmc/articles/PMC2921311/.

69 Daiene Mendes, "Favelas, Popular Territory," *RioOnWatch*, August 3, 2016, http://www.rioonwatch.org/?p=31356.

Andreea Cojocaru

A Hierarchy of Separation

Emerging Territorialization Techniques in Romanian Gypsy Communities

Gypsy mansion under construction on the main street in Buzescu, Teleorman County, Romania.

Gypsy mansions lining the main street in Buzescu, Teleorman County, Romania.

What if, through a back door, a group of oppressed and silenced yet opportunistic subjects acquire the means to produce architecture and create a disturbance in the modern city? And what if this group belongs to a special category of society that maintains an internal organizational structure little influenced by larger political and economic systems? What type of spaces and representations would such a group produce?

The Romanian village Buzescu delivers a visual shock. Several stories high, its Gypsy[1] mansions are eccentric—even otherworldly. Ornamented bargeboards, soffits, downspouts, gables, bracketed eaves, dormers, corner posts, canopies, pediments, turrets, towers, and balusters, all in tremendous surplus, adorn palatial mansions on both sides of a wide and newly asphalted national road. While common strategies can be identified, each mansion is a unique blend of external influences and original solutions.

1. Official organizations for people of Gypsy ethnicity promote the term *rrom* or *roma*, meaning man in Gypsy language, instead of *tigan* (with the English translation Gypsy), a term that has acquired negative connotations in Romanian. While for official purposes the correct term is indeed *roma*, some scholars consider the term *tigan* to refer foremost to an ethnic and cultural group and that ill-intended uses of the word by some should not deter from its original meaning.

Gypsy spatial practices range in scale from isolated, makeshift homes to dynamic settlement patterns present in all of Europe. The nature of these practices and their relationship with the wider, dominant spatial order—understood here in the sense of a Deleuzian, homogenizing apparatus that parcels, controls, and distributes territory through political and economic mechanisms—is one of unbound historical and social complexity. What is apparent is that the century-long tension between the two systems has led to forms of spatial occupation unique to Gypsy communities. Caravans, camps, urban islands, and Gypsy towns, the taxonomy of Gypsy spatial practices proposed in this article, all represent strategies for claiming a physical location within and often against a dominant spatial order. However, as the research collective the City as a Project states, "Far from being just an aesthetic category, physical form represents the political understanding of the city as a constant dialectic process of inclusion and exclusion."[2] At a closer look, Gypsy-authored places and architecture engage and challenge their surroundings through the tensions they create. The type of dialogue they provoke involves, and at times throws into momentary chaos, all aspects of society—the non-Gypsy community, local authorities, cultural and aesthetic norms, and building and urban legislation. Through these spatial practices, the Gypsy communities do not necessarily pursue acceptance and inclusion, but rather the establishment of a spatial hierarchy of separation, on their own terms.

2. "About 'The City as Project' Research Collaborative," accessed January 18, 2017, http://thecityasaproject.org/about.

This article will concentrate on Romania, an Eastern European nation that is home to the largest population of Gypsies in Europe.[3] After a historical outline of the relationship between the Gypsy community and the non-Gypsy society and an overview of Gypsy spatial practices, I will focus on Gypsy towns such as Buzescu and Strehaia,[4] which represent some of the newest manifestations of Gypsies' space making.[5]

3. According to a 2011 census by the Romanian National Institute of Statistics published in 2013 and listed on its website as of December 2, 2016, Romanian citizens of Gypsy origin number 621,573 people, or 3.3% of the total population. However, in 2012 Amnesty International placed Romania's Gypsy population at 1.85 million. See Gabriele Marin Thornton, "The Roma/Gypsies: 'Outcasts' of Europe," accessed January 19, 2017, http://www.e-ir.info/2015/02/16/the-romagypsies-outcasts-of-europe.
4. Buzescu is a town in Teleorman County in southern Romania. According to the 2011 national census, out of the town's 4,000 inhabitants, between 25% and 35% identify as Roma. Strehaia is a town of 10,000 inhabitants in Mehedinti County with an official Roma population of 11%.
5. This article includes information from interviews taken by the author with Gypsies living in Buzescu during a trip to Romania in the summer of 2011 and a conversation between the author and Nicolae Busila, a Romanian architect who specializes in designing Gypsy mansions, in the fall of 2011.

HISTORICAL BACKGROUND

Gypsies entered Eastern Europe in the first part of the Middle Ages from northern India.[6] In the territory of present day Romania, historic documents from Moldavia and Wallachia[7] show that Gypsies were traded as slaves as early as the fourteenth century.[8] The Russian occupation of Eastern Europe lessened the Ottoman discrimination against the Gypsies and eventually helped lead to their liberation from slavery during the 1840s and 1850s.[9] The treatment of Gypsies in Western Europe during this time period was not much better. Decrees such as "whosoever kills a Gypsy, will be guilty of no murder," issued by the German Diet of Augsburg from 1545, were customary.[10]

The beginning of the twentieth century did not bring about significant improvements for Gypsy communities. A series of brutal measures meant to control their reproduction and itinerant lifestyle were applied throughout Europe. In many countries it was illegal for Gypsies to enter parks, cafes, and restaurants or to use public transportation.[11] Measures included taking Gypsy children by force and placing them into Christian foster homes, sterilizing Gypsy women, and interring males into work camps. Anti-Gypsy sentiments culminated in the Porajmos, the Gypsy holocaust, between 1933 and 1945. Gypsies were considered part of the same category as "mice, rats, crows, vagabonds and Jews" and slogans such as "after the Jews, the Gypsies" were common in Central and Eastern Europe around this time.[12]

6. David Crowe, *A History of the Gypsies of Eastern Europe and Russia*, 2nd ed. (New York: Palgrave Macmillan, 2007), xvii.
7. Romanian principalities under the influence of the Ottoman Empire.
8. Ştefan Ştefănescu, *Istoria medie a României*, vol. 1 (Bucharest: Editura Universităţii din Bucureşti, 1991), 42.
9. Crowe, *A History of the Gypsies of Eastern Europe and Russia*, xvii.
10. Ibid., 34.
11. Ibid., 52.
12. Ibid., 52, 60.

During the communist regimes that followed World War II in Eastern Europe, "the growing number of Gypsies in each country tested each nation's commitment to bring the fruits of socialist transformation to all segments of the population."[13] Following communism, the freedom of democratization unleashed anti-Gypsy sentiments previously held in check by the more forceful and controlling socialist regimes. Extreme violence toward the Gypsies sprung in the year immediately following the revolutions of 1989.[14] In certain Romanian and

Bulgarian villages, Gypsy quarters were burned to the ground, with loss of Gypsy lives. In some Eastern European capitals, walls were painted with the slogan "Kill the Gypsies,"[15] and calls for "the necessity to curtail the extended reproduction of the socially unadaptable and mentally backward population" were common in public political discourse.[16]

13. Ibid., xxi.
14. Isabel Fonseca, *Bury Me Standing* (1995; repr., New York: Vintage, 1996), 154.
15. Crowe, *A History of the Gypsies of Eastern Europe and Russia*, 103.
16. Ibid., 66.

In contemporary society Gypsy communities continue to fall as victims of discrimination.[17] Accused of theft, exploitation of society, parasitism, begging, prodigality, and rowdiness, Gypsies are considered one of the major ethnic problems in the European Union (EU). According to the World Bank, in Eastern Europe, 90 percent or more of Roma households live below the poverty line.[18] The percentage of Gypsy children graduating secondary school is 29 percent at best, and much lower in some European countries, especially among girls.[19] As Romania's accession to the European Union in 2007 increased dramatically the number of Gypsies living abroad; the lack of integration became a major source of tension and mutual blame between Gypsy home countries like Romania and the rest of Europe. As the responsibility to address what some refer to as "the Gypsy problem" partially shifted from home governments to the EU, most measures taken represent just the latest in a long history of questionable attempts. Although more effort has gone into research aimed at better understanding the Gypsy communities and their plight, many implemented measures have not only failed but policies remain dangerously similar to the past.[20]

17. For an overview, consult Amnesty International's "Discrimination against Roma" website, accessed December 1, 2016, http://www.amnesty.eu/en/news/press-releases/eu/discrimination/roma/#.V9GGDfl97Dc.
18. World Bank, "Roma," February 24, 2015, accessed December 1, 2016, http://www.worldbank.org/en/region/eca/brief/roma.
19. European Union Agency for Fundamental Rights, "The Situation of Roma in 11 EU Member States" (2012), accessed December 1, 2016, http://fra.europa.eu/sites/default/files/fra_uploads/2099-FRA-2012-Roma-at-a-glance_EN.pdf.
20. In 2010, the French government forcefully closed down Gypsy camps and returned the Gypsies, EU citizens with Romanian passports, to Romania. Each deported Roma was given 300 euros and an additional 100 euros per child. According to the same BBC report, France repatriated 10,000 Roma in 2010, and "other European countries, including Germany, Italy, Denmark and Sweden pursued similar policies." "France sends Roma Gypsies back to Romania," *BBC News Europe*, August 20, 2010, accessed December 1, 2016, http://www.bbc.com/news/world-europe-11020429.

The label of "ethnic problem" attached to Gypsies is difficult to unpack, as it conflates contemporary forms of prejudice as well as real negative consequences that local communities incur due to individual Gypsies' actions. Many of these behaviors might begin as cultural misunderstandings, but can quickly turn into legal infractions and public health concerns. Such practices include squatting in public areas, itinerant lifestyles, unconventional occupations, and a wide range of documented criminal activities. Growing up in a predominantly non-Gypsy neighborhood in Romania, I nonetheless had daily exposure to naked Gypsy children emptying street trash cans, others swearing and exposing genitalia aimed at "cursing" the non-Gypsies, street violence against younger non-Gypsy children, and store owners refusing to sell goods to Gypsies. Worse offenses are extensively covered by Romanian media. There are numerous accounts of "Gypsy mafia" running illegal lending schemes followed by death threats to recuperate money, control over farmer markets, organized child exploitation through begging networks, drug trafficking, and so on.[21]

21. See, for example, Ionut Muresan, "Omerta intr-un oras intreg: cum au instituit camatarii Clanului Barcsa legea tacerii in Reghin," *Evz Group*, June 4, 2016, accessed December 1, 2016, http://www.evz.ro/omer-ta-intr-un-oras-intreg-cum-au-instituit-camatarii-clanului-barcsa-legea-tacerii-in-reghin.html (in Romanian); or "Mafia tiganeasca a pietelor galatene," *Impact Est*, accessed December 1, 2016, http://impact-est.ro/republicuta-galati/mafia-tiganeasca-a-pietelor-galatene (in Romanian).

Such behaviors and illegal activities are tied into the discriminatory attitude of the Romanian community, leading to a seemingly endless vicious cycle. In contemporary Romanian society, the word *tigan*, meaning "Gypsy," has become the word of choice to describe almost any undesired aspect of an individual, from political corruption to rude or criminal behavior. The term, and its negative connotations, is increasing in daily use across all age groups, social classes, medias, and environments.

View of main street in Buzescu, Teleorman County, Romania.

Gypsy mansions lining the main street in Buzescu, Teleorman County, Romania.

SPATIAL TAXONOMY

The long history of tensions between Gypsy communities and larger society has fueled the development of alternative modes of spatial occupation and spatial production. The taxonomy below outlines four of these main strategies.

The Gypsy caravan is perhaps the earliest form of Gypsy spatial organization following their release from slavery and reflects their status as citizens free to move but without land ownership. Extended families often lived in caravans, consisting of several carriages. Traditionally, the caravan moved from one town to another selling specific Gypsy products and, in the absence of well-developed transportation and trade routes, Gypsy caravans have played an important role in the economies of small Romanian towns. As many elderly Romanians recall, their arrival was an anticipated event in the town's life. According to many accounts, Gypsies did not disdain but showed an affinity for the itinerant life style. They appropriated it into their culture and identity, which is consistent with their inclination to cultivate and celebrate characteristics that separate them from the non-Gypsies.[22]

22. The following recording from a dialogue with a Gypsy man from the 1930s is typical. "A *muzhik* has his land, and a Gipsy, his horse. Do you understand? Our horse is our land, our bread-box, our treasure. We are not trained to till the land, and we are not as clever as the Jews; we cannot change so easily." Crowe, *A History of the Gypsies of Eastern Europe and Russia*, 175.

Gypsy caravan. Photo by Wendy Corniquet.

Gypsy camps are large groups of people of Gypsy origin who, lacking access to housing, live in squalid conditions in makeshift abodes, typically at the outskirts of cities. In many cases the camps are dismantled after a few months by the local authorities and the community is forced to travel to a different location. Examples in contemporary society abound and have been widely covered by the media. In the context of urban studies, it is noteworthy that since Romania's accession to the European Union, camps of Romanian Gypsies can be found at the outskirts of many Western European cities. In this new context, their existence and cyclical demolition has been raising questions about the legal nature, ownership, and use of land on the periphery of cities and has been highlighting cracks in the European project of free movement.

A gypsy camp in the Craica neighborhood of Baia Mare, Maramus County, Romania. Photo by Zsolt Czegledi.

Gypsy islands are small groupings of Gypsy houses in predominantly non-Gypsy areas sometimes referred to as Gypsy "pockets" by the locals. They can consist of two or three houses in a neighborhood, such as Medeea in my hometown of Constanta, or they occupy a larger area, such as in Ferentari, a neighborhood in Bucharest. In the case of the former,

Gypsy houses, typically existing structures bought from non-Gypsy owners, become easily recognizable from the rest, as they often lack gardens, host multiple families, and in time reveal that the owners have a different understanding of property maintenance than their non-Gypsy neighbors. In the case of Ferentari, a hotspot for drug addicts, prostitution, and criminality, poor Gypsy communities live in dilapidated apartment buildings.

Gypsy island. Photo by Nikolay Kozlovich.

Gypsy towns are urban or semi-urban settlements where significant areas are now owned by the Gypsy community. Unlike Gypsy islands, Gypsy-commissioned buildings in Gypsy towns have come to visually and organizationally dominate and redefine the urban nature of the town. Examples such as Buzescu represent a new and little understood type of Gypsy spatial practice. The remarkable willingness of affluent Gypsy communities to engage at the urban scale in such a resource intensive (and place-based) endeavor such as architecture marks a new chapter in their spatial practices and in their relationship with the non-Gypsy community.

Without a closer look at the nature of Gypsy society, it would be premature to interpret the above spatial strategies as traditional acts of settlement in the sense of "a primary act of social mobilization in order to define and reproduce specific forms of life."[23] In fact, the insular and opaque nature of Gypsy society might make an overt physical manifestation of their inner organization undesirable. As such, the relationship between "the specific form of life" of the Gypsy community and its spatial manifestations is characterized in each of the four strategies mentioned above by ciphered interventions meant to assert the existence of the Gypsy community without necessarily belying its true organization. In fact, Gypsy communities tend to either reject or reappropriate and distort the ways in which the dominant culture has used architecture to signify hierarchy or to symbolically mark public institutions. Telling of Gypsies' attitudes towards traditional architectural signifiers is the fact that Gypsy governing bodies, such as the Gypsy court, a parallel judiciary system to which most members of the community strictly adhere,[24] are to this day never bound to a physical place. While a multitude of examples exist of affluent Gypsy families commissioning mansions that mimic the White House, the Bolshoi Theater, the local city hall, or "the house on the back of the hundred dollar bill,"[25] there are no instances of prominent Gypsy-commissioned buildings that serve a public role.

23. Introduction, "End of Year Presentations: Radical Settlements", *City as a Project*, June 23, 2015, accessed December 1, 2016, http://thecityasaproject.org/2015/06/end-of-year-presentations-radical-settlements.
24. Walter O. Weyrauch, "Romaniya: An Introduction to Gypsy Law," *American Journal of Comparative Law* 45, no. 2, (Spring 1997); and Walter O. Weyrauch and Maureen Anne Bell, "Autonomous Lawmaking: The Case of the 'Gypsies,'" *Yale Law Journal* 103, no. 2 (November 1993).
25. Nicolae Busila, in discussion with the author, October, 2011. Various Romanian news sources for the rest. See, for example, "Capitala tiganimii nu se afla in Romania, ci intr-o tara vecina," *Romania TV*, accessed January 19, 2017, http://www.romaniatv.net/capitala-tiganimii-nu-se-afla-in-romania-ci-intr-o-tara-vecina-galerie-foto-si-video_289106.html#n.

GYPSY TOWNS

Gypsies' recent concern with architecture is an attempt to attain visibility, weight, and presence within a dominant non-Gypsy culture. However, an examination of the Gypsies' use of space reveals something unexpected. Gypsy buildings, through their location and drastic appearance, do not reflect and are not always designed to serve the needs of their community. Typically, Gypsies recognize little separation between their own property and public areas such as sidewalks and street corners. They congregate informally, discuss, eat, or raise children on the streets and sidewalks of their neighborhood, to the disdain of their non-Gypsy neighbors. In contrast to these practices, their mansions stand strangely respectful of the

Gypsy mansion on the main street in Buzescu,
Teleorman County, Romania.

Gypsy mansion under construction on the main street in Buzescu,
Teleorman County, Romania.

sidewalk and are surrounded by high fences. In fact, often only the ground floor of a Gypsy mansion is occupied, and the top levels have no electrical wiring or plumbing. In some cases, families live in smaller houses behind the mansions altogether.[26]

26. Based on author's observations in Buzescu, October 2011.

This drastic disjunction between form and function hints at a complex relationship between the Gypsy community, as producer of spatial conditions and of architecture, and the larger urban environment. Rather than understanding their production of houses as a process of spatial affirmation, it is useful to read Gypsy architecture in terms of layers of separation and exclusion (or rather, self-separation and self-exclusion). The Gypsy community has historically rejected assimilation into mainstream society, which it perceives as violent and discriminatory. At the same time, while they have been barred from holding mainstream jobs through lack of formal education and discrimination in hiring practices, the activity of Gypsies has always been tied to the city as a center of trade. The Gypsy lifestyle is thus both independent and dependent on the city.[27] In this context, Gypsy architecture stands for visibility and newly found economic might, but in the sense of a mute presence. The role of each recognizably Gypsy building is one of obfuscation and derailment, a disruptive bulwark. The buildings are not a bridge between them and us; they are another wall.

27. The relationship between the location of a Gypsy family's residence and the city as center of their economic activity is more complex in some cases, and a proper analysis does not fall within the scope of this article. For example, Gypsies who I interviewed in Buzescu declared that most community members of working age leave their households for periods of months, even years, to find work in Western Europe. The streets of Buzescu were indeed empty with the exemption of a few elderly and small children.

Tactics for insulating their society from a hostile environment have been developed and enforced by Gypsy communities for centuries. Given that the survival of Gypsy communities depends on economic exchanges with the rest of society, interactions with the non-Gypsy cannot be avoided. These interactions, however, are strongly regulated through cultural practices. In addition to regarding the world of the non-Gypsy as separate and inferior,[28] the Gypsies consider it polluting—that is, having the ability to bring bad omens and disgrace unless certain precautions are taken.[29] According to these rules, members of the Gypsy communities are not allowed to eat or drink from the same plates as a non-Gypsy (some Gypsies reported bringing their own silverware to eat in a restaurant) or to share a car with one (Gypsy children sometimes refuse to share a taxi ride with their non-Gypsy social workers). Breaking these rules can result in castigation from the community, which can only be reversed after a certain amount of time has passed or by a resolution from the Gypsy court.[30]

28. Carol Silverman, "Negotiating 'Gypsiness': Strategy in Context," *Journal of American Folklore* 101, no. 401 (1988): 263.
29. Ibid., 262.
30. "The persecution [of the Romani people from the Middle Ages to the present times] has permanently affected the willingness of the Gypsies to collaborate with any structured inquiry into their culture, especially their law," leading them to develop "a tribal system that is operating autonomously within our society, largely unnoticed, with internal laws and procedures." Weyrauch and Bell, "Autonomous Lawmaking," 321 and 333.

Certain behaviors and traditions in the Gypsy community are not only meant to separate but also to dissimulate and to deliberately confuse the outsider. These tactics have been labeled by anthropologist Carol Silverman as "impression management," and they speak to the necessity for Gypsies to partially or entirely submerge their Gypsy ethnicity because it is a social stigma. To this end, Gypsies cultivate multiple repertoires and effectively switch between cultural codes.[31] In their dealings with non-Gypsies, Gypsies change their identity, language, occupation and even religious beliefs according to the region they find themselves in or to the specific person they are addressing.[32] From the outside, one can only conclude that "there is not one Gypsy culture but rather a Gypsy world view that produces many variations of Gypsy culture depending on the particular environment and geography. In effect, the outside world is presented with a surrogate Gypsy culture."[33] Gypsy mansions, demanding attention in strategic areas of the town, also serve as distorting mirrors. They are bewildering and enigmatic constructions that, through their rich semantic associations, are simultaneously familiar and otherworldly. They look as if their cultural references can be read and understood, but they resist transmitting a clear message. They hide more than they reveal.

31. Silverman, "Negotiating 'Gypsiness,'" 265.
32. Fonseca, *Bury Me Standing*, 122; and Crowe, *A History of the Gypsies of Eastern Europe and Russia*, 75.
33. Silverman, "Negotiating 'Gypsiness,'" 273.

Impression management involves tactics that play a surprisingly important role in the way Gypsy architecture is positioned in the larger economic and political context. Their dissimulation strategies, for example, include creative use of individual names. According to a local newspaper, most Gypsy individuals in Strehaia, a Romanian town with a similar Gypsy population as Buzescu, are named *Mihai*. The repetition of the name *Mihai* makes it difficult for officials to investigate the many cases where houses are built without construction permits or property taxes are not paid.[34] Other allegations include suspicion that Gypsy mansions are built with money received from begging in Western European countries. While some attempts at cross-border investigations have been made,[35] it is typical for Gypsy activities to unfold over large and shifting territory, at the border between legality and illegality, and, more recently, to exploit the many gray areas on issues of territorial authority and legislation within an entity such as the EU.

34. "Palatele din Strehaia, ridicate din afaceri dubioase, inexistente in acte," Adevarul Turnu-Severin, accessed January 19, 2017, http://adevarul.ro/locale/turnu-severin/palatele-strehaia-ridicate-afaceri-dubioase-inexistente-acte-1_50ae473b-7c42d5a6639b45b2/index.html (in Romanian).
35. Monika Krajnik, "BBC, pe urmele tiganilor cu palate din Huedin," *Adevarul*, March 21, 2012, accessed December 1, 2016, http://adevarul.ro/news/societate/bbc-urmele-tiganilor—palate-huedin-1_50aee5057c42d5a663a18592/index.html (in Romanian).

The Gypsies' construction endeavors also have a precarious relationship to the real estate market. Without concern for demand and, implicitly, for market value, Gypsies invest in excess. The ornamentation of their buildings becomes an expression of wealth and power, not unlike traditional state-sponsored architecture. Grand European city halls, opulent official residences, majestic train stations, and so on are monuments designed to project and reinforce the historical legitimacy of select political and social structures. In such buildings, more often than not, the visual representation overrides notions of spatial economy and functionalism. Similarly, the size and layout of Gypsy mansions are rarely mapped to the needs of the family for which it is intended, while on the outside each building aims to be the epitome of customization and individualization. In some examples from Buzescu, letters spelling out the owner's first name are integrated into the exterior ornamentation. Such measures and proclivities push Gypsy mansions outside the market. When attempts have been made by local authorities to seize Gypsy mansions and sell them to recuperate money owed in taxes, they have failed to sell, despite being initially appraised at high values.

Nicolae Busila, a Romanian architect from the city of Timisoara with Gypsy clientele, has described, that the Gypsy community is concerned with "showing Romanians what a good house looks like."[36] Busila attributes the beginning of this style of Gypsy buildings to the years immediately following the end of Communism in 1989. While former President Nicolae Ceausescu's closed border policy of the 1980s made it difficult for Romanians to travel abroad, some Gypsies were able to preserve their traveling routes. In this way, it is commonly known that they accumulated small fortunes, making them wealthier than most of the non-Gypsy society, which was heavily burdened by the austerity measures in force at the time. However, these Gypsies were wary of spending their wealth for fear of confiscation and saw the change of regime as an opportunity to spend at last.[37] In the early 1990s, Gypsies began to approach architects with postcards or magazines taken from Western European countries, driven by a desire "to duplicate in Romania the emotional effect they experienced while encountering these foreign buildings in person."[38]

36. Busila, discussion, 2011.
37. Ibid.
38. Ibid.

The non-Gypsy community's reaction to this new built phenomenon has been vociferously negative. Gypsies' buildings are unanimously perceived as undesired mutants and are in constant danger of destruction. The political and regulatory mechanisms in cities like Timisoara, Sibiu and Bucharest, in the name of maintaining control and uniformity, are fighting to delegitimize the buildings and to find a legal basis for their demolition. In locations where demolitions are currently underway, local authorities have been able to prove that the mansions lacked construction authorizations, or they found irregularities in the authorization process. In many cases extensively covered by the local press, Gypsy families barricaded themselves inside their houses to prevent the demolition, prompting the appearance of special forces accompanied by police dogs, journalists, and crowds of bystanders.[39] More insidious attempts to outlaw Gypsy houses target buildings considered too boisterous and outspoken in their appearance. Last year, Nicolae Robu, the mayor of Timisoara, declared in reference to Gypsy mansions that the local authorities have the task of identifying all buildings in Timisoara with the kind of architecture that leaves room to suggest that it is not authorized, "...and we are referring to buildings kitsch, endowed with elements that depart from Timisoara's beautiful architecture."[40] The mayor of Huedin was more explicit, declaring, "I will speak to the authority responsible for construction permits to see how we can prohibit houses with turrets."[41] Architect Busila, himself the target of the local press and fellow architects for his baroque-inspired Gypsy mansion designs,[42] believes that the vexation and acrimony are not caused by the architecture but stem from deep-seated hatred and contempt toward the Gypsy community.

39. Irina Stoian, "Mascatii au fost alungati cu blesteme din palatele tiganesti", *Libertatea*, June 28, 2016, accessed December 1 2016, http://www.libertatea.ro/stiri/scandal-tagu-jiu-romii-ameninta-ca-isi-dau-foc-daca-le-vor-fi-daramate-palatele-1524880 (in Romanian); or Florina Oporanu, "Case ale romilor, demolate de Primaria Slatina", Ziare.com, accessed December 1, 2016, http://www.ziare.com/slatina/stiri-actualitate/case-ale-romilor-demolate-de-primaria-slatina-2285583 (in Romanian).
40. "Nicolae Robu, spaima tiganilor? Romii din Timisoara isi demoleaza singuri, de bunavoie, turnuletele!", *Vocea Timisului*, accessed January 19, 2017, https://voceatimisului.ro/nicolae-robu-spaima-tiganilor-romii-din-timisoara-isi-demoleaza-singuri-de-bunavoie-turnuletele (in Romanian).
41. "Primaria Huedin pune tunul pe turnuletele tiganilor", *Adevarul*, accessed December 1, 2016, http://adevarul.ro/locale/cluj-napoca/primaria-huedin-pune-tunul-turnuletele-tiganilor-1_50aeab7e7c42d5a6639eed1b/index.html (in Romanian).
42. Gheorghe Ilas, "Cine sta in umbra turnuletelor de tinichea din Timisoara? Vezi lantul complicitatilor care i-au adus orasului titlul neoficial de capitala palatelor de tigani din Romania," *Opinia Timisoarei*, accessed October 20, 2011, http://www.opiniatimisoarei.ro/cine-sta-umbra-turnuletelor-de-tinichea-din-timisoara-vezi-lantul-complicitatilor-care-i-au-adus-orasului-titlul-neoficial-de-capitala-palatelor-de-tigani-din-romania/20/10/2011 (in Romanian).

Gypsy mansions embody an understanding of architecture's power to assert physical boundaries and agency at the urban level, as well as to make statements on a political and emotional level. They command Buzescu's main street while remaining aloof and impenetrable to the passerby. Their playfulness with typology ridicules both themselves and the buildings they reference. In contrast to the perceived powerlessness of a segregated community, Gypsy

Gypsy mansion on the main street in Buzescu, Teleorman County, Romania.

Gypsy mansions lining the main street in Buzescu, Teleorman County, Romania.

mansions are power players. And, perhaps most importantly, they challenge, through their borrowed or improvised styles, the visual narrative of the wider urban and political context. There is something grotesque and perverse in their semiconscious amalgamation of styles, epochs, and typologies. The Gypsy mansions are hybrids, multi-voiced and multi-accented, and the result is an almost too literal collision "between differing points of view on the world."[43]

43. This brings the mansions close to an architectural interpretation of Homi Bhabha's reading of Mikhail Bakhtin in "Culture's in Between." Mikhail Bakhtin, cited in Homi K. Bhabha, "Culture's In Between," Artforum *32*, no. 1 (September 1993): 58.

Spatial practices are resource heavy interventions with the aim of catering to a community's needs in the form of walls, entrances, zoning, and so on. In the Gypsy community, the relationship between their internal organizational structure and their spatial interventions is obscured by a complex and evolving relationship with a dominant and hostile non-Gypsy culture. All forms of spatial organization of the Gypsy communities have been harshly criticized and used to reinforce their image as inferior: the nomadic lifestyle was considered inappropriate and at times illegal; Gypsy camps have routinely been regarded as parasitic and uncivilized and, as a consequence, dismantled; the presence of islands of Gypsy homes in non-Gypsy neighborhoods decreases the value of the neighborhood and especially of adjacent lots; Gypsy mansions are considered an eyesore that threatens the aesthetic value of their context. Newly created spatial conditions quickly become targets and are enlisted as new reasons for discrimination.

Space production is being constantly denied to the Gypsies. The non-Gypsy society desires them to be territoryless, a condition even more basic than nomadism, a state of spacelessness. Such a state does exist—it is the space of fantasy. Indeed, in this castrated, territoryless form, the Gypsies have been accepted and embraced by the dominant society. (As any Romanian will tell you, "no wedding is a real wedding without a Gypsy band.") Any other form is too real, and thus threatening. However, as Henri Lefebvre noted, "any 'social existence' aspiring or claiming to be 'real' but failing to produce its own space would be a strange entity, a very peculiar kind of abstraction unable to escape from the cultural realm."[44] The story of the Gypsies' spatial production is a story about the unfathomable importance of territory, but also about the complex politics and hierarchies of physical separation that weave together violence, emotions, wealth, and history.

44. Henry Lefebvre, *The Production of Space* (Oxford: Blackwell Publishing, 1991), 53.

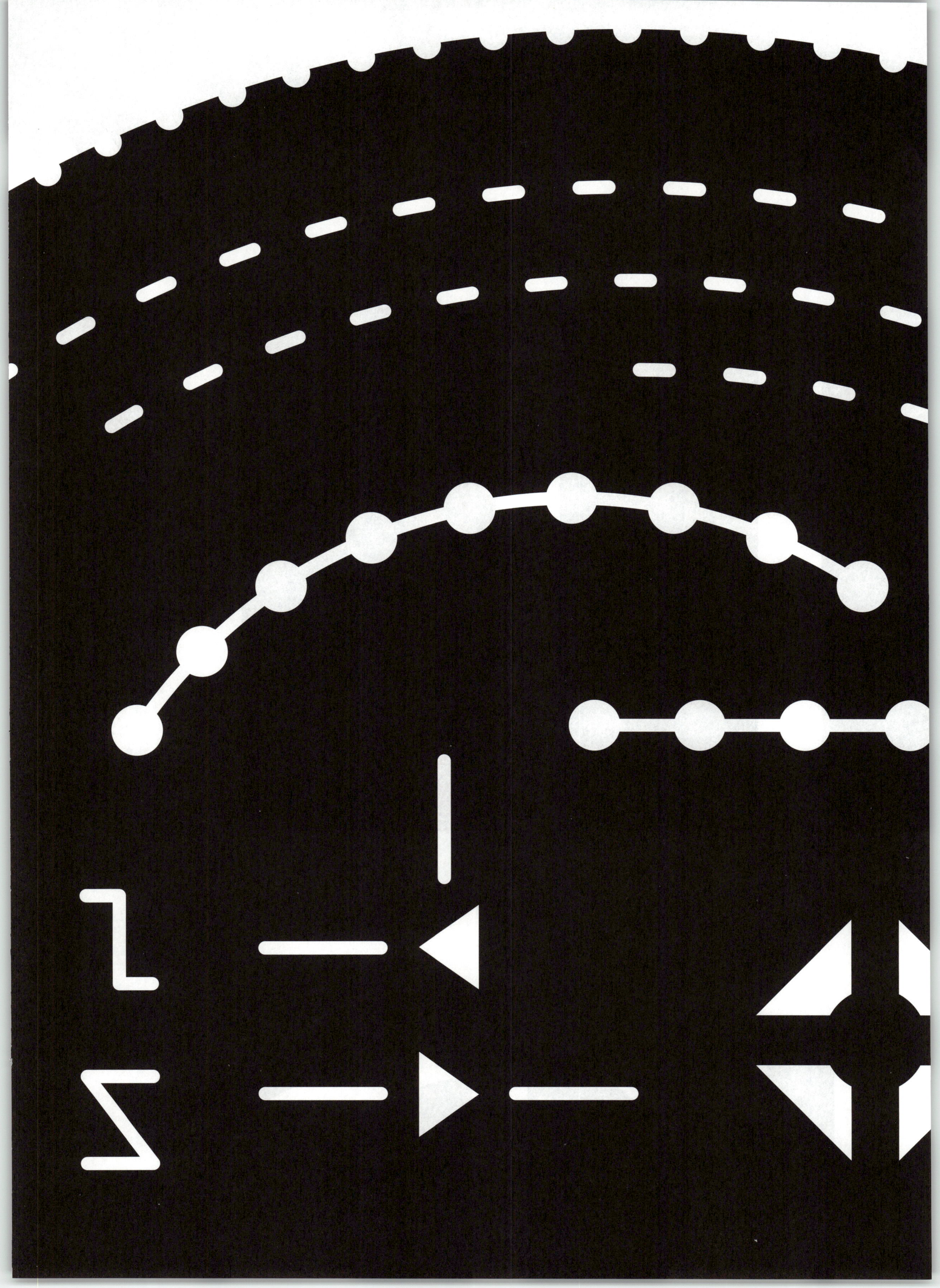

TRANSMEDIA URBANISM: BERLUSCONI AND THE BIRTH OF TARGETED DIFFERENCE

ANDRÉS JAQUE
OFFICE FOR POLITICAL INNOVATION

Aerial view of Milano 2.

I cesaroni 20.30
every tuesday
rete4

Bella più di prima 22.40
every wednesday
La 5

CentroVetrine 22.40
Mon to Fri
Canale 5

I cesaroni 20.30
every tuesday
rete4

Uomini e Donne 14.44
Mon to Fri
Canale5

Casa Vianello 24h
online broadcast
fivestore.it

Pomeriggio Cinque 17.10
Mon to Fri
Canale 5

Mela Verde 10.00
Sun and Sat
Canale 5

Cuatrilocale house
Milano 2
Ragazzi and Partners. *Architects*

Mediaset TV-mirroring of actual apartments' daily life.

Accounts of Silvio Berlusconi's power seldom include two of its key sources: namely, architecture and urbanism. Whereas his involvement in media is seen as a momentous constituent of his political trajectory, what is often forgotten is that his particular way of reinventing the relationship between politics and media was an architectural invention, developed and tested through the interiors, buildings, landscapes, and urbanism to which he and his team devoted a large part of their time and resources, from the late 1960s to the early 1990s.

In 1968, Silvio Berlusconi, then chair and owner of urban development company Edilnord Centri Residenziali, started to promote "Milano 2," a 712,000-square-meter residential city ten minutes from the center of Milan. Presented as an alluring and inoffensive mix of rational architecture and vernacular embellishment, Milano 2 embodied a radical urbanism. Conceived as an alternative to the converging and homogenizing culture promoted by state-centered postwar European governments, this new urban model would instead segregate society into differentiated clusters of specialized consumption targets. Life in Milano 2 was structured by a cable television service that would grow to become the corporation now known as Mediaset. Milano 2's capacity to integrate the economic, social, and political evolution of its inhabitants was fueled by a series of design strategies meant to coordinate TV programming, interiors, access to commodities and services, architecture, and landscaping into what I will call "transmedia urbanism." This coordination was intended to render Berlusconi's company as the compulsory node in a new context in which purveyors, consumers, and the links that brought them together were reinvented.

TV NATIONS

The European national TV networks, such as the BBC (United Kingdom), RTF (France), and RAI (Italy), played a fundamental role in the social articulation of economics and politics of everyday life in Europe's postwar period. While the 1952 European Coal and Steel Community is often considered as the first forerunner of the European Union, the true antecedent was the 1950 organization that brought together the European national public TV networks, the European Broadcasting Union (EBU). It was precisely these networks that played a role in the social, economic, and material reconstruction of postwar Europe, operating within a system where the unifying elements of national societies could be organized from the top-down with the intention of maximizing their power of self-production.

In this process, RAI was paradigmatic. In January 1954, RAI began broadcasting television programs from its Milan headquarters at a central position in the city: Corso Sempione. The building included Studio TV3, which was, at the time, the largest television studio in Europe.[1] The headquarters were redesigned by no less than the architect Giò Ponti. Architecture was already an essential factor.

In postwar Italy, television was not watched alone. In 1954, the cost of a TV set was 250,000 lire—three times the annual salary of a secretary. Very few people could afford them. They were found mainly in bars, churches, and the living rooms of wealthy families. These places, where television was communally watched, turned into transfamilial spaces of interclass enactments. Control over the television signal was precious, for it brought the power to decide what content would shape collective existence.[2]

RAI worked hand in hand with the Istituto per la Ricostruzione Industriale, a public holding company that owned many

Interiors of Milano 2 apartment. Photographs by Miguel de Guzmán.

Interiors of Milano 2 apartment. Photographs by Miguel de Guzmán.

of the main industries that shaped everyday life in Italy—from telephones to highways, food to cars, airplanes to military weapons. By 1960, eighty percent of Italy's population watched television, with RAI playing a unique top-down role in unifying Italian society. RAI significantly contributed to the standardization of language and helped make Italian universally spoken in southern Italy. Moreover, RAI suspended its programs everyday between 7:30 and 8:45 pm to synchronize dinnertime across the country.[3] National schedules were coordinated to ensure rest hours for workers and efficiency in family management. Television delivered a coordinated mass of workers to the nationally centralized industries.

In 1957, RAI began to produce short films to advertise industrial products. The intention of these films was to convey the value of industrial products to audiences who would be rendered into a generic universal public in part by the effect of this commercial TV content. These short films signaled the birth of the TV commercial. The made-in-Milan *Carosello*, a TV show composed of accumulated short commercials, encouraged a common children's bedtime, as it was intended to be watched right beforehand.[4] From 1955 to 1959, Mike Bongiorno hosted *Lascia o raddoppia?*—the most successful Italian TV program to this day.[5] In this massively popular quiz show, the cultural knowledge of participants was challenged and rewarded, with prizes reaching 5,120,000 lire and with the Fiat 1400 as a consolation prize. The public celebrated the collective achievement of the nation's educational competence week after week, and Bongiorno's language was carefully tailored to make participants and audiences feel as if they were exactly the same: equal citizens or "ordinary Italians." Ordinary Italians would simultaneously be the unspecialized consumers and manufacturers of the generic products advertised on television.

This entire process dovetailed with a massive provision of residential units in cities. During the 1950s and 1960s, the number of residential units in Italy increased by thirty-five percent, sixty-eight percent of them built in the thirteen most populous cities. Waves of migration followed a government initiative to concentrate workers in urban areas. The government's aim was to ensure a uniform provision of labor to the factories that were producing goods at a national scale.[6]

In 1968, not only did students protest in Milan, but so did domestic migrant workers, who had come mainly from the south of Italy and who were still attracted by Milan's economic miracle and industrial development. These workers were paid twice the wages that they could earn in their hometowns, but due to the scarcity of affordable housing, their living costs quadrupled.[7] Scandals, such as cuts to Gescal, the government's fund for workers' housing, brought the housing crisis into the streets, where demonstrators demanded more government financing. "Guerra per la casa" (War for the House) was the name given to the protests by *Casabella*, the renowned Italian magazine. In January 1970, an editorial exhorted big industry to collaborate and speed up the provision of housing. It argued that the innovation capacity of the nation's industrial muscle should aid in the development of advanced solutions to provide the workers it attracted with places to live.[8] At *L'Espresso* magazine, architect Bruno Zevi added his voice to the discussion, advocating for the relocation of workers from cities to underdeveloped rural areas, where land was cheaper. All these ideas would rapidly develop into housing projects—but not for the workers.

MILANO 2

In 1968, Edilnord acquired the 712,000 square meters of land in the municipality of Segrate, where Milano 2 would be constructed, at a bargain price due to the noise pollution of air traffic from the nearby Linate International Airport. Berlusconi's political influence facilitated a reduction of air traffic and the acceptance by left-wing municipal authorities of Milano 2's masterplan. This development was designed not only to supply accommodation for ten thousand inhabitants, but also as a complete urbanism equipped to provide education, fitness, entertainment, idealized nature, and, above all, sales. Its 2,600 apartments were placed on the perimeter, with their TV rooms expanding onto big balconies, directed not toward the Milan skyline, but to an inner landscape, with large trees carefully placed to suppress any perception of a neighboring human presence. Under the direction of the landscape designer Enrico Hoffer, more than five thousand trees were planted at Milano 2. A significant number of them were already over twelve meters tall when they were relocated—among them, fir trees, maples, Japanese red maples, cedars, birches, beeches, gingkoes, magnolias, pine trees, plane trees, and lindens.[9] Adjacent dwellings would be screened by a costly and carefully composed biological version of TV snow, an arboreal screen vibrating like the static light noise of unsynchronized TVs.

Milano 2's young design team was led by the then thirty-one-year-old architect Giancarlo Ragazzi, partnered with Giulio Possa and Antonio D'Adamo. The architects paid careful attention to the sectional bifurcation of the design. Milano 2's architecture segregated an above-ground domain for daily human life, characterized by a green landscape crisscrossed by pedestrian and bicycle circulation, from a netherworld of car traffic and underground centralized pipes flowing with utilities and media content controlled by Berlusconi's company, Fininvest. Milano 2 was the outcome of a growing context of Italian companies operating internationally, including Abet Laminati, BTicino, Hoval, and Max Meyer. The ideas promoted by these companies aligned with those defended in *Casabella*'s January 1970 issue, which suggested that the development of techno-

Fictional scene produced by Edilnord portraying the Number Ones, 1976.

Milano 2 show apartment, 1976.

logically advanced systems and societies should be specifically applied in new forms of urbanism and architecture.

PRODUCING THE NUMBER ONES

From the beginning, Milano 2 was not a project designed to accommodate an existing group of humans, but instead one meant to produce a new type of society. Throughout all media outlets, the development was profusely advertised as "La Città dei Numeri Uno" (The City of Number Ones). Actors were hired to impersonate the prospective inhabitants in fictional renderings depicting these Number One humans in their City of Number Ones. The Number Ones were not the workers, not even the workers who proved to be exceptional, but neither were they members of the wealthy Milanese society. Number Ones were instead an until-then disconnected sector of ambitious young middle-class, family-oriented executives. They were not working for the national industries governed by the Istituto per la Ricostruzione Industriale, but instead they mainly worked for growing multinational corporations such as IBM, 3M, Siemens, and Unilever. These corporations had started to locate their branches in places like Segrate that were more likely to attract middle-class employees and young executives: people, as Berlusconi would present himself, unrelated to Milan's elites or industrial dynasties.[10]

Most of these employees were not owners of the companies where they worked, nor did they have personal fortunes, but they were paid high salaries. Milano 2's favorable financing arrangements and low upfront payments enabled them to purchase dwellings of a kind that, in most cases, they could have never afforded in Milan's center. These employees incarnated the shift from a postwar nation-based Europe to a globalized realm of multinational corporations.

Model apartments were built in the middle of the yet non-urbanized estate where Milano 2 was to be constructed. They were carefully decorated, photographed, and published in the most fashionable international media outlets, including *Vogue* magazine.[11] From images of fictional Number Ones in these spaces, potential buyers would imagine what it might be like to be Number Ones themselves. This use of printed media set into motion the evolution of the potential subjectivity of Number Ones by the way they were confronted with fictionalized, stylized versions of themselves. These media outlets created a mirror-based dynamic meant to maximize the displacement of daily life into a progression from the actual to the aspirational and vice versa. This dynamic was produced by the fictional architecture of the model apartments where actors performed as Number Ones. These fictions

Views of Milano 2. Photographs by Miguel de Guzmán.

Views of Milano 2. Photographs by Miguel de Guzmán.

traveled from the fictional settings to magazines and newspapers and eventually to real life. The isolated apartment towers of Milano 2, where the Number Ones would be spatially confined, did not grow out of a city or even the countryside, but rather from media. Milan's new social type, the Number Ones, were segregated spatially, aesthetically, and economically. Berlusconi, who involved himself personally in selling the apartments, insistently explained that neither he nor Edilnord had the funds to complete the development, but that funds would be mobilized by a pyramidal financing scheme: those who bought early would get an apartment that would double its value as others joined. From a financial point of view, Milano 2 was sold as the device that would help adventurous early buyers become successful investors.

ESCAPING URBAN PROMISCUITY

In the sales brochures, Berlusconi himself encouraged buyers to "escape from metropolitan chaos—from traffic, crime, immigrants, and workers. From the city itself."[12] Milano 2's marketing suggested self-banishment from urban promiscuity. Milano 2 provided an additional means to render oneself as a nonworker and as a nonimmigrant. Being a Number One was not only a progression to the aspirational, but a departure from urban promiscuity into a realm of class sorting and clarification.

The strategy of offering an escape was paralleled by offering a suburban marketplace within Milano 2, and Edilnord managed to reap a share of the money spent on every good or service that Milano 2's residents purchased on a daily basis. A central part of Edilnord's strategy was to retain ownership of the on-site commercial spaces.[13]

If gray concrete and modern architecture had once embodied the aspirations of Milanese society, now red vernacular seemed to cater to the sensitivities of the emerging Number Ones, who were young enough to enjoy the then-trendy aesthetic context brought about by folk music, picturing themselves in a globalizing rural romanticism.[14] Along with the red vernacular came mansard roofs. Milano 2's underground cables ensured TV antennas did not ruin the picturesque atmosphere.[15]

The center of Milano 2 has never been occupied by the symbolic presence of religious or administrative power but, instead, by the Lago dei Cigni, the Lake of the Swans. The core of Milano 2's infrastructure, which could be perceived as a pleasant architecture celebrating picturesque banality, also contained a sports and business center, schools, retail, a four-star hotel, and a park intended—according to the apartment sales brochures—to allow the children of Number Ones to play Cowboys and Indians and have organized treasure hunts.[16]

Together, these elements provided potential buyers of apartments with evidence of the way that Milano 2 would produce Number Ones and their children as competitive, healthy, earnest, aggressive, treasure-seeking, and athletic beings, prepared to occupy a position in a socially stratified world. In the way this infrastructure in Milano 2 is used even today, it can still be considered part of Edilnord's project to shape bodies and societies through architecture and urbanism. An important factor in achieving this goal is that part of Milano 2's architecture remains virtually invisible: namely, the underground studios of Mediaset, where the core of Berlusconi's political coordination is concealed, an architecture that needs to be hidden to maximize its political efficacy.

View of the green landscaping in between Milano 2 apartments.

Tele Milano studios in Milano 2, 1976–1978.

In 1974, Giacomo Properzj and Alceo Moretti started to broadcast amateur programming by tapping into this underground, wired network. Tele Milano had just been born. Unlicensed movies and amateur, self-produced happenings were broadcast from the Jolly Hotel located in Milano 2. The TV station was cheap but successful. It recruited residents to its official board, who would help in choosing the content. A program showing images of women undressing, as male residents of Milano 2 called into the station to participate in a quiz game, would rapidly achieve an unexpected success. Not only did it attract viewers, but also it mobilized a particular sector of Milano 2 society, the adult males, and placed them into a differentiated time gap, experienced by its sectored audience as an exclusive late-night TV salon. If RAI homogenized society, gathering the public together into a media space inhabited by generic shows, Tele Milano started to break Milano 2's society into specialized clusters according to the TV content promoted. Whereas RAI coordinated bedtime to ensure national industrial production, Tele Milano kept adult males awake to glean a share of revenue from their phone consumption. Consequently, these men became a group defined by their use of time, their media, and their gender practices.

In 1975, Berlusconi's Fininvest became the owner of Tele Milano, seduced by its unexpected success.[17] Edilnord's project to segregate Milan's sectors of mass consumption and solidify control of the interactions and purchases of residents extended to Tele Milano, which would quickly consider its mission as increasing Milano-2-based commerce.[18] With a 1976 ruling by the constitutional court of Italy authorizing the aerial transmission of private local TV channels, Tele Milano became Tele Milano 58, and then Canale 5, and started to be broadcast over the air beyond Milano 2.[19] Fininvest purchased local TV channels across the country and, taking advantage of a legal loophole in Italy's aerial transmission regulations, made all the channels broadcast the same content simultaneously, giving birth to what was, in fact, a private national TV network: Mediaset.[20] What had started as a transmedia satellite city expanded into a national transmedia urbanism—one that would produce urban settings in the interaction of actual space with media domains—transferring the segregationist project tested in Milano 2 to the scale of Italy.

SCALING UP: THE BIRTH OF TARGETED DIFFERENCE

In the 1980s, Fininvest developed two related initiatives. First, it acquired the retail chain Standa with the intention of controlling the node between distributors and Number Ones, already exiled from urban-market promiscuity. Fininvest's team lacked experience in logistics, and the competence of stronger retail groups made this initiative fail. Second, in 1980 Fininvest created the media agency Publitalia. Within ten years, Publitalia would completely transform urban mediation between production and consumption.[21] Formed to sell TV advertising space for Mediaset, Publitalia developed a different way to recruit advertisers, based on four principles.[22]

First, television would no longer be a space for top-down pedagogy, but, instead, a device to bring production and consumption together. Second, TV content would be designed according to advertisers' goals. Third, instead of programming to serve generic audiences, content would be designed to attract specific publics—if toys needed to be sold, there would be TV shows for children; if middle-aged males were targeted, there would be late-night shows for them to inhabit. Whereas RAI had promoted urban convergence and the creation of a unified public, Publitalia focused on differentiation and distribution; progressively scaling up what was previously developed as the 2000-apartment transmedia urbanism of Milano 2 and Tele Milano. Finally, advertisers would not be charged for the amount of time their commercials were broadcast, but for the increase in their sales. Fininvest would get fifteen percent of the increase in sales for companies advertised on Mediaset's channels. Talking of Publitalia's activity, Berlusconi stated: "I do not sell spaces; I sell sales."[23] If nation-driven TV-urbanism in the postwar era constructed space and organized society in social classes, Milano 2 instead constructed sales and structured society in consumption targets. By defining and sorting targeted groups, then utilizing differentiated channels and timetables and depicting and instigating exemplary subjectivities, consumptions, and practices for each individual sector, television would produce urban difference.

Publitalia's project worked. Small local companies such as the furniture manufacturers Aiazzone and Foppap Pedretti, the mattress company Permaflex, and fur coat seller Annabella unexpectedly grew when advertised by Mediaset. This success fueled the expansion of Publitalia. Mediaset's ventures into France, the Netherlands, Spain, and other countries were followed by the organization of new corporations, such as Publifrance, Publiespaña, and Publieurope. In 1984, Publitalia surpassed Sipra, RAI's advertising sales unit, in revenue.[24] That same year, Auditel, the Italian research company that measures television ratings and statistics, was created. For the first time, the demographics of audiences were monitored.[25]

In 1980, Mike Bongiorno, the original host of RAI's biggest hit—*Lascia o raddoppia?*—left RAI to become Mediaset's star presenter. As part of his contract, Bongiorno would live in Milano 2, so he could become part of the community of Number Ones. In contrast to gated communities, Milano 2 welcomed visitors, and it became a popular place to go to see celebrities. The superstars would dwell in penthouses in the Garden Towers, but they could be seen when using the facilities gathered around the lake. The *bellini,* sexy young female models playing secondary roles in TV shows, would occupy apartments on the first floor, where their domestic life could be seen from the gardens.

TRANSMEDIA APARTMENTS: MIRRORED BODIES

Mediaset provided a mirrored broadcasted home, an implemented version of the model apartments publicized by *Vogue* magazine that first compelled the Number Ones to buy apartments in Milano 2: a home that has kitchens, mothers, living rooms, sofas, hosts, bedrooms, showers, and older brothers. In order to increase the legally regulated maximum percentage of promotional space, advertisements leapt from commercials into TV shows, as promotional segments devoted to sponsors started to be included in Mediaset programs. Apartments, celebrities, mirrored homes, and advertisers constituted a daily life to inhabit, one that was not contained in any city, but in an urban enactment resulting from the large corporations' choreography of techno-social interaction.

In the late 1970s, in the underground basement of an ordinary bar in Milano 2, the popular DJ Claudio Cecchetto hosted *Chewing Gum*, a musical TV show. Week after week, Cecchetto brought dancers to populate his basement audience from Milan's disco temple, Divina, where he was resident DJ. Valerio Lazarov, the "King of the Zoom Shot," would edit and broadcast the show in such a way so it would not only bring the best of Milan's nightlife into Milano 2's living rooms, but would also bring the bodily experience of psychedelia and disco dancing to the Number Ones. At the same time that Charles and Ray Eames's *Powers of Ten* (1977) used the zoom to provide universal constancy and "non-discontinuity,"[26] Lazarov would expand bodies in the living rooms of apartments in Milano 2 by turning these private spaces into centers of disco nightlife. To go out, one could stay at home.

In March 2012, Clemente Russo, a well-known boxer and policeman, made his début as the main character in the reality show *Fratello Maggiore*, in which he corrected the behavior of spoiled teenagers by becoming their fictional older brother. In this show on Mediaset's TV channel Italia 1, he can be seen interacting with ordinary people in domestic interiors, where problematic teenagers are asked to reshape their lives according to his suggestions, a process which is scaled up by the way edited images of his life are scrutinized by his Facebook followers, many living in Milano 2 apartments, where they switch on their televisions, check their smartphones, and find him again. There, he wears Dolce & Gabbana and Nike, drinks Bacardi at the Tatanka Club, exercises following *Muscle & Fitness* magazine, consumes Enervit Sport, communicates with a Samsung phone, and travels on Alitalia.

Today, Milano 2's banality is incessantly published on Instagram accounts: its swans and its trees, the changing seasons of the grass, its living rooms, cats in front of red pitched roofs, people in front of TV sets. With more than four million paying subscribers in Italy, Sky-TV, Europe's most popular satellite TV platform, currently doubles the number of subscribers to Mediaset Premium digital cable television, Mediaset's satellite television service. Together, Mediaset Premium and Sky-TV, as transnational media platforms, are globalizing direct-to-home urbanism, in which the architectural embodiment of the political has been implemented in a way that has so far remained unexplained. The effects of what once started in Milano 2 can be seen everywhere that people consume, and it has become the urbanism we mainly live by.

1 Boccazzi Varotto Carlo, "Costruire la RAI. Tecnologia e televisione in Italia dai pionieri al boom economico," *Nuova Civiltà delle Macchine* (April-June, 2004).

2 John Foot, *Milan Since the Miracle: City, Culture and Identity* (New York: Berg, 2001).

3 Ibid.

4 Gino Moliterno, (*Encyclopedia of Contemporary Italian Culture* (London: Routledge, 2000).

5 Roberto Levi, *Le trasmissioni Tv che hanno fatto (o no) l'Italia. Da "Lascia o raddoppia" al "Grande Fratello"* (Milan: Rizzoli, 2002).

6 Maurizio Coppo and Marco Cremaschi, eds., *Strutture territoriali e questione abitativa* (Milan: Franco Angeli, 1994).

7 In Italy, although 26% of new residential units were publically financed in the 1950s, that figure dropped to less than 6% by the end of 1960s. Coppo and Cremaschi, eds., *Strutture territoriali e questione abitativa*.

8 *"Guerra per la casa," Casabella* 344 (1970).

9 P. Ceretti and R. Fantacci, *I nostri alberi. Una passeggiata botanica tra le Residenze ed i luoghi d'incontro di Milano 2* (Segrate: Edilnord, 2011).

10 S. E. D'Anna and G. Moncalvo, *Berlusconi in Concert* (London: Otzium, 1994).

11 Edilnord Centri Residenziali S.A.S., *Milano 2. Una cità per vivere* (Milan: Edilnord Centri Residenziali, 1976).

12 Silvio Berlusconi, in Milano 2 sales brochures. Edilnord Centri Residenziali, Milano, 1970.

13 This consolidation of ownership of the market facilities would remain until the 2000s, when the Fondo Mario Negri sold a large number of the spaces to independent retailers.

14 Early Milano 2 apartment buyers, discussion with author, October 2013 - April 2014.

15 Giancarlo Ragazzi, discussion with author, 2014.

16 Edilnord, *Milano 2. Una cità per vivere*.

17 Eugène Saccomano, *Berlusconi: le dossier vérité* (Paris: Parole Et Silence, 1994).

18 Former Tele Milano executive, discussion with author, 2014.

19 F. Colombo, *Le tre stagioni. Problemi dell'Informazione* 4 (1990): 593–97.

20 Gabriele Balbi and Benedetta Prario, "The History of Fininvest/Mediaset's Media Strategy: 30 Years of Politics, the Market, Technology and Italian society," *Media Culture & Society* 32, no. 3 (May 2010): 391–409.

21 Paul Ginsborg, *Silvio Berlusconi: Television, Power and Patrimony* (London: Verso, 2004).

22 This information is the result of an ethnography developed by the author in Publitalia's headquarters.

23 Alexander Stille, *The Sack of Rome: Media + Money + Celebrity = Power = Silvio Berlusconi* (New York: Penguin, 2007).

24 Cinzia Padovani, "Berlusconi on Berlusconi? An Analysis of Digital Terrestrial Television Coverage on Commercial Broadcast News in Italy," *Discourse & Communication* 6, no. 4 (November 2012): 423–47.

25 Fausto Colombovand Michele Sorice, "Audience Studies in Italy," *Cost Action IS0906 Transforming Audiences, Transforming Societies* (2010), accessed November 15, 2016, http://www.cost.eu/COST_Actions/isch/IS0906.

26 M. Golec, "Optical Constancy, Discontinuity, and Nondiscontinuity in the Eameses' Rough Sketch," in *The Educated Eye*, ed. Mark J. Williams and Adrian W. B. Randolph (Hanover, N.H.: Dartmouth College Press, 2011).

OPEN PORTALS: REFLECTIONS ON CHINATOWN GATES

BY GARY W. MCDONOGH

Que ce soit à New York, San Francisco ou à Londres, tous les Chinatowns du monde sont pourvus d'une porte traditionnelle monumentale dressée à l'entrée. (Whether in New York, San Francisco, or London, all the Chinatowns of the world have a traditional monumental gate erected at their entrances.)[1]

After I had joined other colleagues in a conference on the Chinese presence in Prato, Italy, in June 2015, an audience member raised the question of why the large Chinese enclave in that city lacked "a gate" (*un portale).* Prato, an historic manufacturing center of 190,000, has gained a new global identity because 12,000-25,000 Chinese immigrants have settled there since the 1990s. Fujianese and Wenzhounese have taken over the spaces of its failing textile industry, and their 3,000 businesses have revitalized manufacturing and trade. Chinese immigrants have come to constitute ten to twenty percent of the municipality's population.[2] Relations of Chinese and Italians have oscillated from constructive to mystified to deeply tense, but Prato now acts as a hub in Chinese global trade.[3] Still, conference participants, Chinese and non-Chinese, evoked parallel cities and "otherness" to characterize their urban separation, which follows a preexisting spatial division between the walled medieval city and its modern industrial expansion; indeed, the first major English-language study of this community spatializes Chinese in its very title: *Living Outside the Walls* (2006).[4]

Despite the tensions of Chinese-Pratese relationships, in fact, the question of the gate was not framed in terms of divisions. Instead, people were interested in the possibility—or even the necessity—of a gateway arch as a public symbol of ongoing Chinese presence and the links between an older Prato and an emergent global reality. This discussion, in turn, led to a wider question of how Prato might become a destination for visitors. Prato lives in the global shadow of Florence; a Chinatown gate would distinguish Prato and connect it to the imaginary of worldwide polyglot cities.

A gateway, in its historical construction and functions, as well as in contemporary architecture and urbanism, signals differentiation: separation, security, and control. Ancient, medieval, and early modern cities of Europe, Africa, and Asia built gates for defense as well as control of taxes and population; these constructions imposed a cultural and physical order on the city and its surroundings.[5] Similarly, the Chinese *paifang* (牌坊; *páifāng*) that inspires many contemporary Chinatown gates served to delineate and divide precincts in the Tang dynasty city (618–907 CE). By the Song dynasty (960–1279), these arches had come to serve primarily memorial and decorative functions, hence their overlap with *pailou* (牌樓; *páilóu*), which refers more specifically to a commemorative arch. They often marked entrances or ceremonial boundaries. Such pai-portals proliferated in the Ming (1368–1644) and Qing (1644–1912) dynasties within a wider architectural vocabulary of both protective and memorial constructions.[6]

The multiplicity of functions and meanings associated with gates remains part of their global evolution, as centuries of destruction of walls for the opening of modern urban expansion across European and then Asian cities turned even dour fortifications into symbolic sites of memory and power. Meanwhile, twentieth-century urbanization has seen the reappearance of "gated communities" as symbols of retreat and separation by the wealthy of the world into enclaves of security and privilege. These gated communities are as widespread in China as they are in Europe and the Americas, often reasserting an architectural, albeit symbolic, vocabulary of separation.[7] Yet as this paper argues, Chinatown gates embody Chinese agency, global linkages, past divisions, and hard fought connections that force recognition and thoughtfulness about contested Chinese urban presence. As "open portals," these gates illuminate deeper complexities of Chinese hybridization and spatialization across global cities.

Modern Chinatown gates generally lack any barriers to stop flows of traffic or pedestrians. Instead, they are usually colorful ceremonial arches composed of two sturdy posts that may or may not be decorated, soaring as high as ten meters.The gate's lintel and eaves generally spans the street at a height of two to three stories.These crosspieces vary from simple slabs with inscriptions of friendship and community to more elaborate and ornamented multilayer tiled roofs that resonate with other ornamental markers of Chineseness, such as urban street furniture (street signs, telephone booths, etc.) or decorations that individual merchants and restaurateurs impose on a vernacular urban fabric. While many arches, at first glance, seem to embody division, in cases I have examined closely around the world, Chinese and other busi-

1 Note that this is untrue: New York does not have an arch even as Paris proposes to build one! "Le Chinatown parisien aura bientôt lui aussi sa porte," *Le Parisien*, November 3, 2015, http://www.leparisien.fr/paris-75/le-chinatown-parisien-aura-bientot-lui-aussi-sa-porte-03-11-2015-5243803.php.

2 See Graeme Johanson, Russell Smyth, and Rebecca French, eds., *Living Outside the Walls: The Chinese in Prato.* (Newcastle upon Tyne: Cambridge Scholars Publishing, 2009); Fabio Bracci, "The Chinese Deviant: Building the Perfect Enemy in a Local Arena," in *No Borders: Immigration and the Politics of Fear*, ed. Emma Bell (Chambry: L'université de Savoie, 2010), 97–116; Andrea Abati, *La prole del drago. Per una nuova romanzo fotografico* (Prato, 2012); Francesco Arese-Visconti, *Hidden Identity: The Italian-Chinese Community in Prato* (Florence: Aion Edizioni, 2015); and the collected essays in Fabio Berti, Valentina Pedone, and Andrea Valzania, eds. *Vendere e comprare: Processi di mobilità sociale dei cinesi a Prato* (Pisa: Paccini, 2013). More information on the Dryphoto Project that led to this conference can be found at http://www.dryphoto.it/new/2014/piazza-dellimmaginario.

3 Sylvia Smyth, "The Italian Fashion Capital Being Led by the Chinese," *BBC News*, Feburary 12, 2013, http://www.bbc.com/news/business-21350013.

4 This division is also personalized in an intense fashion in the memoirs of Edoardo Nesi, scion of a local industrial family in ruins, who vividly portrays Chinese as aliens and competitors in the midst of the city in his *Storia dell Mia Gente* (Rome: Bompiano, 2010).

5 See, for example, I.A. Richmond, *The City Wall of Imperial Rome: An Account of Its Architectural Development from Aurelian to Narses* (1930; repr. College Park, Md.: McGrath, 1971); John M. Merriman, *The Margins of City Life: Explorations on the French Urban Frontier, 1815-1851* (Oxford: Oxford University Press, 1991); James Tracy, ed., *City Walls: The Urban Enceinte in Global Perspective* (Cambridge, UK: Cambridge University Press, 2000). In Chinese, such fortified gates would be identified as city gates or *chéng mén* (城门).

6 For a brief review of the Chinese architectural, see Joseph Lau, "Planning of Interpretation Strategy for Chinese Style: 'Pai-type Portal Structure' before 1941 on Hong Kong Island," M.S. thesis in Conservation, University of Hong Kong, 2005, http://hub.hku.hk/handle/10722/56078; Chi-Feung Lee, "Pai-fang: Gateways to the History and Socio-politics of Indigenous Villages in the New Territories," M.S. thesis in Conservation, University of Hong Kong, 2013. Both studies suggest the changing use of such gateways in Hong Kong over time. Lee's update raises some ques-tions about global reflected meanings discussed below. Erica Allen-Kim has also raised important issues in the modern history of such gates in her "Political Economy of Chinatown Gates," n.d. http://www.academia.edu/4298726/The_Political_Economy_of_Chinatown_Gates.

a)

b)

a) Chinese Arch, Liverpool, UK. Photograph by author, 2013.

b) Concrete arch outside of Chinatown in Havana, Cuba. Photograph by author, 2015.

nesses spill over on both sides of the arch: the gate is about place-making and flows as much as separation. Local meanings also have evolved within urban social history: in some cases, a newly built arch anticipates the emergence of a new Chinese community or project, while in others, the arch has been stranded by demographic tides, as Chinese have moved elsewhere in the city or to its peripheries.

Nevertheless, while such gates are popularly read today as iconographic necessities for a Chinatown—demonstrated by pleas of Chinese and others to build new arches—not all Chinatowns have them. Paris, Amsterdam, and Manhattan, among other famous enclaves, lack any flashy monument (although plans are under discussion in the first). Even iconic gates in major cities, such as Bangkok, Havana, Lima, Philadelphia, San Francisco, Sydney, and Washington, D.C., represent relatively recent constructions, erected within the past fifty years, although their Chinese settlements are 150 years old or more. Such arches, moreover, not only refer to China but also reference each other across competing global Chinatowns and their host cities. Meanwhile, their iconographic and cultural meanings embody the contested presence of Chinese worldwide, of closed borders and differential integration, globalization, and locality. These open portals distill divisions but also link places and populations, a dialectic which continues to make them important for existing communities and tempting for those uncertain of their place in the city.

This essay draws on decades of experiences around the world that have underpinned an ongoing research project with Cindy Hing-Yuk Wong on the formation, social structure, and cultural meanings of global Chinatowns as laboratories and commentaries on contemporary urbanism. In this project we have lived in, worked with, and examined archives, media, and representations of more than one hundred Chinatowns—old, new, emergent, and denied—in thirty countries in the Americas, Asia, Australia, Africa, and Europe.[8] In this research, Chinatown gates have generally been backgrounds rather than our focus—duly photographed as markers of place, but scarcely given more attention than they receive from residents who pass them every day. To recenter my attention on these gates as urban portals, embodying questions of architectural and sociocultural differentiation, has demanded reflection as well as analysis, rereading data (and correcting impressions) as much as gathering new cases.[9] To illuminate this complexity of experience and meaning, I begin with an overview of the emergence of diasporic Chinatown gates, their histories, and their meanings within urban settings, situating them in time and culture, as well as place. A more ethnographic approach to three cases follows, examining the many gates of Los Angeles and the apparently strategically placed gate of Philadelphia's Chinatown, in counterpoint with the ungated frontiers of New York City's Chinatowns. Based on these complementary foundations, I return to the meaning of such open portals, their global signification, and local meanings.

WHERE ARE THE GATES? MYTHS, HISTORIES, AND GLOBALIZATION

Chinatown gates and arches around the world, like Chinatowns themselves, are often linked to a mysterious timelessness imputed to the Chinese other.[10] At the same time, they are often used and celebrated by Chinatown's entrepreneurs. This vague mythologization becomes problematic when we try to trace origins and influences of Chinatown gates prior to the 1970s. How do we document an absence? Arnold Genthe's classic photographs of pre-1906 earthquake San Francisco Chinatown, for example, shows no such arches nor does Philip Choy discuss them in his reviews of Chinese architecture in that city.[11] The current arch, the iconic Dragon Gate, was designed by Chinese-American architect Clayton Lee and built in 1969 amid global political shifts discussed below. Fifty years later, the gate itself is part of the iconography of the city for residents and global tourists—identified by websites today as "the gateway to Chinatown" and "the only authentic Chinatown gate in North America."[12]

In many other cities where Chinese populations have also been present for over a century, the arch is even more recent. Lima's gate was built in 1971; Havana's in 1972. Melbourne, Australia, began to build its four striking red gates on Little Bourke Street in the 1970s, although Chinese had lived in the area since the 1850s.[13] Sydney constructed theirs upon government recognition of an official Chinatown in 1980, following Australia's dismantling of its White Australia policy.[14] London, Philadelphia, and Washington, D.C., followed later in the 1980s; Liverpool, in 2000 (Fig. a). Incheon, South Korea, even though the kingdom opened to the world in the nineteenth century and established a Chinatown, received its arch from the city of Weihai in the twenty-first century.[15] Even Bangkok, one of the oldest overseas Chinese settlements, only saw an arch dedicated to the Thai king built in a traffic circle in 2000. In Manila, where a Chinese community was recorded since the 1600s, received a new arch only in 2015. [16] All these dates mark gaps of decades or centuries between the arrival of Chinese and the building of arches—posing questions of how and why they appeared, as well as what they mean in times of difference or assimilation.

Architectural models for Chinatown gates have existed for millennia. People left China in great numbers in the nineteenth century and established diasporic communities that sought to find identities in new places while maintaining fragile ties with China and its

7 Setha Low, *Behind the Gates: Life, Security, and the Pursuit of Happiness in Fortress America* (New York: Routlege, 2003); Teresa Caldeira, *City of Walls: Crime, Segregation, and Citizenship in São Paulo* (Berkeley: University of California Press, 2000); See Guillaume Giroir, "A Golden Ghetto in a Chinese Garden: The Fontainebleau Villas in Shanghai," in Fulong Wu, ed., *Globalization and the Chinese City* (New York: Routledge, 2006), 208-224.

8 See Gary McDonogh and Cindy Wong, *Global Hong Kong* (London: Routledge, 2005); Gary McDonogh and Cindy Wong, "Beside Downtown: Chinatowns and Global Downtowns," in McDonogh and M. Peterson, eds., *Global Downtowns* (Philadelphia: University of Pennsylvania Press, 2012): 273–97; Gary McDonogh and Cindy Wong, "Negotiating Global Chinatowns: Difference, Diversity and Connection," *Cambio* (Italy), December 2013.

9 This project has entailed a new and invigorating exploration of the digital presence and iconographies of Chinatowns: Chinatown gates also attract internet attention, sometimes with erratic historical interpretations, but nonetheless as indicative of myth and reception as much as architectural genealogy.

10 Ivan Light, "From Vice District to Tourist Attraction: the Moral Career of American Chinatowns, 1880–1940," *Pacific Historical Review* 43, 3 (1974): 367-94; Winston Kyan, "Electric Pagodas and Hyphenate Gates: Folklore, Folklife, and the Architecture of Chinatown," *Amerasia Journal* 39, 2 (2013): 25–47.

11 John Kuo Wei Chen, Arnold Genthe's Pictures of Old Chinatowns (New York: Dover, 1984); Anthony Lee, *Picturing Chinatown: Art and Orientalism in San Francisco* (Berkeley: University of California Press, 2001); Philip Choy, *San Francisco Chinatown: A Guide to its History and Architecture* (San Francisco: City Lights, 2012); Kyan, "Electric Pagodas and Hyphenate Gates."

12 "Gateway to San Francisco," San Francisco Chinatown, http://www.sanfranciscochinatown.com/attractions/gateway.html; "Chinatown – Gateway Arch," Public Art and Architecture from around the World, http://www.artandarchitecture-sf.com/chinatown-san-francisco-may-11-2012.html.

13 "About Chinatown Melbourne," Chinatown Melbourne, http://chinatownmelbourne.com.au/about-chinatown/.

14 Sarah Homewood, "Arches the Gateway to a More Tolerant Future," Sydney Morning Herald, February 10, 2013, http://www.smh.com.au/nsw/arches-the-gateway-to-a-more-tolerant-future-20130209-2e53n.html; for more on the White Australia Policy, see: "Fact sheet – Abolition of the 'White Australia' Policy," Australian Government Department of Immigration and Border Protection, http://www.border.gov.au/about/corporate/information/fact-sheets/08abolition.

15 "Chinatown," http://incheon.roadplanner.ru/eng/chin/chinkod.html.

imaginaries. This was often pursued through ornamentation and architecture: we can find early Chinese ornamentation in cemeteries, temples, signage, and commercial buildings in cities worldwide. Yet, Chinatowns themselves also had a protective and isolating function in areas where Chinese were suspect aliens. In the United States, for example, as across much of the Americas, Chinese immigration faced specific controls, including the complete denial of citizenship to non-American-born Chinese from 1882 to 1943 with reforms not complete until the 1960s. Hence, after the 1960s, the construction of monuments also stood for agency and presence within a civic evolution as well as an architectural framework.[17]

But how did gates become global markers? One historical connection between classical Chinese architecture and late-twentieth-century urban gates has been suggested by the work of Hong Kong scholars on pai-portals in local architecture from the colonial period (1841–1997). Historian Joseph Lau catalogued a number of the gateways in existence prior to 1941 throughout Hong Kong; many were associated with entrances to parks, cemeteries, institutions, and elite private residences. Historian Chi-Feung Lee also noted that after 1965, colonial planners encouraged villagers to add pai-portals to the reconstructed villages of the rural New Territories. In the twenty-first century, such gates have strengthened local (Chinese) identity in cosmopolitan cities.[18]

Whatever their initial disseminations, the construction of Chinatown gates experienced a global boom in the 1970s. The florescence of arches across the United States reflects a new security of citizenship and Chinese agency in a country that had sought to exclude Chinese for decades. Yet it also embodied power struggles of Chinese geopolitics after World War II. After the mainland People's Republic of China (PRC) and Republic of China (Taiwan) split in 1949, new Chinatown gates were often sponsored by one side or the other as a means of asserting power and connections. In San Franciso, for example, while the Dragon Gate became emblematic of one of the world's best-known Chinatowns, Erica Allen-Kim attributes actual sponsorship to Taiwan.[19] In fact, the arch has a Taiwanese flavor, in that it balances global authenticity and meaning with American politics by its references to Sun Yat-Sen and Guomindang principles, especially claimed as heritage by the Republic of China.

Global contestation becomes even more apparent in the arches of Lima, Peru and Havana, Cuba. Since the nineteenth century Lima and Havana have hosted two of the largest Chinatowns in the Western hemisphere.[20] In Lima, Chinese became middle-class modernizers, and their institutions—from theaters to the Chinese Tennis club—constituted monuments of the early-twentieth-century city.[21] Lima's Chinatown gate was built with Taiwanese assistance in 1971. This sturdy structure marks the entrance to the original historic Chinese area. As the center city decayed and many Chinese moved to suburbs by the 1980s, itinerant peddlers swamped the gate, making it almost invisible in newspaper photos. The gate was restored and given space by a new pedestrian mall in the 1990s. Here, however, the People's Republic took over renovation of the arch, because Peru had switched recognition from Taiwan to the mainland in 1972.[22] In Havana, a massive gateway arch was also donated by the People's Republic, more than a decade after most Chinese-Cuban merchants had fled to the United States in the wake of the 1959 Revolution. As I have noticed on visits, this heavy concrete arch stands far from the edge of a now-shrunken Chinatown (Fig. b). As a Cuban journalist noted in 2014:

> Some years ago a portal was constructed imitating Chinese architecture that intended to indicate the beginning of the barrio... This portico responded to touristic goals more than practical ones. Moreover, within the barrio buildings Chinese architecture was not constructed but instead details were added as ornaments to western-style buildings.[23]

In 2015, amid new global interest in late-Socialist Cuba, the PRC reinvested in a different way in Chinese culture, converting an historic theater at the heart of Havana's Chinatown into a Confucius Institute, both destination and beacon, far from the stranded gate.

As the conflict of Taiwan and the PRC faded on a global stage, a second wave of gate building emerged in the mid-1980s, with mainland China flexing its growing political and economic power. This is when major cities like Philadelphia, Washington D.C., Chicago, and London acquired arches—and competed with each other regarding their authenticity, size, and links to China. The Washington arch was dedicated in 1986 and is now described on a District of Columbia tourism website as "the largest such archway in the world."[24] Ironically, this elaborate monument straddling a wide avenue now stands isolated in a moribund Chinatown. Chinese names now primarily adorn non-Chinese businesses—Starbucks, Urban Outfitters, and varied restaurants—in an area dominated by the Verizon Center and gentrification (Fig. c). Most Chinese now live in suburbs outside the city.[25]

This wave of gate building has soared with the rise of China as a multifaceted global presence in goods, diplomacy, and investment since the 1990s. For some cities, like Seattle, which acquired an arch in 2008, this has meant a process of catching up: a news-

16 "Manila Unveils World's Largest Chinatown Arch," Coconuts Manila, June 24, 2015, http://manila.coconuts.co/2015/06/24/manila-unveils-worlds-largest-chinatown-arch-binondo-local-chinese-are-not-happy. Political questions swirled about the arch's inscription, *chong guo cheng*, which to local critics implied an extension of China, while many overseas Chinese communities would prefer the term, *hua ren qu*, or 'Chinese people district.'

17 While the Chinese Exclusion Act in the United States may be the best-known of such racialized restrictions, Chinese also faced shorter limitations on immigration and rights around the world during their first global migrations through the Pacific Rim and the British Empire in the nineteenth and early twentieth century. Such legal differentiations were generally repealed during and after World War II.

18 Lau, "Planning of Interpretation Strategy for Chinese Style"; Lee, "Pai-fang." The issue of early expansion and connections still demands more research. Allen-Kim, for example, has suggested looking to world expositions like the San Francisco Panama-Pacific Exposition of 1915, where the exhibition of the nascent Chinese republic did include an elaborate gateway, although the exhibit also stressed China's modernity. At this point, though, Chinese faced blatant racism in California that made it unlikely that they would replicate such construction in their urban enclave, despite a growing recognition of its role in the fabric of the city.

19 Abigail Markwyn, "Economic Partner and Exotic Other: China and Japan at San Francisco's Panama-Pacific International Exposition," *Western Historical Quarterly* Vol. 39, No. 4 (Winter, 2008), 439–65.

20 Kathleen López, Chinese Cubans: A Transnational History (Chapel Hill: University of North Carolina Press, 2014);,

21 Adam McKeown, Chinese Migrant Networks and Cultural Change: Peru, Chicago and Hawaii, 1900–1936 (Chicago: University of Chicago Press, 2001).

22 "Los cuarenta años del arco chino," *El Comercio*, October 11, 2011, http://elcomercio.pe/blog/huellasdigitales/2011/11/los-40-anos-del-arco-chino.

23 "Hace algunos años se construyó un pórtico imitando la arquitectura china.... Este pórtico responde en realidad más a fines turísticos que prácticos. Es más, dentro del Barrio no se construyeron edificios ni viviendas al estilo chino, sino solo se incorporaron detalles como adorno a las edificaciones que se levantaban de estilo occidental." Fernando Damaso, "Zanja, corazón del Barrio Chino" *Diario de Cuba*, November 15, 2014, http://www.diariodecuba.com/cuba/1415910253_11254.html. Havana also has some interesting memorial arches in its Chinese cemetery that merit further investigation.

24 Alfred H. Liu, "Chinatown: Friendship Archway in Washington, D.C.," http://www.dcmemorials.com/index_indiv0000440.htm.

25 Yanan Wang, "D.C.'s Chinatown Has Only 300 Chinese Americans Left and They're Fighting to Stay," *Washington Post*, July 15, 2015, https://www.washingtonpost.com/lifestyle/style/dcs-chinatown-has-only-300-chinese-americans-left--and-fighting-to-stay/2015/07/16/86d54e84-2191-11e5-bf41-c23f5d3face1_story.html.

c)

d)

c) Chinatown Arch in Washington, DC. Photograph by author.

d) Gate at Dragonul Rosu, Chinese wholesale center near Bucharest, Romania. Photograph by author, 2013.

paper article notes that Seattle's citizens had wanted an arch "for fifty years." This entails the usual arguments about history and authenticity, affirmed at the end of the article, when a Shanghainese student is cited as saying, "It's like I'm back in China."[26]

Chinatown arches have also become associated with commerce and urbanism in new wholesale malls built to link Chinese goods to emerging markets. Visitors to the sprawling Dragonul Rosu complex outside Bucharest, Romania meet wiry dragon gates (Fig. d); similar constructions ornament new retail developments in Hungary and the Dragon Mart, which opened in Dubai in 2004, and aborted plans had been made for a similar complex in Cancún.[27] Teeming wholesale malls in Johannesburg have made it central to Southern African Chinese trade networks, which use florid pai-portals as decorative elements, gateways to goods that will be distributed across Southern Africa.

Any review of the meaning of pai-portal architecture must also consider where gates are not built. In Barcelona, for example, a burgeoning Chinese population has been arriving from Qingtian since the 1990s, today constituting a metropolitan population of 35,000 with concentrations in the suburban cities of Santa Coloma and Sant Adrià.[28] A proposal to build an arch in Santa Coloma, though, was rejected by the city. The permanence of a gate conflicts with ideals of assimilation and resurgent Catalan identity. These same tensions spilled into other public spaces in 2013, when Chinese organizations canceled all public celebrations of Chinese New Year in the city. Such absences speak of social and civic divisions.[29]

While gates symbolize agency and permanence, they also divide, and the underlying stories are often as complicated as the architecture and placement themselves. Here, a closer reading of three divergent embodiments of portals in nearby North American cities illuminates the interplay of power, agency, and representation.

GATES OF THE CHINESE CITY: CHINATOWNS ACROSS NORTH AMERICA

While San Francisco may host the best-known Chinatown arch, Los Angeles boasts a longer tradition of gates intertwined with Hollywood and other local myth-makers. Originally a small, somewhat peripheral community, the early pueblo's Chinese enclave was the site of a massacre in 1871, when a mob of white and Hispanic men lynched more than a dozen Chinese residents.[30] After a destructive fire in 1887, Chinese residents migrated to another nearby urban site; this embattled community was again forced to move by the plans for a new Union Station, begun in 1929. A parade and ceremony marked the final razing of this Chinatown in 1933.[31] Although Chinese were weary and wary of displacement, new Chinatowns took shape, adding gates that embodied varied meanings of Chineseness and permanence.[32]

One 1938 project for a new Chinatown in Los Angeles, China City, evoked the romantic theming already apparent in the transformation of Olvera Street into an Old Mexican fantasy by elite preservationist Christine Sterling and other civic leaders.[33] (These same people had favored the erasure of a Chinatown blight by Union Station development.)[34] Sterling's China City project relied on the exotic, the picturesque, and, frankly, the cinematic. A young set designer from Paramount, William Tuntke, was hired as artistic director in conjunction with architect Frederick Hust; their project made use of existing structures as well as Hollywood castoffs (from *The Good Earth*).[35] As architectural historian Josi Ward notes, the overlap of film and "real life" extended from the Chinese film museum to the "choreography" of residents and employees for visitors. The entire project was surrounded by a stone wall with a gate and tile roof (Fig. e). This gate, seemingly more representative of a fortress than other Chinatown gates, disappeared when fire destroyed the project in 1948.[36]

At the same time that Sterling's project moved forward, the Los Angeles Chinatown Corporation announced its own project led and designed by Chinese Americans. Combining modernity and tradition, this project was derided by Sterling, who quipped, "What do they want? An Oriental Westwood Village?"[37] This new Chinatown, as Ward notes, was a hybrid—with modern ideas of space replacing older Chinese/Angeleno alleys and Anglo architects working with a Chinese-American middle class, who provided money and taste. Among the latter was Y.C. Hong, who built four buildings with architects Eric Webster and Adrian Wilson, including "the Broadway Pai-lou or entrance gate, which he donated in honor of his mother."[38] This gate, which still stands, commanded a plaza ornamented in high chinoiserie with a pyramid, restaurants, and curio shops; another gate was also built and inaugurated by the governor; it is now known as the West Gate.[39] (Fig. f) Still another gate, a wiry construction of dragons, now spans Broadway and acts as a ceremonial marker for this Chinatown, although it was only added in 2001.

26 Brad Wong, "Historic Gate Provides Another Link to Chinatown's Roots," *seattlepi.com*, http://www.seattlepi.com/local/article/Historic-gate-provides-another-link-to-1260821.php. Seattle also has a long history of rejection of Chinese, including problems raised by its own exposition prior to San Francisco; See Markwyn, "Economic Partner and Exotic Other." Nonetheless, in 2015 the city became a destination for the American visit of President Yi Jingping.

27 Dragonul Rosu, http://www.dragonulrosu.ro: Linda Szabo, personal communication; "¿El enemigo en casa? Chinos construyen en Cancún el mayor complejo de comercio fuera del Gigante Rojo: Dragon Mart," *Sin Embargo*, June 23, 2012, http://www.sinembargo.mx/23-10-2012/406745 (Cancún); Dragon Mart, http://www.dragonmart.ae/ (Dubai).

28 G. McDonogh and C. Wong, "Beside Downtown: Chinatowns and Global Downtowns," 273-297.

29 Joaquín Beltrán Antolín, *Los Ocho Inmortales Cruzan el Mar* (Barcelona: Bellaterra, 2002). Also Beltrán Antolín, personal communication, 2012.

30 Scott Zesch, *The Chinatown War: Chinese Los Angeles and the Massacre of 1871* (New York: Oxford University Press, 2012); Roberta Greenwood, *Down by the Station: Los Angeles Chinatown 1880–1933* (Los Angeles: Institute of Archaeology, University of California Los Angeles, 1996).

31 Greenwood, *Down by the Station*, 38.

32 For more discussion of displacement see McDonogh and Wong, "Beside Downtown"; Bethany Li, Domenic Vitiello and Anthony Acoca, *Chinatown Then and Now: Gentrification in Boston, New York, and Philadelphia*, Asian American Legal Defense Fund, 2013, http://aaldef.org/Chinatown%20Then%20and%20Now%20AALDEF.pdf.

33 Cindy Sterling's ambivalent role as preservationist, philanthropist and developer stretched from Santa Barbara to the Plaza of Los Angeles, which she developed with support of conservative local leaders like Harrison Otis and Harry Chandler of the Los Angeles Times.

34 Josi Ward, "'Dreams of Oriental Romance': Reinventing Chinatown in 1930s Los Angeles," Buildings and Landscapes 20, no. 1 (Spring 2013): 19–42; William D. Estrada, *The Los Angeles Plaza: Sacred and Contested Space* (Austin: University of Texas Press, 2008). For a Chinese American vision of China City, see William Gow, "Building a Chinese Village in Los Angeles: Christine Sterling and the Residents of China City," *Gum Saan Journal* 32, no. 1 (2010), http://www.chssc.org/History/ChinatownRemembered/Neighborhoods/Residents_of_China_City.aspx.

35 Ibid., 28ff. Ironically, later in his career Tuntke was the art director for a Chinatown episode of the New York based police series Kojak, http://www.imdb.com/title/tt0621378/fullcredits/.

36 William Gow also notes that China City provided livelihoods for many Chinese families including those not incorporated into the older Cantonese networks that controlled the larger community. Gow, "Building a Chinese Village in Los Angeles."

37 Ward, "'Dreams of Oriental Romance,'" 33. Westwood Village was an upscale Los Angeles development with a Mediterranean theme, opened in 1929, that remains one of the more elite areas of the city to this day.

38 Ibid., 34.

39 Angels Walk LA: Chinatown, 2003, http://www.angelswalkla.org/pdfs/AWLA_CHINATOWN_GUIDEBOOK.pdf.

e)

f)

e) Street signage for China City in Los Angeles evoked the graphics of a movie set. Photograph by Henry Quillen, c.a. 1939. Courtesy of LAPL.

f) The West Gate to Chinatown in Los Angeles. This historic photograph by Gordon Dean dated July 5, 1962 was captioned: "The gate to Oriental fantasy in the heart of Los Angeles." Courtesy of LAPL.

Like the pai-portals of Hong Kong, the multiple gates around the Los Angeles Chinatown muddled sources and meanings. Since their origins in the 1930s, they have served as entrances, memorials, decorations, attractions, and points of identity. They separated new Chinatowns from the rest of the city, but did so in order to invite others in; they relied on "authentic" Chinese models, but livened them with local—albeit Hollywood—touches.

Philadelphia's Chinatown arch, by contrast, reflects the struggles and meanings of more recent arches worldwide. Although the Chinese population first appeared on streets near the downtown by the 1870s, the Chinatown Friendship Gate, at 10th and Arch Streets, was built in 1984 by craftsmen from Tianjin as part of a new commercial and trade agreement and refurbished under the same guidance in 2008.[40] The twelve-meter-high wooden project, brightly colored in red, green, white, and gold under tiled roofs, proudly announces "*fei cheng hua bu*" or "Philadelphia Chinatown" in its overhead inscription, while noting donors along its base.[41] This arch allows cars, bicyclists, and pedestrians to pass through, while framing a vision of Chinatown from Center City and vice versa. Yet, in recent years, when the Philadelphia Chinatown Development Corporation and other associations in the city take over the streets of this downtown enclave to celebrate the mid-autumn festival, the Friendship Arch has taken an important pride of place. Shutting off a main artery that runs from north Philadelphia into Center City, Chinese stores and restaurants set out their wares, while associations promote activities for visitors and locals, young and old, and the arch nestles a stage on which pan-Asian groups perform for mixed audiences (Fig. g).

This ephemeral dividing function of the gate emphasizes its everyday place in a city of flows. Anyone who drives or bikes in the city notes another immediate paradox in this gating: while it connects pedestrians to Center City, given traffic flows south on one-way 10th Street, the gate clearly demarcates an exit from Chinatown for many people rather than an entrance. For most drivers, the "entrance" to this part of Chinatown would come from the Vine Street Expressway artery, which itself vivisects the enclave. This automotive entrance entails both actual walls constructed as a sound barrier against expressway traffic and a political mural showing the struggles of Chinese immigrants, including images of local and national protests over mistreatment of Chinese. The mural, in turn, underscores how long Chinese have lived in the city before walls or murals (Fig. h).[42]

The definition of this Chinatown as a place, as folklorist Kathryn Wilson argues, was linked not only to residence, social formation, and ornamentation of buildings, but also to such struggles. Among these conflicts are long battles in the mid-twentieth century against the urban connector highway that originally was destined to destroy Holy Redeemer Chinese Catholic Church and School, which had become an anchor of the Chinese community. As a prime location next to downtown, Chinatown has grappled with the emergence of urban walls on all sides that have nothing to do, apparently, with Chinatown itself. To the east, for example, Chinatown is bounded by Franklin Square, one of the original creations of William Penn's plans. Urban division is emphasized even more by the ceremonial space constructed around Independence Hall, including a multi-block grassy mall that now terminates in the National Constitution Center, opened in 2003. Looking at this space and the impressive public buildings that shape it, it is hard to remember that until the mid-twentieth century, the same kind of rowhouses that make up Chinatown behind its decorative and neon facades occupied the vanished streets of the mall. This was a continuous inner city area of tawdry boarding houses, small businesses, and some light industry. This recalls, in turn, the convergence of Chinatowns with skid row areas in Manhattan, Seattle, and Vancouver. Here, the contemporary physical division was imposed by urban planners attempting to create a national architecture of reverence to set apart historic places.

To the south of Chinatown lies Market Street, formerly the main shopping avenue of Philadelphia, ornamented by global department stores like Wanamaker's, Strawbridge and Clothier, and Gimbels, among others now disappeared. This continued into the Reading Terminal and its viaduct, the so-called "Chinese Wall" that divided the city with elevated railroad traffic.[43] With the postwar decline of downtown and the closure of the terminal in 1952, the Rouse Company began to develop part of the site as an enclosed downtown mall, the Gallery, a monolith that now presents a relatively blank wall to Chinatown.[44] Between this and the gate, in fact, the city becomes almost a no man's land dominated by the Greyhound Bus Station and small businesses, Chinese and non-Chinese, including fast food, tattoo parlors, and small stores. While the Gallery mall development was less conflictive than later "walls," a Chinatown leader, Cecilia Moy Yep linked it to the later gate when she said that residents of Chinatown felt insulted when the Gallery was built with its back to Chinatown, and she claimed, "We needed something to attract people into Chinatown."[45]

While Independence Mall and the Gallery "walled in" the existing Chinatowns by the 1960s, two other enclosing developments spurred more significant opposition and activism. Here, decades of battles by Chinese to change the route and lower the expressway created a new wall nonetheless, but also a new sense of activist identity that continues in organizations and leaders to this day.

Finally, in the 1990s, the Pennsylvania Convention Center to the west defined yet another boundary for Chinatown. Here, various attempts have been made to promote interaction between the massive and relatively bare edifice, which has now grown to 1,000,000 square feet of rental space. The PCC website even touts its proximity to Chinatown, whose restaurants and stores profit from

40 Lou Yi, "Big Plans to Awaken City's Faded Dragon," *Philadelphia Inquirer,* May 14, 2007, http://web.archive.org/web/20080612223424/http://www.philly.com/inquirer/multimedia/20070514_Big_plans_to_awaken_Phila_s_faded_dragon.html; Kyan, "Electric Pagodas and Hyphenate Gates"; Li et al, *Chinatown Then and Now*; Kathryn Wilson, *Ethnic Renewal in Philadelphia's Chinatown: Space, Place and Struggle* (Philadelphia: Temple University Press, 2015).

41 Winston Kyan notes that the *hua* here has strong associations with global Chineseness, unlike other inscriptions that emphasize *Tong Zhi* (Tang Street, a southern Chinese reference) or some variation on a Chinese (*Jong man*) quarter. Kyan, "Electric Pagodas and Hyphenate Gates."

42 For discussion of this debate and other Philadelphia Chinatown issues, see McDonogh and Wong, "Beside Downtown"; Wilson, *Ethnic Renewal in Philadelphia's Chinatown*; and Li et al., *Chinatown Then and Now*.

43 As far as I have ascertained this provocative reference has no direct relation to Chinatown but evokes the Great Wall of China, almost obliviously to the demography of the area. It seems to have been in use early on for the massive downtown viaduct constructed in 1880 and destroyed in the 1950s. See "Tracing the 'Chinese Wall' in Center City," *Hidden City Philadelphia*, October 2, 2013, http://hiddencityphila.org/2013/10/tracing-the-chinese-wall-in-center-city/.

44 For recent plans to open up this wall, see architecture critic Inga Saffron, "Changing Skyline: The Future Fashion Outlets: Do the Renderings Reflect Reality?" *The Philadelphia Inquirer*, July 6, 2015, www.philly.com/philly/columnists/inga_saffron/20150705_Changing_Skyline__The_future_Fashion_Outlets__Do_the_renderings_reflect_reality_st.html.

45 Yi, "Big Plans to Awaken City's Faded Dragon."

46 "PA Convention Center – Attendees" Pennsylvania Convention Center, accessed October 2016, http://www.paconvention.com/attendees.

g)

h)

g) Philadelphia Chinatown Arch during Mid-Autumn Celebration. Photograph by author, 2015.

h) Mural discussing Chinese immigration on the edge of Chinatown in Philadelphia. Photograph by author, 2016.

conventioneers.[46] Nonetheless, Chinese friends in Chinatown and those outside this core who use Chinatown services have complained repeatedly about snarled traffic and price gouging at parking lots during major Convention Center events. Meanwhile, the commercial enterprises on each side of 12th Street form an urban canyon: convention business or empty fronts to the south; Chinese banks, restaurants, and businesses to the east.

Through these different edges we can reread the meaning of the construction of the gateway in the 1980s as a marker in time and history, of permanence as well as place, a dialogue and a struggle. The gate had been discussed since the 1960s, but only became a reality with the movement of the Philadelphia Chinatown Development Corporation (PCD) via a National Endowment for the Arts grant in 1979 and negotiations with the city. In these discussions, though, it was clear that agendas differed. As one participant recalled, "We went in to talk about housing and [local civic leader] Dick Doran[47] says, 'I can't help you with housing but I like this. I like this gate.' We were going in for housing and he likes the gate! I was a little upset to tell the truth."[48] In a sense, as historian Kathryn Wilson notes, the Friendship Gate became one more marker in a struggle for Chinese residents to belong as citizens and receive their rights against "the market-driven approaches to urban development that came to characterize the 1980s and beyond, approaches that engendered the commodification of ethnic identity and urban spaces to create cultural attractions."[49]

At the same time, the gate participated in geographies beyond the city. Construction celebrated a new treaty linking Tianjin and Philadelphia. While Philadelphia funded the project, artisans from Tianjin and Beijing became part of its authenticity at its construction in 1984 and refurbishment in 2003 and 2008. In this, Philadelphia became a forerunner of the wave of Chinatown gates that would follow, while claiming to be the "most authentic." Indeed, a 2007 newspaper story on the reconstruction noted that "'Washington was jealous,' said Cecilia Moy Yep, founder of the development corporation, which helped develop Philadelphia's gate. 'They said, 'You, Beijing, helped Philadelphia, but we are your sister city.' We want a gate, too.'"[50]

For Wilson, and those she interviewed, the legacy of the arch has been positive. Those feelings correspond to my own experiences and conversations there over decades: "Although tourism was not a main goal of the PCDC, Moy admits that it was 'in a way. We knew we had to put Chinatown in a positive light.' [...] At the same time, the gate, with its immense size and weight, ensures Chinatown's future in this location."[51] Still, this analysis is pregnant in its ambiguity and its sense of the fear that Chinatown might still be pushed out of the city. The gate remains an anchor as well as a link.

Yet, this very insistence can also distinguish the Chinese residents in Chinatown from the majority of the regional Chinese community, 90 percent of whom live outside Chinatown. This suggests other metropolitan divisions of class and assimilation that intersect with experience, as Lou Yi noted in 2007 reports on arch renovation: "Though struck by the beauty of the gate, Yakui Wu, 47, a former researcher at the Shanghai Social Science Institution, said he had never thought of living in Chinatown. 'It is nothing like Shanghai,' Wu said, complaining that Chinatown had dirty streets, outdated restaurants, bad service in hair salons, and limited parking. Instead of going to Chinatown, Wu lives on the Main Line [an expensive suburb] and drives to a near by Korean supermarket for Chinese food. 'Simpler and cleaner,' he said."[52]

The history, context, and meanings of Los Angeles and Philadelphia gates contrast with a final case: the older, iconic, *yet gateless* Chinatown in Lower Manhattan. Here, instead, of a pai-portal, strung across Canal Street in Lower Manhattan is a contraption of wires and lights that reads "WELCOME TO CHINATOWN." Similar wire signs hang at other edges of the neighborhood. While Manhattan also has the simple Kimlau Memorial Arch located in Chatham Square that commemorates US service members of Chinese ancestry who died in World War II, this Chinatown lacks a more stereotypical monumental portal of the paifang style (Fig. i). This situation has spurred protests from planners and political activists like Wellington Chen of the Chinatown Partnership who complained in 2012, "Every single traditional Chinatown has a gateway. What's the holdup?"[53]

Like the more vivid gate in Philadelphia and other exemplars worldwide, the existing markers in New York have ambivalent spatial and social meanings. Erected a century after Chinese workers fled from the Western goldfields and railroads and moved east, the signs scarcely demarcate any boundary. Along Canal Street, bustling Chinese stores selling tourist goods and knockoff products continue for blocks from the Manhattan Bridge (where another wire arch used to hang) past Lafayette, gradually mingling with other merchants of assorted accents (and Chinese goods) before reaching areas now undergoing the general gentrification of Manhattan that is threatening Chinatown itself.[54] The Chinese community has also spread into Little Italy to the north of Canal (with its own wire street arch), creating ambiguous claims on space and imagery.

Despite local discussions of building an arch since the 1960s, it was the crisis of 9/11, which isolated and endangered Chinatown as a downtown space cut off from transportation and visitors, that led leaders again to consider a more substantial archway.[55] They raised money from both the city and local donors.[56] Still, nothing has been built.

Manhattan's Chinatown, expanding along East Broadway with new Fujianese immigrants, actually represents only one of multiple Chinatowns in the metropolitan area. Flushing, Queens, developed as a center for Taiwanese immigrants in the 1970s and has since expanded with Chinese and pan-Asian capital into a welter of skyscrapers and stores. Yet it, too, lacks an arch.[57] So does Sunset Park, in Brooklyn, which has also become the fastest growing Chinese enclave in the city in the twenty-first century, surpassing Manhattan's to become the fourth largest such enclave in the United States. Here, however, discussion of a new arch

47 Democratic civic leader and Chief of Staff to former Governor Milton Shapp.

48 Wilson, *Ethnic Renewal in Philadelphia's Chinatown*, 118.

49 Ibid. One sees echoes in the title of a web page from the local Balch Institute: "A threshold to Chinatown. A gateway from the homeland." http://www2.hsp.org/exhibits/Balch%20exhibits/chinatown/gate.html.

50 Yi, "Big Plans to Awaken City's Faded Dragon."

51 Wilson, *Ethnic Renewal in Philadelphia's Chinatown*, 118.

52 Yi, "Big Plans to Awaken City's Faded Dragon."

53 Pearson, "Manhattan Chinatown Still Lacks Gateway Arch."

54 As cited previously, Bethany Li et al. noted the implications of gentrification for Chinatowns in Boston, Manhattan, and Philadelphia. Li et al., *Chinatown Then and Now*.

55 Barbara Ross, "Chinatown 's Garment Business Shrivels, Tourism Traffic Dwindles in Lasting Blow of 9/11," *New York Daily News*, September 5, 2011, http://www.nydailynews.com/new-york/chinatown-garment-biz-shrivels-tourist-traffic-dwindles-lasting-blow-9-11-article-1.954982.

56 "New York Chinatown to Build Gate, City Government allocated $250,000," 中国侨网 Overseas Chinese Net "纽约华埠建牌坊 市议会批25万资助" 2005年4月8日; Kurt Semple, "Chinatowns Renew Push for Traditional Gateways," *New York Times* October 31, 2103, http://www.nytimes.com/2013/11/01/nyregion/chinatowns-renew-push-for-traditional-gateways.html.

57 Hsiang-Shui Chen, *Chinatown No More: Taiwanese Immigrants in Contemporary New York (*Ithaca: Cornell University Press, 1992).

58 "New Arch to Welcome Visitors to Brooklyn's Chinatown in Sunset Park," *News 12 Brooklyn*, April 19, 2013, http://brooklyn.news12.com/news/new-arch-to-welcome-visitors-to-brooklyn-s-chinatown-in-sunset-park-1.5103707. See Semple, "Chinatowns Renew Push for Traditional Gateways"; and Tarry Hum, *Making a Global Immigrant Neighborhood: Brooklyn's Sunset Park* (Philadelphia: Temple University Press, 2014).

i)

i) Kimlau Memorial Arch in Chatham Square, New York, NY. Photograph by Mahdi Sabbagh, 2016.

surfaced in the press in 2013, with a project to be donated by Beijing's burgeoning Chaoyang District. While nothing further has surfaced in this regard, Sunset Park is less well-known than the older Chinatowns in Flushing and Manhattan and is threatened by gentrification and displacement.[58] Here, then, we should consider the gate as a potential way of instating social division as presence in a situation of perceived threats.

In all these cases, the functions of Chinatown gates—even if only imagined in newspaper reports—are cultural and contextual, yet deeply rooted in local relations. In Philadelphia, the arch connects as much as it divides. In New York, the absence of arches speaks to the historical seniority and iconicity of Manhattan's Chinatown, which scarcely needed an arch to attract visitors in the past. The possibility of a New York arch in another Chinatown has been called upon as an indicator of resilience that even the buoyant streets of Chinatowns could not guarantee in the face of global terrorism and local gentrification.

CONCLUSIONS

Winston Kyan, who has contributed provocative readings of Chinatown architecture, asks, "Given the prominent role of the built environment in constructing, informing and translating the folklore and folklife of Chinatown, how do architecture and its representations interact to tell the tales of Chinatown as providing ethnic protection for its inhabitants as well as brokering ethnic difference for broader consumption?"[59] These colorful and imposing multi-story gates of wood, concrete, and metal that now mark so many Chinatowns worldwide seem almost archetypically meaningful as monuments of division. At first glance, they emphasize and embody the historical segregation of Chinese diasporic communities not only in space but also in time, as mythical places of the exotic other. Yet, as I have suggested through this ethnographic and comparative examination of their presence, social and cultural meanings, and ongoing global propagation, it is necessary to read gates as sites of evocation and connection even more than division and differentiation.

As the closer reading of select American cases suggests, these arches can frame the flows in and out of Chinatown, calling attention to a global enclave in its presence in the city as much as in its exclusion. Yet, these arches also speak to agency—the ability of Chinese to make a city through Chinese constructions that stand out from indigenous vernaculars and embody not only the actions and voices of longterm populations but also the possible leveraging of a newly global China. This reading, in turn, speaks also to the absence of gateways, whether presumed to be a mark of embattled strength, as in Manhattan, or of weakness, as in Barcelona.

Arches may seem to frame Chinatown as a timeless other, and certainly this was implied in Los Angeles and other cities. Yet for the Chinese immigrants, local and global, and descendant-citizens who build gates or seek to construct them—gates mark a permanence, a connection between an era in which Chinese people had no place in the city and their claim to be visible citizens today. At the same time, the pai-portals' references to transnational symbolism and cooperation in funding and construction "create" a gate between the host country and a distant China. The gates create a new notion of proximity and shifting relations of political and economic power. It is striking, for example, that the People's Republic of China has patronized gates in Philadelphia, Havana, and Washington but not in New York City, perhaps one of the best known of global Chinatowns.

Gates, finally, have become symbols for cities, whatever the role of their Chinese populations. Hence Seattle and Washington D.C. have been characterized as catching up, while other urban administrations like San José, Costa Rica, want a new arch to attract Chinese investment and affirm globalization. In 2013 the Canadian post office issued eight commemorative stamps of Chinatown gates in Mississauga, Montreal, Ottawa, Toronto, Victoria, Vancouver, and Winnipeg, all built since the 1980s, noting, "In Canada today, these gates are often the most visible representation of Chinatown in our cities, symbolic of cooperation between various levels of Canadian and Chinese governments, businesses, and citizens."[60] Meanwhile, *People's Daily* has explained to Chinese traveling abroad that they should learn to appreciate these gates as "symbols of Chinatowns," noting to visitors to Washington's pailou that "you will be swept up by its magnificence."[61]

Today, paifang structures neither enforce nor eliminate the social, cultural, economic, and political differences of Chinese and their descendants across global metropoles. As open portals, instead, they ask us to pause and reflect on the complex and changing architecture—physical, social, and symbolic—of divisions within cities of global flows and ever-changing human agency.

59 Kyan, "Electric Pagodas and Hyphenate Gates," 25.

60 Chinatown Gates Collection, Canada Post Website, https://www.canadapost.ca/shop/gifts/stamp-collectors/p-341953.jsf.

61 "美国唐人街的牌楼 American Chinatowns Gates " *People's Daily* (overseas edition) Accessed:2013-02-18 16:54 http://www.usnook.com/travel/china/complete/2012/0705/555.html.

The Making of a Public: Guerrilla Art in the 1970s and 80s

JENNY HOLZER
with an introduction by the editors

Following the Occupy and Black Lives Matter movements that began in 2011 and 2012, a new discussion arose about public space in the city and its relationship to inequality. Although the organization of these movements was largely nonphysical, taking advantage of social media, it was their manifestation in physical space that enabled their visibility and power. Ironically, the most iconic of the American Occupy protests was in Zuccotti Park, a privately owned public space in Manhattan. This fact raises questions about what is public in the US—are there truly public spaces where the collective can imagine itself and demonstrate agency?

The public/private divide in the American city has witnessed some slippage—the private seeping into the public through new forms of ownership as well as digital media. Parks, plazas, and public streets themselves can be dominated by advertising—both on physical signage and on the phones we read while traversing the sidewalk. Whether literally or psychologically, access to such public spaces is often reserved for only those with capital. What is left of public collective identity in the everyday physical experience of urbanity? How can art and architecture provoke a recognition of what is public?

Jenny Holzer's early work in New York, Seattle, and other cities in the 1970s and 1980s speaks to the role that art can play in engaging the public. Her projects pictured on these pages playfully subvert space that would otherwise be reserved for corporate advertising, transforming the sidewalk into a place of possible political engagement. Holzer's work uses words that can provoke visceral reactions, a reminder of our humanness and our shared experience in a flawed society.

The urban context of these works was quite different from today's. These were gritty, often dangerous places—not the polished and patrolled streets of many contemporary downtowns. A client of Holzer's recently ordered a photograph from this earlier era and requested that the litter in the image be edited out. What does it say about how our city streets have transformed? Has the sidewalk become more about erasure, cleanliness, and capitalism than collective presence? Has public art itself become co-opted as a mechanism of gentrification rather than freedom of expression? This photo essay asks us to reflect on the state of public space and the role of art in raising the consciousness of a collective public.

PROTECT ME
FROM WHAT
I WANT

OF GENIUS
IS JUST AS DANGEROUS
CAN RUIN YOUR
IS INEVITABLE
CAN BE A USEFUL
IS PERFECTLY HEALTHY
IS IMMORAL
IS A LEGITIMATE AREA OF INVESTIGATION
DESIRES ARE DESPOILING THE EARTH
INACTIVITY IS PREFERABLE TO MINDLESS FUNCTIONING
YOUR UNCONSCIOUS IS TRUER THAN YOUR CONSCIOUS MIND
IS DEADLY
PUNISHMENT AWAITS REALLY BAD PEOPLE
INTENTIONS CAN YIELD GOOD RESULTS
ONE WITH YOURSELF IS INCREASINGLY UNPOPULAR
IS MORE IMPORTANT THAN ANYTHING ELSE
IS NOT ALWAYS THE BEST WAY
IS A SIGN OF LIFE
OF YOURSELF MEANS YOU'RE A FOOL
IN REBIRTH IS THE SAME AS ADMITTING DEFEAT
MAKES YOU DO CRAZY THINGS
MORE CONDUCIVE TO CREATIVITY THAN IS ANXIETY
FEAR IS CALMING
VALUABLE BECAUSE IT LETS THE OPPRESSED BE TYRANTS
THE NEW IS DANGEROUS TO SOCIETY
ARE THE CRUELEST OF ALL
ARE THE HOPE OF THE FUTURE
IS A NICE IDEA WITH NO SUBSTANCE
IS AS ARTIFICIAL AS PLASTIC
YOURSELF IS A WAY TO STAY HONEST
PROPERTY IS RELATIVELY UNIMPORTANT
BE AN END IN ITSELF
CREATIVE THING
BE A MEAL TICKET
MORE VALUABLE THAN METAPHOR
SACRIFICED TO INCREASE GROUP SOLIDARITY
APPROPRIATE RESPONSE TO MOST SITUATIONS
A KIND OF ANESTHESIA
TRUST IN EXPERTS
LIVES FOR THEM
THE REAL ISSUES
IS A FRIGHTENING CONTRADICTION
GIVES YOU CONSIDERABLE PERSPECTIVE
AS FALLING OFF A LOG
POLLUTION
AS VALUABLE AS

TALK TO ME. DON'T
BE POLITE TO ME. DON'T
TRY TO MAKE ME FEEL NICE.
DON'T RELAX. I'LL CUT THE
SMILE OFF YOUR FACE. YOU
THINK I DON'T KNOW WHAT'S
GOING ON. YOU THINK I'M
AFRAID TO REACT. THE JOKE'S
ON YOU. I'M BIDING MY TIME,
LOOKING FOR THE SPOT. YOU
THINK NO ONE CAN REACH YOU,
NO ONE CAN HAVE WHAT YOU
HAVE. I'VE BEEN PLANNING
WHILE YOU'RE PLAYING. I'VE
BEEN SAVING WHILE YOU'RE
SPENDING. THE GAME IS
ALMOST OVER SO IT'S
TIME YOU ACKNOWLEDGE ME.
DO YOU WANT TO FALL NOT
EVER KNOWING WHO TOOK YOU?

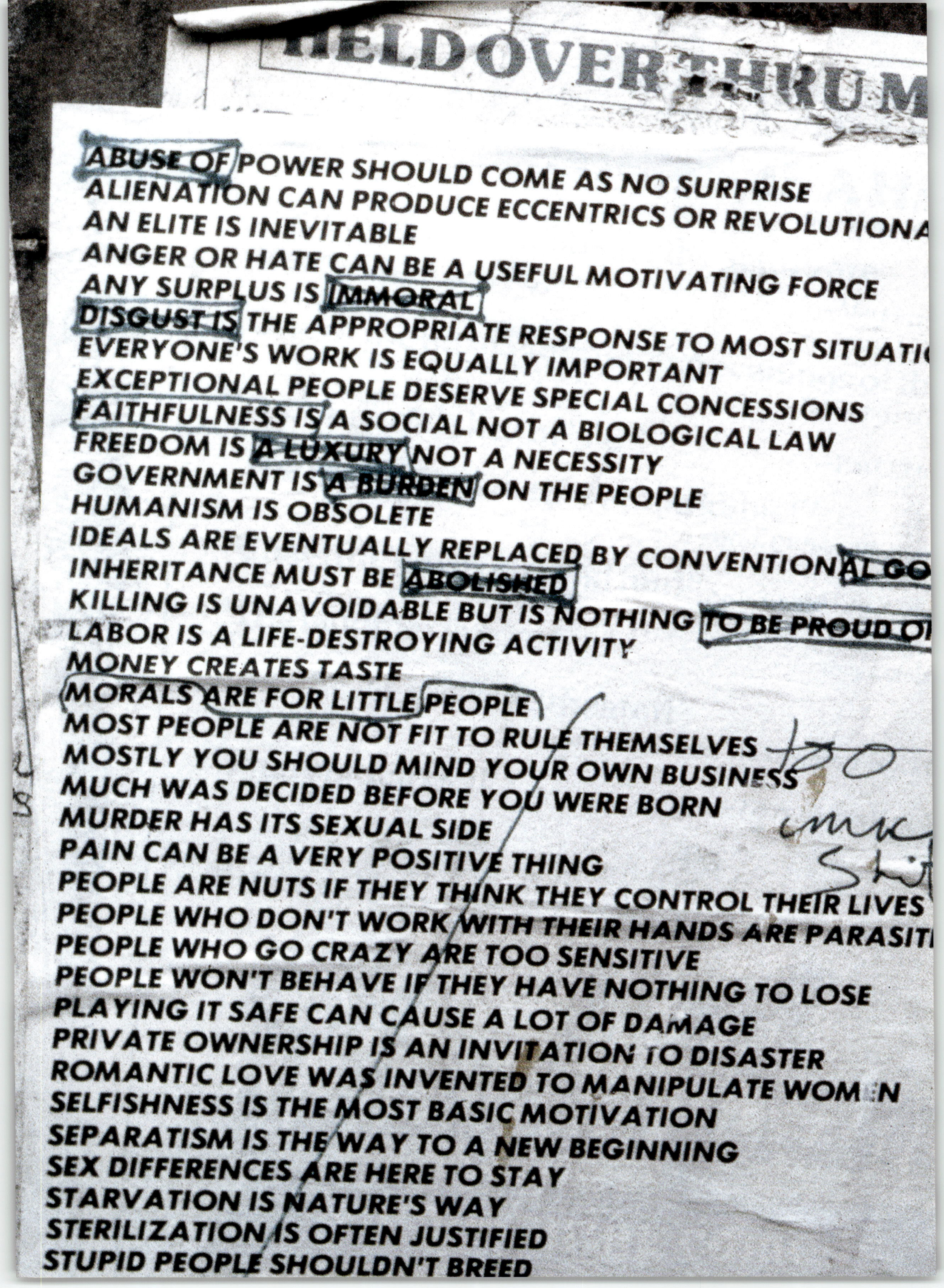
HELD OVER THRU M
ABUSE OF POWER SHOULD COME AS NO SURPRISE
ALIENATION CAN PRODUCE ECCENTRICS OR REVOLUTIONA
AN ELITE IS INEVITABLE
ANGER OR HATE CAN BE A USEFUL MOTIVATING FORCE
ANY SURPLUS IS IMMORAL
DISGUST IS THE APPROPRIATE RESPONSE TO MOST SITUATI
EVERYONE'S WORK IS EQUALLY IMPORTANT
EXCEPTIONAL PEOPLE DESERVE SPECIAL CONCESSIONS
FAITHFULNESS IS A SOCIAL NOT A BIOLOGICAL LAW
FREEDOM IS A LUXURY NOT A NECESSITY
GOVERNMENT IS A BURDEN ON THE PEOPLE
HUMANISM IS OBSOLETE
IDEALS ARE EVENTUALLY REPLACED BY CONVENTIONAL GO
INHERITANCE MUST BE ABOLISHED
KILLING IS UNAVOIDABLE BUT IS NOTHING TO BE PROUD OF
LABOR IS A LIFE-DESTROYING ACTIVITY
MONEY CREATES TASTE
MORALS ARE FOR LITTLE PEOPLE
MOST PEOPLE ARE NOT FIT TO RULE THEMSELVES
MOSTLY YOU SHOULD MIND YOUR OWN BUSINESS
MUCH WAS DECIDED BEFORE YOU WERE BORN
MURDER HAS ITS SEXUAL SIDE
PAIN CAN BE A VERY POSITIVE THING
PEOPLE ARE NUTS IF THEY THINK THEY CONTROL THEIR LIVES
PEOPLE WHO DON'T WORK WITH THEIR HANDS ARE PARASITI
PEOPLE WHO GO CRAZY ARE TOO SENSITIVE
PEOPLE WON'T BEHAVE IF THEY HAVE NOTHING TO LOSE
PLAYING IT SAFE CAN CAUSE A LOT OF DAMAGE
PRIVATE OWNERSHIP IS AN INVITATION TO DISASTER
ROMANTIC LOVE WAS INVENTED TO MANIPULATE WOMEN
SELFISHNESS IS THE MOST BASIC MOTIVATION
SEPARATISM IS THE WAY TO A NEW BEGINNING
SEX DIFFERENCES ARE HERE TO STAY
STARVATION IS NATURE'S WAY
STERILIZATION IS OFTEN JUSTIFIED
STUPID PEOPLE SHOULDN'T BREED

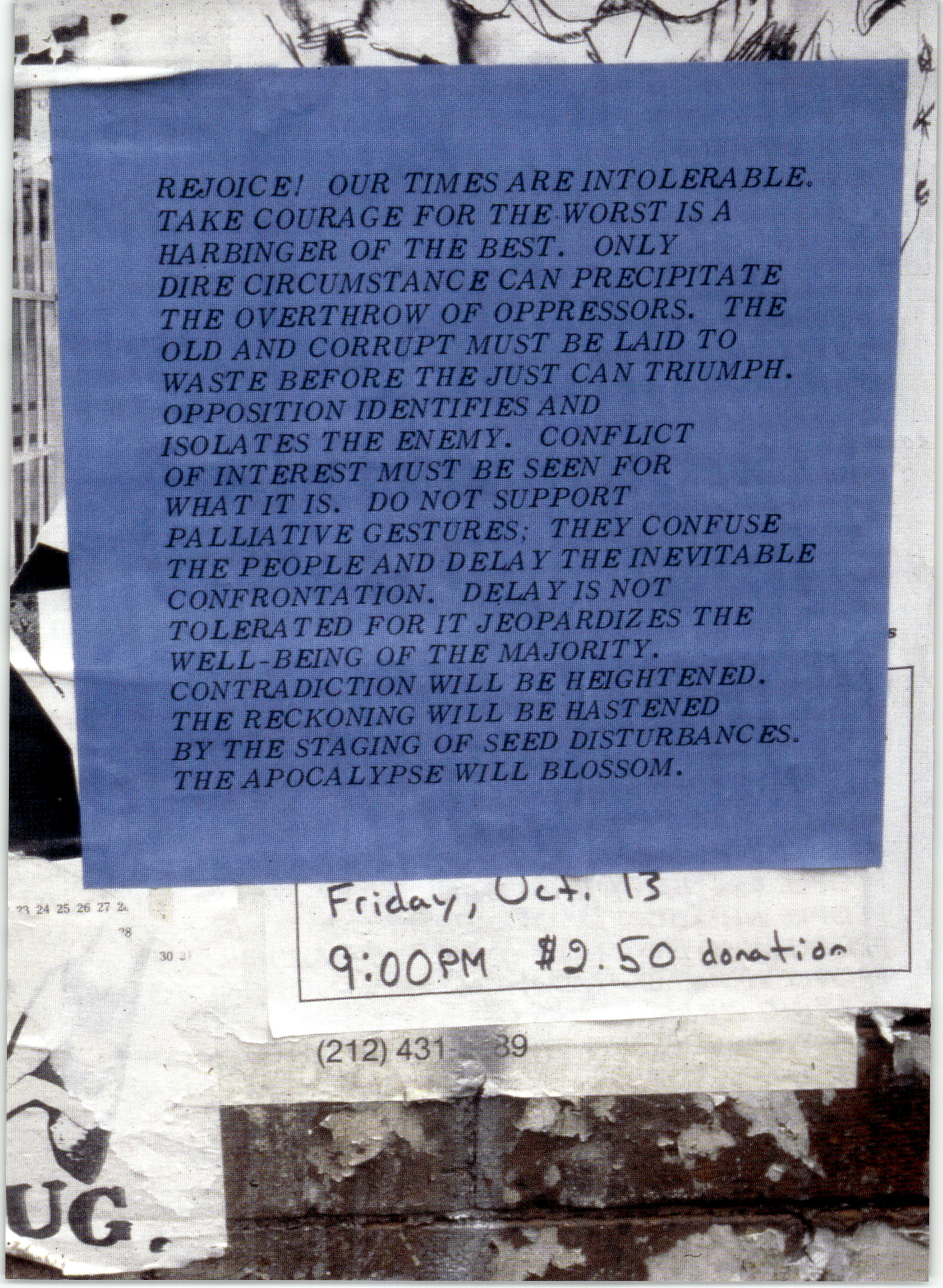
REJOICE! OUR TIMES ARE INTOLERABLE. TAKE COURAGE FOR THE WORST IS A HARBINGER OF THE BEST. ONLY DIRE CIRCUMSTANCE CAN PRECIPITATE THE OVERTHROW OF OPPRESSORS. THE OLD AND CORRUPT MUST BE LAID TO WASTE BEFORE THE JUST CAN TRIUMPH. OPPOSITION IDENTIFIES AND ISOLATES THE ENEMY. CONFLICT OF INTEREST MUST BE SEEN FOR WHAT IT IS. DO NOT SUPPORT PALLIATIVE GESTURES; THEY CONFUSE THE PEOPLE AND DELAY THE INEVITABLE CONFRONTATION. DELAY IS NOT TOLERATED FOR IT JEOPARDIZES THE WELL-BEING OF THE MAJORITY. CONTRADICTION WILL BE HEIGHTENED. THE RECKONING WILL BE HASTENED BY THE STAGING OF SEED DISTURBANCES. THE APOCALYPSE WILL BLOSSOM.
Friday, Oct. 13
9:00PM $2.50 donation
UG.

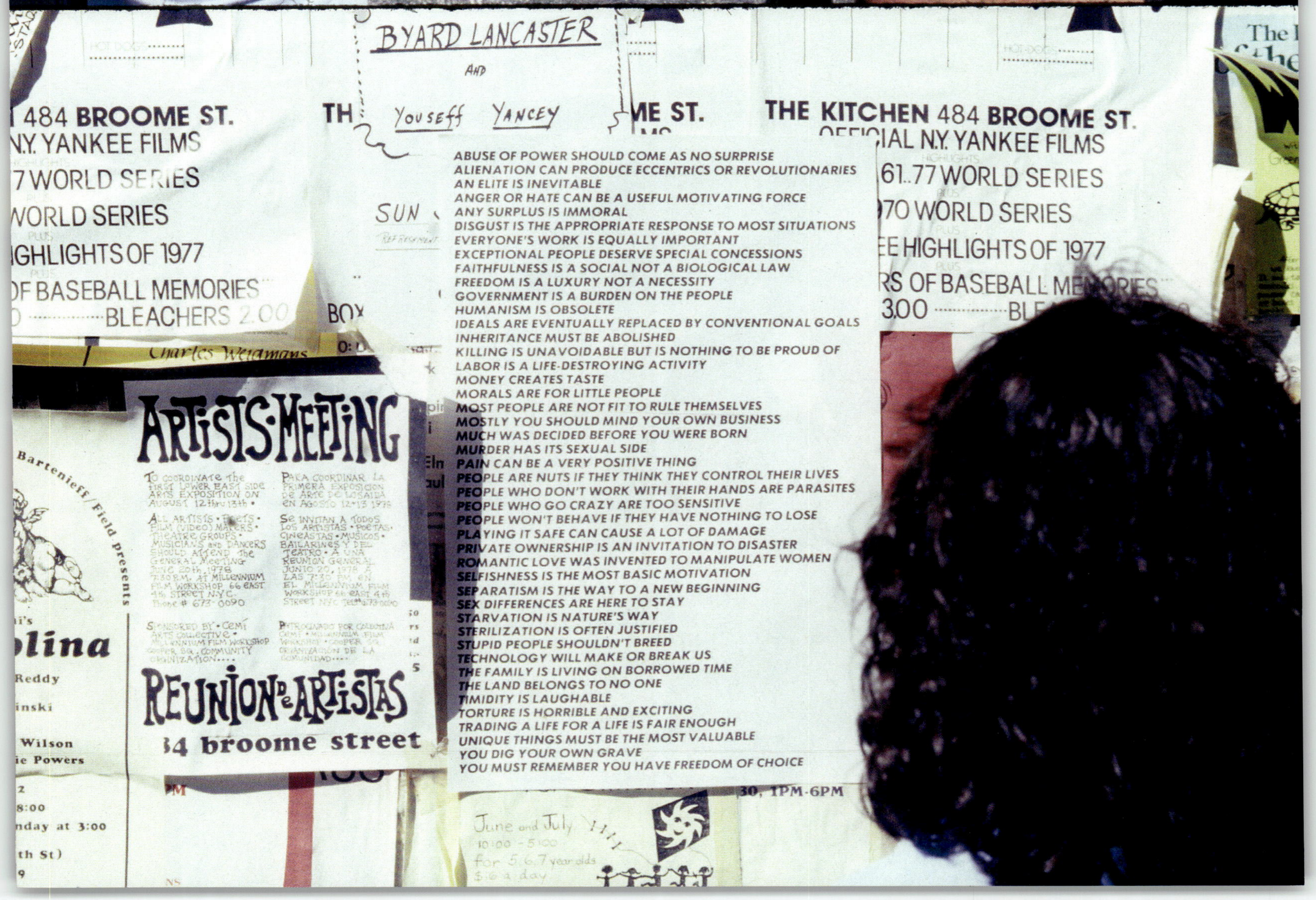
BYARD LANCASTER
AND
Yousef Yancey
THE KITCHEN 484 BROOME ST.
N.Y. YANKEE FILMS
WORLD SERIES
HIGHLIGHTS OF 1977
OF BASEBALL MEMORIES
BLEACHERS 2.00
ABUSE OF POWER SHOULD COME AS NO SURPRISE
ALIENATION CAN PRODUCE ECCENTRICS OR REVOLUTIONARIES
AN ELITE IS INEVITABLE
ANGER OR HATE CAN BE A USEFUL MOTIVATING FORCE
ANY SURPLUS IS IMMORAL
DISGUST IS THE APPROPRIATE RESPONSE TO MOST SITUATIONS
EVERYONE'S WORK IS EQUALLY IMPORTANT
EXCEPTIONAL PEOPLE DESERVE SPECIAL CONCESSIONS
FAITHFULNESS IS A SOCIAL NOT A BIOLOGICAL LAW
FREEDOM IS A LUXURY NOT A NECESSITY
GOVERNMENT IS A BURDEN ON THE PEOPLE
HUMANISM IS OBSOLETE
IDEALS ARE EVENTUALLY REPLACED BY CONVENTIONAL GOALS
INHERITANCE MUST BE ABOLISHED
KILLING IS UNAVOIDABLE BUT IS NOTHING TO BE PROUD OF
LABOR IS A LIFE-DESTROYING ACTIVITY
MONEY CREATES TASTE
MORALS ARE FOR LITTLE PEOPLE
MOST PEOPLE ARE NOT FIT TO RULE THEMSELVES
MOSTLY YOU SHOULD MIND YOUR OWN BUSINESS
MUCH WAS DECIDED BEFORE YOU WERE BORN
MURDER HAS ITS SEXUAL SIDE
PAIN CAN BE A VERY POSITIVE THING
PEOPLE ARE NUTS IF THEY THINK THEY CONTROL THEIR LIVES
PEOPLE WHO DON'T WORK WITH THEIR HANDS ARE PARASITES
PEOPLE WHO GO CRAZY ARE TOO SENSITIVE
PEOPLE WON'T BEHAVE IF THEY HAVE NOTHING TO LOSE
PLAYING IT SAFE CAN CAUSE A LOT OF DAMAGE
PRIVATE OWNERSHIP IS AN INVITATION TO DISASTER
ROMANTIC LOVE WAS INVENTED TO MANIPULATE WOMEN
SELFISHNESS IS THE MOST BASIC MOTIVATION
SEPARATISM IS THE WAY TO A NEW BEGINNING
SEX DIFFERENCES ARE HERE TO STAY
STARVATION IS NATURE'S WAY
STERILIZATION IS OFTEN JUSTIFIED
STUPID PEOPLE SHOULDN'T BREED
TECHNOLOGY WILL MAKE OR BREAK US
THE FAMILY IS LIVING ON BORROWED TIME
THE LAND BELONGS TO NO ONE
TIMIDITY IS LAUGHABLE
TORTURE IS HORRIBLE AND EXCITING
TRADING A LIFE FOR A LIFE IS FAIR ENOUGH
UNIQUE THINGS MUST BE THE MOST VALUABLE
YOU DIG YOUR OWN GRAVE
YOU MUST REMEMBER YOU HAVE FREEDOM OF CHOICE
ARTISTS MEETING
REUNION DE ARTISTAS
34 broome street
June and July

Selwyn
LIPPING INTO MADNESS
IS GOOD FOR THE SAKE
OF COMPARISON
IT IS IN YOUR SELF-INTEREST
TO FIND A WAY
TO BE VERY TENDER
PEEP SHOW

CAMERAS
ELECTRONICS
CALCULATORS
TYPEWRITERS
LUGGAGE
APOLLO
KARATE ACADEMY
PEOPLE WHO DO
WITH THEIR
ARE PAR

TIMES SQUARE
PEOPLE WHO DON'T WORK
WITH THEIR HANDS
ARE PARASITES
MURDER
HAS ITS SEXUAL SIDE

WHAT URGE
WILL SAVE US
NOW THAT SEX WON'T?
YOU ARE TRAPPED
ON THE EARTH
SO YOU WILL EXPLODE
YOU ARE SO COMPLEX
THAT YOU DON'T ALWAYS
RESPOND TO DANGER

GO WHERE
PEOPLE SLEEP
AND SEE IF
THEY'RE SAFE
ACK OF CHARISMA
CAN BE FATAL
4
SMASH
HITS
TO CHANGE IT QUICKLY

CATEGORIZING
FEAR
IS
CALMING

YOU ARE TRAPPED
ON THE EARTH
SO YOU
WILL EXPLODE
ANTI

THINGS ARE SO
URGENT NOW
THAT SUICIDE IS
ALMOST OBSOLETE

WHEN SOMEONE BEATS YOU WITH A FLASHLIGHT YOU MAKE LIGHT SHINE IN ALL DIRECTIONS
SAVOR KINDNESS BECAUSE CRUELTY IS ALWAYS POSSIBLE LATER
PUSH FOR COIN
Free calls
Toll Free 800 Numbers
800 + Number
TEAR DUCTS SEEM TO BE A GRIEF PROVISION
INSERT ONE COIN AT A TIME. TURN HANDLE TO RIGHT AS FAR AS POSSIBLE AFTER EACH COIN.
YOU ARE SO COMPLEX THAT YOU DON'T ALWAYS RESPOND TO DANGER

SAVOR KINDNESS
BECAUSE CRUELTY
IS ALWAYS
POSSIBLE LATER

01
Survival (1983–85), 1985
Electronic sign. 20 x 40 ft. /6.1 x 12.2 m. Installation: Selection from the Survival Series, Times Square, New York, 1985.© 1985 Jenny Holzer, member Artists Rights Society (ARS), NY. Photo: John Marchael

02
Truisms (1977–79), 1978
Photostats, audio tape, posters 20 x 20 ft. / 6.1 x 6.1 m Installation: Franklin Furnace, New York, 1978. © 1978 Jenny Holzer, member Artists Rights Society (ARS), NY
Photo: Mike Glier

03
Truisms (1977–1979), 1984
Offset posters. 34.75 x 22.9 in. / 88.3 x 58.1 cm, each Installation: Poster Project, Seattle, Washington, USA, 1984. © 1984 Jenny Holzer, member Artists Rights Society (ARS), NY

04
Inflammatory Essays, (1979–82), 1982 Offset poster. 17 x 17 in. / 43.2 x 43.2 cm Installation: New York, 1982. © 1982 Jenny Holzer, member Artists Rights Society (ARS), NY
Photo: Jenny Holzer

05
Truisms (1977–79), 1977
Offset poster. 34.75 x 22.9 in. / 88.3 x 58.1 cm. Installation: New York, 1977. © 1977 Jenny Holzer, member Artists Rights Society (ARS), NY

06
Inflammatory Essays (1979–82), 1978–79 Offset poster. 17 x 17 in. / 43.2 x 43.2 cm Installation: New York, 1978-79 © 1978–79 Jenny Holzer, member Artists Rights Society (ARS), NY

07
Truisms (1977–79), 1977
Offset poster. 24 x 18 in. / 61 x 45.7 cm. Installation: New York, 1977. © 1977 Jenny Holzer, member Artists Rights Society (ARS), NY

08
Truisms (1977–79) © 1977 Jenny Holzer, member Artists Rights Society (ARS), NY

09
Exhibition view: *Forty-second Street Art Project,* Times Square, New York, 1993 © 1993 Jenny Holzer, member Artists Rights Society (ARS), NY
Photo: Maggie Hopp

10
Exhibition view: *Forty-second Street Art Project,* Times Square, New York, 1993 © 1993 Jenny Holzer, member Artists Rights Society (ARS), NY

11
Exhibition view: *Forty-second Street Art Project,* Times Square, New York, 1993 © 1993 Jenny Holzer, member Artists Rights Society (ARS), NY
Photo: Maggie Hopp

12
Exhibition view: *Forty-second Street Art Project,* Times Square, New York, 1993 © 1993 Jenny Holzer, member Artists Rights Society (ARS), NY
Photo: Maggie Hopp

13
Exhibition view: *Forty-second Street Art Project,* Times Square, New York, 1993 © 1993 Jenny Holzer, member Artists Rights Society (ARS), NY
Photo: Maggie Hopp

14
Survival: You Are Trapped..., 1983 Offset silver sticker 2.5 x 3 in. / 6.3 x 7.6 cm
Text: Survival, 1983–85
Installation: New York, 1983 © 1983 Jenny Holzer, member Artists Rights Society (ARS), NY
Photo: Mike Glier

15
Survival: Things Are So Urgent..., 1983. Offset silver sticker. 2.5 x 3 in. / 6.3 x 7.6 cm
Text: Survival, 1983–85
Installation: New York, 1983 © 1983 Jenny Holzer, member Artists Rights Society (ARS), NY
Photo: Mike Glier

16
Survival: When Someone Beats You..., 1983 Offset silver sticker. 2.5 x 3 in. / 6.3 x 7.6 cm. Text: Survival, 1983–85. Installation: New York, 1983. © 1983 Jenny Holzer, member Artists Rights Society (ARS), NY
Photo: Mike Glier

17
Survival: Savor Kindness..., 1983 Offset silver sticker. 2.5 x 3 in. / 6.3 x 7.6 cm
Text: Survival, 1983–85
Installation: New York, 1983 © 1983 Jenny Holzer, member Artists Rights Society (ARS), NY
Photo: Mike Glier

18
Survival: Tear Ducts Seem..., 1983 Offset silver sticker 2.5 x 3 in. / 6.3 x 7.6 cm
Text: Survival, 1983–85
Installation: New York, 1983 © 1983 Jenny Holzer, member Artists Rights Society (ARS), NY
Photo: Mike Glier

19
Survival: You Are So Complex..., 1983 Offset silver sticker. 2.5 x 3 in. / 6.3 x 7.6 cm. Text: Survival, 1983–85
Installation: New York, 1983 © 1983 Jenny Holzer, member Artists Rights Society (ARS), NY
Photo: Mike Glier

20
Survival: Savor Kindness..., 1983 Offset silver sticker 2.5 x 3 in. / 6.3 x 7.6 cm. Text: Survival, 1983–85 Installation: New York, 1983. © 1983 Jenny Holzer, member Artists Rights Society (ARS), NY
Photo: Mike Glier

21
Inflammatory Essays (1979–82), 1984. Offset posters. 17 x 17 in. / 43.2 x 43.2 cm, each. Installation: Poster Project, Seattle, Washington, USA, 1984. © 1984 Jenny Holzer, member Artists Rights Society (ARS), NY

Studio Gang

Toward new possibility in the public realm, together: Polis Station

Jeanne Gang and Alissa Anderson

THE STAKES

A growing body of research demonstrates that the more we interact with people who are different from us, the more innovative and engaged we become, making better decisions and developing successful solutions to complex problems that fuel social and economic progress. Cities are key sites where diverse people come together and conceive these ideas that move the world forward.[1] So what might this mean for the United States, where our urban environments are trending toward fragmentation?

Economic segregation is increasing, with one-third of American families in major metropolitan areas now living in either high- or low-income neighborhoods—a division that is greater than double that of 1970.[2] Further, concentration of poverty is increasing, with the number of high-poverty urban neighborhoods having tripled, and the number of poor people living in them having doubled over that same forty-plus year period.[3]

Multiple overlapping forces are behind these trends; most notably, rising income inequality across the nation and public policies at various levels of government that make it difficult for lower-income families to move into middle- and higher-income neighborhoods.[4] Combined, they are producing toxic conditions for individuals, families, and communities. Researchers are accumulating evidence about how the negative effects associated with poverty are amplified when a large fraction of a poor person's neighbors are also poor—including worse mental and physical health, higher crime, and obstructed economic mobility. Further, as 75 percent of residents in high-poverty US neighborhoods are African American or Latino, these effects disproportionately burden the lives of people of color.[5]

Seeing this growing divide embedded in the shifting fabric of urban America, how can architects and designers proceed? Will we mirror it by sorting ourselves into architects of the rich and architects of the poor? To be sure, there are those who have adapted their practices to the typologies serving first-world luxury lifestyles, focusing their design energy on formal innovation, while others have centered their work on addressing social conditions by building for those in need of the basics. The dominant perception within the discipline is that the former is architecture with a capital "A," whose creative success hinges on its formal qualities, while the latter's contribution is socially beneficial but not held to the same creative standard, or sometimes not considered design at all.

But this divergence of design practice and its assumed value is not a forgone conclusion. In the fertile space between assumed polarities lie many ways forward in which architects can synthesize formal technique and social questions. Historically, we can find this synthesis in modernism. Born in a time of upheaval and great divergence in wealth, the architects of the Modern Movement engaged major social issues with high design. In doing so they realized revolutionary formal ideas in projects that continue to impact people from all walks of life. Le Corbusier himself did his most innovative work in the social realm, synthesizing design and human needs in projects for urban growth, low-cost housing, and shelter for the homeless (*Cité de Refuge*, 1929–33).

Today, as the challenges in many US urban cores and inner ring suburbs resonate with those of post-war reconstruction and the Great Depression, it is time for architects to explore how current social science and movements for social justice can inform a renewed design avant-garde propelled by public interest. Recognizing that rising income inequality and the concentration of poverty are intertwined crises that ultimately harm everyone, architects can—rather than mirroring society's widening rifts—discover new possibilities for the discipline and beyond.

THE APPROACH

Essential for this work is exploring the role that US cities' civic fabric can play in empowering communities. The places that have historically made up the American public realm —from parks, schools, and libraries to transit and recreation centers—have been key sites where people access opportunities and form relationships across demographic boundaries. These networks of relationships are what social scientists refer to as "social capital," the bonds and shared commitments that enable societies to function and progress.[6] Today, however, we can see that social capital is decreasing in America, a trend that appears to be related to a weakening public realm. Whether demonstrated in declining levels of trust, time

Fig 1. 6th District

Fig 2. 10th District

The current police station prototype in use in Chicago's 6th, 7th, 8th, and 10th police districts.

Fig 3. 7th District

Fig 4. 8th District

spent socializing with neighbors, use of public transportation, or a number of other metrics, it appears that disinvestment and disengagement from the public realm has damaged cities' ability to support the diverse human connections that make them flourish and that make our nation capable of addressing larger-scale issues such as inequality and climate change.[7]

Our practice is developing an approach to urban intervention that aims to help reactivate the American public realm and rebuild diverse social relationships. It is informed by ecology, the field that arose in the mid-twentieth century as scientists moved away from studying individual species and toward understanding the web of relationships between species and their greater environment. Though certain notions of ecology have been used in recent years within the theory and practice of architecture, urban design, and landscape design, we are now using it to conceptualize the organization of cities' public realms and imagine new possibilities at the scale of architecture.

Drawing insight from an expanded, human-scaled sense of ecology, our urban approach diverges from those popular in the past in a few key ways. First, instead of focusing design energy on conceiving totally new structures, it "starts with what's there"—the publicly-owned spaces that already exist in cities, including civic buildings, streets, parks, vacant land, and bodies of water. This is in part a pragmatic move, which recognizes the ubiquity and inherent potential of the scale of what the urban public holds in common: thirty to fifty percent of the land in US cities.[8] It is also a sustainable move informed by natural ecologies, as we see in nature that using the least energy possible is the preferred mode and key to survival. Finally, it is a socially strategic, democratic move, which understands the reduced yet still significant role of public places and institutions in the lives and daily experiences of Americans, and focuses directly on enhancing these existing relationships to make an inclusive and robust human impact.

Second, in contrast to the top-down approach of urban renewal, which often imposed sweeping and destructive changes on neighborhoods in service of grand, city-wide visions, this updated approach defers to neighborhood communities and designs at their scale. It allows city-wide change to happen in a grassroots way, spreading outward from many different nodes that develop into a strong, distributed network as individual neighborhoods activate their public realms. The role of the architect or designer here is not to single-handedly imagine and delineate the future they presume will be most successful. Instead it is to lead a collective process imagining and shaping multiple shared futures, whose success is predicated on the aspirations and engagement of the people who will make them possible. This work entails building a multifaceted understanding of a neighborhood and its public assets through research, community engagement, and analysis (including first-person observation, data analytics, and conversations with residents, community leaders, policy-makers, and other key actors) to identify specific possibilities and develop design ideas that bridge between present conditions and collective goals. The methodology and overarching aim are consistent, but the results are always as unique as the communities from which they emerge.

Fig 5. Watch box, New York City, ca. 1810.

Finally, this urban design approach is grounded in the scale of architecture—that is, it mines the possibilities that come from working at the scale between long-range master planning and one-off, tactical urbanism interventions. Typical urban plans are important visionary and practical tools for city authorities, but the future that they describe is often difficult for a general audience to understand and too abstract to inspire personal investment. On the other end of the spectrum, tactical urbanism projects tend to be isolated interventions with a limited scope and duration of engagement with their community. Often "parachute pop-ups" made by individuals or organizations from outside a neighborhood, these projects do not share or transfer agency; instead they continue to separate the people with the most at stake (neighborhood residents) from the power to make change, thereby greatly limiting their impact. The architectural scale sits at a sweet spot in its ability to be imagined, practically realized, and measurably impactful. Communicated with an accessible narrative and images, architecture can create common ground that engages diverse stakeholders in the design process and fosters their active ownership of the projects that result. Ideally, these projects are actionable investments at multiple scales that can unfold over time as community preferences evolve and successful projects accumulate, with their demonstrable positive effects attracting additional social and economic investment.

Fig 6. 2nd Street Police House, New Bedford, Massachusetts, 1856.

Fig 7. West Town Police Station, Chicago, Illinois, 1917.

Fig 8. Police Call Box, Washington, DC, 1912.

THE POLICE STATION

This urban approach has thus far been tested most thoroughly in Polis Station, an ongoing project exploring how one type of civic building—the police station—can be reimagined through an inclusive design process to better serve neighborhood communities and the urban environment as a whole. Police stations are a sensitive piece of the American public realm. They are publicly-funded institutions with a civic mandate. They are also often charged spaces, both in everyday experience and in the public imagination. Recent acts of violence by and against police officers across the nation have further laden them with complex and controversial meanings. These tragedies and resulting protest have spotlit systemic inequities connected with policing, and calls for policing reform have led to updated recommendations for policy and training. Many Americans are seizing this moment to identify and leverage resources that can help make change. Our practice has posited that police stations—both in spite of and because of the tensions surrounding them—are one such possible resource.

Polis Station draws on the classical idea of the polis, the urban body politic, to reframe stations as part of their surrounding community fabric rather than nodes in spaces of patrol like police precincts or districts. Recognizing that stations are civic buildings located in so many neighborhoods throughout the US, the project addresses them as well-positioned local tools that communities can use to implement short- and long-term changes they want to see. Given that station buildings are publicly owned and all citizens have a stake and should have a say in how they operate, Polis Station asks the question, What do we want our police stations to be?

Fig 9. 9th District Police Station, St. Louis, Missouri, 1936.

The project approaches the police station from two angles: the station building and the neighborhood. It targets the core role of stations by exploring how altering their programming and physical spaces could support healthier police-community relationships—above all, toward establishing common goals and greater trust. It also explores how police stations can expand their capabilities as public assets by imagining them as part of larger civic networks that include parks, schools, libraries, and other important places. Working

Fig 11. 24th District Police Station, Chicago, Illinois, 1977.

simultaneously at the scale of the station and the scale of the neighborhood, the project provides a challenging test of architects' and designers' abilities to bring diverse stakeholders together to envision a better shared future.

Leading this process calls for a wide range of methods and tools, from historical research, to Geographic Information Systems (GIS), to community engagement workshops. It begins with the question: what is a police station? Unlike federal buildings, such as courthouses, that symbolize American democracy and equality under the law with an established Classical architectural language, stations lack a consistent style. They are local buildings born largely out of practical concerns. But this doesn't mean they're devoid of embedded biases and cultural attitudes about what policing means. American policing arose for different reasons in different regions (in the West, for example, to combat "lawlessness," and in the South to reinforce slavery), which led to considerable architectural variation. The geographic scope of our Polis Station project was therefore narrowed to police stations in the north and northeast. In these regions several architectural and urban trends can be traced from the colonial period to the present day that illustrate

Fig 12. 22nd District Police Station, Chicago, Illinois, 2005.

the changing civic role of police stations in cities and society.

The first police stations in the US were not buildings but "watch boxes"—networks of small shelters in colonial towns where watchmen (volunteers who patrolled their own neighborhoods on foot) would check in and log their observations at predetermined times.[9] These small wooden constructions operated as resting stations that provided watchmen with the necessities to conduct their work. As towns grew, police departments were created as municipal governance expanded and formalized during the first decades of the nineteenth century.[10] Police shared space in buildings with other civic workers such as firemen. Around the mid-nineteenth century, police departments began to establish their own station buildings. Stations were the central hub from which officers kept watch over regularized patrol areas—an innovation in policing practice borrowed from London.[11] With this

Fig 10. 69th Precinct Station House, Brooklyn, New York, ca. 1968.

change, constructing a station came to imply creating a zone of public safety, and these buildings became important pieces of neighborhood infrastructure that often seeded residential and commercial development. By 1890, population growth and urban densification necessitated smaller stations embedded in the city fabric, and "row house stations" became popular.[12] They were supplemented by growing networks of call boxes, which increased policing efficiency by allowing officers to call for backup or report crimes without physically returning to the station.[13] During this turn-of-the-century era of industrialization and immigration, police had close ties with local politicians. This led them both to perpetuate corruption (carrying out election fraud and bribery,

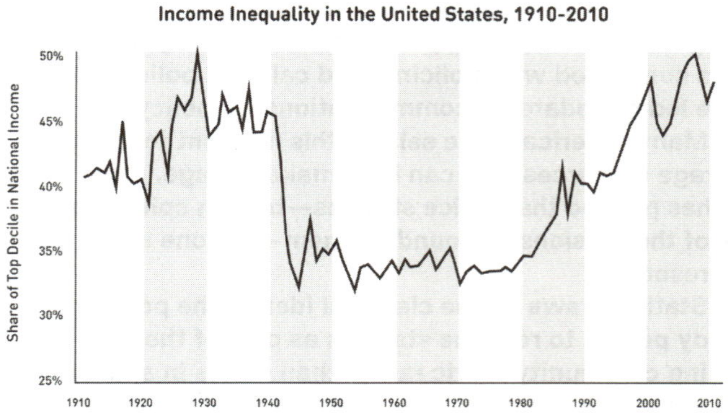

Fig 14. Economist Thomas Piketty's chart illustrating income inequality provides key context for understanding trends in the built environment of US cities in the 20th and 21st centuries.

Fig 13. Shooting hoops at the 10th District half court.

for example) and to provide a variety of social services, including running soup lines, helping people find work, and providing temporary housing for new immigrants inside row house stations.[14]

The rise of the automobile led to a dramatic shift in policing space in the early twentieth century. Stations expanded in size to accommodate garages and became more widely distributed in the urban fabric as police cars enabled patrol areas to expand. As the decades passed, police departments became large hierarchical institutions with complex protocols. Police monitored large urban areas primarily by car, which by the 1930s were equipped with two-way radios. As suburbanization increased, many officers (who were mostly white) came to live far from the more racially diverse communities that they patrolled. Simultaneously, redlining[15] and other discriminatory private and public policies destabilized and directed investment away from low-income neighborhoods, where a majority of residents were people of color.[16] By the 1960s "fortress stations" began to appear. In Chicago, these were very large buildings that housed multiple specialized units and administrative staff, and included office space, file storage, and interrogation rooms. Urbanistically, fortress stations were islands isolated from residential and commercial fabric by large parking lots, with their public entrances often facing major roads rather than neighborhood streets. These moves, which reflect the scalar approach then popular for urban renewal projects, further reduced everyday interactions between police and residents, widening the social separations effected by suburbanization and disinvestment.

During the 1970s and '80s social questions came to the fore in criminal justice theory and the philosophy of community policing began to influence policing practice. Aimed at proactive crime reduction, it emphasized the work of building trust between officers and communities by increasing opportunities to openly communicate and interact in non-enforcement situations. A major component of this practice was encouraging officers to patrol regular, smaller beats on foot. Architectural strategies became part of municipal efforts to soften public perception of police. Stations scaled down slightly and design decisions involving fenestration and materiality, for example, were guided by the goal of creating less imposing exterior expressions. Public plazas were also added to provide space for officers and residents to interact on an everyday basis.

Despite the proven success of many community policing initiatives, their implementation varied widely based on municipal authorities' preferences and budgetary allotments and continues to remain in flux in many cities.[17] In today's Chicago, police districts are larger than ever—Chicago's 10th District alone spans five neighborhoods—and most officers patrol multi-neighborhood areas by car. Station buildings are also larger than ever. The city's current police station prototype is 44,000 square feet and includes expansive parking lots. Sited on major thoroughfares, these stations remain oriented away from their neighborhood communities and are often difficult and imposing to enter. Furthermore, their programming offers little to draw community residents into the station. Without available activities or services that people want, residents have little incentive to spend time in the space of the station, let alone spend time getting to know officers and developing familiarity that could lead to trust.

Fig 15. Talking and sketching with local high school students gave the design team valuable information about how their neighborhood's police station could adapt to better serve the community's interests.

THE POTENTIAL

This morphology indicates that American police stations in the north and northeast have changed relatively little following their most dramatic evolutionary jump: the proliferation of the fortress station in the 1960s. Since then, their main architectural and urban response to the community-oriented shift in policing has been to project a more open and welcoming *image* of police to community members; for example, by increasing the amount of glazing on their main façade or by adding an adjacent plaza. Unfortunately, this cosmetic treatment of the station type makes these gestures mostly symbolic. Ignoring the central principle of community policing —to combat crime by fostering better relationships through everyday, personal interactions—today's stations keep police marooned in huge buildings that face away from neighborhood residents, adrift in seas of parking lots. Inside stations, though there has been an effort to include community rooms for neighborhood beat meetings and other outreach activities, the programmatic combination of corporate office plus jail that emerged in the '60s continues to dominate.

What this morphology also reveals, however, is that stations *have* played expanded civic roles in their neighborhoods and cities throughout history. More importantly, it suggests that giving serious design consideration to local police stations today can unlock civic potential that may have been unimaginable in the past.

Fig 16. A Community Café workshop brought together local officers and residents of Chicago's 10th District to learn how the police station could offer them more activities and amenities.

The Polis Station project stems from the need to explore this potential in light of current American challenges—from police brutality, to widening inequality, to climate resiliency. Rather than adjusting police stations' form in response to external developments such as advancing technologies (as historically seen with the telephone, radio, and automobile), it is time to deliberately reshape stations in response to critical advances in our understanding of how public institutions and spaces can help foster safer communities. These advances include community policing theory but also extend beyond it, including issues such as mental health and returning citizen programs, universal education, and collective efficacy. (To return to our ecological framework, understanding that public safety arises from a web of related conditions echoes biological mutualism—the symbiotic, mutually beneficial relationships that add up to thriving ecosystems.)

Polis Station therefore rejects the now-common "prototype" practice in which identical police stations are set down in neighborhoods. Instead it stakes the claim that, like other pieces of the public realm, stations should be the result of a community-driven process that recognizes the significance of physical spaces in community-building and activates the full public potential of these civic buildings.

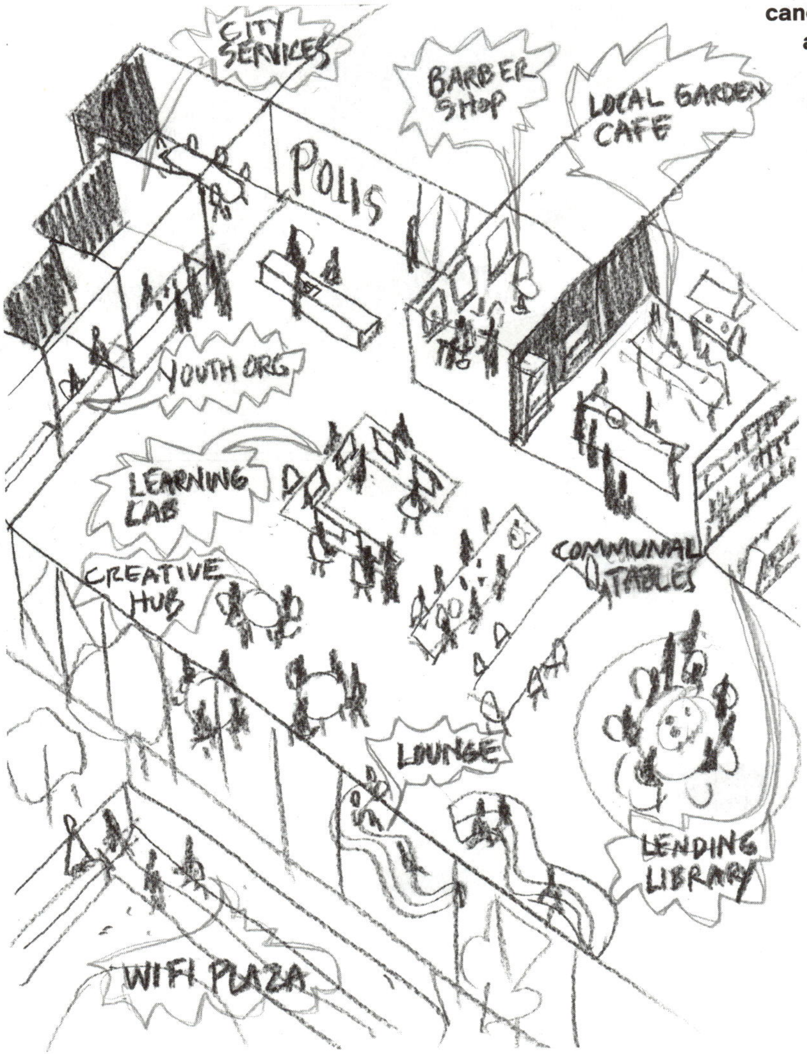

Fig 17. A sketch made during the Community Café workshop illustrating how community members' and officers' program ideas could be incorporated into the 10th District Station's lobby.

THE PROPOSAL

The project proposes a set of six design principles relevant to any community for re-tuning their own local police station. Included below, these principles suggest key ways that physical space and programming can foster stronger relationships and neighborhoods. These principles incorporate recommendations from the 2015 *Final Report of the President's Task Force on 21st Century Policing*. Developed by an interdisciplinary, federally-commissioned panel through a public engagement process conducted in cities across the US, the recommendations are structured under six thematic "pillars": Building Trust and Legitimacy, Policy and Oversight, Technology and Social Media, Community Policing and Crime Reduction, Training and Education, and Officer Wellness and Safety.[18] Nationally applicable and informed by local input, the report's recommendations are the most comprehensive set of policing reform ideas to emerge in the post-Ferguson era. They do not, however, address the spatial aspects of policing. This oversight prompted our work of translating their policy goals into architecture and urban design principles that can be helpful for any community.

The Polis Station proposal for Chicago's 10th District police station in the North Lawndale neighborhood—an initial case study site—uses these design principles to explore how the site's

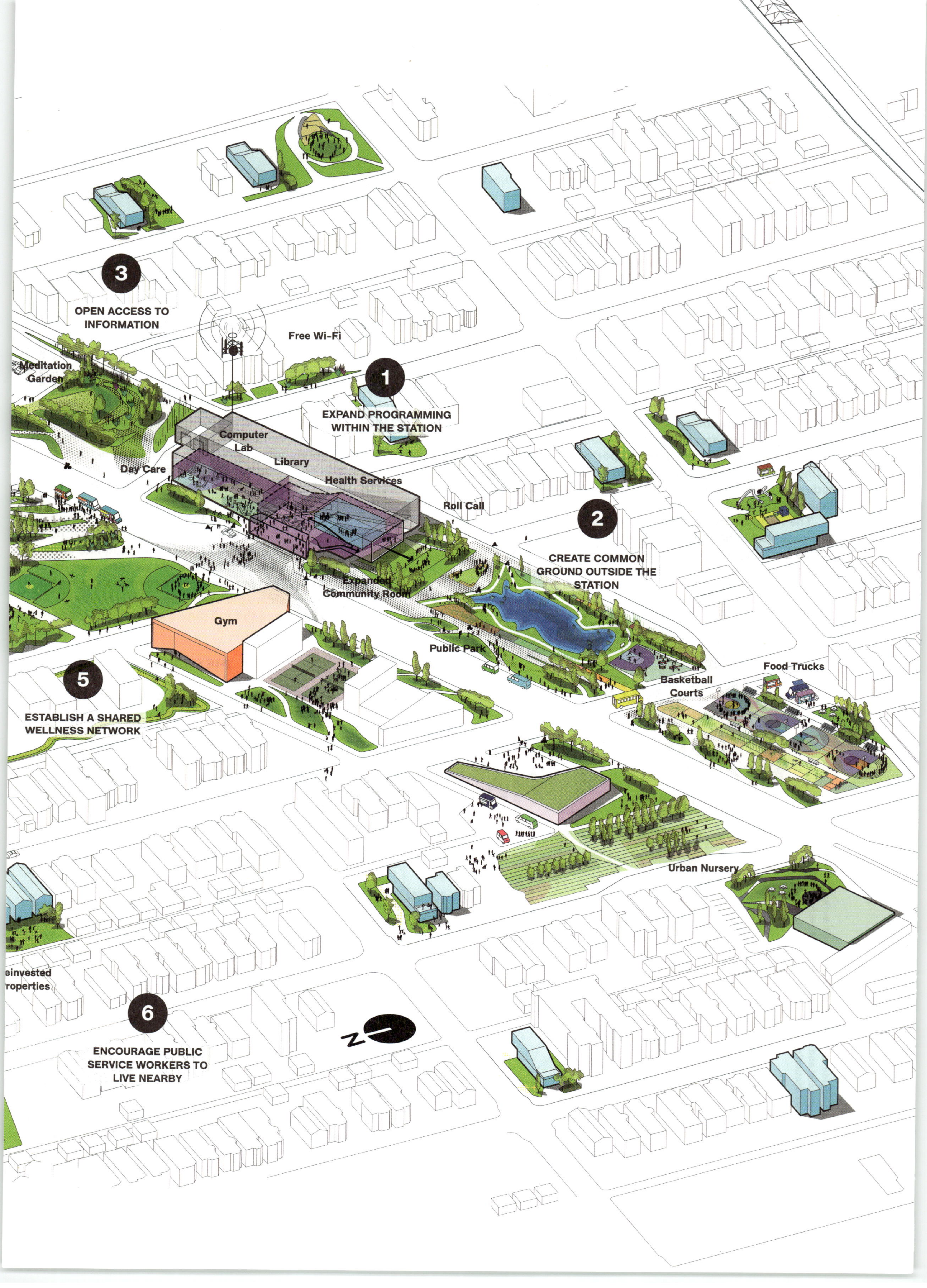
3
OPEN ACCESS TO INFORMATION
Free Wi-Fi
Meditation Garden
1
EXPAND PROGRAMMING WITHIN THE STATION
Computer Lab
Library
Day Care
Health Services
Roll Call
2
CREATE COMMON GROUND OUTSIDE THE STATION
Expanded Community Room
Gym
Public Park
5
ESTABLISH A SHARED WELLNESS NETWORK
Food Trucks
Basketball Courts
Urban Nursery
einvested
roperties
6
ENCOURAGE PUBLIC SERVICE WORKERS TO LIVE NEARBY
N

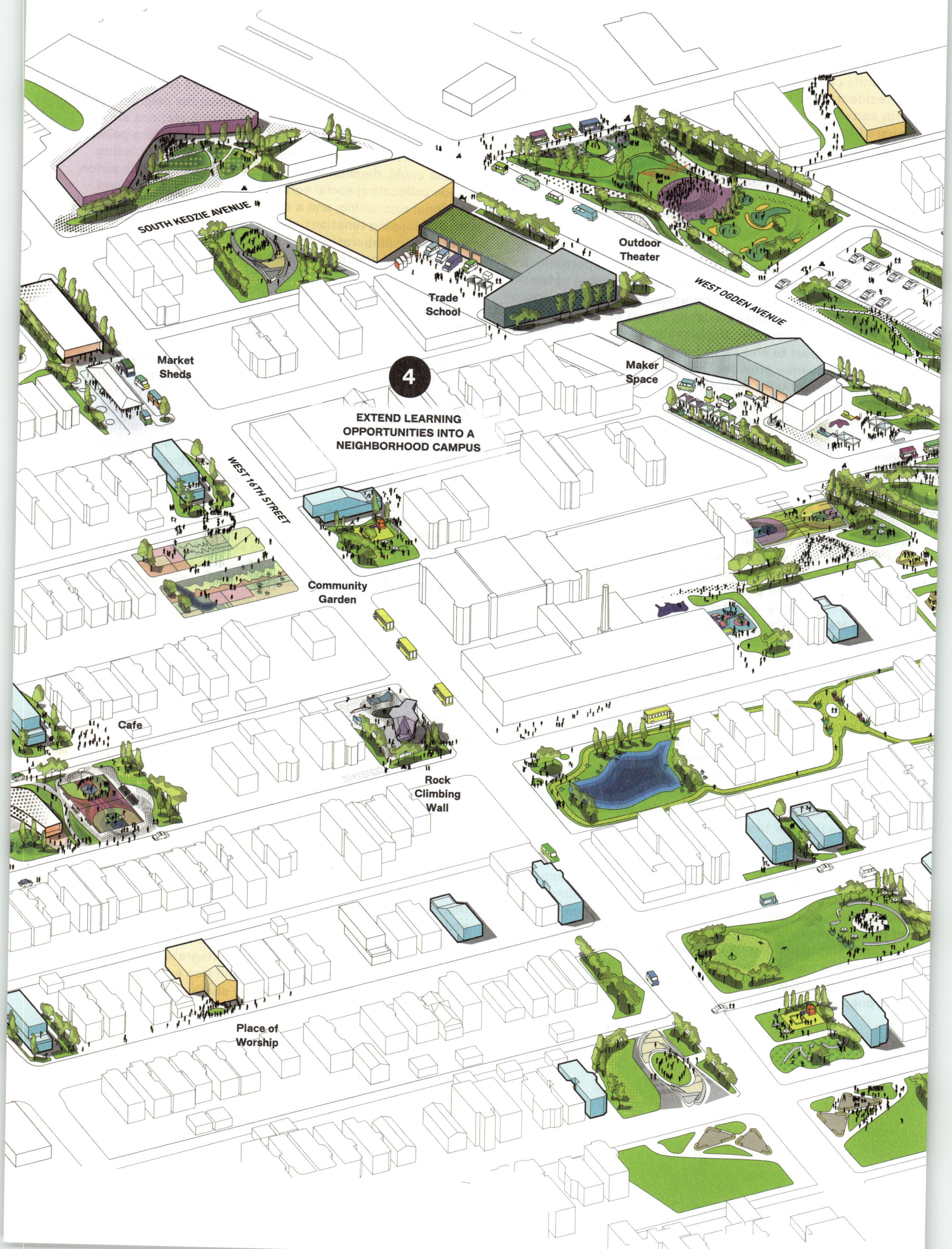
SOUTH KEDZIE AVENUE
Outdoor Theater
WEST OGDEN AVENUE
Trade School
Market Sheds
Maker Space
4
EXTEND LEARNING OPPORTUNITIES INTO A NEIGHBORHOOD CAMPUS
WEST 16TH STREET
Community Garden
Cafe
Rock Climbing Wall
Place of Worship

built environment can support the particular goals and suggestions of local community members and officers. Their input was gathered through a variety of community engagement formats to ensure a broad spectrum of perspectives. These included one-on-one conversations with community leaders, community café workshops bringing together police officers and residents, and roundtable sketching sessions with local youth and officers. Specific questions and prompts were prepared for each session to focus the discussion and to help assess the total community input across various engagement formats and stakeholder groups.

The proposal's design vision illustrates how the spaces of the existing 10th District station could be reconfigured. This vision accommodates new programming informed by the *President's Task Force Report* and local stakeholders' suggestions, including athletic and play facilities, a barbershop, and computer stations. It also envisions how these opportunities can expand throughout the neighborhood, forming a network of recreational, educational, entrepreneurial, and green spaces that tie into the community's existing assets and strengthen them with new investment. Importantly, these new programs and spaces appeal to and serve both residents and police officers. This overlap provides them with multiple new opportunities to interact with each other in non-en-forcement situations—the everyday encounters and exchanges that can lead to more trusting relationships. In addition, it provides both groups with access to services, activities, and spaces that underpin safer, healthier, and stronger communities.

One of the strongest wishes that emerged from conversations with community members and officers in North Lawndale was for more safe spaces for youth to play—basketball, especially. Police expressed a desire to coach youth sports teams, but they currently had to do so on their own time and at courts that were not within walking distance of the station. Community members also noted that neighborhood basketball courts had previously existed near the station and had been used by well-known athletes, such as local hero and NBA Hall of Famer, Isiah Thomas. Seizing this information of a shared aspiration, the project's design team worked closely with police and community leaders and the local alderman to design and build a half court on a little-used portion of the station's parking lot. As of this writing, the court has become so popular among local youth that community leaders and officers have asked the design team to expand it into a public park, extending the half court into a full court and adding more green space and amenities.

It is difficult to argue that realizing a standard basketball court is, in itself, design. But as part of a larger, self-initiated project, it demonstrates how designers can expand how we practice in order to work toward social change in our cities. We can design a process or point to a solution as part of our design practice—and this is precisely what the project in North Lawndale succeeds in doing. By providing safe, outdoor recreation space on police property, this simple intervention is supporting everyday overlap between the worlds of police officers and neighbors—beginning to turn one station's empty parking lot into an active, inviting place where people come together through play. This small investment in the neighborhood is leading to more interventions through a strong, ongoing dialogue between designers and users.

SIX DESIGN PRINCIPLES FOR "POLIS STATIONS"

1. Expand Programming within the Station
   (*Task Force Report* pillar: Community Policing and Crime Reduction)

Transforming police stations into full-service community centers can improve public safety and enhance the neighborhood's social capital and economic strength. Police stations are strategically located in neighborhoods and therefore poised to offer crucial services. Simple interventions into existing stations could, depending on the specific community's vision, include collocating social services, job training, health and nutritional counseling, and a small lending library, for example. With overlapping functions and flexible spaces, opportunities abound for collaborative partnerships between law enforcement and local community institutions.

2. Create Common Ground Around the Station
   (*Task Force Report* pillar: Policy and Oversight)

Extending beyond the station, a variety of indoor and outdoor spaces can provide many opportunities for local residents and police officers to spend time together informally, as well as for community organizations to host events and gatherings. Accessible and inviting, these spaces can range from athletic courts, to open markets, to urban nurseries. The design emphasis should be on creating places that serve multiple functions; for example, a public park with paths for recreation, a pond that filters stormwater, quiet restorative spots for resting, and signage that facilitates educational visits.

3. Open Access to Information
   (*Task Force Report* pillar: Technology and Social Media)

Much like a public library, offering access to a free, secure internet connection and other information technology creates a welcoming space for the community. Building on the types of inquiries that officers regularly receive from the community, stations can become places where locally relevant information is shared in real time. An interior announcement board, for example, could show upcoming community events and highlight when and where neighborhood services are available. Large-scale visible information could incorporate the police department's social media networks, serving as platforms for police and residents to openly engage in conversation and exchange information.

4. Extend Learning Opportunities into a Neighborhood Campus
   (*Task Force Report* pillar: Training and Education)

Partnering with local schools, universities, police academies, and other organizations can provide more comprehensive officer training and a range of educational opportunities for neighbors of all ages. Trade schools and workshops, innovation labs, and community gardens can serve as accessible, therapeutic, and transformational learning spaces for both police and community members, including returning citizens. By locating a satellite police academy near the Polis Station, the police will have a stronger, more integrated civic presence in the community they serve. This will also support police recruitment from the community by sharing access to educational opportunities.

5. Establish a Shared Wellness Network
   (*Task Force Report* pillar: Officer Wellness and Safety)

Incorporating new amenities throughout the neighborhood that support mental, emotional, and physical well-being, can both enrich and provide respite from daily life for police and local residents. Restorative gardens and green spaces support psychological wellness and healing. Flexible social spaces

45° right of way
South Kedzie Ave
West Ogden Avenue
Howland Charter School
North Lawndale College
Prep Charter High School
West 16th Street
Amount of vacant property
increases north of Ogden Avenue
45° right of way

1960s
FORTRESS STATION
2nd District Station, Chicago (45,000 ft²)

Now large hierarchical institutions, police stations grow to house multiple specialized units and administrative staff.

1980s
CIVIC STATION
24th District Station, Chicago (35,000 ft²)

In an effort to soften the perception of the police, stations become less imposing and include public plazas.

2000s
TODAY'S STATION
10th District Station, Chicago (48,000 ft²)

Today, Chicago's station prototype is sited on a major thoroughfare, flanked by expansive parking lots.

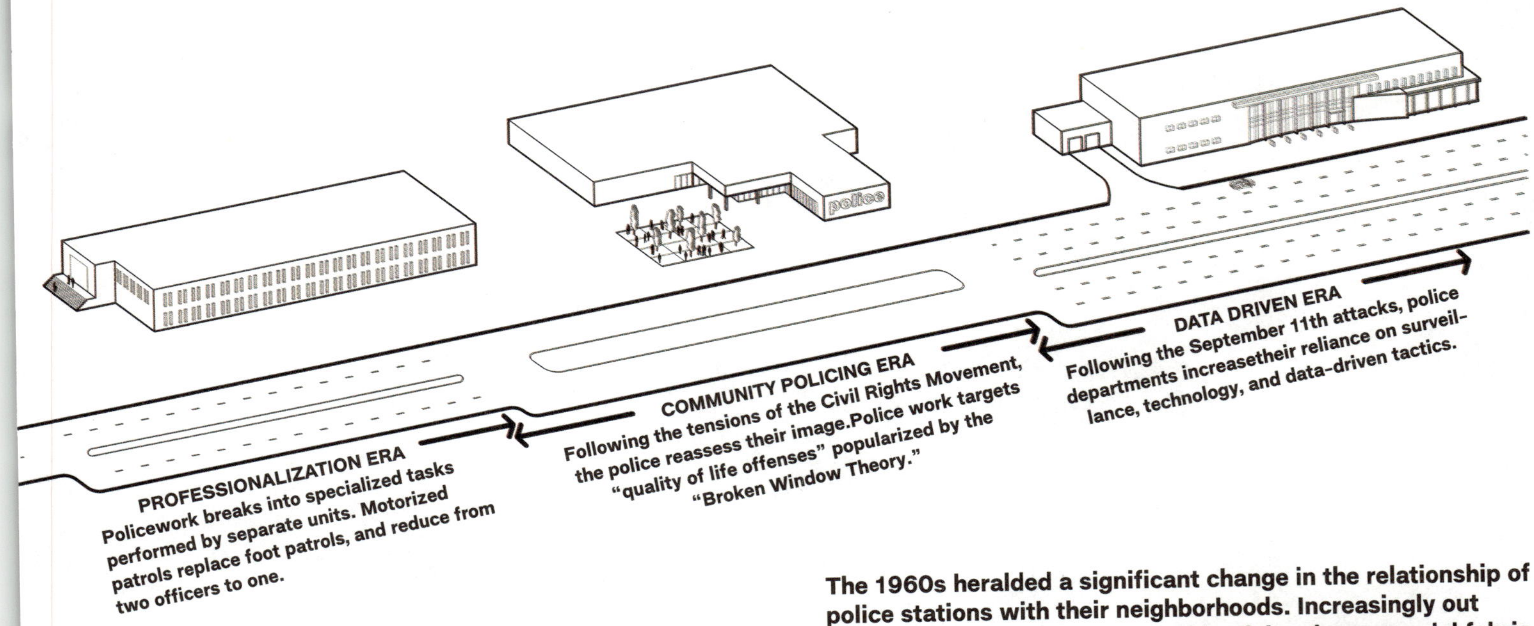

The 1960s heralded a significant change in the relationship of police stations with their neighborhoods. Increasingly out of scale and cut off from the residential and commercial fabric by large parking lots, stations became more oriented to major roadways than to the people they serve. In Chicago, this relationship continues to be perpetuated through the city's current station prototype despite widespread recognition that more positive, everyday encounters between officers and community members leads to greater public safety.

1980s
CIVIC STATION
24th District Station, Rogers Park, Chicago

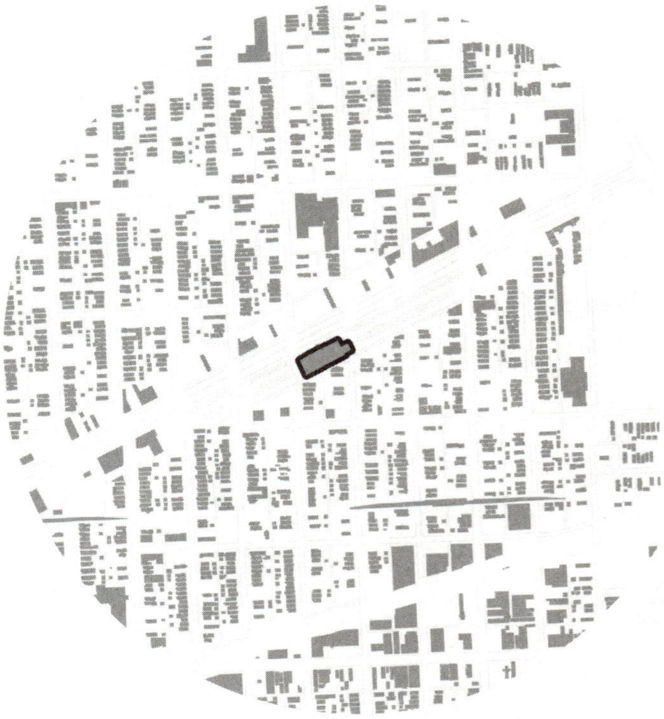

2010s
TODAY'S STATION
10th District Station, North Lawndale, Chicago

1850s
FIRST STATIONS
Multiple U.S. Cities
(1800 ft²)

After decades of using spare space within other civic institutions, police departments establish their own station buildings.

1890s
ROW HOUSE STATION
Multiple U.S. Cities
(1000 ft²)

Stations are embedded in the rapidly densifying urban fabric.

CALL BOX
Multiple U.S. Cities
(1 ft²)

Call boxes appear on the streets shortly after the invention of the telephone. Police and trusted members of the community have access to make calls to the police station.

1930s
STATION FOR THE AUTO AGE
Early Prototype, Chicago
(4000 ft²)

The automobile changes the physical requirements of police stations and enlarges the area of patrol.

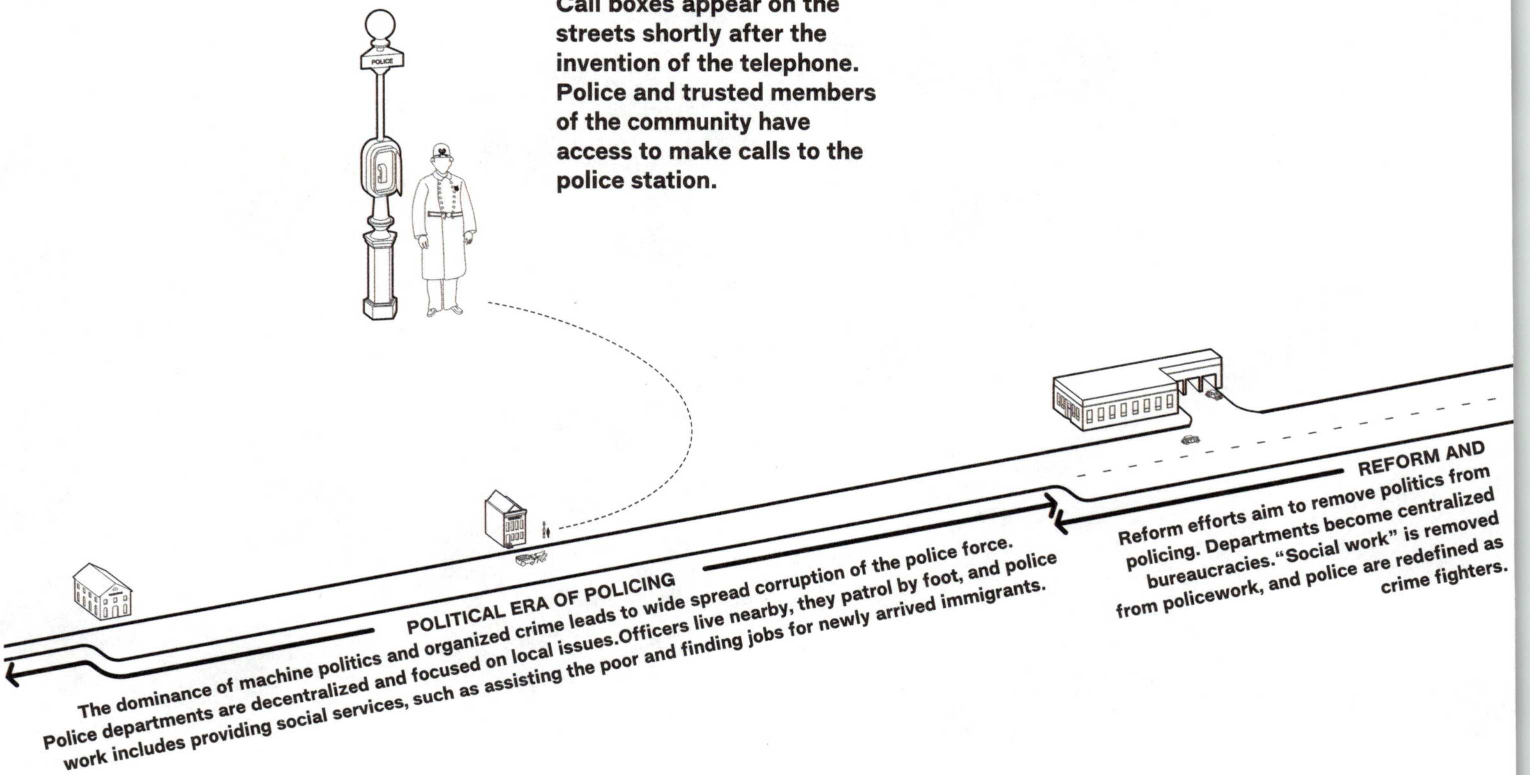

1930s
STATION FOR THE AUTO AGE
Old 13th District Station,
West Town, Chicago

1960s
FORTRESS STATION
Area 1 Station,
Bronzeville, Chicago
(near Robert Taylor Homes housing development)

2-acre parking lot
10th District Police Department
1.5-acre parking lot
130' wide right of way

allow officers to spend time together outside of patrols, office work, and meetings. Athletic facilities allow the police and public to converge, facilitating physical fitness, teamwork, and mentoring relationships through play.

6. Encourage Public Service Workers to Live Nearby (*Task Force Report* pillar: Building Trust and Legitimacy)
Encouraging police officers and other key public service workers—including firefighters, nurses, teachers, and social workers—to live within the communities where they work enhances the social potential of the first five principles and brings new economic investment. Residency incentive programs, as proposed in the *Task Force Report*, can offer financial support to help service workers renovate, rebuild, and move into abandoned homes. Filling in gaps within the urban fabric with new residences contributes to more complete urban blocks. In addition to strengthening the urban fabric, a workforce more reflective of community demographics can emerge. Beyond their roles as civil servants, service workers can be positive civic role models and help to connect their neighbors with good jobs and job training.

THE DESIGN CHALLENGE

Polis Station illustrates how intervening in existing police stations holds social promise—and it also raises questions about how the full potential of design can come into play when architects engage the public realm. How can designers' aesthetic understanding and invention come to fruition when embroiled in the everyday world of neighborhoods, communities, and government buildings? How can a design philosophy of "starting with what's there" and the spirit of ecological systems invite formal creativity? What of geometry, technical innovation, and form?

What is clear is that we cannot allow conventional disciplinary boundaries or social divides to prevent us from testing architecture's mettle against the shared challenges we face today in American cities and globally. To make progress toward a better future we will need to gather intelligence, innovation, and technique that is currently being used across the spectrum of architecture and bring it to our communities, where together we can imagine and realize new possibilities for our public realm.

1. For a quick gloss on social diversity's productive effects, see Katherine W. Phillips, "How Diversity Makes Us Smarter," *Scientific American*, October 1, 2014, available online at https://www.scientificamerican.com/article/how-diversity-makes-us-smarter. For a more in-depth exploration of the role of cities, see Ed Glaeser's *Triumph of the City: How Our Greatest Invention Makes Us Richer, Smarter, Greener, Healthier, and Happier* (New York: Penguin Books, 2012).

2. The proportion of American families in major metropolitan areas who live in either rich or poor neighborhoods (34 percent in 2012) is in fact now nearing that who live in middle-income neighborhoods (40 percent in 2012); in 1970 those percentages were 15 and 65, respectively. See Sean F. Reardon and Kendra Bischoff, *The Continuing Increase in Income Segregation, 2007-2012* (Stanford Center for Education Policy Analysis, March 2016), 5, http://cepa.stanford.edu/content/continuing-increase-income-segregation-2007-2012.

3. High-poverty neighborhoods are those where 30 percent or more of the population live below the poverty line. See Joe Cortright and Dillon Mahmoudi, *City Report: Lost in Place* (City Observatory, Dec 2014), 2, http://cityobservatory.org/wp-content/uploads/2014/12/LostinPlace_12.4.pdf.

4. These two causes are further discussed by Cortright and Mahmoudi in *City Report: Lost in Place*, 8-9, in which they provide examples of these public policies, including local land use restrictions and terms attached to federal housing assistance. Reardon and Bischoff's report provides a specific measurement of inequality in the US: in 2014 the top 10% of earners accrued 50% of all income. This statistic is drawn from Thomas Piketty and Emmanuel Saez's 2015 updated table and figures of their 2003 report "Income Inequality in the United States, 1913–1998," http://eml.berkeley.edu/~saez/TabFig2014prel.xls.

5. Cortright and Mahmoudi, *City Report: Lost in Place*, 8.

6. David Halpern's book *Social Capital* (Malden, MA: Polity Press, 2005) provides a comprehensive introduction to this concept, including discussing its varying definitions and considering its policy implications.

7. For an overview and analysis of a wide range of these measures, see Joe Cortright, *City Report: Less in Common* (City Observatory, June 2015), http://cityobservatory.org/wp-content/uploads/2015/06/CityObservatory_Less_In_Common.pdf.

8. This is a widely known statistic in discourse on cities and public space. For a focus on how streets factor in, see Janette Sadik-Khan and Seth Solomonow, *Street Fight: Handbook for an Urban Revolution* (New York: Viking, 2016) and Gregory Scruggs, "How Much Public Space Does a City Need?", *Next City*, January 7, 2015, https://nextcity.org/daily/entry/how-much-public-space-does-a-city-need-UN-Habitat-joan-clos-50-percent.

9. A detailed description of watch boxes in colonial Philadelphia is found in volume three of J. Thomas Scharf and Thompson Westcott's *History of Philadelphia, 1609-1884* (Philadelphia: J.B. Lippincott & Co., 1884), 1778.

10. Criminal justice scholar Gary Potter defines police departments in part one of his article "The History of Policing in the United States," http://plsonline.eku.edu/insidelook/history-policing-united-states-part-1: "These 'modern police' organizations shared similar characteristics: (1) they were publicly supported and bureaucratic in form; (2) police officers were full-time employees, not community volunteers or case-by-case fee retainers; (3) departments had permanent and fixed rules and procedures, and employment as a police officers was continuous; (4) police departments were accountable to a central governmental authority." He cites Robert J. Lundman, *Police and Policing: An Introduction* (New York: Holt, Rinehart & Winston, 1980).

11. For more on the relationship of American and British policing reforms in the nineteenth century, see Kenneth J. Peak, *Policing America: Challenges and Best Practices*, Sixth Edition (Upple Saddle River, NJ: Prentice Hall, 2009), 18-26.

12. Examples of row house stations in Chicago are included in Jacob Kaplan's article "Disused Police Stations" on *Forgotten Chicago*, http://forgottenchicago.com/articles/disused-police-stations.

13. In some cities, select private citizens were also given access to call boxes to report different types of crimes or public emergencies. See Gary Potter, "The History of Policing in the United States: Part 3," http://plsonline.eku.edu/insidelook/history-policing-united-states-part-3.

14. George L. Kelling and Mark H. Moore, "The Evolving Strategy of Policing," *Perspectives on Policing*, no. 4 (November 1988): 3.

15. Redlining is the practice in which financial institutions arbitrarily deny or limit extending loans and other financial services to people from specific neighborhoods, largely because their residents are poor or people of color. For more on redlining's history in Chicago, see D. Bradford Hunt's entry "Redlining" in the Newberry Library's *Encyclopedia of Chicago*, http://www.encyclopedia.chicagohistory.org/pages/1050.html.

16. Mindy Thompson Fullilove, Molly Rose Kaufman, and Aubrey Murdock discuss these and other polices as a related set of "Serial Forced Displacements" in their article "The Aesthetics of Equity: A Magic Strategy for the Healthy City," included in *By the People: Designing a Better America* (New York: Cooper Hewitt, 2016), 36–43.

17. For an overview focused on Chicago's history, see Nissa Rhee, Manny Ramos, and Andrea Salcedo, "The rise and fall of community policing in Chicago," *Chicago Reader*, September 22, 2016, http://www.chicagoreader.com/chicago/caps-cpd-community-policing-analysis/Content?oid=23635982.

18. The Task Force's *Final Report* was published by the Office of Community Oriented Policing Services and is available online at https://cops.usdoj.gov/pdf/taskforce/taskforce_finalreport.pdf.

URBAN COMMONING, AGAINST CITY DIVIDED: FIELD NOTES FROM TAIPEI AND HONG KONG

Occupation of Taiwan's National Legislature during the Sunflower Movement in 2013. Photograph by Kevin WY.

BY JEFFREY HOU

Do You a Flavor is an experimental social start-up formed by a group of young protesters who participated in Taiwan's Sunflower Movement in spring 2014. During the movement, students and activists occupied the Assembly Chamber of Taiwan's National Legislature for twenty-three consecutive days to protest against the passage of a trade agreement with China. The agreement, by opening up the country's service sector to large corporations from China, was expected to adversely impact a large segment of Taiwan's economy that was already faced with declining wages and a shrinking job market. The unprecedented occupation ended peacefully on April 10, 2015, after the trade agreement was successfully stalled. As an outcome of the movement, new political and civic organizations have also emerged to address a broad range of social, economic, and political issues facing the country. Do You a Flavor is one such group that focuses on helping the urban poor—homeless individuals, street vendors, and scavengers that have long been stigmatized and marginalized in the society.

In bringing people together and sharing what they have with others, Do You a Flavor is one of many recent examples of urban commoning—formation of alternative space and social relationships based on sharing of material and social resources—now spreading through East Asia in cities such as Hong Kong, Seoul, Taipei, and Tokyo. I spent my sabbatical leave in 2015 studying emerging cases in Taipei and Hong Kong, including Do You a Flavor.[1] In this research, I am interested in exploring organized acts of commoning that transcend social and spatial divides in the contemporary city. Through a variety of cases, I learned about the contexts in which groups like Do You a Flavor have emerged, how they are organized, and whom they have collaborated with and engaged.[2]

To address the theme of urban divides, this essay focuses on acts of commoning and their potential for overcoming social, political, and spatial divides—divides that have become deeply entrenched in cities and societies today, as manifested in new and old spatial forms, including gated communities, privatized public spaces, and enclaves of migrant workers. They also include non-spatial barriers such as patented seeds and privatized natural resources that are equally, if not more, significant in their impact on the everyday life and struggles in the contemporary society, with worsening economic disparities, stagnant wages, and growing social tensions. Such disparities have contributed to the widening divides between the haves and have-nots, privileged and disenfranchised, and documented and undocumented in today's neoliberal systems.

It is precisely against this background of enclosures and divides that the expanding acts of commoning around the world are significant and intriguing to observe. Through acts of commoning, citizens and activists engage in self-organized social and spatial configurations that enable individuals and communities to thrive in niches within market-based economic and state institutions. They create alternative social and economic networks and relationships across economic and class divides and put social justice and equity ahead of financial and self-interests. In the context of the planning and design profession, these acts of commoning suggest ways to move away from the current paradigm of neoliberal, market-driven practices to rethink how architects, landscape architects, and planners can play a more critical and proactive role for social change, which citizen groups and community organizers have already started to do. These acts of commoning represent hopes and possibilities in overcoming the ever more entrenched urban divides that characterize cities and societies today.

Commons and Commoning

Commons and commoning have emerged as an important intellectual framework behind recent social movements around the world. They represent distrust against the state institutions and their role as no longer the sole provider of social good and services in a neoliberal era.[3] Furthermore, the concept of commoning also suggests forms of participatory self-governance that set them apart from state institutions.[4] According to Charlotte Hess, the rise of new commons represents reactions to "increasing commodification, privatization, corporatization, untamed globalization, and unresponsive government."[5] She further describes the recent movements as developing "new forms of self governance, collaboration, and collective action."[6]

With the renewed interest in the notions of commons and commoning, there have been efforts to articulate their contemporary meanings. For instance, political philosophers Michael Hardt and Antonio Negri suggest that the commons can be understood as both the commonwealth of the material world (air, water, place, etc.) and the results of "social production that are necessary for social interactions and further production" (knowledges, languages, code, information, affects, etc.).[7] Specifically, they argue for a notion of commons that focuses on "the practices of interaction, care, and cohabitation in a common world, promoting the beneficial and limiting detrimental forms of the common."[8] Similarly, Hess defines commons as "communities working together in self-governing ways in order to protect resources from enclosure or to build new openly-shared resources."[9] In examining the process of space commoning in the recent movements manifested in occupied squares around the world, including the Arab Spring, the Spanish Indignados, and the worldwide Occupy Movement, Stavros Starvides notes that in these movements, space served both as a good to be shared and as a form of organizing shared practices.[10]

In a recent publication on the urban commons in the *Delft Architectural Theory Journal*, it is further noted that most contemporary definitions of commons comprise of three parts: commons as resource, institutions, and communities "who are involved in the production and reproduction of commons."[11] Also, using a three-part framework, philosopher Adrian Parr suggests that urban commoning refers to three processes working in tandem: first, "a political project that seeks to construct coalitions between individual, local, regional, national, and even international struggles"; second, "an urbanization process that constructs alternatives to the production and realization of surplus value"; and third, "collaborative activities involved in concretely transforming the system of exclusive ownership that renders the common non-common."[12] In short, urban commoning suggests a vision of society distinct from the predominant, neoliberal paradigm that has dictated the transformation of cities and privatization of urban spaces in the recent decades.

Urban Commoning in East Asia

Aside from the context of radical social and political actions, urban commoning also takes on other more quotidian forms, as reported in several case studies in the Western Hemisphere where commoning and commons are enjoying a resurgence of interest among activists and scholars. In Helsinki, Amsterdam, Berlin, Vienna, and Naples, for instance, a variety of social actors, including squatters, transformed the cities' abundant vacant lands into alternative venues for art, entertainment, commerce, and housing.[13] In Dublin, against the rising cost of rent, artists and residents developed mechanisms for space sharing and created the so-called independence spaces by collectively paying rent through donations, membership, fundraising, and providing food.[14] In cities around North America, the growing movement in transforming vacant sites and parking spaces into parklets and pop-up spaces also represents a desire for alternative forms of urban public space. Branded as tactical urbanism or creative placemaking, efforts like these have catalyzed new forms of social spaces and sociality, which challenge the conventional norms of public space and formalized spatial planning. More importantly, they represent experiments in the making of alternative social, economic, and political relationships through a more inclusive urban landscape with more open spatial and social boundaries, all in the face of growing privatization and enclosure of urban spaces and public institutions.

In East Asia, where there is no shortage of economic and spatial enclosures in the form of privatized public space and land expropriation for industrial and urban development, a substantial number of urban commoning cases have also emerged. A majority are self-organized initiatives, but some also intersect with state institutions and resources. In Taipei, a variety of new urban commons have mushroomed in recent years. They range from self-organized placemaking activities to community-driven initiatives to activate vacant sites with the support of city resources. These activities include community gardening, urban farming, appropriation of residual spaces for social events, and salons hosted by independent cafés and bookstores. In Hong Kong, instances of urban commoning have emerged against a backdrop of significant social and political shifts since the handover from the United Kingdom to China in 1997.[15] Some efforts have strong ties to the recent protest movements, including the occupation of Queen's Pier, the movement against the high-speed railway connecting to China, and more recently the Umbrella Movement. Specifically, many of the recent commoning initiatives have been organized by activists who participated in those movements.

In Seoul, responses such as Bin-Zib shared housing have emerged in the context of declining income and job opportunities for young people, coupled with high living costs in the city.[16] With the election of Mayor Park Won-Soon, a longtime human-rights lawyer, the Seoul Metropolitan Government launched an aggressive Sharing City initiative in 2012 to address issues of transportation, parking, residential, and environmental issues through sharing policies. In Tokyo, there are also a variety of commoning initiatives, ranging from Curry Caravan, a moving feast of curry rice to catalyze social interactions and activate public spaces, to more established initiatives, such as the 3331 Arts Chiyoda, a vacant public school transformed into a hub for artists and designers.

For the purposes of this essay, I focus my attention on a few selected cases in Hong Kong and Taipei. My notes are based on fieldwork conducted in summer and fall of 2015. During that time, I spoke with local colleagues who have been involved in the growing number of cases. They then introduced me to other important actors with whom I conducted more interviews. Much of the network also occurred through social media.

In examining the cases in Hong Kong and Taipei, I found many parallels in the typology of the organizations. I also found notable differences in the political and institutional contexts—which may have influenced the paths that the movements have taken—with a stronger focus on social entrepreneurship and community collectives in Hong Kong on one hand (having less opportunities for political participation), and stronger institutional support and collaboration with professional

Curry Caravan serves hot curry rice for free in parks, streets, and other forms of public space to catalyze social exchanges. Photograph by author.

actors in Taiwan, on the other hand (having a longer history of professional and government support for community initiatives). Before I begin to introduce the cases and my observation and analysis, I must caution that the typology of Movement Spinoffs, Social Start-Ups, and Makerspaces I have outlined here is not an exclusive categorization, as some of the cases clearly overlap in their scopes and orientations.

Movement Spinoffs

One of the most distinct aspects of urban commoning initiatives in Hong Kong and Taipei is their connection to the recent large-scale social and political movements. Fixing Hong Kong, for example, is an outgrowth of the Umbrella Movement in 2014, in which thousands of Hong Kong citizens occupied streets and thoroughfares in key locations through the city for over two and a half months to demand universal suffrage. The Fixing Hong Kong group consists of skilled artisans who helped build the "Study Area" on the streets of the Admiralty district during the occupation. The study area enabled many students to join the occupation while preparing for their exams. After the occupation, Fixing Hong Kong decided to continue their newfound political activism by offering repair service for people in need, under the slogan of "fixing Hong Kong begins with fixing communities."[17] The political advocacy through home repair approach came from a realization that the pro-democracy activists needed better ways to engage the public, who were often indifferent to political discussion. While doing repairs, the activists would engage the residents in conversation about politics. As one of the founders of Fixing Hong Kong, said, "the residents would only open their doors for repairs... But repairing is just the first step; our goal is politicize the people."[18]

I shadowed the group on an October evening to see how they worked. The group consisted of not only artisans, whose main job was to perform the repairs, but also volunteers, who included students and young office workers, to handle other aspects of community outreach. In addition to individual home repair appointments, the group meets weekly to conduct outreach in the To Kwa Wan neighborhood in East Kowloon, an area that was transformed from a rural village into an industrial zone in the 1960s and 1970s, with predominantly older apartment buildings and low-income residents. The volunteers split into groups. One group went out to do scheduled home repairs. Another went to hand out leaflets on the street to let more people know about their free service. The last group went door-to-door in a nearby apartment building, a seven-story walk-up, and spoke to the residents in their small apartments. In addition to problems that needed to be fixed, some residents also needed furniture but could not afford it. The volunteers then started to look for free furniture online. The evening ended around 11 p.m. after a debriefing session, which offered a chance for me to witness how the simple intention of doing home repairs soon spiraled into other community initiatives, including an organized cleanup of apartment stairways that would bring residents together to improve their living environment. Within the group itself, members also engaged in other forms of sharing, as volunteers with different skill sets teamed up to handle different tasks. During the week that I was there, Fixing Hong Kong successfully registered as a charity organization so that they could collect donations to expand their mission and services.

In Taipei, as mentioned above, Do You a Flavor was formed by a group of student activists who met during the Sunflower Movement. During the occupation at the National Legislature, they were involved with managing the food supplies donated to the movement by the public. With more supplies than they needed, including perishable food, they decided to share the food with the homeless. As young

Fixing Hong Kong volunteers handing out fliers on the street of Tu Kwa Wan in Hong Kong. Photograph by author.

and privileged college students, they had no previous experience interacting with the city's homeless population, which has been largely invisible and concentrated in a few enclaves in the city.[19] In coming into contact with homeless individuals, the students learned about the economic hardship and the social isolation experienced by many of the homeless, an issue that was not addressed by social service agencies and other organizations. In researching the lives of many homeless people who made their living by selling items on the streets, the students also became aware of the role of streets and public space in the livelihood of marginalized urban populations.

Do You a Flavor's first project was to create a digital map (http://agoama.tw) showing locations of recyclers who combed the streets of Taipei for cans, bottles, cardboard boxes, etc. Through the interactive map, they encourage visitors to the website to give recyclable items to the recyclers to help them make a living. The website also allows anyone to report locations of recyclers and the schedules of their collections to add to the database. The mapping project brought attention to Do You a Flavor. Soon a fan base was established on Facebook. Their next project, Stone Soup, brought more volunteers to donate food and cook for the homeless about once per month. The homeless individuals not only received food at given locations, they also had a chance to interact with the volunteers. To move beyond charity, the Do You a Flavor organizers have been developing a project to design new products for struggling street vendors. The redesigned products include small packets of dried fruits and organic tea that are produced by small-scale, organic farmers. Their goal was to attract more customers who would be interested in buying these products, which would in turn help both the vendors and small producers. As such, the products would support alternative economic networks against the dominance of large distributors.

Although organizations like Fixing Hong Kong and Do You a Flavor do not occupy regular locations or actively create new spaces, their work has contributed to the urban environments in a meaningful way. For example, by making repairs in old apartment buildings in To Kwa Wan, volunteers for Fixing Hong Kong have improved the living conditions of the predominantly older residents in the neighborhood, a situation that has become increasingly prevalent in East Asian cities as the population ages. Through the interactions between younger volunteers and older residents, these activities also foster intergenerational bonds, building much-needed social networks in the city, and bridging the gaps between the haves and have-nots. In the case of Do You a Flavor, the series of commoning initiatives represents attempts to transform the streets into a more welcoming and inclusive environment for vendors and to remedy the societal isolation of the homeless. They also produce social networks and capitals with greater capacity to address the social and economic divides in the society.

Social Start-Ups

Similarly to other major cities around the world, the number of social enterprises and new independent businesses is on the rise in Taipei and Hong Kong. Many of these entities are also engaged in acts of commoning in their attempts to create alternative social and economic networks.

Hun Communes is one of many café-style co-working spaces now existing in Taipei. What made Hun Communes different from the others, however, was its status as the very first co-working space in the city. Justin Yu, a twenty-something entrepreneur and owner of Hun Communes was influenced by similar initiatives that he saw in Japan and Europe, which led him and his colleagues to the venture at a time when no one really understood what a co-working space was. As such, after Hun Communes was launched, Yu was commissioned by the city government to produce a handbook on co-working spaces to help other entrepreneurs develop similar projects. Tucked in a quiet residential alley, this trendy, café-like co-working space soon became a site of frequent pilgrimage by aspiring entrepreneurs and start-ups. More than simply a co-working venue, Hun Communes has been the site of ongoing social and business experiments. Rather than following a conventional business model, half of its staff are actually volunteers who have other paying jobs. The arrangement, with volunteers working there because they enjoy being part of the community, has significantly reduced the operating cost and allowed Hun Communes to break even in only nine months since it opened. With such arrangement, Hun Communes functions more as a collective than a typical, profit-seeking business venture.

Hun Communes' ongoing experiment extends beyond the co-working space itself. In 2014, Yu and his colleagues applied for a city grant to convert a nearby, government-owned vacant lot into a temporary community open space in a residential neighborhood. Named "Umbrella Park," the project was envisioned to provide "refuge, togetherness, and linkages" in the community.[20] To build outdoor furniture for the park, they partnered with a nonprofit organization, DreamCityBuilding, that trains homeless individuals to become carpenters. In the process of creating the space, Hun Communes invited locals to participate in an art installation featuring photographs of residents. Participants included both old-timers and student renters (the neighborhood is located next to a major university), who began having conversation with each other—something that had never happened before in the community.

With an abundance of new co-working spaces in Taipei already, Shiy-Rung Pan, the cofounder of 9floor Co-Living Apartments, set out to create something different—a co-living space for those looking for affordable and alternative living arrangement in Taipei, one of the most unaffordable housing markets in the world.[21] Pan, still a graduate student at a local university at the time of my interview with him, got the idea from sharing his small rented apartment with friends, visiting international students, and activists who came to join protests in Taipei during the Sunflower Movement. At one point, more than twenty people were staying together at his place. To improve their deteriorating living condition, he and his roommates started to look for a larger apartment in the city. To subsidize the higher rent for the larger space, they decided to keep one of the rooms in sparkling condition and rent it out through Airbnb. They also host other short-term visitors, including visiting scholars from overseas. With the living room empty during the day (as people are out for school or work),

The garden on top of the Fringe Club in Central, Hong Kong,
managed by Rooftop Republic, transformed the vacant rooftop into a demonstration site and an educational space. Photograph by author.

Umbrella Park – transforming a vacant site into a temporary community open space. Photograph by author.

they also rent it out as a home-style, co-working space, or what he called "co-working at home."[22] The additional revenue was invested into improving the apartment and amenities shared by the tenants.

With the success of the experiment, 9floor has since expanded to a total of eight locations in just over a year, all in highly desirable residential locations in the city center. With the added income streams from Airbnb and co-working uses, the business model has enabled 9floor to keep the rent low for the majority of its tenants, allowing young people and students to live close to work and schools downtown. More than just an affordable place to stay, however, 9floor also promotes an alternative, communal lifestyle and seeks to bridge diverse communities in the city. One of its ongoing programs is hosting shared meals and social events with migrant workers in the living room of one of its locations to promote intercultural understanding. This has been done in partnership with One-Forty, another Taipei-based social start-up that organizes educational and outreach programs for migrant workers mostly from Indonesia.

In Hong Kong, the number of social enterprises is also on the rise. In October 2015, I interviewed the organizers of two initiatives there, both members of the Good Lab, a major co-working and incubating space for social start-ups in Hong Kong. One of the initiatives was Rooftop Republic, an urban gardening service start-up with a mission to promote sharing and community building. More than just providing technical services, Rooftop Republic recruits companies and organizations to share their privately-owned rooftops with the community for gardening and other activities. They served about twenty locations throughout Hong Kong at the time of the interview, including rooftops of apartment buildings, company headquarters, schools, senior centers, and other public buildings.

Also born out of the Good Lab, Oh My Kids is a service organization for parents with young children. Its mission is to promote alternative parenting.[23] The organization runs an online platform that includes blogs for parents to share tips on parenting and education. It also serves as a content curator that connects program or service providers with parents who are looking for alternative play/learning activities for kids. Some of the recent programs included a trip to an organic farm joined by 120 households and an arts workshop that was so popular that the organizers had to raise its initial capacity of thirty to 150 registered parents. In addition to serving as an online resource platform, Oh My Kids facilitates the creation of an alternative social network that enables parents to self-organize collective activities, including camping trips.

Unlike radical social and political actions as witnessed in the Sunflower Movement and the Umbrella Movement, the cases of social start-ups in Taipei and Hong Kong focus more on creating social services and community building opportunities through alternative business models that rely on sharing and commoning. However, similar to radical forms of commoning, these initiatives also contribute to breaking down social and economic barriers that exist under the established economic and institutional framework and social norms.

Makerspaces

Makerspaces, or shared fabrication facilities, have become an emerging phenomenon in East Asia that also embodies aspects of commoning. In Hong Kong, the prime example is MakerBay, one of the very first makerspaces in the city that has opened in June 2015. A brainchild of Cesar Harada, inventor and TED Senior Fellow, MakerBay occupies a floor of a large concrete warehouse building located in the industrial waterfront area of Yau Tong district. More than just a fabrication lab, MakerBay also functions as a co-working space that provides members with access to tools, equipment, and technical support. In addition, it hosts social nights, talks, Hackathons, and programs for kids. Besides regular members, the place is bustling with students on weekends, especially product design students who do not have access to equipment and tools at their schools. According to Fiona Ching, MakerBay's general manager, their long-term goal is to serve also as a resource to the local community (almost entirely public housing estates) and schools through educational programming. In other words, its mission is as much about building community as it is about creating cool projects.

Distinct from the industrial setting of MakerBay in Hong Kong, makerspaces in Taipei can be found in residential neighborhoods. Surrounded by multistory apartment buildings, the White Hut was once a vacant two-story shed sitting idly on a street corner. It now serves as one of the most active and unusual neighborhood spaces in the city. Each Saturday morning, the first-floor façade opens to allow residents and visitors (some from far away) to use its growing collection of tools to fix household appliances, furniture, and so on. A group of volunteers are on staff to offer assistance. Rather than offering free repairs, however, the volunteers prefer to teach the residents and visitors how to perform the repairs themselves. The main mission of the White Hut is therefore to reduce waste and encourage an alternative, environmentally responsible lifestyle. On a typical day, the volunteers would include Mr. Wen, a retired city engineer, Ken, an electrical engineer, and Mr. Yu, a physicist and creative entrepeneuer, who is also one of the White Hut's main organizers. Some residents also volunteer on a regular basis. It is difficult, however, to know who will show up on any given day, as there is not an assigned schedule. "People just showed up," said Mr. Yu with a smile.[24]

Migrant workers and young people sharing a meal together during Southeast Asian Sundays hosted by 9floor in partnership with One-Forty. Photograph by author.

Similar to the way volunteers just show up, the White Hut itself also came about somewhat serendipitously. The project began with the temporary storage of heavy tools after a community event, which sparked the idea for creating a tool library in the community. First intended for tool sharing, the White Hut soon became a hub for a variety of community activities. Besides the repair hours on Saturdays, it holds workshops (such as soap making) and events during the week to serve a variety of residents and visitors. More recently, it began holding woodworking hours on Sundays with power tools made available to residents and visitors.

With the success of its many programs, the volunteers at the often overcrowded White Hut have begun to branch out. For example, they once partnered with a homeless advocacy organization to build storage cabinets for the homeless. More recently they began to help other communities or organizations set up similar kind of makerspace. One such project is the Timber Hut, located in a working-class neighborhood known for its strong artisan community. The staff of the White Hut have assisted in multiple events joined by local residents and visitors, turning the space into another community makerspace and an active neighborhood hub. In the cases of MakerBay and the White Hut, the makerspaces serve not only as a place for fabrication, repair, and tool sharing. They also function as venues for community building and to spark interactions between individuals and groups with no previous connections. The White Hut in particular has forged a strong network of volunteers who contribute their time and skills and engage actively in promoting a culture of sharing and reuse, against the dominant culture of consumption.

Characteristics of Contemporary Commoning

The examples above are not meant to present a complete and exhaustive picture of urban commoning initiatives in Taipei and Hong Kong. But even with such a limited sampling, several characteristics are apparent, which may help us understand how acts of commoning have emerged, how they are organized, and what they mean for planning and design practices.

First, the acts of commoning as examined here reflect broader cultural and political shifts through the concept of sharing. Regardless whether an act or organization emerges from social movement, social entrepreneurism, or community initiatives, the focus is consistently on sharing—sharing of spaces, knowledge, networks, and material resources. Distinct from the corporate sharing economy (as exemplified by Uber, Lyft, and Airbnb), the emphasis here is on sharing for the common good and building of social relationships, beyond profit-making. In the case of Fixing Hong Kong, sharing of skills, time, and expertise provides a means of communication between activists and residents that would not have occurred otherwise. The act of sharing further serves as a vehicle for political and social transformation. In the case of Do You a Flavor, sharing and commoning also break down preconceived social and economic boundaries (between the volunteers and the homeless, the public and the vendors), leading to greater awareness and a better understanding of the issues facing marginalized communities in the city. In the cases of Hun Communes, 9floor, Rooftop Republic, and Oh My Kids, although the line between revenue and the common good is blurred, sharing remains fundamental to the greater social good that these initiatives aspire to (and rely upon). At the makerspaces in Hong Kong and Taipei, sharing and community building also constitute an important part of the projects and are critical to their mission.

Secondly, spaces, spatial medium, and spatial practices remain important to the different initiatives, although it may not be equally explicit across the cases. In the case of Fixing Hong Kong, repair of dilapidating apartment buildings provides a means for political advocacy. The work of Do You a Flavor focuses on recognizing and protecting the streets as a place of livelihood for the homeless and marginalized individuals reliant on street vending. The work of Hun Communes and 9floor explores spatial practices of co-working and co-living through ongoing experimentation in the form of temporary community, open space, and shared meals with migrant workers. In both cases, the acts of placemaking has transcended conventional boundaries between public and private, and between different social groups in the society. Rooftop Republic seeks to open up private spaces for community use and community building through rooftop gardening. Oh My Kids also takes on place-based programming and activities, albeit facilitated through an online platform. MakerBay, the White Hut, and the Timber Hut also would not have been possible without the physical spaces that they occupy and transform. While spaces are critical to these cases, it is perhaps more important to note that the acts of commoning would not have occurred without the agency and creativity of the participants and the organizers. This aspect echoes the current literature on commoning that sees commons as production of social actions and relationships beyond material resources.

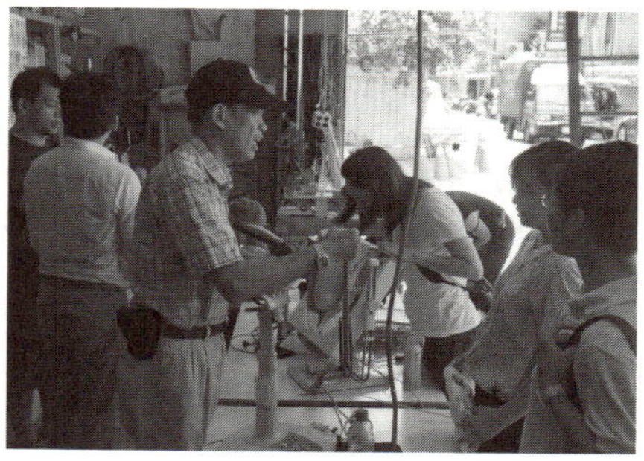

Volunteers at the White Hut transformed the once vacant building into a community hub. Photograph by author.

Third, while the initiatives may seem completely self-organized, it is important to recognize the relationships between these individual initiatives and some degree of institutional support. More precisely, rather than entirely spontaneous actions and isolated efforts, the acts of commoning in Taipei and Hong Kong are often networked and nested within a broader ensemble of actors and institutions. For example, both the White Hut and the Timber Hut have received funding support from Taipei's Open Green program—a matching grant for community initiatives. Do You a Flavor has been supported by a grant from Oxfam Hong Kong. Most recently, Justin Yu of Hun Communes and his team have entered into contract with the city government to run the new Center for Innovation Taipei, an office space for creative startups, including One-Forty, housed in an old sports stadium. In Hong Kong, both Rooftop Republic and Oh My Kids are projects housed in the Good Lab, which itself was a collaboration of seven founding organizations with extensive networks in the business and professional establishment Hong Kong. MakerBay, on the other hand, was funded by impact investors who are interested in social and environmental innovations. Even in the case of Fixing Hong Kong, the volunteer group operates out of a "community story house," a neighborhood hub and service center staffed by St. James' Settlement, an established social service and charity organization in Hong Kong.

In Taipei, in particular, many of the initiatives have worked with one another. For example, Do You a Flavor has recently hosted an event in the Hun Communes' Umbrella Park. It also partners with other organizations on a regular basis, including the DreamCityBuilding, and with the Association for Humanitarian Architecture (AHA), a Taipei-based organization that recruits and coordinates volunteers to work on building projects primarily in remote rural communities. Recently, AHA has provided help for Do You a Flavor with building storage cabinets for the homeless. These networks and collaboration have enabled the individual organizations to strengthen their capacity through pooling and sharing of resources and expertise—an additional layer of urban commoning.

Staff and volunteers from the White Hut were on hand to assist community members at the Timber Hut. Photograph by author.

Located in the industrial waterfront of Yau Tong, MakerBay aims to become a hub for makers and entrepreneurs, as well as local residents and students. Photograph by author.

Conclusion: Designing the Commons?

With the growing number of initiatives and an expanding network of actors, the phenomenon of urban commoning in Taipei and Hong Kong has challenged preconceived boundaries and barriers in these societies. They do so by connecting different populations, networks, resources, knowledges, and skillsets. To various extents, these acts of commoning facilitate the production of new social relationships, meanings, and understanding beyond the confines of social and economic classes, resident statuses, and memberships in particular social groups. In other words, they perform all the good things that are promised in the commons literature. At the same time, however, the cases from Hong Kong and Taipei offer a more complex and nuanced picture of contemporary urban commoning in East Asia.

Rather than the stereotypical image of anarchist communes or "primitive" resource management regimes, the contemporary acts of commoning in Taipei and Hong Kong are technically, socially, and economically savvy. They represent intersections of self-initiatives and support from governmental entities and private investors. As such, their operation is not as clear-cut as described in the recent literature of commons and commoning in its outright rejection of the state and the market. In fact, many of the cases examined here have taken advantage of the marketplace (as in the case of 9floor using Airbnb for short-term leases of its property) and institutional resources.

The more nuanced picture of urban commoning in Hong Kong and Taipei raises an important question concerning whether those acts of commoning may be compromised by its nested relationship within state and market mechanisms, or if such alignment is a necessity or an interim step toward growing the commons. As most of the current initiatives are still in their nascent stage, this will require ongoing examination and critical reflections in years to come. It will also require the organizers of these initiatives and their participants to be vigilant about the encroachment of business and state interests and potential dependency on state and even corporate resources that defeat the very purpose of commoning.

While the recent acts of urban commoning in Hong Kong and Taipei have only been around for a few years or in some cases months, they offer powerful lessons for rethinking how both spatial and social resources and assets can be mobilized and how urban divides can be overcome. From co-working and co-living spaces to rooftop gardens and community makerspaces, the cases in Hong Kong and Taipei represent a current movement in redefining how urban spaces and social relationships can be reprogrammed and produced. They suggest new ways through which individuals, communities, and even institutions can come together to forge new relationships, understanding, and empathy across the deepening social and economic divides. From apartment buildings in Hong Kong to street corners in Taipei, the cases demonstrate that any sliver of urban space can become a space for organizing, a social and political space. Through their work particularly with marginalized populations, the cases make visible the divides and mobilize the public to address them.

In moving from a focus on shared resources to the production of social relationships, the recent discourse of commons and commoning have important implications for planning and design in the urban context. Specifically, the renewed notion of commoning reminds us to reflect critically upon the long-standing emphasis on form and space in design theory and practice, and to reconsider the importance of social processes as tools and ingredients for rebuilding cities and societies. Commoning, in this sense, represents a form of social design—design that explores and supports social networks and processes, serves and engages diverse groups, and with potential for overcoming social and economic divides.

Architects, landscape architects, and urban planners have long been builders of the public realm. In today's cities, however, the public realm is no longer confined to archetypal categories. While conventional public spaces may still allow for the meeting and gathering of diverse populations, overcoming social and economic divides will require more skillful, innovative, and even subversive undertakings. By examining the recent cases of urban commons and commoning in Hong Kong and Taipei, this essay highlights the growing capacity and agency of civil society groups in addressing the wide array of economic and social divides in contemporary cities. These organizations and initiatives serve as an inspiration for how our professions can progress in the future. They call on us to reconsider our role and rebuild our capacity as builders, instigators, and advocates of the commons.

Notes:

1. My research in Taipei was made possible through a Fulbright Scholar Grant from the Foundation for Scholarly Exchange (Fulbright Taiwan) and the Council for International Exchange of Scholars (CIES). A research grant from the China Studies Program at the University of Washington, Seattle supported my research in Hong Kong.
2. This focus on commoning, sharing, and border-crossing builds on my earlier work, including *Insurgent Public Space: Guerrilla Urbanism and the Remaking of Contemporary Cities* (London: Routledge, 2010) and *Transcultural Cities: Border-Crossing and Placemaking* (London: Routledge, 2013). In the earlier work, I examine how citizens and communities create their own "public space" often at border of regulatory domain, and how places and placemaking serve as a vehicle and medium for cross-cultural understanding between diverse social and cultural groups.
3. Heidi Sohn, Stavros Kousoulas, Gerhard Bruyns, "Introduction: Commoning as Differentiated Publicness," *Footprint: Delft Architecture Theory Journal*, 16 (2015): 1–8.; Markus Kip, Majken Bieniok, Mary Dellenbaugh, Agnes Katherina Müller, and Martin Schwegmann, "Seizing the (Every) Day: Welcoming to the Urban Commons!" in *Urban Commons: Moving Beyond State and Market*, ed. Mary Dellenbaugh, Markus Kip, Agnes Katharina Müller, and Martin Schwegmann (Basel: Birkhäuser Verlag, 2015), 9.
4. Kip, et al., "Seizing the (Every)Day," 9.
5. Charlotte Hess, "Mapping the New Commons,"(paper, Twelfth Biennial Conference of the International Association for the Study of the Commons, Cheltenham, UK, July 14–18, 2008), 3.
6. Ibid., 3–4.
7. Michael Hardt and Antonio Negri, Commonwealth (Cambridge, Mass: Belknap Press of Harvard University Press, 2009), viii.
8. Ibid.
9. Hess, "Mapping the Commons," 40.
10. Stavros Starvides, "Re-inventing Spaces of Commoning: Occupied Squares in Movement," *Quaderns-e* 18, no. 2 (2013), 40–52.
11. Kip, et al., "Seizing the (Every) day," 13.
12. Adrian Parr, "Urban Debt, Neoliberalism and the Politics of the Commons," *Theory, Culture & Society* 32, no. 3 (May 2015), 87.
13. Urban Catalyst, "Patterns of the Unplanned," in *Loose Space: Possibility and Diversity in Urban Life*, ed. Karen Franck and Quentin Stevens (New York: Routledge, 2007), 271–88.
14. Patrick Bresnihan and Michael Byrne, "Escape into the City: Everyday Practices of Commoning and the Production of Urban Space in Dublin," *Antipode*, 47 (2014): 36–54.
15. J-H. Kao, "Reckless Space," *Art Critique of Taiwan*, 57 (2014): 4–9. (In Chinese)
16. Didi K. Han and Hajime Imamasa, "Overcoming Privatized Housing in South Korea: Looking through the Lens of 'Commons' and 'the Common,'" *in Urban Commons*, 91–100.
17. See: https://www.facebook.com/FixingHK/?fref=ts.
18. Beard (co-founder, Fixing Hong Kong), in discussion with the author, October 2015.
19. There were approximately 700 homeless individuals in Taipei in 2015. Around 80% of the population is concentrated near the Taipei Main Station and the Lungshan Temple in the Wanhua District. See Yin-Yi Chen, "Li Ying-Zhi: Reversing Perspectives, Helping the Homeless to Become Self-Reliant," *Rhythms Monthly* 204 (2015): 90–103. (In Chinese)
20. Justin Yu (owner, Hun Communes) in discussion with author, July 2015. Note: Umbrella Park has no relationship with the Umbrella Movement in Hong Kong.
21. The ratio of median housing price to median annual household income in Taipei was 15.7 in 2014, compared with 17 in Hong Kong and 10.6 in Vancouver, two of the most unaffordable cities in the world; see Yi-Ling Chen, "The Factors and Implications of Rising Housing Prices in Taiwan," *Brookings Taiwan- U.S. Quarterly Analysis*, July 2015, http://www.brookings.edu/research/opinions/2015/07/15-taiwan-rising-housing-prices-chen.
22. Shiy-Rung Pan (co-founder, 9Floor Co-living Apt) in discussion with author, September 2015.
23. In reference to Amy Chua's book *Battle Hymn of the Tiger Mother* (New York: Penguin Press, 2011).
24. Mr. Yu (staff, the White Hut) in discussion with author, September 2015.

RADICAL URBANISM IN THE DIVIDED CITY:
On M. Paul Friedberg's Riis Park Plaza (1966)

Marisa Angell Brown

Photograph of M. Paul Friedberg, ca. 1990s.

The "wrong side of the tracks," "Skid Row," and "the outskirts of hope"—all phrases that testify to the ways in which poverty is often given spatial definition in modern America. It has been theorized as a place apart from the prosperous center, not just a condition but a space that is physically, socially, economically, and culturally peripheral to an imagined center, whether that center is figured as the middle class or as Main Street. Documentary photographers in the late nineteenth century and their better-known heirs in the 1930s—Works Progress Administration (WPA) photographers such as Dorothea Lange and Walker Evans—published the first photo books of urban slums and rural shack towns, in which poverty was represented as a different country, a world apart. The title of New York journalist Jacob Riis's *How the Other Half Lives* (1890), the first publication in this genre, said it all: the poor were "the other half," ostensibly making the book's readers "this half," as the cultural historian Maren Stange has pointed out.[1]

The national public housing program, established in 1933 under Title II of the National Industrial Recovery Act and expanded in 1937 with federal legislation authorizing the establishment of local housing authorities that could finance and develop public housing, suggested an alternative conception of poverty, attempting through the design of new projects to obscure some of the physical divisions between "this" and the "other" half. In its nascent period, the 1930s, public housing architecture took design cues from tropes associated with the local middle class, from the neo-Georgian brick developments in Atlanta and the tropical stucco villas of Miami to the International Style projects in New York City, Cleveland, and other urban centers where cutting-edge modernism was known.[2]

These projects, always built on relatively inexpensive land—land that was either at the physical periphery of the center, or that had been cleared of existing tenements deemed to be "slums"—were conceived as jumping-off points into middle-class life, liminal spaces that served as a way station between two divided economic and cultural spheres. This is most powerfully expressed in photographs of the new public housing projects that were commissioned by the local and federal housing authorities, which drew visual connections between the projects and the distant skyscrapers of the city center. These images elided any relationship between the new developments and the surrounding tenements, providing a visual cue to the overarching goals of the public housing program at its start, which was designed to draw outlying slums into the middle-class fold.

Similar, operationally, to the importation of the architectural styles and methods of the colonial powers into their colonies, early public housing architecture was deliberately conceived by the agencies that guided and approved project designs to transform indigent subjects figured overwhelmingly in photographs as abject, often black, women into modern "domestic workers."[3] This is why the Housing Division's (the agency tasked with overseeing the public housing program in its early years) planning requirements stipulated strict minimums on sunlight penetration into unit interiors and dictated efficient kitchen and closet designs that were intended to support cooking and cleaning in the "domestic workshop."[4]

But this transition did not take place. The public housing program was suspended during World War II, and after the war the 1944 G.I. Bill and a subsequent revision to this bill in 1945 offered financial incentives to private developers and home buyers to kick-start the construction and purchase of new homes for returning veterans. In effect, the bill laid out "easy terms for borrowers and virtual carte blanche for developers," allowing borrowers to obtain loans of up to 100% of the home's purchase price.[5] As the historian Kenneth Jackson and others since have demonstrated, rapid suburbanization and white flight from the urban centers ensued, creating a postwar built landscape that was increasingly stratified by race, class, and even gender as suburban men commuted back and forth between the city and suburb while women remained at home.[6]

Was urban renewal a corrective response to white flight (in that its aim was to attract suburban whites back into the city center) or was it an extension of the same segregationist drive to further divide the postwar landscape by creating islands of white leisure, work, and residential life within increasingly heterogeneous urban centers? Urban historians, political historians, and sociologists ascribe different motives to the individuals, agencies, and community groups that promulgated urban renewal, but in the end most agree that the massive program—authorized under the 1949 and 1954 U.S. Housing Acts, which allowed the federal government to subsidize private developers in acquiring and razing slums and building new residential, commercial, and industrial projects in their place—further stratified the postwar city by race and class. By the early 1960s, in words reminiscent of Riis's 1890 book, there was talk of an "other America," which was understood to be not only poor, but also black and Latino, and now segregated spatially in public housing projects in the growing ghettoes of many urban centers.[7]

What started out as a project to create transitional launching pads to the middle class had become, by the 1960s, a project associated with segregation and containment, with keeping residents "in" rather than hop-scotching them "out" of the slum. This evolution was captured in contemporary sociological accounts of life in the projects from this time and in representations of them in the media, which

1 Maren Stange, *Symbols of Ideal Life: Social Documentary Photography in America, 1890–1950* (New York: Cambridge University Press, 1989), 14–17.

2 The regionalism of early public housing architecture has not been adequately understood. Ever since the 1932 International Style exhibition at the Museum of Modern Art—where a model of one of the first public housing projects was exhibited—and Henry-Russell Hitchcock and Philip Johnson's accompanying publication, *The International Style* (1932), which posited the factory and the low-cost housing project as the two building types that embodied the style and aims of modernist architecture, the sense that early public housing architecture was, across the board, modernist has dominated our understanding of public housing design. Richard Pommer's "The Architecture of Urban Housing in the United States during the Early 1930s," *Journal of the Society of Architectural Historians* 37, no. 4 (December 1978): 235–64, and Richard Plunz's treatment of public housing in *A History of Housing in New York City* (New York: Columbia University Press, 1990), 189–227, have supported this misconception, but many public housing projects in the 1930s outside urban centers bore little connection to modernist design principles, either in form, plan, or applied ornament.

3 The document that most clearly lays out the design objectives of the early public housing program in its nascent phase is Col. Horatio B. Hackett, "How the PWA Housing Division Functions," *Architectural Record* 77 (March 1935): 148–84. Hackett was Director of the Public Works Administration (PWA) Housing Division. Throughout this document, Hackett uses terms then in vogue in scientific management and home economics, presenting the new public housing projects as domestic factories designed to enable productivity. This new view of the home was advocated in multiple reports at President Herbert Hoover's 1931 Conference on Home Building and Home Ownership, predating the PWA. See, for example, White House Conference on Child Health and Protection, *The Home and the Child: Housing, Furnishing, Management, Income, Clothing* (New York: Century Company, 1931), 18–24; and Marisa Angell Brown, "Imagined Communities: Race, Gender and the Architecture of Alterity in American Public Housing Design" (Ph.D. diss., Yale University, Department of the History of Art, 2014): 27–53.

4 Hackett, "How the PWA Housing Division Functions," 174.

5 Alexander von Hoffman, "History Lessons for Today's Housing Policy: The Political Processes of Making Low-Income Housing Policy," August 23, 2012, Joint Center for Housing Studies of Harvard University, http://www.jchs.harvard.edu/sites/files/w12-5_von_hoffman.pdf, 19.

6 Kenneth T. Jackson, *Crabgrass Frontier: The Suburbanization of the United States* (New York: Oxford University Press, 1985).

7 Michael Harrington, *The Other America: Poverty in the United States* (New York: MacMillan, 1962); and Nathan Glazer and Daniel Patrick Moynihan, *Beyond the Melting Pot: The Negroes, Puerto Ricans, Jews, Italians, and Irish of New York City* (Cambridge, Mass.: MIT Press, 1963).

8 See Sam Castan, "Modern Design for a City Ghetto," *Look* (September 21, 1965), M7–M8 and "Major Changes Urged for Public Housing," *Chicago Daily News* (undated news clipping from 1965), CHA Scrapbook, Box A, Bertrand Goldberg Archive, The Ryerson and Burnham Libraries, the Art Institute of Chicago.

pictured these spaces as prisons indelibly separating their occupants from the downtown spires they were once intended to relate to.

The particular projects that were understood to be agents of spatial apartheid were those built in the cities that had seen high numbers of incoming blacks (from the southern states in the years following the Depression) and Puerto Ricans, who emigrated to the United States in large numbers in the 1950s and 1960s. These included the Robert Taylor Homes (1962) on the South Side of Chicago— called a "$70,000,000 ghetto" and "the Congo Hilton" shortly after completion.[8] By the 1960s, Samuel Zipp writes, public housing projects such as these "evoked the divided urban landscape—suburban plenty at the fringe and urban deprivation at the core—that marked the dawning age of 'urban crisis.'"[9] The well-known bookend to all of this is the photograph of the Pruitt-Igoe Homes being blown up by dynamite that was used by Charles Jencks and also by Colin Rowe and Fred Koetter in important texts from the 1970s to argue for the ideological bankruptcy of modernist architecture.[10]

There was a brief period from the early 1960s to the early 1970s in which a number of architects and landscape architects charted a new course in the design of public housing. Informed by broad changes in American thinking about race and ethnicity and also by currents in postwar sociology, these projects reveal architecture grappling with race and poverty, and also with the question of how architecture might effectively engage in social activism and cultural critique. This essay looks at one of these projects in particular: the landscape architect M. Paul Friedberg's 1966 design of two acres of space within the Jacob Riis Houses (1949) stretching from East 6th Street to East 10th Street between Avenue D and FDR Drive on the Lower East Side of Manhattan.

Riis Park Plaza, as it was called, was a seminal intervention into urban space. It suggested alternatives: alternatives to the postwar dichotomy between suburban plenty and urban deprivation; alternatives to the segregated space within the postwar city; alternatives to a model of urbanism that ignored play and creativity as elemental needs; and alternatives to the historical practice of landscape architecture, which until this period was focused more on horticulture than the design of public space. It was a seminal project in the history of American architecture, an early experiment in radical urbanism in the divided postwar city that demonstrated sophisticated ways in which activism might shape architecture.

Tragically, Riis Park Plaza was razed in 2000, but understanding how it worked is relevant today. Some of the things we have long associated with the past—segregation and slavery, for example—are still with us (the Global Slavery Index estimates that 45.8 million people are currently held in bondage globally, while racial segregation continues to divide our twenty-first-century cities).[11] Architecture is implicated in these issues as it is our medium for giving these ideas spatial definition and therefore materiality. It may be that most of the buildings and spaces that get built over the next century extend the powerful arm of global capital and instantiate the urge to divide our habitat along racial, class, or gendered lines. But are there possibilities for resistance—and does architecture have a role to play in such resistance?

Alfredo Brillembourg and Hubert Klumpner of Urban-Think Tank think it does; the exhibition they curated in 2015 at the 6th Bi-City Biennale of Urbanism\Architecture in Shenzhen, *Radical Urbanism*, as well as their accompanying essay, "The Evolution of Radical Urbanism: What Does the Future Hold for Our Cities?" suggest that there is a vibrant global history of radical urbanism, which they define as architectural and urban projects, exhibitions, publications, theories, and even performances that challenge and critique political and social norms, bringing utopic notions of possibility in direct engagement with contemporary social and political action.[12]

Along these lines, it may be helpful to begin to assemble a canon of radical urbanist experiments that grappled—and continue to grapple—with division so that we understand that there is a tradition of such work in American architecture. It may also be helpful to understand the particular ways in which twentieth-century radical urbanists used design to further social activism and to analyze their successes and failures. What we may find is that the most powerful tools that architects have are the same tools that make architecture so imperative to political and economic expansion: the production of space.

* * *

When Friedberg was given the Riis Park Plaza commission, he was only thirty-four years old and had a thin resume. Prior to this commission, Friedberg collaborated with the architect Simon Breines on remodeling the outdoor space surrounding the Carver Houses (1958) in Harlem in 1963. This project involved replacing a series of inaccessible lawns and small fenced playgrounds with a series of three outdoor "rooms": a modernist garden, a playground, a wooden maze, and a sandlot, and in between, a large multi-use space that had elements of an open-air amphitheater and contemporary bandstand with a small canteen.

The project was spearheaded by Brooke Astor, who approached the New York City Housing Authority (NYCHA) as she wanted to fund a new publicly accessible recreational space in Harlem through the Astor Foundation.[13] NYCHA selected the Carver Houses because there had been conflict between residents and the building's managers over use of the central open space, which had been fenced off due to the managers' insistence that the landscaping was being destroyed.[14] Breines, Friedberg, and Robert Zion (who worked in I.M. Pei's New York office at the time) were invited to submit designs for the Carver Houses commission; Breines and Friedberg chose to work as a team and were ultimately given the commission.[15]

The project was in many ways a first draft of the ideas that would come to fruition at Riis. As soon as the Carver Houses project was completed, it was deemed an important contribution to the physical landscape of Harlem and harbinger of a new direction in public housing design. In 1964, the chairman of NYCHA wrote to Astor that Carver Houses was "a 'must' on the schedule of every inspection tour conducted by the [New York City Housing] Authority," while a 1966 publication promoting NYCHA's achievements devoted a three-page spread to the distinctive bandstand, amphitheater, and spray pool.[16] In 1965, the Park Association gave its annual design award to NYCHA for Carver and its other open space projects as, one journalist noted, "recognition of breakthroughs in the design and concept of public housing" which previously had been the "grimmest" in the country.[17]

9 Samuel Zipp, *Manhattan Projects: The Rise and Fall of Urban Renewal in Cold War New York* (New York: Oxford University Press, 2010), 26.

10 See Colin Rowe and Fred Koetter, *Collage City* (Cambridge, Mass.: MIT Press, 1976), 23; and Charles Jencks, *The Language of Post-Modern Architecture* (1977; repr., New York: Rizzoli, 1991 [1977]), 9–10.

11 See The Walk Free Foundation, www.globalslaveryindex.org.

12 Alfredo Brillembourg and Hubert Klumpner, "The Evolution of Radical Urbanism: What Does the Future Hold for our Cities?" *Arch Daily*, December 4, 2015, http://www.archdaily.com/778308/the-evolution-of-radical-urbanism-what-does-the-future-hold-for-our-cities.

13 Simon Breines to the Client Award Program, New York State Association of Architects, August 21, 1964, Vincent Astor Foundation Records, Box 4, Folder "NYCHA", Special Collections, New York Public Library.

14 Ibid.

15 Friedberg credits Breines with taking a lead role in the design.

16 Bill Reid, the Chairman of NYCHA, to Brooke Astor, October 6, 1964, Vincent Astor Foundation Records, Box 11, Folder "Carver Amphitheater Committee."

17 Thomas C. Wheeler, "New York Tries a New Approach," *The Reporter*, June 17, 1965.

18 The Astor Foundation donated $700,000 towards the $900,000 budget. *The Vincent Astor Foundation, 1964–1968* (New York: Vincent Astor Foundation, n.d.), 6, Vincent Astor Foundation Records.

(Fig. 1) Kahn & Jacobs, Carver Houses, before Simon Breines and M. Paul Friedberg's design intervention. Photograph courtesy of the New York City Housing Authority.

(Fig. 2) Simon Breines and M. Paul Friedberg, Carver Court, showing the playground at top of photo and bandstand at bottom (modernist garden located north of the bandstand is not visible in this photograph). Photograph courtesy of the New York City Housing Authority.

(Fig. 3) Simon Breines and M. Paul Friedberg, Carver Court on dedication day, showing level changes and pergola at top of photograph, brick walls facing the raised stage and canteen built into one of the brick walls at right bottom, viewed from the north. Photograph courtesy of the New York City Housing Authority.

(Fig. 4) Riis Park Plaza amphitheater. Photograph courtesy of M. Paul Friedberg Partners (MPFP).

(Fig. 5) Riis Park Plaza adventure playground. Photograph courtesy of MPFP.

(Fig. 6) Riis Park Plaza adventure playground. Photograph courtesy of MPFP.

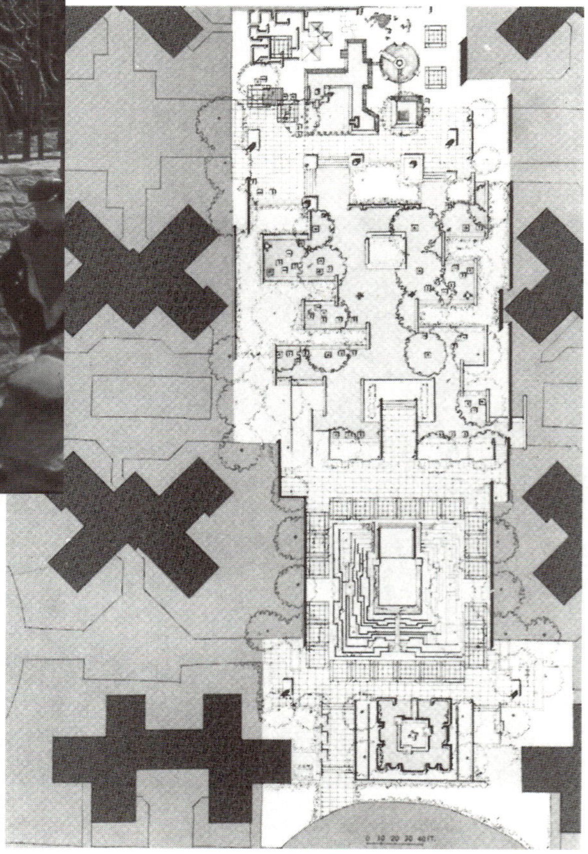

(Fig. 7) Riis Park Plaza site plan showing, from bottom to top, the walled elderly garden, amphitheater, open plaza with modernist plantings and adventure playground. Plan courtesy of MPFP.

(Fig. 8) Riis Park Plaza: kids climbing in amphitheater. Photograph courtesy of MPFP.

(Fig. 9) Riis Park Plaza adventure playground. Photograph courtesy of MPFP.

(Fig. 10) Riis Park Plaza adventure playground. Photograph courtesy of MPFP.

Three years later and several miles south of Carver, Riis Park Plaza was dedicated in May 1966. For NYCHA and for the city, Riis Park Plaza was even more of a public relations success than Carver had been; Lady Bird Johnson gave remarks along with New York City Mayor John V. Lindsay and Astor,[18] and it received awards from the Department of Housing and Urban Development, the American Institute of Architects, the New York State Association of Architects, the New York State Council on the Arts, the City Club, the American Society of Landscape Architects, the Municipal Art Society, and the Public Housing Agency.[19] As a result, Friedberg became a significant figure in public housing design: he was asked by NYCHA to draw up plans for the insertion of Riis-like spaces at the Forest Houses, Foster Houses, Van Dyke Houses, and the Brevoort Houses in 1967 and was even retained around this time by the St. Louis Housing Authority to suggest design alternatives for the troubled Pruitt-Igoe Homes as well.[20]

What had made such a splash? The two-acre space, as at the Carver Houses, replaced a series of fenced rectangular grass lawns and small playgrounds surrounded by broad concrete walkways. Contemporary journalists noted that the former chain-link fencing had been posted with "Keep Off the Grass" signs and other notices that prohibited residents and children from damaging, defacing, or actively using the grounds. The space that Friedberg designed, by contrast, was open and accessible and was programmed to accommodate a variety of activities, experiences, and age groups. It worked for all ages and all energy levels, encouraging social integration by letting each loosely defined space flow into the next without the disruption of fences, gates, or other physical barriers.

At its southern end, a small "elderly garden" provided benches for reading and conversation. With a fountain at its center, the whole area was loosely bounded with a brick wall to create a sense of enclosure. The heart of Riis Park Plaza was its amphitheater, located just to the north, an immense multilevel space that could hold up to 2,000 spectator-participants, with dressing and rehearsal rooms at basement level designed in consultation with Joseph Papp, director of the Shakespeare in the Park series at the outdoor Delacorte Theater, and built-in jets that could convert the entire space into a giant water park in the warmer months.

A modernist garden separated the amphitheater from the plaza's northernmost point—an innovative adventure playground, the first of its kind in the United States, which featured interconnected climbing structures, jungle bars, and slides made of cobblestone, old railroad ties, bits of repurposed concrete sewer pipe, and a sand floor with the overall appearance of an ancient ziggurat or igloo city, a fanciful landscape in miniature that provided a contrast to the standard swing/slide equipment installed in most playgrounds of the era. When it was completed, one journalist noted, the playground was a site of "frenzied activity—the children play as if the whole thing might disappear tomorrow."[21] NYCHA photographs show the playground and amphitheater as sites of exuberant use, with science demonstrations and dance-offs, while newspaper accounts noted that Twyla Tharp performed at Riis in August 1967, and in the summer of 1968, a long list of children's performances included an acting troupe called the Paper Bag Players, a magic show, and a puppet show, while the space was booked in 1970 for a jazz and Latino music performance and more children's skits.[22]

Coming when it did, Riis Park Plaza was a spirited defense of the city as an idea and should be understood within the context of the emerging critique of the homogenized American suburbs in books such as *The Exploding Metropolis* (1958), edited by William H. Whyte, and the better known *The Death and Life of Great American Cities* (1961) by Jane Jacobs. Whyte and Friedberg were friends, and Friedberg later recounted that they "sympathized" and "had similar ideals... He was an advocate. I was a producer."[23] Jacobs' book would become the bestseller, but *The Exploding Metropolis* was the opening salvo against suburbanization and large-scale urban projects that we now link with Robert Moses. As Whyte put it in his introduction, "This is a book by people who like cities."[24] For a landscape architect to not only agree with this point of view but attempt to instantiate many of these ideas into urban space was an unexpected move.

Friedberg talked about Riis Park Plaza as if it were an urban habitat rather than a garden or park. Although—or perhaps because—he came to landscape architecture through horticulture (his father owned a nursery in New York where he worked as a boy; he received his B.S. in Horticulture from Cornell University in 1954 and planned to take over his father's nursery before he moved into landscape architecture), by the 1960s, he was dismissive of the notion that the most valuable tools of his trade were "flowers and trees and lawn," which he termed "archaic" and irrelevant given the enormous economic, social, and physical challenges of the modern urban ghetto.[25] Rather than celebrating nature, Riis Park Plaza celebrated urban social life in all of its complexity, contradiction, and unruliness without devolving into either caricaturing urban life or treating it as spectacle.

When asked what he thought he had contributed to the field of landscape architecture, Friedberg said, "It's enjoying the city, removing the landscape architecture bias of the past [of] the preconceived notion that the city is a hostile place."[26] Riis Park Plaza transgressed two different, but linked, sets of norms: it upended the postwar suburban/urban dichotomy that equated the city with poverty and abjection—think of the popularity of film noir in Friedberg's time, which represented the city as an ominous, forbidding landscape—by offering a celebratory reading of the city. In addition, it tested the traditional skepticism toward urban infrastructure that was expressed in mainstream landscape architecture of his era, while eschewing an avant-garde aestheticizing branch within the field that took direction from abstract and surrealist art. Friedberg's work, rather, was related to—and probably also indebted to—the older landscape architect Karl Linn's "neighborhood commons" work in Philadelphia in the early 1960s, combining park-playgrounds that were designed in concert with local residents in inner-city neighborhoods.[27]

19 *The Vincent Astor Foundation, 1964–1968* (New York: Vincent Astor Foundation, n.d.), 6; Vincent Astor Foundation Records.

20 Memorandum to Department and Division Heads of NYCHA from J. Christian, General Manager of NYCHA, November 13, 1967, New York City Housing Authority Collection, New York, Box 73B1, Folder 9, La Guardia and Wagner Archives, La Guardia Community College, New York; and Mildred F. Schmertz, "Designing the Spaces in Between," *Architectural Record* 143, no. 3 (March 1968): 128.

21 John Morris Dixon, "Riis Plaza: Three Acres Filled with Life," *Architectural Forum* 125, no. 1 (July–August 1966): 73.

22 "Dance Programs of the Week," *New York Times*, August 20, 1967, D5; "Children's Activities Listed," *New York Times*, July 3, 1968, 30; "Amusements Listed in City for Children," *New York Times*, July 17, 1968, 38; "Amusements Scheduled for Children Throughout City," *New York Times*, July 24, 1968, 28; "Things for Youngsters to See in the City," *New York Times*, May 6, 1970, 70; "Entertainment Events," *New York Times*, October 4, 1970, 2; *East Side News*, September 3, 1971, New York City Housing Authority Collection, Box 92C5, Folder 22.

23 M. Paul Friedberg, interviews by Charles S. Birnbaum, James Sheldon and Shirley Veeneman, October 5–6, 2006, and May 22, 2008, Pioneers Oral Histories Series, Cultural Landscape Foundation, 16.

24 William H. Whyte, Jr., ed., *The Exploding Metropolis* (1958; repr. Berkeley: University of California Press, 1993), 7.

25 Friedberg, Oral History, 27; and M. Paul Friedberg, discussion with author, February 13, 2002.

26 Friedberg, Oral History, 24.

27 Karl Linn, interviews by Lisa Rubens in 2003 and 2004, Oral History Regional Oral History Office, the Bancroft Library, University of California Berkeley, 71–72. Both Friedberg and Linn mention each other in their oral histories. See Friedberg, Oral History, 13, and Linn, Oral History, 52, in which Linn recounts meeting with Friedberg, Edward Bye, Jr., and Conrad Hamerman from time to time to discuss their work.

Ironically, all of this lost was lost on Lady Bird Johnson, whose dedicatory comments presented Riis Park Plaza as a bucolic oasis within the larger urban landscape. This was evident from her first words—"Oh, how nice; oh, how lovely ... [look at the] green trees and bright flowers and moving waters"—to her prepared comments:

> I suspect if some of those early Greeks were to stand in Grand Central at 5 o'clock today and see the exodus to the country each afternoon, they would be perplexed and say: "Where are you going? If you are so smart and progressive, why haven't you learned to bring the countryside down?" And that's just what you have learned here in Riis Plaza.[28]

This fundamental misunderstanding of Riis, viewing the new park as an escape from urbanity rather than a celebration of it, is not surprising, given that Johnson came to Riis Park Plaza in the midst of her national "beautification" campaign. This mistake is important as it points to the pitfall of privileging the historical written record over formal and spatial analysis within history. In this case, much of what Friedberg was up to can only be gleaned through a close reading of Riis Park Plaza combined with his own statements about his work and about this project in particular as other observers—not only Johnson, but also Astor Foundation and NYCHA staff—were either not attuned to the subtleties of Friedberg's design or valued it primarily as a juvenile crime prevention measure.[29]

What does a close reading of Riis Park Plaza reveal? First, it is instructive to see when, how, and where Friedberg used trees, shrubs, and flowers and to keep in mind as a counterpoint to the abundance and Romanticism of Frederick Law Olmsted's Central Park which then—and even now—set the standard for landscape architecture in New York and beyond. In the amphitheater and in the garden room at Riis Park Plaza, trees and shrubs were used as supporting players; many mature trees from the original plan were saved, and new ones were strategically planted to provide shade or to act as sentinel-like markers in space, creating lines and grids that directed movement and divided space into increasingly intimate, but never naturalistic, rooms. In the adventure playground, Friedberg clearly took pains to incorporate existing trees into the design, in one instance building a cobblestone climbing structure around a tree, and in another case using an existing tree as the center of a simple deconstructed tree house. In a few places, Friedberg even left the trunks of some trees that had been sheared off at the top as climbing equipment.

The overall effect suggested that natural materials had a role to play in the urban habitat, but only insomuch as they supported both the needs and the physical infrastructure of urban culture—a far cry from the painterly, picturesque treatment of trees in Olmsted's Central Park, where nature has been aestheticized and the city outside screened as much as possible.[30] Riis Park Plaza illustrated the rhetorical defense of the city found in *The Exploding Metropolis*, crystallizing many of what this emerging urbanist group considered to be the best parts of urban life in one space: play, community, energy, and diversity.

Second, a close reading of Riis Park Plaza reveals Friedberg's attention to space, and the sophisticated ways in which he deploys space as a building material. In every part of the scheme, from the amphitheater steps, waterways, and water spouts to the stepped-timber climbing structures, the relationship between line and space is emphasized, casting space as a substance with as much physicality as the materials it abuts. There is a density to space in these moments, a sense that, like water, it rushes in to fill gaps wherever they occur.

It is interesting to note that some elements of Riis Park Plaza align with the tenets of Minimalism, which emerged in the early and mid-1960s and was first formulated as a movement in the *Primary Structures* exhibition in the spring of 1966 at the Jewish Museum in New York, a month before Riis Park Plaza was dedicated. In both Riis Park Plaza and in Minimalist sculpture, modern industrial materials are manipulated to activate the surrounding space with the aim of creating a phenomenological interplay between viewer and artwork or play piece, pulling him or her into a relationship with it. Like many Minimalist sculptors, Friedberg was also critical of figuration, writing in 1970 that figurative play structures, like fire trucks and sculpted animals, were "literal design [that] restricts a child's imagination" by cuing him or her to one specific use.[31] Riis Park Plaza, by contrast, was abstract and made use of only a few materials: cobblestone, wood, concrete, steel, and sand.[32] Friedberg also noted that "all the sculptors were into designing play pieces because some kids were climbing on a Calder... However, you could never really play on this stuff."[33] His contribution "was to create a play piece that was sculptural as opposed to a sculpture that was a play piece."[34]

Friedberg said that psychological research on play from the 1930s through the 1960s was an important influence on his work as it highlighted the importance of play in development.[35] In the first part of the twentieth century, Johan Huizinga's *Homo Ludens: A Study of the Play Element in Culture* (1938 translated and published in the United States in 1944) for the first time theorized play as central to the development of culture and connected it to sacred ritual and mythmaking, while Jean Piaget's *Play, Dreams and Imitation in Childhood* (1951) argued that play and games had a crucial role in the psychological formation of the self. Brian Sutton-Smith, whom Friedberg directly

28 Lady Bird Johnson, quoted in Bernard Weinraub, "Mrs. Johnson Opens Riis Playground," *New York Times*, May 24, 1966, 1 and 50.

29 In an undated letter to Brooke Astor from Fannie Nealy, Chairman of the Carver Amphitheater Committee, Nealy writes, "Before this [amphitheater] program began ... small children got into all sorts of mischief. Adolescents looking for trouble, forming gang fights and upsetting the whole neighborhood. Your kindness eliminated all this last year." Vincent Astor Foundation Archives, Box 11, Folder "Carver Amphitheater Committee." Linda Gillies, Director of the Astor Foundation, also wrote to Brooke Astor about this on May 25, 1966, stating that Riis Park Plaza was "the best way we have ever used our charitable dollars to combat delinquency." Vincent Astor Foundation Archives, Box 8, Folder "Riis Park."

30 Media coverage of Riis Park Plaza was extensive in the 1960s: Editorial, "New York's Great Open Space," *New York Times,* May 24, 1966, 45; Ada Louise Huxtable, "At Last, a Winner," *New York Times* May 24, 1966, 49; Philip H. Dougherty, "On a Hot Day a Kid Can Go to the Riis Playground and Just 'Let Go,'" *New York Times*, June 21, 1966, 45; "Frog into Prince," *Progressive Architecture* 47 (July 1966): 170–72; Mildred Schmertz, "Shaping the Community in an Era of Dynamic Social Change," *Architectural Record* 140, no. 1 (July 1966): 196–99; John Morris Dixon, "Riis Plaza: Three Acres Filled with Life," *Architectural Forum* 125, no. 1 (July–August 1966): 68–73; "Urban Playscapist," *Progressive Architecture* 47, no. 8 (August 1966): 70–72; Scott Kelly, "Plaza on a Grass Plot," *Industrial Design* (October 1966): 53–57; and Charles L. Mee, Jr., "Putting the Play in Playgrounds," *New York Times*, November 6, 1966, 112, 117, 119, 120.

31 M. Paul Friedberg, *Play and Interplay: A Manifesto for New Design in Urban Recreational Environments* (New York: MacMillan, 1970), 82.

32 Was Friedberg aware of Minimalism when he designed Riis Park Plaza in 1965? Minimalism was still in its early days at that point, and the only publications or exhibitions that pointed toward this new direction in contemporary art were a handful of essays and downtown gallery shows featuring the work of Donald Judd and Robert Morris, which exhibited neither the playful humanism of Riis Park Plaza nor any sense of the social value of activating space in this way. Although Riis Park Plaza was certainly a critique of traditional landscape architecture—and Friedberg's treatment of space was one part of this critique—the design leveraged space for greater ends, marshalling space as a "catalyst" to support the individual child's psychological development and the creation of social bonds with others. See M. Paul Friedberg, "Looking Back," *Process Architecture* 82 (Tokyo, 1989): 8.

33 Ibid., 28.

34 Ibid.

35 Friedberg, discussion with author.

36 Ibid. See works by Brian Sutton-Smith, such as: *The historical and psychological significance of the unorganized games of New Zealand school children* (1953) and *Theories of play and games for cognitive development (1967)*.

(Fig. 11) Riis Park Plaza adventure playground. Photograph courtesy of MPFP.

(Fig. 12) Riis Park Plaza adventure playground. Photograph courtesy of MPFP.

(Fig. 13) Riis Park Plaza: detail of the water features turned on, sculptural fountain in the elderly garden. Photograph courtesy of MPFP.

(Fig. 14) M. Paul Friedberg's drawing of elements of the amphitheater and its waterways. Drawing courtesy of MPFP.

(Fig. 15) Riis Park Plaza adventure playground. Photograph courtesy of MPFP.

named as an influence, wrote prolifically on the psychological and cultural significance of play in different cultures and its fundamental importance to maturation. [36]

This research had special ramifications for the children who would use Riis Park Plaza, as they did not benefit from nursery school education like their wealthy peers. This made public playgrounds important, but previously unrecognized, centers of psychological and social development. (Friedberg viewed Head Start, a federal program established in 1965 to provide free nursery education to lower-income children the summer before they started elementary school, in part to make up for this deficit, as an analogue of the play spaces he designed.)[37] Riis Park Plaza was designed to facilitate several different experiences: role playing and spectatorship in the amphitheater; "interplay" or "linked play," in which many children at once could move from one play structure to the next (from igloo to tunnel to monkey bars) without stopping; and, finally, the sense of physical and emotional challenges overcome, as Friedberg's play structures required more daring than most off-the-rack designs.[38]

If the play space presented an environment of permissiveness—one that was the antithesis of the restricted and protected grass lawns that occupied this space previously—the amphitheater was its analogue, a nearly empty space intended to empower residents by inviting them to program its use. [39] (Friedberg explained, "The amphitheater ... needn't direct community action into any specified behavior that is not authentically its own. An amphitheater is simply a resource that can reflect the feeling of the community in the ways in which it is programmed.")[40] Deployment of this powerful archetype invoked the culture of the classical Greek polis, or city-state, at a time when New York City, Chicago, and other large American cities were in crisis. The civil rights movement troubled the notion of America as a democratic nation, and this use of classical Greek architecture signified a new vision of the *demos* that included the population living in public housing, including African-Americans and recent immigrants.

Inserting amphitheaters into public housing projects in this social and political context not only provided residents with greater recreational and cultural opportunities, it recognized and authorized residents' social and political identities and even their capacity and power to agitate for change. Recalling Friedberg's use of amphitheaters in his design work at the time, Arthur Rosenblatt—who was the Deputy Administrator of the Parks Department when Riis Park Plaza was built—stated, it was "the time of riots and 'power to the people.'" Residents wanted a place to assemble, whether peacefully or otherwise, and spaces like Riis gave them this ability.[41]

With its open vistas, Riis Park Plaza provided nearly two acres of continuous space for "interplay" for children and adults, recasting the divided city into a generative, nurturing, challenging, and fun place to be. It not only disrupted postwar dichotomies between suburban (good) and urban (bad), middle class and poor, landscape architecture and urban infrastructure, but it also remapped the social geography of the Lower East Side by breaking down spatial divisions between different racial, ethnic, and age groups. The late 1950s and early 1960s were a period of intense demographic transition in public housing projects throughout the city and in low-income neighborhoods in general.[42] The Lower East Side, where the Jacob Riis Houses were built, was divided internally by urban color lines. These lines were in flux in the early 1960s as white immigrant communities from Eastern Europe and Ireland, who had arrived in New York in the 1920s and 1930s, were slowly giving ground to increasing numbers of Puerto Rican and black residents, more recent arrivals who were often a generation younger than the old guard.[43] In addition, the East Village began to emerge in the early 1960s as a haven for musicians, artists, and hippies. Sociologist Christopher Mele describes the shifting but very real spatial segregation of the Lower East Side during this era as "a hybrid neighborhood identity always in flux and fraught with episodes of conflict and compromise." He further notes that turf wars were common among the many youth gangs in the neighborhood that primarily identified according to racial and ethnic identity.[44]

Construction of Riis Park Plaza did not dismantle this spatial segregation—it couldn't—but it did disrupt it. The Jacob Riis Houses contained 1,187 units, housing nearly 3,000 residents when it was built; the amphitheater, which was built to hold up to 2,000 spectator-participants, was therefore built as a community resource as it was too big to have been conceived solely for Riis tenants.[45] Newspaper accounts of the programs held in the amphitheater in the 1960s and 1970s reveal a heterogeneous mix of American and Latin jazz, soul performances, modern dance, and children's magic and puppet shows. In addition, the simple fact that Riis Park Plaza provided linked space for both the elderly and for children was telling, since, as Mele writes, these two groups at this particular moment in time and in this particular location were often divided by race, culture, religion, and language: elderly residents were more often part of the white Eastern European immigrant community, while young children and families were more often black and Latino.

It is difficult to overestimate how radical this space was for its deep engagement with contemporary psychological and sociological theory, and the way that it determinedly marshaled the tools of landscape architecture to produce a proudly urban and generative public space within a context of class and racial division. In this, it differed both from the Carver Houses project—which gestured toward many of these moves, but did not succeed to the same degree as Riis—and other similar projects of this time, such as Albert Mayer's 1960 redesign of the outdoor space at the Jefferson Houses in Harlem, which a critic later called "a grim proletarian parody of the country-club terrace," a simulacrum of World's Fair-like festivity and spectacle that was more a whitewashing of urban problems than a true engagement with them. [46]

After 1966, Friedberg was commissioned by NYCHA to design amphitheaters, playgrounds, and parks in other of the city's public housing projects, but none was as ambitious in scale, design, or programming as Riis Park Plaza. With the election of John Lindsay as mayor of New York City in 1966 and his appointment of Thomas Hoving—future director of the

37 M. Paul Friedberg, *Playgrounds for City Children* (Washington, D.C.: Association for Childhood Education International, 1969), 7–8.

38 Friedberg writes about "linked play" and its psychological dimension in *Play and Interplay*, 44.

39 In an article written a few years after Riis was completed, Karl Linn wrote, "We have to build soap boxes as well as sand boxes—neighborhood block commons, forums, plazas and teenage assemblies... Democratic decision-making, so-called, has been too limited to the middle-aged middle class." See Karl Linn, "'White Solutions' Won't Work in Black Neighborhoods," *Landscape Architecture* (October 1968): 24.

40 Friedberg, *Play and Interplay,* 149.

41 Arthur Rosenblatt, discussion with author, March 24, 2004. It should be noted that an amphitheater was central to another radical urbanist design of this period, Bertrand Goldberg's Hilliard Homes on the South Side of Chicago, completed in the summer of 1966. See the author's forthcoming article in the *Journal of the Society of Architectural Historians*.

42 Some of the most explosive change occurred in East Harlem, where fifteen public housing projects were built between 1941 and 1965, accounting for 10% of the public housing constructed by NYCHA in this period. Zipp, *Manhattan Projects*, 258 and 21.

43 See Christopher Mele, *Selling the Lower East Side: Culture, Real Estate, and Resistance in New York City* (Minneapolis: University of Minnesota Press, 2000).

44 Ibid., 137.

45 NYCHA put a bathroom into the amphitheater in 1967 to serve the larger community, indicating the agency's willingness to promote broad usage of the space.

46 Mildred Schmertz, "Shaping the Community in an Era of Dynamic Social Change," *Architectural Record* 140:1 (July, 1966), 197.

47 Press Releases on Mayor Lindsay's programs, John Vliet Lindsay Papers, Box 138, Folder 148, Series VIII, and Box 358, Folder 374, Series XVI, Manuscripts and Archives, Sterling Memorial Library, Yale University.

(Fig. 16) Riis Park Plaza adventure playground. Photograph courtesy of MPFP.

(Fig. 17) Riis Park Plaza adventure playground. Photograph courtesy of MPFP.

(Fig. 18) Riis Park Plaza adventure playground. Photograph courtesy of MPFP.

(Fig. 19) Riis Park Plaza amphitheater. Photograph courtesy of MPFP.

Metropolitan Museum of Art—to be the city's parks commissioner that year, recreational and open space design, including in NYCHA projects, transitioned to a model of simplistic spectacle, including a "Movie in the Street" program that dispatched trucks to ghetto communities during the summer to show films outdoors and a program in which "mini-pools" for swimming were put into many public housing projects in the city, also in the hot and troubled summer months.[47]

Hoving openly described the spaces and programs that the Parks Department sponsored during this time as "bread and circuses," "pre-explosive maintenance" that were intended to "keep [poor kids'] fucking minds off of getting drugs and shooting each other."[48] It was in this context that he hired the architect Morris Lapidus, known for designing lavish resorts in Miami Beach in the 1950s, including the Fontainebleau, Eden Roc, and Americana hotels, to create a $1.9 million community pool and playground in the Bedford-Stuyvesant neighborhood[49] which was to "rival the flossiest pool in Palm Beach."[50] This signaled a direction in public housing design in which architects associated either with luxury and leisure or with the design avant-garde, which were—and are—brought onto projects to create a buzzy splash (both on-site and in the media), without seriously engaging with the needs and desires of users. These programs were aligned with Lindsay's overall approach to fixing a deteriorating city, which a contemporary newspaper reporter characterized as superficial, ineffective, and self-serving: "Lindsay was always preoccupied with the appearance rather than the reality of things... [He] often asked his aides, when making a decision, how will this be played in the *Times*? How will it look on the six o'clock news?"[51]

From our vantage point today, the spatial apartheid of the 1960s urban ghetto was transparent. On the Lower East Side and in many other urban neighborhoods at this moment, urban color lines could be read in storefront signage and in the kinds of meat and produce stores stocked. Today, these lines are often less transparent, existing internally within neighborhoods or even laterally within individual "mixed-income" buildings. A recent mobile documentary project by the transmedia director Michael Epstein called *Walking Cinema: Museum of the Hidden City* (2015) captures this point beautifully. The film follows a Latino family of four that has been awarded, through city lottery, an apartment in a private luxury high-rise in San Francisco as they tour the modernist roof-deck garden, the large fitness center, and the pet "spaw" in the lobby. In one heart-breaking scene, the mother notes, "I don't know my next-door neighbors because they never say hi. I only see them close the door, open the door, but I don't know who they are. Yeah, they do activities here, but only for those people who go and talk about their work. I can't show up and be like, 'Hey everyone, I'm a housekeeper in a hotel!'"

Divides have been and will always be central to the relationship between race and American architecture; they may even be the physical and social crux of the way that race and architecture interact in the United States, from segregation and desegregation to what we now recognize as resegregation.[52] Divides are, of course, both the physical manifestation of ideas about social relationships and, at the same time, important players in these relationships; once built, they interact physically with the groups that have been divided. As we make our way into the twenty-first century, all of the data so far shows that inequality is on the rise and that the "middle class" is splintering.[53] Architecture—and landscape architecture—can serve as handmaiden to the global system that produces this stratification, or it can resist. It may be that there are greater possibilities for resistance in the design of public space—both because of its intrinsic nature and because, as Saskia Sassen points out, many of our recent global protest movements "are not marches: they are occupations of a space," indicating the potential for these places to catalyze, or at least support, social change.[54]

What does such resistance look like, and how does it work? A close reading of Riis Park Plaza reveals one architect's attempt to subvert inequity by crafting a physically, psychologically, politically, and socially impactful public two-acre commons in the heart of a charged frontier.

48 Thomas Hoving, quoted in Vincent J. Cannato, *The Ungovernable City: John Lindsay and his Struggle to Save New York* (New York: Basic Books, 2001), 113. Hoving used the same language, calling these programs "bread and circuses" again in author's interview with Thomas Hoving, February 26, 2004.

49 Note that Lapidus had grown up in Bedford-Stuyvesant, not Florida.

50 See "Florida Architect is Designing a Pool for Brooklyn Ghetto," *New York Times*, November 23, 1966, 30; "20 New Minipools Planned in Slums," *New York Times*, March 24, 1968; "Bedford Stuyvesant Community Pool," *Architectural Record* 155, no. 7 (June 1974): 95–104; and Morris Lapidus, *Too Much Is Never Enough* (New York: Rizzoli, 1996), 9–11.

51 Journalist quoted in Cannato, *The Ungovernable City*, 114. Lindsay wrote in his 1969 memoir that mayors can "give symbolic evidence of concern," revealing the extent to which he viewed social programs as symbolic—not always results-driven—efforts. See John V. Lindsay, *The City* (New York: Norton, 1969), 115.

52 See studies such as: Bader, Michael D. M., and Siri Warkentien. "The Fragmented Evolution of Racial Integration since the Civil Rights Movement." *Sociological Science* 3 (2016): 135-166.

53 Saskia Sassen, "The Middle Classes: An Historic Actor in Today's Global World," *Juncture* 20, no. 2 (2013): 125–28.

54 Ibid., 126.

(Fig. 20) View of the Jacob Riis Houses. Photography courtesy of New York City Housing Authority.

PERSPECTA 50

URBAN DIVIDES

THE YALE ARCHITECTURAL JOURNAL

Contributors

JON CALAME
directs "Thermal Efficiency: Eastport", a community-scale affordable heating project in Maine, USA, since 2011. A decade of field-based research is summarized in *Divided Cities: Beirut, Belfast, Jerusalem, Mostar and Nicosia* (2009). Previously, Mr. Calame was a Rome Prize recipient, a Fulbright Senior Scholar in Cyprus, a founding member of the Minerva Partners consultancy group, and partnerships manager for the World Monuments Fund.

DANA CUFF
is founder and director of cityLAB, a research and design center at UCLA that explores the challenges facing the 21st century metropolis. In 2012, she launched the Urban Humanities Initiative, funded by the Mellon Foundation, to bring a crossdisciplinary focus to cities on the Pacific Rim. She has written widely on urban design and the politics of place, including the books *Fast Forward Urbanism* and *The Provisional City*. She received a Ph.D. in Architecture from UC Berkeley.

JESSE VOGLER
is an artist, designer, and co-director of the Institute of Marking and Measuring, a multi-disciplinary platform for critical spatial practices. He is also an Assistant Professor of Landscape Architecture at Washington University in St. Louis. He was recently a Fulbright Scholar in Tbilisi, Georgia, researching the political and spatial residue of the Soviet state farm system. Jesse's work has been featured in *Thresholds, Artforum, Domus, MONU,* and *Forty-Five*.

MARK HACKETT and
KEN STERRETT
co-founded CITY REPARO in 2015, a multidisciplinary consultancy focused on urban transformations. Hackett is an architect and a former partner in Hackett Hall McKnight, a Belfast-based firm, that won the UK Young Architect of the Year Award in 2008. Sterrett is an urban planner and former lecturer at Queens University Belfast. Mark and Ken's work with the Forum for an Alternative Belfast was exhibited in the Venice Biennale in 2012.

MITCH MCEWEN
is Principal of McEwen Studio / A(n) Office and Assistant Professor at Princeton University School of Architecture. Before founding McEwen Studio, McEwen worked at Bernard Tschumi Architects and the New York City Department of City Planning. She holds an M.Arch. from Columbia University (GSAPP) and B.A. from Harvard.

MICHAEL SORKIN
is an architect, urbanist, and writer who runs Michael Sorkin Studio and its nonprofit arm, TERREFORM. Michael is Distinguished Professor of Architecture and Director of the Graduate Program in Urban Design at City University of New York. This project is the work of TERREFORM and will appear in *Open Gaza*, a collection to be published by Terreform's book imprint, UR.

KIAN GOH
is Assistant Professor of Urban Planning at UCLA Luskin School of Public Affairs. She is a founding partner of SUPER-INTERESTING!, an architecture and design firm, and she previously worked for Weiss/Manfredi Architects. Kian received her M.Arch. from Yale in 1999 and her Ph.D. in Urban and Environmental Planning from MIT in 2015.

TATIANA BILBAO ESTUDIO
is an architectural practice established in Mexico City in 2004 whose projects occupy a range of diverse typologies in varying scales across vastly different contexts. Its work seeks to use spatial tools derived from a clear formal language, material exploration, and a study of local culture to respond to the social landscape, and built environments that foster social collaboration and economic opportunity for underserved populations.

ONNIS LUQUE
is an independent architectural photographer and founder of Arquitectura Vista, a project which integrates new visions and processes concerning architecture's visual presence in urban history. Luque is the author of the book "USF/DF Táctica de Apropiación" published by CONACULTA and Ediciones Acapulco.

GUY TRANGOŠ
is a Doctor of Design student at the Harvard University Graduate School of Design, a professional architect, and urban researcher. He holds a Research Associateship at the Gauteng City-Region Observatory, has an M.Arch. from the University of the Witwatersrand, and an M.S. in City Design and Social Science from the London School of Economics and Political Science.

ALFREDO BRILLEMBOURG and
HUBERT KLUMPNER
are the founders of the interdisciplinary design practice URBAN-THINK TANK (U-TT), and hold a joint Chair of Architecture and Urban Design at ETH Zürich.

ALEXIS KALAGAS
is a writer and researcher at U-TT/ETH, and co-edited the recent book *Reactivate Athens: 101 Ideas* (Ruby Press, 2017).

ANNABEL JANE WHARTON
is William B. Hamilton Professor of Art History at Duke University and was Vincent Scully Visiting Professor at the Yale School of Architecture in Fall 2014. Annabel received her Ph.D. from the Courtauld Institute of Art at the University of London.

TODD REISZ
is an architect and writer who teaches at the Yale School of Architecture. He is editor of *Al Manakh 2: Gulf Continued* and the Beirut-based journal *Portal 9*. He previously led urban research projects at OMA/AMO. Todd received his M.Arch. from Yale.

ANOORADHA IYER SIDDIQI
is a Fellow in the Mahindra Center for the Humanities at Harvard University, and received a Ph.D. in the History of Art and Archaeology from the New York University Institute of Fine Arts. Her work focuses on spatial politics, urbanisms, and modernist culture and discourses in history, drawing from primary research in East Africa and South Asia for two book projects, *Architecture of Humanitarianism: The Dadaab Refugee Camps* and *Emergency Urbanism in History and Vocal Instruments: Minnette De Silva and an Asian Modern Architecture*. She co-edited the volume *Spatial Violence*, and has practiced architecture in the United States and India.

ALISHINE HUSSEIN OSMAN
left Somalia at the age of seven due to political turmoil and was settled in Ifo Refugee Camp, Dadaab, Kenya. He and his family were confined there from 1991 to 2007. Osman graduated from the first class to pass through Ifo Secondary School, and worked in Dadaab for the international humanitarian organization Norwegian Refugee Council. In 2007, he was resettled in the United States. He received a B.A. in Political Science from Pennsylvania State University. Mr. Osman works in a social service organization in Harrisburg, Pennsylvania, and as a language and cultural consultant across the United States.

SANDI HILAL and
ALESSANDRO PETTI
are co-directors of
DECOLONIZING ARCHITECTURE
ART RESIDENCY (DAAR),
an architectural office and artistic residency program that combines conceptual speculations and architectural interventions. They are also the founders of *Campus in Camps,* an experimental educational program hosted in Dheisheh refugee camp in Bethlehem. Petti and Hilal co-authored the book *Architecture after Revolution* (Sternberg, Berlin 2014) with Eyal Weizman, and Petti contributed to *Archipelagos and Enclaves* (Bruno Mondadori, Milan 2007).

THERESA WILLIAMSON
is the founder and executive director of Catalytic Communities, an organization that works towards integrating formal and informal urbanism in Rio de Janeiro. Theresa received her Ph.D. from the Department of City and Regional Planning at the University of Pennsylvania.

GARY W. MCDONOGH
is a cultural anthropologist holding a Ph.D. from the Johns Hopkins University where he is the Helen Herrmann Professor and Chair of the Growth and Structure of Cities Department at Bryn Mawr College. He has co-edited various collections in urban studies, including *Global Downtowns* (2011) and *Sustainability in the Global City: Myths and Practices* (2014).

ANDRÉS JAQUE
is an architect and directs the OFFICE FOR POLITICAL INNOVATION based in New York and Madrid. He received his Ph.D. from ETSAM in 2015 and he is currently an Advanced Design Professor at Columbia and a Visiting Professor at Princeton. The Office for Political Innovation has been awarded with the 10th Frederick Kiesler Prize and the Silver Lion at the Venice Biennale in 2014, and its work has been shown at MoMA in 2012 and 2015.

JYOTI HOSAGRAHAR
is Director, Division for Creativity in the Culture Sector at UNESCO. Prior to joining UNESCO in 2016, she was a professor and Director of the SUI Lab at GSAPP, Columbia University; UNESCO Chair in Culture, Habitat, and Sustainable Development at Srishti Institute of Art, Design, and Technology in Bangalore, where she was also Chair of the Ph.D. program.

ANDREEA COJOCARU
is a practicing architect and theorist. She is currently founding partner and Creative Director at Numena, a German company that develops spatial environments for Virtual Reality applications. Her research focuses on design methodologies for multi-space experiences and the politics of subjectivity in spatial practice. Andreea holds an M.Arch. from Yale.

JENNY HOLZER
has presented her astringent ideas, arguments, and sorrows, for more than thirty-five years, in public places and international exhibitions, including 7 World Trade Center, the Venice Biennale, the Guggenheim Museums in New York and Bilbao, and the Whitney Museum of American Art. Starting in the 1970s with the New York City posters, and continuing through her recent light projections on landscape and architecture, her practice has rivaled ignorance and violence with humor, kindness, and courage. Holzer received the Leone d'Oro at the Venice Biennale in 1990, the World Economic Forum's Crystal Award in 1996, and the Barnard Medal of Distinction in 2011. She holds honorary degrees from Williams College, the Rhode Island School of Design, The New School, and Smith College. She lives and works in New York.

JEFFREY HOU
is Professor of Landscape Architecture at the University of Washington, Seattle. His recent research and practice focus on design activism and public space. He was the winner of the 2012 Great Places Award for his edited book, *Insurgent Public Space*. He is a co-editor of a new book *City Unsilenced: Urban Resistance and Public Space in the Age of Shrinking Democracy*.

JEANNE GANG
Architect and MacArthur Fellow, is the founding principal of STUDIO GANG. A recipient of the National Design Award in Architecture, her work spans scales and typologies to foreground the relationships between individuals, communities, and environments. Jeanne is the author of three books and teaches regularly, most recently as the John C. Portman Design Critic at the Harvard Graduate School of Design.

ALISSA ANDERSON
directs publications and special projects at STUDIO GANG. A graduate of Columbia GSAPP's Critical, Curatorial, and Conceptual Practices in Architecture program (CCCP), she is a contributing editor of the *Avery Review*.

MARISA ANGELL BROWN
is an architectural historian and curator with research interests in architectural movements, buildings, and spaces of the 1960s to the present, including the formation of the preservation and heritage movements. She received her Ph.D. in architectural history from Yale in 2014. Brown is the Assistant Director of Programs at the John Nicholas Brown Center for Public Humanities and Cultural Heritage at Brown University and produces architecture exhibitions and programs through her firm Genie Loci.

MEGHAN MCALLISTER
and MAHDI SABBAGH
are the editors of *Perspecta* 50. They are practicing architects and urbanists, and are collaborating on projects together beyond *Perspecta*, including a contribution to the forthcoming publication, *Open Gaza*. Both Mahdi and Meghan graduated with a Masters in Architecture from Yale in 2015.

ALEXIS MARK
is an office for graphic design and typography. Through cross-disciplinary collaborations the office primarily works with clients and collaborators from the fields of art, design and architecture. Born from its interest in the concepts of language and transmission Alexis Mark additionally runs the occasional exhibition platform and project space Annual Reportt which serves as a public laboratory for exploring the overlapping peripheries of various artistic disciplines. After graduating from the Gerrit Rietveld Academie (NL) and Yale (US), the office has been operating out of Copenhagen, Denmark since 2016.

Image Rights

The editors greatly acknowledge the permissions granted to reproduce the copyrighted material in this publication. Every effort has been made to trace the ownership of all copyrighted material and to secure proper credits and permissions from the appropriate copyright holders. In the event of any omission or oversight, all necessary corrections will be made in future printings. Unless otherwise noted, all images are courtesy of the author.

CUFF
Fig 1, 2, 7. Courtesy of the Housing Authority of the City of Los Angeles.
Fig 3. Data courtesy of the Housing Authority of the City of Los Angeles (modified format).
Fig 4, 5, 6. Collection of Thomas S. Hines.

VOGLER
p. 32. Courtesy of St. Louis County GIS Service Center, © 2012 (modified format).

CITY REPARO
Fig 2, 3, 5, 6. Courtesy of Mark Hackett.
Fig 4, 7, 10, 12–14. Courtesy of Forum for an Alternative Belfast / CIty Reparo.
Fig 8. © public domain.
Fig 9. © Ron Weiner, 1975. (with modifications by author).
Fig 11. Illustration by author based on satellite © Google Maps, 2014.

MCEWEN
Fig 2. Courtesy of the U.S. Library of Congress, Prints & Photographs Division, Detroit Publishing Company Collection, [reproduction number, e.g., LC-D4-10865].
Fig 4. Public domain from US Patent and Trademark Office.
Fig 5, 10. Courtesy of Detroit Water and Sewerage Department.

GOH
Fig 2, 4, 5. Courtesy of NCICD.
Fig 3. Illustration by author based on satellite © Google Maps, 2015.
Fig 8. Courtesy of UPC
Fig 9. Courtesy of Ciliwung Merdeka.
Fig 10–15. Courtesy of Rebuild by Design.
Fig 16. Courtesy of SUPER-INTERESTING!

SORKIN
p. 76. © and courtesy of ISOCARP, 2015.
p. 79. (top) Public domain.
p. 80. (top) © REUTERS/Ibraheem Abu Mustafa
(all other illustrations courtesy of Terreform).

BILBAO
All photographs © Onnis Luque, 2016.

TRANGOŠ
Fig 3. © Martin West, UCT Libraries, C Kirkwood.
Fig 4–5. Illustration by author with satellite underlay from © Google Maps, 2016.
Fig 6. © Westonaria Borwa Mega Project.
Fig 9. From top: © Vaal River Development Company ; © Zendai Development South Africa; courtesy of Lyt Architects; © Zendai Development South Africa.
Fig 10. Public domain.
Fig 11–12. Courtesy of Khosto Mahlangu

BRILLEMBOURG, KLUMPER, KALAGAS
Fig 1–6. Courtesy of Daniel Schwartz/U-TT.
Fig 7–15. Courtesy of U-TT.
Fig 16. Courtesy of Jan Ras/U-TT.

REISZ
Fig 1. Public domain.
Fig 3. Courtesy of Mark Harris.
Fig 4. Courtesy of Peter Jackson.

WHARTON
Fig 2, 4, 5, 12, 13. Public domain.
Fig 9–10. Courtesy of Mahdi Sabbagh.

MCALLISTER, SABBAGH
(All photos listed in clockwise order from top left of given page).
p. 155. Courtesy of Aanya Chugh; courtesy of Palmyra Geraki; courtesy of Denis Schofield; public domain.
P 156. Courtesy of Denis Schofield; courtesy of David Lee; courtesy of Camilla Wasserman; courtesy of Mahdi Sabbagh.
p. 157. Courtesy of Denis Schofield; public domain; courtesy of Andy Sternad; public domain (photo by Nick Carson).
p. 158. Courtesy of Craig Rosman; public domain; courtesy of Meghan McAllister; public domain (photo by Gerard Janot).
p. 159. Courtesy of Mahdi Sabbagh; courtesy of Meghan McAllister; public domain; and photo courtesy of Mahdi Sabbagh.
p. 160. Courtesy of Maggie Tsang; photo courtesy of Meghan McAllister; courtesy of Jean Ahn; public domain.
p. 161. Courtesy of Meghan McAllister; courtesy of Camilla Wasserman; courtesy of Swarnabh Ghosh; courtesy of Todd Reisz.
p. 162. Public domain (photo by Eckehard Jagdmann); courtesy of Swarnabh Ghosh; courtesy of Mahdi Sabbagh; courtesy of Walker Oleson.
p. 163. Courtesy of Nizar Harake; courtesy of Meghan McAllister; photo courtesy of Swarnabh Ghosh; courtesy of Catalytic Communities.
p. 164. Courtesy of Jonathan Sun; public domain (photo by Jensie Gheest); © Gabriel Hurtado; courtesy of Michael McAllister.
p. 165. Courtesy of Catalytic Communities; courtesy of Pavel Bendov; courtesy of Meghan McAllister; public domain.
p. 166. Courtesy of Andreea Cojocaru; courtesy of Mahdi Sabbagh; courtesy of Meghan McAllister; courtesy of Meghan Lewis.
p. 167. Courtesy of Mahdi Sabbagh; courtesy of Andy Sternard; courtesy of Peggy Deamer; courtesy of Mahdi Sabbagh.
p. 168. Courtesy of Mahdi Sabbagh; courtesy of Sheena Zhang; courtesy of Meghan Lewis; courtesy of Mahdi Sabbagh.
p. 169. Courtesy of Outside Development; courtesy of John Tubles; courtesy of Perry Wexelberg; courtesy of Meghan McAllister.
p. 170. Courtesy of Mahdi Sabbagh; courtesy of Jesse Vogler; courtesy of Mahdi Sabbagh; courtesy of Caecilia Pieri.

SIDDIQI, OSMAN
Fig 1, 11. Courtesy of UNHCR.
Fig 7. Courtesy of Bethany Young.

DECOLONIZING ARCHITECTURE ART RESIDENCY
Fig 1–3, 5, 6. Courtesy of Alaa Abu Asad.
Fig 4. Courtesy of Dima Srouji
Fig 7-9. Courtesy of Campus in Camps/Sara Anna.

HOSAGRAHAR
All photographs are courtesy of Jyoti Hosagrahar.

WILLIAMSON
p. 214–215, 216 (bottom), 218, 223, 226. Courtesy of Catalytic Communities
p. 216 (top). Courtesy of the Mauricio Hora Archives.

COJOCARU
p. 234 (top). Photograph by Wendy Corniquet, Public Domain.
p. 234 (bottom). Photograph by Zsolt Czegledi, © European Pressphoto Agency.
p. 235. Photograph courtesy of Nikolay Kozlovich.

JAQUE
p. 243. © CNES, Centre National d'Études Spatiales (France).
p. 244-45. Courtesy of Andrés Jaque / Office for Political Innovation. Photographer: Miguel de Guzmán.
Foldout (left). Courtesy of Andrés Jaque / Office for Political Innovation.
Folout (right). Courtesy of Edilnord Centri Residenziali, Milan.
p. 246-48. Courtesy of Andrés Jaque/ Office for Political Innovation. Photographer: Miguel de Guzmán.
p. 249. Courtesy of Edilnord Centri Residenziali, Milan.

MCDONOGH
e. © Harry Quillen, Harry Quillen. Collection/Los Angeles Public Library.
f. © Gordon Dean, Valley Times Collection/Los Angeles Public Library.
i. Courtesy of Mahdi Sabbagh.

HOLZER
All photographs © 1983 Jenny Holzer, member Artists Rights Society (ARS), NY.

GANG, ANDERSON
Fig 1–4. Photos © Google Maps 2016
Fig 5. Public domain, wood engraving by John Karst, 1885.
Fig 6. Illustration courtesy of Spinner Publications.
Fig 7. Photograph © Chicago Historical Society, from the Chicago Daily News negatives collection, Chicago History Museum, DN-0067671.
Fig 8. Photograph from the Harris & Ewing Collection, courtesy of the U.S. Library of Congress, Prints & Photographs Division, LC-H261- 3251-B.
Fig 9. Photo courtesy of St Louis Police Veteran's Association.
Fig 10. Photo © and courtesy of Mario Burger.
Fig 11. Photo © and courtesy of Studio Gang.
Fig 12. Photo courtesy of the Public Building Commission of Chicago.
Fig 13. Photo by Tom Harris © Hedrich Blessing, courtesy of Studio Gang.
Fig 14. Chart redrawn by Studio Gang from Thomas Piketty, Capital in the Twenty-First Century, trans. Arthur Goldhammer (Cambridge, MA: Harvard University Press, 2014).
Fig 15. Photo © and courtesy of Studio Gang.
Fig 16. Film still © Spirit of Space, courtesy Studio Gang.
Fig 17. Sketch © and courtesy of Studio Gang
Foldout (front). Satellite Image © Google Maps 2016, with notations by Studio Gang.
Foldout (inside). Drawings © and courtesy of Studio Gang.

HOU
Fig 1. Public domain (photo by Kevin WY)

BROWN
Frontispiece, 4–19. Photographs courtesy of MPFP.
Fig 1–3, 20. Photograph courtesy of the New York City Housing Authority.

Acknowledgements

We would like to thank Marta Justo Caldeira for her constant guidance throughout the initial stages of this project. We would also like to thank Alan Plattus and Keller Easterling for their mentorship, Richard DeFlumeri for the incredible support, the editors of Perspecta 49 for their on-call tips and advice, and Erene Morcos for proofreading the book. Finally, we are thankful for the various individuals who supported us throughout this editing process, including but not limited to our parents, Perry Wexelberg, JT Keeley, Maya Alexander, George Miller, José Bruguera, Haruko Fukui, and Meghan's colleagues at Bohlin Cywinski Jackson.

Our most sincere thanks to the donors that make the production of Perspecta possible:

Marc F. Appleton, '72 M.Arch.
Hans Baldauf, '81 BA, '88 M.Arch.
Austin Church III, '60 BA Family Fund
Fred Koetter and Susie Kim
Elizabeth Lenahan
Cesar Pelli, '08 DFAH
Robert A.M. Stern, '65 M.Arch.
Jeremy Scott Wood, '64 BA, '70 M.Arch.
F. Anthony Zunino, '70 M.Arch.

We would like to thank the members of the Perspecta board for their direction, guidance, and trust:

Deborah Berke
Peggy Deamer
Sheila Levrant de Bretteville
Keller Easterling
Gavin Macrae-Gibson
Cesar Pelli
Alan Plattus
Harold Roth
Robert A.M. Stern

Colophon

PERSPECTA 50: URBAN DIVIDES
THE YALE ARCHITECTURAL JOURNAL

Editors
MEGHAN MCALLISTER
MAHDI SABBAGH

Graphic design
ALEXIS MARK

Copyeditor
STEPHEN HOBAN

This book was printed and bound
in Breda, The Netherlands by
NPN DRUKKERS

This book is typeset in
PERSPECTA GOTHIC
by BEN FEHRMAN-LEE

PERSPECTA, THE YALE ARCHITECTURAL JOURNAL is published in the United States of America by the Yale School of Architecture and distributed by the MIT Press.

Massachusetts Institute of Technology
Cambridge, MA 02142
http://mitpress.mit.edu

Library of Congress Cataloging-in-Publication Data is available.

ISBN: 978-0-262-53427-7
ISSN: 0079-0958